Studies in Eighteenth-Century Culture

VOLUME 28

Studies in Eighteenth-Century Culture

VOLUME 28

Edited by

Julie Candler Hayes
University of Richmond

and

Timothy Erwin
University of Nevada at Las Vegas

Published by The Johns Hopkins University Press for the
American Society for Eighteenth-Century Studies

The Johns Hopkins University Press
Baltimore and London

The Johns Hopkins University Press
2715 North Charles Street
Baltimore, Maryland 21218-4363
www.press.jhu.edu

ISBN 0-8018-6247-7
ISSN 0360-2370

Articles appearing in this annual series are abstracted and
indexed in *Historical Abstracts* and *America: History and Life*.

DANIEL GORDON / History / University of Massachusetts
KENNETH W. GRAHAM / English / University of Guelph
RICHARD GRAY / German / University of Washington
ANITA GUERRINI / History of Science / University of California at
    Santa Barbara
SUSAN GUSTAFSON / German / University of Rochester
GEORGE E. HAGGERTY / English / University of California at Riverside
MAUREEN HARKIN / English / Stanford University
PHILIP HARTH / English / University of Wisconsin at Madison
CLEMENT HAWES / English / Southern Illinois State University
CHARLES H. HINNANT / English / University of Missouri at Columbia
ROBIN IKEGAMI / English / Xavier University
CATHERINE INGRASSIA / English / Virginia Commonwealth University
JOHN ISBELL / French / Indiana University
ANNIBEL JENKINS / English / Georgia Institute of Technology
HERBERT JOSEPHS / French / Michigan State University
SUVIR KAUL / English / Stanford University
THOMAS KAVANAGH / French / University of California at Berkeley
DEBORAH KENNEDY / English / Saint Mary's University
BETH KOWALESKI-WALLACE / English / Boston College
ELIZABETH KRAFT / English / University of Georgia
MARIE-PAULE LADEN / French / University of California at Davis
ELIZABETH LAMBERT / English / Gettysburg College
DONNA LANDRY / English / Wayne State University
NANETTE LECOAT / French / Trinity University
WILLIAM LEVINE / English / Sul Ross State University
ROGER LUND / English / LeMoyne College
DEIDRE LYNCH / English / State University of New York at Buffalo
ELIZABETH MACARTHUR / French / University of California at
    Santa Barbara
ROBERT MANIQUIS / English / University of California at Los Angeles
LOUIS MARCHESANO / History / Cornell University
ANDREW MCCLELLAND / Art History / Tufts University
ALAN MCKENZIE / English / Purdue University
HEATHER MCPHERSON / Art History / University of Alabama
LINDA MERIANS / English / LaSalle University
JEFFREY MERRICK / History / University of Wisconsin
JERRINE MICHELL / Art History / Independent Scholar

WENDY MOTOOKA / English / Oberlin College
RICHARD NASH / English / Indiana University
ANTHONY PAGDEN / History / Johns Hopkins University
CATHERINE PARKE / English / University of Missouri
ELLEN POLLAK / English / Michigan State University
DAVID RICHTER / English / Queen's College
SOPHIE ROSENFELD / History / University of Virginia
TREADWELL RUML / English / California State University at
   San Bernadino
PETER SABOR / English / Université Laval
THOMAS P. SAINE / German / University of California at Irvine
STEVEN SAND / History / Maryhill College
MONA SCHEUERMAN / English / Oakton Community College
BETTY SHELLENBERG / English / Simon Fraser University
RICHARD SHER / English / New Jersey Institute of Technology
SANDRA SHERMAN / English / University of Arkansas
ANN B. SHTEIR / Humanities and Women's Studies / York University
FRANK SHUFFELTON / English / University of Rochester
JOHN H. SMITH / German / University of California at Irvine
JEFFREY SMITTEN / English / Utah State University
ANTOINETTE SOL / French / University of Texas at Arlington
RAYMOND STEPHANSON / English / University of Saskatchewan
KRISTINA STRAUB / English / Carnegie Mellon University
RAJANI SUDAN / English / University of Texas at Arlington
GEOFFREY SYMCOX / History / University of California at Los Angeles
JAMES THOMPSON / English / University of North Carolina at
   Chapel Hill
LINDA TROOST / English / Washington and Jefferson College
RANDOLPH TRUMBACH / History / Baruch College
ELEANOR TY / English / Wilfrid Laurier University
ANNE VILA / French / University of Wisconsin at Madison
CYNTHIA WALL / English / University of Virginia
STEPHEN WERNER / French / University of California at Los Angeles
HUGH A. WEST / History / University of Richmond
ANNE WILLIAMS / English / University of Georgia
LAUREL WILSON / History of Textiles / University of Missouri
CAROLYN WOODWARD / English / University of New Mexico
BETH WRIGHT / Art History / University of Texas

Contents

Editor's Note

Over the past ten years or more, eighteenth-century scholars have taken a lively interest in the question of the "public sphere." Spurred initially by Jürgen Habermas's early *Strukturwandel der Öffentlichkeit*, especially following its translations into French (1978) and English (1989), an increasingly diverse and nuanced body of work has explored the material and discursive conditions under which, in Habermas's words, "private people came together as a public" in the early modern period. Habermas's own work, after these social-historical beginnings, led him to the more abstract philosophical texts of the 70s and 80s, significant public debates with Hans Georg Gadamer and Niklas Lühmann, and his elaboration of "communicative action" as a means of reconciling the "unfinished project" of Enlightenment with the demands of modernity. Although eighteenth-century studies has been less quick to assimilate these later developments, there would doubtless be real value in a historicized reflection on the idea that "the rational is what emerges from a free and unfettered dialogue among all concerned," in philosopher Lorenzo Simpson's succinct formulation *(Technology, Time, and the Conversations of Modernity*, 1995). There has been much fine work produced in the pursuit of a deeper understanding of public and private. But, if on the one hand the public/ private distinction offered a powerful conceptual tool, it sometimes encouraged reified dichotomies on the other. Thus it comes as a positive development that scholars are turning their attention to the multiple ways in which these categories are connected.

Such were the thoughts that came to me as I was flying from Boston to Richmond in early December, 1997, my attention divided between thoughts of the NEASECS conference I'd just left, and the pile of revised *SECC* submissions on my lap. The essays in this volume, as in previous years, were presented at different places and at different times during the academic year 1996–97, at the meetings of the American Society for Eighteenth-Century Studies and its affiliates. They were read by separate editorial readers; each was selected for its significance within its own field as well as for its potential interest to scholars in other areas. Few, if any, of the authors here would have expected to find themselves in a volume prefaced with remarks on the public/private distinction. And yet, looking over the final selection, connections suggested themselves, as did the idea of giving a single title to the entire volume and asking readers to think about the pieces in that light.

Reading these essays together replicates one of the great strengths of the national and regional meetings of ASECS, where one can walk into a room and be unexpectedly struck by the connections among, say, Italian literary academies, British chinoiserie, and prostitution (to take the first three essays in the volume) and realize their relevance to a study on Voltaire . . . In addition to their individual merit, these articles bespeak a subtle sea-change in the way that we have come to conceptualize public and private; or, to put it differently, the ways in which our professional discourse has subsumed those categories and proceeded on: here, public and private are not so much separate "spheres" as complexly connected zones. Certainly, as Peter Reill's concluding essay emphasizes, the Enlightenment was no stranger to mobile and criss-crossed categories and "systems." A number of the essays that follow look at the shared discursive formations that structure the most intimate forms of subjectivity, while others consider the affective and temporal dimensions of place and public space. The private ambitions and passions of public writers (and vice versa), the entwinement of the personal and political in advertizing, fiction, and historiography—all these suggest ways in which local and historically punctual studies can help us refine our larger theoretical paradigms. Ultimately, I would argue, such projects as these, with their careful focus on the sites and conditions of discourse, will help us situate, analyze, and redefine what we mean by such terms as "unfettered conversation" and even "rationality."

I take my leave of *SECC* with an expression of profound gratitude toward all who lent their time and talent to this project: Associate Editor Tim Erwin, the members of the Editorial Board, and the hundred-plus members of ASECS who participated in the review process this past year. Special thanks to Charles H. Hinnant, who also rotates off the board with volume 28, and whose professionalism, critical acumen, and wit have been a great source of strength. Thanks too to my graduate assistant, Catherine Constantino, for her help with the copy-editing, and to the members of the ASECS Executive Board for their ongoing support. *Bonne continuation.*

Julie Candler Hayes
University of Richmond

Studies in Eighteenth-Century Culture

VOLUME 28

The Ridiculous, the Sublime, the Modern: Aspects of Italian Culture in the Early Eighteenth Century

SUZANNE KIERNAN

In 1725, when the *Accademia degli Arcadi* was thirty-five years old, the first stone was laid on its new and permanent site in Rome for the little amphitheater that can still be seen there today in its garden setting by anyone who knows where to look for it and how to gain admission. The elaborate decorum of "pastoral" simplicity assumed by the Arcadian academicians decreed that wherever they met, that place—no matter what its temporary location—was always the "Parrhasian Grove." The Academy's foundational "Custodian," Giovanni Mario Crescimbeni, had published the account of its various sites in *L'Arcadia* (Rome: Antonio de' Rossi, 1708), in *Storia dell'Accademia dell'Arcadia* (Rome: Antonio de' Rossi, 1712), and in his *Stato della Basilica di S. Maria in Cosmedin in Roma 1719* (from the same printer-publisher). In his view, the progressive elaboration of locations reflected a regrettable loss of "prisca semplicità"—a primitive simplicity that was implicitly a guarantee of the probity of the institution. Most commonly, the theater of the Arcadians' recitations took the form of a simple grassy declivity ("un semplice fosso ritondo"), or of a "teatro verde" in a tradition described by an enthusiastic proponent of their restoration for theatrical use in the present century:

> These "topiary theaters," laid out symmetrically with evergreen plantings,
> are the main theme of the Italian—that is to say Roman, Mediterranean,

or "antique"—style of architectonic garden. "Parrhasian Groves," or small enclosed gardens drawing their inspiration as much from a geometric as from a Romantic ideal, are reminiscent of those ordered, well-groomed medieval gardens described in Boccaccio's *Decameron,* intended for small-scale performances, dramatized dialogues, dances and "conversations." The "Parrhasian Grove" in Rome on the slopes of the Janiculum. . . . is a reconstruction of a small Graeco-Roman theater, seating between 100 and 200, and framed by greenery.[1]

While it embodies, in a particularly lovely way, Arcadian aesthetic-ethical ideals that have evolved in the first two decades of the century, the creation of a permanent *Bosco Parrasio* nevertheless coincides with the "sclerosis" discernible in Arcadia as an instutition (as distinct from the literary-aesthetic movement named for it), and with its definitive co-option to pontifical politics. Following the death of Pope Clement XI in 1721, his notional "Campagne" (his metaphoric pastoral holdings) and pastoral name of "Alnano" were devolved upon the King of Portugal.[2] It was the King's subsequent endowment of the Academy, which had never had financial resources, that made possible the purchase of the steeply sloping site on the Janiculum, its landscaping and planting, and the building of an amphitheater. In his account of the Arcadia's political affiliations throughout the eighteenth century, Antonio Cipriani concludes that the King of Portugal's gift of 4,000 *scudi* can be understood only in view of the closeness obtaining from the Academy's inception between it and the Papal Court, making the Academy a suitable pawn in the regal-papal strategy of the early 1720s.[3]

At the end of 1723 the King's gift was a firm enough promise for a special meeting to be convened to select a site for the Bosco. Those available were inspected by Antonio Canevari ("Elbasco" in Arcadia, and also a member of the affiliated Fine Arts Academy in Rome, the *Accademia di San Luca*), assisted by Nicola Salvi ("Lindreno"), whose reports were duly entered in the registers of the *Fatti degli Arcadi.*[4] The money became available the following year, and the site was purchased in July 1725. An entry dated 6 August 1725 bears out Crescimbeni's cause for despondency in years gone by: there is evidently a continuing concern among members with questions of rank, since mention is made of a need to provide special seating for academicians who are also cardinals. Within a week, the Pope's Master of Ceremonies and an archbishop are on record as having visited the site to determine "how and where the Cardinals' seating ought to be constructed," ensuring it was more comfortable, more elevated and commanding a better view than the rest.[5]

An official account of the whole project subsequently appeared in 1727: Vettorio Giovardi's *Notizia del nuovo Teatro degli Arcadi aperto in Roma l'anno MDCCXXVI.* In an undistinguished piece of writing, Giovardi is at pains to observe that what Crescimbeni termed the "prisca semplicità" of the Arcadia's origins has now of necessity been surpassed:

> Modest were its beginnings, yet so rapidly did it grow in both the number and degree of its Shepherds, that it soon became one of Rome's—and indeed Italy's—chief Ornaments, and the gathering of Auditors having grown out of all measure, Necessity decreed it must abandon the cramped site where it was wont to meet, and in divers Villas in divers places make its home according to Chance and Circumstance. . . . It was ordained, however, that where the Gathering of the Arcadians had its origin, there should it have its dwelling place. The munificence of Don John V, most glorious King of Portugal, was the occasion and the means of it. . . . The commission for the fabric had long been entrusted to Elbasco, second to none among modern Architects, a man of ready Wit and original Ideas befitting such a meeting of Minds, for the most part of a Poetic cast, dedicated one and all to Letters.[6]

The ceremony of the laying of the foundation stone for the theater, set for the anniversary date of October 5, had to be postponed, Giovardi reports, on account of the "extravagant intemperance" of the weather. From the *Fatti degli Arcadi*, it seems that it rained, but four days later,

> no words could describe the joy of the goodly number of Arcadians present at the laying of the first stone by the Custodian's own hand, which all the others followed suit by casting other stones into the Foundations amid joyful acclamation and the recitation of not a few Compositions, which on this Occasion, were delivered on joyous impulse, and, in a novel manner, without an appointed order, and simply from that very place where the speaker stood.[7]

Though nothing was complete by September the following year, the *Fatti* record that the Academy "felt itself duty bound to carry out its obligations towards the King of Portugal."[8] Rather than delay "the public proofs of Gratitude that the Gathering owed to its Royal Benefactor," Giovardi relates, it was decided to inaugurate "all Academic Functions with the celebration of the Olympic Games" on 9 September, 1726.[9] Canevari's theater, he continues,

> is constructed upon an oval Plan, with seating provided in accordance with a new Fashion, since it was foreseen by Elbasco that the provision of five rows of seats, as the Commissioners had resolved, would have taken up too great a portion of the ground space, reducing the theater to a species of sunken Well; retaining the original number of levels, he devised a means of not raising the steps to too great a height, thus allowing the untrammelled enjoyment of the open Air equally to those seated, Pastoral fashion, on the

ground, which has been planted with fragrant Herbs. The aforementioned steps are thus so arranged that they constitute an admittedly small, yet delightful, Amphitheater.[10]

A *casino* (assembly rooms) designed by Canevari was opened in 1730,[11] although Giovardi's description (below) ambiguously suggests a finished building in 1726–27. It would not have been this structure that appeared to Vernon Lee as "a damp, decaying casino in the suburbs" when she "discovered" the *Bosco Parrasio* in the late 1870s;[12] Giovardi is most likely referring to rooms flanking the entry portal at the foot of the hill. No longer there, they can be seen in the engraving included in his 1727 book and accompanying the present article (see n. 16).

The Amphitheater was to be the place for the enunciation and enactment of the Arcadia's principles and ideology in *ragionamenti* and *orazioni* whose didactic (and frequently encomiastic) intentions could here be given theatrical expression. Also given clear expression is the confused utopianism implicit in their organization on principles of social equality, emerging as a dissimulated conservatism, or at best, as velleity and uncertainty. Concern with the question of the seating arrangements for those members admitted by acclamation rather than on their specific literary merits—which Crescimbeni surely need not have put such weight on in 1708, and later, had he not wished to give expression to the existence of a problem that could not be discussed in political terms—evidently persists throughout the following two decades. It surfaces finally in the neurotic attention lavished on the construction of the seating in the most permanent, highly elaborated, and expensive habitation yet—or ever—of the *arcadi*. The solution is so masterful that the untutored eye can scarcely be aware of the problem that faced this miniature *societas*: how to dissimulate all appearance of social hierarchies while keeping them intact. The solution lies in a balance between the demands of modern taste— *buon gusto* given architectural expression as "amenity," simplicity, and charm—combined with obedience to the authority of a classical model. Insofar as the Arcadian "utopian" ideal achieves a final visible and tangible architectonic representation, it can finally be seen as itself a dissimulation, as Amedeo Quondam remarks in a thorough and dispassionate analysis of Arcadia—the institution and its imaginative projection in the realm of ideas: "Arcadia is a counter-utopia; the republic of equals is a playful masking of the real society of the day."[13]

The remark arises from a consideration of Crescimbeni's 1708 "libro-manifesto," *L'Arcadia*,[14] while in fact it applies rather more closely to that other emblematic work of the "Arcadian movement" which is the *Bosco Parrasio*, twenty years later. Characteristics of Crescimbeni's text are its

Figure 1. *Bosco Parrasio*. Engraving from Vettorio Giovardi, *Notizia del nuovo Teatro degli Arcadi aperto in Roma l'anno MDCCXVI* (Rome: Antonio de' Rossi, 1727), 11.

"virtuality" and lability, despite formal properties to do with the plot and its closure. In Crescimbeni's book, Arcadian society is a "democratic Republic of Letters" on a model of a network whose boundaries are indeterminate, constituted by exchanges of ideas (concretized at nodal points in texts) among members. In the *Bosco Parrasio*, and especially in the focal point of its theater, it is the members themselves, replete with outward signs of their position in the *res publica reale*, who constitute the *Repubblica letteraria*. The difference between these two representations is not explained simply by the penuriousness of Arcadia before the gift of the regal four thousand *scudi*. Though not enunciated, poverty (as simplicity) was a founding principle of the Academy, and a proposal in the first decade of Arcadia's existence to levy a small annual fee on members was a cause of bitter dissent, clearly voiced by Gian Vincenzo Gravina at time of the "schism" that it partly occasioned in 1712. In any case, an extraordinary reluctance on the part of many members to disburse, attested in various places by the *Fatti* . . . . meant that the three *giulii* levy went largely uncollected. Giovardi relates that there was rejoicing in 1726 that, since it was now embodied in stone and marble, Arcadia henceforth would not be "soggetta agli oltraggi del tempo" (by which he may have been referring equally to the depredations of time and the outrages of the weather).[15] But Crescimbeni's unease and regret at the mounting structural elaboration and permanence of the Arcadian theaters indicates that some Arcadians at least would have seen *any* attempt to represent their social ideals in stone and marble as a travesty of them.

The Arcadian amphiteatre of the mid-1720s, then, is an historical point of arrival, and of closure. The disposition of the elements making up the "Parrhasian" complex expresses this trajectory (as process, or progress) in an extraordinarily articulate way. Extracts from Giovardi's contemporary account can be called into service at this point:[16]

> The visitor first beholds an imposing entry Portal, approached by an octagonal Stairway composed of raised kerbstones, judiciously dispos'd. Four Statues adorn the entry Pilasters, two relating to the Arcadians, and two to the World of Letters: Pan and Syrinx to the one side, and to the other, Pallas Athena and Mercury; flanking the entry are two handsome edifices taking up the entire width [of the site], affording the pastoral Gathering a retreat in the event of rain. On entering, to either side our visitor sees nascent Laurels, trees essential to the celebrated and ideal Parrhasian Grove of old, flanking the foot of a vast double staircase, it too consisting of well-placed kerbstones and adorned with a hedge of the same nascent laurels taking the place of a parapet. In the space encircled by the two arms of the staircase are two Fountains whose gushing waters commingle, representing the Tiber and the Arno, symbols of the Latin and Tuscan schools of

Poetry practised in Arcadia. Surmounting them, and facing the Portal, is a magnificent slab of white Carrara marble, sculpted with pilasters and cornice and adorned with a mask, the whole a support for the Young Apollo, sculpted likewise in white marble, holding aloft in one hand a Crown of Laurel, and indicating with the other the Inscription engraved upon the aforementioned stone, commemorating the Munificence of the Benefactor and the Gratitude of its recipients.[17]

Terminating this terrace is an ample Grotto composed of towering blocks of Tufa which, with the Water gushing amid the stones and grasses, makes for an Object arousing at once horror and delight; within this lies a noble Statue pouring waters from an Urn, representing [the river god] Alpheus, symbol of that Greek Poetry believed to be the source of all Poetry. On either side of the Grotto two more encircling flights of steps rise, quite different, and taking an opposite direction from the former, meeting at the top to form a capacious Assembly-place from which, leaning on an imposing balustrade surmounting and surrounding the aforementioned Grotto, the visitor takes in the greater part of Rome and not a little of the surrounding Countryside. . . . This Assembly-place allows for pleasant diversion before passing into the contiguous Theater, and is moreover required to take the overflow in the event of a crowd, since the Performers' voices may be heard equally from here, as the most recent, and crowded, Gathering has prov'd.[18]

Entrance to the Theater is by means of two openings giving off the aforementioned Assembly-place, containing the seating for those Shepherds waiting to recite their Orations and Eclogues, the remainder being seated, as is the Custom among the Arcadians, scattered at random among the audience. Facing the Entrance, and raised by four steps, is the bench, adorned with its fine solid back-rest, intended for Their Eminences the Cardinals. Flanking this are two further openings leading to the imposing entry Portal of the sumptuous Edifice behind the Theater, constituting a point of arrival for the entire place, and crowning the noble Prospect[.][19]

What Giovardi's pedestrian account fails to make clear is that the landscaping of the *Bosco* site takes the form of a double baroque staircase, notably close in design to the "vasta scenografia" of Francesco de Sanctis' well-known stairway linking the Piazza di Spagna and the Church of the Trinità de' Monti.[20] The "Spanish Steps" were under construction in those very years in which the *Bosco Parrasio* was laid out, their first stone being laid on 25 November 1723 and the official opening taking place in 1725.[21] Just as the rustic "ripiani" that are a prelude to the Arcadia's neoclassical Amphitheater are scenographic in a way which will be discussed below, so the larger-scale public equivalents on the *Scalinata di Spagna* were—and remain—theaters

Figure 2. Francesco di Sanctis, *Scalinata di Spagna* [Spanish Steps], 1725 (ground plan). Courtesy of the Fine Arts Department of the University of Sydney.

of social life. The contemporary Roman diarist Francesco Valesio relates in the early 1730s that they were known as "teatro o anfiteatro" and "teatrino o anfiteatrino" respectively, where public dances sometimes took place by moonlight.[22]

The scenographic quality of the successful design for the approach to the church of the Trinità de' Monti presents some interesting contradictions in a time when theater itself—especially public theater—was subject to rigid control and censorship. The curious document that is Lione Pascoli's *Testamento politico* bears witness to many aspects of social experience in Rome in the 1720s,[23] and gives an insight into the beginnings of the economic depression characterizing the next decade.[24] Pascoli voices misgivings over the consumption of those dangerously stimulating luxury beverages tea, coffee, and chocolate ("which I strongly suspect may even be the cause of the sudden deaths that have become so frequent in these days in Rome among Persons of civil condition"),[25] and over the scandalously high cost of snow. He touches, too, upon legislation affecting the contemporary theater:

> Would it be accounted a good thing if the inhabitants of our State, and of Rome its Capital (the former being subject to, and the latter being outside the jurisdiction of the Ruler of the Church, while at the same time being his Seat) should be organized in accordance with a Monastic or Religious rule, or some quite different system of Conduct from that obtaining among men in other places in the civilized World? Those who have no religious Vocation, while not being in a position to have any other manner of Education, must yet be permitted in all good faith to seek out those same honest and licit Amusements available to others elsewhere in the Catholic World. I do not say that Theaters should remain open for the greater part of the Year, as is the case with our Neighbours on the other side of the Alps, for public Balls, and general merrymaking, nor that Masquerades ought now be permitted as they are in other Places, for that assuredly would never be accounted a good thing. In my Opinion, the last 10 days of Carnival are sufficient for such; nevertheless, the Theaters might properly be kept open from the beginning of October until the beginning of Advent, and from the end of the latter until the beginning of Lent; allowing women, too, to take part in performances, in conformity with the practice elsewhere; for it is well known that they do not at all give rise to that Scandal nor cause the Harm, the fear of which induced the Pontiff to prohibit it . . . . Who can fail to see, therefore, how essential to Rome and to the State are the Theaters and Carnival? Who can deny the Detriment, the Damage and the Prejudice abounding while such remain under prohibition? And who, in setting his mind to it, can fail to find [such prohibition] inscrutable?[26]

But the appeal to the church commissioners of the "theatricality" of the Spanish Steps had nothing to do with the general appeal of theater in Rome. Rather, the fact that the whole considerable scene could be taken in at a single glance was an aid to social control of their immediate precinct, in which, under the conditions preceding the steps' construction, they reported being able to witness "gross obscenities on the very steps of the Church" in broad daylight.[27] Before the *Scalinata* was built, there was no architectonic disposition at all of the site: illustrations post-dating Bernini's *barchetta* fountain, and pre-dating the Steps, show a great avenue of elms.[28]

Despite a similarity of ground plan between the *Scalinata di Spagna* and the *Bosco Parrasio*, so close as to have given rise to a "vulgar" tradition that both were by the same architect,[29] the two could not be more dissimilar in intention. This is not simply a matter of their respective origins. Though an ecclesiastical commission, the Steps are essentially secular in spirit: from the bottom, the focus is themselves rather than the church at the top, and from the top, they move in a powerful tidal motion into the city. The essential difference is rather that the "Parrhasian Grove" *cannot* be taken in at a glance; the Amphitheater at the top as a point of arrival cannot be seen from the bottom: more importantly, cannot be *fore*seen. The sinuous ascending passage has a strong lateral pull exerted upon it, especially in that tract immediately preceding the entry to the theater. The layout is conducive to distraction, divagation, diversion. The *Bosco* is the very place of that "civil conversation" by which the eighteenth-century culture liked to define itself. Where the grand late-Baroque *Scalinata* is public and rhetorical and strongly unified, the *Bosco* is intimate, conversational, and must be experienced as pleasurably fragmented. Its perfect symmetry and the precise disposition of its permanent architectonic elements are softened and confused with the vegetation, which includes "lofty" trees provided for in the original design (those described by Giovardi as "nascenti" in 1726–27). Everything here is calculated to *prevent* a unified view and a consistent aesthetic experience, while inducing curiosity as to the outcome and ensuring pleasure and "amenity" on the way. With its playful contradictions and its resort to "quotation" in an essentially nostalgic vein of irrecoverable classical antecedents, there seems to be no way to describe the *Bosco Parrasio* other than as a *rococò* work. The fact that it is completed ("crowned") by a neoclassical theater by way of solution seems a perfect expression of the tensions in "Arcadian" culture discernible in the earlier ("proto-*rococò*") literary work by Giovanni Mario Crescimbeni, *L'Arcadia*.

In the plastic arts, Italian *rococò* is a special case. Playful *rocaille* decoration never seemed to "take" in Italy with the aeriness of its French original, if one may judge by the Palazzo Doria Pamphilj in the center of Rome, as well as a number of Venetian examples dating from what is usually considered the high season of Italian *rococò* in the mid-century. Accretion and addition of decorative elements is the general guiding principle in Italian *rococò*, rather than suggestion and subtraction, elision and allusion. This is particularly noticeable in the case of interiors. As an early apostle of *rococò* in Italy (though without the benefit of the term),[30] Pier Jacopo Martello observes in 1718 that Italian architects are hopelessly inept when it comes to interiors, building houses with rooms that are more like roofed-over town squares ("coperte piazze") than residences. His character, a "Parisian Italian," explains how differently these things are ordered in France:

> All Citizens, including those of the Merchant class, have a place set aside where they eat, another where they receive (and for the most part they receive in the quarters where they sleep), and the Cabinet where they write. In this way, several household members and their children may be decently and comfortably accommodated in a House of average size, since . . . the internal walls are made out of wood and fashioned as folding doors, creating different Apartments according to need, as you will have remarked even from your brief sojourn among that Nation; and these Panels are either resplendent with a coat of brilliant coloured lacquer, or are covered with painted fabric in the guise of Tapestries, and copiously adorned with Mirrors; and on the very day in which the Builder puts the finishing touches to his Work, on that same day the Owner is at liberty to move in and enjoy it, without cause to fear for his Health, a circumstance certainly not obtaining in Rome nor, for that matter, in the rest of Italy, where he must needs leave his new House open to the winds and the sun for years on end, and then fumigate the rooms, and have great fires blazing the grates, and then consult his doctors, before at long last he can take up residence (the Novelty, and the Pleasure it might have afforded, having quite worn off), blaming hence forth every Headache or Cough he might be so unfortunate to suffer, whatever its cause, on the building: with the result that, even when no such thing afflicts our state of Health, the mere Thought that we might be so afflicted, makes us fancy we have Complaints that in fact we do not have at all.[31]

The architectural expression of interiority has been externalized in the Piazza S. Ignazio, realized in 1727–28 by Raguzzini, the architect championed in Rome by Pope Benedict XIII Orsini from the beginning of his reign in the early 1720s, when the first plans for the *Bosco* were being discussed. As the "*rococò* Pope" he did not always have the approval of those in the circle of the former "Arcadian Pope." Within six years of Clement XI's death (in 1721, after a twenty-one-year reign), Raguzzini had been the ruin of Rome with his architecture,[32] according to an acidulous caption to a caricature of the architect by Pier Leone Ghezzi (former Secretary of the Accademia di S. Luca, and an *arcade*). The austere Francesco Milizia, much later in the century, is quoted as saying that, thanks to Raguzzini, Piazza S. Ignazio was quite "debased by those ridiculous houses resembling chests-of-drawers."[33] Raguzzini's design, taking in the late-*Seicento* church façade by Algardi, is a signal instance after the *Scalinata di Spagna* of architectural scenography, and an exposition *par excellence* of an interpenetration of public and private space to create a theater for "civil conversation."

In just such a way, the *Bosco Parrasio* presents the double aspect of a bosky salon, its architectonic solidity and clarity of form subject to the transformations of nature. Given the site, the project might have been conceived as a grandiose one, in thrall so to speak to the imposing view of St. Peters and the greater part of Rome that is to be had from the topmost point (where the Cardinals were specially seated). Instead, the ideal route through the grove is one travelled with the wayfarer's back to the grand prospect of Imperial and Papal Rome, with no imperative to reach the neoclassical summit, offering no vistas exceeding a scale calculated to conform to the personal and the intimate.

In his Dialogue on style, Martello had lightly proselytized in favor of a taste in conformity with what would come to be regarded as Enlightenment imperatives: utility, pleasure, and rationality. Even more than by a dining-room wall-fountain that squirts water into the diners' glasses, his Frenchified Italian is captivated by the modern Gallic man-of-letters' study:

> But what think you of these little Cabinets, my dear Martello? Can the human mind conceive of any lovelier and more jocund Thing than a study in the French style? Miniatures, pottery, porcelain, with mirrors all about to multiply these charming, ordered small *objets*: all therein conspiring to luxury and delight. And those little book-cases, so cunningly recessed and arranged with their gilded and painted shelves all tricked out from one side to the other with little furbelows [*falpalà*] which at once protect the Books from dust while they afford a pleasing unity to the Eye. The spacious table with its *escritoire*, its binding-press, sealing-wax, paper and pens, all these in Order, without clutter, suggestively invite to the gentle recreation of Study, while the sun in the daylight hours, and at night, the light from crystal lamp, are centuplicated by as many mirrors above, beside, below, cunningly recessed and variously configured, all to dazzling Effect. What man is there so rude in temperament as could not find a place such as this—so amenable, untrammelled and undisturbed—conducive to sweet Thought?[34]

The attention to detail in the matter of the *falpalà* is significant, for it is at such points that the utilitarian and the aesthetic intersect in "Arcadian" taste, though they can manage to give rise to a paradigmatic form only in the realm of the trivial. Determining factors in the choice of the site for the Bosco were that it should have healthy air ("aria sana," on which some Arcadian medical experts were consulted) and ample parking nearby.[35] Like the "gabinetto franzese," the *Bosco Parrasio* is on a scale conducive to withdrawal, to recreation, to privacy—for which last no word was available to Martello in Italian, any more than he could have found one for *falpalà*. Enlarging the scale, the *Bosco* is the scene of intersubjectivity in the world conceived *sub specie pastoralis*, providing for the perfect accommodation of the personal and social, the social and the civic, this last looming in all its concrete ineluctability at the back of the traveller through the Parrhasian Grove.

The *Bosco Parrasio* must surely be recognized as the master-work and definitive manifesto of "Arcadia." Significantly, its first stone was ceremoniously laid in the year of the publication of Giambattista Vico's *Scienza nuova*: 1725. The recognition that it belongs in the same historical conspectus as the one arguably indispensable and truly great book produced in early eighteenth-century Italy requires some effort, and it may seem that the present study, beginning with a consideration of "Arcadia" to arrive at Vico, is a perverse attempt to accommodate the sublime to the ridiculous (given that it involves an exercise in taking "Arcadia" seriously and, in an earlier chapter of the work-in-progress from which this essay is extracted, proposes Vico as a parodist). As canonical space, the *Bosco* seems the complete obverse of the *Scienza nuova*'s limitless vistas for the play of the historical imagination. Where Vico conceives the social world *sub specie civili*, the *Bosco* is an image of the social world *sub specie pastorali*, at the same time representing a field of aesthetic experience. Its dynamics provoke curiosity, distraction, isolation of detail, and superficiality (as attention to surface), all of which set up a conflict with its symmetrical classicizing plan. It is from just such conflict, for which the imagination fails to find a solution while refusing to experience that failure as crisis, that the spirit of *rococò* derives, expressed in lacunae, the broken frame and the wistfully etiolated line. The *Bosco*'s layout conforms to the plot of Crescimbeni's romance *Arcadia*, which is a series of deferrals of short-term goals *en route* to a single long-term one. For it is precisely the propensity of Crescimbeni's group of women to spend time in apparently idle social gatherings ("oziose adunanze" of the kind that Crescimbeni's severe critic, Gravina, scorned), to "read" the surface of the culture of their day as if it were a mere "libro di diporto," to be literally sidetracked, that guides them through, and, finally, takes them to the heart of that culture. Crescimbeni's book is a "manifesto" in more than the way recognized by the present-day critic Amedeo Quondam. In its compilation of a map of contemporary knowledge as the result of the play of a diffuse attention, and as an exposition in the mode of curiosity as a means to knowledge, it is an early manifesto of the experience of modernity. In his inconclusive and provocative essay "The Work of Art in the Age of Mechanical Reproduction," Walter Benjamin has adduced the sports-spectator's vicarious "expertise," or the "distracted attention" of the cinema-goer as types of an essentially modern aesthetic experience.[36] Earlier, insisting that "the mainspring of his genius is curiosity," Baudelaire had chosen to see in a decidedly minor illustrator, Constantin Guys, the foremost painter of modern mid-nineteenth-century life in all its panoramic triviality. The particular value in Baudelaire's essay "The Painter of Modern Life" consists in its suggestion that works that come into being as "occasional," "minor"—terms applying by general agreement to all of Crescimbeni's output—may be witnesses to the profoundest truths about their time. In that undeniably "minor" and "occasional" work, *L'Arcadia*, it is the glancing attention to manners and dress, the conversational exchange of conceptual flotsam, diversions, the asides and parentheses which yet carry major theses, that all bear the burden of the work's quite self-conscious intention to represent "modernity" in that very sense that Baudelaire undertook to explain when he wrote that "by 'modernity' I mean the ephemeral, the fugitive, the contingent, the half of art whose other half is the eternal and the immutable."[37]

A contemporary *fable à clef*, and at the same time a Utopian fiction, Crescimbeni's book is a literary sport, without identifiable antecedents and without issue. Its very eclecticism says a great deal about the impossibly Utopian political and social ideals that the Arcadia sought to represent. It completes, in 1708, a thesis on poetry and taste begun in *La bellezza della volgar poesia* of 1700, while the new Dialogue in the 1712 edition of *La bellezza . . .* sets the seal on it (with the endorsement of Pier Jacopo Martello, clearly one of the most interesting writers of that "proto-Enlightenment" generation, as one of the *dramatis personae*).[38] A novel aspect of *L'Arcadia*, however, consists in its steps towards a philosophic feminism as a propaedeutics to a political feminism, as it extends the thesis on taste to take in the question of knowledge and its relation to power. Crescimbeni's "feminine curiosity" *(curiosità muliebre)*, this trivial impulse to small-scale knowledge, contemned by "Ancients" and "Moderns"—or "Aristotelians" and "Cartesians", or Thomists and Calvinists—alike, is made analogous to the grander impulse of the mind to accede to wisdom.

Alone among Crescimbeni's contemporaries, it is Vico who places "curiosity," seen as both "primitive" and fundamental, in a continuum with the highest wisdom:

> Humankind, ignorant of the Causes of things, while every extraordinary event in Nature arouses its sense of Wonder, is by its natural curiosity naturally impelled to desire to know the Meaning of such things.[39]

It is nothing less than the root cause of human history under its double aspect of the history of the Chosen People and of the "nazioni gentili" since religions, the precondition of civilization, have their roots in "that desire, innate in all Men, which is to have eternal Life . . . [which makes them] curious as to the future. This curiosity, which Nature cannot appease, since it regards a thing belonging to the infinite and eternal Mind of God, is the root cause of the Fall of the two Branches of the human Kind."[40]

The point of coincidence of the "ridiculous" Crescimbeni and the "sublime" Vico in the matter of the cognitive status of curiosity is the place where both can be located in relation to their time and to each other—one usually considered too lofty, the other too puny, to figure in a coherent cultural history. Often styled a "reactionary," Vico is a "modern" in his recognition of the fragmentary and discontinuous nature of contemporary knowledge *circa* 1700. In *De nostri temporis studiorum ratione*, in 1708 (the same year as Crescimbeni's *Arcadia*), his perception of this as the precondition of a crisis in contemporary knowledge seems a "post-modern" moment in modernity at its inception. His resort to the "sublime" in the *Scienza nuova* comes at points where epistemology fails, in striking conformity with an account of twentieth-century "modern sublime" offered under the rubric "Some Answers to the Question: 'What is Postmodernism?'":

> It takes place . . . when the imagination fails to present an object which might . . . match a concept. We have an Idea . . . but [not] the capacity to show an example of it . . . . Those are Ideas of which no presentation is possible. Therefore, they impart no knowledge about reality (experience); they also prevent the free union of the faculties which gives rise to the sentiment of the beautiful; and they prevent the formation and the stabilization of taste. They can be said to be unpresentable.[41]

Everything that can be postulated about an aesthetics and an epistemology deriving from "Arcadia" stops well short of the threshold of the "sublime." The kind of thrilling bafflement Vico invokes is put to the test in "Arcadia" by a "stabilized taste" whose foundation is the movement's very purpose; the kinds of expression typically sought by seventeenth-century "baroque" artists to represent "wonder" and the "sublime" are found to be "barbaric" or "depraved" or otherwise offensive to *buon gusto*. The art of *rococò*, to which "Arcadian" aesthetics tends, is an art of the anti-sublime, in which the imagination retires gracefully in the face of an incommensurability of Idea to representational capacity.

And yet, a curious failure to define *buon gusto* is surely symptomatic of conditions finally *un*favourable to any "stabilization" of taste. Though "anti-sublime," *rococò* is no less a negation of the rational normative view, expressed by the asymmetry, the interrupted line, and the elliptical gesture that are among its characteristic signs. These gaps are the correlatives, on an intimate scale and superficial plane, of Vico's unimaginable spaces filled with endless time. The resort to the intimate perspective, to ephemera, detail, and even to "good taste" with all its reductive connotations, is a response to the mind's inadequacy to encompass its own works (as knowledge accumulated in time). This—to appropriate the attractively vatic term—is the unmistakably modern experience of "incommensurability." Vico's response is twofold: he testifies to it, in passages of grandiose prose-poetry, and then finds a way to overcome it by "discovering" in the *etym* a measure enabling the mind to see itself reflected back from the awful endless vistas of the past *(le sterminate antichità)*.

Elaborated on other grounds, Crescimbeni's solution reveals no less an awareness of the critical momentum of the growth of knowledge. Such is the rate of growth in these years, with its imperative of increased consumption, that the "digest" becomes a necessity: several periodicals undertaking this task begin publication in Venice in the 1720s.[42] The logically absurd end to the "digestive" process made necessary by the proliferation of print is the visionary prospect of the "one-book man"—an idea emanating from the nation of the *falpalà*, translated into Italian and published in Padua in 1718 as

The One-book Man,

    OR:

an entire Library in one Small Book devis'd expressly for those Persons of Wit who yet lack Time, Opportunity, even a Life sufficiently long to read the thousands of Authors who have written to date on the State of the Nations of the World, on the chief Religions, on the Progress of the Sciences and the liberal Arts, and who are Concern'd not to appear Ignorant in civil Conversation; all of which they will find within, in Summary form, from the Beginning of the World until the Year of Our Lord 1715. [43]

If superficial knowledge obtained in the mode of curiosity is the order of the day, this is because knowledge in the present has very much more "surface" than ever before, and it falls to Crescimbeni properly to take account of this operative factor in modernity. To a far greater extent than the undeniably more significant Vico, he recognizes, in *L'Arcadia*, that the growth of contemporary knowledge is accompanied by a growth in the number of *knowers*, prophetically represented by his group of scheming women. Dissembling their true objective, which is to enter into possession of this knowledge, they thus act politically to achieve it. In two remarkable episodes of his inexplicably neglected fable of cultural change, Crescimbeni shows that a proliferating cultural production may be kept to "commensurable" proportions—through consumption. The women looking through the keyhole take in just as much of the vast culture on the other side as is within their power from their limited view from the threshold. It is a post-Enlightenment truism that cultural liberation and a culture of consumption have proceeded *pari passu*. And so it is that Crescimbeni is not merely ingenious but perhaps wiser than he knew when, in the scene of the "banquet of wisdom" declined to suitably modern proportions in a fashionable *veglia*, he shows poetry—which for the *Arcadi* was metonymous with culture at large—being consumed as *Conforto* (comfits). No less significantly, the recipe for this English dish is supplied in *L'Arcadia*—by Lorenzo Magalotti (1637–1712), who both prepares and serves it to a group of literary ladies, and who evidently had collected it while abroad in the service of the grand-duke of Tuscany in the latter years of the seventeenth century.

Crescimbeni's inclusion of women in the "Republic of Letters" is both a recognition of the fact of their presence in its economy of consumption and—increasingly—production of culture, and is a proto-feminist *prise de position* rare in its time. Different though their works might be in value, purpose and stature (not to mention reputation), Crescimbeni and Vico both recognize that what they have to deal with is modernity, and that it is problematic (as we like to say now), though only Crescimbeni gives full weight to the trivial and contingent through which it is revealed. If these intentions are acknowledged for a writer who has never been allowed any seriousness of purpose, and if they are acknowledged as significant in the generically "Arcadian" culture of the Italian eighteenth century, then Arcadia as a movement does represent a change in cultural outlook. And this despite its inability to realize its Utopian charter as a "democratic Republic of Letters," and the velleities and equivocations revealed by a persistent use of old forms—like the sixteenth-century imitation of the Petrarchan sonnet—for content that was new.

N O T E S

Translations into English of quoted passages are the author's, except as indicated otherwise.

1. "I 'Teatri di Verdure,' costruiti simmetricamente con piante sempreverdi, sono il soggetto principale del Giardino Architettonico all'Italiana—cioè romano, mediterraneo, detto di 'stile antico'. . . . I Boschi Parrasi, piccoli giardini conchiusi,

ispirati tanto all'ideale geometrico, quanto a quello romantico, ricordano i giardini ordinati, pettinatissimi, medioevali, descritti dal Decamerone e destinati ad accogliere spettacolini, dialoghi, danze, conversazioni. Il Bosco Parrasio romano, alle falde del Gianicolo. . ., è la ricostruzione d'un teatrino greco-romano, per 100 o 200 posti, nel quadro di verdura[.]" Anton Giulio Bragaglia, "Teatri all'aperto," *Capitolum* 31 (1956): 230–36; quotation at 232.

2. Vettorio Giovardi, *Notizia del nuovo Teatro degli Arcadi aperto in Roma l'anno MDCCXVI* (Rome: Antonio de' Rossi, 1727), 11.

3. Antonio Cipriani, "Contributo per una storia politica dell'Arcadia settecentesca," in Arcadia: Accademia Letteraria Italiana: *Attie Memorie* , 3rd ser., 5: 1–2 (1971), 101–66; quotation at 112.

4. Extracts from volume 4 of the *Fatti degli Arcadi* relating to the purchase of the site for the Bosco Parrasio and to the discussions preceding its opening have been conveniently included by Cesare D'Onofrio in his *Storie Romane tra Cristina di Svezia, piazza del Popolo e l'Accademia d'Arcadia: Roma val bene un'abiura* (Rome: Palombi, 1976), 285–90. References are to this source.

5. "Avendo Elbasco nostro architetto esibita in Collegio l'intenzione, o prospetto del Teatro, e altri ornamenti che pensa fare del sito già compro, se vogliono approvarla e ordinarne l'effettuazione. Fu lodata; e furono deputati Semiro [Antonio de Felici] e Filacidio [Francesco Lorenzini], perché stabilissero il posto, dove e come dovesse fabbricarsi il sedile per li SS.ri Cardinali, e dissero che andava fabbricato al piano del Teatro in faccia al prospetto della Città, elevato almeno per due scalini, colla sua spalliera; alzato degli altri ordini de' sedili, per un tratto considerabile" (D'Onofrio, 286).

6. "Umili furono i suoi principi, ma crebbe cosí presto e di numero, e di qualità i Pastori, che divenne uno dei principali ornamenti di Roma anzi d'Italia, ed essendo oramai immenso il concorso degli Uditori, fu duopo abbandonare l'angusto sito, ove a principio solevansi ragunare, e in altre Ville d'uno in un'altro Colle secondo i vari accidenti, e le varie fortune . . . . Ma egli era prefisso, che ove la Ragunanza degli Arcadi aveva avuto il suo principio, avesse il suo stabilimento. La munificenza di D. GIOVANNI V gloriosissimo Re di Portogallo ne diede l'occasione, ed il modo . . . . Fu commessa la cura della Fabbrica ad Elbasco Arcade già da gran tempo, e tra gli Architetti moderni a niuno certo inferiore, Uomo di pronto spirito, d'Idee pellegrine, e qual conveniasi ad una unione di ingegni per la maggior parte Poetici, e tutti letterarj" (Giovardi, 10–11).

7. ". . . indicibile fu il giubilo, che dagli Arcadi tutti in buon numero presenti fu provato nel getto della detta prima pietra fatto di sua mano dal Custode, ed imitato da tutti gli altri col getto d'altre pietre ne' Fondamenti in mezzo alle fauste acclamazioni, ed alla recita di non pochi Componimenti, che in tale occasione per impulso d'allegrezza furono cosí in piedi, e alla rinfusa con nuovo costume recitati" (Giovardi, 12).

8. ". . . si stimò in obbligo la Ragunanza . . . di compire a suoi doveri verso la Maestà del Re di Portogallo" (cited by D'Onofrio, 288).

9. ". . . si proseguí in tanto la Fabbrica, e benchè non del tutto ridotta al suo termine, pure per non più ritardare quegli attestati di giubilo, e di gratitudine, che la

Ragunanza doveva al suo Regio Benefattore fu destinato, che a i nove dello scorso mese di Settembre si aprisse il nuovo Teatro, e si desse principio alle Funzioni Accademiche, conforme fu fatto, celebrandovisi i Giuochi Olimpici" (Giovardi, 16–17).

10. "È il Teatro composto di forma Ovata, ed ha i sedili in nuova foggia costrutti, poiché vedendosi da Elbasco, che per innalzare cinque ordini di sedili, come da i Deputati era stato risoluto, sarebbe venuto a restare il piano del detto Teatro troppo occupato, ed a maniera di Pozzo; serbando egli il numero delle dette gradinate trovò la maniera di non alzare soverchiamente i gradini, e far godere liberamente dell'aria anco a quelli, che nel suddetto piano di odorifere erbe ripieno, e coltivato si fossero posti (come spesso succede) Pastoralmente a sedere. Sono dunque i detti gradini talmente collocati, che ci rappresentano la vera forma d'un piccolo sí, ma delizioso Anfiteatro" (Giovardi, 17).

11. Gustavo Brigante Colonna, "Il Bosco Parrasio," *Capitolum* 11 (1938): 553–60; quotation at 553.

12. Vernon Lee [Violet Paget], *Studies of the Eighteenth Century in Italy*, (1880; reprint, New York: Da Capo Press, 1978), 18. According to an account in the Philadelphia *Evening Telegraph* of 14 March, 1879 ("Miss Anne Brewster's letter: Representatives of the Catholic journals congratulate the Pope; the Pope and Arcadian; the Society of Arcadia and its origin [etc.]", 3–4) the classicizing reception rooms that are presently on the site of the Bosco are entirely a work of the mid-nineteenth century, designed in 1836 by an architect named Azzurri. The state of the Bosco Parrasio at the time of the bicentenary of Arcadia in 1890 presented a dismal picture ("fosco quadro") to bourgeois Roman eyes:

"By degrees ivy wrapped the trees, brambles choked the avenues, and the weather took its toll on the building. In this sorry state the grove became a den of vice and crime, and thieves and prostitutes made it their meeting-place . . . The bannisters were stolen from the inside stairs, likewise the water-pipes and the flag-stones from the villa; even a prostitute's appointment book was found in the grass that had now become a lascivious bed for lubricious *amours*," wrote Francesco Barberi in the opening of "Arcadia inquieta" in *Strenna dei Romanisti* 14 (1953): 1–8.

13. "Quella dell'Arcadia è una contro-utopia: la repubblica di eguali è un travestimento giocoso della società reale"; Amedeo Quondam, "Gioco e società letteraria nell'*Arcadia* del Crescimbeni", in Arcadia: Accademia Letteraria Italiana: *Atti e Memorie*, 3rd ser. 6 (1975–76): 165–95; quotation 191.

14. G[iovanni] M[ario] Crescimbeni, *L'Arcadia* (Rome: Antonio de' Rossi, 1708).

15. Giovardi, 16.

16. Pictorial material for the *Bosco Parrasio* from published sources is not plentiful. The engraving of Canevari's design for the entire site included in Giovardi's book is therefore particularly valuable. The reproduction accompanying this essay is taken from the enlarged edition of Crescimbeni's *Storia dell' Accademia degli Arcadi* (1712), reprinted along with later material, including extracts from Giovardi, in 1804 (London: T. Beckett of Pall-Mall), where it appears opposite page 83. No provenance is given for the illustration in Vernon Lee's book (2nd ed.) last century; she notes it has been "chosen by Dr Guido Biagi, of the Laurentian Library, Florence." The *Arcadia* entry in the *Enciclopedia Italiana* is accompanied by a photo-

graph of the amphitheatre and a view of the *Bosco*, neither seen to much purpose. In "Gli sviluppi del giardino classico," Chapter 6 of his work on gardens (Rome: Edizioni dell'Ateneo, 1967), Francesco Fariello gives a ground plan and section on p. 127. In "Il 'gregge pecoraio', ovvero: l'Accademia d'Arcadia", 261–90 in his *Storie Romane . . .* , Cesare D'Onofrio reproduces some contemporary sketches of earlier realizations of the Bosco, as well as the elevation given in Giovardi's 1727 book. There are no recent studies of any account; Daniela Predieri's short 1990 monograph, the most recent known to the present writer, is disappointing.

17. "Si vede a principio un Maestoso Portone, a cui si ascende per una gradinata ottangolare di rilevati, e ben disposti Cordoni. Sopra i Pilastri del quale rendono un vago adornamento, quattro Statue, due attenenti allo stato degli Arcadi, e due a quello de' Letterati, mirandosi da una parte Pan, e Siringa, dall'altra Pallade, e Mercurio, ed accanto al detto Portone occupano da ambo i lati tutta la larghezza della facciata, due vaghi Edifizj, che al di dentro devono avere i loro ingressi, ed apprestare un comodo ricetto alla gente adunata in caso di pioggia. Appena entrati, a destra, e a sinistra si scorgono i nascenti Lauri, Alberi necessarj a formare il celebre, e già ideale Bosco Parrasio; accanto a questi si partono due vaste gradinate distinte parimente a cordoni, ed ornate invece di sponda d'una vaga spalliera del medesimo sempre verdeggiante lauro. Nella centina che fanno le dette gradinate si apre un vasto ripiano, dove due fonti, che scaturiscono delle Urne del Tevere, e dell'Arno, simboli della Latina, e Toscana Poesia, che si professano in Arcadia, vanno a confondere le loro acque. Sopra di esse nel prospetto, che riguarda il Portone si alza una magnifica Lapida di Marmo bianco carrarese di basi, Pilastri, Cornice, e Maschera vagamente adorna, e tutta centinata, sovra la quale posa il Giovine Apollo, che scolpito ancor esso in bianco marmo sostiene con una mano una Corona di Alloro, e coll'altra indica l'Iscrizione, che a perpetua memoria contesta ivi nella sottoposta già descritta Lapida la Munificenza del Benefattore, e la gratitudine dei Beneficati[.]" (Giovardi, 18–19).

18. "Nel terminare del detto ripiano si vede un' ampia Grotta composta di smisurati Tufi, che colle acque grondanti fra i sassi, e fra l'erbe rende un' orrido insieme, e delizioso oggetto, e dentro a questa si vede giacere, e diffonder l'acque dalla sua Urna effigiato in nobile Statua il celebratissimo Alfeo Simbolo della Greca Poesia, e creduto principio delle altre maniere di poetare. Di quà, e di là dalla Grotta si alzano due altre gradinate a cordoni di centina in tutto diversa, e contraria alle prime, che nella sommità si uniscono, e formano una capace Platea, d'onde appoggiandosi ad una maestosa Ringhiera, che s' alza in giro sopra l'accennata Grotta, si vede perfettamente la maggior parte di Roma, e gran parte della vicina Campagna. . . . La suddetta Platea serve per dare un comodo trattenimento prima di passare nel contiguo Teatro, ed è un necessario sfogo in caso di troppa moltitudine di popolo, potendosi ancor da essa ascoltare le voci de' Recitanti, come nell' ultima numerosissima Adunanza vedemmo accadere" (Giovardi, 33).

19. "Si entra nel Teatro per due aperture, che hanno l'ingresso dalla sopraccennata Platea, e racchiudono in mezzo il sedile per li Pastori. che sono destinati a recitare le Orazioni, e le Egloghe, sedendo gli altri, come è costume degli Arcadi sparsi, e alla

rinfusa fra gl' uditori. Incontro a questo resta elevato sovra a quattro gradini un' ampio, e ben distinto sedile adorno di una soda, e vaga spalliera, destinato per gli Eminentissimi Cardinali. Accanto ad esso due altre aperture si scorgono, che guidano alla magnifica Porta del sontuoso edifizio, che restando dietro al Teatro viene a formare un come termine di tutto il luogo, e dà compimento alla nobil veduta [....] (Giovardi, 34).

20. D'Onofrio writes of the use of the steeply raked site of the Bosco Parrasio that "recurring to a particular typology of Roman steps starting with Torriani's for [the Church of] Sts Domenico & Sisto, developed subsequently in a series of late-seventeenth-century proposals for the slope of the Pincio beneath Trinità de Monti, and given an almost archetypal formulation in the flight of steps actually built by [architect Alessandro] Specchi at Porto di Ripetta, which then became de Sanctis' starting-point for the vast stage-set that is the present stairway to the Trinità de' Monti —Canevari, influenced above all by this last example, [the "Spanish Steps"], laid out the Janiculum slope in three super-imposed planes[.]" (*Storie Romane,* 273) D'Onofrio also writes on the *Scalinata di Spagna* in *Scalinate di Roma* (Rome: A. Studerini, 1973). Vincenzo Golzio's compilation of notes from the eighteenth-century *Diario* of Francesco Valesio (see n. 3) remains useful for an insight into contemporary responses to the *rococò* style, even after the appearance of the two-volume edition of 1978 (see n. 22 below). A tradition that de Sanctis followed a hastily-done sketch by Filippo Juvarra is not borne out by the documentation sifted by Pio Pecchiai in "La grande Scalinata di Piazza di Spagna," in *L'Urbe* 17–18 (1939): 9–24; Pecchiai nevertheless finds the tradition "verosimile," in that no other work is known by de Sanctis, who was evidently a civil engineer working mainly in repairs and restoration. Mario Rotili, describing him as an "agrimensore" (73), ascribes the façade of the Church of the Trinità dei Pellegrini to de Sanctis in his *Filippo Raguzzini e il rococò romano* (Rome: Palombi, 1951), 29. When part of the retaining wall of the *Scalinata* fell down on 26 September 1728, among the distinguished architects called upon to advise on repairs was a "cav. architetto Filippo Rauzino [*sic*]," of whom Pecchiai observes that "non ci è nota alcuna opera architettonica di fama" (20). This seems a curious remark, since Filippo Raguzzini was in Rome at that time, and if he did not actually supervise the repairs to the Spanish Steps, he was certainly an interested party in the matter.

21. Pecchiai, 13; 15.

22. Francesco Valesio, cited by Pecchiai, 21; see also Valesio's *Diario di Roma (1700–1742),* ed. G. Scano, 2 vols. (Milan: Longanesi, 1978).

23. Lione Pascoli, *Testamento politico d'un Accademico Fiorentino in cui con nuovi, e ben fondati principj si fanno varj, e diversi progetti per istabilire un ben regolato commerzio nello Stato della Chiesa e per aumentare notabilmente le rendite della Camera* (Cologne: Egmond, 1733). Though the *Testamento politico* was pub-lished in 1733, the Censor's approval is dated 30 May 1728 ([vii]). The publisher's Preface refers to unspecified painstaking measures *(diligenze, e ricerche)* neces-sary before he was able to obtain Pascoli's MS; it seems plausible, therefore, to consider Pascoli's report as referring to the 1720s.

24. See Franco Venturi, "Gli anni '30 del Settecento," in *Miscellanea Walter Maturi*, ed. Gianfranco Torcellan (Turin: Giappichelli 1966), 89–153.

25. ". . . che dubito forte non sia anche cagione delle morti improvvise, che sono oggidí divenute cosí frequente in Roma tra gli uomini civili"; Pascoli, 62.

26. Pascoli, 68–69: "Qualora gli abitatori del nostro Stato, e di Roma, che n' è la metropoli, perché quello è soggetto, questa oltre la soggezione è anche sede di principe ecclesiastico ridur si potessero a monastica, e religiosa regola, o a educazione tutto affatto diversa dagli altri, che bella cosa sarebbe? Ma perché quelli che non hanno vocazion religiosa, e che educar non si ponno diversamente dagli altri bramano all' uso degli altri divertirsi, permetter loro di buona voglia si dovranno tutti que' divertimenti leciti, e onesti, che permessi sono altrove nel mondo cattolico. Non dico, che stieno aperti i teatri la maggior parte dell' anno, come nell' Oltramontane regioni, che vi si facciano pubblici balli, e festini, o che ora vi si permettano le maschere, come in altri luoghi; perché certo troppo disconverrebbe. Dico ben sí che bastano per queste le ultime 10 giorni di carnovale; ma tener si dovrebbero aperti quelli dal principio d'ottobre fino al principio dell'Avvento, e dal fine di questo, come già si costuma fino al principio di quaresima; potendosi permettere anche le donne nelle recite, conforme si fa da per tutto altrove; perché si è ben conosciuto, che non danno quello scandalo, né fanno quel male, che indusse il principe a proibizione. . . . Chi non vede dunque, quanto necessarj siano a Roma, e allo Stato i teatri, e il carnovale? Chi non ne confesserà lo scapito, il danno, il pregiudizio allorché questi si proibiranno? E chi non ne comprenderà il misterio, se vi porrà mente?"

27. ". . . delle oscenità grandi sopra le scale della medesima loro chiesa"; cited by Pecchiai, 12.

28. In his *I viventi diritti dell'Italia a Palazzo Farnese alla Scalinata ed alla Trinità de' Monti* (Rome: Bruno Fogar, 1965), C. A. Ferrari has collected some interesting illustrations of *L'Olmata*—some with grazing cows.

29. According to Georgina Masson: "This [architect of the *B. P.*] is said to have been Francesco di Sanctis, co-designer of the famous Spanish Steps[.]" *Italian Gardens* (London: Thames and Hudson, 1961), 157.

30. Walter Binni, writing on the concept of *rococò* transferred from the plastic and decorative arts, gives an account of the term's derivation. Also illuminating is the chapter "The Interrupted Supper," in Erich Auerbach's 1946 *Mimesis: The representation of Reality in Western Art,* trans. Willard Trask (New York: Doubleday, 1957), 347–82, as well as Santino Caramella, *L'estetica italiana dall'Arcadia all'Illuminismo: Momenti e problemi di storia dell'estetica,* ed. Mario Fubini (Milan: Marzorati, 1959); Helmut Hatzfield, "Rococo motives in Settecento litera- ture," *Forum Italicum* 6 (1972): 467–87; Ilaria Magnani, "Primi accenni di rococò nelle liriche di Paolo Rolli," *Studi e problemi di critica testuale* 16 (1978): 225–42.

31. "I cittadini poscia e i mercanti han dove mangino, dove ricevano (e per lo più ricevono dove dormono), e il gabinetto ove scrivono. A questa guisa, e più fratelli decentemente, e più figli, senza che l'uno all'altro dia soggezione, si possono in una mediocre casa adagiare, con tanto maggiore facilità, quanto, comeché abbondino di pietre da edificare, all'interna parte delle abitazione somministrano le pareti di legno

il ripiego di framezzare diversamente, e a misura della bisogna, gli appartamenti, siccome avrete nel vostro quantunque brieve soggiorno osservato; e questi legni, o coperta di lucida e colorata vernice risplendono, o sotto a tele dipinte in guisa di arazzi vagamente, e di specchi adorne si cuoprono; e quello stesso giorno nel quale il maestro alza la mano dal lavoro, il padrone vi si caccia dentro a godersele, senza temere della propria salute, lo che in Roma e per quanta è l'Italia non addiviene, dove egli è d'uopo lasciarle per anni abitate dai venti e dal sole, e poi profumarle, e farvi per entro delle gran vampe ai cammini, e poi consultare i medici, e poi finalmente vi si comincia a stanziare, senza il piacere della novità, tolta dal tempo, incolpando di ogni emicrania o d'ogni tosse la fabbrica, se per isventura od a caso qualcuno di cotai malanni per tutt' altra cagione ci soprarriva: conciossiaché, quando anche il nostro temperamento non ne patisse, l'apprendere che ne possa forse patire, fa sentirci que' mali che per verità non abbiamo[.]" Pier Jacopo Martello, *Il vero parigino italiano*, in *Scritti critici e satirici*, ed. Hannibal S. Noce (Bari: Laterza, 1963), 340. The work originally appeared as *Il parigino italiano*, in *Prose degli Arcadi*, vol. 2 (Rome: Antonio de' Rossi, 1718).

32. ". . . ha rovinato Roma con la sua architettura." Cited by Rotili, 7.

33. ". . . deturpata da quelle ridicole case a foggia di canterani." Cited by Rotili, 53. As source of both this quotation and that in n. 32, Rotili gives vol. 5 of Francesco Milizia's collected *Opere* (Bologna, 1827), which I have not been able to see. In the 4th ed. of Milizia's *Memorie degli architetti antichi e moderni* (Bassano: Remondini, 1785) there is no entry for Filippo Raguzzini, nor for Francesco de Sanctis. Milizia's entry for Filippo Ivara [*sic*] scotches the legend (undocumented) that de Sanctis utilized a sketch by him for the Scalinata di Spagna. Juvarra had been approached to prepare designs for the steps of S. Trinità de' Monti, and when asked for them on the eve of his departure for Portugal to work for the King (benefactor of the Arcadia), "he proceeded to scribble on a piece of paper, coming up with a perspective drawing of a flight of steps, of which it is said that, had it been followed, had been a magical staircase [*un incanto di scalinata*], entirely different from that subsequently built by Roman Architect Francesco de Sanctis" (2: 241).

34. "Ma tu che dici di quei gabinetti, Martello mio? Può immaginarsi da mente umana cosa più vaga e ridente di un gabinetto franzese? Pitturette, buccheri, porcellane e specchi che d'ogni intorno moltiplicano i leggiadri, ordinati e piccoli oggetti, spirano lusso e delizia. E quelle piccole libreriette, sí ben cantonate e disposte nelle indorate ed inverniciate scanzie, tutte abbigliate di piccole falpalà che, da un canto all'altro scorrendo, ornano, eguagliano la vista de' libri e dalla polvere li salvano. La spaziosa tavola con lo scrittoio, col torchietto di forbito acciaio per soppressare le lettere, i sigilli, la carta, le penne, che in ordinanza, la qual non ingombra, guarnisconla, non invitano, non violentano, ma dolcemente a ricrearsi studiando, mentre ne' giorni il sole e nelle notti la lampada di cristallo sono alla vista di chi vi siede centuplicati da quanti specchi, e sopra e a' fianchi abilmente annicchiate e variamente configurati, abbarbagliano. Qual genio sí ruvido può in luoghi cosí gentili, con quiete, con silenzio, con solitudine amenamente non occuparsi?" Martello, 338–39.

35. *Fatti degli Arcadi* 4 (December 1723): 116–17; also D'Onofrio, *Storie Romane*, 285.

36. Walter Benjamin, "The Work of Art in the Age of Mechanical Reproduction" (1936), in *Illuminations*, trans. Harry Zohn (London: Jonathan Cape, 1970), 242.

37. Charles Baudelaire, *"The Painter of Modern Life" and Other Essays*, trans. and ed. Jonathan Mayne (London: Phaidon, 1964), 7.

38. G[iovanni] M[ario] Crescimbeni, *La bellezza della volgar poesia* (Rome: Francesco Buagni, 1700; rev. and enlarged, 1712). Following Crescimbeni's death in 1728, the book had a 1730 Venetian edition, and there were several reprints.

39. "[G]li uomini, ignoranti delle cagioni, ogni cosa straordinaria in natura che richiami la loro meraviglia, sono dalla lor natural curiosità naturalmente destati a desiderare di sapere che quella tal cosa voglia significare." Giambattista Vico, *La Scienza nuova prima; con la polemica contro gli "Atti degli Eruditi" di Lipsia*, ed. Fausto Nicolini (Bari: Laterza, 1931), 212. The work referred to as *Scienza nuova prima* appeared in 1725, at the author's expense; a rewritten version was published in 1730, while the definitive version of 1744, best known today and often referred to as the *Scienza nuova seconda*, was so substantially revised and enlarged as to constitute a different work. Best among translations into English is *The New Science of Giambattista Vico*, trans. from the third edition of 1744 by Thomas Goddard Bergin and Max Harold Fisch (Ithaca: Cornell University Press, 1948); 2nd rev. ed., intro. Max Harold Fisch, 1968, repr. with corrections 1976.

40. ". . . quel desiderio che hanno naturalmente tutti gli uomini di vivere eternalmente; . . . essi sono curiosi dell'avvenire. Tale curiosità, per natura vietata, perché di cosa propria di un Dio mente infinita ed eterna, diede la spinta alla caduta de' due principj del genere umano[.]" Vico, 172.

41. J.-F. Lyotard, *The Postmodern Condition: A Report on Knowledge* (1979), trans. Geoff Bennington and Brian Massumi (Minneapolis: University of Minnesota Press, 1984), 78. See also my article "J.-F. Lyotard's *The Postmodern Condition* and G. B. Vico's *De nostri temporis studiorum ratione,*" *New Vico Studies* 4 (1986): 101–15.

42. Among the Venetian periodicals offering a "digest" of recent European publications are the following: *Giornale de' Letterati d'Europa di Giovanni Angeli per servire di continuazione alla Storia letteraria d'Europa*, ed. Angelo Calogerà, 2 vols. (Venice: Cristoforo Zane, 1727); *Novelle della Repubblica Letteraria*, ed. Angelo Calogerà, 33 vols. (Venice: Albrizzi; Simone Occhi, 1729–62); *Storia letteraria di Europa; tradotta dalla lingua francese nell'Italiana da Giovanni Angeli* [Angelo Calogerà], ed. Angelo Calogerà, 2 vols. (Venice: Antonio Bortoli, 1726–27). In *Impolite Learning: Conduct and Community in the Republic of Letters, 1680–1750* (New Haven: Yale University Press, 1995), Anne Goldgar deals very ably, largely from the viewpoint of French culture, with the cultural situation to which the "digest" is a response.

43. "*L'uomo di un libro*; ovvero Libreria in un sol piccolo libro fatto apposta per le persone d'ingegno, che non ponno avere né tempo, né comodità, nemmeno una vita bastevolmente lunga per leggere migliaia d'Autori, che hanno scritto del governo

degli stati, del culto delle erenti religioni, di ciò che è accaduto circa le scienze, e le arti, che perciò averanno il contenuto di non comparire affatto ignoranti nella conversazione; del che troveranno qui la sostanza universalmente prodotta, benché in modo conciso, dal primo anno del mondo, fino all'anno di Cristo 1715." (Padua: Gio[vanni] Manfré, 1718).

Chinoiserie and the Aesthetics
of Illegitimacy

DAVID PORTER

Plates and tea wares have made us better acquainted with the Chinese than we are with any other distant people.

— Robert Southey, *Letters from England* (1807)

From the time Jesuit missionaries began sending back reports on Chinese culture at the end of the sixteenth century, the European attitude towards China gradually evolved from the fairy-tale fascination with distant images of unimaginable grandeur, wealth, and strangeness evoked by the romances of Marco Polo and John de Mandeville into an informed curiosity about an increasingly variegated geographic and cultural entity. Scholarly interest peaked in the late seventeenth century with panegyrics—inspired by the Jesuits—on the wisdom of Confucian ethics and government and protracted speculations on the origins of the Chinese people and language.[1] European interpreters of the signs and emblems of Chinese culture—linguistic, theological, political—often, in this period, ascribed to them a groundedness and authenticity derived from their great antiquity and supposedly unchanging nature. Philologists and language reformers from Bacon and Wilkins to Leibniz and Swift, for example, found in the ancient, non-alphabetic script of the Chinese living evidence of the perfectibility of language and the possibility of grounding it on universally valid, rational foundations.² Followers of Matteo Ricci and his policy of accommodationism, meanwhile, claimed to find evidence of divine revelation in the classical Confucian canon and argued strenuously for the essential compatibility of its religious precepts with those of the Catholic Church.³ During a period of intense conflict and upheaval at home, such interpretations of Chinese culture provided Europeans with reassuring images of the possibility of stability and legitimacy in the troubled realms of language, religion, and government.

A second wave of interest in things Chinese, this time focused primarily on the aesthetic offerings and consumer goods of the Far East, followed in the eighteenth century. Imports of Chinese porcelains, lacquerware, furniture, and wall hangings had risen steadily since the mid-seventeenth century, and the new, strikingly exotic design motifs they brought with them stimulated the growth not only of domestic porcelain manufactures but of an entire industry of designers and producers of chinoiserie from the Beauvais tapestries to Chippendale furniture and the "Chinese" temples and pagodas of the English landscape garden. In England especially, the "Chinese taste" reached heights of popularity unmatched in any other era before or since. Extravagant spectacles featuring Chinese costumes and ornaments drew crowds to the theaters. Chinese plays were adapted and widely performed. A craze for chinoiserie furnishings and architecture transformed sitting rooms and gardens across the country and fueled the flames of Classicist satire on the degradation of contemporary taste.⁴

The collectors and consumers of the vast quantities of Chinese or Chinese-inspired porcelain, wallpapers, lacquerware, silk and furnishings that circulated through all of Europe in the eighteenth century remained generally oblivious of the ambitions of an earlier generation of missionaries and philologists to "know" China, to render legible its vast universe of endlessly perplexing signs. Rather than approaching China as a cultural terrain to be mapped and mastered through a paroxysm of heroic hermeneutics, the majority were content simply to enjoy a delicious surrender to the unremitting exoticism of total illegibility. To luxuriate in a flow of unmeaning Eastern signs, to bask in the glow of one's own projected fantasies, such were the pleasures afforded by China's arrival in the marketplace of contemporary taste.

Chinoiserie, in other words, was an aesthetic of the ineluctably foreign, a glamorization of the unknown and unknowable for its own sake. If the philologists' approach to language in China had entailed an excavation of the deep structure of hieroglyphic writing, the consumerist response to "the Chinese taste" in housewares and garden architecture was a celebration of superficies, a fixation on the glossy sheen of the porcelain vase and the surface play of images in the willow-pattern worlds it conjured up for the viewer's eye. China became in chinoiserie a flimsy fantasy of doll-like lovers, children, monkeys and fishermen lolling about in pleasure gardens graced by eternal spring. There was no substance to such a vision and indeed no desire for substance: the entire movement was a rejection of the very principle of substantiality that had attended the earlier ideal of China as a privileged site of linguistic and religious authenticity. In the decorative arts that expressed the new style, the manifestos that championed it and even the satires that lampooned it, chinoiserie comes across as a bold celebration of disorder and meaninglessness, of artifice and profusion, an exuberant surrender to all that remains unassimilated by rationalist science and classical symmetries.[5]

My purpose in this article is to consider how the European production and reception of chinoiserie might be interpreted as a form of cross-cultural representation and to compare the images of China that informed and in turn were elaborated and aestheticized by chinoiserie with those images evoked by other broadly contemporary discourses on China. When viewed in the context of these other discourses, I argue, chinoiserie represents far more than a mere exotic twist on the rococo style that emerged in tandem with it. Rather, it suggests a dramatic reversal of those tropes and assumptions that had largely defined the European idea of China over the preceding century. As I have suggested, both the Chinese written language and the Confucian belief-system had been venerated as emblems of stable, legitimate forms of representational authority. Chinoiserie, by aestheticizing the idea of this authority, effectively eviscerates it, transforming symbols of awe-inspiring cultural achievement into a motley collection of exotic ornamental motifs. After tracing the aesthetic deflation of the cultural authority of the Chinese in the political, religious, and sexual spheres through a number of representative examples of the chinoiserie style, I will offer an analysis of the hostile response to the style among English satirists of the mid-eighteenth century and, finally, suggest how my interpretive method might be applied to chinoiserie motifs in English literature of the period.

As the bulk of what follows concerns the vision of Chinese culture implicit in chinoiserie, two clarifying remarks on the nature of the paradigm shift represented by this new vision may be in order. First, the transformation I suggest in prevailing attitudes towards China is a gradual one, occurring over the course of several decades during which there is some degree of overlap. A characteristically eighteenth-century treatment of Chinese porcelain, for example, occurs as early as 1675 in Wycherley's *The Country Wife*; quasi-mystical interpretations of the Chinese language persist until the death of the Jesuit figurist Joseph de Prémare in 1736. The new view, in other words, does not so much displace or actively repudiate the old as progressively supersede it as the image of China comes to be deployed for an altogether different set of cultural purposes.

Second, the shift in attitudes corresponds to a shift in the prevailing genres of representation from scholarly writings to the decorative arts. One might argue that a comparison between a Jesuit tract and a porcelain vase would inevitably yield conflicting representations of their foreign other simply as a result of this generic incongruity, and indeed my argument would falter were the two genres historically coterminous. But in fact they are not: the comparison is justified on the grounds not only that the two types of "texts" are the products of largely distinct historical periods (roughly 1600–1740 in the first case and 1675–1775 in the second), but also that they typify the predominant ways in which China was imagined and represented in their respective periods. This shift in the prevailing modes of representation of China from the scholarly to the aesthetic is itself an essential component of the transformation I describe, and one that justifies my premise that the decorative arts can legitimately be read in such a context as a site of cultural representation. While Robert Southey's remark that "plates and tea wares have made us better acquainted with the Chinese than we are with any other distant people" may not reflect favorably on the depth of this acquaintance, it does suggest the degree to which such objects were perceived as being "about" the place to which, however reductively, they referred.

A tradition of significant allusions to chinoiserie runs through English literature of the Restoration and eighteenth century from Wycherley and Pope to John Gay and William Beckford. The literary work, however, that best captures the spirit of chinoiserie as a cultural phenomenon is Oliver Goldsmith's *Citizen of the World*. First published serially as *Letters from a Chinese Philosopher* in the *Public Ledger* beginning in 1760, Goldsmith's satire draws upon the well-worn device of a foreigner resident in a European city to comment on local customs and mores. Prominent among these are the contemporary fashion for anything and everything Chinese and the propensity of the English to flatten the idea of Chineseness into a merely aesthetic arena for the surface play of signs.

Colorful *mis*conceptions about the Chinese abound throughout the work. Invited for a meal, the visitor Lien Chi is offered a cushion in lieu of a chair, and a choice of bear's claws or bird's nests as an entrée. When he objects that he is unacquainted with these dishes and would prefer roast beef instead, he is rebuked with the assertion, "The Chinese never eat beef." His hosts inform him that the "true eastern sense" consists of nothing more than "sublimity," and "lay it down as a maxim, that every person who comes from thence must express himself in metaphor; swear by Alla, rail against wine, and behave, and talk and write like a Turk or Persian."[6]

But the most striking among these fantastic notions are those that deny Chineseness any meaningful content at all. A lady of distinction who has invited Lien Chi for an interview remarks on first seeing him, "What an unusual share of *somethingness* in his whole appearance," and seems to value the knickknacks in her Chinese porcelain collection only in so far as she believes them to be "of no use in the world." A certain "grave gentleman," after discoursing learnedly on the use of chopsticks and Chinese geography, finally sums up the appeal of the Orient as that place "where all is great, obscure, magnificent, and unintelligible," while a connoisseur of the popular genre of Eastern tales explains that the authenticity of their style lies in the privileging of sound over sense: "[they] should always be sonorous, lofty, musical, and unmeaning." Finally, a little beau praises "Asiatic beauties" as "the most convenient women alive," on the grounds that "they have no souls."[7] The English sinophiles' insistence on the vacuity of their object of admiration constitutes precisely the kind of "flattening" of cultural value that is the hallmark, I argue, of the chinoiserie style. Confronted with the potentially disturbing prospect of foreignness, these admirers of the Chinese exotic consistently dissolve it into a glimmering, inarticulate spectacle "somethingness," "uselessness," or plain "unintelligibility."

The repeated conflation in the minds of Goldsmith's English characters of the cultures of Near and Far East into a generic "orient" raises the question of the degree to which chinoiserie more generally can be read as being specifically and distinctly "about" China at all. Part of the contemporary fascination with the style, without a doubt, partook of a generalized interest in the exotic, a category in itself inherently inimical to nuanced distinctions among points of origin. Furthermore, chinoiserie appears, in many of its incarnations, to owe as much to European as to "oriental" stylistic influences. The chinoiserie designs of Watteau and Pillement, for example, might easily be classed as quaintly exotic variations on rococo themes; across the Channel, architectural design books published in England in the 1750s regularly intermingled Chinese and Gothic motifs.[8]

The undeniable hybridity of the chinoiserie style does not, however, detract from its legibility as an emblem of contemporary responses to Chinese culture. In the case of the Goldsmith passage, I would argue, the conflation of cultures does not so much efface the difference of Chineseness as attach the principle of cultural effacement as a quality particular to it. The interchangeability of "Eastern" cultural attributes, in other words, reinforces the notion that Lien Chi's culture is characterized by an essential quality of indeterminacy that echoes, indeed, the indescribable air of "somethingness" about his own appearance. The myriad artistic currents that contribute to the development of the chinoiserie style in Europe can, likewise, themselves be read as emblematic of the domestic reception of a foreign cultural influence. To recognize the rococo influence in a Watteau chinoiserie is not to deny the Chineseness of the inspiration behind the theme, but rather to acknowledge an inevitable process of stylistic translation between two very different cultural milieux. In interpreting such an artifact, then, the rococo cast that emerges from this process of translation can in itself be read as one component of the vision of China implicit in the work.

Goldsmith's *Letters* appeared at the height of the classicist backlash against the Chinese taste in the mid-eighteenth century. As a satire against the shallow extravagance of the virtuoso and connoisseur in their reception of a newly exoticized East the letters hit their mark: Lien Chi's London seems a world apart from the urgent controversies over the language and religions of China of only a half century before. But it is the content of these new images of China and the reaction to them that provides the most striking contrast with the scholarly paradigms promoted by the missionaries and philologists of an earlier age. In its relation to themes of authority, nature and sexuality, chinoiserie overturns the dominant, rationalist conceptions of the sinophilic intelligentsia to replace them with a new aesthetic exalting the very principles of semiotic chaos and illegitimacy they had so deplored. In rejecting the imperative of legibility in their reception of the foreign, the purveyors and consumers of the Chinese fashion discover a mode of encounter and of "reading" that prizes irreverent laughter over mastery and that revels in the playfully anarchic fantasies of an unintelligible world.

The earlier, analytic response to the seemingly inassimilable foreignness of the Chinese entailed the projection of highly structured models of authority on the unruly confusion of Eastern linguistic and religious signs. These hierarchical structures, legitimated in the European view by their ancient historical derivation, provided a crucial interpretive framework—and a precondition of legibility—for early proto-sinologists. Both the rationalist linguistics of the language philosophers and the accommodationist precepts of the Jesuits presumed an absolute authority on the part of the earliest founders of Chinese civilization that guaranteed its intelligibility to—and eventually mastery by—its western interpreters.

Chinoiserie, however, forgoes the will to interpretive mastery. Through its kaleidoscopic lenses, the once venerated emblems of Chinese authority disintegrate into a parodic pastiche of gaudy fragments. In the tapestries, drawings, and architectural plans that set the tone of the Chinese rage in the decorative arts, "Chinese" temples, palaces and even the Emperor himself succumb to the trivializing exigencies of ornamental design. There was little space on a teacup to evoke four millennia of cultural achievement, let alone the respectful awe such a prospect had once inspired. With the reduction of an empire into a series of miniaturized motifs and the aestheticization of the very concept of the foreign into an excuse for decorative extravagance, the ideal of a deep-rooted epistemological authority native to Chinese culture degenerated into brazen self-parody. No longer the home of ancient and universal truths, China becomes in these images the site of capriciousness, folly, and illusion, its philosopher's stone nothing more than a glittering shard of pottery.

The process by which the idea of Chinese authority is delegitimized in chinoiserie stands out most clearly in the depictions of the Chinese Emperor that seem to have been especially popular in turn-of-the-century France. The paramount link in the rigidly hierarchical Confucian chain of being, the person of the Emperor embodied in the political arena those qualities of Chinese culture that Europeans had long sought to discover in Chinese language and religion. The absolute power and legitimacy of the sovereign appeared to be grounded firmly in both a patrilineal line of descent and heavenly mandate. According to the account of Johan Nieuhof, a member of the Dutch East India Company's embassy to Peking of 1655,

> The King or Emperour of China, commands the Lives and Estates of all his Subjects, he alone being the Supream Head and Governour; so that the Chinese Government, as we have said, is absolutely Monarchical, the Crown descending from Father to Son . . . Their Emperour is commonly called Thienfu, which signifies the Son of Heaven . . .[9]

In the portrait of the Emperor on the frontispiece of Nieuhof's *Embassy* (fig. 1), the Son of Heaven cuts an awesome figure well in keeping with this description. Seated erect upon a raised throne, his arm extended nonchalantly across a large globe at his side, he gazes out at the viewer with an air of imposing majesty. Gathered close around him are a large number of fierce-looking guards (112 on each side, according to the account) armed conspicuously with all manner of weaponry, while kneeling at his feet are a number of abject supplicants in chains and a supine monk with his head locked in a wooden stock. The Emperor is shaded by a parasol held over his head, but apart from this there are few concessions to regal opulence in the decor: the image conveys all the strength and self-assurance of an ambitious Manchu warrior-king. In both the portrait and descriptions of the court and imperial bureaucracy in his account, what seems most to impress Nieuhof is the sheer power of the sovereign together with the ordered efficiency of his administration: a political system in perfect harmony with the philosophical writing system and ancient Confucian theology of the Chinese.

Nieuhof's richly illustrated account first appeared in Dutch in 1665 and was quickly translated into Latin, French, and English. It was a standard

Figure 1. Frontispiece to Johan Nieuhof, *Embassy to China* (London, 1669).

source of information on China through the end of the seventeenth century, and its more than one hundred engravings were endlessly adapted and reproduced by the first creators of European chinoiseries. The best-known adaptations of the Nieuhof imperial portrait appeared in a series of wool and silk tapestries manufactured in Beauvais in the early eighteenth century and known as the first *Tenture chinoise*.[10] Small details in the rendering of the Emperor himself—the identical position of the hand upon the waist, the same necklace, head position, and drooping moustache—establish the influence of the Nieuhof frontispiece. But any stylistic resemblance ends here: these later images convey a radically different conception of the Chinese imperial court than did the stoic severity of their model.

Probably the best known of the series and the one most closely comparable to the Nieuhof engraving in its setting is *The Emperor's Audience* (fig. 2). Once again the Emperor is seated on a raised throne with supplicants at his feet and attendants behind him. One's first impression on seeing the image, however, is less that of a counsel of state than of a sumptuously appointed menagerie. Winged dragons and peacock feathers adorn the intricately carved throne, while a large elephant glares out menacingly from behind it. A stork struts across the foreground, a peacock looks on attentively, and a dozen exotic birds flutter conspicuously overhead. The soldiers that crowded Nieuhof's drawing, in contrast, have retreated into the background. A single languid guard stands at the Emperor's side, his shield resting on the ground, his banner sagging beside his drooping head. A second attendant glances distractedly off to the side as he holds the elephant's rein. Several other guards in clownish caps joke among themselves as they peer around a curtain from behind the main platform. Overhead stands an extravagantly ornamented pavilion on spindly columns, while a luxurious oriental carpet spills sumptuously down the steps before the throne.

The Emperor seated amidst all this clutter still strikes an impressive pose, but the overwhelming decadence of the decor ultimately distracts from his own glory. Not only do the various animals and attendants seem oblivious to the ostensible gravity of the moment, the viewer too is invited to wander intrepidly about the scene, sharing in the audacity of the strutting stork and the hilarity of the royal guards. The Emperor occupies the focal point of the image as is his due, but he has some difficulty sustaining the dignity that it should confer. The opulence and activity all around him seems rather to reduce him to the status of just another curio in the pastiche of exotic splendor that the scene presents. His once absolute authority degraded into parodic decadence, the majesty of his court into sheer spectacle, the Chinese sovereign has been reduced under the weaver's loom to the ruler of a large, lavishly illustrated wall hanging—and no more.

Figure 2. *The Audience of the Emperor,* tapestry from *The Story of the Emperor of China* series, French (Beauvais), before 1732. Courtesy of the Fine Arts Museum of San Francisco, Roscoe and Margaret Oakes Collection, 59.49.1.

Eventually, the eviscerated token of Chinese legitimacy that was the Emperor vanishes from such scenes altogether. In many of the remaining tapestries of the series he does not appear at all, while in the other media favored by chinoiserie he makes at best a rare appearance. In general, the only allusion to Chinese imperial majesty in these works is literally a hollow—architectural—shell. The design books for furniture and garden structures "in the Chinese taste" that were popular in England in the mid-century are full of fanciful illustrations of royal garden seats, triumphal arches, and even an "Imperial Retreat for Angling."[11] The royal personage implied by such titles is of course never pictured: these designs represent the final stage in the distillation of an aestheticized aura of Chinese authority that was begun by the weavers of Beauvais. The plan for a "Royal Garden Seat" is pure ornamental context, a sanitized setting for play and leisure intended for the pleasure gardens of the rich (fig. 3). Any vestige of the actual basis of that legitimacy to which the artist whimsically alludes has evaporated from the scene, leaving only decorative lattice-work, layer upon layer of exotically curved awnings and the quaint little bells that hang from each of them, jangling in the wind. A triumphal arch which in China, according to Nieuhof, would have been "made of Stone or Marble, with great Art, Cost, and Ingenuity" and "erected in honour of some famous Act, Thing, or Person . . . to eternize their Memory" becomes in English garden architecture a flimsy wooden structure that serves only as "a proper Termination of a grand avenue leading from a Gentleman's seat to a road or navigable river."[12] The English gentleman in his country seat has, in other words, replaced the Chinese Emperor in his throne and, in the process, reduced the honor of his rival to an incidental ornament in a panoramic view.

The much vaunted religious and moral authority of the Chinese proves equally vulnerable to the whimsical fancy of chinoiserie. William Chambers' designs for the Kew Gardens include a "House of Confucius" which, with its intricate lattice-work and roof-top bells would seem a not-too-distant cousin of Decker's "Royal Garden Seat." Although it appears alone in some illustrations such as the one in the *Gentleman's Magazine* of June 1773, Chambers' own depiction of its garden setting leaves no doubt as to its function there (fig. 4). Published in his *Plans, Elevations, Sections, and Perspective Views of the Gardens and Buildings at Kew* in 1763, the plate shows "a view of the Lake and Island, with the Orangerie, the Temples of Eolus and Bellona, and the House of Confucius." In the Jesuit pantheon Confucius might well have stood Christ-like and alone, but for the English garden architect he is just another heathen god among many, his temple just another quaint attraction in the theme park of a princess.

Figure 3. *Royal Garden Seat,* engraving from P. Decker, *Chinese Architecture* (London, 1759).

Figure 4. *A View of the Lake and Island, with the Orangerie, the Temples of Eolus and Bellona, and the House of Confucius,* engraving from William Chambers, *Gardens and Buildings at Kew* (London, 1763).

But it was the critics of chinoiserie who most explicitly repudiated an earlier generation's conception of the cultural authority of the Chinese. China, viewed through the now prevailing lens of chinoiserie, appeared to these critics as a breeding ground for grotesque and barbarous forms that in their flagrant disregard for classical precepts of measured simplicity and grace threatened to corrupt the untrained eye and with it the moral fiber of the nation. By denouncing the rival Chinese taste as, in effect, an illegitimate usurper of the public gaze, the style's critics concluded the reassessment of the idea of Chinese authority that the *tapissiers* of Beauvais had begun. If the aesthetic of chinoiserie stripped prevailing images of Chinese culture of their aura of dignity in the name of exotic charm, its critics compounded the disgrace by vilifying the aesthetic, in turn, as a sign of complete cultural degradation.

While in France it was Fénelon in his *Dialogues des Morts* who led the attack on sinomania in the opening years of the eighteenth century, the most influential critic of chinoiserie on the other side of the channel was the third Earl of Shaftesbury.[13] Shaftesbury wastes few words denouncing the Chinese style *per se* as a specific instance of aesthetic depravity, preferring, like Lien Chi's English hosts in *The Citizen of the World*, to lump it indiscriminately together with those other varieties of gaudy and grotesque foreign extravagance that seemed to exercise a particular fascination for his contemporaries. His remarks on the subject are sufficient to suggest, however, that like Fénelon he drew a parallel between the depraved and superficial aesthetic and moral values of the East and perceived on both counts a Chinese threat to established forms of cultural authority at home.

Shaftesbury's great contribution to contemporary discussions on matters of taste, of course, was his contention that the faculties of aesthetic and moral judgement were inextricably linked. By conscientiously training one's eye in the appreciation of the most exemplary paragons of classical beauty, "right models of perfection" that might include on a visit to Rome, for example, "the truest pieces of architecture, the best remains of statues, the best paintings of a Raphael or a Caraccio," one might learn properly to distinguish "merit and virtue" from "deformity and blemish" and thereby aspire to "the character of a man of breeding and politeness." Examples of false taste, by the same token, were to be studiously avoided if one was not to bear the imprint of their deformity upon oneself.[14]

The art of the East clearly falls into this latter category. Like Fénelon, Shaftesbury acknowledges the seductive charm of its surface splendor. Yet to linger among superficial charms is to cloud one's appreciation of true and lasting beauty. He offers the following hypothetical case:

> Effeminacy pleases me. The Indian figures, the Japan work, the enamel strikes my eye. The luscious colours and glossy paint gain upon my fancy . . . But what ensues? . . . Do I not for ever forfeit my good relish? How is it possible I should thus come to taste the beauties of an Italian master, or of a hand happily formed on nature and the ancients?[15]

The lack of depth and verisimilitude in Chinese art reflects for Fénelon the philosophical standing of the Confucian notion of virtue. It falls to Shaftesbury, though, to posit a causal connection between the ethical and artistic domains and to implicate the Oriental taste directly in the corruption of moral authority among its western consumers. In doing so he sets the stage for a sustained satirical attack on chinoiserie that would challenge not only the questionable aesthetic standards that it embodied, but also the frightening vision of cultural anarchy that it seemed to portend. China had been transformed, for these critics, from an unassailable seat of cultural legitimacy to a wellspring of depravity that threatened to unravel the very fabric of a well ordered society, one enchanted viewer at a time.

The poet laureate William Whitehead, a frequent contributor to *The World,* perhaps best captures the prevailing sense of alarm among classicist critics with a fictional anecdote. Having warned in general terms that the fashion for chinoiserie threatened "the ruin of that simplicity which distinguished the Greek and Roman arts as eternally superior to those of every other nation," he hammers his point home with a poignant illustration of the kind of calamity that lay in store. A certain Lady Fiddlefaddle, he ominously reports, who had inherited a collection of Italian masterpieces from her grandfather, cast them out to make room for Indian paintings,

> and the beautiful vases, busts, and statues, which he brought from Italy, are flung into the garret as lumber, to make room for great-bellied Chinese pagods, red dragons, and the representation of the ugliest monsters that ever, or rather never, existed.[16]

By conflating the figure of the forsaken patriarch with the fallen icons of classical beauty, Whitehead portrays chinoiserie as an illegitimate usurper of the cultural authority of the classical tradition. Although the Chinese statues figuratively displace the western patriarch, as a form of representation they are, like the image of the Emperor in the Beauvais tapestries, utterly without substance: the ancient, originary truths of the Chinese sages have collapsed into a motley assortment of absurd phantasms and abominable depictions of, as it turns out, nothing at all.

The cultural topographies of chinoiserie, however unruly, made their most conspicuous and lasting impact among the compliant hills and dales of the

English landscape garden. Triumphal arches, temples, and pleasure houses "in the Chinese taste" imparted, as we have seen, a quaintly exotic flavor to the hilltops and lakesides of country estates even as they trivialized those forms of authority to which they playfully alluded. It was in the representation of nature itself, however, that chinoiserie revolutionized the very idea of the garden, and in so doing set forth a radically altered conception of the representational status of the Chinese sign. The doctrine of legitimacy that informed early research on the written language of China from Bacon onward presumed an absolute, originary grounding of the meaning of its "characters real" in the true nature of things in themselves. With the proliferation of treatises on Chinese gardening in the eighteenth century, however, this notion of a privileged basis for Chinese representation began to unravel.

A Chinese character appealed to language reformers such as Wilkins, Leibniz, and Swift because it was guaranteed to mean something, and because that meaning was stable, unambiguous, and reliably grounded. Unlike the words of modern western languages that were constantly subject to the vagaries of careless usage, relentlessly shifting meanings and rhetorical indulgence, an ideograph embodied etymological purity, historical continuity, and a sense of rational, even philosophical truth. The modes of representation that prevailed in chinoiserie presented an entirely different scenario. Nature in this new aesthetic was little more than a vehicle for the most extravagant flights of imagination, exercises in pure fantasy that seemed to repudiate the possibility of representation itself. If nature had once served as an original, unshakable foundation for the language and philosophy of the Chinese, it emerged now in the art of the Chinese as the negation of that role, as a purely aesthetic principle that rejected mimesis in the name of a new conception of exotic beauty.

The critics, predictably, denounced chinoiserie's revolt against nature and propriety with the same vigor that they had condemned its assault on established cultural authority. As the lawyer and politician Sir James Marriott railed in *The World* of March 27, 1755, Chinese

> paintings, which, like the architecture, continually revolt against the truth of things, as little surely deserve the name of elegant. False lights, false shadows, false perspective and proportions, gay colours . . . , in short, every incoherent combination of forms in nature, without expression and without meaning, are the essentials of Chinese painting.[17]

The standard against which chinoiserie appears as false, incoherent, and meaningless is an idealized conception of classical simplicity, a pure, literal mode of representation that captures the beauty of nature without distortion or adornment. "Simplicity," wrote the critic and poet Joseph Warton in the same periodical, "is with justice esteemed a supreme excellence in all the performances of art, because by this quality, they more nearly resemble the productions of nature." His contempt for collectors of chinoiserie stems from their perverse predilection for disfigured forms that undermine the very precept of natural resemblance and the precondition of aesthetic legitimacy.

> If these observations are rightly founded, what shall we say of the taste and judgment of those who spend their lives and fortunes in collecting pieces, where neither perspective nor proportion, nor conformity to nature are observed; I mean the extravagant lovers and purchasers of China, and Indian screens. . . . No genuine beauty is to be found in whimsical and grotesque figures, the monstrous offspring of wild imagination, undirected by nature and truth.[18]

The "unnaturalness" of Chinese depictions of nature continued to excite impassioned responses on both sides as its distorted scenes spread from porcelain plates to the planted terraces of country manors. Gardening, as Arthur Lovejoy suggests, "was perhaps the eighteenth-century art *par excellence*," and its incorporation of principles of Chinese garden design gave rise to the notion of *le goût anglo-chinois*. Sir William Temple introduced the Chinese principle of *sharawadgi,* or artful disorder, in an essay on gardening of 1692.[19] But it was William Chambers, royal architect and designer of the gardens at Kew, who first interpreted *sharawadgi* as a variation on the familiar motifs of eighteenth-century chinoiserie, and in doing so elaborated the idea of the Chinese garden into a full-blown cross-cultural fantasy.

Chambers authored three substantial works on Chinese garden design, the best known of which was his *Dissertation on Oriental Gardening* of 1772. What emerges in all three of these texts is an extravagant vision of the Chinese garden as a vast pleasure-house of the senses, replete with horrid and enchanted scenes, imported tigers, Tartarian damsels, and artificial waterfalls. Chambers ascribes to the Chinese a wildly hedonistic conception of nature that turns classicist pieties on their head and celebrates the irreverence towards ideals of verisimilitude that characterized so much chinoiserie. In creating this imaginary landscape, Chambers expands the flattened splendor of the Beauvais tapestries into a three-dimensional virtual world that engulfs the entire body of the spectator within its glittering surfaces. The superficial becomes all-consuming, representation becomes reality, the ungrounded vacuity of the Chinese sign is transformed into a universe of rarified perception, unmediated and unrestrained.

These transformations begin with Chambers' presentation of the idea of nature in the Chinese garden. The Chinese, like the classicists, hold up nature as a model for their art. But where the classicists venerate nature as a fount of ordered grace and simplicity and the touchstone of a highly cultivated sense of beauty, Chinese gardeners relish its unpredictability and sensuality. Nature here is no longer an idealized paradigm to be revered and imitated, but a medium to be shaped and arranged by art so as to maximize its impact on the imagination of the viewer. "Inanimate, simple nature," he writes, "is too insipid for our purposes." In the *Explanatory Discourse* published soon after the *Dissertation* appeared, he adds a stinging riposte to Shaftesbury and his ilk:

> If I must tell you my mind freely, Gentlemen, both your artists and connoisseurs seem to lay too much stress on nature and simplicity; they are the constant cry of every half-witted dabbler, the tune by which you are insensibly lulled into dullness and insipidity. If resemblance to nature were the measure of perfection, the waxen figures in Fleet-street, would be superior to all the works of the divine Buonarotti . . .[20]

Chinese gardening, by replacing the tired classical doctrine of imitation with an emphasis on variety, contrast, and surprise, frees the Chinese artist from those constraints of representational legitimacy that had seemingly shaped the formation of his written language. The successful gardener, after all, aspires not to the wisdom of the philosopher but to the genius of the poet:

> Gardeners, like poets, [he writes,] should give a loose to their imagination, and even fly beyond the bounds of truth, whenever it is necessary to elevate, to embellish, to enliven, or to add novelty to their subject.

This, I propose, is a view of Chinese cultural activity unlike any that came before. Chambers credits the Chinese with the creation of a new species of aesthetic pleasure that subverts traditional western categories of beauty. Their gardeners traffic in representational forms that share with other types of chinoiserie the mantle of symbolic illegitimacy in their groundlessness, sensuality, and unbounded proliferation. But Chambers breaks from the classicist critics in celebrating the achievement. In his iconoclastic revery he overturns the long-standing paradigm that had stigmatized the bacchanalian tendencies westerners back to Matteo Ricci's day had found in certain aspects of Chinese culture, elevating them into an art form that could rival, in his words, "the great productions of human understanding."[21]

In doing so, I would like to suggest, Chambers fundamentally rewrites the script of the European encounter with the foreignness of the Far East. The mark of the foreign, whether in the impenetrable cipher of a Chinese character or the convoluted doctrines of a Buddhist scroll, had hitherto provoked attempts to neutralize the perception of difference through either admiring gestures of assimilation or contemptuous shrugs of disdain. Chambers is the first significant writer of the period to exalt this experience of cultural strangeness as a worthy end in itself. His revised version of the script of encounter immerses the western visitor in a landscape calculated to mislead and confound but also ultimately to thrill and delight. The Chinese garden and by extension China itself is no longer a terrain to be rationally mapped and mastered, but one in which to lose oneself in the sensual allure of foreignness and to take respite from the dullness and insipidity of the everyday.

If Chambers reconfigures the encounter with Chinese foreignness through an aesthetic re-mapping of cultural anxiety, he simultaneously transforms that foreignness from a site of intellectual assimilation and mastery to the object of a less ethereal form of desire. The landscape garden, like other forms of chinoiserie, renders the signs of unmanageable difference into an exotic spectacle. Where the potent combination of mystery and sensuality exceeds the bounds of more traditional aesthetic categories, it spills happily into the domain of erotic fantasy. Drawing on the well-established genre of seraglio tales that flourished in France and England following the translation of the *Arabian Nights* at the beginning of the century, Chambers seeds his Chinese garden with pornographic possibilities, titillating vignettes that promise the reader, like the wide-eyed traveller he or she accompanies, a taste of those pleasures that can only accompany a thorough submission to the unknown.

The very description of the grounds frequently calls to mind a well-constructed erotic narrative, with its emphasis on suspense, concealment, voyeurism and variety and its masterful modulation of curiosity and the progressive revelation of the object of desire. The art of Chinese gardening at times would seem to resemble more closely the arts of seduction than those of porcelain painting or lacquerware:

> Another of their artifices is to hide some part of a composition by trees, or other intermediate objects. This naturally excites the curiosity of the spectator to take a nearer view; when he is surprised by some unexpected scene, or some representation totally opposite to the thing he looked for. The termination of their lakes they always hide, leaving room for the imagination to work; and the same rule they observe in other compositions, wherever it can be put in practice.

The pleasures of the imagination are sustained by "a continual state of fluctuation" in gardens "that leaves no room for satiety," unlike "pictures, statues, [and] buildings," which "soon glut the sight, and grow indifferent to the spectator."[22]

The centrality of these pleasures to the ethos of the garden is mirrored in the garden's topography. "In the center of these summer plantations," Chambers writes, "there is generally a large tract of ground set aside for more secret and voluptuous enjoyments." Artful concealment once again enhances the pleasures of discovery: the tract "is laid out in a great number of close walks, colonnades and passages, turned with many intricate windings, so as to confuse and lead the passenger astray." Hidden among the thickets between these paths are "many secret recesses," each one containing "an elegant pavilion" inhabited by the owner's "fairest and most accomplished concubines." Should the traveller's wanderings lead him to the enchanted scenes in another corner of the garden, he will find himself soothed not only by "the singing of birds, the harmony of flutes, and all kinds of soft instrumental music," but also by a variation on the voluptuous theme better suited to this ambiance:

> sometimes, in this romantic excursion, the passenger finds himself in extensive recesses, surrounded with arbors of jessamine, vine and roses, where beauteous Tartarean damsels, in loose transparent robes, that flutter in the air, present him with rich wines, mangostans, ananas, and fruits of Quangsi; crown him with garlands of flowers, and invite him to taste the sweets of retirement, on Persian carpets, and beds of camusath skin down.[23]

If the Chinese garden provides Chambers an occasion to fantasize on the luxuriant sensuality of a Turkish sultan's court, it is no less "Chinese" for this indulgence. The aesthetic of the Chinese garden, for Chambers, is fundamentally about the indulgence of every extravagant pleasure of the imagination, an extravagance that can only be supplied by subsuming within the idea of "Chinese" the more generalized experience of exquisite foreignness. The China of the Chinese garden and chinoiserie, in other words, represents the essence of pure foreignness distilled into an aesthetic *frisson*.

Chambers's erotic twist on the exotic motifs of chinoiserie frames the issue of their representational status in a provocative new light. The "monstrous forms" of chinoiserie, I have argued, in their departure from classicist definitions of artistic merit, violated implicit codes governing the legitimate representation of nature. The Chinese taste bore the stigma of illegitimacy in so far as its objects flaunted their anarchic contempt for any natural derivation. Brazenly ungrounded, absurdly meaningless, and dangerously popular, they threatened an established hierarchical order of taste with their shameless extravagance.

But the leisurely, playful, almost hedonistic spirit that animates many of the creations of chinoiserie from the Beauvais tapestries to Chambers's three-part manifesto on the pleasures of Chinese gardening raises another kind of

concern for their classicist critics: namely, the incompatibility they saw between the experience of true beauty and mere sensual delight. "Grotesque
and monstrous figures often please," Shaftesbury admonished his readers,
"but is this pleasure right?" The discerning viewer turns his eye from all that
is "gaudy, luscious, and of a false taste," having realized that "'tis not by
wantonness and humour that I shall attain my end and arrive at the enjoyment I propose," but rather by submission to the rigid rules of art.[24] Chinoiserie
is suspect not only because it deviates from nature, but because it is too much
fun, too "wanton," offering immediate gratification and frustrating virtuous
restraint.

The skillful concubines and Tartarean damsels that inhabit the Chinese
garden of an Englishman's dreams embody the forbidden aesthetic of wanton sensuality taken to its most literal extreme. The pleasures they proffer
are as boundless and sublime as the plunging cataracts outside their abodes,
and equally alien to reasoned, rational modes of representation. Chambers
was not the only writer, though, to draw upon sexualized imagery of
chinoiserie. The mid-century critic James Cawthorn, in his attack on the prevailing "luxury of taste" in contemporary English cuisine, gardening, and
architecture, condemns the reigning mode of church-building as "loose and
lascivious," and attributes the decline of the "August and manly" style of the
ancients to an insidious Eastern influence.

> Of late, 'tis true, quite sick of Rome and Greece,
> We fetch our models from the wise Chinese:
> European artists are too cool and chaste,
> For Mand'rin only is the man of taste.

The Chinese artist, by implication, tends towards a feverish licentiousness.
He lays out his gardens "without the shackles or of rules or lines"; as the
contagion of his designs spreads to Europe and "our farms and seats begin /
To match the boasted villas of Pekin," so too must his idolatry and moral
laxity invade the English sitting room.

> On ev'ry shelf a joss divinely stares,
> Nymphs laid on chintzes sprawl upon our chairs;
> While o'er our cabinets Confucius nods,
> Midst porcelain elephants and china gods.[25]

These sprawling nymphs, close cousins of Chambers's sylvan concubines,
can be read, surely, as the symbolic progenitors of "the monstrous offspring
of wild imagination" that Joseph Warton had decried. The unbridled sensuality of chinoiserie comes to be coded, in other words, as an aesthetic ana-

logue of illegitimacy in the sexual sphere. Signalled by a proliferation of bastard forms, ungrounded in nature and truth, it overturns the immaculate genealogies of that earlier model of Chinese representation that was the Chinese script in an orgy of anti-representational exuberance.

The earliest literary antecedent for these sexualized constructions of chinoiserie is William Wycherley's *The Country Wife* of 1675. In this classic Restoration comedy, the young libertine Mr. Horner gains access to the married women of the town by passing himself off as a eunuch. The erotic climax of the play draws upon a curious metaphor:

> (*Enter Lady Fidget with a piece of china in her hand, and Horner following.*)
> Lady Fidget. And I have been toiling and moiling, for the prettiest piece of china, my dear.
> Horner. Nay she has been too hard for me, do what I could.
> Mrs. Squeamish. Oh Lord I'll have some china too, good Mr. Horner, don't think to give other people china, and me none, come in with me too.
> Horner. Upon my honour I have none left now.
> Mrs. Squeamish. Nay, nay I have known you deny your china before now, but you shan't put me off so, come— . . .[26]

As in the Chambers and Cawthorn texts, a Chinese artifact stands in here as a symbol of extravagant and illegitimate sexuality. If Tartarean damsels and sprawling nymphs conveyed a sense of generalized licentiousness, the porcelain phallus in this passage evokes a vivid scene of rampant cuckoldry and voracious female desire. The ladies' husbands, after all, are not the only losers here: Horner, whose transformation from a eunuch to a man hangs on the invocation of a metaphor, finds himself figuratively emasculated as the scene begins. Lady Fidget possesses the china now, and her apparent delight in its acquisition gives one ample cause to believe his claim—uttered, one presumes, in a high-pitched whine—to "have none left." Her pleasure, that is, entails his symbolic unmanning as the piece of china that passes between them sheds its mantle of phallic authority for a shudder of pure jouissance. This transformation from potency into pleasure echoes the displacement of Mr. Fidget's legitimate paternity at the hands of his wife's illegitimate desire. At the same time, it prefigures the classicist critique of chinoiserie as a site where firmly grounded, established forms of aesthetic knowledge are undermined in the pursuit of passing sensual delights.

It is clear, then, that over the course of this century the sexualization of chinoiserie partakes of a rich array of interconnected imagery. We have seen the critics repeatedly decry a monstrous proliferation of illegitimate forms and the corruption of the moral and aesthetic codes of artistic reproduction. These, in turn, would appear to follow from the style's overt sensuality and in particular from its depictions of highly eroticized femininity. The Wycherley text, finally, suggests that this emphasis on female sexuality is by no means fortuitous: the mechanism of illegitimate reproduction, whether of bastard sons or misshapen porcelain idols, is one in which pleasure triumphs over knowledge and phallic certainty succumbs to the vagaries of (female) desire. Chinoiserie emerges, then, as a token of an emasculating feminine libido that strips art of its classical patrimony in the service of an aesthetic of immediate and irreverent sensual appeal.

Literary and artistic allusions to chinoiserie throughout the first half of the eighteenth century corroborate such a reading. The narrative climax of Pope's *The Rape of the Lock* centers on a piece of porcelain that establishes Belinda as a direct descendent of Lady Fidget. When the Baron's scissors finally dissever the sacred hair from her fair head,

> Then flashe'd the living Lightning from her Eyes,
> And Screams of Horror rend th' affrighted Skies.
> Not louder Shrieks to pitying Heav'n are cast,
> When Husbands or when Lap-dogs breathe their last,
> Or when rich *China* Vessels, fal'n from high,
> In glittring Dust and painted Fragments lie![27]

The image of the shattered porcelain vase clearly functions on one level to dramatize the loss of Belinda's innocence. But it works simultaneously on another level as part of a satirical deflation of a husband's standing in an ungrateful lady's eyes: his demise, after all, appears of no more consequence than that of a lap dog or a vase. All three are objects of vanity and sources of fleeting and superficial pleasures. Belinda, violated by the "fatal engine" of a brazen male, effectively avenges the assault in a rhetorical riposte that repeats Lady Fidget's transformation of phallic authority into an aestheticized and insubstantial fragment. Although it is the Baron who wields the scissors, on the rhetorical plane it is Belinda, through the poet's satirical contextualization of her scream, who does the cutting, reducing the *vertu* of emboldened manhood into the glittering dust of a collector's *virtu*.

Eight years later in 1725, John Gay once again invokes a piece of china as a lover's rival in the poem "To a Lady on her Passion for Old China." Though the poem satirizes a woman's misplaced affections—along with the follies of virtuosos more generally—the speaker is hardly a disinterested observer.

> What ecstasies her bosom fire!
> How her eyes languish with desire!
> How blessed, how happy should I be,

Were that fond glance bestowed on me!
New doubts and fears within me war:
What rival's near? A China jar.

He addresses his coy mistress with all the frenzied passion of an Andrew Marvell ("Love, Laura, love, while youth is warm"), but her "coyness," mediated through her own all-consuming passion for chinoiserie, renders her oblivious to his appeals. How this mediation comes about is suggested by the lover's own accolade to antique jars later in the poem, in which he compares them in their purity, polish, and fragile beauty to "the types of womankind." The simile suggests a sufficient motive for coyness, for as he concedes, "She who before was highest prized, / Is for a crack or flaw despised." He finds himself excluded from her affections, in other words, by her identification with an immaculate, untouchable form of beauty and the pleasure she takes in contemplating it rather than "the strong earthen vessel" of "courser stuff" that is the male of the species. Whether her preference for a china jar over her suitor is a token of narcissistic virtue or homoeroticism, it represents a troublesome libidinal self-determination that threatens not only to "break a faithful heart" but also to subvert the sexual economy that sustains its hopes. A woman in possession of china, these last three works imply, has little need for a man. Encompassing the iconography of both virgin and whore, chinoiserie represents for these women an emancipation of pleasure from the confines of patrilineal legitimacy. If as an aesthetic chinoiserie privileges surface play over a firm basis in nature and truth, as a sexual metaphor it proclaims the freedom of desire from the dictates of both the law of the father and of the pining lover's laments.[28]

The violation of these dictates, then, is from a male perspective the source of both sexual and aesthetic illegitimacy. Chinoiserie, as we have seen, appears as a fundamentally transgressive and anarchic perversion of true taste. In a venomous diatribe against the Chinese taste published in *The World* in 1753, William Whitehead insists that:

> Taste, in my opinion, ought to be applied to nothing but what has as strict rules annexed to it . . . People may have whims, freaks, caprices, persuasions, and even second-sights if they please; but they can have no Taste which has not its foundation in nature, and which, consequently, may be accounted for.[29]

Chinoiserie, by disregarding classical rules prescribing for art the natural foundation that can alone provide a legitimate basis for representation, gives rise to a profusion of fatherless forms and foolish pleasures that defy any genealogical accounting. To the extent that maleness or at least masculine authority, in a broadly symbolic sense, is premised on the enforcement and enforceability of the rules of taste and of representational and biological descent, their wanton transgression in chinoiserie suggests a boldly emasculating gesture. The rampant cuckoldry effected by a piece of china and the male impotence occasioned by its surrender in *The Country Wife* are literary allusions to such a gesture, as are husbands' rhetorical humiliation in *The Rape of the Lock* and the lover's frustration in Gay's poem.

Corollaries to these scenes occur in the visual arts of the period. Hogarth, in particular, repeatedly links the extravagant excesses of chinoiserie with a figural unmanning of male characters. Consider, for example, the second plate of *Marriage à la Mode* (fig. 5). Exhausted and disheveled after a night of wild partying, husband and wife repose amidst the cluttered disarray of an elegant sitting room. The decor suggests that among their other troubles the couple has fallen victim to the Chinese taste. There is a Chinese firescreen, a porcelain tea set, and over the fireplace a motley assortment of squatting pagods and clumsy mandarines straight out of Oliver Goldsmith or the satirists of *The World*. In typical Hogarth fashion, these ornaments reflect the moral tone of the scene, in this case one of generalized debauchery. The wife stretches out her foot enticingly from under the tea setting in a pose reminiscent, perhaps, of Cawthorn's sprawling nymphs as well as of the reclining figure in the risqué painting in the next room. On the firescreen, meanwhile, a woman with a Chinese parasol peers out from behind the husband's chair while the family dog extracts a telltale bonnet from his coat pocket. In spite of his recent conquests, though, he conveys an air of abject defeat. In contrast to his wife, who seems game for another frolic, he stares listlessly at the floor, oblivious to the remonstrances of a steward come to collect on a sheaf of unpaid bills and, most crucially, to the shameful spectacle of a sword lying broken at his feet. Like Horner before him, he has sacrificed his manhood at the altar of a porcelain fantasy. Unable to pay his debts, win his fights, or even respond to his wife's advances, he slumps dejectedly in his chair, while over his head "Confucius nods, midst porcelain elephants and china gods."

The sheer extravagance demanded by the Chinese style had clear financial repercussions that very often mirrored its perceived moral and aesthetic effects. Hogarth's young Squanderfield, after all, had not only a broken sword to show for his wife's love affair with chinoiserie, but also a growing mountain of unpaid debts. Debtors, then, increasingly joined the sorry assembly of cuckolds, eunuchs and fops that seemed to be all that remained of British manhood in the wake of the China craze. The torrents of desire the style unleashed unmanned not only those who, like Horner, gave up their precious china in the flood, but also those who sustained the craze on the open marketplace.

The issue of September 20, 1753 recounts the woeful tale of a man who, having married a "woman of taste," watches on as she redecorates his home

Figure 5. Bernard Baron, 1696–1762, British, after William Hogarth, 1697–1764, *Marriage à la Mode, Plate II,* 1745. Etching and engraving, platemark: 38 x 46.6 cm. Courtesy of the Cleveland Museum of Art, 1998, Gift of Mr. and Mrs. Milton Curtiss Rose, 1759.312.

under the guidance of a Chinese upholsterer by the name of Mr. Kifang. By the end of several months, he finds his house

> entirely new furnished; but so disguised & altered, that I hardly knew it again. There is not a bed, a table, a chair, or even a grate, that is not twisted into so many ridiculous and grotesque figures . . . The upper apartments of my house, which were before handsomely wainscotted, are now hung with the richest Chinese & Indian paper, where all the powers of fancy are exhausted in a thousand fantastic figures of birds, beasts & fishes, which never had existence . . .
>
> The chimney piece also (and indeed every one in the house) is covered with immense quantities of china of various figures; among which are Talapoins & Bonzes, and all the religious orders of the east.
>
> As my furniture increases, my acres diminish, and a new fashion never fails of producing a fresh mortgage.[30]

Even as the undifferentiated profusion of kitsch on the mantlepiece mocks the once vaunted religious authority of the Chinese, and the wallpaper degrades nature from a wellspring of truth and beauty to a handmaiden of monstrous deceit, the meaningless abundance of hollow images that characterizes the new decor enacts a radical subversion of an implicit ideal of legitimacy in representation. The reckless fantasy of a woman of taste spawns an uncontrolled proliferation of groundless signs that drags their nearest referent, China, with them into a swamp of aesthetic, moral, and finally cultural illegibility. The husband gains a mortgage in the process, but what, after all, is a mortgage if not a gaping void where his patrimony should be, a eunuch's scar patched over with a glimmering illusion.

NOTES

1. See, for example, the useful collection of articles in Julia Ching and Willard Oxtoby, eds., *Discovering China: European Interpretations in the Enlightenment* (Rochester: Univ. of Rochester Press, 1992) as well as *Appréciation par l'Europe de la tradition chinoise à partir du XVIIe siècle*, Colloque International de Sinologie, Chantilly 1980 (Paris: Les Belles Lettres, 1983). A more comprehensive treatment of the intellectual history of the encounter can be found in René Etiemble, *L'Europe chinoise* (Paris: Gallimard, 1988), while G. F. Hudson provides a helpful though somewhat dated general overview in *Europe and China: A Survey of Their Relations from the Earliest Times to 1800* (London: E. Arnold, 1931).

2. For an overview of European interpretations of the Chinese written language during this period, see David Porter, "Writing China: Legitimacy and Representation 1606–1773," *Comparative Literature Studies* 33 (1996): 98–122.

3. On the Jesuits in China and Ricci's policy of accommodationism, see David Mungello, *Curious Land: Jesuit Accommodation and the Origins of Sinology* (Stuttgart: Franz Steiner, 1985), George H. Dunne, S.J., *Generation of Giants: The Story of the Jesuits in China in the Last Decades of the Ming Dynasty* (Notre Dame: Univ. of Notre Dame Press, 1962), and Arnold Rowbotham, *Missionary and Mandarin: The Jesuits at the Court of China* (Berkeley and Los Angeles: Univ. of California Press, 1942).

4. The best introductions to chinoiserie are Hugh Honour, *Chinoiserie: The Vision of Cathay* (New York: Dutton, 1962), and Dawn Jacobson, *Chinoiserie* (London: Phaidon Press, 1993). For a comprehensive overview of this period of British fascination with China, see William Appleton, *A Cycle of Cathay* (New York: Columbia Univ. Press, 1951).

5. In this respect, chinoiserie bears a clear relation to other important developments in eighteenth-century culture. The parallels with the rococo aesthetic have been thoroughly documented. See, for example, Jacobson, *Chinoiserie,* 59–88. The chinoiserie aesthetic also bears clear resemblances to, and may have served some of the same cultural functions as the carnivalesque, which enjoyed a considerable vogue in England in this period. See Terry Castle, *Masquerade and Civilization: The Carnivalesque in Eighteenth-Century English Culture and Fiction* (Stanford: Stanford Univ. Press, 1986).

6. Oliver Goldsmith, *Citizen of the World* (London: J.M. Dent and Sons, 1934), letter 33.

7. Goldsmith, letters 14, 33, 99.

8. See, for example, Watteau's *Divinité Chinoise* or *Idole de la Déesse Ki Mao Sao,* William and John Halfpenny's *Chinese and Gothic Architecture Properly Ornamented* (London, 1752), and Thomas Chippendale's *The Gentleman and Cabinet-Maker's Director* (London, 1754).

9. Johan Nieuhof, *An Embassy from the East-India Company of the United Provinces, to the Grand Tartar Cham, Emperor of China* (London, 1669), 149–50.

10. For helpful discussions of the Beauvais tapestries, see Edith A. Standen, "The Story of the Emperor of China: A Beauvais Tapestry Series," *Metropolitan Museum Journal* 11 (1976): 103–17 and Madeleine Jarry, *Chinoiserie: Chinese Influence on European Decorative Art, Seventeenth and Eighteenth Centuries* (New York: Vendome Press, 1981), 15–31.

11. See, for example, Thomas Chippendale, *The Gentleman and Cabinet-Maker's Director* (1754), William Halfpenny, *Rural Architecture in the Chinese Taste* (London, 1755), and P. Decker, *Chinese Architecture* (London, 1759).

12. Nieuhof, 197; Halfpenny, notation to plate 20.

13. Arthur O. Lovejoy, "The Chinese Origin of a Romanticism," in *Essays in the History of Ideas* (New York: George Braziller, 1955), 107.

14. Lord Shaftesbury, "Advice to an Author," in *Characteristics of Men, Manners, Opinions, Times, etc.*, ed. John Robertson (London, 1900), 1: 217–18.

15. Shaftesbury, "Advice," 219.

16. William Whitehead, *The World* no. 117 (March 27, 1755), quoted in B. Sprague Allen, *Tides in English Taste (1619–1800)* (Cambridge: Harvard Univ. Press, 1937), 241.

17. *The World*, no. 117 (March 27, 1755).

18. *The World*, no. 26 (June 28, 1753).

19. See Lovejoy, "Chinese Origin," 101, 110–112 and William Temple, *Upon the Gardens of Epicurus* (1692) in *Works* (London, 1757) 3: 229–230. This and a number of other essential primary texts on eighteenth-century English gardening are reprinted in John Dixon Hunt and Peter Willis, eds., *The Genius of the Place: The English Landscape Garden 1620–1820* (London: Elek, 1975). For useful discussions of the English adaptation of the Chinese style in gardening, see Cunzhong Fan, "China's Garden Architecture and the Tides of English Taste in the Eighteenth Century," *Cowrie: A Chinese Journal of Comparative Literature* 1 (1984): 21–34; Liangyan Ge, "On the Eighteenth-Century English Misreading of the Chinese Garden," *Comparative Civilizations Review* 27 (1992): 106–126; and Shou-yi Ch'ên, "The Chinese Garden in Eighteenth-Century England," *T'ien Hsia Monthly* 2 (1936): 321–339.

20. William Chambers, *A Dissertation on Oriental Gardening* (London, 1772), 19; William Chambers, *An Explanatory Discourse* (London, 1773), 145.

21. Chambers, *Dissertation*, 19, 11.

22. William Chambers, *Designs of Chinese Buildings, Furniture, Dresses, Machines, and Utensils* (London, 1757), 18; Chambers, preface to *Dissertation*.

23. Chambers, *Dissertation*, 25–27, 40.

24. Shaftesbury, "Advice," 218–219.

25. James Cawthorn, *Of Taste: An Essay* (London, 1771).

26. William Wycherley, *The Country Wife*, in *Restoration Drama*, ed. Ronald Berman (New York: Signet, 1980), 86.

27. Alexander Pope, *The Rape of the Lock*, canto III, lines 153–60.

28. Such an analysis might be elaborated further by a reading of a long pornographic poem published in 1740 under the title *A Chinese Tale*, ostensibly written by "a celebrated mandarine of letters," Sou ma Quang. The frontispiece depicts the Chinese maid of honour Chamyam masturbating before a mirror in a room cluttered with chinoiserie while her frustrated (male) lover looks on from his hiding place in a large china jar. The poem is a lavishly long-winded meditation on this scene.

29. *The World*, no. 12 (March 22, 1753).

30. Ibid., no. 38 (Sept. 20, 1753).

Pictorial Prostitution: Visual Culture, Vigilantism, and "Pornography" in Dunton's *Night-Walker*

JAMES GRANTHAM TURNER

This essay traces a recurrent topos—the brothel masquerading as a culturally respectable if mildly erotic gallery of paintings—as it migrates between various genres that might historically be called "pornographic." Across a surprising range of discourse, including bawdy tales, lawsuits protesting against sexual defamation, political satires, and crusading journalism, this motif exploits the ambiguous relationship between two etymological elements that would eventually combine: *porné* (signifying the prostitute openly revealed and reviled) and *graphé* (the expressive mark or engraved sign, verbal as well as visual). Everything depends on who is making that mark and who controls its interpretation. Each of these narratives pits a woman's autographism or self-representation (as genteel art collector or respectable matron) against efforts by the narrator/defamer to pry open or cut into this high-cultural exterior, to reveal the expected story of sexual exposure and conquest—the "pornographic" moment in the modern sense. My principal example, however, suggests a third usage of the term, partway between the modern meaning and its etymological roots, corresponding more closely to the eighteenth-century word *pornographe* coined by Restif de la Bretonne: the collective portrait of urban vice brought to light by a private citizen who blends into the murky demimonde and extracts its most salacious truths. John Dunton predates Restif by a century, but he creates a similar persona in his ostensibly factual monthly *The Night-Walker*, part detective and part sociologist. Both of these faintly sinister secret agents proclaim a larger moral purpose—indeed, Dunton's eponymous "night-walker" presents himself as a contributor to the great Reformation of Manners—but both clearly revel in their familiarity with the illicit counter-culture and their ability to simulate the fashionably lascivious *flâneur*.

Dunton clearly plays a game of appearances that resembles (in reverse) that of the prostitutes he endeavors to expose: these cultured courtesans display the forbidding exterior of the *virtuosa* and the *connoisseuse* (only revealing the sexual interior at strategic moments), while Dunton adopts the costume and manner of a Restoration rake scenting the night air for sexual opportunity, driven by titillated curiosity (only revealing his reformist zeal at the last minute). The origins of his vigilante project suggest a deeper investment in voyeurism and vicarious appetite, however. Several years before the launch of *The Night-Walker* it emerges as just another curious item in the popular journalism that Dunton helped to found: in summer 1691 several issues of the *Athenian Mercury* (the English equivalent of the *Mercure galant*) whet the reader's appetite by promising the "Six Nights Rambles" of a Gentleman in search of whores, to illustrate its ongoing discussion of the efficacy and ethics of the "present offers at a Reformation"; the anonymous writer first solicits the editor ("desires to know whether it be convenient to insert" his account), who then tantalizes the reader with hints of "the Confessions he has got from several *lewd Women* (some of 'em of no mean Rank)." (Dunton himself was of course the publisher, and quite probably the author-confessor too.) On August 4 these "Rambles" actually appear, conveying the porno-biographical revelations that come to light when the young spy "imitates" flesh and blood (exactly the style of the Night-Walker five years later). The entire passage is repeated, incongruously, in Dunton's *The Ladies Dictionary, Being a General Entertainment for the Fair-Sex*, with the title "Six Nights Rambles of a Young Gentleman through the City, for the detection of lewd women," and passages are again recycled in *The Night Walker* itself—though they are now presented as the author's own direct experience.[1] This speck of mercury is thus heated and stretched into an autonomous serial publication, one which (despite its "design to expose Vice" and thereby extirpate prostitution) could continue to sell *ad infinitum*, for as long as London provides stylish courtesans and salacious-indignant readers.

Each of the following episodes chooses visual culture as the battleground where one kind of "design" maneuvers to outwit another. The weapons of this confrontation are not only actual pictures but hermeneutic modes of understanding the visible surface. The whoremaster/vigilante must negotiate a finely-wrought representation that could variously be interpreted as a pure art-object or as a commercial "sign" leading directly to the person it depicts.

The best known (and least ambiguous) example of this trope is Angellica's display of her portrait in Aphra Behn's *Rover*, which the author herself uses as an emblem of her literary practice; here the high-cultural status of the portrait (given to Van Dyck in Killigrew's *Thomaso*, the original of Behn's play) directly signifies the colossal price that Angellica demands for her favors, but she makes no attempt to conceal her courtesan status, and exhibits the painting in the public square rather than indoors.[2] In Dunton's London the device has turned inward, literally and metaphorically installed behind a façade of *politesse* that requires new techniques for the extraction of pleasure. Dunton's adoption of those techniques for police work throws into question the attempt to separate or cordon off the various masculine drives for "satisfaction," sexual, epistemological, and vigilante-reformist. The deflection of those desires onto the simulacrum, the portrait, and the disguise, I shall further argue, renders the male searcher himself an object of sexual-visual appraisal and exchange.

I. The Night-Walker

Sometime in January 1697 John Dunton (if we can believe a word he says) insinuated himself into a rather fancy bawdy-house at the "Court end of the Towne," not at all the usual haunt of the puritanical City tradesman and gutter journalist.[3] He had become a Night Walker, a Rochesterian "ramble[r] . . . after Lewd Women," as his title page titillatingly proclaims (fig. 1); only the sepulchral black letter hints at the moralistic, vigilante purpose of this prowling, which we can term "pornographic" in the original sense of the word coined by Restif de la Bretonne. Dunton normally operated down-market (in Bartholomew Fair or Cheapside), but like Rochester he would sometimes ramble in St. James's Park and the West End. He would not only pick up women on the street "to *sound their Inclination*" by wheedling them into a tavern, but would try to penetrate fashionable-looking houses and maintain his gallant disguise right up to the moment of sexual avowal or surrender, when he would whip out his Bible and start preaching reformation. (In one such encounter his victim sighs, bursts into tears, and cries she is "undone," at which moment Dunton declares himself "willing to push on to the Conviction.") Dunton's monthly publication replicates this masquerade of seduction-conversion. The framing devices most visible to the casual browser—title-pages and lists of contents—suggest prurient adventures and facetious mock-encomia: a dedication "to the Whore-Masters of London and Westminster," an episode summarized as "A ramble to *S. James's Park*, with what happen'd 'tween the *Night-Walker* and a young Crack."[4] Like the 1658 *L'Escole des filles*, which simulates that celebrated pornographic text only

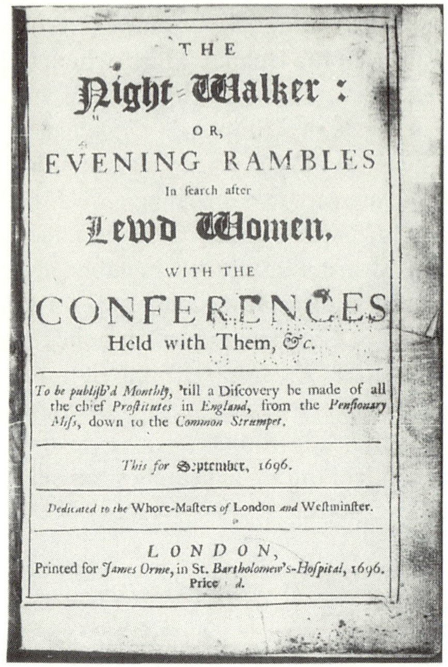

Figure 1. John Dunton, *The Night-Walker* (September, 1696), title page

to inveigle the lewd reader into a defense of traditional chastity, Dunton perpetrates a pious fraud.[5]

Several critics have noted the peculiar congruence between Dunton's covert operations and the illicit sexuality they purportedly expose, and his near-obsession with what we might call porno-semiotics, the *signs* (both literal and metaphorical) that turn the great trading city into a vast sexual marketplace. A typical passage of *The Night-Walker*, purportedly sent in by a correspondent but transparently Duntonian, denounces citizens' wives who "sit Trickt and Trim'd, and Rigg'd in their Shops as if they had more mind to expose themselves to Sale, than their Goods."[6] These Cheapside tradeswomen act "as if they had more Confidence that their Modish Dresses and Wanton Glances would attract more Customers than either their Signs or the Pictures and other Representations of their Merchandise could do; and being thus exposed to the Eye of the *Lascivious Sparks*, they take the thing in its natural signification, and come to *treat with them for themselves*, and not for the Goods in their Shops." Dunton's swivelling syntax suggests his inability to decide who is the subject and who the object of this "ex-position," and where the writer stands in this visual exchange. Though the voyeur-informer tries to dissociate himself from "the Eye of the *Lascivious Sparks*," it is obvious that he shares the same prurient vision and imposes the same "natural signi-fication" upon fashionable display; indeed, "no man can well put any other Construction upon it, when he sees a fine Woman exposed in a Shop" that sells bacon or coal. He transfers the blame from his own gaze to the woman's visual agency: to avoid temptation, "a Man" would have to pull out his eyes or "walk hoodwinkt in our Streets." The "lascivious spark" and the visually-fixated reformer share the same "Construction," splitting the fashionably dressed Citizen's wife into the figure visible from the street and the secret sexual interior—then further interpreting that public aspect as a *sign*, more real than the actual painted board that identifies her shop. In a grim if uncon-scious pun on the etymology of "prostitute," Dunton constructs a "natural" interpretation of the female figure as duplex, the image that "stands in front" and the whore who awaits customers in the rear.

In this January 1697 episode of *The Night-Walker*, semiotic complexity is further increased by the need to maintain social appearances and by the related use of paintings as a mediating device. In order to hunt out the whores who look "like Ladies" (23) the Night-Walker must look like a gentleman, perform as a libertine, and give signs of the insider knowledge that will al-low him access to the erotic interior. The stories he has already gathered now serve as tokens for admission, as he names one of the procuress's genteel clients: she concedes that he looks like "a Gentleman" but to ensure against "Tricks" insists on repeating the question "Who recommended you to me?"; he responds, "seeing you press me to it, I know that you helpt Esq. ———— to an handsome Mistress." Once inside, however, he must negotiate and decode another fictive surface. Instead of women he finds a gallery of Titianesque portraits and mythologies, a room "hung round with Pictures representing all the Amours of *Ovid*'s Heathen Gods, and amongst them were Intermixt the Pictures of her Ladies of Pleasure, set off to the best advantage, one of them had her Golden Tresses dis-shevell'd upon her Shoulders, and her Breast exposed to view; another was drawn putting on her Smock; a third tying her Garters; and a fourth in the Arms of her Gallant" (24).

These paintings obviously appeal to the sensuousness of the viewer, but where should that arousal be directed? Is this a museum or a shop? As we shall see in other versions of this porno-pictorial topos, the high-cultural status of painting meant that it could be used to conceal as well as advertise, by deflecting desire from the represented object to the artefact. Art turns the naked into the nude, the scene of lewd "Company" into *genre* or *conversa-tion galante;* Titian's full-length nudes, among the most erotic paintings ever made, were happily bought from Charles I's collection by the Puritan Colo-nel Hutchinson and taken to adorn the virtuous country retreat celebrated by his widow.[7] Dunton must negotiate this ambiguity by deciding which "Construction" to adopt for these images, the conventional or the "natural" (which means the sexual). He shows his appreciation of the visual "Entertainment" but then asks to compare "the Originals"; he chooses from this picture gallery the figure "set off to the best advantage"—that is, the dishevelled blonde whom he had already described most sensuously in his ekphrasis—and then insists on applying his new found connoisseurship to "the Person" as well as the canvas, "that I may be satisfied whether the Painter has not flattered her" (24). The "satisfaction" of the art-historical researcher, comparing this particularized painting with the generically named "Mistress *Betty*" when she appears, anticipates and focuses the search for physical satisfaction. When he tells the two women that "I must discourse 'em a little before we entred into any further Familiarity" he reminds us of the "familiarity" already established in the picture-viewing scene and the intimacy that his detective method requires. Only when further bargaining with "the Person" breaks down does Dunton break his disguise—"Well Ladies, I will now pull off my Mask" (25)—and launch into his fiery sermon, which he ironically calls an "Entertainment" as if to match his earlier appreciation of the visual display ("Madam, I perceive you have such Entertainment as is sufficient to provoke the dullest Appetite").

The two women recover their confidence after the initial shock of Dunton's self-exposure, denouncing his ungentlemanly, scatological language and his puritanical hypocrisy even after he cries "you don't know who I am" and pulls out a constable's staff. Already infuriated by his gross attacks (the mistress is a "private Close Stool" and the procuress the chambermaid who empties it), they rise to heights of affronted gentility after his display of constabular authority: "the old Bawd told me, *That she did not value my Fanatical Cant, there were men of better Sense than I that thought it no sin; that she knew the opinion of the Greatest Wits of the Town, in those things, and car'd not what a parcel of Canting Coxcombs said.*" Suddenly the staged confrontation of godly reformer and cowering slut turns into the rout of the lower-class "fanatic" by the voices of fashionable secular hedonism. Rather implausibly, given the heat of the argument, the madam then describes their mode of life and explains how they attract gallants in church and read "Play-Books, that we may know how to Entertain the Gallants with Witty Discourses" (January 1697, 26–27). (Dunton reverts so frequently to the formative role of the theatre that Catherine Gallagher infers, from a typical *Night-Walker* episode, that theatricality and prostitution were wholly interchangeable, that "the clients themselves . . . seem in search of a dramatic, as much as a sexual, experience.")[8] In short, when Dunton tries to awe his courtesan-victims by revealing "who I am" they counter by insisting on who *they* are, on the legitimacy of their profession and its congruence with the values of polite society as formed by the "Greatest Wits" and the most brilliant "Play-Books." Dunton has to fall back on the kind of vigilante violence that the "Greatest Wits" themselves indulged in, symbolically breaking through the upper-class façade by threatening "to have their Quarters beat up, upon which in a Day or two after they removed their Lodgings for fear" (27).

This trivial-seeming episode connects Dunton to several important cultural moments. Expanding into an autonomous publication the experiment begun in his *Athenian Mercury*, the *Night-Walker* founds a kind of journalism still prevalent in the English tabloid—the undercover exposé of "vice" that mingles prurient fascination with moralistic indignation. Dunton's covert operation of course resembles the work of the Reformation Societies, to whom he dedicates the issue of December 1696. The mediation of prostitution through the iconic objects of high consumer culture—the respectable-looking house, the expensive portrait gallery—obviously draws it closer to the nexus of sex and money in upperclass marriage, driving a wedge between "property" and "propriety" and posing with some urgency the problem of the role to be played by sexual passion in a "polite" culture founded on commerce. More specifically, the gallery invites specular possession and assigns a performative position to the male spectator, a solicitation apparently explicit and straightforwardly phallocentric. I will argue, however, that this "porno-pictorial" arrangement destabilizes the straightforward equation of masculine possession and masculine identity with the gaze, and complicates the relation of "Original" and simulacrum. By revealing the vigilante's complicity with the simulation that maintains the secret economy of pleasure, Dunton's self-representation dissipates the authority that he claims by unmasking. Indeed, he lays bare crucial similarities between the *agent provocateur* and the libertine he impersonates—the phallic impudence of the moralist who pursues penetration and "satisfaction," the violence of the rake who enjoys the whore and then "beats up her quarters" or "kicks her out of doors" (to use a vocabulary shared by Rochester and Dunton).[9] Zeal-to-expose is here revealed as analogous to the sexual drive in that both are constructed and inauthentic. And this brings in for questioning what we might call the "originary myth," the notion that male agency (and hence male authority) stems from genuine primal drives that must break through and triumph over mere appearance.

II. The Portrait in Restoration Narratives of Prostitution

Already in the *Wandring Whore* pamphlets of 1660 the London brothel seems obsessed with visual display: the visiting Venetian courtesan describes the paintings displayed on her own walls and disparages those of a rival, and the bawd stages *tableaux vivants* for her customers. But the images described are grotesque and cartoonish, as if illicit sexuality could only enter visual culture at the "low" carnivalesque level. Though Julietta (the *puttana errante* who gives the series its title) claims to own sophisticated Italian erotic art—*"Peter Aretines* postures curiously painted, with several beautiful pictures stark-naked"—the details she supplies are extremely crude: in her gallery of beauties "one [is] holding a Chamber-pot betwixt her Legs, another striving might and main to enlarge the Orifice of her Mysterium magnum that unfathomed bottom, a third laughing at the large pair of cheeks and haunches she hath got," and so on.[10] In contrast, the paintings described by Dunton sound like an actual collection of Titians and Correggios such as the one Charles I assembled in the private rooms of Whitehall, the nude alongside the clothed, mythologies and *conversazione* mingled with those equivocal *belle donne* and scantily-clad "half-lengths" that art historians still find it difficult to interpret.[11] Are they portraits of courtesans, court ladies, or goddesses? do they represent individual persons, or generalized illustrations of beauty?

The *Wandring Whore* records one exception to its lower-stratum treatment of sexual culture, however—a brief but prophetic allusion to a London entrepreneuse who was already exploiting the uncertain significance of the *bella donna* painting. Mrs. Cresswell in Upper Moorfields is congratulated for recruiting, not plebeian professional whores, but "Citizen's wives, whose Pictures you keep in readiness for your best Customers to chuse on, and trade with."[12] This ambiguous "trading" depends on something culturally and epistemologically amphibious in the nature of portraits. Though portrait-gallery brothels may well have existed—a traveller describes them as normal in Amsterdam in 1681—household inventories show that perfectly respectable collectors could own and display portraits of "famous courtesans."[13] Such portraits can be displayed for the beauty of the painting alone, or stand in for some "Original." Furthermore, that "standing in" can be interpreted as a purely cerebral and visual process, an act of recognition that enhances connoisseurship without implying any course of action, or it may be "constructed" as an invitation to desire. Desire in turn may be channeled towards the absent and unattainable (as in the museum), or towards "the Person" in the flesh (as in the shop or brothel), constituting the "fronting" relationship of sign to body that provides the earliest meaning of "prostitution." Portraits can thus participate both in the clandestine sexual economy (by virtue of their sensuous content) and in official culture, proclaiming the sitter's social consequence and conferring the aura of high-aesthetic connoisseurship associated with oil painting. Several early Restoration whore-pamphlets refer to "lady"-like prostitutes commissioning their own portraits, to improve their social cachet and so to "meliorate their commodities."[14] By exhibiting such prestige objects Mrs. Cresswell meliorates herself—displaying the prosperity and taste of an aspiring "Citizen"—and at the same time protects her "Citizen's Wives."

The semiotic ambiguity and high-cultural status of the portrait is nicely summed up in another version of the citizen's-wife-in-the-brothel story, retailed in *The London-Bawd:* by using the portrait-gallery device, the bawd explains, "we are sure that none but Persons of Quality can be admitted; and the Ladies Honours are thereby secur'd."[15] Were they secured, one wonders, by the well-known discretion of the "Quality" customer or by the portrait medium itself, which can convey appearance and yet conceal identity by mythologizing, idealizing, or imposing the fashionable standard? (Van Dyke and Lely had already established the generic appearance of the Court portrait which "shows" and yet conceals, luxuriously clothed but displaying a voluptuous decolleté; as contemporary observers complained, the facial features increasingly conformed to the sleepy-eyed "look" modeled after, or required in, the latest royal infatuation.)[16] These "Pictures" that Mrs. Cresswell keeps could thus be suitable for her public rooms, a "front" or line of defence against the Duntonesque spy. Only by insisting on the "natural construction" could these images of citizen's wives be translated into bodies available for "trading."

Mrs. Cresswell's citizen portraits, reserved for her "best" customers, must have been quite different from the explicitly erotic paintings that pornographic texts recommend in the bedroom, to stimulate or "authenticate" the sexual act itself. Ferrante Pallavicino's *Retorica delle puttane* for example, which insists on a scrupulously-maintained impression of luxury and respectability on the exterior of the house and in the courtesan's public entertainments, recommends her to display in her private quarters "le figure dell'Aretino in unico quadro raccolte"—that is, the "*Peter Aretines* postures curiously painted" of which the wandering whore would later boast. The customer is assumed to need stimulation and guidance, to derive his ideas and feelings from the painting which "must be imitated" in performance and which "authenticates" the fiction of spontaneous natural desire; the picture is the "Original" and the human subject a mere simulacrum here. In much the same way, the courtesan herself must visualize the mental image of a "vaghissimo giovine," an absolutely gorgeous boy, so that she can simulate desire when coupling with a repulsive client (who believes, of course, that *he* has inspired this passion).[17] The English adaptation of this Italian text is in some ways even more dependent on pictorial stimulus, though the individual images become more timid. *The Whores Rhetorick* (1683) suggests "the best draughts of Men and Women naked" to "operate on" the customer, and for the courtesan herself an actual painting of a *"Ganymede"*: "you must frame in your mind the Idea of some comely Youth who pleases you best, whose shadow will create a greater gust than could be raised by a nauseous though real enjoyment. The Picture of this charming Boy may very fitly be placed near your Bed, to imprint the fancy deeper in your imagination" (166–70). "Aretino's Postures" are rejected as too sodomitical for the English climate, however (171–72). And even in the bedroom, erotic images must be covered with a curtain or concealed inside an anamorphic puzzle-picture that looks completely innocent until it is rotated to reveal its sexual meaning (169, 172). A similar "rotation," conceptual-hermeneutic rather than physical, occurs in the portrait gallery. Significantly, the old bawd who gives this advice in the English *Whores Rhetorick* is the very same Mrs. Cresswell who developed discreet pictorial pornography over twenty years earlier.

The *Wandring Whore*'s recreation of the Cresswell house—the externally visible portrait gallery rather than the clandestine posture-gallery—derives instead from works like Crispin de Passe's *Miroir des plus belles courtisanes*, a book-length collection of alluring but not indecent portrait engravings. English readers might especially notice countrywomen like "My lady of Oxon" or "Margery of Richmonde" (fig. 2), whose loose smock and cascading blonde hair anticipates the image that Dunton picked out. Including these aristocratic figures presumably exploits a potential ambiguity in the word *courtisanes*, which an inexperienced reader might construe as "Court Ladies."[18] (The English title, which appears on the engraved but not the printed title-page, actually translates the word as "Courtiers.") As the artist himself explains in his preface, his "design" was not to "attract anyone to debauchery" (a concession that clearly identifies these images as prostitutes) but to show "the changes of fashion" and to amuse the viewer with "nayves representations de vices"—*naive* in the nonpejorative sense of fresh and spontaneous. In such collections the connoisseur can enjoy these "representations" on paper, appreciating the engraver's "art" and "seeing the World without leaving his room."[19] To assist the imaginary transition from the viewing-closet to the "World," de Passe created a scenic title-page (fig. 3) in which a Cavalieresque customer scrutinizes the portraits—accurately copied from the images within the book that follows. Just as the reader moves from this viewing-scene to the individual vignettes, so the depicted client choses a painting and then, to judge from the activity at the rear, procures what Dunton rather naively calls the "Original." In this iconic construction of sexuality, desire quite literally originates in the image and passes on to "the Person" as a secondary phenomenon. Like the bawd-curator in the foreground, the engraver-publisher brings the depiction of the courtesan forward into the domestic space, without actually breaking the frame of decorum.

Figure 2. Crispin de Passe II, *Miroir des plus belles courtisanes de ce temps* (Amsterdam?, 1631), portraits 19–20, "Margery of Richmonde" and "Dority her chambermaide."

The fullest prototype of Dunton's "meliorated" and graduated encounter expands de Passe's engraved frontispiece into a fictionalized version of Mrs. Cresswell's portrait house.[20] Shortly after his first success as a card-sharp, the picaresque hero of Richard Head's 1665 *English Rogue* visits a "new-fashion *Bawdy-house*," where business is run on hedonistic rather than mercenary principles and the aspiring customer must pass through a series of visual testing stages in which *he* is objectified as much as the "Ladies." The visual appraisal staged in de Passe's frontispiece—which places the swaggering male sustomer securely at the centre of consumption, smoking by the fireside while choosing the porno-pictorial delights offered by a deferential hostess—remains a future promise, and in the meantime the evaluative gaze must be turned upon the appraiser.[21] At each step he is subject to a "stricter view" to see if he displays the signs of wealth and status, scrutinized first by the porter, then by the "grave Matron," then by the "Gentlewomen" themselves, concealed behind "peeping-holes"; since many of them are persons of quality, this vantage-point is necessary to preserve the "security" promised by the London bawd. If the *belle de jour* likes what she sees, she "would appear and tender herself as the subject of his pleasure" (actively performing the passive role "with much freedom"); if she recognizes someone who might

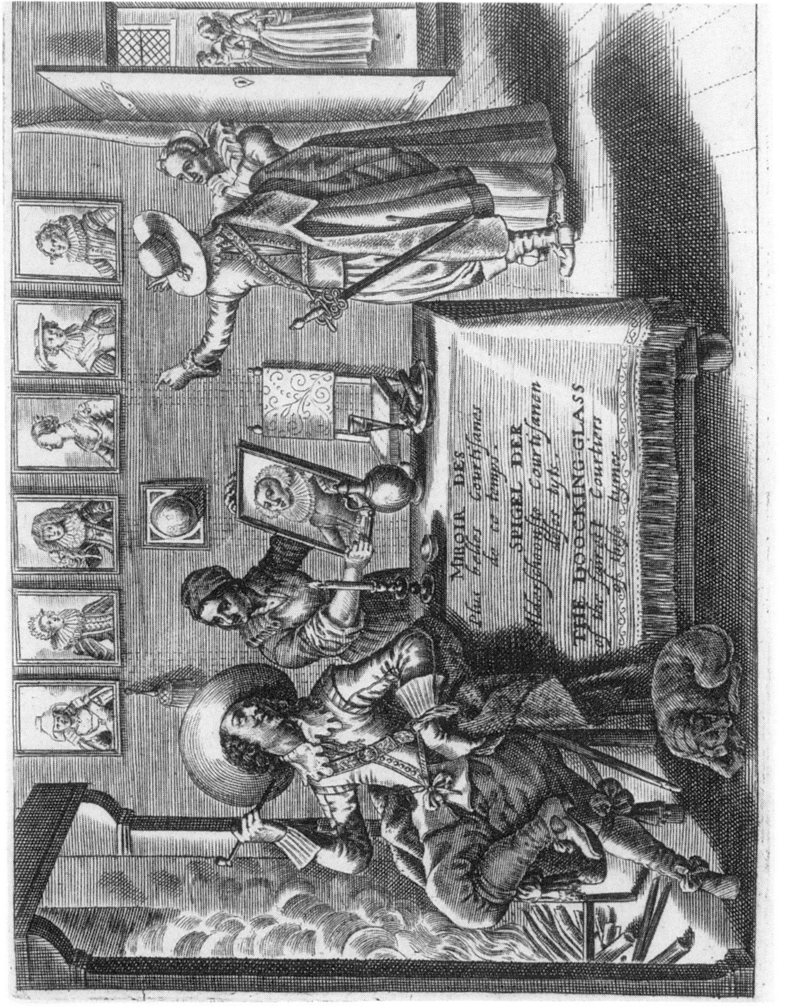

Figure 3. de Passe, *Miroir des plus belles courtisanes*, title page.

recognize her, such as a husband or relative, she can remain protectively hidden while "Madam Bawd" explains the picture as an artefact "bought casually at second-hand" or given by a collector-friend, an *objet de virtu* rather than a coded "representation of vice." As in the steps that Dunton has to pass through to gain *his* "satisfaction," the matron must be "satisfied in *me*" before she takes him to what we might call the gallery-stage, "a very large and fair dining-room hung with rich Tapistry, and adorned round with excellent pictures, the effigies of divers Ladies (as I took them to be) renowned and celebrated in all ages, for the fairest and most beautiful of that sex" (35). The low-life criminal apprentice appears to have stepped into a gallery of historic beauties of the kind established in Renaissance courts.

Like the disguised reformer, the disguised "English rogue" must not only look right but perform properly, putting into play the gallant turns of phrase and high-cultural aesthetic concepts that maintain the fiction that distinguishes this from a common brothel. The hostess invites him to show his upper-class credentials by an aesthetic critique of these pictures: "as you are a Gentleman, you may have some knowledge in that noble Art of Limning . . . much studied by the Gentry of this Nation." Like Dunton he responds with a descriptive analysis of the image he chooses, fleshing out the facial features of the portrait, itemizing and evaluating them according to prescriptive standards derived from treatises on beauty ("passing her cheeks, which carry in them an excellent air, and her nose, which is neither too long nor too short, view her lips, whose plumpness and redness resemble a double Cherry"). Significantly, he endows the eyes with an erotic agency that places *him* in the passive position: "by their intuitive faculty" they "seem to penetrate that which they look on" (36). While thinking to exert his powers, he subjects himself to a property of the portrait that had already been articulated (and eroticized) in the Renaissance: its capacity to seem active, to fix and impose an identity upon the viewer. In one *cinquecento* dialogue, for example, the courtesan-speaker explains that in the amorous gaze the lover becomes "a portrait of that which he loves"; the eroticized female, far from remaining the passive object of male desire, actively wields "love's stylus" and thereby "portrays herself" in her admirer's face and heart.[22]

The rogue-connoisseur attempts to counteract the "penetrating" force of visual representation by a "discourse" both complimentary and complementary, blazoning and filling in ("for the dimples in her cheeks and chin, I could make them the subject of an whole dayes discourse: what might be said more of this representation, I shall waive," etc.). Discourse offers the possibility of endless deferral, but it also allows him to accelerate the courtship ritual. The conversation leads, via the conceit of shadow and "real substance," to a request for the person represented; the bawd agrees, but in terms that reassert the primacy of the visual (to meet the original "is not impossible, Sir, if you can have but the faith to believe your own eyes"). He awaits more in terror than pleasurable anticipation, evidently insecure in this new ocular "faith," torn between two kinds of visual compulsion intensified by a class-anxiety which threatens to ruin the gentlemanly pretense that brought him to this point. The originary myth takes another beating. The apprentice-libertine is already smitten or "penetrated" by the picture—an old romance motif transferred to the libertine pornosphere—and now, "Hearing a rushing of silks, I drew my eyes off the Picture" only to be visually transfixed and dumbfounded by a "celestial" icon. He remains "at a distance, admiring, or rather adoring her person"—as if the Person were yet another artefact, alienated and exalted to high art. After half an hour of silence and social diffidence, however, "confidence had repossest her ancient seat in me." This regaining of the seigneurial position allows him to "come to my self," to perform sexually and to recuperate the dominant language: the next morning, he gloats over his own prowess, dismisses the former "angels" as "cattel," sneers at women's "insatiate lusts," and finally reasserts his aesthetic control by completing in verse the verbal portrait he had improvised to gain access to this realm of pleasure—extending it from a portrait to a full-length nude. This verbal-plastic composition of itemized "delights" simultaneously *creates* his desire and *responds* to it, like inanimate matter stirring under the "warm hand" of a plebeian Pygmalion.[23]

In the *English Rogue* and in other bawdy tales circulating during the Restoration, the "picture-gallery" motif combines with other, older narratives of secret lust and cunning exposure. In the *London-Bawd* version, which we could call the "St. Antholin's Bells" variant, the husband himself tries to expose the wife by sleeping with her in disguise—precisely the danger that the "new-fashion Bawdy-house" guards against by providing "peeping-holes." The wife of a prominent citizen has inscribed herself into a secret economy of visual pleasure, evidently modelled on Mrs. Cresswell's house; not only is the dining room lined with individually-commissioned portraits, but each bedroom contains a mirror, "for some take as much delight in seeing as in doing." Her alibi is the Puritan lecture at St. Antholin's Church, where the suspicious husband follows her (luckily she *does* go to church on this occasion, since the painter has not yet finished her portrait, and so unwittingly allays suspicion). Thereafter she attends the brothel every morning, clearly reassured by the "Quality" and security promised by the picture-gallery arrangement (63 above). Nevertheless, the fashioning of appearances turns out to increase her danger. Her painting attracts so many customers that a jealous rival writes a Duntonesque anonymous letter to the husband, providing him with the private entry-code that allows him past the "genteel" exterior:

he is to pose as a connoisseur who wishes to view "the Ladies in the Dining-Room." He alters his appearance exactly as Dunton does, by wearing "a very Beauish Suit, Wig, and Hat," and once inside the picture-gallery he can select his own wife by nominating the canvas that "pleases my Eye better than any of the rest." He performs his gentlemanly role so well, "Counterfeiting his Voice" and adopting the aesthetic language of "Shadow" and "Substance," that his wife fails to recognize him even in bed. She clearly lacks not only the "peeping-hole" that lets her screen customers in advance, but the "intuitive faculty" that the English Rogue projects into the very portrait. Anonymous enjoyment distracts her from "the Person," though her senses remain open to the sounds of the urban landscape around her: "whilst they were a Dancing and Acting the delights of *Venus*, the Bells of St. *Antholins* Rung very sweetly, which made her say, whilst she was thus incountring her suppos'd Gallant, *O how sweetly St.* Antholin's *Bells Ring!* Which she Repeated over as oft as they renew'd their Pleasures."[24]

The elements of this story predate the importation of the Italianate picture gallery. Though its influence had waned long since, the lecture at St. Antholin's (or St. Anthony's, Budge Row) had been perceived as the main source of radical ideology during the civil wars, "the grand nursery from whence most of the Seditious Preachers were after sent abroad throughout all England to poyson the people with their anti-monarchical principles."[25] Following the logic of "porno-political" satire, that church and its bells became synonymous with the secret sexuality of City wives; a royalist pamphlet of 1642, for example, jeers at women's devotion to "that *Tinckle tanckle* bell [of Saint Antholing] that rayses them in a morning to a stirring exercise," though they really "love the bell for the Clapper sake."[26] (The luxurious brothel-picture-gallery also features in underground royalist satire against the Puritan leaders.) Decades earlier, in an astonishing legal case of 1629, the widow Elizabeth Smith brings a defamation suit against two malicious neighbors who destroyed her marriage-prospects by circulating a story very like the one in *The London-Bawd*, minus the portrait-gallery: her first husband shaved off his beard, disguised himself as a gallant customer, and followed her to a brothel in St. Swithin's Lane, round the corner from her supposed destination St. Antholin's; after a generous payment the bawd ushers them together, but she runs off in panic once she recognizes his voice, and he dies of grief and shame.[27] Such variations on the ancient device of the bed-trick—used eight times in Boccaccio's *Decameron* and over thirty times in seventeenth-century English comedy—may seem wholly conventional to us. But in fact they crossed easily from entertainment into allegation, from printed "merry tales" into oral slander so damaging that Elizabeth Smith felt compelled to sue the narrators in court. Later in the century, Dunton's true stories would exploit precisely this uncertain borderline between fiction and fact, entertainment and exposé.

Like all bed-trick narratives, the St. Antholin's tale hinges on the malleability or conventionality of exterior appearance. In every version except the "picture-gallery" variant retailed in *The London-Bawd*, however, it is only the men who are deceived. The assumption is that women can always infer individual identity from bodily sensation, but that males' arousal renders their perception generic and obtuse. In some cases (for example in *Measure for Measure* or Aphra Behn's *The Lucky Chance*) the man never once recognizes his partner during a night of love-making. The bawd may be taken in by the genteel-seeming stranger, or the husband may deliberately smuggle in another man under cover of darkness (as in a later scene of *The Lucky Chance*), but the female participant always realizes whom she is touching. In the 1629 defamation-trial narrative, Elizabeth Smith recognizes her disguised husband the moment she hears his voice. In *The London Jilt* of 1683, the citizen's wife who wants to enjoy an anonymous night in the brothel is terrified to see her own husband coming in as a customer, and only escapes by substituting her maid (II.30). In Middleton's comedy *The Family of Love*, where the husband inveigles himself into the nocturnal orgies of that religious sect, the wife appears to enjoy the stranger's embraces but later disarms criticism by exclaiming "Husband, I see you are hoodwinked in the right use of feeling and knowledge—as if I knew you not then as well as the child knows his own father! . . . hath not fellow-feeling taught us to know one another as well by night as by day?"[28] In the pictorially-conscious world of *The London-Bawd*, this "fellow-feeling" has been replaced by a visual régime of seductive appearances. The wife makes love to her "suppos'd Gallant" to the tune of St. Antholin's bells, and they part without her realizing his true identity. The dénouement is deferred to that night, when they are once again in bed together. We are led to expect a vigilante showdown à la Dunton, an indignant exposé mingled with self-applause for his own mastery of appearances and adroit performance in the prurient role. Ironically, however, the wife's nonperception wins the day, since she is able to turn her husband's disguise into a critique of his conventionality. The truth comes out because "he had a mind to try whether he cou'd with the same briskness manage things at home as he had done abroad: But finding it on both sides much more Dull, he told her St. *Ant'lin*'s Bells didn't Ring half so sweetly then as they did i'th'Morning" (78–79/80–81). Her reply (after an initial moment of confusion) regains the mastery by suggesting that, judging identity by "performance," he truly *was* a different man in the brothel than in the marriage-bed: "if you wou'd be but as brisk at home as you are abroad, I should be very well Satisfy'd without going abroad, with your own performances at home. I see you can do better if you will; and if you don't, blame your self and not me, if you are made a Cuckold" (80/82).

Incorporating pictorial self-consciousness thus adds a new twist to these narratives of bawdy escapism and penetrating cleverness, literally and juridically "pornographic" since they seek to demonstrate the whoredom of women trying to live within the customary roles assigned them by the patriarchy (as "citizen's wives" or genteel landladies). Appearances and inferences can be manipulated by cunning subjects at each end of the transaction, to baffle or compel; the visual cone can be grasped and fashioned into a "hood." To be sure, none of these petty tales demolishes the larger structures of male dominance or deeply challenges that "double standard" that should more accurately be called a triple standard, since it discriminates by class as much as gender: not only is the husband's attendance at the brothel considered venial, but the sexual misadventures of "City" couples are regarded as intrinsically comic. But the order of things is unsettled, nevertheless. Once endowed with aesthetic allure and social prestige, once it becomes a shining exemplar of "cultural capital," the visual representation seems to exert its own fascinating agency. The portrait looks back, and the viewer cannot look away. The "gaze" is not necessarily unidirectional, nor coincident with the source of power. The masculine "rambler" may be visually "fixed" against his will (like Dunton in Cheapside), or "hoodwinked in the right use of feeling and knowledge" (like the husband at the Familist orgy), or he may become the object of class-identifying scrutiny (like the English Rogue under the "stricter view" of the *patronne*) or the awestruck witness of "celestial" iconicity (like the Rogue in the presence of his chosen "original"). He can be separated from his husbandly identity and appreciated as a "beau" and performing stud (as the "St. Antholin's" wife does, first unwittingly and then deliberately). And the visual-prostitutional relation itself may be reversed, as we shall see in some of Dunton's night-walks; having donned his rake-identity, redesigned himself for the "detection of lewd women," he finds *himself* the pleasure-commodity to be bought and traded by "lascivious dames," subject to *their* "natural construction."

III. "Looking Like a Gentleman": Dunton's Libertine Simulacra

The history of Restoration visual "pornography" that I have just outlined, a history that operates in both the fictional and the legal realms, provides the motive for Dunton's confrontational visit to the portrait-gallery, and perhaps even its source. The picture-collection stands as a marker of social status and "genteel" whoredom, of course, but it also emblematizes the subsumption of eros into appearance, and thereby extends a tantalizing challenge to the "supposed gallant": now, perhaps, he might beat the courtesan at her own game of visual mastery, "hoodwink" the secretive City wife, reveal the *porne* that underlies the *graphe*. The vigilante, like the libertine, applies his "Briskness" to the game of cracking and penetrating the multiple layers of exteriority coded as respectable. In Dunton's version, the social stakes are further raised by transposing the house from the City back-street to "the Court end of the town." As in *The London-Bawd*, however, entrusting himself to "performances" can reveal his own shortcoming and his own implication in the system of libertine visuality.

In order to impose his "stricter view" on the prostitutes, Dunton must turn *himself* into an ambiguous portrait, subject to *their* testing gaze. And he takes evident pleasure in this campaign against the women of pleasure. Dunton presents himself as a kind of Protestant Horner, equally eager to sniff out "the game" and equally proud of the tricks, disguises, and displays of libertine expertise that get him past the fashionable-respectable exterior. Like the picaroon in the *English Rogue* or the cunning husband posing as libertine gentleman in the *London Bawd*, he *looks right* in both senses—evidencing the right appearance and the right "eye." He deploys the right "discourse" and knows the proper climactic moment to move from discourse to action. Like the genteel rogue, he enjoys the chance to display his own erotic connoisseurship and procurative skills as he luxuriates in his description of the pictures and selects his favourite courtesan. As we have seen, these are no longer the crude caricatures described by the supposedly Venetian "wandering whore" but sophisticated Titianesque courtesans and *bellissime donne*. Dunton participates in this high-cultural game of erotic appearances, *investing himself* in it quite literally, and this suspiciously intense involvement reflects back upon his own artefactuality, his own constructedness, undermining the moral and judicial authority that he claims when he pulls off the mask.

Dunton's double dealing is supposed to maintain a rigid distinction between his original core identity (virtuous, steely, indignant) and the gentrified and dissolute simulacrum that he scarfs about him in order to subvert and explode a hidden libertine system which exactly reverses this interior-exterior dichotomy. But something happens to this fixity when he dresses up in the disguise that allows him to penetrate the economy of desire. "For the better Accomplishment of my design," he explains, "I equipt my self like a Ruffling Spark, with" not only his "Hat Cockt up" but his long wig, "the hinder part of [which] bore an exact resemblance of those parts, which the *Lascivious Dames* come in Quest of, and tho' nature has not been wanting in her part, I thought it best to improve my Shoulders with an Addition of *Flannel*" (December 1696, 3). Dunton's slippery syntax throws the emphasis onto the "part" that Nature has supplied him with, which echoes the "part" explicitly figured in the outrageous dangling wig even as it looks forward to other bulges that Dunton does not need to simulate, yet "adds" anyway in the form of a stuffed toy. "Nor was I wanting," Dunton continues with equal ambiguity, "to make use of those contrivances with which Sparks use to supply their Calves"; does this mean that he felt no desire to use this artificial supplement, or that he did not fail to supply it? In either case, the wig-passage already flaunts in the reader's face the assurance that he does not need a simulated "Addition," the hint that he really is fashioned for this sport and thus not wholly in disguise. In both incarnations—in the "true" vigilante self verbally revealed to the reader, as well as in the flannel-padded rake-character that he displays to the unsuspecting world—he becomes a walking phallus "rambling" in search of satisfaction.

Dunton was almost forty years old, heavily pock-marked, and just as heavily committed to the Whiggish and nonconformist "reformation of manners" that revived the old puritan fury against Stuart immorality; nevertheless, his crusading self-promotion seems perpetually compromised by sexual vanity. A recurrent theme in his autobiographical publication is his pursuit by the lust-crazed wives of other "Citizens."[29] When he issues forth for his night walk, resplendent in powder, perfume, and jewels, he congratulates himself on "looking Fresh and Brauny" (imagining himself through the eyes of the "lascivious dame" impressed by the length of his wig). He exults in the attention of these ladies (whom he "ogles" in return), and enters readily into the prostitutional exchange. One of them slips him a guinea and makes an assignation, which in turn leads to a bedroom-scene where she sprawls "in a very wanton posture" and he provides the climax, an equivocal unmasking and a stern revelation of identity: "you do not know who I am." Having thoroughly terrified her and exposed her to her husband by means of an anonymous letter, he maintains the sexual-economic exchange with the parting promise to "bestow her Guinea better than she intended it"—though we never actually learn its fate (December 1696, 3–5). When Dunton picks up another and more socially exalted "Gentlewoman" in St. James's Park (who feeds his vanity by calling him "a very Complaisant Gentleman and fit to be a Courtier"), his reformist zeal noticeably softens (October 1696, 22). Even in his most ferocious and radical-Puritan rhetoric he reminds us of the display of phallic significance that he shares with the libertine, the gentlemanly "Addition" that allows his acts of penetration. Immediately before his ramble into the picture-gallery, for example, he indulges in an extraordinary Good Old Cause diatribe that returns irresistibly to the convergence of male appendage and aristocratic privilege, the "part" that he himself "does not want": "if all the Gallants who walk our Streets and are guilty of this Beastly Pollution should have their Wigs served as the *Grecians* used to serve the Beards of their Fornicators, that is to say, have their long Taggs and monstrous Locks cut off with a sharp Ax, we should have abundance of Gentlemen become Round-Heads, who now hate the Name on't" (January 1697, 22).

Dunton's fierce declarations of self-identity—"I will now pull off my Mask!" "you don't know who I am!"—turn out to be as equivocal as the painted ladies themselves. And the staff he produces to reinforce his authority hardly confounds the libertine system of signification he claims to be destroying. On several occasions he whips it out at the precise moment that the city-wife slips her hand into his breeches with a comment like "Its not Preaching but a —— that I expect from you"; Dunton trusts the reader's sense of alliteration to fill in the dash (January 1697, 29). Only two pages after the picture-scene, when another recalcitrant victim confronts him with her own secular-hedonistic integrity, declaring him a "Canting Coxcomb" and threatening to have him kicked downstairs, he replies "Why such a passion Madam? I know which way to lay it"; then, "pulling out a short Staff, *like a Constables*, which I carried with me on purpose, in case of any such Adventure," he promises to carry her before a Justice (December 1696, 7, my emphasis). When he jeers at her for being as inauthentic as the "Frothy and Filthy" plays she takes as model, she reminds him of his triple incongruity: she "should little have thought to have met with a Constable in a Beaux Habit, or with a preacher and a Constables Staff in his Pocket" (9). On a similar occasion, after Dunton unmasks a whore and her pretended "aunt" (and threatens them with the "Entertainment" of Bridewell), "the young slut ... beginning to show her immodest tricks, said she would quickly bring me off from those severe Morals, upon which"—predictably—"I pull'd out my *short Constable Staff.*" This implement, less a "Constable Staff" than a staff "in the manner of Constable," is clearly as fictitious as the prostitute's cloaking narrative and apparently just as effective for "bringing him off" (December 1696, 15). Yet Dunton seems unconcerned by either the fictiveness or the phallicity of this little wand, which corresponds in both respects to the dangling tail of his wig. Indeed, he exploits the parallel of these different tools for "laying passion." Preaching and prick become interchangable, and both are simulacra.

The question of Dunton's self-identity and originality is further complicated when we turn from the *Night-Walker*—a moral crusade authenticated by direct personal reportage—to contemporary bawdy and pornographic fiction, the "Wicked Books" that Dunton himself blames for spreading the "Poyson" of libertinism, "the raging sin of Uncleanness" (February 1697, 19). As I have shown, the "porno-pictorial" device allegedly encountered in a real West End assignment-house in January 1697 was already illustrated (and exemplified) in the Franco-Flemish *Miroir des courtisanes*, and the motif recurs in Interregnum royalist satire, in the literally pornographic *Wandring Whore*, and in the picaresque *English Rogue*. The disguising and unmasking impulses combine with the pictorial-brothel theme in the "St. Antholin's Bells" story recycled in *The London-Bawd*, a publication by Dunton's wealthy colleague John Gwillim.[30] The City husband in this St. Antholin version seems especially close to Dunton's vigilante masquerade; he simulates the foppish appearance of the gentleman so effectively that his own wife fails to recognize him, and he penetrates the equivocal exterior by deploying expert insider information. Like Dunton he fails in his opening gambit by asking too coarsely for a "Fleshly Convenience." The landlady responds with affronted respectability—"I hope you don't take me for a Bawd?"—but relents when he names his secret contact: "I was directed hither by *Tom Stanhop*, to take a Survey of the Ladies in the Dining-Room" (76/78). Dunton likewise triggers a rejection with his first request for a tasty morsel (*"I hope you don't take me for a Bawd"*) but wins entry by naming her customer, Squire ——. In the "St. Antholin" version, as we have seen, the unmasking climax rebounds on the husband's own head: in a sense, the dull Cit really *had* become a different person when he put on the periwig and the phallic activism of the libertine, and the married couple remain friends as long as he can resume that "person" in bed. But the tragic version returns towards the end of *The London-Bawd*, when the title-character herself describes a visit from a libertine customer who turns out to be a spy for the Society for the Reformation of Manners.

Until this intrusion the narrator of *The London-Bawd* had led a life of quiet professionalism in a respectable-looking house "in St. *Thomas Apostles*" (151/153); the earlier "genteel" brothel had been precisely located when the wife crosses over from St. Antholin's to "the Back-side of *St. Thomas Apostles*, and there go[es] into a House" (75/77), the implication being that both episodes involve the same residence. (Since the church was destroyed in the Fire and never rebuilt, this detail suggests that both stories circulated long before 1697.)[31] Here she trains the younger generation in the techniques she had learned in her youth (discreetly seductive behavior in church, conversation improved by reading plays), and builds a collection of paintings: Ovidian Loves of the Gods mingle with portraits of "those Ladies of Pleasure I keep in my House, drawn in very amorous and inviting Postures," for example "one with her Golden Tresses dishelv'd upon her Shoulders, and her Breasts naked." Suddenly "a Gentleman in a very good genteel Habit knocks at my Door." At first he is rebuffed ("I hope you don't take me for a Bawd?"), but gains credence by naming the élite customer Squire —— and by showing his appreciation of the visual "Entertainment" (153–56). Does this sound familiar? The whole of Dunton's account, including the lush description of the pictures and the final threat to "beat up their quarters," appears virtually word for word, page after page, though here it is told from the London bawd's point of view. Who has plagiarized whom? Which is the "Original" here, pornographic fiction or vigilante witness to the sober truth?

The *London-Bawd* passage *reads* like the original and *sounds* like a publication of the 1680s or early 1690s, when allusions to Mrs. Cresswell and Posture Moll, the reigning queens of pornopictorial representation, would still have felt topical. Unfortunately only the third edition of 1705 and the verbally identical fourth edition of 1711 seem to have survived, so precise antedating is impossible. Gwillim's work bulges with plagiarism, but always from sources earlier than Dunton.[32] Moreover, certain details in the bawd's story work more plausibly there than in the *Night-Walker*: the house has a more precise location that matches earlier references to St. Thomas Apostle's; the chosen courtesan has the specific name "Gertrude" rather than the generic "Betty"; the account of how they would make themselves alluring on the way to church and read plays to improve their conversation, which the bawd tells to describe their way of life before the vigilante comes to break up her house, is awkwardly inserted into the furious and emotional argument that Dunton reports. The description of the pictures in *The London-Bawd*, slightly more explicit than Dunton's, fits the character and the occasion better, since the bawd is entertaining a sensually-inclined goldsmith's wife and softening her up as a recruit. The violent ending is better integrated with the narrative structure, as the bawd goes on to describe her anxious move and the heightened security she was forced to adopt (no strangers without written letters of reference). Nevertheless, without an extant first edition we simply cannot know whether Gwillim plagiarized Dunton or whether Dunton's entire truth-claim—he actually did this, went there, confronted those people, and only refrains from publishing their names and addresses because his goal is to reform rather than to expose—is just another dangling appendage made from someone else's hair.

The *possibility* of plagiarism, suggested by resemblences between the *Night-Walker* and texts like the *English Rogue* that certainly predate 1697, is confirmed by a revealing admission that seriously compromises Dunton's claim to be delivering unmediated, first-hand reportage. In the "Conclusion to the Criticks" that closes the February 1697 issue he defends himself against the accusation that the *Night-Walker* actually *teaches* innocent readers "the way of being Lewd" rather than reforming them (18–19). Lunging for the high moral and epistemological ground, he insists not only that he is relating "matters of fact" but that exactly the same criticism could be leveled against the Bible itself. In the same breath, however, he reveals that he drew his "matter" from a quite different kind of scripture. Those Wicked Books are indeed to blame for England's corruption, yet readers who have perused them "with but too much intention" might now be "entice[d]" to read Dunton's publication; "it was thought that a Design of this Nature"—that is, *The Night-Walker* itself—"recounting the same Intrigues in a more modest manner, . . . might [promote] the design of a Reformation." Like the prostitutes themselves he "entices" by "Design." His self-justifications draw attention to the danger of his stratagem, his attempt to reverse the relationship between *porn* and *graph* while keeping both fully visible; he dissociates himself from the Society for the Reformation of Manners (claiming to pursue the same goal by a different method) precisely because they refuse to publish the details of the lewdness their agents uncover (20). Dunton admits in this "Conclusion" that in effect he is recycling the very books that cause the wickedness in the first place, but "with the reproofs annexed," with an "Addition" or "front" of morality. And he even names his sources, "the *London Jilt*, and other of the Sort, which are spread through the Nation like so much Poyson." Indeed, the principal example that Dunton cites, what we might call the "Original" of his enticing illusion, is the *"English Rogue."*

To create a "Conclusion" is particularly difficult in this infinite regress of simulacra, this endless mutually-productive cycle of prostitution and prosecution; the plagiarist of the libertine subculture passes himself off as a crusading tabloid journalist disguised as a constable disguised as a beau preying on the libertine subculture. Each episode in Dunton's serial stalker-narrative concludes with its more or less brutal climax, more or less tactlessly revealing the congruence of the whoremonger and the vigilante. But the process of enticement-and-publication itself can only end when the goal of Reformation is actually achieved, illicit sexuality entirely abolished, dangling wigs cut to the root, reversible spy-holes stopped up, and the demand for "Wicked Books" reduced to zero. (Given Dunton's recycling economy, the supply as well as the demand would have to dry up, too.) *The London-Bawd*, in contrast, ingeniously combines voyeuristic-vicarious pleasure and reformist terror into a novelistic ending—though once again it is impossible to decide whether bawdy narrative expropriates pseudo-pseudopornographic journalism or vice versa. This closure is achieved by giving the last word to the citizen's wife, a device rehearsed in the surprise ending of the "St. Antholin's Bells" story.

After the London bawd finishes her autobiography the goldsmith's wife takes over the narrative reins, placing the procuress in the audience-position. She recounts her clandestine affair with a Mr. Bramble, but under an increasing cloud of anxiety. What makes her particularly fearful of exposure to her husband—and what makes her story more like that of the London Jilt than the St. Antholin's lady—is a change in the domestic configuration; the happy bourgeois couple has been infiltrated by a new kind of entertainer, a neighbor who regales them with scenes from his undercover work as a *pornographe*. This "Constable that lives hard by us, and is one of the Society for Reformation," visits to tell them about the enormities he has discovered, but apparently his intention is to amuse more than to horrify. Secretly the wife feels a "Consternation" that inhibits her enjoyment, but this soon melts into relief at not being discovered, and she can then articulate—finally—the faintly sadistic thrill that such exposés really elicit: she was now "better satisfy'd," and found these stories "diverting enough, as long as it did not concern me. For tho' we care not to be expos'd our selves, we are yet ready to take a kind of pleasure in hearing that others are so." To cap the entire narrative the reformed wife, converted from one kind of "satisfaction" to another, recounts to her bawd-listener a specimen of these newly-pleasur-able "diversions" (which also "divert" attention from her own rambles). She retells a lewd episode that, like the gallery-visit, also appears almost verba-tim in Dunton's *Night-Walker*. It is, in fact, the very scene in which he ex-poses the "aunt" and lugs out his Constable staff when the "niece" promises to "bring him off" (74 above). Confirming Dunton's confession that he has been retailing low-libertine literature "in a more modest manner," this clos-ing narrative of *The London-Bawd* contains details more specific than the night-walker's version; rather than coaxing out the baton with unspecified "immodest tricks," for example, the younger woman "pluck'd up her Coats, and told me she'd find me other Business to do. I seeing that pull'd out my Short Constables Staff" (175). (The fictional version is also more definite about his constabular status.) The book thus ends with a distinct turn in the fortunes of everyone involved: the wicked wenches beat hemp in Bridewell prison; the bawd crosses the threshold from creator to consumer of moral "pornography"; the erring but undetected wife inwardly resolves never to take such a risk again; and the entire cast acknowledges the vigilante-figure who has provided the feast of stories. As a ringing finale, "my Husband and I both applauded the Constable."[33]

In these multiple exchanges of role and purpose, narrative itself takes on the mobility and semiotic ambiguity of oil painting. These tales of seduction, penetration, and exposure may be *retailed*, passing from collector to collec-tor "at second hand." They float away from their supposed original inten-tions: bawdy fictions resurface as moralistic reportage, which in turn becomes "a general entertainment for the Fair Sex" (as in Dunton's entrepreneurial launching of his Rambles, or the reappropriation of risky story-telling by the goldsmith's wife). Led by what Dunton calls the desire to "insert," these stories themselves ramble into different sites of "construction," different modes of "satisfaction," and different genderings of narrative authority. Originality dissolves into simulation, Reform into "Design," detection into "diversion." The paintings in the brothel, like "pornography" in the book trade, simultaneously reveal and conceal. They "rotate" (like the anamorphic picture in *The Whores Rhetorick*) from lens of truth into enjoyable peepshow, slipping back and forth between procurement and connoisseurship. For the citizen's wife diversion means camouflage, a protective "investment" in storytelling that deflects or hoodwinks the Duntonian drive to identify the "sign" with the body of the shopkeeper, to pin "roguish" wandering narratives onto particular persons. Applauding the Constable defuses his vigilante hermeneutics, and turns the danger of identification into pleasure in the exposure of Somebody Else.

N O T E S

The place of all publications cited below is London, unless otherwise specified. I would like to thank Katherine Inman, Joanna Picciotto, and Eric Chandler for their comments on an earlier draft of this essay.

1. *Athenian Mercury*, Vol. 3, Number 3 (4 Aug. 1691), verso of unpaginated broadside, and cf. Numbers 1 and 2 (28 July, 1 Aug. 1691) for the anticipatory announcements; N. H., *The Ladies Dictionary* (1694), 454–56. Stephen Parks, *John Dunton and the English Book Trade: A Study of His Career with a Checklist of His Publications* (New York: Garland, 1976), 317, notes the *Dictionary* article (though not the *Mercury* passage), and suggests that the idea of turning it into an independent periodical came from *The Wandring Whore*. Only in the *Life and Errors* (quoted by Parks here) does Dunton explicitly identify this "design to expose Vice" as his own work.

2. Thomas Killigrew, *Thomaso, or The Wanderer*, in *Comedies and Tragedies* (1664), Part One, II.i (p. 326) and II.ii (p. 333); Aphra Behn, *The Rover, or the Banished Cavaliers*, Part One, II.i and Postscript.

3. *The Night-Walker: or, Evening Rambles in Search after Lewd Women* (January, 1697), 23; subsequent references will likewise cite the month and page.

4. In the "Contents of the first Volume" appended to the December 1696 issue. For "sounding" and other aggressively probing detective techniques, see Dec. 1696, 26, and Sept. 1696, 17. For the recurrent use of "ramble" and "frolick" in Dunton's own accounts of his life and publications, see J. Paul Hunter, *Before Novels: The Cultural Contexts of Eighteenth-Century English Fiction* (New York: Norton, 1990), 102, 298, 335.

5. R. D. V., *L'Escole des filles* (n. pl., 1658); references to the "Vit" and "Con" (1: 6) and the "Art foutatique" (1: 12) show how far this undercover work of morality is prepared to go in ensnaring readers for the "Seconde Partie, ou sont contenus les vrays et solides enseignments d'une Fille."

6. *The Night-Walker* (October, 1696), 12. This passage is discussed in Shawn Lisa Maurer, "Reforming Men: Chaste Heterosexuality in the Early English Periodical," *Restoration* 16 (1992): 49–50, and in Melissa Mowry, "(Re)Productive Histories: Epistolary Fiction and the Origin of the English Novel," Ph.D. diss., Univ. of Delaware, 1993, 98–102.

7. Arthur MacGregor, ed., *The Late King's Goods: Collections, Possessions and Patronage of Charles I in the Light of the Commonwealth Sale Inventories* (Oxford: Oxford Univ. Press, 1989), 227.

8. Catherine Gallagher, *Nobody's Story: The Vanishing Acts of Women Writers in the Marketplace, 1670–1820* (Berkeley and Los Angeles: Univ. of California Press, 1994), 29, citing a long passage from the Nov. 1696 issue.

9. Cf. John Wilmot, Earl of Rochester, *Poems*, ed. Keith Walker (Oxford: Blackwell, 1984), 92 ("*Witts* are treated just like common *Whores*, / First they're enjoy'd, and then kickt out of *Doores*") and 98 ("I'll tell of *Whores* attacqu'd, their Lords at home, / *Bawds Quarters* beaten up, and *Fortress* won, / *Windows* demolisht, *Watches* overcome, / And handsome ills, by my contrivance done").

10. [John Garfield], *The Wandring Whore Continued* (1660), 13. This periodical also combined bawdy entertainment and titillating glimpses of the sexual underworld with an ostensible claim to be reforming the vices of London; Garfield, unlike Dunton, actually prints lists of names.

11. MacGregor, ed., *Late King's Goods*, esp. 204; the long-standing controversies over the specificity of Titian's "Venuses" are usefully summed up in Mary Pardo, "Artifice as Seduction in Titian," in James Grantham Turner, ed., *Sexuality and Gender in Early Modern Europe: Institutions, Texts, Images* (Cambridge: Cambridge Univ. Press, 1993), 59–60.

12. [John Garfield], *The Wandring Whore: A Dialogue between Magdalena a Crafty Bawd, Julietta an Exquisite Whore, Francion a Lascivious Gallant, and Gusman a Pimping Hector* (1660), 10.

13. Alison McNeil Kettering, *The Dutch Arcadia: Pastoral Art and Its Audience in the Golden Age* (Montclair: Allanheld and Schram, 1983), 144 n. 32, 145 nn. 42, 45. Jean-François Regnard, in a generic account of Amsterdam brothels that does not claim eye-witness status, describes a somewhat regimented system in which a portrait is posted over each bedroom door; the customer must pay in full on the basis of the picture alone, "tant pis pour vous si la copie a été flattée" (*Voyage de Flandre et de Hollande, commencé le 26 avril 1681* [Amsterdam: Menno Hertzberger, 1935], 34).

14. Cited from *Select City Quaeries* (1660), 3: xv, in Roger Thompson, *Unfit for Modest Ears* (London: Macmillan, 1979), 181 (referring to "the ladies regent at the Bell and Falcon by Moorgate," evidently a class oxymoron). The inflated reckoning in *Wandring Whore* 1: 14 includes the sum of 5s. "for dress-

ing perfuming and painting [Julietta's] picture as *B: S:* does." This is evidently supposed to be an outrageous sum (though twice as much is charged for pickled oysters and anchovies); it would be extremely low, however, for a portrait in oils from a recognized artist, and Garfield seems to be confusing cosmetic and artistic "painting."

15. *The London-Bawd, with her Character and Life, Discovering the Various and Subtle Intrigues of Lewd Women*, 3rd ed. (1705), 69; subsequent page references will be followed where possible by that of the 4th ed. (1711), since that has become accessible in facsimile ([New York: Garland, 1985], 71).

16. Lely "put something of Clevelands face as her Languishing Eyes into every one Picture . . . all the Eyes were Sleepy alike"; unidentified contemporary author cited from MS in Oliver Millar, *Sir Peter Lely, 1618–80* (London: National Portrait Gallery, 1978), catalogue entry 45.

17. Ed. Laura Coci (Parma: Ugo Guanda, 1992), 84–85, 96.

18. Though French historical dictionaries do not record the usage, Randle Cotgrave's *Dictionarie of the French and English Tongues* (1632 ed.) still defines "Courtisane" as "A Ladie, Gentlewoman, or waiting-woman of the Court; also (but less properly) a curtizan, a professed strumpet, famous (or infamous) whore."

19. Crispin de Passe II, *Miroir des plus belles courtisanes de ce temps; Spiegel des alderschoonste cortisanen dises tyts; Spieghel der alderschónsten Courtisanen diser Zeyt* (Amsterdam?, 1631), unsigned f. after engraved title page. This work has three distinct prefaces in each of three languages, the Dutch more moralistic, the German more verbose, and the French more chic and worldly: de Passe assures us that he intended only "representer les divers changemens des habites et Modes," though not all "espritz" are capable of appreciating these "nayves representations de vices qui s'y voyent comme dans un miroir. Ce n'est que jaye dessein d'attirer quelque personne a la debauche, mais seulement pour achever le dessein de mon Livre, qui n'a esté qu'a bonne fin, et pour servir a des Personnes de nostre art, et a ceux qui veullent voir le Monde sans partir de leur Chambre." In the engraved title page (fig. 3), and only there, an inexpert form of English has been substituted for German, and in portrait 22 the abbreviation "Oxon" has been miswritten "Oxm" (then expanded, accoustically, to "Oxsom" in the French poem opposite). A reversed copy of 1635, its engraved title page easily distinguished by the additional errors in the English ("Doocking," "Cortiers"), has sometimes been confused with de Passe's original (e.g. in the Folger catalogue). A 1635 edn with English verses (referring explicitly to "this game" of prostitution) is cited in Kettering, *Dutch Arcadia*, 52. For de Passe and French collections that expropriate several of his images (some circulating under the same title and some as single sheets with verses that identify them as courtiers rather than prostitutes), see also Elise Goodman, *Rubens: The Garden of Love as Conversatie à la Mode* (Amsterdam: John Benjamins, 1992), 50–55; the supposed Countess of Oxford ("a lady of great beauty" according to *DNB*'s life of Henry de Vere, 18th earl) is illustrated in her figs. 37 (from the anonymous reversed copy) and 46 (an engraving by Jean I Leblond). De

Passe seems to have based his engraved books of respectable ladies (in identical format) on the courtesan series, rather than vice versa; cf. *Les vrais Portraits de quelques unes des grandes dames de la chrestianite, desguisees en bergeres* (Amsterdam, 1640), which is bound at the front of the 1635 copy of *Courtisanes* in BL 685.d.27.

20. Richard Head, *The English Rogue Described* (1665), 3rd pagination, 34–40 (ff. ccc1v–4v). Earlier in his career as lewd apprentice the rogue does visit "Mother *Cr*— formerly famous for the Citizen's wives that frequented her house" (1st pagination, 76); evidently Head here cites the *Wandring Whore* allusion, but now presents Cresswell's as a more conventional bawdy-house. The narrator hears "a ruffing of Silks" as in the gallery-house (68 above), but the women themselves appear (not their pictures), and they act impudently rather than genteelly; the pictorial motif has been split off from Cresswell to form the later "new fashion" episode.

21. I use the term *gaze* with some hesitation, since it has acquired an associative superstructure that threatens to obliterate its standard English meaning. One anonymous reviewer of this essay argues that in this scrutinizing of the potential customer "the gaze is not *at all* reversed, since the ideological apparatus appropriate for the gender politics operating here doesn't seem disturbed" (my emphasis). (It is loosely true that the courtesan is "still inscribed in a patriarchal position"—women are still the objects of consumption, though they are also the owners of the business and the controllers of the scenography—but the specific argument seems unconvincing, i.e. that the security-holes really protect the male family members from having their cuckoldry publicly displayed.) I would agree entirely with this reviewer that intensified forms of looking (what Head calls the "stricter view") involve "a whole complex of social and erotic meanings," indeed that the gaze is always bound upon *some* kind of ideologically-driven work (though it rarely stays still enough to carry out this work with exemplary success); in this case it passes *from* the porter and the proprietress *to* the newly-arrived apprentice, objectifying and placing him according to class criteria. The point is to analyse the working of the gaze precisely, frame by frame, rather than to restrict discussion by insisting that the word can *only* be used as a synonym for the entire structure of patriarchy.

22. Speroni Sperone, as cited by Pardo, "Artifice as Seduction," 57. Cf. Richard Brilliant, *Portraiture* (Cambridge: Harvard Univ. Press, 1991), 129, commenting on a letter of Claudio Tolomei to Sebastiano del Piombo: "if life should imitate art, then the portrait was not only to be drawn from him; it was also to be imposed on him, to fix him as a moral being amid all the conflicting contingencies of existence [and] give coherence and meaning to his life."

23. The verse itself rarely rises above doggerel: "Nay, all delights do here in one combine / To raise mens fancy, that he may do o're / That thing he did but even then before. / How could I do it, and enlarge my bliss, / But that I view'd her parts, as well as kiss? / Her rosie dimpled cheeks, vermilion lips, / Did blush to see her ivory thighs and hips: I could forbear no longer, nor could wait / The tyde, but sail's into the mouth i'th'streight / Her round soft belly swell'd with pride below, /

Like a small Hill 'twas overspread with snow: / Let a warm hand but touch it, and it will / Its moisture into pearly drops distill" (39–40).

24. *The London-Bawd*, 69–78/71–80. The anonymous letter is addressed to "Mr. R—d S—n."

25. Cited from Dugdale (1681) in Henry B. Wheatley, *London Past and Present* (London: John Murray, 1891), *s.v.*; this article also cites a 1684 pamphlet that declares the lectures out of fashion (even though the church itself, destroyed in the Fire, had been rebuilt by Wren in 1682–83).

26. J. H., *A Strange Wonder, or A Wonder in a Woman* (1642), 4; the version cited in Sharon Achinstein, "Women on Top in the Pamphlet Literature of the English Revolution," *Women's Studies*, special issue ed. Achinstein, 24 (1994): 145, allegedly spells the church *"Saint Amholing"* (either a misreading by Achinstein or an excruciating pun). In John Crouch's *The Man in the Moon* (5–12 Sept. 1649), 172, the leaders of the "Junto" enter an élite brothel in St James's, using the password "Liberty," and find themselves in a "spacious Room" whose panelling slides down to reveal a series of previously-concealed internal "windows," each one framing a courtesan engaged in some high-cultural activity ("one Singing, another playing on the Lute, another on Virginals, another reading a Lecture of Lust out of *Ovid*"). Only after the client has chosen his partner (with an imperious nod) is he led into "a Room hung with all manner of Lacivious Pictures"; the pictorial element is here a supplementary detail rather than the central testing-device.

27. Cited in Laura Gowing, "Gender and the Language of Insult in Early Modern London," *History Workshop* 35 (Spring 1993): 4 (the deponent might have meant the side street that passes St Antholin's, St Sithe's, written "Sizes" in John Ogilby's map of London and Westminster [1677] so evidently of variable pronunciation and orally confusable with "Swithin's"). For a survey and numbered catalogue of bed-tricks in European fiction and English pre-Restoration comedy, see Marliss C. Desens, *The Bed-Trick in English Renaissance Drama: Explorations in Gender, Sexuality, and Power* (Newark: Univ. of Delaware Press; London: Associated University Presses, 1994).

28. (1602), cited in Desens, *Bed-Trick*, 75.

29. For his appearance, see Parks, *Dunton*, 9; for his pursuit by lewd ladies, cf. *The Dublin Scuffle*, summarized in Hunter, *Before Novels*, 333–34, and *Dunton's Whipping Post* (1706). The October 1696 *Night-Walker* is dedicated to the still-living Duchess of Cleveland, who is blamed in a scalding diatribe for "polluting" the entire nation; direct condemnation of Charles II is avoided only by blanks and dashes.

30. Dunton and Gwillim seem to have cooperated by putting each other's names on reprints of Quaker tracts; see Parks, *Dunton*, 201.

31. Wheatley, *London*, *s.v.* "Thomas (St.), The Apostle" (nothing in *The London-Bawd* suggests that St. Thomas Apostle, Southwark is meant). Ogilby's map shows the relation of "St. Anthony Church" to the street named "Back of St. Thomas Apostles," reached by "go[ing] by [St Antholin's] Church, and

cross[ing] over the way" (according to *London-Bawd*, 75/77); between this back street and "St. Thomas Apostles" is the church-yard where the burned-out church stood. The phrasing in the "Bells" episode ("the Back-side") suggests reference to an actual building, however.

32. The dialogue in which whore, pimp, pandar, bawd, and prodigal argue over precedence is transposed from Humphrey Mill, *A Nights Search, Discovering the Nature and Condition of All Sorts of Night-Walkers* (1640), 20–25, 47–52, with one passage directly lifted from John Taylor the Water Poet, *A Bawd, a Vertuous Bawd, a Modest Bawd* (1635), 18; the tale of the Irish footman (55–58/57–60) and the two sparks who try to hire a whore for one year (140–45/142–47) likewise come from Mill's *Nights Search* (56–59, 42–45); the episode of the husband who mutilates a woman he thinks is his wife (26–34/28–36) comes from Boccaccio (VII.viii); the poem by "a Learned Author" (113–15) is by Thomas Randolph; the bawd's family background—*arriviste* Parliamentarian parents grow rich on confiscated crown lands under Cromwell, send her to Hackney School, but lose everything at the Restoration (117–18/119–20)—is lifted from *The Ape-Gentle-Woman, or the Character of an Exchange-Wench* (1675), 3 (with the minimal change from "Crown" to "Bishops Lands"). The bawd puts on a show better than "whatever has been either done, or related to be done, by Madam *Creswel*, Posture *Moll*, the Countess of *Alsatia*, or any other German Rope-dancer whatever" (147/149); the third person I cannot trace, but is clearly related to the popularity of Shadwell's 1688 play *The Squire of Alsatia* (i.e., the criminal haunt of Whitefriars).

33. 3rd ed., 168–76; the BL exemplar of the fourth edn., unfortunately chosen for the Garland facsimile, is defective and lacks these final pages.

Fallen Men: Representations of Male Impotence in Britain

JUDITH C. MUELLER

When Pope compares bad writers to impotent would-be lovers in his *Essay on Criticism*, he invokes a familiar complex of attitudes and assumptions about male impotence for his readers. In keeping with convention, he treats sexual impotence not as a morally neutral physical disability, but as an object of contempt and source of disgrace, pronouncing in a revealing comparison, that in writing, "*Dulness* with *Obscenity* must prove / As Shameful sure as *Impotence* in *Love*."[1] Needless to say, in Pope's day, as now, to call a man impotent is to say much more than that his penis is incapable of erection, penetration and ejaculation.[2] The label, *impotent* relentlessly signifies beyond the unperforming organ to the entire man—his mind, his character, his will, his very manhood.

Such certainly seems to be the case during the late seventeenth and early eighteenth centuries in England. A 1674 hoax entitled, *The Women's Petition against Coffee, Representing to Public Consideration the Grand Inconveniences Accruing to Their Sex from the Excessive Use of that Drying, Enfeebling Liquor*, reflects a prevalent nostalgia for a bygone day when men were men and thus virile. The writer claims in jest what is asserted elsewhere in earnest: That the current crop of Englishmen falls far short of the gallants of "former Ages [who] were justly esteemed the *Ablest Performers* in Christendome."[3] Whether or not Great Britain experiences a "crisis of masculinity,"[4] as some have argued, the period sees an uneasy and indeterminate renegotiation of gender roles, during which the male body becomes a common site for anxious deliberation about the nature, and possible decline, of manliness.

Given its composition, the late seventeenth- and early eighteenth-century "masculine ideal" appears intrinsically disposed to crisis. As Carolyn D. Williams has shown, notions of manliness in the period embody significant contradictions. Whether masculinity is conceived in the "hard" or "soft" terms she discusses,[5] however, virility remains an absolute requirement; yet this too renders the ideal precarious. Sexual potency functions as a kind of literalized symbol for other kinds of masculine power in the period. The virile penis, conventionally figured as, and standing for, the *pen*, the *sword*, the *scepter*, grants men privileged access to the domains of power which these objects represent; the supposed exclusivity of male intellectual, military, political (and consequent economic) power could be said to rest upon figures of speech—hardly firm ground. In exposing the instability of that ground, the impotent male might even appear "dangerous to government."[6] Pierre Darmon's phrase, "the myth of virility," applies well to the notion of a stable and absolute phallic authority undergirding male privilege.[7] The impotent male's body effectively belies the myth and seals his shame.

Disruptive to cherished notions, the impotent male enjoys a marked flurry of anxious attention from the late seventeenth to the mid-eighteenth centuries when fears of male "feminization" and the loss of *"Old English Vigour"*[8] seem to run high. He serves as frequent metaphor for other kinds of failure, bad writing the most common among them; his self-lashing or self-justifying voice rages in the imperfect enjoyment poems of the Restoration; he occupies the best and worst medical minds; he is the frequent brunt of jokes in the pamphlet wars of the late seventeenth century in which women and men debate the contested and shifting ground of gender; as fumbling husband, he spurs the sexual adventures of the libidinous heroines of bawdy verse; he titillates a voracious readership of divorce court proceedings sold to a large popular audience.[9] And this list barely mentions his many manifestations in canonical literature. Drawing from such various discourses, this essay finds that, from the late seventeenth to the mid-eighteenth centuries, in diverse contexts, the impotent male is invested with several distinct, identifiable features. All of these features reveal aspects of the "masculine ideal" in marking perhaps the most shameful deviation from that ideal.

Of course, to some degree, shame can accompany illnesses and deviations of all kinds during the period—a time of transition from spiritual to material explanations for physiological phenomena. Gideon Harvey echoes a fairly common view even in the introduction to a self-consciously empirical medical treatise of 1678, *The Family Physician, and the House-Apothecary*: "Diseases and Death are marks of the Divine Justice in the punishment of Sin."[10] But the assumption that physical problems, in some way, reflect spiritual corruption has particularly ominous implications for the impotent male. Since Augustine (and perhaps before), sexual impotence has served the West as a shameful signifier of human fallenness.[11] This convention is echoed in the best-selling 1719 reprint of the early seventeenth-century trial in which the Lady Frances Howard sued her husband, the Earl of Essex, for divorce on the grounds of impotence. There, the Lord Chamberlain speculates, "That, perhaps, the Father's Sin" (the older Earl had been beheaded as a traitor) "was punish'd upon the Son: [and] That it was Truth, that the Earl had no Ink in his Pen."[12] Such reasoning makes impotence a lurking danger to all the sons of Adam, that original traitor.[13]

Although male impotence is sometimes met with compassion as writers offer supposed cures, the language of much medical discourse confirms assumptions that impotence indicates moral corruption. Since *seed* is often treated as the source of *soul* in the period, and its emission the work of "spirits" ("animal" though they be),[14] a man who fails to deposit it where he ought has a much graver than physical problem. Assumptions of "ought" and moral obligation bleed through countless efforts to describe objectively male anatomy and sexual performance. James Drake declares, in his anatomy of the human body, that "without an Erection it were impossible to emit and lodge the *Seed* where it ought to be."[15] The moral imperative imbedded in this otherwise seemingly plain fact, recurs with remarkable frequency in this text and others of its kind. Medical writers repeatedly affirm that to have sexual intercourse with his wife is a man's "Duty."

While describing, much medical literature ends up rigidly prescribing not only a man's sexual behavior (that it be heterosexual intercourse of a certain frequency, duration, intensity and generativity) but his very physiology (the measure and responsiveness of his reproductive organs) in terms that carry ethical weight. Many writers of the day describe in striking detail the "most proper" dimensions of a penis, in states of both flaccidity and erection.[16] John Marten insists that the "laws of nature" dictate the constitution of the "yard," as it is called.[17] Given his numerous anecdotes about "imperfect" males, deviance seems almost as common as the norm; his catalogue of kinds of impotence and genital abnormalities in men is remarkably long and detailed.[18] Nevertheless, the laws of nature remain firm and here seem as much ethical as physical. When preceded by admonitions to duty, words such as *imbicile* and *vicious*, frequently applied to male genitalia that depart from the norm, seem to retain all of their metaphysical connotations.

Of course, the prescriptive thrust of language used in discussions of male sexuality reflects not only a pervasive desire for a stable category of "manliness," but also a strong pronatalism in the period.[19] As many scholars have noted, medical and sexual advice literature of the day reveals a deep assumption that procreation is the ultimate end of sex, rendering noble, "so filthy, so contemptible and base a thing as *Venery* is."[20] Even the radical proposal outlined in the 1735 *Essay upon Improving and Adding, to the Strength of Great-Britain and Ireland, by Fornication* treats reproduction as the best reason for extramarital sex, for at times, marriage itself obstructs that greatest good:

> How often may one see a handsome, jolly, sprightly Girl, join'd for Life, to a poor decripit, aukward, silly, sour, ill-natured Fellow, that is not capable of acting his Part to purpose, or giving *due Benevolence* to that pretty Creature, who is so proper a Subject to work upon, and bring forth abundantly? What prodigious Loss is it to Mankind, that so lovely an Object, capable of producing Numbers of wholesome, beautiful Children, should lie idling by this impotent Fumbler.[21]

Though one might question the author's motives and candor here, he effectively appeals to popular concerns. The importance placed on procreation leads to John Marten's harsh judgment of the impotent in his widely read *Gonsologium Novum*:

> [I]f there be no Erection that Man may certainly be said to be Impotent, and by being Impotent, will always, till that be removed, be Unfruitful, and not able to Generate, and in that respect is a useless Member to the Common-wealth in which he lives.[22]

But the value of reproduction cannot entirely account for the contempt that the impotent male inspires, which seems especially intense surrounding his presumed place as head of a household. Indeed, so great is a man's responsibility in that role that, according to some authors, he must answer not only for his own sexual and reproductive condition, but also for that of his wife. The anonymous 1679 *Treatise of Marriage* assumes that a man's moral history will determine the fruitfulness of his wife; his wickedness, of whatever sort, will result in her barrenness.[23]

Most disgraceful, however, is the situation of the married impotent male who must answer for his wife's probable wantonness, which can only be bridled by male potency. An unperforming husband exacerbates a woman's natural lechery, compounding his own guilt nightmarishly. Marten attempts a medical explanation for this convention; calling excessive female desire a

"Disease" (common though it may be), he explains that in women this disease is,

> incident to *Virgins*, but peculiarly to young Widows, and such Women that have *impotent* Husbands that they don't affect, whereby their *Seminary* Vessels are not sufficiently disburthened, or their amorous Affections duly satisfy'd.[24]

Like the anonymous *No Way More Delightful than the Conjugal*, many sources take for granted that a wife's infidelity, though condemnable, is "seldom known . . . where the Husband behaves obligingly and amorously."[25] Given the importance placed on satisfying female desire, the premature ejaculator fares no better than the utterly "frigid" man; both are termed impotent.[26] Whatever the precise nature of his disability, the impotent man poses a moral danger to his wife since he cannot provide for her the sexual satisfaction that ensures female virtue. Citing the authority of an "Eminent and Learned Surgeon," John Marten claims,

> no Man was ever made a *Cuckold*, but from a deficiency in one of the *Pieces*, the *Head-Piece*, or the *Cod-Piece*; for the Husband was either a *Fool* or a *Fumbler*, and the first is as odious at *Board*, as the other in *Bed*. So that . . . *Fathers* cannot be too careful in matching their Daughters to Men of untainted Reputation and Honesty, and also of promising *Ability*.[27]

While the impotent man might carry the burden of a wife's sin, his condition contaminates even the most chaste of wives, as one defender of divorce notes: "[H]ow impossible it were to save the Honour and Conscience of Women, if their Union with the Impotent form'd indissoluble Bonds." For a woman, an impotent husband is "a continual Source of Scandal and Disorder."[28]

The pressure such attitudes place on men prompts some counter-measures in the discourse of the day. The dependency of proper manhood on the satisfaction of female desire surely provokes representations of that desire as monstrous. In *The Men's Answer to the Women's Petition against Coffee*, the men describe the lengths to which they have gone to satisfy women:

> [H]ave we not condiscended to all the Methods of Debauchery? Invented more Postures than *Aretine* ever Dreamed of! Been Pimps to our own Wives . . . . Nay, have we not forced languishing Nature by preparations of Cantharides, spiced Meats, Anchoves, Cullises, Jelly broths, Lambstones, Diasatyrion, Bononia Sawsages, &c. All to answer the height of your Amorous Passions.[29]

If satisfying woman's desire requires such extreme measures—some of which were actually recommended by medical doctors of the day—surely not even the most potent of men can be blamed for failure.

But anxiety still runs high, and impotence, with all its shameful associations, stands as a warning to the potent of the period. Indeed, no man could feel securely virile reading the medical and sexual advice literature of the late seventeenth and early eighteenth centuries since virility proves to be a less stable category than one might expect. Potency is alleged to require not only a "proper Conformation," but also a difficult exercise of will.[30] Impotence is often treated as a consequence of the prodigal misuse of potency. But restraint poses as much danger as indulgence: a man must avoid too little and too much "venery," ejaculate neither too early nor too late, have neither too long nor too short a "yard," eat foods neither too warming nor too chilling, avoid fatness and thinness, too much and too little exercise.[31] Any of these "extremes" threatens potency and thus manhood. As these dangers reveal, double binds and difficult balances characterize prescriptions for virile masculinity. Masturbation, the very act that might assure a man of his potency, threatens to destroy it.[32] And social proof of manhood, which, as many historians of sexuality have noted, depends on sexual conquest, threatens that same manhood by way of enfeebling disease and exhaustive expenditure from "excessive venery."[33]

Such double binds may have their source in a problematic conception of male sexuality itself as something both glorious and utterly base. Like other writers of the period, Pierre Dionis treats male reproductive organs as "Noble Parts," even above the brain and heart, because of their function in preserving the species.[34] But just as often, and usually in the same paragraph, writers treat the penis as "Mans more obscene part."[35] Like Dionis, Samuel Collins, and other writers on the subject, John Marten, betrays a prevailing ambivalence in his description of the male genitals:

> [They] are clad with Hair . . . [which] serves as a Veil to hide or cover the obscenity of those Parts, which Parts are indeed wonderfully and curiously made, and which we ought to admire the handywork of the Almighty in, when we consider that these Parts, above all the Parts of a Man's body, should feel in the Act of Copulation such exceeding Tickling and Pleasure, as if the Soul was at once sallying out of the Body, to communicate it self to another.[36]

Unfit for such erotic/spiritual transport, the impotent man's genitals retain, and underscore, all of the obscenity and none of the glory that Marten suggests here.

In fact, impotence is frequently associated with obscenity. After all, sexual efforts not legitimized by procreation are presumed obscene. But, ironically, impotence becomes particularly associated with the obscenity of "excessive venery." Wycherley's notorious rake, Horner, effectively capitalized on the association of impotence with debauchery in his effort to gain the trust of the London husbands he would cuckold.[37] John Cleland draws on this association seven decades later in *Fanny Hill* in the pitiful character of Mr. Norbert, reduced to virtual impotence by his "over-violent pursuit of the vices of the town."[38] Most medical writers of the period assume that man has a limited store of seed, which enlivens the body and mind and is replenished by blood transformed in the brain.[39] Both impotence and too frequent intercourse, therefore, accompany or cause a variety of physical and mental problems. Nicholas Venette's famous *Conjugal Love* claims that from both excessive venery and the "self-pollution" common in a long virginity, a man not only loses his ability to copulate, but

> the brain will melt like ice before the fire, the eyes will grow dim and runny, the head will ache in the morning, and be afflicted with frequent meagrims . . . the whole strength of the body will be greatly enfeebled and diminished, in as much as the seed is specifically the vigor thereof. . . . the spirits are lowered, the appetite lost, and the memory obstructed. In a word, a man in this miserable circumstance, becomes slow in action, heavy in gait, dull in his conversation, stupid in his comprehension, unadvised in his labour, and apt to believe every thing.[40]

As well as excessive venery, impotence can conjure images of deviant venery. Lacking or having lost his manhood, the impotent male allegedly employs perverse means to awaken or restore it. Cleland's Fanny Hill assumes that old and impotent men require stimulation from beating for the purpose of,

> quickening the circulation of their sluggish juices, and determining a conflux of the spirits of pleasure towards those flagging, shrivelly parts that rise to life only by virtue of those titillating ardours created by the discipline of their opposites.[41]

Whether succumbing to exhaustion or requiring perverse titillation, the impotent male's body points up the precariousness of virile masculinity. Perhaps his dishonor ultimately derives from the uneasiness he produces in his more able brothers who anxiously set out to demonstrate their manhood. He may provoke so much contempt because he challenges the comfortably familiar opposition between (to use Thomas Laqueur's words) "a problematic, unstable female body that is either a version of or wholly different from a generally unproblematic, stable male body."[42] Since, as R. W. Connell observes, "True masculinity is almost always thought to proceed from men's bodies,"[43] a man's body that fails to meet performative expectations poses an obvious threat both to anyone's individual potency and to gender arrangements at large. Indeed, popular divorce court materials concentrate attention not only on the shame of a limp penis, but also on the dubious status of an erect one as a reliable sign of potency, problematizing what ought to be an unambiguous physical category. Although men in England who were accused of impotence could successfully defend themselves by masturbating before examiners, not everyone accepted the morality or the reliability of such performances. In the famous French de Gesvres trial, translated in 1714 and read voraciously in England,[44] the pleader for the Lady (whose argumentation the English editor applauds in the "Advertisement") insists that even if the Marquis were to achieve erection before examiners, his potency could not be presumed, since perfect proof "depends on the Interior": that which takes place inside his wife during intercourse, that which cannot and should not be seen.[45] Of course, impotence—or, rather, the charge of impotence—occasions this assertion; the possibility of failed virility brings to light the inadequacy of even an apparently functional penis as a reliable public signifier of manhood. The impotent male becomes the locus of shame, a scapegoat, for the indeterminate signification of all male bodies.

The easiest, most obvious and common solution to the problems the impotent man exposes in the notion of a stable and comprehensible male body is to project that instability on him and then insist he is no man at all. Given its frequent repetition, the assertion that manhood and all its essential attributes depend on potency becomes virtually tautological in the medical literature: all real men are virile. The "fumbler," like the eunuch, should pose no threat to the assumption that men are unequivocally "masculine" if one assumes that he is not quite a man. His one advantage over eunuchs is that he might be cured, and often medical literature kindly promises as much. But like others who do not conform to the "fierce order of virility,"[46] the impotent male is frequently conceived as effeminate, diminished, close to a woman, without strength, wit or moral will.

The "fumbler" is perhaps most "feminine" in failing to control his emotions, which can lead to a multitude of sins. His excessive passion and eventual rage are virtual clichés of the Restoration imperfect enjoyment poems. Indeed, the kind of impotence lamented in those poems, premature ejaculation, is portrayed as having its source, without exception, in to too great passion.[47] The unperforming lover is consistently disabled by excessive desire, and once his failure is sealed, his passion shifts to uncontrollable rage, which only disables him further. Behn's Lysander is both enraged by his own impotence and made more irredeemably impotent by his "Rage and Shame" which "left no Spark for New Desire."[48] In divorce court cases published for popular readership in the early eighteenth century, a man's rage serves almost to prove his impotence.[49] Pope can refer to dull writers who "Rhyme with all the Rage of Impotence,"[50] confident that his readers have encountered representations of the raging "fumbler" many times before.

For all his rage and passion, however, like a woman, the impotent male is hardly a man of action. The common association of manly action in the public domain with a healthy sexual drive emerges in Bernard de Mandeville's *A Modest Defence of Publick Stews*, written for the benefit of "Men of Business":

> If there are some Men of a particular Constitution, whose puny Desires may be easily block'd up with the Assistance of *three small Buttons*; or else endow'd with such an extraordinary Strength of Reason, that they can master the most *rampant* Sallies of this raging Passion; I heartily congratulate their happy Conquest, but have nothing more to do with them at present, the *Publick Stews* not being design'd for such. I am here speaking of those Men of Business, who, notwithstanding their abstinence or the Regularity of their Lives, are sometimes prevailed upon to quench these amorous Heats; and, I say, in such Men the Passion is much stronger than in Men of Pleasure.[51]

Exhibiting similar assumptions about the dependency of manly action on a robust libido, *The Women's Petition against Coffee* uses conventional metaphors that associate sexual impotence with a failure of masculine performance generally: of the male coffee drinkers, the women complain,

> so unfit are they for Action, that like young Train-band-men when called upon Duty, their *Amunition* is wanting; peradventure they *Present*, but cannot give *Fire*, or at least do but *flash in the pan*, instead of doing Execution.[52]

The impotent male's lack of valor in bed reflects and is figured by failure in other male spheres.

No man of action, the impotent male sometimes appears as a passive (non)man of too many words, connecting him to conventions of female garrulousness.[53] Ironically, whereas woman's excessive speech supposedly derives from her excessive sexual desire, the impotent man's garrulousness derives from his inability to satisfy that desire. The women petitioning against coffee complain that although their over-caffeinated men

> frequently have hot contests about most Important subjects; as what colour the Red Sea is of; whether the Great Turk be a Lutheran or a Calvinist; or who Cain's Father in Law was, &c. yet they never fight about them with any other save our weapon, the Tongue.[54]

The women betray mock jealousy that the men "will usurp on our prerogative of *Tatling*, and soon learn to exceel [*sic*] us in *Talkativeness*: a Quality wherein our Sex has ever Claimed preeminence."[55] As I argue elsewhere, Swift draws on the convention of the garrulous "fumbler" in his "Epistle to a Lady."[56] Dryden and Pope both associate prolific bad writing with sexual impotence.[57] While often accused of having "no ink in his pen,"[58] the impotent male tends to produce a gross surplus of words.

Although the "fumbler" may be dismissed as a passive, weak, overly passionate, sometimes jabbering, womanish thing, such dismissal hardly relieves anyone's anxiety. Despite his alleged reduction in all areas—body, mind, spirit—the most disarming thing about an impotent (non)man is that he might appear in every other way a man entire. For this reason, impotence (like femininity) becomes associated with deceit and disguise. This association clearly works against husbands sued for divorce on the grounds of impotence, and consequently, such cases often have the flavor of witch trails. For one commentator cited in *Cases of Divorce for Several Causes*, the Earl's "guilt" in the Essex case is predicated on the assumption that, in marriage, "the Impotent deceives, the Potent Mistakes."[59] In the de Gesvres case, the Lady's pleader cautions that although the Marquis, her husband, "appear[s] to be a Man, he is not presently to be concluded such, because there are some whose Ensign of Manhood is a mere Cheat, giving mighty Hopes, but performs nothing."[60] The pleader uses the analogy of "a Picture of a Man, so like one, it could do every thing but speak," suggesting that the Marquis had organs for generation, but not the ability to use them as he "ought." But this metaphor also likens the Marquis to something deceptively resembling a man, an imitation man. His very speech appears imitative: "the Language of a Parrot, *I have consummated, I have consummated*, and that's all."[61]

A number of Thomas Hamilton Haddington's bawdy poems draw on the stereotype of the deceitful "fumbler," the imitation man who seduces or marries a woman only to disappoint her. In "The Rebuke," he writes, as if it were a common situation,

> I always thought it want of sense,
> And the worst kind of impudence,

In men who are for love unfit,
Yet ever are attempting it,
Since women, when they find the cheat,
Can never pardon the deceit.[62]

Haddington goes on to narrate the humiliation of an inept, if "well known rake," who attempts to prove his manhood with an experienced woman; she promptly humiliates him for his likeness to "a vile Italian singer." Cleland extends the convention of the deceptive impotent to encompass self-deception in the dissipated rake, Mr. Norbert. As his mistress, Fanny must affect a fraudulent virginity to arouse his illusory virility. Although he absolutely requires a virgin to stimulate him, his raptures seem less sexual than psychological; he is aroused by the lie of his "manly" conquest, which Fanny effectively (and profitably) sustains.

No matter how a man endeavors to hide his sexual failing from himself and others, as Haddington's poem suggests, women *will* "find the cheat," even if they are too polite or too well paid to announce it. Not only does a woman know from her private experience of a man whether he be potent, but her body stands as evidence—sometimes public evidence. As Lawrence Stone observes, "In normal impotence suits the issue was settled by a physical examination of the wife by experienced midwives and doctors to see whether or not her hymen was intact."[63] The Marquis de Gesvres battles to keep the examiners away from his wife, which only compounds the impression of his "guilt." Some husbands, such as the cuckolded Duke of Beaufort, "chose to masturbate to erection and ejaculation" in the presence of the "leading judge of the ecclesiastical court, two physicians, and three surgeons."[64] But as the pleader for the Marquis de Gesvres observes, such an audience "would be more likely to check than raise" motions of "manhood."[65] Although this test could not perfectly reveal what occurs in the bedroom between husband and wife, its successful completion meant a decision in the husband's favor, despite criticisms of the obscenity of the test itself. But finally, as in the Essex and de Gesvres cases, the wife's virginity becomes the only proof when a man refuses or fails to perform before examiners.

Of all the issues that surround male impotence, nothing seems to threaten gender arrangements more than a woman's power to decide whether or not a man is virile. Doctors peddling their cures for impotence often refer to wives' satisfaction as *proof* of medical efficacy. Marten boasts of a surgical technique by which a patient of his "was cured and was afterwards so capable of satisfying his Wife, that she never had Cause again of Complaining of her Husband's Impotency."[66] The question of male impotence makes clear a kind of authority that women have over manhood itself, if manhood requires (heterosexual) potency. Such authority in the hands of women produces understandable fears among men. In the "Batchelors'" response to the 1693 *Petition of the Ladies of London . . . [for] Husbands*, the men express concern that women, possessing the power to measure male potency, "may think no Measure enough."[67]

Peter Wagner argues that the authority of female judgment may account for popular trial records,

> almost always includ[ing] implicit attacks on women who dared to question their husband's sexual powers. Thus, after an initial shock, the masculine pride is restored by a section in the book which attempts to prove "that there are no certain signs of virginity in women."[68]

In 1732, John Crawfurd, who compiles for publication the court documents from a 1731 suit, denies the very existence of the hymen and appeals to legal, medical, and church authority in his argument "That There are no Real Natural Marks of Virginity, and That All Pretended Ones May Be Effected by Art."[69] Crawfurd transfers the taint of deceitfulness from the allegedly impotent husband to his "troublesome" wife, for "The Physicians and Canonists agree, that there are a great many *made-Virginities,*" and "it is easy to so contract the Parts by astringents, that the most profligate Strumpet may pass for a Maid."[70] Like the signs of manhood, the signs of virginity prove unreliable, though here that unreliability produces less anxiety than relief as it serves to undermine female authority. Indeed, tests of virginity appear perfectly acceptable when a man's virility is not at issue; in the case of "a Man, who had engag'd himself to marry a young Woman, upon Condition she was a Virgin," Crawfurd agrees with one authority "that he is oblig'd to marry her, if she can prove her Virginity" because "the question is not concerning *Virginity,* as a Proof of the *Impotency* of her Husband."[71] In impotency suits, Crawfurd defends the husband's right—indeed, his obligation—to oppose the examination of his wife. Divorce and men's reputations are too grave matters to be decided by the signs that a variable female body provides.

Despite such assurances, however, the impotent male exposes the extent to which men of the period are at the mercy of women for proof of their masculinity. The "fumbler" reveals the dependency of man on woman for his domination over her. In so doing, he becomes a kind of traitor to his sex. Perhaps for this reason, female judgment underlies much of the intense derision that the impotent male inspires in other men. In discussing eunuchs and impotents, John Marten repeatedly notes how "ridiculous" women perceive them to be. Masturbation "renders [a man] (to Women ridiculous, because) Impotent."[72] The impotent man is "One whom the Fair Sex would avoid, unless it were to Look at him, Point and Laugh with their Fans before their Faces, as not fit for that Conversation."[73] One can hardly imagine women having quite so strong an aversion as Marten himself betrays here. Yet Marten also reveals sympathy: he sings the praises of one impotent man's wife,

> a very modest Person, [who] behav'd her self with great complacency and discretion, without upbrading him, &c. which he spoke much to her Honour, but yet not without a great concern for his own Misfortunes and Inability.[74]

This oscillation between contempt and occasional compassion, not at all unique to Marten, perhaps reflects the potent man's uneasy identification with the impotent, at the mercy of women's judgment. Though associated with deceit himself, the impotent man exposes the lie of the masculine ideal, its sham authority and contingent superiority. His betrayal of the brotherhood, however involuntary, no doubt accounts for representations of the impotent man, so fraught with shame, that obscure the ways in which hegemonic masculinity denies the diverse experiences, abilities and desires of actual men.

NOTES

1. Alexander Pope, *Essay on Criticism*, in *Poetical Works*, ed. Herbert Davis (Oxford: Oxford Univ. Press, 1966), 532–33.

2. Pierre Darmon refers to "erecting, entering, and emitting," as "the eternal trinity which confirms a man's virility," in *Trial by Impotence: Virility and Marriage in Pre-Revolutionary France*, trans. Paul Keegan (London: Hogarth Press, 1985).

3. *The Women's Petition against Coffee, Representing to Public Consideration the Grand Inconveniences accruing to their Sex from the Excessive Use of that Drying, Enfeebling Liquor* (London, 1674), 1.

4. Michael S. Kimmel argues for such a crisis. See his "The Contemporary 'Crisis' of Masculinity in Historical Perspective," in *The Making of Masculinities: The New Men's Studies*, ed. Harry Brod (Boston: Allen and Unwin, 1987), 121–53. See also Kimmel's introduction to *"Mundus Fopensis: or, the Fop Displayed" and "The Levellers,"* in Augustan Reprint Society publication 248 (Los Angeles: William Andrews Clark Memorial Library, University of California, Los Angeles, 1988), iii–xiii. Carolyn D. Williams questions Kimmel's notion of a crisis—in the seventeenth century and today: "In the face of the evidence he presents, it would be foolish to deny the existence of these crises. Yet it would be rash to assume that men at other times are consciously serene, or that there is ever a precise correlation between anxiety levels and verifiable data." *Pope, Homer, and Manliness: Some Aspects of Eighteenth-Century Classical Learning* (New York: Routledge, 1993), 3.

Particularly compelling is Mark Breitenberg's argument, in his study of an earlier period, that given its purpose of maintaining the rights of male privilege within patriarchy, "Masculinity is inherently anxious." See the Introduction to his *Anxious Masculinities in Early Modern England* (Cambridge: Cambridge Univ. Press, 1996), 1–34. For discussions of the economic and social changes that precipitated the gender turbulence of the period, see Lawrence Stone, *The Family, Sex, and Marriage in England, 1500–1800* (New York: Harper and Row, 1977); Felicity Nussbaum, *The Brink of All We Hate: English Satires on Women, 1660–1750* (Lexington: Univ. Press of Kentucky, 1983); Antonia Fraser, *The Weaker Vessel: Woman's Lot in Seventeenth-Century England* (New York: Knopf, 1984); Jerome Nadlehaft, "The Englishwoman's Sexual Civil War: Feminist Attitudes towards Men, Women, and Marriage, 1650–1740," *Journal of the History of Ideas* 43 (1982): 555–79.

5.   Williams explains that masculinity could be viewed either "purely in terms of physical courage and stoical endurance," or in a "softer" manner, "as a balanced state in which courage is exercised only at the bidding of reason and virtue" and which includes "the capacity to feel and express a fully human range of emotions" (*Pope, Homer, and Manliness*, 27–28).

6.   Although the women petitioning against coffee claim that the reduced men of England cannot be "dangerous to government" because they are "too tame and too talkative to make any desperate Polititians," the list of men's weaknesses that follows this claim suggests a significant menace to the nation; in the end, the men are unable to so much as "Lifeguard a Cherry-tree" (*Women's Petition against Coffee*, 4–5).

7.   See the final chapter of Darmon's *Trial by Impotence*, 210–29.

8.   I take this phrasing from *Women's Petition against Coffee*, 1.

9.   Although there were many fewer instances of women filing for divorce on the grounds of impotence in England than in France in the period, the British public was fascinated by such cases. Curll published divorce court proceedings, beginning in 1714 with the tremendously successful *Case of Impotency Debated in the Late Famous Tryal at Paris; Between the Marquis de Gesvres, (Son to the Duke de Tresmes, Present Governor of Paris) and Mademoiselle de Mascranny his Lady, Who after Three Years Marriage, Commenc'd a Suit against Him for Impotency*, 2 vols. (London, 1714). The popularity of this volume lead to the publication of *Cases of Divorce for Several Causes* (London, 1715); *The Case of Impotency, As Debated in England, in that Remarkable Tryal, 1613, between Robert Earl of Essex, and the Lady Frances Howard, who, after Eight years Marriage, commenc'd Suit against him for Impotency*, (London: Curll, 1719). That such cases retained popular appeal into the thirties is suggested by the publication of *The Cases of Impotency and Virginity Fully Discuss'd. Being the Genuine Proceedings in the Archescourt of Canturybury Between the Honorable Catherine Elizabeth Weld, Alias Aston, and Her Husband Edward Weld, Esq. of Ludsworth-Castle in Dorsetshire,* John Crawfurd, LL.D., ed. and reporter (London: Thomas Gammon, 1732). Because of the popularity of these volumes, all of which treat impotence at some point, they often appeared in multiple editions. For a discussion of French cases, see Jeffrey

Merrick, "Impotence in Court and at Court," *Studies in Eighteenth Century Culture* 25 (1996): 187–99.

10. Gideon Harvey, introduction to *The Family Physician, and the House-Apothecary* (London, 1678). Such views are commonly found in the prefatory material to medical literature of the time.

11. Augustine argues that with the Fall came the separation of will and sexuality. Before the Fall, man could will his own erection, and copulation did not depend on desire. See *The City of God*, trans. Marcus Dods, D.D. (New York: Modern Library, 1950), 472–73.

12. *The Case of Impotency, As Debated in England*, 3.

13. I take the Fall as the original for all Biblical instances of the sins of a father being punished upon his children.

14. The influential mid-seventeenth-century figure William Harvey asserts this position about seed and soul most explicitly in *Anatomical Exercitations Concerning the Generation of Living Creatures: To Which Are Added Particular Discourses, of Births, and of Conceptions, &c.* (London, 1653), 548. References to spirits and animal spirits as essential to sexual function appear in the majority of works on the subject. Michael Ettmüller asserts the view that "Impotency, or the Defect of Erection of the Yard" results from "inactivity of the Spirits" in *Etmullerus Abridged: or, A Complete System of the Theory and Practice of Physic Being a Description of All Diseases Incident to Men, Women and Children* (London, 1699), 573. Walter Charlton affirms the notion that these spirits inform the activity of the "soul," which moves the body to action, in *Natural History of Nutrition, Life, and Voluntary Motion* (London, 1659), 183.

15. James Drake, *Anthropologia Nova: or, A New System of Anatomy. Describing the Animal Œconomy, and a Short Rationale of Many Distempers Incident to Human Bodies* (London, 1717), 133. Drake lifted some of his observations about male anatomy directly out of John Marten's *Gonsologium Novum: or, A New System of All the Secret Infirmities and Diseases, Natural, Accidental, and Veneareal in Men and Women* (London, 1709). See page 58, where he says much the same thing in the same language that Drake uses here. Such lifting is not uncommon in medical texts of the period.

16. See Samuel Collins, *A Systeme of Anatomy, Treating of the Body of Man, Beasts, Birds, Fish, Insects, and Plants* (London, 1685), 534–35; Thomas Gibson, *The Anatomy of Humane Bodies Epitomized* (London, 1697), 160. The most detailed account may be Marten's in *Gonsologium Novum*, 13–19.

17. Marten, *Gonsologium Novum*, 14.

18. Marten, *A Treatise of all the Degrees and Symptoms of the Venereal Disease, in Both Sexes* (London, 1708).

19. Roy Porter refers to "a social economy of procreation," in the period, based in part on fears of a declining population. "The Literature of Sexual Advice Before 1800," in *Sexual Knowledge, Sexual Science: The History of Attitudes to Sexuality*, ed. Roy Porter and Mikulás Teich (Cambridge: Cambridge Univ. Press, 1994), 146.

20. Marten, *Gonsologium Novum*, 1.

21. *An Essay upon Improving and Adding, to the Strength of Great-Britain and Ireland, by Fornication, Justifying the Same from Scripture and Reason* (London, 1735), 19.

22. Marten, *Gonsologium Novum*, 59.

23. *A Treatise of Marriage with a Defense of the 32th Article of Religion, of the Church of England* (London, 1679), 38.

24. Marten, *Treatise of all the Degrees*, 424.

25. *No Way More Delightful than the Conjugal* (London, 1753), 24.

26. The general belief that female orgasm is necessary for conception reinforces the perception of the premature ejaculator as thoroughly impotent.

27. Marten, *Treatise of all the Degrees*, 431.

28. *The Case of Impotency Debated in the Late Famous Tryal at Paris*, 1: 37, 40. Although this is a French case, its publication in English proved so enormously popular as to prompt Curll to seek out and publish the other so-called "impotency volumes" (see n. 5). The details of the de Gesvre case, though French, were firmly planted in English popular consciousness. For an account of the popularity of the "impotency volumes" see Ralph Straus, *The Unspeakable Curll* (London: Chapman and Hall, 1927), 40, 116.

29. *The Men's Answer to the Women's Petition against Coffee, Vindicating Their Own Performances, and the Vertues of That Liquor, from the Undeserved Aspersions Lately Cast upon Them by Their Scandalous Pamphlet* (London, 1674), 1–2.

30. Explanations of impotence as resulting from witchcraft had mostly lost their credibility by the late seventeenth century.

31. These assumptions are so widespread as to be almost universal. The following sources are fairly representative: On the frequency of copulation, see Nicholas Culpeper. *Culpeper's School of Physick, or, the Experimental Practice of the Whole Art* (London, 1696), 195–96. On the timing of ejaculation, see Ettmüller, *Etmullerus Abridged*, 571–72. On the proper length of the penis see Marten, *Gonsologium Novum*, 13, 19. On proper diet and the warming/chilling effects of food, see, Lazare Rivière, *The Universal Body of Physick, in Five Books; Comprehending the Several Treatises of Nature, of Diseases and Their Causes, of Symptoms, of the preservation of Health, and of Cures* (London, 1657), 17, 379. On fatness as well as exercise, again see Ettmüller, *Etmullerus Abridged*, 558. On extremes of fatness and thinness, see *Aristotle's Last Legacy, Unfolding the Mysteries of Nature in the Generation of Man* (London, 1741), 50. On thinness, see Culpeper, *Culpeper's School of Physick*, 195–96.

32. In a twentieth-century study, Leonore Tiefer refers to the work of psychologists who explain how, "during adolescent masturbation, genital sexuality (that is, erection and orgasm) acquires non-sexual motives such as the desire for power, achievement, and peer approval that have already become important during preadolescent gender role training." "In Pursuit of the Perfect Penis: The Medicalization of Male Sexuality," in *Changing Men: New Directions in Research on Men and Masculinity*, ed. Michael S. Kimmel (London: Sage Publications, 1987), 166. John Marten has much to say about the ill effects of masturbation in *A Treatise of all the Degrees* (esp. 395–98).

33. See John Archer, *Every Man His Own Doctor* (London, 1673), 75–76.

34. Pierre Dionis, *The Anatomy of Humane Bodies Improv'd, According to the Circulation of the Blood, and all the Modern Discoveries* (London, 1716), 163.

35. Samuel Collins, *A Systeme of Anatomy*, 534.

36. Marten, *Gonsologium Novum*, 12. Similar ambivalence is apparent in the language Samuel Collins uses to describe male sexual pleasure: "The Glans or Head of the Penis . . . is endued with the most exquisite Sense; which is so far hightned in Fruition, that it giveth us a kind of transport of Sensual Delight, to court us and amaze us in the meaner act of Coition, where we engage into the *Vagina Uteri*, seated between two receptacles of Excrements, to which we are earnestly sollicited by the most acute sense and Pleasure seated in the Glans" (*A Systeme of Anatomy*, 536). This example suggests that part of the discomfort with male sexuality derives from its association with the female body.

37. William Wycherley, *The Country Wife* (Lincoln: Univ. of Nebraska Press, 1965).

38. John Cleland, *Fanny Hill: or, Memoirs of a Woman of Pleasure* (New York: Signet, 1996), 161.

39. Find this common view in *Aristotle's Last Legacy*, 51, and in Marten, *Gonsologium Novum*, 41. See Thomas Laqueur for an extended discussion of this view, which derives from the ancient notion of the "interconvertibility" of bodily fluids, *Making Sex: Body and Gender from the Greeks to Freud* (Cambridge: Harvard Univ. Press, 1990).

40. Nicholas de Venette, *Conjugal Love; or, The Pleasures of the Marriage Bed Considered. In Several Lectures on Human Generation* (London, 1750), 46–47.

41. Cleland, *Fanny Hill*, 177.

42. Thomas Laqueur, *Making Sex*, 22.

43. R. W. Connell, *Masculinities: Knowledge, Power and Social Change* (Berkeley and Los Angeles: University of California Press, 1995), 45.

44. See note 27.

45. *Case of Impotency Debated in the Late Famous Tryal at Paris*, 1: 8.

46. I take this phrasing from the subtitle of Michel Leiris's autobiography, *Manhood: A Journey from Childhood into the Fierce Order of Virility* (Chicago: Univ. of Chicago Press, 1992).

47. A partial list of imperfect enjoyment poems would include Rochester's "The Imperfect Enjoyment," Wycherley's "The Unperforming Lover's Apology," Etherege's "The Imperfect Enjoyment," and Behn's "The Disappointment."

48. Aphra Behn, "The Disappointment," *The Works of Aphra Behn*, ed. Janet Todd (Columbus: Ohio State Univ. Press, 1992), 1: 97–98.

49. See, for instance, the popular translation, *Case of Impotency Debated in the Late Famous Tryal at Paris*, 1: 39, 132, 195.

50. Pope, *Essay on Criticism*, 609.

51. Bernard de Mandeville, *A Modest Defence of Publick Stews: or, an Essay upon Whoring, as It Is Now Practised in These Kingdoms* (London, 1724), 24.

52. *Women's Petition against Coffee*, 3.

53. For a discussion of the rhetorical tradition of *dilatio*, which associates female garrulousness with excessive sexual desire, see Patricia Parker, *Literary Fat Ladies: Rhetoric, Gender and Property* (New York: Methuen, 1987).

54. *Women's Petition against Coffee*, 5.

55. *Women's Petition against Coffee*, 3–4.

56. Judith C. Mueller, "Imperfect Enjoyment at Market Hill: Impotence, Desire, and Reform in Swift's Poems to Lady Acheson," forthcoming in *ELH*.

57. See Pope's *Essay on Criticism*. His *Epistle to Arbuthnot* and *Dunciad* also suggest a relationship between questionable sexuality and bad writing. See Dryden's *MacFlecknoe*, where the prolific Shadwell has beer instead of ball and other characteristically impotent associations.

58. An apparently common metaphor, found not only in the Essex trial, but in other sources as well, such as in the collection of bawdy jokes and stories, *Apollo's Feast: or, Wit's Entertainment* (London, 1718), 10.

59. *Cases of Divorce for Several Causes*, 3.

60. *Case of Impotency Debated in the Late Famous Tryal at Paris*, 2: Appendix.

61. *Case of Impotency Debated in the Late Famous Tryal at Paris,* 1: 69.

62. Thomas Hamilton Haddington (1680–1735), *Forty Select Poems on Several Occasions* (London: J.H. Bell, 1769).

63. Lawrence Stone, *Broken Lives: Separation and Divorce in England 1660–1857* (Oxford: Oxford University Press, 1993), 132.

64. Stone, *Broken Lives*, 134.

65. *Case of Impotency Debated in the Late Famous Tryal at Paris*, 2: 46.

66. Marten, *Gonsologium Novum*, 18.

67. *An Humble Remonstrance of the Batchelors, in and about London, to the Honourable House, in Answer to a Late Paper, Intituled a Petition of the Ladies for Husbands* (London, 1693), 3.

68. Peter Wagner, "The Pornographer in the Courtroom: Trial reports about Cases of Sexual Crimes and Delinquencies as a Genre of Eighteenth-Century Erotica," in *Sexuality in Eighteenth-Century England*, ed. Paul-Gabriel Boucé (Manchester: Manchester University Press, 1982), 125. For an example of such an attempt to undermine female authority, see *"An Account of the Intrigue between* Robert Car, *Earl of* Somerset, *Viscount* Rochester, &c. *and the Lady* Frances Howard" by Arthur Wilson, Esq., appended to *The Case of Impotency, As Debated in England.*

69. *Cases of Impotency and Virginity Fully Discuss'd*, 62, 58.

70. Ibid., 65–66

71. Ibid., 65.

72. Marten, *Treatise of all the Degrees*, 395.

73. Marten, *Gonsologium Novum*, 59.

74. Marten, *Treatise of all the Degrees,* 398.

"No Cure, No Money," or the Invisible Hand of Quackery: The Language of Commerce, Credit, and Cash in Eighteenth-Century British Medical Advertisements

LISA FORMAN CODY

Everybody knows that eighteenth-century medical concoctions were made of nothing and good for nothing, at least nothing that a little rum or a sugarcube couldn't cure on its own. Balm of Gilead was but brandy, and the omnipresent anodyne necklace beads of peony wood. A few pennies' worth of ingredients, and the rest was sheer profit for the ingenious quack vendor. How, when contemporary critics knew this and warned the public of the uselessness of such goods, did quacks ensnare the public? The question they faced, as they advertised their wares, was then how to put something into nothing, or how to make gold out of tin.

This essay will examine how quack medicines—perhaps the most worthless of consumer goods in the eighteenth-century marketplace—defined themselves as valuable. Exploring this problem in part illuminates the most common form of eighteenth-century popular medical culture and the strategies of vendors battling widespread public skepticism about the trustworthiness of all doctors—not just quacks—and the efficacy of their products. Not surprisingly, practitioners under siege publicly portrayed themselves as accomplished altruists, but they also invoked a melange of popular cultural trends presumably attractive to a public in search of effective medical remedies. Although quacks invariably represented wretchedly afflicted bodies cured by their special nostrums' awesome powers, they also tried to attract customers by attaching their products to astronomy, astrology, *causes célèbres*, statesmen, popular figures, hoop-skirts and patches, the family, prostitutes, politics, nationalism, the exotic and foreign, commerce, money, gold, God; in short, everything. Some of these promotions shouting "Eronania. On the Misusings of the Marriage-Bed"[1] of course caught the eye or titillated; others announcing "An Article out of a Letter from a Gentleman at Paris, to his Correspondent here in London"[2] tricked a reader into seeing the advertisement as news, elevating a commodity to the realm of public and political discourse. Both devices inflated quack remedies' values, suggesting that a consumer got more than opium for his gout; he was also able to participate in the public events of the day.

But even if they received a "free" gift, say, an engraving of Farinelli the Castrato or Peter the Wild Boy when purchasing an anodyne necklace, consumers still parted with quite sizable numbers of shillings in the transaction. Critics of quackery always portrayed this as a mercenary business, as low as thievery and as clever as a con-job. Indeed, like most con artists, some quacks promised to offer a striking deal that would make their customers rich not only in health, but also in the marketplace. All advertisements, whether for bogus medical goods or a real house to let, were designed to confer value and worth on the commodity, but a particular subset of quack promotions and strategies employed monetary imagery and promises to compensate for the customer's loss of cash. These quack advertisements capitalized on positive images of cash, credit, and commerce to underwrite their goods' value while subordinating the economic fact that the quack-merchant was the more enriched player.

That many Georgian quacks vending pap disguised as gold became very rich suggests that their promotional strategies succeeded; in turn, the apparent success of these marketing ploys reveals a public not always economically "rational" about the "real" worth of medical nostrums. I am not arguing here that the public was stupid, but rather that the quack's depiction of the consumption of medicines as the consumer's gain helped structure and reinforce an economic logic that made "rational" sense elsewhere: investing in a stock company, for example, demanded that the investor believe that parting with cash in the present equalled later profit. The economic language of certain medical advertisements reiterated and naturalized participation in the new kinds of investment opportunities, credit and commodity arrangements of the long eighteenth century. But more than simply echoing the "rational" discourse of investment, value, and circulation, these advertisements—and the medical commerce they facilitated—actually enabled this financial and economic revolution.

Advertising, Commerce, and the Public Sphere

Newspapers helped create the "financial revolution" of the seventeenth century in Britain[3] because they reported and disseminated the economic news of shipments, investments, sales, purchases, tariffs, insurance, and fluctuating exchange rates to investors and consumers geographically separated. When a London newspaper reported news of cargo returning from the West Indies, for example, the report's value relied on the reader imagining and trusting in something far away. Training readers' imaginations in the reality and relevance of the geographically distant primed investors to have faith in temporally distant commodities and profits too. Such faith was absolutely necessary for private individuals and public ministers not only to invest in such (actually risky) schemes as joint-stock companies, the Bank of England, and floating loans—all the key structures of the financial revolution—but also to purchase and try out the goods and services advertised in newspapers.

And it was advertisements, particularly for medical goods and services, which helped underwrite the costs of these newspapers.[4] From the beginning of the periodical press in the 1620s, advertisements gave publishers their profits. The penny or so charged for each copy of a paper helped cover the costs of paper, ink, labor, and capital investment, but the two shillings or more charged for running each advertisement in each issue made the printer's endeavor worthwhile. As newspapers flourished in the eighteenth century, three categories of goods dominated advertisements: other printed goods, commerce, and medical products. One study of the *Salisbury Journal* figures that about 10 to 14 percent of ads were for medical goods,[5] but some metropolitan papers relied much more heavily on such ads. A February 1722 London paper had thirty ads, five of which were for books or pamphlets, including one on gonorrhea; seventeen ads were for medical products for humans, and two for horses, one touting Markham's Cordial Horse Balls, the other lauding Gibson's Cordial Horse Balls.[6]

The three categories dominating eighteenth-century ads (print, commerce, medicine) composed the central activities of coffeehouses and such public spaces as fairs and streets; a person read the papers, perhaps invested in a financial scheme, and possibly purchased a bottle of elixir when at Lloyd's. Although the public has long been depicted as an idealized bourgeois "rational-critical" sphere, the reality was rougher and much more bodily.[7] Quackery and quack medicines littered real coffeehouses, newspapers, bookshops, streets, markets, and fairs. Quack medicines were simply among the most "public" of goods being offered up for "the benefit of the public," as their vendors always proclaimed. But despite these high-minded and altruistic boasts made to downplay quacks' private interests, quacks' main concern remained diseased flesh.

Warts, worms, tooth-aches, and tumors—and all the wretched cures doctors devised—overtook early modern peoples' bodies, as well as their print and public culture. One correspondent to *The Spectator* remarked that there were more ads and bills in a Westminster Coffeehouse for "elixers, tinctures, the anodine fotus, English Pills, electuaries . . . than . . . there are diseases."[8] Not just print-ads, but also live medical advice and demonstration could be found in public, with elite physicians frequenting The British Coffee House while lower-status practitioners and their products could be found almost everywhere else. For example, according to a 1731 notice, not only could Christopher Kelly's Curing Drops which remedied breast cancer be purchased at John's Coffee House in Mitre-Court, the man himself could be found there "perform[ing]" an "account of the wonderful cures . . . constantly from one to three."[9]

Diseases and remedies were omnipresent, but not every medical practitioner advertised in the press or on handbills, or demonstrated his wares in coffeehouses. Many elite and traditional practitioners, namely physicians, surgeons, and midwives, less often promoted their services in print, choosing to rely instead on word-of-mouth and recommendations among a private clientele. Most medical ads were placed by marginal practitioners or even book and printsellers who sold quack or patent medicines on the side. These vendors, even when they did possess a legitimate medical degree or treated an elite private clientele, were universally considered quacks by critics. Quack vendors often copied physicians' accoutrements, or deliberately linked their cures to eminent doctors' names, but this did not increase their stock among skeptics and critics. Perhaps needless to say, no advertisers labelled themselves "quacks," but they were quick to accuse competitors of fraud. In fact, a common tactic was to publish a pamphlet ostensibly attacking quackery or patent medicines in general, but then appending descriptions of and testimonials attesting to the excellence of the author's particular cure.[10]

Both elite practitioners and quack vendors recommended many of the same cures—mercury, for example—but the physician did so in private transactions with patients at home, while quacks and medical vendors offered their cures publicly, whether in print or at fairs. Although both elite and quack doctors frequented coffeehouses, it seems that the former did so to be simply located by their clientele, while the latter actually set up shop by handing out bills, seeing the sick, vending cures, and collecting fees. In the eighteenth century, when formal practitioners had few pharmaceutical miracles at hand, the difference between the physician and the quack was not so much what might be prescribed, but the form of the medical transaction. The entirely public and transparently venal nature of the quack's venture was exactly what made him a quack, according to critics.[11]

Despite its dubious cultural standing, quack advertising enabled the flourishing of a public print culture because eighteenth-century printers gained their profits not from subscriptions and sales, but selling advertising space. Ads allowed publishers to make newspapers relatively inexpensive and widely available, but ads still had to be affordable. Vendors of goods could only place ads if their products were highly marketable and seemingly within reach of a wide clientele—which might explain why luxury goods (jewelry and furniture) were far less often advertised than items costing only a few shillings (medicines, books, pamphlets, prints, almanacs) or requiring only one buyer (property, slaves, labor).

Even though medical ads were thus in reality an economic strut and lacked the supposed transparent truthfulness of such real news as reports of parliamentary discussion or the weather, for example, many observers apparently treated ads as the news itself. Joseph Addison remarked of this phenomenon in *The Tatler*: "I consider as accounts of News from the little world, in the same Manner that the foregoing Parts of the Paper are from the great. . . . A man that is by no Means big enough for the Gazette, may easily creep into the Advertisements; by which Means we often see an Apothecary in the same Paper of the News with a Plenipotentiary . . . ." Continuing to mock how ads mimicked the function of legitimate public news, Steele noted that advertisements contributed to "the Management of controversy, insomuch that above half the advertisements one meets with now-a-Days are truely Polemical." For example, "[t]he Inventors of *Strops for Razors* have written against one another this Way for several Years, and that with great Bitterness. . . . I need not mention the several Proprietors of Dr. *Anderson's Pills* . . . ."[12] Addison himself, perhaps inadvertently, demonstrates the permeability of the boundaries between public news and private profits, "rational" observations and bodily matters in the *Tatler* essay by introducing the entire text of a paid-for advertisement into his critique of advertising. He explains that because the elegantly described "Compounded Spirit of Lavender" "is a Pattern of good Writing . . . I shall give it a Place in the Body of my Paper." The prose of advertising infects the "rational-critical" prose of *The Tatler* when Addison injects into the main body of the *Tatler* essay this advertisement's copy.[13] Blurring distinctions even further, Addison follows with the more vulgar, redundantly named "Carmininitive Wind-Expelling Pills," whose pretty Latin name politely envelopes, but is nonetheless undermined by the scatological English adjective defining what "carmininitive" actually is. Historians and critics have credited the polished style of Addison and Steele with smoothing the way for a polite public culture. But the focus on *politesse* has disguised the way in which the process of creating a public sphere accommodated both the seemingly counterpoised characteristics of elegant, intellectual criticism, and the intestinal concerns of the body, disease, and medicine.[14]

One correspondent to *The Spectator*, less concerned with the ambitions of apothecaries hobnobbing with ambassadors on paper, saw this melange of high and low as destroying distinctions. He complained that "Men who frequent Coffee-houses, and delight in News, are pleased with every thing that is Matter of Fact . . . . They read the Advertisements with the same Curiosity as the Articles of the Publick news . . . . In short, . . . they are Men of a Voracious appetite, but no Taste."[15] The threat here is partly about class boundaries being broken because those who lack taste and the means to discern are (unfortunately) admitted into the reading and coffee-drinking public; but it is also about the difficulty of discernment itself when newspapers publish items both public and private. The placement of news next to ads allows the unlearned to mix up the factual, reasonable, and valuable with the fraudulent and worthless. Ads thus reveal the reality of the eighteenth-century public sphere as a complex space of both fact and con, reason and dissimulation.

All advertisements dissimulated, especially when they tried to pass themselves off as equivalent to news, or denied self-interest or private advantage. Quack advertisements conned, not only because they touted medically worthless goods like peony-wood beads, but because they presented their vendors and their readership as something other than they were. *The Spectator*'s correspondents may have found fellow readers lowbrow for treating ads as fact rather than con, but purveyors of quack medicines flattered their audience as more sophisticated. Advertisements appealed to their readers as if they were gentry, perhaps indicating that eighteenth-century consumerism promoted and played on class emulation.[16] The most prosaic problems—chafing, for instance—were said to result from more elegant causes, as in a 1734 ad appealing to the upwardly mobile riding bareback: they would be relieved to buy "the famous chymical powder, so highly esteem'd by the nobility and gentry of both sexes . . . [and] those gentlemen and ladies whose skin being of a finer texture than ordinary, are . . . subject to chafing or soreness upon riding . . . or otherwise."[17] The public sphere of print culture relied on a fiction where participants acted as if they were elite, and their problems genteel, whether they actually were or not. But this was more than editors and readers politely tolerating the trite and bumpkinish; when ordinary things like lavender water could be elevated through classical rhetorical devices, Addison applauded, and in doing so endorsed the banal and bodily as topics fit for polite criticism.

Medicine and the Marketplace

Once it flattered its readers, the typical medical ad got down to business and reveled in its audience's intestinal worms, scrofulous craws, and venereal sores. Advertisers hardly downplayed disease; if anything, they magnified and invented afflictions (including of course the evil of onanism).[18] It is no surprise that bodies and disease dominated many medical ads, not just because medicines redressed the imbalances of the body, but also because bodily detail worked novelistically, conjuring up an image of living customers.[19] These bodily descriptions appeared in third-person accounts, as well as in first-person testimonials. More frequently used than any other device in quack and patent medicine advertisements, the testimonial described a supposedly satisfied customer's diseased condition and recovery in great detail, often appending a name, address, and occupation. A real person willingly consigning his private *vita* to the public marketplace was meant to provide a credit-worthy account and an imaginable face in the marketplace. This, then, is the paradox on which the quack ads played: in an appeal to an audience for whatever reason disinclined to consult a physician or surgeon and thus craving *anonymity*, the quack ad publicly invoked fellow (private) sufferers who in their specificity and authentic individuality could guarantee the efficacy of the cure and the anonymous transaction.

Anonymity, and thus distance, particularly marked the quack transaction, but these features resembled some aspects of traditional private practices. For instance, quack vendors' reliance on communication through advertisements and the mail was similar to how the very well-respected Scottish physician William Cullen ran his practice through the post by answering patients' letters in which they described their ailments. Both the quack transaction at the coffeehouse and the eighteenth-century physician's private consultation relied on patients verbally describing, even self diagnosing, their ailments rather than the medical practitioners' physical examinations. Early modern medical transactions, unlike modern ones, were mediated by respecting distance. The doctor asked permission even to take a patient's pulse; he might diagnose entirely through writing.[20]

Unlike the medical transaction which respected physical distance, other early modern transactions relied on proximity. In the case of the medieval and early modern marketplace more generally, commercial exchanges occurred in actual places between individuals who physically presented their goods and payment to each other. The typical early modern exchange demanded the physical and concrete; if actual specie were not handed over, a contract would be written and witnessed in the marketplace. Even in the case of such early forms of credit as thirteenth-century bills of exchange, it was guaranteeable personal relations that built the necessary "mutual confidence." Here, bills only passed between established purchasers and sellers along well-traveled commercial routes.[21] Seventeenth and eighteenth-century credit transactions were also facilitated by material underpinnings of trade (roads and canals). Yet these credit relations, on the other hand, were more elaborate, allowing for the *circulation* of credit between more than one seller and one buyer. Furthermore, modern credit depended less on imaginatively overcoming geographical separation between two points (Antwerp and Florence, for example), than on exploiting, yet trusting in the entirely abstract temporal separation between the present and the future. With the rise of modern capitalism and seventeenth-century financial revolutions of national banks, credit, cheques, lotteries, floating payments, and long-term investments, the eighteenth-century market increasingly developed as an imaginary space and an unseen process which relied on suspending disbelief to trust that real people—and real commodities and real values—were on the other side of representational transactions only as immediately concrete as paper.[22]

Perhaps paradoxically, during the eighteenth century the opposite trajectory occurred in more formal medical practices, with the respectful space between practitioner and patient compressed as doctors touched, examined, and enquired more aggressively. In the eighteenth century, even such physically invasive practices as pediatrics and man-midwifery became quite routine. The quack transaction which occurred between a self-diagnosing sufferer reading an ad resisted this trend towards physical contact. Unlike the private encounter between a patient and his physician, or even apothecary, the quack medical transaction happened in an abstract space: reading ads, the sufferer diagnosed himself by matching his symptoms to the ones described. He might not see the vendor of medicine: sometimes goods would be ordered, paid for, and sent through the post or a servant. That the process was anonymous, and that the quack promised to respect his customers' privacy obviously greatly attracted venereal sufferers and worried masturbators. In fact, quack vendors exploited the inherent advantages of this imaginary, geographically splayed marketplace, and in doing so helped establish the circulation of news, commodities, money, and credit. The eighteenth-century quack transaction, unlike that between physician and private patient, embodied the anonymity and trust required of the eighteenth-century financial and commercial marketplace more broadly. The quack advertisement faced the same problem as any one of these new financial innovations since both depended on investors trusting that real value backed their stock.

Unlike the physician or apothecary, the quack capitalized on customers wishing *not* to have face-to-face encounters, but he still needed to show that his product responded to real individuals suffering from similar afflictions. Though largely an anonymous relationship between vendor and customer, the vendor had to convince customers of the reality and value of the product. One strategy for bringing the market to life was the testimonial supposedly from satisfied customers. These testimonials, dolled up with supplementary signatures from "witnesses," purported to be real affidavits and occasionally promised to send potential customers to veritable "people of undoubted credit" who would testify to "the great and good effects" of, in this case, Dr. Rock's Viper Drops.[23] To give testimonials the ring of truth, vendors often included, or invented, statements that spoke of a client's initial doubts, their skepticism regarding quackery, or fear of appearing in print. For example, the lengthy advertising pamphlet, *Turlington's Balsam of Life* (c. 1750), compiled hundreds of testimonials, many of which echoed the mixed feelings that brought sufferers to the medical marketplace:

> I have sometimes perus'd the list of extraordinary and surprising cures said to be perform'd by your balsamic tincture, but could never be induced to believe one half of what you are pleased to urge in behalf of its efficacy and use, till I was convinced by ocular demonstration. The public papers are daily stuffed with quack advertisements, sufficient to persuade a credulous person that he may secure immortality in the midst of corruption. . . . I am not fond of appearing in print, but this acknowledgement I would chuse to make public, that the use of this grand specifick may still become more universal. I am sir, your most obedient and humble servant. John Derway[24]

Here, John Derway's initial skepticism, experimental spirit, and sound reason not only constructed a believable story which the presumably dubious newspaper reader would respond to, but also invoked the experimental attitude of Enlightenment and natural philosophy.

Marketing Quackery

Quacks established their own authority by, on the one hand, conferring intelligence on their customers for cautiously experimenting with the nostrum, as we see in Derway's reflections, and on the other, invoking their own scientifically sound explanations for their goods. The true power of the amuletic anodyne necklace, for instance, emanated from microscopically visible creatures "which . . . ha[ve] been Discovered by some curious Gentlemen, Who affirmed that they nicely viewed it thro one of those Microscopes that discover Mites in Cheese to be real Living Animals, ... and they plainly saw infinite Numbers of Particles all in a Hurry and Motion, . . . in a Perfect Cloud coming from the necklace . . . ."[25] Later in the century, the Prussian quack Gustavus Katterfelto who vended his medicines on stage while performing experiments with microscopes, electricity, balloons, as well as flashy magic tricks, suggests that the "legitimate" tools of scientific inquiry were deployed for quacks' private profit.[26] The mock-quack speech explaining that the Universal Solutive "operate[s] seven several ways viz. Hypnotically, Hydrotically, Cathartically, Propysinatically, Hydragogically, Plumatically, and lastly Synecdochically, by corroborating the whole Oeconomia Animalis" was a satire,[27] but not far from the latinized and bloated vocabulary doctoring up many notices. Where the testimonial sought to bring a believable fellow sufferer into the reader's mind, the turn towards fancy medical and scientific explanations was designed to distinguish the quack's knowledge from the reader's, establishing value by placing the cure in the realm of arcane learning.

Value and worth beyond the reach of the ordinary reader was signified by a university education, a royal patent, membership in the Royal Society. Not surprisingly, quacks displayed certificates, endorsements, diplomas, patents, letters of royal appointment, any and all official documents to validate their authority especially in their public performances and presentations. Many also included supposed facsimiles of these documents in their print ads and pamphlets. Addison complained, "I have seen the whole Front of a Mountebank's Stage . . . faced with Patents, Certificates, Medals, and Great Seals, by which the several Princes of *Europe* have testified their particular Respect and Esteem for the doctor. Every great Man with a sounding Title has been his Patient. I believe I have seen Twenty Mountebanks that have given Physick to the Czar of *Muscovey*. The Great Duke of *Tuscany* escapes no better. The Elector of *Brandenburg* was likewise a very good Patient."[28] And if observers thought quack medicines had been commodified, how about the certificates themselves, sneered Swiss physician-cumanti-onanist quack, Samuel Tissot:

> it cannot be repeated too often, that whatever ostentatious Dress and Figure some of these Impostors make, . . . they have no scientific Knowledge; . . . their Titles and Patents are so many Impositions, and inauthentic; since, by a shameful Abuse, such Patents and Titles are become Articles of Commerce, which are to be obtained at very low Prices; just like the second-hand laced Cloaks which they purchase at the Brokers . . . .[29]

Tissot vilified quacks' accoutrements, reminding his readers that "their Certificates of Cures are so many Chimeras or Forgeries" because a credulous public (falsely) believed that the things surrounding a quack—diplomas, dress, and figure—represented the quack's worth and credit. Yet what the public mistook for his capital was simply no more than the *quack's* ability to consume, to buy "at very low Prices" the representation of some greater worth. Tissot condemned quacks' phony devices not just because they were frauds, but because they commodified things like knowledge that should be above commerce.[30]

Tissot issued the warning because quacks and medical vendors enjoyed tremendous success in the century. Science, diplomas, real faces, and details helped build a reality effect, a guarantee that the vendor's goods possessed a verifiable value and that he engaged in real transactions in a real market-place, even if it was visible primarily in the imaginative spaces of advertising columns and handbills. But the quack attached more than an imagined worth to his goods and his business. The quack offered real gifts, guaranteed value for the penny.

Gift Economies

Many medical vendors promised that consumers would receive not only the nostrum, but also a "free" gift. The most famous and certainly omnipresent quack treatment of the eighteenth century was the anodyne necklace, advertised in virtually all newspapers. The anodyne necklace's real *caché* was not its healing effluvia, but the topical almanac, print, or pamphlet which always accompanied it for free. Anodyne Necklace newspaper ads often began with the header "This Day Published," making them initially indistinguishable from other notices for printed goods; most of the ad was composed of text intriguingly describing some pamphlet or printed ephemera given with an anodyne necklace. Like other quack goodies, the anodyne necklace was expensive—five shillings, the same price as a week's wages. Described as "gratis," yet only available as gifts to those who bought the necklace, the pamphlets and prints must have been imagined to be worth something making up for the high cost of the necklace itself.

No doubt even healthy people were attracted to the necklace in order to receive pamphlets like these: In 1726 before the case was exposed, the curious could read how Mary Toft "could have 18 real, true, and living Rabbets within her, and of which she was really and truly delivered,"[31] but later in the month they would received an account of "the pretended Deliveries."[32] In 1746, one could receive "gratis" "Pro, and Con. —— For, and against. Old Maids."[33] In 1735, salacious sufferers could receive "Curious Letters, from A gentleman at Constantinople . . . [and] of the two sorts of eunuchs that guard . . . ladies, viz. those eunuchs who have but half cut off, and those who have all clean cut off." And in 1745, one could receive, "The interpretation of women's dreams . . . . The 35th [dream], tells what children she'll have —— but, if she dreams the 34th Dream, She may as well wed FARINELLI, all one. With a curious print of FARINELLI, finely engrav'd. Plainly shewing, to open, and clear view, the apparently Visible MARKS of his CASTRA-TION . . . ."[34] Such pamphlets' value only increased given the occasional accompanying nota bene that "This curious book will NOT be given to any Boys, nor Girls, Nor any *Paultry Persons*, notwithstanding the most Plausible Pretence they may make for their being sent for it." Such a warning also implicitly guaranteed the upstanding morality of the person who did receive the titillating pamphlet since "paultry persons" were banned from ownership, and once again helped construct an imagined community of worthy citizens.[35]

Spending Money, Making Money

In addition to these exciting products, including an entire line of antionanism essays,[36] many other anodyne give-aways explicitly created patriotic, commercial, and financial themes, from a treatise on sign language to one on shorthand, from the pamphlet "Gibralter, Reasons why we ought not on any Account give it up"[37] to one describing "the CHARACTERS of the English, Welch, Scots, Irish, French &c. For Example THREE Frenchmen, TWO cooks. THREE Italians, TWO fiddlers."[38] Even one of the anti-venereal pamphlets, *A Practical Plan* was promoted in 1720 London advertisements in French, Swedish, Castilian, Dutch, and German editions, the foreign languages simultaneously titillating by signifying the naughty and paving an international market by supposedly appealing to foreign readers.[39] There were several annual almanacs, including in 1737 the crypto-critical sounding "Hanover Almanack, Containing those things which the common almanacks ought to mention yet none of them speak a word of."[40] In 1728 the anodyne vendors boldly offered "The English Man's Two Wishes: One, That Hanover was Farther. The Other, That ———, &c." It turns out that the second wish, a standard attack on effeminacy and luxury, was "that foreign singers had no encouragement here to amass by their squeeking and squalling, such vast sums of our English money, as many of them have of late years done. 'Tis well known what a vast sum a certain Half-Man sent from London to the bank of Venice: And another of those Things (for what to call them, one scarce knows) sent almost as much to the bank of Genoa, which mony wou'd otherwise have circulated amongst our tradesmen."[41] Some anodyne pamphlets echoed the latest speculative trends, like the 1745 promotion involving "a lottery, for husbands, for young maids . . . not one blank, but ALL prizes."[42] But many more preached the virtues of sound savings, like the 1742 "The Worth, and Value, and TWENTY BY-Uses of a PENNY,"[43] which seems to have emphasized the importance of saving many pennies in order to buy an anodyne necklace.

A favorite anodyne pamphlet was *The Travels of a Shilling*, a greatly expanded version of a *Tatler* episode.[44] Addison's talkative (male) shilling begins his autobiographical narrative as South American ore who finds himself forged into a coin during Queen Elizabeth's reign, and then passes through dozens of hands and pockets, sometimes hidden away, occasionally reminted and restamped, and only twice taking part briefly in medical exchanges, first into the hands of an apothecary for a bottle of sack, and then into the pocket of an old herb woman. The anodyne necklace's chatty shilling, on the other hand, naturally gravitated in his eight-page journey towards anyone in need of an anodyne necklace or a Sugared Worm Pill. The autobiographical little coin describes how he passed through mints and exchequers, treasuries and coin-clippers; in between these episodes he describes the goods and services he is "sent for," including "a pack of cards; very often for twelve penny worth of oysters, and frequently . . . after dinner to a waiting servant." He experiences international commerce, witnessing his value shift, for instance when he "was carried to Holland, where I was much vexed to be changed for 11 paltry Dutch Stuyvers. But the person that took me . . . to Dublin, I there had the joy to see my self valued at thirteen pence." Late in his travels, the shilling finally encounters human consumers like

> one Mr. Hull a clockmaker [who] . . . coming to London bought with me & four more of my own rank an Anodyne Necklace. Of whose success he sent (of his own accord, & unknown to the author) the following account in a letter to London, to be published for the general good of children: 'Hearing the fame of the Anodyne Necklace recommended by Dr Chamberlain for Children's teeth, & having buried two children before, who died with the hard breeding and cutting of their teeth, [etc. etc.] . . . .'

And so continues the testimonial embedded in the shilling's autobiographical narrative, and on the shilling travels through more transactions inspiring testimonials to necklaces and sugar-plums and elixirs along the way.[45] Where Addison's shilling described being reminted as "chang[ing] my sex," the anodyne shilling, keeping with his proprietor's distaste for Farinelli and effeminacy, remained a hard-working male shilling, traded among men, strengthening the great English economy.

The happy story of the travelling coin inciting commercial exchanges over and over helped create the imaginary eighteenth-century marketplace. The shilling's movements simultaneously etched the physical lines of commerce across (and beyond) the nation and promoted the fiction that each transaction enriches the nation, that one shilling has an economic power equivalent to itself multiplied by the number of its exchanges. *The Travels of a Shilling* has an immediate and practical purpose, too, for it tells the buyers of anodyne necklaces what happens to their particular (five) shillings when they send them to London, to the anodyne vendors' shops. The anodyne advertisers, like most quack vendors, explained to the public how the commercial exchange would work, how a consumer could send money by carriage or post and be guaranteed a commodity in return.[46]

The Travels of a Shilling—like the second part of *Two Wishes*—informs its reader how commercial transactions work, what the value of money is, and all the places coins go once they slip out of our hands.[47] What on earth is a shilling worth? What on earth is an anodyne necklace or a curative sugar plum worth? *The Travels* gives an answer to both questions which solidifies the abstract and seemingly arbitrary worth of both money and quack medicines. By describing the valuable and pleasurable things he can be traded for—packs of cards, oysters, a servant's labor —the shilling establishes values for himself which are comparative with, but not quite equivalent to the incredible healing anodyne necklace. The sense of cumulative riches as each transaction with the shilling brings escalating pleasure and joy culminates in the ultimate purchase of anodyne necklaces at the end of the travelling coin's tale, placing the necklace at a narrative peak. But what was this actually worth? One 1748 anodyne necklace ad which gorily described infants' pains and potential death from teething warned that "a mother . . . would never forgive herself, whose child should DIE. Purely for want so DIVERTING a thing, to ease, and Please it,—and that for such a trifle of expence, as only six pence."[48] In other words, a baby's life was given a price: it was worth at least six pence, and so was an anodyne necklace. Because a baby's life should be above price, the anodyne necklace in its ability to save lives also acquired inestimable value.

In 1733, the vendors of the anodyne necklace exploited public anxiety regarding a recoinage of pre-1663 gold coins. In April 1732, "many merchants and traders in London" petitioned the Treasury to prohibit gold "broad . . . and quarter pieces" because of excessive "wear, clipping and filing"; their petition was successful, and the Treasury ordered in gold coins reimbursing people not the face value of the coinage, but the weight of the gold.[49] Given that a severely clipped coin might be worth less than its face value naturally was distressing. The anodyne proprietors offered an attractive solution: they promised to guarantee the "real" value of the gold by exchanging the old gold coins for anodyne products at the rate of the coins' face (rather than "pure") value. By structuring the transaction as if they would take a *loss*, the anodyne vendors infused the necklaces with a pure value too:

> ANY of the Call'd-in Pieces of Gold will be taken for their Former usual WHOLE Value, . . . For Anodyne Necklaces . . . . Note, 'Tis scarce worth any one's while to go to the Mint to receive Current Money for Only One or Two such Pieces of Call'd-in Gold, whereas by this proposed way, Any Person who may want an ANODYNE NECKLACE &c. will not lose any

thing at all . . . . And whatever is thus received, will be exchanged at the Mint all together afterwards, and the Author of the Anodyne Necklace will take all the Loss to himself.[50]

Although the offer to trade peony-bead necklaces for old specie may seem a joke, or may imply that the anodyne proprietors took their clients for rubes, such an exchange would have had reasonable associations for consumers. For one, assigning an exchange-value, as well as an implied use-value, to a thing like an anodyne necklace was merely barter, a familiar form of exchange in economies lacking adequate currency; older customers might also have been familiar with the seventeenth-century custom of proprietors stamping and issuing trade tokens for small goods like cups of coffee, also in lieu of small currencies.[51] For another, the proprietors may have echoed the thaumaturgic associations between a sufferer's coin and the healing power it was given when the monarch touched and blessed it for the king's evil.[52] But what the "Call'd-in Gold" campaign really attempted to do was transmogrify the nature of commercial exchange by suggesting that the money used to buy a good was a less stable currency than the necklace itself, and that the only person to part with anything was the vendor.

Testimonials throughout the century reinforced this equation as letter writers gushed that the nostrum was always worth more than its cost. For example "a respectable Gentleman at Litchfield, who, for family reasons, requests his name may not be made public" wrote to Dr. Samuel Solomon in 1798: "I inclose . . . a bank note for five pounds, and shall be glad you would send . . . nine or ten bottles of your Cordial balm of Gilead, a *proportion* infinitely more valuable than the inclosed."[53] Unlike the anodyne necklaces' financial narratives which fixed a specific comparative value for their goods, Solomon instead emphasized that the value of his Balm was beyond quantification, but unquestionably of greater worth than the money he received.[54] Solomon even claimed that his Cordial Balm was indeed equivalent to gold because "the most learned physicians of the age . . . have been unable to discover [in it] the least particle of either mercury . . . iron, or any other mineral except *Gold! pure virgin Gold! and the true Balm of Mecca.*"[55] Medical knowledge, a gift beyond price, was passed down from master to initiate for generations, but Solomon presented himself as kind enough to translate that treasure into an economic value by placing the balm on the same plane as *"Gold!"*

Turning Medicine into Money

Solomon, with at least one other late eighteenth-century vendor (of "Gowland's Lotion" for scurvy and pimples),[56] creatively reconfigured the traditional quack certificates and affidavits which accompanied nostrums to resemble bank-notes, stock certificates, and even Bank of England pound notes (figs. 1–3).[57] Solomon's certificate, like many seals and pieces of paper attached to other medical products, is described as being "For Public Security against counterfeits." Quacks warning the public against the dangers of fraudulent versions of their products circulating in the medical marketplace of course implied that their own products possessed true, and specific value if others would copy them.[58] But Solomon and Gowland transformed these standard guarantees which vouched for the worth of the accompanying product by imbuing the guarantee itself with monetary value.[59] With their layout, space for a number and signature, and placement of seals, these guarantees of authenticity designed to distinguish the products they accompanied from the supposed plethora of counterfeit balms and lotions, themselves resemble counterfeit bank-notes. By implying that the balms are valuable enough to inspire counterfeits, the original product guarantees its real value, mimetically becoming a thing worth emulating—just as bank-notes were worth copying to confer worth.

Although Solomon turned to both specie and paper credit to validate the worth of his balm, he and other late eighteenth-century quacks capitalized on a public's growing faith in representational currency, that *real* monetary value backed the piece of paper called a "cheque" or a Bank of England note. The quack doctor Martin van Butchell did not issue fake bank-notes with his elastic trusses. But he did flag his advertisements with observations about money, including the power of paper currency. One 1796 notice described various medical ailments, and then hopped to the Prime Minister, currency, the wonders of compound interest:

> Hint to BIL-ly Pit: My eldest boy (—aged fifteen—) has shewn me on paper that twenty shillings, at five percent per annum, compound interest, 999 years, will yield 74 trillion, 106,976 billion, 294,838 million, 206,464 pounds sterling. . . . Bank-of-England Notes! Save Time and trouble:—Vastly important: to-useful-people! ten millions of men, would be twenty years, counting the above sum; if each man counted two hundred pounds a minute, ten hours a day, six days a week, and fifty weeks a year. One could count it: —In a few hours, with Bank-of-England-notes![60]

The real wonder van Butchell acclaims has less to do with compound interest than with the power of print currency to represent value and thus save (while representing) human labor. The revolution in print which permitted the development of a viable public sphere also spurred a financial revolution where money could be printed; in time, people trusted that "real" value did back

Figure 1. Samuel Solomon, M.D. Cordial Balm of Gilead. Certificate of Authenticity. J.J. Coll. Patent Medicine, Box 4. Bodleian Library, Oxford.

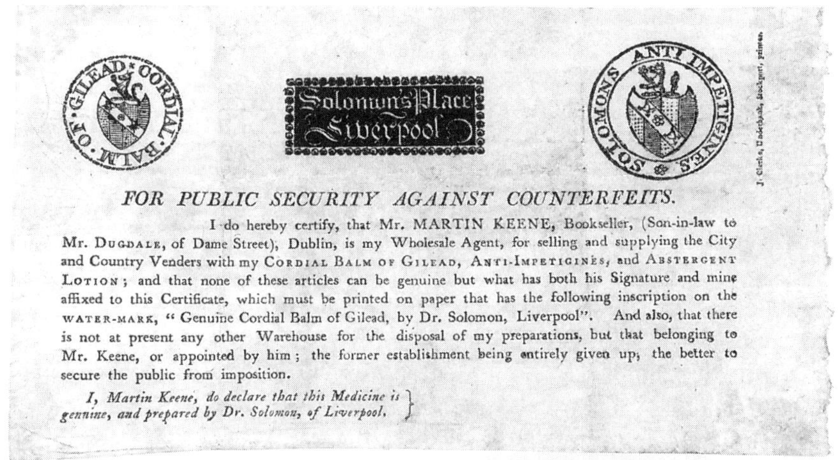

Figure 2. Mr. Martin Keene, Bookseller and vender of Dr. Samuel Solomon's Cordial Balm of Gilead. Certificate of Authenticity. J.J. Coll. Patent Medicine, Box 4. Bodleian Library, Oxford.

Figure 3. Gowlands Lotion (sold at 55 Long Acre, London). Certificate of Authenticity. J.J. Coll. Patent Medicine, Box 4. Bodleian Library, Oxford.

English bank-notes and representational currency. The anodyne necklace's "Call'd-in Gold" campaign of 1733 had exploited the early eighteenth-century public's fear that money was a concrete object rather than a representation of value, perhaps possessing a use-value somehow equivalent to the use-value of an (actually useless) anodyne necklace. The *faux*-notes of Solomon, Gowland, and van Butchell, printed out later in the century in countless quantities—with each bill described as individually representing enormous amounts of money—purported to represent astronomical value, but actually demonstrated inflation. Solomon's invocation of "Gold!" possessed an inestimable value just like the apparently unlimited exchange value of paper currency, which the public was slowly coming to trust by the 1740s.[61]

Not only did more and various forms of representational currency—from "notes of the private bankers" to "cheques" and "Bank of England 'bills' and notes," from "Exchequer bills" to "malt tickets and lottery tickets"—flood the eighteenth-century economy, these paper currencies also floated out into the most ordinary and everyday commercial transactions by mid-century. Originally only cash-laden merchants, sellers, nobles, and gentry used credit and paper currency to replace transporting heavy, unwieldy amounts of specie in large transactions. Since most early eighteenth-century exchanges using paper money still occurred among the well-off (rather than the majority of customers to whom quacks advertised), paper promises may have lacked the advertising appeal that Solomon and Gowland saw in them in the late eighteenth century. By the 1750s some London shopkeepers began accepting bills, and parliamentary acts passed in 1765 and 1777 indicate that private banks and persons were issuing paper bills in denominations as slight as six pence. These paper moneys, many of which were entirely worthless as their issuers were frauds or collapsed in bankruptcy, circulated among the lower and middle orders for common and daily transactions. Although it was the failure of credit and paper money in 1763 and 1772 which inspired the legislation, these two acts forced issuers to back their notes with real monetary value, and in doing so, helped concretise paper claims. The 1777 Act "provided that all notes of . . . less than £5, should specify the names and places of abode of the persons to whom . . . they were made payable" which "destroy[ed] for all practical purposes their negotiability and therefore their character as currency," yet this act had the effect of imbuing representational currency and paper transactions with guaranteeable value backed by a real person's name and address.[62]

Jean-Christophe Agnew describes how commodity exchange is subsumed by capital-exchange in capitalistic markets: "What begins as a bounded process of the circulation of commodities through the medium of money (C-M-C) ends as the boundless circulation of money via the medium of commodities (M-C-M)." Agnew then quotes Marx's very bodily metaphorical description: "'Circulation sweats money from every pore.'"[63] We would think that many eighteenth-century quacks had exactly this image in mind as they conjugated sweating, oozing bodies with copious and regenerative financial imagery. By invoking money not as the exchange value of the commodity, but as equivalent to the commodity itself, quacks were in part attempting to confer a real value on a commodity concocted out of worthless ingredients. By claiming the Balm of Gilead was actually gold (or making its certificate of authenticity resemble a Bank of England note or offering to turn outdated, clipped gold coins into anodyne necklaces) quacks conveyed that medicines were not the endpoints in commodity exchange, but a medium of exchange and thus at least metonymically equivalent to cash itself.

Of course, no one could possibly have thought that anodyne necklaces would be better items of exchange than an old gold sovereign or that the Balm of Gilead could be exchanged for other goods. But I would argue that these figurative transmutations, like *The Travels of a Shilling*'s explanation of what shillings and goods were worth, attempted to reassure a particular public with few shillings and little experience in the most imaginative spaces of the eighteenth-century financial market. It would seem that quack ads were aimed at the lower and middle reaches of society, groups particularly eager to make their way in the new marketplace and public sphere, but especially easily duped by lotteries and other risky schemes. Critic John Tennent lamented how quacks so easily succeeded because customers willingly suspended disbelief and trusted fabulous claims, but he warned, "Such Thoughts are equally absurd with those of *Lottery Adventurers,* every one thinking that they are to have Capital Prizes, when they can but fall to the Lot of a few."[64]

By turning the act of spending money into receiving money, or at least a representation of money, the quack transformed consumption into a seemingly safe financial investment. Critics gawked at the public's willingness to be taken in by such an equation. *The Spectator*, for instance, had attacked quacks for falsely disavowing their "private interest" and the foolish crowds who believed

> one of these public-spirited artists at Hammersmith, . . . [who] told his audience, 'that he had been born and bred there, and that having a special regard for the place of his nativity, he was determined to make a present of five shillings to as many as would accept of it.' The whole crowd stood agape and ready to take the doctor at his word; when putting his hand into a . . . bag, as everyone was expecting his Crown-piece, he drew out an handful of little Packets, each of which he informed the spectators was constantly sold at five shillings and six pence, but that he would bate the odd five shillings to every inhabitant of that place: the whole assembly immediately closed with this generous offer, and took off all his physick, after the doctor had made them vouch for one another, that there were no foreigners among them, but that they were all Hammersmith men.[65]

Where Addison and Steele depicted quacks' profits resulting from *legerdemain* foisted on gullible and irrational consumers, later economists like Adam Smith rationalized the transaction, correcting the assumption that "[a]pothecaries' profit is become a bye-word, denoting something uncommonly extravagant." In fact, aside from the fact that the market tolerated apothecaries' prices, Smith explained that what critics considered inflated prices were actually natural prices which incorporated an apothecary's education, stock, expenses, labor, and "the trust which is reposed in him." The public may have been able to understand that "the part of the apparent profit is real wages, disguised in the garb of profit" when considering pharmacists in their splendid, stock-rich shops.[66] But quacks were certainly less likely to receive such credit, particularly since their stock was imagined, described only in handbills and advertisements, and their shop often nothing more than the table they occupied at a coffeehouse.

Adam Smith may have argued that the "invisible hand" controlled the medical marketplace as much as any other economic arena, but quacks themselves devised their own sleight of hand which allowed them to manipulate the checks and balances of the marketplace. Recognizing that certificates and science might lure the sick and curious, but could not guarantee an actual sale, many quacks offered a "No Cure, No Money" clause promising to refund money to the dissatisfied.[67] But given the feeble powers and inherent worthlessness of most quack goods, there must have been many unhappy customers.

This paradoxically is exactly how quacks generated so many glowing testimonials: quacks were happy to refund money, so long as the displeased customer signed his name and offered his good credit in a bogus testimonial. Some contemporaries went farther, describing this as extortion and the pivot in the quack transaction. The critic P. Coltheart claimed that once patients realized that the quack's cures had not healed

> ... often too late, [their] Eyes ... are open, and see plainly the dangerous Ambuscade they are led into; and being willing to extricate themselves, by applying to some judicious and regular Practitioner, yet are frequently interrupted by the Menaces and Threats of their depredating Doctor, who tells them he will either expose their Affairs ... he demands a Sum of Money. Upon Non-Payment, possibly for wants of Ability, the Consequence that frequently follows, is, that the Person of the Patient is destroy'd.[68]

In other words, the sufferer who so craved anonymity that he chose a quack vendor rather than a real physician in a face-to-face transaction was publicly exposed, with his name, occupation, residence, and details of bodily pain used in advertisements and handbills. If Coltheart is to be believed, the patient lost all his private person to the quack, not only his money and his body, but his good name and honor. A person's name, address, and "creditable behavior" were exactly what guaranteed credit relations more generally (including the post-1777 transactions of small paper bills); by calling in and publicizing private persons' credit to assign value to his nostrums, the quack may have lost a little hard currency, but he gained credit which he could never acquire on the basis of his own worthless goods. Publicly humiliated, the patient was silenced, but his body, fraudulently described as healed, conferred healing powers on the quack-extortionist and value beyond price on the quack concoction. The invisible hand in the quack's deck was this ability to turn loss into profit by transforming the consumer's credit into his own, and making the desperate complicit in publicizing the supposedly "great and good" public benefits of his quack arsenal.

N O T E S

Grateful thanks to Julie Anne Lambert and the staff of the John Johnson Collection at the Bodleian Library, Oxford who guided me through the collection and generously made reproductions of rare materials for me. I would also like to thank Eric Chandler, Bill Forman, Meg Jacobs, Steve Pincus, Rob Rodgers, Jane Shaw, Simon Stern, Aviva Tuffield and the anonymous readers for their helpful insights, and John Brewer for telling me many years ago about the John Johnson treasures.

1. *Eronania: On the Misusings of the Marriage-Bed by Er and Onan Judah's two Sons: Genesis 38* (London: H. Parker, 1724), British Library, T. 420 (7); this is a "free" pamphlet given with the Anodyne Necklace. See also Francis Doherty, *A Study in Eighteenth-Century Advertising Methods: The Anodyne Necklace* (Lewiston: Edwin Mellen Press, 1992), 154–55. Since Doherty collates almost all known Anodyne Necklace pamphlets and promotions, my citations cross-reference his *Study*; for an overview of the product, see Francis Doherty, "The Anodyne Necklace: A Quack Remedy and Its Promotion," *Medical History* 34 (1990): 268–93.

2. *The Universal Spectator and Weekly Journal*, 25 July 1730. The advertisement continues: "Paris, July 20, 1730. The King of France's four Children wear each of them one of the famous ANODYNE NECKLACE which has greatly added to their Respect here. And of whose Effect on his Royal Highness the DAUPHIN OF FRANCE, the Publick News-Papers throughout all Europe, gave an Account in March last, that he had cut several teeth, without any Notice at all of Pain (he being six Months old) to the agreeable Surprize of all that were about him, and goes on cutting his Teeth with all desirable Safety, wearing still his ANODYNE NECK-LACE . . . ." Doherty, *Study*, 48, 64–65.

3. For the financial revolution more broadly see P. G. M. Dickson, *The Financial Revolution in England: A Study in the Development of Public Credit, 1688–1756* (1967; reprint, Aldershot, England: Gregg Revivals, 1993); John Brewer, *The Sinews of Power: War, Money and the English State, 1688–1783* (New York: Knopf, 1989); Colin Nicholson, *Writing and the Rise of Finance: Capital Satires of the Early Eighteenth Century* (Cambridge: Cambridge Univ. Press, 1994); Patrick Brantlinger, *Fictions of State: Culture and Credit in Britain, 1694–1994* (Ithaca: Cornell Univ. Press, 1996).

4. On the costs of printing and profit of advertisements, see Michael Harris, *London Newspapers in the Age of Walpole: A Study in the Origins of the Modern English Press* (London: Associated University Presses, 1987), 49–64; R. M. Wiles, *Freshest Advices: Early Provincial Newspapers in England* ([Columbus]: Ohio State Univ. Press, 1965), 95–146; Jeremy Black, *The English Press in the Eighteenth Century* (Philadelphia: Univ. of Pennsylvania Press, 1987), 61–64. For advertising medicine in particular, see Roy Porter, *Health for Sale: Quack Medicine in Eighteenth-Century England* (Manchester: Manchester Univ. Press, 1989); the relatively few other works examining medical advertisements during the period include: P. S. Brown, "The Venders of Medicines Advertised in Eighteenth-Century Bath Newspapers," *Medical History* 19 (1975): 352–69; P. S. Brown, "Medicines Advertised in Eighteenth-Century Bath Newspapers," *Medical History* 20 (1976):

152–68; Colin Jones most provocatively links medical advertising to broader political and cultural meanings: see his "The Great Chain of Buying: Medical Advertisements, the Bourgeois Public Sphere, and the Origins of the French Revolution," *American Historical Review* 101 (1996): 13–40.

5. C. Y. Ferdinand, "Selling it to the Provinces: News and Commerce Round Eighteenth-Century Salisbury," in *Consumption and the World of Goods*, ed. John Brewer and Roy Porter (New York: Routledge, 1993), 393–411; see also Henry Sampson, *A History of Advertising from the Earliest Times: Illustrated by Anecdotes, Curious Specimens, and Biographical Notes* (London: Chatto and Windus, 1874), 373–421, on quackery and medicine.

6. Unidentified newspaper, (but publisher is "J. Peele," February 1722, so the paper could be *The London Journal* [Harris, *London Newspapers*, 71]). Clipping in the John Johnson Collection, Patent Medicines, Box 14, the Bodleian Library, Oxford; hereafter cited as J. J., P. M.

7. Jürgen Habermas, *The Structural Transformation of the Public Sphere*, (Cambridge: M.I.T. Press, 1989); for analyses of the public relevant here, see Steve Pincus, "'Coffee Politicians Does Create': Coffeehouses and Restoration Political Culture," *Journal of Modern History* 67 (1995): 807–34; Greg Laugero, "Infrastructures of Enlightenment: Road-making, the Public Sphere, and the Emergence of Literature," *Eighteenth-Century Studies* 29 (1995): 45–68; Margaret C. Jacob, "The Mental Landscape of the Public Sphere: A European Perspective," *Eighteenth-Century Studies* 28 (1994): 95–113; David Zaret, "Religion, Science, and Printing in the Public Sphere in Seventeenth-Century England," in *Habermas and the Public Sphere,* ed. Craig Calhoun, (Cambridge: M.I.T. Press, 1991), 212–35; Nancy Fraser, "Rethinking the Public Sphere," in Calhoun, *Habermas*, 109–42.

8. Joseph Addison and Richard Steele, *The Spectator*, ed. Donald F. Bond, 5 vols. (Oxford: Clarendon Press, 1965), no. 572 (26 July 1714), 5: 551–55.

9. Unidentified newspaper (1731), clipping in J. J., P. M., Box 14.

10. For example, *Free Thoughts on Quacks and their Medicines Occasioned by the Death of Dr. Goldsmith and Mr. Scawen* (London, 1776); see Jonathan Barry, "Publicity and the Public Good: Presenting Medicine in Eighteenth-Century Bristol," in *Medical Fringe and Medical Orthodoxy, 1750–1850*, ed. W. F. Bynum and Roy Porter (London: Croom Helm, 1987), 29–39.

11. Roy Porter, "The Languages of Quackery in England, 1660–1800," in *Language and Society*, ed. Peter Burke and Roy Porter (Cambridge: Cambridge Univ. Press, 1987), 73–103; W. F. Bynum "Treating the Wages of Sin: Venereal Disease and Specialism in Eighteenth-Century Britain," in *Medical Fringe*, 5–28; Roy Porter, "'I think Ye Both Quacks': The Controversy between Dr. Theodor Myersbach and Dr. John Coakley Lettsom," in *Medical Fringe*, 56–78.

12. Joseph Addison, *The Tatler*, ed. Donald F. Bond, 3 vols. (Oxford: Clarendon Press, 1987), no. 224 (10 Sept. 1710), 3: 166–71.

13. I am especially grateful to an anonymous reader for drawing my attention to this paradox in Addison's essay.

14. For an evaluation of the reading public's interest in medicine and the body see Roy Porter, "Lay Medical Knowledge in the Eighteenth Century: The Evidence of the *Gentleman's Magazine*," *Medical History* 29 (1985): 138–68 and "Laymen,

Doctors and Medical Knowledge in the Eighteenth Century: The Evidence of *Gentleman's Magazine*," in *Patients and Practitioners: Lay Perceptions of Medicine in Pre-Industrial Society*, ed. Roy Porter (Cambridge: Cambridge Univ. Press, 1985), 283–312.

15. *The Spectator*, no. 452 (8 Aug. 1712), 4: 90–94. That readers apparently considered ads to be facts like news apparently was not lost on advertisers, who often designed their ad copy to look like "real news," as we saw with "A Letter from France."

16. Neil McKendrick, John Brewer and J. H. Plumb, *The Birth of a Consumer Society: The Commercialization of Eighteenth-Century England* (Bloomington: Indiana Univ. Press, 1982); see also John Brewer and Roy Porter, introduction to *Consumption and the World of Goods*, 1–15.

17. Unidentified newspaper (1734), clipping in J. J., P. M., Box 14.

18. A typical, even restrained description of the afflicted body: "R. Rock's Restorative Viper-Drops . . . restore greatly in weak habits, strengthen weak backs, warm and invigorate parts that are languid and weaken'd by gleets, or other injuries; they help digestion, comfort a cold stomach, and expel wind both from thence and the bowels, and help the effects of hard drinking, cleanse the ureters from slimy or sabulous matter, thereby taking away gravel pains in the back, compose hurry'd spirits, and take off flutterings and lowness; comforting the brain and causing chcarfulness; they are a noble balsamick also for all inward or outward wounds, consolidating the part injured, almost instantly; cure burns or scaldings, applied immediately, in a surprising manner, and without leaving disagreeable marks or scars." Unidentified newspaper (1752), clipping in J. J., P. M., Box 14; on quacks inventing diseases, see Thomas W. Laqueur, "Credit, Novels, Masturbation," in *Choreographing History*, ed. Susan Leigh Foster (Bloomington: Indiana Univ. Press, 1995), 119–28.

19. Thomas W. Laqueur, "Bodies, Details, and the Humanitarian Narrative," in *The New Cultural History*, ed. Lynn Hunt (Berkeley and Los Angeles: Univ. of California Press, 1989), 176–204.

20. Dorothy Porter and Roy Porter, *Patient's Progress. Doctors and Doctoring in Eighteenth-Century England* (Stanford: Stanford Univ. Press, 1989), 16–52, 70–95; Guenter Risse, "Doctor William Cullen, Physician, Edinburgh: A Consultation Practice in the Eighteenth Century," *Bulletin of the History of Medicine* 48 (1974): 330–51; for the dominance of verbal description before the development of a "medical gaze," see Michel Foucault, *The Birth of the Clinic: An Archaeology of Medical Perception*, trans. A. M. Sheridan Smith (New York: Pantheon, 1973).

21. Peter Spufford, *Money and Its Use in Medieval Europe* (Cambridge: Cambridge Univ. Press, 1988), 254.

22. Jean-Christophe Agnew, *Worlds Apart: The Market and the Theater in Anglo-American Thought, 1550–1750* (Cambridge: Cambridge Univ. Press, 1986); Dickson, *Financial Revolution;* Nicholson, *Writing;* on the interpersonal effects of modern capitalism, see Thomas L. Haskell, "Capitalism and the Origins of the Humanitarian Sensibility," *American Historical Review* 90 (1985): 339–61, 547–66.

23. Unidentified clipping (1752), J. J., P. M., Box 14; for contemporary charges of fraudulence, see *The Spectator,* no. 572 (26 July 1714), 5: 551–55.

24. *Turlington's Balsam of Life* (c. 1750), 65, pamphlet in J. J., P. M., Box 4.

25. *Concerning the Gout* (London: T. Parker, 1730), British Library, T. 420 (15); Doherty, *Study*, 208–13. Other scientific (and frequently reprinted) Anodyne Necklace pamphlets include: *A Philosophical Essay upon the Celebrated Anodyne Necklace . . . . In this Essay therefore is clearly shewed from the Principles of the New Philosophy* (London: H. Parker, 1717) which was dedicated to the "Most Illustrious the Royal Society" and interlarded claims about the Anodyne Necklace with Robert Boyle's work in natural philosophy; *A Philosophical Essay Upon Actions on Distant Subjects: Wherein are Clearly Explicated, According to the Principles of the New Philosophy, and Sir Isaac Newton's Laws of Motion, All Those Actions Usually Attributed to Sympathy and Antipathy*, 3rd ed. (London: H. Parker, 1715), which developed its own spin on Newton's laws to provide proof for the necklace's invisible, healing effluvia: "Chap. 1. Three universal Laws of Nature, necessary to be premis'd to the following Essay. Ist. Law. Out of the Pores of all Bodies whatsoever, tho' never so hard and solid, there is more or less a constant Effluvium and Exhalation of Volatile subtle Steams and Atoms (almost *Always* sensible to our Smell), caused by the Attractive Influence of the Sun, and Crowding and Pressure of other Atoms. . . , " 3–4.

26. Sampson, *History of Advertising*, 403–5; Porter and Porter, *Patient's Progress*, 26; Roy Porter, "Before the Fringe: Quack Medicine in Georgian England," *History Today* (Nov. 1986): 16–22.

27. *Pharmacopola Circumforaneous; or, the Horse Doctor's Harangue to the Credulous Mob* (Dublin, [1739]), British Library, 1890 e. 5 (133); passage also quoted without citation in C. G. S. Thompson, *The Quacks of Old London* (London: Brentano's, 1928), 140.

28. Addison, *The Tatler*, no. 240 (21 Oct. 1710), 3: 232–36.

29. [Samuel Auguste David] Tissot, *Advise to the People in General, with Regard to their Health . . . with a Table of the most cheap, yet effectual Remedies*, trans. J. Kirkpatrick, (London, 1771), 554.

30. Many of the quacks even boasted that they had come by these "medical *Insignia*" simply by buying, rather than earning, them; see for example, John Taylor (oculist), *The Life and Extraordinary History of the Chevalier John Taylor*, 2 vols. (London: M. Cooper, 1761), 1: 50–51.

31. *The Daily Post*, 8 Dec. 1726.

32. Advertised in *Mist's Weekly Journal*, 31 Dec. 1726; Doherty, *Study*, 395. During the following summer, buyers could receive "pictures Engraved of the Pretended Rabbit-Breeder her self Mary Tofts, and of the Rabbits, and of the Persons who attended her during her pretended deliveries, shewing who were, and who were not imposed upon by her," *Mist's Weekly Journal*, 14 July 1727; on Mary Toft, see Lisa Cody, "'The Doctor's in Labour; Or a New Whim Wham from Guildford," *Gender and History* 4 (1992): 175–96; for a similar interpretation, see Dennis Todd, *Imagining Monsters: Miscreations of the Self in Eighteenth-Century England*, especially his chapters "A New Whim Wham from Guildford" and "The Doctor's in Labor," (Chicago: Univ. of Chicago Press, 1995).

33. Unidentified newspaper, 3 May 1746, in Daniel Lysons, *Collectanea: or, a Collection of Advertisements* (1828), British Library, 1881. b. 6., vol. 1, part 2.

34. Unidentified newspaper advertisement (1745) in Douce Adds. 138, 212, the Bodleian Library, Oxford; this campaign was also run a decade earlier in *The Universal Spectator and Weekly Journal* 23 Aug. 1735; Doherty, *Study*, 396–97.

35. Nota bene inserted in the 1735 advertisement for *Curious Letters*.

36. Doherty, *Study*, 129–181, 402–5.

37. *The British Journal*, 25 March 1727.

38. Unidentified newspaper advertisement (1750) in Douce Adds. 138, 228.

39. For this campaign, see Doherty, *Study*, 170–71.

40. Unidentified newspaper advertisement (1737) in Douce Adds. 138, 202; Doherty, *Study*, 288–92.

41. *The English Man's Two Wishes: One, That Hanover was Farther: The Other, That ——, &c.* (London, 1728?), 2; Doherty, *Study*, 346–48.

42. Unidentified newspaper advertisement (1745) in Douce Adds. 138, 212; Doherty, *Study*, 78.

43. Doherty, *Study*, 313.

44. Addison, *The Tatler*, no. 249 (11 Nov. 1710), 3: 269–73.

45. *The Travels of a Shilling, from Queen Elizabeth's Reign to K. George the IId's Time* (London: H. Parker, 1728?), 1–8.

46. Doherty, *Study*, 164–65; see also Laugero, "Infrastructures."

47. On the genre of narrating inanimate objects later in the century, see Aileen Douglas, "Britannia's Rule and the It-Narrator," *Eighteenth-Century Fiction* 6 (1993): 65–82. Although Douglas does not include the earlier *Shilling* stories in her account since she focuses on post-1760 literature, her argument that such stories "whimsically register England's transformation into a consumer society turning a troubling, if exciting phenomenon into a harmless game" (69), suggests how these fictional narratives functioned to assign (positive) values to the invisible aspects of the new marketplace.

48. Unidentified newspaper advertisement (1748) in Douce Adds. 138, 231; this copy is also advertised earlier in *The Universal Spectator and Weekly Journal* 27 October 1737; see also Doherty, *Study*, 63.

49. *Calendar of Treasure Books and Papers, 1731–1734*, ed. William Shaw, 5 vols. (London: Eyre and Spottiswoode, 1898), 2: 222, 369–70.

50. The "Call'd-in Gold" advertisement ran in *The Universal Spectator and Weekly Journal* 10 March through 30 June 1733; see also Doherty, *Study*, 407–8.

51. John Yonge Akerman, *Tradesmen's Tokens, Current in London and Its Vicinity between the Years 1648 and 1672* (London: John Russell Smith, 1849) and Jacob Henry Burn, *A Descriptive Catalogue of the London Traders, Tavern, and Coffee-House Tokens Current in the Seventeenth Century* (London: for the Corporation, 1853).

52. Helen Farquhar, *Royal Charities: Angels and Touchpieces for the King's Evil* (London: Harrison and Sons, 1922).

53. Samuel Solomon, *Guide to Health; or Advice to Both Sexes* (Stockport: J. Clarke, 180–?), 55.

54. Solomon, like many other quacks, promised that the public could "save" when purchasing his wares. For instance, "A Saving of £1.6. The Cordial Balm of

Gilead is sold in bottles, price half-a-guinea each; there are also boxes, price £5. containing equal to twelve bottles at 10.s.6d," Solomon, *Guide*, 255–56.

55. Solomon, *Guide*, 36–37.

56. The anodyne vendors, according to Francis Doherty, offered customers purchasing a necklace the gift of silver and copper metals which would, at least symbolically, invoke monetary value. Since I have not seen these particular promotions or items myself, I am hesitant to analyze them alongside these *faux* paper notes (Doherty, *Study*, 87). Later in the century, Gowland's, like so many quack medicines of the day, seems to have been used for an array of visible afflictions from morally neutral freckles and blemishes to morally laden pock marks and ulcerated flesh. In Jane Austen's *Persuasion* (vol. 2, ch. 4) Anne Elliot's father praises the concoction: "I should recommend Gowland, the constant use of Gowland, during the spring months. Mrs. Clay has been using it at my recommendation, and you see what it has done for her. You see how it has carried away her freckles." Tony Tanner suggests that contemporary readers would have also known using Gowland's could signify having syphilis as the concoction included "corrosive sublimate of mercury" which helps build Mrs. Clay's unsavory character in the novel. (I am grateful to an anonymous reader for these references; see Tony Tanner, *Jane Austen* [Cambridge: Harvard Univ. Press, 1986], 237, where he cites a letter from Nora Crook to *The Times Literary Supplement,* 7 Oct. 1983, for the medical evidence.)

57. The three certificates resemble a private bank cheque, a Bank of England note, and a stock certificate; all are in J. J., P. M., Box 4. The *faux* note for fifty-five pounds, dated 1795, may have been a promotion exploiting that year's debates about the Bank's printing small denominations (see note 60 below). Solomon's *Guide to Health* also described how a consumer could identify true, authentic versions of the product with their accompanying certificates: "The Cordial Balm of Gilead is in flint glass square bottles, with these words impressed on the glass, 'The Cordial Balm of Gilead, prepared by Dr. Solomon, Solomon's Place, Brownlow Street, Late of Marybone, Liverpool.' And with each bottle is given the following copper-plate certificate, signed by the Doctor himself, which is chequed and numbered, and will detect a counterfeit sort immediately: Solomon's Place, Brownlow Street, late of No. Marybone, Liverpool, I certify that this Cordial Balm of Gilead is genuine, and was truly prepared . . . by me, S. Solomon, MD Entered by [blank for 'Clerk's Name']. Observe also, on the outside of the wrapper is a fac-simile of the Doctor's hand-writing, which must correspond with the *real* signature to the certificate, sealed up *within* the said wrapper, with a seal bearing the Doctor's arms and crest. . . . Each bill of directions contains a copy of Dr. Solomon's Diploma or Degree of Doctor of Medicine as a regular Physician, granted to him by the University and College of Physicians. All such as do not answer this description are assuredly counterfeits; and the Doctor will pay a reward of FIFTY GUINEAS, on the conviction of any person vending a spurious sort of the Cordial Balm of Gilead." Affidavits, facsimiles of the arms, the diploma etc. follow. Solomon, *Guide*, 230–32.

58. Doherty describes the specific, complex battles between competing vendors of the anodyne necklace several of whom accused the others of counterfeiting. An especially heated ad reads: "You may Easily know the SLY COUNTERFEITS at

the Royal-Exchange made by the Woman . . . . Note, Those Persons who have been *Unthinkingly Trick'd* at the ROYAL EXCHANGE, in having Bought the *Pernicious* COUNTERFEITS of the Remedies belonging to Dr. Chamberlain's Famous ANODYNE NECKLACE, which the grossly *Ignorant Illiterate* WOMAN makes, have been so Imposed upon by those *Counterfeit* Medicines, that they have *afterwards* most heartily CURS'D both *the Doctoring* WOMAN for so basely Tricking them, and her SLY *Counterfeit* Medicines together . . . ." *The Universal Spectator and Weekly Journal*, 5 July 1735.

59. Solomon in fact promised to *give* consumers fifty guineas—if they helped him prosecute competitors counterfeiting his balm (see note 57 above). Given that apparently nobody was passing off copies of his products, Solomon's promise was valueless, but designed, like the anodyne proprietors' "Call'd-in Gold" campaign, to fix a monetary value to his wares.

60. Unidentified newspaper advertisement (1796) in Douce Adds. 138, 226; for other examples of Van Butchell's invoking money, see Sampson, *History*, 401. Van Butchell's 1796 campaign (for trusses) advertises the utility of one-pound notes replacing all those unwieldy piles of twenty heavy shillings; the Bank of England did not, until the following year, issue notes in sums lower than five pounds; see A. E. Feavearyear, *The Pound Sterling: A History of English Money* (Oxford: Clarendon Press, 1931), 162–70.

61. Nicholson, *Writing*, 4–7, 13.

62. Feavearyear, *Pound Sterling*, 147–52, 161–63; Julian Hoppit, "Attitudes to Credit in Britain, 1680–1790," *The Historical Journal* 33 (1990): 305–22; J. G. A. Pocock, *Virtue, Commerce, and History* (Cambridge: Cambridge Univ. Press, 1985).

63. Agnew, *Worlds Apart*, 42.

64. John Tennent, *Physical Enquiries: Discovering the Mode of Translation in the Constitution Of Northern Inhabitants . . . the mercenary Practice of Physicians, by an Impartial State of Dr. Ward's Qualifications for the Practice of Physic* (London: T. Gardner, 1742), 45; for several contemporaries who laid blame on the credulity of the English people in falling for quacks' claims, see Porter, "'I Think Ye Both Quacks,'" 65.

65. *The Spectator*, no. 572 (26 July 1714), 5: 551–55.

66. Adam Smith, *An Inquiry into the Nature and Causes of the Wealth of Nations*, 2 vols. (Oxford: Clarendon Press, 1976), 1: x.b., 128–29.

67. "No Cure, No Money" is an exceedingly common medical promise; the pithy retort made by critics of quackery was: "No Money, No Cure." For various examples, see Thompson, *Quacks*, 80, 167.

68. P. Coltheart, *The Quacks Unmask'd, Which Detects, and sets in a true Light, their Pernicious and Destructive Practice; with some reasons why it ought to be entirely abolished* (London, 1727), 14.

"Imaginary Productions" and "Minute Contrivances": Law, Fiction, and Property in Eighteenth-Century England

ELEANOR F. SHEVLIN

Power, right, prohibition, duty, obligation, burthen, immunity, exemption, privilege, property, security, liberty—all these with a multitude of others that might be named are so many fictitious entities which the law upon one occasion or another is considered in common speech as creating or disposing of. Not an operation does [the law] ever perform, but it is considered as creating or in some manner or other disposing of these its imaginary productions.

. . . the customary law is a fiction from beginning to end: and it is in the way of fiction if at all that we must speak of it.

(Jeremy Bentham, *Of Laws in General*, c. 1782)[1]

The contention that Common Law consisted of "a fiction from beginning to end" would have elicited indignant surprise if not scorn in eighteenth-century England. Even the era's most inveterate novel-readers—long accustomed to temporarily suspending disbelief—would have had difficulty accepting for a moment that such deeply cherished tenets of English culture as individual rights, property, security, or liberty were actually "imaginary productions" or that the law operated as a system enmeshed in fabricating and eliminating phantasmal products. "Imaginary productions" and "the mere work of the fancy" held no truck with the tradition of Common Law or the hallowed place of property in eighteenth-century English culture. Instead, charges of fantastic indulgences were reserved for those eighteenth-century prose narratives now called novels which, despite their typical insistence on being based in truth and reality, were almost always recognized as fictional constructions.

Today we are still far more likely to recognize how law operates in fiction than how fiction operates in law. True, some connections between the law and the English novel have received attention.[2] But we are not accustomed to speaking of Common Law as fiction about property relations or the early English novel as a cultural court in which the law and its fictions of property are discussed and debated. By engaging in such a conversation, I wish to draw attention to how fictional fashionings of self and land in early English novels closely resemble those fictional procedures employed by Common Law in articulating property relations and determining property rights. Changing conceptions of property and the way it structured social relations spurred the growth of both legal fictions and the fictions known today as novels. In post-1688 England, the conventions surrounding the law's according a right to liberty and property to English citizens generated a cultural consciousness ripe for fostering fictions of individuality and ownership—fictions that the novel as a form has retrospectively been seen to champion. Understanding the development and place of fictions in English law will underscore how cultural conceptions of land and law, specifically English in nature, shaped the English novel during its formative years. My examination of fictions in law, moreover, proposes that the novel developed in England as a logical outgrowth of the ideologies informing Common Law.

Fictions of law, the reasons for adopting such fictions, and many of the procedures by which these fictions operate become reworked in the fictional conventions employed by the eighteenth-century narratives we now call novels. Making such an argument necessarily entails the introduction of other threads, most importantly, that of property. For not only do the law's strategies and rationales for employing fictions resurface in realistic narrative, but the early English novel's thematic preoccupation with property is part and parcel of its reworking of the law. Before proceeding to similarities in procedures, the first part of this essay will therefore clarify the importance of property in thematically coupling novels and law.

A look at the use of fictions in Common Law will provide a preface for discussing legal fictions and the traits that make their relationship with the early English novel distinctive. After detailing the ways in which fictions in law inform the fictional strategies employed by early novels, I will use the legal fiction of "ejectment" as a specific, extended example of how the practices of fiction in the legal realm correspond to the practices of fiction found in novels. Although remarks by Jeremy Bentham open this essay, it is the work of jurist William Blackstone which dominated eighteenth-century understanding of English law and its regulation of property. Thus Blackstone's *Commentaries on the Laws of England* (1765–69) will figure prominently in these discussions.

My emphasis on the intersections between fictions in law and the fictional strategies of early English novels shifts attention away from the search for the novel's origins, an investigation J. A. Downie has recently likened to the "quest for the Holy Grail."[3] Yet it does so without relinquishing the important cultural and historical work that has accompanied many of these endeavors. By showing how the early novel's fictional procedures incorporated and extended the strategies of fictions in law, this firmly grounded sociohistorical analysis will not only advance our understanding of the cultural work novels performed, but it also will provide a renewed justification for recovering the era's now forgotten novels.

"There is nothing which so generally strikes the imagination, and engages the affections of mankind, as the right of property."[4] So declared William Blackstone in his *Commentaries on the Laws of England.* For eighteenth-century English society, Blackstone spoke a political, social, psychological, and literary truth. Drawn from a series of lectures Blackstone gave at Oxford in the 1750s, the *Commentaries* did not address the established legal community but instead made English law accessible to the literate lay population at large.[5] In this sociopolitical context, nothing—not the love of one's fellow creatures, not the spectacle of royalty, not even an awe of the Almighty[6]—could exercise so strong a hold on English people's imagination as property and the right to it. It should come as no surprise, then, that as the "novel" was gaining ground as an interpretative vehicle of everyday life for a growing segment of the population, its subject matter embraced property as an overriding theme.

While property constitutes a thematic component of virtually all the era's novels, it also serves as the *raison d'être* of eighteenth-century English law.[7] This interest in property and its regulation is what binds together English law and novels. In some instances, when actual legal cases spawned fictional counterparts, these ties are readily observable. *Memoirs of an Unfortunate Young Nobleman* (1743), for example, offers a fictional account of the events leading up to and those surrounding *Annesley* v. *Anglesea* (1743), a case brought by James Annesley to reclaim his inherited title and its accompanying estates in Ireland from his uncle, the Earl of Anglesea.[8] Although omitted from the Garland reprint, the "novel's" original third volume consisted of "trial transcripts" and actual legal arguments used in hearing the case, thus materially yoking law to the novel in the form of a three-volume edition. *The*

Widow of the Wood (1755), written at the request of Sir William Wolseley, relates an equally complicated case through the use of legal affidavits.[9] The sixty-year old Wolseley's private marriage to his widowed, but much younger neighbor, Anne Whitby (who was already pregnant with another man's child, and who later made the unfounded claim that she had married this man before her union with Wolseley) gave rise to a series of suits and charges which the novel charts. *The History of a Late Infamous Adventure, Between a Great Man and a Fair Citizen* (1768), an epistolary novel, recounts the events leading up to Lord Baltimore's trial for the abduction and rape of Sarah Woodcock, a milliner.[10] In all three of these novels derived from legal cases, property questions clearly form the heart of each work: Who actually owns the Annesley property? Was Wolseley defrauded of the property he should have held in Whitby through his marriage to her? Were Whitby's actions driven by her desire to preserve the property that she had in her good name and that she wished her unborn child to inherit? Did Lord Baltimore violate the property Sarah Woodcock had in her own person by invading the ultimate form of personal property, one's body?

Such questions, while less visible without the pointing finger of an actual legal case to indicate them, are not unique to fictional works tied to factual accounts. Rather these same concerns with acquiring, preserving, and reassigning property are posed again and again across the wide spectrum of works that are known today as eighteenth-century novels. For even when novels lacked direct links to a bona fide trial or specific legal debate, property concerns forged implicit bonds between these fictional narratives and the law. Put less abstractly, the novel's fascination with marriages made, inheritances lost, estates restored, identities reclaimed, bankruptcies endured, and fortunes earned, all bespeak eighteenth-century English society's ubiquitous concern with property and its legal regulation. Whether we consider Robinson Crusoe's desire to acquire more and more property, Pamela's pleas to preserve her most prized property, Tom Jones's securing of his rightful property, or Peregrine Pickle's fallings in and out of property, what we quickly see is how much the right of property governed the imagination of these works.

The idea that eighteenth-century novels furnished fictions about property relations makes sense, especially given the genre's retrospective associations with creating believable worlds of everyday matters and given eighteenth-century English society's obsession with property. In contrast, it seems incongruous to couple imagination or fiction with the law's regulation of property relations. Yet the law also employed imagination and fictions in explicating and sorting out property rights and relationships. The presence of these imaginative productions and fictional procedures in both the literary and legal realms establishes several functional links between the early English novels and the law that make their relationship more than simply a matter of shared themes.

These functional links, as the remainder of this essay will detail, manifest themselves in several ways and on several levels. Yet they all demonstrate that property offers not just a means of dividing up the world but that it also furnishes a way of viewing it.[11] By deciding how property should partition the world, one is also deciding how the world and relationships within that world should be imagined. It is through this notion of property that imagination enters both the law and early English novels as a functional device. In achieving what Lord Mansfield had recommended when he declared that "[r]ules of Property ought . . . to be *generally known,* and not left upon loose Notes, which rather serve to *confound* Principles, than to *confirm* them,"[12] Blackstone's *Commentaries* imagined a particular vision of the world, one governed for and by the propertied. While the *Commentaries* produced a particular view about the way property structured English society, realistic fictional narratives were ideally positioned not only to replicate this view but also to imagine contesting visions. Yet no matter what world-view Blackstone's work and eighteenth-century novels disseminated, both in the *Commentaries* and the fictional narratives known now as novels, the fictions of self and land engendered by the way property structured society derived their power from the tradition of Common Law.

England's legal tradition of Common Law fostered a distinctive cultural consciousness in its people which paved the way for the fictions of land and self that early novels constructed. As part of an island complex, England partook in a geography that physically distinguished its territory from that of its Continental counterparts, making it in many senses a land unto itself. England's national rootedness in terra firma extends to the country's very name. Even across linguistic boundaries, this nation's tightly held connection to the land was sustained.[13] Consider its French appellation, *Angleterre,* a verbal underscoring of the nation's coupling with the earth itself. With its sometimes slow, often violent political yoking together of the lands of Wales (1536) and Scotland (1707) to its destiny, England solidified its island character. Mirroring this geographic distinctiveness was the country's sense of its unique legal heritage, a sentiment which dominated post-1688 national accounts of England's past and which the French political philosopher and lawyer, Montesquieu, indirectly cites in his *The Spirit of the Laws* (1748). In a chapter entitled "Of the Inhabitants of Islands," Montesquieu declares that the "people of the isles have a higher relish for liberty than those of the continent."[14] And indeed, from the *Doomesday Book* (1086) to the *Magna Carta* (1215) to the *Bill of Rights* (1689), law, land, and self were inextricably intertwined in English conceptions of its history as a people.

Specific sociohistorical events, moreover, furnished a material basis for England's distinctive sense of itself as a nation. Unlike the rest of Europe, England experienced a major upheaval in property relations during the reign of Henry VIII. In the 1530s the King's seizure of monastic lands, his appropriation of the Church's guild and chantry holdings in 1547, and his subsequent re-parcelling out of this land resulted in a wholesale reconstruction of land ownership in England. This sequence of events hastened the end of feudalism in England and spurred the nation closer to an industrial capitalist mode of operation far earlier than in France and the rest of the Continent.[15] Less than a century later, the English Civil War ushered in forty some odd years of confiscation, redistribution, and restitution of land and government that did not subside until 1688. Both as an element and result of these events, English law during the seventeenth and eighteenth centuries retrenched its commitment to Common Law as it solidified legal principles such as protection against self-incrimination and the right to a jury trial (Tigar, 258–59). All of these developments honed a sense of England's uniqueness as a nation.

By the eighteenth century the triad of law, land, and self had also become complexly interwoven with conceptions of property as a particular English treasure. As one poet proclaimed, "A wheaten garland does her head adorn / O *Property!* O goddess, *English-born!*"[16] Crowned with a wheaten garland, a symbol of the land and its bounty, "Property" is hailed here as specifically English in birth and landed in nature. Such strong sentiments regarding land were intimately connected with property and a sense of England's national self and often lauded in the era's verse and prose. The ties binding law, land, and self to property not only appeared as frequent subjects of imaginative literature, but these concepts themselves often developed as the products of fictions. Significantly in terms of the novel's relationship to the law, the Common Law acted as a prime vehicle for producing fictions of land, self, and property which, in turn, were all essential elements in the imaginary productions novels created.

While the legal narratives surrounding the rights of English subjects involve many examples of such fictional constructions, the belief that English liberties as rights date from time immemorial ranks as perhaps the most familiar of these. This notion, tightly related to property,[17] contributed significantly to the idea of England's legal uniqueness in the aftermath of the Revolution of 1688. From this point on, in most circles, liberties ceased to be something that the king gave to the people but instead became firmly ensconced as God-given rights which were never constitutionally part of the king's jurisdiction.[18] By the time the *Commentaries* were published, constitutional fiction had become legal fact. Blackstone's narrative of the rise and progress of feuds—that is, landed estates that a lord held in return for service—furnishes one instance of how the past was reinterpreted to suit post-1688 ideas of liberty and constitutional history. More important to the discussion here, it does so explicitly by way of fiction.

Blackstone first stresses that feudalism was not imposed on England by its Norman conquerors but instead adopted "at once, . . . by the common consent of the nation" (2: 4.50). He explains that deeming the king the sole, original owner of the kingdom's lands became "a fundamental maxim and necessary principle (*though in reality a mere fiction*)" once the English acquiesced to feudalism (2: 4.51; my emphasis). (And, as the original owner of all the kingdom's lands, the king was consequently deemed the source from whom all subsequent possession must stem, thus instituting a double fiction of ownership.) The English, he tells us, probably espoused this principle only in order to establish a military system as a defense measure. Yet the Norman lawyers unfortunately "gave a very different construction to this proceeding . . . *as if the English had in fact, as well as theory*, owed every thing they had to the bounty of their sovereign lord" (2: 4.51; my emphasis). After tracing further the history of English liberty, Blackstone concludes by asserting:

> the liberties of Englishmen are not (as some arbitrary writers would represent them) mere infringements of the king's prerogative, . . . but a restoration of that antient [*sic*] constitution, of which our ancestors had been defrauded by the art and finesse of the Norman lawyers, rather than deprived by the force of the Norman arms. (2: 4.52)

Ironically, as Blackstone's verbal maneuvers between the actual and theoretical intentions of the English display, the "restoration" of English liberties depended as much upon "art and finesse" as the means employed by the Norman lawyers. Or, put more directly, Blackstone replaced one fiction with another. Here words and their power to reconstruct events muscle out military might, reshaping the original Norman Conquest into a verbal contest in which the English emerge victorious, unconquered with their liberties intact.

That Blackstone could state that a "fundamental maxim," a "necessary principle" on which a past mode of the nation's political behavior was based, was "in reality a mere fiction," and seem confident that his assertion would not appear questionable or paradoxical, deserves pause. Although this particular instance—constructing the king as the original proprietor of the nation's lands—does not technically represent a true "*legal* fiction,"[19] it does closely resemble such fictions by illustrating how they offered convenient, efficient solutions to situations not otherwise easily negotiated. It also points to how other forms of discourse could readily adopt the strategy of fiction as a respected, accepted technique of the law to suit their own specific needs. Blackstone's narrative about feudal origins posits the practical efficacy of suspending disbelief in the fictional, an efficacy that is duplicated in the eigh-teenth-century marketplace's acceptance of and the growing audience for plausible fictional narratives.[20] In much the same way that Blackstone's fiction reconstructs the nation's past to suit prevailing views about English rights, many of the period's fictional narratives reconstruct a wide range of pressing contemporary concerns—courtship and marriage, landed versus commercial interests, newly acquired wealth, debtors' prisons, crime and servants—to render given perspectives toward these issues all the more credible and acceptable. Both in Blackstone's text and the texts we have come to call novels, the pragmatic power of suspending disbelief derives from the important cultural work of property regulation that such fictions of the real perform.

Elsewhere in the *Commentaries*, Blackstone directly addresses the usefulness of suspending disbelief:

> . . . these fictions of law, though at first they may startle the student, he will find upon farther consideration, to be highly beneficial and useful: . . . [their] proper operation being to prevent a mischief, or remedy an inconvenience, that might result from the general rule of law. (3: 4.43)

In this passage "these fictions of law" with their "highly beneficial and useful" effects refer to established *legal* fictions (the court's assumption of fiction as fact to decide a legal problem) that English courts had institutionalized, in this case ones involving trespass. Allowing "parties to allege . . . incontrovertibly, if fictionally, that foreign places were in England" in order to secure jurisdiction over disputes outside of England offers another example of an accepted fiction used in English law (Tigar, 13). Although Blackstone is speaking strictly of *legal* fictions here, his remarks about their usefulness nonetheless elevate the idea of fiction in general and correspond to the cultural work that the narratives now known as novels are performing by mid century.[21]

The utility of fiction alone, however, hardly accounts for the bonds between the novel and the law that I am proposing. Functional similarities between law and imaginative literature based on fiction's serviceability date back to Aristotle, as does the need to recuperate fiction from Plato's sense of its harmful effects and incompatibility with ethics.[22] In England the law's long tradition of incorporating fictions as a means of expediting legal procedures and justice had been set in motion during the reign of Henry II.[23] Since a span of several hundred years separates the English law's adoption of fiction as a technical tool from the novel's emergence in the English marketplace, we cannot turn to a coinciding chronology as a basis for linking the two. Still, it is interesting that after citing 1590 as the first time the phrase "legal fiction" occurs, the *Oxford English Dictionary* does not offer another citation until its appearance in Blackstone's *Commentaries* in 1767. After 1767, moreover, the *OED* lists increasingly frequent occurrences of this phrase up until the third quarter of the nineteenth century, at which point the novel was firmly established as a respected, recognized genre. This etymological history is, of course, only suggestive, and it would be imprudent to make too much of it. What does distinguish the novel's functional relationship with the law from other literary forms, however, is a shared set of characteristics ranging from ontological links with altered social circumstances and property to a mutual employment of land and fictional persons.

A key trait differentiating the novel's ties to fictions in law from ties between other literary genres and legal fictions is an ontological need to address changing social situations and cultural conditions. English law adopted legal fictions as a procedural technique for responding to such changes. When Common Law's existing rules could not accommodate new circumstances that arose in society, proceeding by means of a fiction offered a way to handle these situations without making any literal changes to the law.[24] Such an approach, as previous commentators on English law have noted, provided the added advantage of maintaining the time-honored fiction that Common Law is unchanging. As Blackstone explains,

> When therefore, by the gradual influence of foreign trade and domestic tranquillity, . . . the whole [feudal] structure was removed, the judges quickly perceived that the forms and delays of old feodal [*sic*] actions [i.e., the legal procedures], . . . were ill-suited to that more simple and commercial mode of property which succeeded the former, and required a more speedy decision of right, to facilitate exchange and alienation. Yet they wisely avoided soliciting any great legislative revolution in the old established forms [i.e., refrained from tampering with Common Law], . . . but left them as they were,. . .and endeavored by a series of minute contrivances [i.e., legal fictions] to . . . answer the purpose of doing substantial and speedy justice . . . (3: 17.267–68)

These legal fictions, or "minute contrivances" as they are termed here, provided the means for "doing substantial and speedy justice" but "wisely avoided soliciting any great legislative revolution in the old established" laws.

Blackstone's synonym for a sequence of legal fictions—"a series of minute contrivances"—aptly describes the twists and turns that the plots of novels took as they worked out particular versions of property relations against the backdrop of ongoing eighteenth-century social changes. Just as legal fictions in law serve as narrative devices that enable action within the guise of unchanging procedures, so, too, do the "minute contrivances" of novels act as narrative devices that advance storylines about property within the guise of dramatic events. For instance, the plots and subplots of *Clarissa* (1747–48), driven by desires to acquire or secure property, offer an example *par excellence* of minute contrivances that intricately inch the novel's narrative toward to its tragic conclusion.[25] A series of minute contrivances, ranging from his first rash departure from home to his shipwreck en route to Guinea, not only lands Robinson Crusoe on an uninhabited island, but an ensuing set of contrivances also results in his achieving dominion over this property in land and the property that Friday has in himself. And Tom Jones comes into his estate and true identity through a series of minute contrivances.

Like the minute contrivances of law, novels were also often poised to deliver "speedy decision[s]." Whether or not they adopted or rejected the appellation "novel," these works promoted themselves as tackling new situations and new issues as they arose. From Fielding's prefatorial claim that *Joseph Andrews* (1742) presents a "species of writing . . . hitherto unattempted in our language"[26] to novel titles proclaiming "new and uncommon events," no other literary genre had purported to deal in new and unusual situations the same way that early novels did. This genre-in-the-making's constant reach for the new encouraged timely responses to topical problems. As one contemporary review of the 1767 novel *The Adventures of a Kidnapped Orphan*[27] makes clear, a novel's attempts to address an issue could easily coincide with the same issue arising in the courts of law: "We should have dismissed this publication with a very indifferent character, had not certain recent proceedings in our courts of law furnished us with the melancholy certainty, that the . . . practice of kidnapping young persons . . . , is or very lately was, frequent in this metropolis."[28]

The significance of the law's and the novel's shared habit of incorporating "minute contrivances" in timely ways is enhanced by a linguistic cross-fertilization. Among literary genres, only the novel possesses a specific definitional correlative in the law. Although "novel" as the term for a certain kind of fictional work would not achieve stability until the late eighteenth century, the word "novel" had been used in law for hundreds of years by the time Blackstone published his *Commentaries*. In legal parlance, "novels" referred to supplementary laws—"new constitutions"—made in response to new situations which could not be handled by previous statutes (Blackstone 1: 3.81). *Novellae*, to use the Latin form often employed in legal texts, had originated with the Emperor Justinian who published them as a supplement or an addendum to his Codes of Law in order to legislate new matters of public and ecclesiastical concern that his previous laws either did not cover or had handled incorrectly. Just as legal "novels" were instituted to handle situations that recorded law could not address, early English literary "novels" embodied the word's legal meaning by operating as cultural extensions of recorded law. As a cultural supplement to the official law, these novels enacted a means of positing, championing, and dismissing competing notions of property relations outside such institutional frames as the Court of Common Pleas, Chancery, and the Inns of Court. Equally striking, the definition of "novel" as a legal term uncannily echoes the rationale given for the adoption of fictions in law. The literary novel's linguistic correlative in the legal realm further tightens and distinguishes the literary novel's ties to the law in its mirroring of the role of legal fictions. Whether by "minute contrivances" or in the form of "new constitutions," fiction in both instances (albeit literally for law and more metaphorically for novels as a literary genre) served the same function: to supplement existing laws in the face of new situations.

Besides acting as an appeals court for existing legislation, novels also acted as supplements to the official law by serving as hearings to urge the passage of new laws. In *The Adventures of a Kidnapped Orphan*, the protagonist, an impressed seaman, explicitly ties the publication of his plight to legal remedies: "O could I possibly represent to one compassionate patriot of influence the state of my case, . . . surely I should not only obtain deliverance, but rouse the legislature to take the most effectual methods, in order to prevent the growth of so crying an evil" (110–11). Abduction in the form of impressment fuels this novel's plot and is viewed throughout the work as a theft of the property one has in one's self, illustrating another instance of how property concerns pervade these eighteenth-century novels. In terms of fiction's functional role here, the novel continually cloaks the orphan's fate in discussions about the need to monitor property and curb the invasion of the property one has in one's self from rapacious commercial interests (79–82; 173; 213; 249). That the *Critical Review*'s dissatisfaction with the work stems from the novel's failure to present "the precise methods . . . for proceeding against [the kidnappers], with the utmost rigour, in our courts of law"[29] points to contemporary expectations that novels generate public hearings in which opinions and solutions about how English society should regulate itself are rendered.

The sociohistorical contexts advanced by Ian Watt and reinforced by forty years of additional theoretical work on the novel's origins[30] provide another, cogent dimension of the ties between novels and legal fictions. Despite the shortcomings lodged against different versions of these theories[31]—the failure to consider the persistence of romance, the omission of gender issues, an overly determined teleology, and the like[32]—the basic sociohistorical strands that this critical legacy has identified with the novel remain intact: a growing emphasis on philosophical and economic individualism, changing gender and class relations, the increased presence of a credit-based economy, major alterations in the book trade, and an expanded market for print. The way theorists have applied these sociohistorical developments to the novel's origins parallels the explanations given for the appearance of legal fictions. Put in the terms we have been considering, just as legal fictions emerged to meet needs that could not be met by existing laws, so too did early novels become a presence in the eighteenth century by addressing and representing changes in society that orthodox literary forms either could not accommodate or could not do so as effectively.

Although the new situations that prompted novels and legal fictions to each develop were separated by different moments in time, they nevertheless share a common characteristic that traverses their specific sociohistorical distinctions. The changes in society that generated legal fictions and novels almost always stemmed from changes involving property.[33] In the case of legal fictions, for example, the full-scale revamping of land ownership that King Henry VIII's seizure of monastic property generated gave rise to new situations (what Blackstone deemed the "more simple and commercial mode of property") that "old feodal actions . . . were ill-suited" to handle (3: 17.267–68). This major upheaval in real-property relations contributed to the proliferation of legal fictions later in the century.

In a similar vein, most of the sociohistorical developments linked to the novel relate to property's changing role in regulating social relations. By the end of 1688, property in land had assumed a place of paramount importance as a determinant of social and political power in England.[34] To paraphrase one historian of the period, the divine right of landed property owners had replaced the divine right of kings.[35] As is well known, however, the advent of paper money, stock speculation, and other trappings of a credit economy (whose institutional debut was marked by the establishment of the Bank of England in 1694 and the creation of the National Debt between 1694 and 1696) gave rise to "new situations"—new forms of personal property that were challenging and complicating the authority of property in land or "real property" as the law tellingly termed it.[36] During the eighteenth century the tensions between real property (land and other immovables) and personal property (movable goods as well as the property one has in one's self) as a means of structuring social relations increased. The tensions between these two forms of property, moreover, act as a shorthand for many of the socio-economic and philosophical changes long associated with the novel's "rise." The novel's harnessing of fictions to address and sort out these changes in property relations marked not so much a new development, but rather a new context for the fictional procedures, long at work in the culture, for dealing with changes related to property. The narratives we now call novels responded to these new circumstances by plotting resulting social tensions within imagined venues that claimed to be "true" if not also real. In short, they employed fictions to imagine how property and what types of property should structure the world.

Although legal fictions and novels share ontological ties to new situations and property, they differ in the way they interact with these ties. This difference in approach, moreover, suggests reasons for the different receptions that marked the respective appearances of legal fictions and novels. That legal fictions offer a means of dividing up the world that preserves the status quo of property relations helps to explain why such fictions generally met with acceptance in responding to new situations.[37] Law, after all, was an arm of those who held property. That early novels, in contrast, offer a means of viewing the world from a spectrum of property structures, including other possible arrangements than the ones already in place, furnishes a retrospectively plausible explanation for why these narratives encountered hostility, especially from more traditional quarters, when they first appeared.

Depending on their individual orientations, these fictional narratives bolstered or contested the institutionalized law of English courts and legislatures because they saw law as either weakening in the face of personal property's power or becoming recalcitrant in the face of real property's power. As one novel, *The Fool of Quality* (1765–70), describes the fate of property disputes in the hands of the law, "Soberly and seriously speaking, English property, when once debated, is merely a carcase of contention, upon which interposing lawyers fall as customary prize and prey during the combat of the claimants."[38] Antagonistic to lawyers but a champion of the British constitution, this novel displays an ample willingness to assume control of property debates through its use of fictions, as evidenced by the discussions ranging from liberty, property, personal rights, and individual responsibilities to discourses on the evolution of the English constitution, paper money, and a credit economy that fill its pages.

Dr. John Shebbeare's *The Marriage Act. A Novel* (1754),[39] which proclaims its ties to the legal realm in its very title, exemplifies even more forcefully how novels often contested the laws set up to regulate property relations. Shebbeare explicitly glosses the functional role of his fictions when he has a character near the end of the novel propose:

> that the preceding Parts of our Lives, added to these Accounts, might furnish out a Novel not undiverting, and certainly useful; as by that means a great many Evils, naturally attending this Marriage-law, might be brought to View, which now lie unobserved by most People. (2: 297).

Within the novel's larger narrative that relates the history of a Mr. and Mrs. James Barter and their two daughters, this work presents scenario after scenario in which the justice, effectiveness, or soundness of the actual Marriage Act of 1753 (26 Geo. II c. 33)[40] is severely questioned. Among other purposes, the Bill was aimed at preventing heirs or heiresses from becoming duped into marriages with persons (ostensibly fortune-hunters) who were socially and/or economically inferior. It was intended by its supporters, in short, to better regulate property. When a character early on in the work depicts marriage as "a kind of taking Money with the Mortgage of a Wife to pay off a Mortgage on an Estate" and adds that "indeed the Legislature seems to have look'd upon it in the same Light, and contrived the Marriage Bill for the Emolument of the Nobility" (1: 93), he articulates a prime reason for this novel's hostile attitude toward the Bill: commercial attitudes toward marriages had caused property in land to become entangled to its detriment with self-interest and commercial aggrandizement, an entanglement that was now being sanctioned by this Bill. As one twentieth-century historian of the period has echoed, "The financial details of the marriage settlement, so often the sacrament by which land allied itself with trade, provided the best lawyers with a good part of their fees."[41]

Over and over again the novel's characters inveigh against the Act and its results and do so by framing the issue in terms of property and individual rights:

> For surely this new Law has rendered Wards more in the Power of their Guardians than before, and more than it ought; if they are prevented from marrying themselves, they are render'd the Property of their Guardians; and of their Parents too . . . (1: 189–90)

and

> there appears to me to be infinite Injustice in the Law itself, or something which I have never yet heard has caused the Clergy of *Great-Britain* to be considered an inferior Race to other Men of this Island, a Set of Slaves and not free Men, . . . excluded from an equal Privilege and Right to Liberty with other *Britons*. (1: 264)

These excerpts, the second of which is taken from a speech extending over eight pages (1: 263–70), offer a glimpse of the novel's typical indictments against the Bill.[42] Collectively, these denunciations rendered a dissenting opinion of the Act in a forum that was perhaps all too public, for shortly after the novel's publication Shebbeare was jailed.[43]

The most cogent way to illustrate the early English novel's intersections with legal fictions is through an extended look at a specific legal fiction and the ways in which novels replicated its procedures. That the creation of fictional characters and of imagined relationships with land figure prominently in the legal fictions used in "ejectment"—a legal action undertaken to recover real property—makes it an ideal choice for demonstrating the novel's adoption of fictional procedures in law. After all, the two major fictional procedures that novels employ are fictional constructions of land and selves. To detail the intricate and often convoluted nature of ejectment, however, would provide a tedious lesson in law that would not serve our express purposes. Thus, a fairly simplistic summary of this legal action will suffice.[44]

Before legal fictions were adopted as the means of determining the rightful ownership of a freehold,[45] trying to lay claim to a freehold meant seemingly never-ending writs and trips through various assizes or county courts. As opposed to freeholders, leaseholders during this time had the much smoother, swifter action of ejectment by which to pursue their claims. To gain access to the legal action of ejectment, freehold cases began to adopt a series of fictions that included imagining that the freehold was a leasehold and that physical force was actually exercised.[46] The person bringing the action would lease the property to a fictitious lessee, "Richard Roe," who would "remove" the fictitious tenant, "John Doe," who would in turn bring suit against "Richard Roe"; at this point, the courts could decide which of the real persons actually had the right to lease the property.[47] Such "make-believe of John Doe and Richard Roe was necessary," as one social historian of the law tells us, "if procedures were to keep up with social needs."[48] Consequently, this make-believe, which "replaced the old real actions," meant that in England "for nearly three centuries . . . the usual action to recover real property . . . involved two non-existent parties."[49] The widespread use of these legal fictions in ejectment between the reigns of Elizabeth I and Queen Victoria should have made these fictions a familiar technique even among the non-affluent and certainly a commonplace one to most of Blackstone's readers. For centuries it proved the most common means of settling contested land disputes.[50] Ejectment's recognition as a well-known legal fiction, its lengthy endurance, and its central role in settling land disputes combine to form a useful basis for comparisons with the early novel and its fictional strategies.

To see the early English novel's use of fictional characters, its creation of imaginary land, and its representations of property disputes as being *intentionally* modeled upon ejectment's formulation of "make-believe" would be an exaggeration. Typically, the early English novel was culturally representing the contested nature of property relations in society at large, while the law was officially addressing specific instances of real property claims between two parties. Exceptions do exist, of course, especially when the novel was directly linked to an actual legal case as in the examples discussed near the start of this essay. In most cases, however, novels engaged in these fictions of land and self to effect general statements about property's role in structuring society and not to render a verdict on a specific situation.

The real import of ejectment's particular formulation of make-believe to the novel rests in the mode of behavior it establishes for fictions involving persons and lands. By presenting "Richard Roes" and "John Does" who do not exist but who are nevertheless crucial to the proceedings, by transforming freeholds into leaseholds and thus making an imaginary construction out of land, by replacing the violence and danger of physical removal with the safety of a removal occurring purely on paper, and by positing the principle that fictions can determine truths—especially truths so important as property ownership—ejectment, in its capacity as English society's leading means of settling particular land claims, interjected these fictional operations into England's cultural consciousness. In other words, fictions of land and persons served as ways of thought for the English in dealing with property.

Like legal fictions which made real what the established law could not, the greatest fiction of novels was their claim to be "true." That these early narratives created self-contained worlds purporting to be, in truth, "real" made their fictions so all-encompassing. Within this large fictional framework, moreover, we can find parallels to the specific fictions used in ejectment. For example, many of the fictional characters found in early novels start out as "Richard Roes" of sorts. The disclosure of their "real" identities forms part of the process by which they recover their rightful inheritance and/or place in society. Tom Jones or Evelina readily come to mind as well-known instances. Even in the cases of characters such as Moll Flanders or Roxana who remain as "John Does," fictional identities still operate as a means for acquiring and claiming property.

Early novels also replicate behaviors found in ejectment's imaginative reconstructions of land and its substitution of physical danger with the safety of paper actions. These narratives created a far safer means of airing views about the nature of property[51] than actually speaking to a public crowd or undertaking other forms of physical action. In the worlds they made, novels reconstructed land's relationship to society in ways that spoke to the diverse opinions about the nature of property. Novels whose fictions idealized landed wealth and the worthiness of those who possess such ties and employ them well—Henry Fielding's *The History of Tom Jones* (1749), for one—reinforced or redefined cultural tenets such as the equation of virtue and public disinterestedness with landed wealth. Often novels served as a forum for elevating personal property—both in the sense of an individual's worth and in the sense of wealth acquired from trade and credit exchanges—with the result that personal property was placed alongside or above real property in social value and esteem. Daniel Defoe's *The Life and Strange and Surpris-*

ing Adventures of Robinson Crusoe (1719) and Samuel Richardson's *Pamela* (1740) serve as just two examples. The retirement to the country of characters with ties to trade, usually as owners of landed property and usually in conjunction with a marriage, that frequently marks the conclusion of so many early novels—Edward Kimber's best-selling *The Life and Adventures of Joe Thompson* (1750) offering a case in point—exemplifies one way this elevation of personal property's value was achieved. In some cases, such conclusions also worked to bolster the cultural fiction that real property in the form of land had remained untouched by moves toward a credit economy. For although land, through mortgaging and other forms of financing, was becoming increasingly intertwined with an economy in which signifiers stood in for absent property that consequently could only be imagined, the fiction that landed wealth possessed an integrity based on its immovable, permanent nature still registered as a truth for many.

Especially for readers who lacked specific ties with the land, these narratives' fictions of land and self furnished alternate ways of imagining one's connections to a society which championed landed property and its civilizing effects. As Joseph Addison proclaimed, "A Man of a Polite Imagination . . . meets with a secret Refreshment in a Description, and often feels a greater Satisfaction in the Prospect of Fields and Meadows, than another does in the Possession. It gives him, indeed, a kind of Property in every thing he sees."[52] For eighteenth-century "novel" readers, long exposed unwittingly to fictions in law, we might revamp Addison's assertion about imagination, land, and property and say that early fictional narratives allowed their readers a property in every kind of world these works imagined.

The parallels between the legal fictions used in ejectment and the fictional procedures employed by early novels are rooted in their functional similarities rather than their thematic content. Yet, on occasion, the subject matter of ejectment and function do cross paths in a novel, and when this happens, as it does in *The Adventures of Emmera* (1767),[53] the results can be instructive. Although the term "ejectment" is never explicitly mentioned in this novel, a series of events surrounding claims to an estate strongly suggests that this estate is a freehold and thus subject to the legal fictions ejectment employs. That the novel's heroine, Emmera, grew up in the wilds of America is directly attributable to her now deceased father's loss of this estate through lawsuits probably involving ejectment. Near the end of the novel "a series of minute contrivances" brings this estate into the novel's immediate sphere of action through another lawsuit in which ejectment, once again, probably forms part of the procedure.

While this essay is not the place for a detailed reading of this work, two points are germane to our focus on ejectment's fictions of self and land. The first concerns fictions of self. The novel's second lawsuit over this estate results in its loss by another worthy family, a loss that duplicates the one endured by Emmera's father: "[the] antagonist is the friend of a former owner of the estate [that is, Emmera's father], for want of whose heirs my father [that is, Miss Hervey's] possesses the estate. *This man carried it* [the lawsuit] *on for a daughter of his friend, the reality of whose being was the disputed point*—but he proved it sufficiently . . ." (2: 145; my emphasis). As it turns out, however, this "daughter" is an imposter who is pretending to be Emmera who, in turn, is an "Incognita," not knowing her surname until the estate is discovered to be hers (2: 172). Like ejectment's fictions of self, the novel's fictional lawsuit features persons acting in the place of others. Yet, unlike ejectment, these stand-ins and fictitious selves in the form of impostors and an incognita do not restore the rightful owners but instead lead, in the case of the stand-ins and impostors, to fraud and, in the case of the Incognita, to the estate, "which has occasioned the practice of so much villainy" and "in the wretchedness which my father escaped when he lost it," being given away by Emmera (2: 175). Secondly, much of the action takes place in the American colonies, a real land that is nevertheless only an imaginary production for most living in England. Such a setting enables not only a critique of property relations as structured through the laws of England, but also an imagining of a new set of property relations in a new world that the novel made "real." Given this critique and Emmera's rejection of England in favor of America, the novel clearly prefers the new land with its new visions of property relationships. In the end, then, *The Adventures of Emmera* through its fictional strategies "ejects" the fictions of English law in favor of system where simplicity and straight-forwardness reign over property relations and lawyers are banished.

Although Blackstone certainly did not intend to suggest that property constituted a fiction when he asserted that nothing struck the imagination so forcefully as property and the right to it, his later critic, Jeremy Bentham, whose disdain for fictions in law we have already encountered in the opening epigraphs, clearly saw things differently: "Now property before it can be offended against must be created: and the creation of it is the work of law."[54] Through "a series of minute contrivances," early English novels and Common Law did indeed create property. In their fictions they produced a plethora of imaginings about how property should construct society. At times, actual law cases inspired the "imaginary productions" of novels, a form whose emphasis on generating believable worlds, intensified the blurring of factual and fictional realms. But even when novels did not reproduce specific proceedings, they nonetheless served as a cultural court in which public hearings on property concerns were aired. The early English novel's links to law courts and legal fictions manifest themselves most forcefully in the period's non-canonical novels. That these pronounced ties occur in novels now forgotten should not be surprising; with the literary values we have inherited, didacticism rarely coincides with aesthetic worth, and overtly didactic novels rarely become candidates for canonization. In providing much of the explicit evidence for establishing the functional ties between fictions in law and early novels, these virtually forgotten works teach us to read the established texts of the eighteenth-century novel canon in a different light. Reading the era's canonical and non-canonical novels in tandem and alongside the fictions that operate in law enables us, in turn, to imagine the properties, in the many senses of this word, of these novels in previously unimagined ways.

N O T E S

I wish to thank Jeanne Fahnestock, Jim Heenehan, and Liza Child for their helpful, insightful comments on earlier drafts of this essay, and to express my deep appreciation to Cal Winton and Paula McDowell for their unfailing, generous support of the larger project from which this essay is drawn.

1. Jeremy Bentham, *Of Laws in General,* ed. H. L. A. Hart (London: Athelone Press, 1970), 251; 193. Although Bentham had finished most of *Of Laws in General* by 1782, it was not published until the twentieth century (xxxi).

2. Of particular note are Alexander Welsh's *Strong Representations: Narrative and Circumstantial Evidence in England* (Baltimore: Johns Hopkins Univ. Press, 1992) and John Zomchik's *Family and the Law in Eighteenth-Century Fiction: The Public Conscience in the Private Sphere* (Cambridge: Cambridge Univ. Press, 1993). For an overview of how imaginative literature and law are paradigmatically linked, see Martin Kayman, "Lawful Writing: Common Law, Statute, and the Properties of Literature," *New Literary History* 17 (Autumn 1996): 761–84.

3. J. A. Downie, "The Making of the English Novel." *Eighteenth-Century Fiction* 9 (April 1997): 249–66; for the citation, 249.

4. William Blackstone, *Commentaries on the Laws of England: A Facsimile of the First Edition of 1765–1769,* 4 vols. (Chicago: Univ. of Chicago Press, 1979), 2: 1.2. All subsequent citations will refer to this edition and will appear parenthetically in the text.

5. As S. F. C. Milsom explains, "Blackstone was addressing laymen, trying to make sense of the formal structure and rules of society for those who would play laymen's parts, and also for those who might decide to become lawyers" (198). See Milsom, "The Nature of Blackstone's Achievement," in *Studies in the History of the Common Law* (London and Ronceverte: The Hambledon Press, 1985), 197–208.

6. In the July 13, 1706 issue of his *Review*, Defoe, while arguing against the divine right of kings, asserts, "Even God himself holds by this Tenure [the Right of Property]; his Right to rule over us, is founded upon his Property in us—" (3: 84.334). See *Review*, 22 vols. Publication No. 44 of the Facsimile Text Society, Facsimile Book 7 of vol. 3 (New York: Columbia Univ. Press, 1938).

7. As one legal historian has noted about the eighteenth century, "The purpose of English law was not even to put down violence, but—as all the world knew—to defend the Englishman's property." See Alan Harding, *A Social History of English Law* (Harmondsworth, Middlesex: Penguin, 1966), 297.

8. [Annesley], *Memoirs of an Unfortunate Young Nobleman* (London, 1743; reprint New York: Garland, 1975).

9. Benjamin Victor, *The Widow of the Wood* (London: C. Corbett, 1755). Its use of depositions anticipates by over a hundred years the narrative technique used in Wilkie Collins's *The Moonstone* (1868).

10. *The History of a Late Infamous Adventure, Between a Great Man and a Fair Citizen* (London: W. Bingley, 1768).

11. I echo explicitly Paul Langford's memorable assertion, "Property is a way of looking at the world, as well as a means of sharing it out" (4–5). See Langford, *Public Life and the Propertied Englishman, 1689–1798* (Oxford: Clarendon Press, 1991).

12. Lord Mansfield, *Goodtitle* v. *Duke of Chandos* (1760). See Sir James Burrow, *Reports of Cases Adjudged in the Court of King's Bench, since the Time of Lord Mansfield's Coming to Preside in it,* 5 vols. 3rd ed. (London: Printed for Edward Brooke, 1777), 2 Burr. Part 4: 1076.

13. Although "Deutschland" may seem, on one level, to mirror "England" in verbally calling attention to a rootedness in the land, the German stem "land" carries different primary connotations than its English counterpart. This difference is illustrated by the German phrase *auf das Land* (or *aufs Land*) which translates as "to the country." In other words, the German term *Land* generally refers to locale, while the English word "land" is used frequently to signify not just locale (in the sense of "this land is ours") but earth as well (as in "the land which we till").

14. Montesquieu, *The Spirit of Laws*, ed. David Wallace Carrithers (Berkeley and Los Angeles: Univ. of California Press, 1977), 18.5.283.

15. Michael E. Tigar, *Law and the Rise of Capitalism* (New York: Monthly Review Press, 1977), 203–5. All subsequent citations will refer to this edition and will appear parenthetically in the text.

16. Ambrose Philips, Esq., "An Epistle to the Right Honourable Charles Lord Halifax" (1714), *The Poems of Ambrose Philips, Esq.*, ed. M. G. Segar (Oxford: Blackwell, 1937), 93, lines 15–16.

17. "Property and Liberty" acted as a rallying cry of the Glorious Revolution, a cry that soon became what Paul Langford has rightly termed "a hackneyed slogan" (4). See G. E. Aylemer, "The Meaning and Definition of 'Property' in Seventeenth-Century England," *Past and Present* 86 (Feb 1980): 87–97; Tim Harris, "'Lives, Liberties and Estates': Rhetorics of Liberty in the Reign of Charles II," in *The Politics of Religion in Restoration England*, eds. Tim Harris et. al. (Oxford: Basil Blackwell, 1990), 217–41; Henry Horwitz, "Lib-

erty, Law, and Property, 1689–1776," and Howard Nenner, "Liberty, Law, and Property: The Constitution in Retrospect from 1689," in *Liberty Secured? Britain Before and After 1688*, ed. J. R. Jones, (Stanford: Stanford Univ. Press, 1992), 265–98 and 88–121; Angus McInnes, "The Revolution and the People," in *Britain after the Glorious Revolution, 1689–1714*, ed. Geoffrey Holmes (New York: St. Martin's Press, 1969), 80–95; and Andrew Reeve, "Debate: The Meaning and Definition of 'Property' in Seventeenth-Century England," *Past and Present* 89 (Nov. 1980): 139–42.

18. Nenner, 88–89.

19. "Any assumption which conceals or affects to conceal the fact that a rule of law has undergone alteration, its letter remaining unchanged, its operation being modified. In short, case A is pretended to be and treated legally as if it were an instance of Case B." See David A. Walker, ed., *The Oxford Companion to Law* (Oxford: Clarendon Press, 1980), 468. Also see, *Black's Law Dictionary*, 6th ed., ed. Joseph R. Nolan et. al. (St. Paul, MN: West Publishing, 1990), 894.

20. The number of works produced and sold for this "growing audience" was nonetheless quite small in comparison to other material produced. According to James Raven, fiction represented about 4 percent of all books and pamphlets issued during the 1740s, 1750s, and 1760s. See Raven, *British Fiction, 1750–1770: A Chronological Check-List of Prose Fiction Printed in Britain and Ireland* (Newark: Univ. of Delaware, 1987), 10.

21. For instance, as we shall see, on one level the author of *The Marriage Act* and the reviewer of *A Kidnapped Orphan* certainly seem to have viewed the "proper operation" of these works as "being to prevent a mischief, or to remedy an inconvenience."

22. Kathy Eden identifies Aristotle as the first to define fiction "to include both the poetic and legal fiction." For a detailed look at Aristotle's articulation of poetic and legal fictions and later interpretations up through Sydney's *Apology for Poetry* (c.1580), see Eden, *Poetic and Legal Fiction in the Aristotelian Tradition* (Princeton: Princeton Univ. Press, 1986), especially chapters 1 and 2. Although not specifically addressing legal fiction, see also Martin T. Herrick, *The Poetics of Aristotle in England* (1930; New York, Phaeton Press, 1976) for how Aristotle's *Poetics* influenced English writers and critics.

23. Alan Harding suggests that the "fictional plea may have been used first in the case of debt" during the reign of Henry II (53). For an explanation of legal fictions through literary example as well an overview of its occurrences in Roman and English law, see Roscoe Pound, *The Spirit of the Common Law,* Classics of the Law 169 (1921; Boston: Beacon Press, 1966), 166–70, 172.

24. This explanation of legal fiction's origins offers perhaps only part of the story. R. S. White has convincingly suggested that competition among courts in the sixteenth century also contributed to the proliferation of such a device. See White, *Natural Law in English Renaissance Literature* (Cambridge: Cambridge Univ. Press, 1996), 87–92, especially 89.

25. The desire for more and more property revealed in the Harlowes' greediness in increasing the family's wealth at all costs, Lovelace's obsession with making Clarissa his property, and Clarissa's struggle to maintain the personal property she

has in herself, all depict "the most important concerns of private life" as property struggles and demonstrate "the distress that may attend the misconduct both of parents and children" when property interests conflict. See Samuel Richardson, *Clarissa, or the History of a Young Lady: Comprehending the Most Important Concerns of Private Life and Particularly Showing the Distress That May Attend the Misconduct Both of Parents and Children, in Relation to Marriage*, ed. with intro. and notes by Angus Ross (London and New York: Penguin, 1985).

26. Henry Fielding, *The History of the Adventures of Joseph Andrews*, ed. Martin C. Battestin (Boston: Houghton Mifflin Company, 1961), 12.

27. *The Adventures of a Kidnapped Orphan* (London: Printed for M. Thrush, 1747 [*sic*]; New York: Garland, 1974). All subsequent citations will refer to this edition and will appear parenthetically in the text. For information about the misprinted date of "1747," see Philip Babcock Gove, *The Imaginary Voyage in Prose Fiction* (New York: Arno Press, 1974), 357.

28. *Critical Review* 24 (Nov. 1767): 345.

29. Ibid., 349.

30. Specifically, I am referring to Ian Watt, *The Rise of the Novel: Studies in Defoe, Richardson and Fielding* (Berkeley and Los Angeles: Univ. of California Press, 1957); Lennard Davis, *Factual Fictions: The Origins of the English Novel* (New York: Columbia Univ. Press, 1983); Michael McKeon, *The Origins of the English Novel, 1600–1740* (Baltimore: Johns Hopkins Univ. Press, 1987); Nancy Armstrong, *Desire and Domestic Fiction: A Political History of the Novel* (New York: Oxford Univ. Press, 1987); John Bender, *Imagining the Penitentiary: Fiction and the Architecture of Mind in Eighteenth-Century England* (Chicago: Univ. of Chicago Press, 1987); and J. Paul Hunter, *Before Novels: The Cultural Contexts of Eighteenth-Century English Fiction* (New York: Norton, 1987). As for the influence of Watt's study, the words of Hunter are worth recalling: "Everyone in the past thirty years who has written about the beginnings of the English novel has been engaged in rewriting Watt" (xx).

31. For critiques of these studies, see Jerry Beasley, "The History of the Novel Writ Large—and New," *Eighteenth-Century Fiction* 8 (Oct. 1995): 73–80; Homer Obed Brown, "Of the Title To Things Real: Conflicting Stories," *ELH* 55 (Winter 1988): 917–54; Robert Folkenflik, "The Heirs of Ian Watt," *Eighteenth-Century Studies* 25 (Winter 1991–92): 203–17; and John Richetti, "The Legacy of Ian Watt's *The Rise of the Novel*" in *The Profession of Eighteenth-Century Literature: Reflections on an Institution*, ed. Leo Damrosch (Madison: Univ. of Wisconsin Press, 1992), 95–122.

32. Among the recent studies seeking to redress one or more of these faults, see Ros Ballaster, *Seductive Forms: Women's Amatory Fiction from 1684 to 1740* (Oxford: Clarendon Press, 1992); Catherine Gallagher, *Nobody's Story: The Vanishing Acts of Women Writers in the Marketplace, 1670–1820* (Berkeley and Los Angeles: Univ. of California Press, 1994); and Homer Obed Brown, *The Institution of the English Novel* (Philadelphia: Univ. of Pennsylvania Press, 1997).

33. Although some legal fictions on the surface may seem distant from issues arising out of the changing nature of property, the new circumstance typically stemmed from something to do with property, even if only at a very basic level.

34. Much has been written about how landed proprietors were viewed as inherently unprejudiced and objective and how, as such, they alone deserved to participate in public affairs. See J. G. A. Pocock's "Authority and Property: The Question of Liberal Origins" and "The Mobility of Property and the Rise of Eighteenth-Century Sociology" in *Virtue, Commerce, and History* (Cambridge: Cambridge Univ. Press, 1985), 51–71 and 103–23, and also his *Machiavellian Moment: Florentine Political Thought and the Atlantic Republican Tradition* (Princeton: Princeton Univ. Press, 1975). For an alternative position to this civic humanist interpretation, see Joyce Oldham Appleby, *Economic Thought and Ideology in Seventeenth-Century England* (Princeton: Princeton Univ. Press, 1978) and *Liberalism and Republicanism in the Historical Imagination* (Cambridge: Harvard Univ. Press, 1992).

35. David Ogg, *England in the Reigns of James II and William III* (Oxford: Clarendon Press, 1955), 546.

36. Reconstructions of English constitutional history were not this era's only revamping of the relationship between property and the imaginative. The past few years have seen increasing attention accorded the relationship between financial imaginary property and literary imagination. See Colin Nicholson, *Writing and the Rise of Finance: Capital Satires of the Early Eighteenth Century* (Cambridge: Cambridge Univ. Press, 1994). For a gendered consideration of these issues, see Catherine Ingrassia, "Paper Credit: Grub Street, Exchange Alley and the Feminization of Culture in Early Eighteenth Century England," (Ph.D. diss., Univ. of Texas at Austin, 1992) Microfilm available from UMI, 1992. For a discussion of these issues in terms of value and political economy, see James Thompson, *Models of Value: Eighteenth-Century Political Economy and the Novel* (Durham: Duke Univ. Press, 1996).

37. Legal fictions were faulted by many, including Blackstone, for their risk of being arbitrary and for their circuitous path. Yet their longstanding incorporation into the daily business of law simultaneously indicated a feeling that their benefits outweighed their inconveniences. Blackstone, for one, emphasized that legal fictions enhanced the courts' ability to render justice. In this sense he echoes Aristotle's linking of equity and fictions. But exceptions, as always, do exist. For instance, Jeremy Bentham, as this essay's opening epigraphs affirm, was notoriously opposed to legal fictions. See David Lieberman, *The Province of Legislation Determined: Legal Theory in Eighteenth-Century Britain* (Cambridge: Cambridge Univ. Press, 1989), 47.

38. Henry Brooke, *The Fool of Quality; or, The History of Henry Earl of Moreland,* 5 vols. rev. ed., with biographical preface by Rev. Charles Kingsley (London: Smith, Elder and Co., 1859), 1: 249.

39. Dr. John Shebbeare, *The Marriage Act: A Novel,* 2 vols. (London, 1754; reprint New York: Garland, 1974). All subsequent citations will refer to this edition and will appear parenthetically in the text.

40. The Act required that banns be announced, licenses secured, parental permission to marry for minors, and the recording of the union in a Marriage Register. See Eve Tavor Bannet, "The Marriage Act of 1753: 'A Most Cruel Law for the Fair Sex,'" *Eighteenth-Century Studies* 3 (1997): 233–54; Randolph Trumbach, ed., *The Marriage Act of 1753: Four Tracts; Marriage, Sex, and the Family in England, 1660–1800.* (New York: Garland, 1984); and Katherine Sobba Green, "The Blazon and the Marriage Act: A beginning for the Commodity Market," in *The Courtship Novel 1740–1820* (Lexington: Univ. of Kentucky Press, 1991), 69–79.

41. See Douglas Hay, "Property, Authority, and the Criminal Law," in *Albion's Fatal Tree: Crime and Society in Eighteenth-Century England* (New York: Pantheon, 1975), 22.

42. Other lengthy examples include 1: 174–89, 1: 222–24, and 2: 46–58. At times, the criticism takes the form of irony as in 1: 143–44.

43. As the *Monthly Review* recounts, "our political novelist has treated the legislature with a freedom that has produced a warrant for taking him into custody, which was executed a few days after the appearance of his work." See *Monthly Review* 11 (November 1754): 395.

44. This account is drawn from Blackstone's *Commentaries,* 3: 11.198–207; White, 89–90; J. H. Baker, *An Introduction to Legal History,* 3rd ed. (London: Butterworths, 1990), 341–43.

45. "An estate for life or in fee . . . to be a freehold must possess these two qualities: (1) Immobility, that is, the property must be either land or some interest issuing out of or annexed to land; and (2) indeterminate duration, for, if the utmost period of time to which an estate can endure be fixed and determined, it cannot be freehold." (*Black's,* 665).

46. Originally, the process involved physically removing the disputed party before the title was even decided.

47. I rely heavily here on White's concise description which employs "Roe" and Doe" as does Baker. Blackstone, in contrast, uses "John Rogers" and "John Smith," names which seem particularly novelistic.

48. Harding, 219.

49. Baker, 342.

50. Ibid., 342.

51. Dr. Shebbeare's experience with *The Marriage Act* exemplifies an exception.

52. Donald F. Bond, ed., *The Spectator* (Oxford: Clarendon, 1965), No. 411; 538.

53. [Arthur Young], *The Adventures of Emmera,* 2 vols. (London, 1767; reprint New York: Garland, 1974). All subsequent citations will refer to this edition and will appear parenthetically in the text.

54. Bentham, 255.

"To Sing the Town": Women, Place, and Print Culture in Eighteenth-Century Bath

ELIZABETH CHILD

To sing the Town, where balmy Waters flow,
To which AMELIA's Health the Nations owe,
My muse aspires; while conscious Blushes rise,
And her weak Pinions tremble, ere she flies;
Till, drawing Vigour from those living Springs,
She dares to raise her Voice, and stretch her Wings.

—*The Description of Bath*[1]

Writing about "the Town where balmy Waters flow" made Mary Chandler's literary reputation. She published *The Description of Bath* anonymously in 1733; by 1767 it had gone into eight editions. The poem earned Chandler praise from Pope, inclusion in Mary Scott's 1774 *The Female Advocate*, and life-long local celebrity.[2] As a resident of Bath, Chandler could speak confidently about town history, the local scenery, the spa's life-giving waters, the social diversions of the tourist population, and the accomplishments of prominent citizens. Later editions of *The Description of Bath* added both a dedication to Princess Amelia and Chandler's name. But it was Chandler's mastery of the local scene, rather than the trope of royal patronage, that authorized her to write, to work in a difficult poetic form, to publish her work and to reveal her authorship. Her poem offers a paradigm for a particular condition of authorship: the condition of place.

To date, geography has played little role in feminism's treatment of eighteenth-century English women's writing. Instead, the recovery of most female authors has been unselfconsciously London-centric, privileging the metropolis as the only significant site of literary production.[3] While performing valuable recovery work, the resurgence of critical interest in authors like Behn, Manley, Haywood, Lennox, Burney and Wollstonecraft at the same time has implicitly fostered a metropolitan (and thereby exclusionary) narrative of women's writing. All of these writers spent major parts of their lives— or at least their professional careers—in London. They had good reason to do so: London was enormously important to eighteenth-century English cultural life for men and women alike. To conflate London with England, or metropolis with nation, however, promotes a homogenous sociocultural geography at the expense of actual historical heterogeneity. One result of our metropolitan bias has been a skewed narrative of women's involvement in print culture. For eighteenth-century English women, less mobile and more constricted than their male peers in terms of access to London's literary culture, the transformation of provincial towns that occurred across the century was a determining condition of authorship.[4] Even a cursory review of provincial urban locales such as Bath immediately begins to challenge the extant historiography, uncovering a significant record of women's literary production that has been obscured by London's long shadow.[5]

Margaret Ezell has recently urged feminist scholarship to practice a much more "self-conscious historicism," arguing that "existing assumptions about modes of literary production and about historiography can be challenged and . . . important texts by women writers can be recovered by a re-visioning of the literary past."[6] A locational model for women's literary history offers such a revisioning. Feminist attention to Chandler, for example, has tended to focus on the influence of Alexander Pope.[7] Reading Chandler specifically as a *Bath* woman writer, on the other hand, inscribes her into a community of eighteenth-century authors ranging from better-known figures such as Sarah Scott, Sarah Fielding, Catharine Macaulay and Sophia Lee, to lesser known authors like Jane Bowdler, Esther Lewis, Lady Anna Miller and Ann Thicknesse. These women belonged to different social classes, worked in different genres and held diverse ideological positions. Considering such authors on the basis of place, however, promotes new patterns of inquiry that challenge previous assumptions about those very categories and propose new ways of reading their texts.

Focusing primarily on women engaged in Bath's print culture in the eighteenth century, I will argue that the town's urban dynamics fostered women's writing in ways distinct, both materially and conceptually, from the metropolitan scene. Key factors in this differentiation included the rapid growth of local publishing as a commercial enterprise, town-specific models of both social relations and the organization of public space, and the availability of civic rhetoric and civic ideology as authorizing agents. In each of these areas, Bath offers a useful case study of the ways in which eighteenth-century women's writing grows out of, and responds to, the local.

It might be said that the literary history of England rests upon a spatial metaphor: London as the hub of a wheel, radiating culture out to the provincial towns and beyond. Taken collectively, however, the trajectory of the careers discussed below decenter metropolitan hegemony, emphasizing instead the increasing feasibility of literary enterprise for women outside of London. Remapping this terrain provides a more contextual literary history, one that resists essentialist claims about gender and foregrounds instead the multiple and complex conditions of authorship shaping women's literary production.

Social historians have dubbed the eighteenth century England's "urban Renaissance," referring to the tremendous socioeconomic growth and burgeoning prosperity that encompassed not only London but also the provinces.[8] Towns like Bath, Bristol, Norwich, Exeter and the new industrial sites, while admittedly only a fraction of London's size, still became large enough, and wealthy enough, to support sweeping architectural renovation, permanent theaters, printers, multiple bookshops and libraries, and even scholarly societies.

That women began to "live by the pen" early in the long eighteenth century is well known. The causal role of newly vigorous local economies in that process, however, has been largely overlooked. During the Restoration and early eighteenth-century, as Paul Hunter has shown, living in London was probably a necessary condition for financially successful female authorship.[9] But as the century wore on, more and more provincial women supported themselves by writing. Bath was a particularly important site by sheer dint of the number of women authors who lived, wrote and published there. The productivity of authors in Bath like Sarah Fielding, Sarah Scott, Catharine Macaulay, Sophia Lee and less familiar figures like Lady Anna Miller suggests that the widespread urban vitality that was transforming small towns like Bath from provincial backwaters into important commercial and cultural centers played a significant role in shaping an increasingly professionalized literary culture.

The decentralization of publishing was a crucial factor in this professionalization. Following the lapse of the Copyright Act in 1695, provincial printers and booksellers enjoyed nearly a century of growth equal to, or even exceeding, that occurring in London.[10] Even though copyrights remained largely in the hands of London cartels throughout much of the century, the eagerness of London publishers to secure provincial distribution agreements attests to the commercial potential offered by extra-metropolitan sites. By 1730, most of the important English towns boasted at least one newspaper; by the mid-1740s, booksellers and stationers were conducting business in approximately 174 towns across the nation, responding to rapid growth in both provincial leisure and provincial literacy.[11] By the end of the century, Bath's ten bookstores and several newspapers were typical of the kind of print apparatus operating in larger provincial towns.[12]

This diffusion of print culture out of London had clear material ramifications for women. Whereas metropolitan publishers were usually highly selective, local businesses were eager enough for material, especially texts targeted to regional audiences, to actively solicit manuscripts. Local patterns of demand and consumption fostered a new enabling subject free of gender constraints: the town itself. Loco-specific literature became particularly important in Bath and other spa towns, where writing witty verses on the available pleasures and pastimes formed a popular social activity among tourists and residents, male and female.[13] Chandler's *Description of Bath* helped inaugurate the local demand for place-specific literary commodities; one critic has suggested that "[h]ers is . . . the first work to choose the city of Bath as its subject."[14] Of obvious local appeal, the poem was actively promoted by Bath's leading bookseller, James Leake. In its description of local attractions, Chandler's poem devotes a whole stanza to Leake's bookshop, a savvy marketing strategy that probably accounts for the significant role Leake played in keeping the poem before the public eye; it advertised both the town and Leake himself.[15] Leake's name appears on the imprints for the first seven editions of *Description of Bath*. Initially listed in a subsidiary position to London booksellers, Leake took over as the primary publisher with the second edition. While *Description of Bath* earned Chandler a national reputation, it was local promotion and distribution that kept her work in circulation for so many decades—local promotion that the poem itself helped orchestrate.

Local authors Hannah More and Ann Yearsley, both from nearby Bristol, were equally quick to exploit regional market opportunities in a different genre, that of drama. While neither engaged in loco-specific theatrics *per se* (although a number of such works were performed, such as the popular local piece, *Bladud),* each recognized the emergence of local theater in Bath as a lucrative and prestigious venue for literary production. Bath's Orchard Street Theater opened in 1750 and quickly came to be recognized as the site of some of the best theatrical work in England, becoming in 1768 the first "Theatre Royal" outside of London.[16] The Bath theater shared its company with Bristol, twelve miles away, meaning that aspiring local playwrights had potential access to audiences in two important urban centers, without the difficulties and degradations suffered by many metropolitan women playwrights.[17] More eventually made her fortune from didactic tracts, while Yearsley's reputation rested primarily on verse. But the availability of high quality local theater (not all eighteenth-century provincial towns could even boast a permanent playhouse) played a pivotal role in both of their careers.

While the Orchard Street company tended to reprise London hits, it also sponsored original work and the management was clearly receptive to the efforts of local women. More's first public venture into the theater, a translation of Pietro Metastasio's *The Inflexible Captive*, debuted in Bath in 1775.[18] The performance launched her theatrical and professional literary career; she went on to have a spectacular London debut with *Percy* in 1777. More moved thereafter in more glamorous metropolitan literary circles, but she never relinquished her personal or professional west country connections.[19] The result was a faithful hometown audience eager to embrace one of its own: "when *Percy* was remounted in Bristol in September 1778, a crowd threatened to storm the building to secure seats."[20]

A decade later, the Bath/Bristol company provided More's erstwhile protegee Yearsley with *her* theatrical debut, a historical drama entitled *Earl Goodwin*, a choice of form perhaps inspired by More's success with *Percy*. The play ran for seven nights in the two towns in the fall of 1789.[21] *Goodwin* never reached the London stage, but local interest in Yearsley, nicknamed "the Bristol milkwoman," was enough to generate the respectable sum of 80£ in authorial profits from the performances alone.[22] The play received metropolitan as well as local notices, and was "well reviewed" when published two years later.[23] The availability of a local venue thus provided Yearsley with the opportunity to experiment with a new literary form, and to be well compensated for that experimentation.

Bath's best-known female playwright was Sophia Lee, who "sought a humble home in Bath" after her first play, *The Chapter of Accidents*, was humiliatingly rejected by Covent Garden's Thomas Harris sometime between 1774–77.[24] *Chapter* was eventually produced by George Colman at the Haymarket in 1780, achieving enormous popular success, but Lee chose to remain in Bath where she continued to write plays as well as fiction and poetry, and, like More, to run a successful girl's school with her sister. That choice suggests that Bath offered Lee both psychological and material advantages over London as a working environment. Her circle in Bath included prominent thespian figures such as Sarah Siddons, who got her start on the Bath stage, as well as Lee's sister Harriet, herself a playwright although never as successful as Sophia.[25]

The spread of sophisticated cultural tastes into the towns, and the emerging mechanisms for feeding those tastes, enabled successful London writers like Sophia Lee to relocate without committing professional suicide. Bath was particularly attractive as an alternative to London because it also offered the hydrotherapeutic benefits of its famous waters and a lower cost of living, important considerations for the many women too sick or too poor to sustain professional literary careers in the capital.

Bath's well-known mid-century "bluestocking" circle coalesced around women who had fled there because of health problems, financial straits, or both. Catharine Macaulay's prefatory comments to her *A modest plea for the property of copy-right* (printed in Bath in 1774) noted the "heavy oppression of sickness, and languor of body" that had driven her to Bath.[26] Macaulay recovered from that immediate crisis, but continued to suffer from poor health and accordingly stayed in Bath for several years where she presided over a circle of admirers both local and metropolitan. Although Macaulay set aside her ambitious, multi-volumed *History of England from the Accession of James I to that of the Brunswick Line* while in Bath, she did produce the first volume in a planned series on *The History of England from the Revolution to the Present Time in a Series of Letters to a Friend*, published in Bath in 1778.[27]

Twenty years earlier, Sarah Fielding had also retreated to Bath in desperation over her failing health. Shortly before leaving London, she wrote to Samuel Richardson complaining of the damp metropolitan air, saying, "Surely I am as weak as a Feather everything strikes me down . . ."; her suffering was so acute that it rendered her unable to write.[28] A few weeks later, she wrote Richardson from Bath that "the waters agree so well with me, that I hope in time they will work as perfect a cure from diseases as an old woman can expect."[29] Fielding's professional output during her years in Bath's environs included *The Lives of Cleopatra and Octavia* (1757), *The History of the Countess of Dellwyn* (1759), *The History of Ophelia* (1760) and *Xenophon's Memoirs of Socrates* (1762)—a level of activity that equals her literary production in London.

Fielding's move apparently was facilitated by Leake, who in addition to being Bath's leading bookseller was also Richardson's brother-in-law. While Fielding continued to rely primarily on London firms for publication, Leake's name appears on the imprints for both the first and second editions of *Cleopatra*. She also used Bath printer Cornelius Pope for the first edition of her translation of *Xenophon*, explaining in a letter that the book "is to be printed here, for I could not undertake a Journey to London, and here is an ingenuous young Man lately set up that I believe will do it very well."[30] In other correspondence, Fielding refers several times to doing business with her London publisher, Andrew Millar, in Bath: "I expect Millar in Bath tomorrow if he keeps to the time appointed, and will then settle it with him, but if he should not come will write to him next week."[31] For Fielding, Bath afforded the physical well-being to continue writing, local resources for production and distribution when she was too ill to travel, and even, on occasion, local access to metropolitan business connections.

The fact that high-profile literary women were able to sustain careers in Bath is significant both in terms of the diffusion of female literary professionalism as a national, rather than purely metropolitan, phenomenon, but also in the collective implications for local culture. Female authors like Fielding, More, Macaulay, Lady Miller and Sarah Scott, whom I will discuss at greater length below, wielded a great deal of cultural authority on the local scene, attracting and inspiring other like-minded men and women. London's eighteenth-century literary culture, by contrast, tended to revolve around powerful male figures like Richardson, Johnson and Garrick, creating a paradigm of literary influence that relegated women writers to peripheral status. In London, the Sarah Fieldings and Hannah Mores orbit like lesser stars around a chosen sun, the narrative of their textual production insistently referential rather than autonomous.[32] Outside of London, however, alternative patronage relationships emerged,[33] relationships that expose the metropolitan paradigm as place-specific rather than hegemonic. Scott and Fielding, for instance, prospered in Bath because they were able to form an almost exclusively female network there of emotional, intellectual and financial support.[34] For Fielding, the Bath circle gradually superseded the male-dominated literary circles central to her professional development in London. She continued to correspond with Richardson, but increasingly it seems to have been Scott and her "bluestocking" circle in Bath, as well as Scott's wealthy sister Elizabeth Montagu on a more long distance basis, who looked after Fielding's physical, financial and literary welfare. Fielding was also befriended by Ralph Allen, Bath's well-known entrepreneur and literary patron, whose beneficiaries included Alexander Pope and Henry Fielding. While Allen bequeathed Sarah Fielding £100 in his will, however, her female friends in Bath felt he could have extended himself more on her behalf, and exerted themselves to oversee her welfare on a more daily basis.[35] Rizzo has suggested that Elizabeth Montagu's patronage in general tended to be exceptionally self-serving and focused primarily on writers from the lower classes,[36] but in this case Montagu appears to have quite generous, quietly funneling food and gifts to Fielding through Scott for several years, and eventually providing her with an annuity. Fielding was not in a position to offer financial assistance to her literary friends, but the relationship with Scott was reciprocal in other ways. Scott's best known novel *Millenium Hall*, for instance, may have been inspired by Fielding's *Countess of Dellwyn*; a subplot in the latter describes a rural charitable institution very evocative of Scott's benevolent female community.[37]

The attempt of the Bath circle to institutionalize their informal network via the creation of a kind of commune of enlightened women has been described elsewhere.[38] While the Hitcham community failed, it could be argued that the Scott-Fielding circle *did* succeed in creating a tradition of female literary authority and agency in Bath that survived them. The activities of Lady Miller, for example, reveal the degree to which women in Bath were able to appropriate cultural authority that might not have been available to them in London, and use it to sponsor female authorship.[39]

Lady Miller, editor of the three-volumed *Poetical Amusements at a Villa near Bath* (1775–81) and a daughter of Scott's Bath friend Margaret Riggs, positioned herself publicly and aggressively as a literary patron in Bath in the 1770s and 1780s. While mocked by such contemporaries as Horace Walpole, and, more gently, Frances Burney, Miller nonetheless instituted a popular salon at her villa "Parnassus," in the village of Batheaston just outside Bath.[40] The poetry competitions held there became a popular diversion for aspiring Bath writers and established metropolitan figures alike, and Miller welcomed not only the ungrateful Walpole, but also Burney, Mary Delany and Hester Thrale to her literary salons. In addition to her role as a tourist attraction for visiting gentry, Miller also actively encouraged the literary endeavours of other provincial women. Miller's salon gave Bath's Jane Bowdler the opportunity to develop as a poet; published posthumously, Bowdler's verses went into multiple editions. Miller also supported the fledgling efforts of Anna Seward, who was later to write a loving elegy for her Bath friend.[41]

Patronage played an important role in the literary culture of the eighteenth century, serving as a vehicle to both sustain and to bestow cultural authority on its practitioners. As a citizen of Bath, Miller had access to a local cultural capital that enabled her to follow in the footsteps of her bluestocking predecessors by appropriating the authority of literary patron, and using it to make a name both for herself and for her protégées.

Social benevolence, of which patronage is a particular manifestation, was central to the way the resident Bath community understood itself in the eighteenth century. While today we largely form our notion of eighteenth-century Bath through the social satire of writers like Smollett and Austen, it is important to remember that the community constructed by satiric discourse is, in the case of Bath, primarily a transient rather than civic one. Citizens of Bath were, however, an increasingly large and prosperous group, many of them deeply invested in various forms of local improvement. The town undertook numerous worthy projects, perhaps most importantly the construction of a charity hospital, a relative innovation for that era. The hospital project was administered by men. Nonetheless, projects like the hospital offered local women an opportunity to participate simultaneously in both the ethos of civic benevolence and the print marketplace through the attractive rhetorical position of publication as an act of local altruism.

The career of Esther Lewis offers an exemplary case. A regular contributor to the *Bath Journal* in the 1750s, Lewis published her collected works in Bath in 1788. The title, *Poems Moral and Entertaining, written long since by Miss Lewis, then of Holt, now and for 30 years past, the wife of Mr. Robert Clark, of Tetbury*, insists on Lewis' local connections. Her literary connections included a friendship with Sarah Fielding, which Lewis invokes (along with their mutual love of snuff) in the introduction to *Poems*. The reference to Fielding helps to inscribe the author into Bath's mid-century bluestocking community of talented and high-minded women. But Lewis also engaged with present-day features of civic life. On the title page, she dedicated the proceeds from the book, at the request of her husband, to public charities in Gloucester, Bath and Tetbury. This rhetorical strategy positioned her as both obedient, and philanthropic—a contributing member of a benevolent civic community rather than a seeker after personal gain. The worthy causes noted on the title page legitimated her publication by tying it to local enterprise. Lewis is relatively unknown today, and philanthropic publications play little role in women's literary histories, perhaps in part because feminism's recovery of eighteenth-century women writers has tended to privilege "professional," self-supporting figures. But the local popularity of philanthropic publications—Bowdler's collected poems were published for the benefit of the Bath hospital in 1786 and quickly went into sixteen editions, and Mary Scott published a two-part poem entitled "Messiah" to benefit the same cause in 1788—testifies to the powerful role local altruism could play in legitimating women's writing, as well as the ways in which women conceived of themselves as active, influential local citizens.[42]

Lewis's work, like that of Chandler, makes forthright her civic ties and agendas. In the remainder of this essay, I will argue that civic ideologies specific to Bath exerted an equal claim, although a less explicit one, on the fiction of Fielding and Scott. The literary production of both women reveals a longstanding mutual concern with the formation of productive communities in the midst of fast-changing social relations and social economies. Bath's civic commitment, at least theoretically, to altruism, benevolence and carefully structured social order, suggests that works like Fielding's *The History of the Countess of Dellwyn* and Scott's *Millenium Hall* can be read as *Bath* novels as well as British novels, their authors "Bathonians" as well as British gentlewomen.

The very existence of the Fielding/Scott relationship speaks to the intimacy of Bath society and its deviations from metropolitan norms. In London,

Fielding had moved in different social circles than the better born, and better connected, Scott. Scott's longtime companion in Bath, Lady Barbara Montagu, was the daughter of an earl and according of much higher social standing than Scott, although Scott was certainly a gentlewoman. But in Bath itself, subtle class distinctions were subordinated to neighborly community—a community forwarded by the town's own efforts to produce new models of social space and social relations that could accommodate a wide range of backgrounds and tastes. The great increase in attractive public spaces in eighteenth-century Bath, along with the entertainments offered therein, fostered a different kind of social hierarchy than London's, where the elite entertained each other primarily at home, and public places like the theater tended to be segregated by rank. In Bath, precedence was still observed, but a much greater degree of social interaction prevailed.

Beau Nash's "Rules" for behavior at the assembly rooms, for instance, dictated a "polite intercourse" between strangers, regardless of station. Nash was hardly a social radical. Yet his rules chipped away at the rigid hierarchies of social intercourse for the middle and upper classes, hierarchies that remained much more firmly entrenched elsewhere, for much longer.[43] Fielding seems to have greatly admired Nash's approach to social regulation; a character in her *Familiar Letters* writes of a public ball in Bath that

> the Appearance of Chearfulness which reigned in the whole Company, seemed to me a Picture of social Happiness . . . I never saw anything better regulated, or conducted with less Confusion, than this whole Scene, which, I was told, was entirely owing to a Gentleman, who for many years has had the Management of all public Diversions here . . . "[44]

Her encomium encapsulates the concern with social relations that lies at the core of both her own fictional work, and that of Scott. Their novels share a teleological orientation towards carefully ordered communities and communal solutions as the best response to individual problems. In their fictive explorations of a more perfect social union, both draw heavily on civic structures and values specific to Bath.

Many recent readers have commented on the fundamental conservatism of Scott's utopian community, which predicates its "reforms" on a firmly entrenched hierarchical socio-economic structure. While hardly utopian by contemporary standards, the concentration of power in the hands of a small elite would, however, have been very familiar to any eighteenth-century resident of Bath, a town almost completely controlled by a "close" corporation of about thirty councilmen and aldermen. As Penelope Corfield has noted, "Such a system, which looked oligarchic even in 1700, when the city of Bath housed 3,000 inhabitants . . . had by 1800, when its total population had risen to nearer 35,000, become a scandal."[45] But in mid-century Bath, town government was working well, at least for the middle and upper classes. The close control of political power aligned with the energy of a booming local economy produced at least superficially a well regulated and philosophically sound social order, one enlightened enough to undertake civic projects like the hospital. The organization of the latter is consistent with both the oligarchic structure of Bath's political culture and the conservative benevolence of *Millenium Hall*; while intended to offer a refuge to poor cripples and other sick people, the hospital administrators also required a referral from a physician, certification by the hospital's officers and an entry fee of thirty shillings. The hospital offered inmates a chance at wellness, or a better life, but under carefully codified conditions, evoking the closely controlled social benefactions practiced at *Millenium Hall*.

Fielding's reconsideration of withdrawal, isolationism and unworldliness as a theory of social practice roughly coincides with her permanent relocation to Bath in 1754.[46] *David Simple Volume the Last*, published the year earlier, details the collapse of the idyllic rural community Fielding had envisioned in *David Simple* (1744). While *Volume the Last* appears to advocate a philosophy of Christian resignation to the inevitable evils of human existence, the novel is not Fielding's last word on the attainability of social happiness. She returned to this issue a few years later in *The Countess of Dellwyn* (1759), a cautionary tale ostensibly concerned with the socially and materially ambitious Charlotte Lucum. Charlotte weds for wealth and social standing, and is punished with a miserable marriage, divorce and social ostracism. Paralleling this story, however, is that of Mrs. Bilson, a gently born character who becomes acquainted with the Dellwyns at Bristol. Mrs. Bilson has also grappled with marital misery, due to her husband's extravagent expenditures which at one point reduce the family to debtor's prison. Unlike Charlotte, however, Mrs. Bilson remains a faithful and devoted wife, rescuing the family fortunes via her entrepreneurial success with a millinery business.

Fielding's novels make clear that she deplored the frivolity of fashionable life, whether in London or in the resorts of Bath and Bristol. At the same time, however, in *The Countess of Dellwyn*, Fielding also acknowledges the economic potentiality of worldliness and the value of bourgeois entrepreneurialism: an ideological shift hinted at in the concluding pages of *David Simple, Volume the Last*. While the latter is generally pessimistic about human nature, suggesting at its most extreme the complete incompatibility of benevolence with power or agency, in the last chapter an exemplar of disinterested kindliness *does* emerge, in the form of a character modelled after Bath's leading citizen, Ralph Allen.[47]

An astute businessman who rose from obscure origins to one of England's great fortunes, Allen was well known for his generosity to civic projects and the relief of individual need. Six years after the publication of *David Simple, Volume the Last*, Fielding suggests in *The Countess of Dellwyn* that the civic exemplar offered by Allen could be appropriated by a woman—Mrs. Bilson—and that the commercial opportunities available in the mercantilist culture of England could lay the cornerstone for an equally virtuous, but more prosperous, community than the model of naive idealism offered in David Simple. Whereas David Simple naively trusts his financial affairs to others, Mrs. Bilson takes charge of her own fortunes, both literally and metaphorically. Ultimately her acumen results in both a successful business and a substantial inheritance from a relative who admires her industry. The family not only prospers itself, but can turn its altruistic energies outward, implementing a refuge for the elderly, a home for distressed gentlewomen, facilities for the sick, and innumerable other benevolent projects. The family chooses to settle in Bristol, for its salubrious air, where they represent a model of social and economic success that works to reform the dissipations of visitors from London.

I have argued above that Scott and Fielding make figurative use of Bath's civic typologies and ideological structures in various of their works, and suggested that exposing these structures opens up new ways of reading these texts. I want to conclude by turning to a less figurative appropriation, examining an element of *Millenium Hall* that many readers have found puzzling but which becomes less opaque when read as a specific response to Bath life.

One of the oddest features of Millenium Hall is the mini-community of congenitally impaired "wretches" who reside there, hidden from the casual eye. Mrs. Mancel characterizes their enclosure as "an asylum for those poor creatures who are rendered miserable from some natural deficiency or redundancy"—that is, who suffer from manifest deformities.[48] The gentlewomen of Millenium Hall evidence particular concern over the exposure of the inmates to the public gaze, "the contemptuous curiosity of the unthinking multitude."[49] In this episode, Scott implicitly critiques the phenomenon of "illness as spectacle" so prominent in Bath daily life. The very mythology of Bath originates in the figure of a deformed prince, Bladud, leperous son of King Hudibras. Commentators from Mary Chandler ("Hither foul scurvy, odious to the Sight; / And Vapours, which, in ev'ry Form, affright . . .") to Tobias Smollett's Matthew Bramble ("the first object that saluted my eye, was a child full of scrophulous ulcers, carried in the arms of one of the guides, under the very noses of the bathers") dwell with a kind of horrified relish on the parade of the afflicted into the baths.[50] In enclosing the "monsters" in Millenium Hall, Scott stingingly rebukes the treatment of sickness as public spectacle. Rather than satirize the afflicted, as did so many other commentators on the Bath scene, Scott opts instead for a rhetoric of benevolence that both reproaches an unfeeling public and rescues its victims.

Scott chose to spend much of her adult life in Bath, leading a relatively independent life in the company of sympathetic, reform-minded women. *Millenium Hall* reiterates the rejection of fashionable life that characterizes so much of Scott's work. And Bath, that eighteenth-century "province of pleasure," was nothing if not fashionable. Yet at the same time, the particular social and economic dynamics of the town helped enable Scott and many other women to pursue meaningful, sustaining work. Local culture promoted cross-class friendships, literary production and social benevolence: an intersection of circumstances that for the women living there, bore fruit in a myriad diverse acts of cultural production.

In *A Room of One's Own*, Virginia Woolf famously posited as a historical milestone that "towards the end of the eighteenth century . . . [t]he middle-class woman began to write." The ongoing recovery of early modern women writers has long since led us to revise that claim backwards by at least one hundred years. What a locational model shows us is that by the middle of the eighteenth century, women across the nation were both writing and publishing. Women's literary history in Bath helps to deconstruct "Englishness" as a monolithic core identity, foregrounding instead the agglomeration of distinctive urban and regional localities that were in dialogue with, rather than exile from, eighteenth-century London. The socioeconomic, religious, political and cultural topographies of these localities exerted a strenuous force on women writers. Their words are marked by a place.

NOTES

I am grateful to Eleanor Shevlin and Paula McDowell for their thoughtful comments on earlier drafts. I would particularly like to thank Susan S. Lanser both for her generous and insightful contributions to this essay and for her sustaining enthusiasm for the larger project, a study of eighteenth-century provincial women writers and English print culture, from which the paper derives.

1. Mary Chandler, *The Description of Bath. A Poem Humbly Inscribed To Her Royal Highness the Princess Amelia*, 3rd ed. (London: Printed for J. Leake, 1736), 1. All future references to *Description* will cite this edition by page number.

2. Accolades for Chandler (1687–1745) in local print culture included an eulogy by Jacob Axford in *Poems on Various Subjects* (Bath, 1764). While Chandler has generated little critical attention in the twentieth century, Theophilus Cib-

ber's inclusion of Chandler in his 1753 *Lives of the Poets*, along with Scott's references in *The Female Advocate*, suggest a wider renown in her own era.

3. An important recent exception is John Brewer's *The Pleasures of the Imagination* (New York: Farrar, Straus & Giroux, 1997), which devotes an entire chapter to the influence of Anna Seward, the "largely forgotten" Lichfield writer and patron, on England's literary life (573–612).

4. In one of the few critical examinations of women and print culture in provincial towns, Cheryl Turner notes that provincial publishers "were instrumental in promoting women's publications on a national scale, thereby familiarizing those living in areas remote from London with that contentious phenomenon, the 'Petticoat Author'" (*Living by the Pen: Women Writers in the Eighteenth Century* [London: Routledge, 1992], 85). In general, however, Turner locates female authorship primarily in the London marketplace.

5. Betty Rizzo has drawn attention to the important community of women writers in Bath in both *Companions Without Vows: Relationships Among Eighteenth-Century British Women* (Athens: Univ. of Georgia Press, 1994), especially 306–19 and the introduction to her edition of *The History of Sir George Ellison* (Lexington: Univ. Press of Kentucky, 1996), xiii–xxx. Rizzo focuses exclusively on the Bath circle around Sarah Scott and Lady Barbara Montagu.

6. Margaret Ezell, *Writing Women's Literary History* (Baltimore: Johns Hopkins Univ. Press, 1993), 9–11.

7. See, for example, Linda Troost's essay "Geography and Gender: Mary Chandler and Alexander Pope," *Pope, Swift, and Women Writers*, ed. Donald Mell (Newark: Univ. of Delaware Press, 1996), 67–85, an investigation of Chandler's indebtedness to Roman and English traditions of landscape poetry.

8. In *The English Urban Renaissance: Culture and Society in the Provincial Town, 1660–1770* (Oxford: Clarendon Press, 1989), Peter Borsay coined the term "urban Renaissance" to refer to "a new wave of prosperity, the most striking sign of which was the cultural refinement and prestige it brought to those towns which were affected" (viii). See also R. M. Wiles, "Provincial Culture in Early Georgian England," in *The Triumph of Culture: 18th Century Perspectives*, ed. Paul Fritz and David Williams (Toronto: A. M. Hakkert, 1972), 49–68. Jonathan Barry's "Provincial Town Culture, 1640–1780: Urbane or Civic?" in *Interpretation and Cultural History*, ed. Joan Pittock and Andrew Wear (New York: St. Martin's Press, 1991), 198–234, offers a critique of both Borsay and Wiles in arguing for new methodological approaches to provincial culture studies.

9. "Once writers . . . became 'professionalized'—that is, writing as a vocation became somewhat detached from patronage and older 'man of letters' notions—women who sought employment in the profession found London as necessary as men. Behn, Manley, and Haywood, for example, made careers there, not necessarily going specifically to write, but certainly finding that, once economic necessity took over their lives, London was the only possible place." Paul Hunter, *Before Novels: The Cultural Contexts of Eighteenth-Century Fiction* (New York: W. W. Norton, 1990), 116.

10. John Feather, "The Country Trade in Books," in *Spreading the Word: The Distribution Networks of Print, 1550–1850*, ed. Robin Myers and Michael Harris (Winchester: St. Paul's Bibliographies, 1990), 165–83.

11. Feather, *The Provincial Book Trade in Eighteenth-Century England* (Cambridge: Cambridge Univ. Press, 1985), 19, 29. Wiles, "Provincial Culture," argues that the profusion of regional newspapers demonstrates, among other things, a provincial literary culture that in many ways equalled that of London.

12. See R. S. Neale, *Bath 1680–1850: A Social History* (London: Routledge and Kegan Paul, 1981), 25, for a brief discussion of Bath bookshops; Borsay, *English Urban Renaissance*, 221, for rival newspapers in Bath; and G. A. Cranfield, *The Press and Society* (London: Longman, 1978), 178–203, for the development of the provincial press in the eighteenth century.

13. Barbara Benedict, in "Consumptive Communities: Commodifying Nature in Spa Society," *The Eighteenth Century: Theory and Interpretation* 36 (1995): 203–19, discusses at length the complex social and cultural work performed by spa literature in Bath and other English resort towns.

14. Troost, "Geography," 67.

15. "But see thro' yonder Door a safe Retreat; / There rest secure, amidst the Wise, and Great: / Heroes of antient, and of modern Song, / The bending Shelves in comely Order throng, / Hither, ye Nymphs, attend the leading Muse, / With her the Labours of the Wise peruse; / Their Maxims learn, their Precepts be your Guide. / Think Virtuous Knowledge Woman's truest Pride. / One hour thus spent, more solid Joys shall give, / Than the gay Idler knows, or Fools conceive" (Chandler, *Description*, 15). A footnote identifies Leake's as the shop in question.

16. For both an overview of the theater's history and a meticulously compiled schedule of specific performances, see *Theatre Royal Bath: A Calendar of Performances at the Orchard Street Theatre, 1750–1800*, ed. Arnold Hare. (Bath: Kingsmead Press, 1977), vi–xv.

17. For examples of specific metropolitan women playwrights and their struggles with the London "system," see Betty Rizzo, "Depressa Resurgam: Elizabeth Griffith's Playwriting Career," in *Curtain Calls: British and American Women and the Theater, 1660–1820*, ed. Mary Anne Schofield and Cecilia Macheski (Athens: Ohio Univ. Press, 1991), 120–42, and in the same volume, Ellen Donkin, "The Paper War of Hannah Cowley and Hannah More," 143–62.

18. Patricia Demers, *The World of Hannah More* (Lexington: Univ. Press of Kentucky, 1996), 24. I have also relied on *Theatre Royal Bath* for information about specific performances; see page 240 for references to performances of *The Inflexible Captive*.

19. Demers, *Hannah More*, 4–6. More maintained a girl's school in Bristol with her sisters for decades, and also invested much of her personal income in a nearby home for herself and siblings.

20. Ibid., 24.

21. Mary Waldron, *Lactilla, Milkwoman of Clifton: The Life and Writings of Ann Yearsley, 1753–1806* (Athens: Univ. of Georgia Press, 1996), 186–87.

22. Ibid., 186.

23. Ibid., 188.

24. Ellen Donkin, *Getting into the Act: Women Playwrights in London, 1776–1829* (Routledge: London 1995), 81.

25. According to the *Theatre Royal Calendar*, Harriet Lee's play *The New Peerage* debuted in Bath in the 1787–88 season (243). *Peerage* does not appear to have been performed in London.

26. Macaulay, *A modest plea for the property of copy-right* (Bath: For Edward and Charles Dilly, in the Poultry, London, 1774), v, reprinted in *The Literary Property Debate: Eight Tracts, 1774–1775* (New York: Garland Publishing, 1974).

27. Bridget Hill suggests that Bath in many ways was an unproductive setting for Macaulay, in part because it lacked the kind of radical political circles so much a part of her London life (*The Republican Virago: The Life and Times of Catharine Macaulay, Historian* [Oxford: Clarendon Press, 1992], 78–104). Barbara Brandon Schnorrenberg characterizes *History of England from the Revolution* as a "thank-you" to Macaulay's Bath friend Reverend Dr. Thomas Wilson; it was poorly received by reviewers. See "An Opportunity Missed: Catherine Macaulay on the Revolution of 1688," *Studies in Eighteenth-Century Culture* 20 (1990): 231–40.

28. Sarah Fielding, Letter 81 in *The Correspondence of Henry and Sarah Fielding*, eds. Martin Battestin and Clive Probyn (Oxford: Clarendon Press, 1993), 127.

29. Ibid., Letter 82, 129.

30. Ibid., Letter 105, 169. *Cleopatra* imprints identify London firms A. Millar and R. and J. Dodsley as well as Leake as publishers. Millar published the 1762 edition of *Xenophon*.

31. Ibid., Letter 99, 158–59.

32. The changing dynamics of eighteenth-century literary patronage, including gender roles within patronage systems, have generated several interesting recent studies, although none focuses on a London/provinces divide *per se*. See, for example, Betty Rizzo's "The Patron as Poet Maker: The Politics of Benefaction," *Studies in Eighteenth-Century Culture* 20 (1990): 241–66, which argues that female patronage had the subversive agenda of undermining a patriarchal definition of literary excellence that was predicated upon formal training in the classics. Dustin Griffin's *Literary Patronage in England* (Cambridge: Cambridge Univ. Press, 1996) provides a brief account of women authors' involvement in eighteenth century patronage systems, through the experiences of novelist Charlotte Lennox and poet Mary Leapor (189–219).

33. The most notorious example of an extra-metropolitan female patronage relationship is that of Hannah More and Ann Yearsley, the poetry-writing milkwoman of Bristol. In *Lactilla*, Waldron offers an interesting account of the way Bristol's local social and economic dynamics inflected More and Yearsley's interactions (48–78).

34. Rizzo, *Companions*, 295–319, offers a detailed look at female friendships in Bath. For a fuller account of Montagu's relationship with other women writers, including financial support, see also Sylvia Myers, *The Bluestocking Circle* (Oxford: Oxford Univ. Press, 1990), 177–206.

35. See Battestin and Probyn, Introduction to Fielding, *Correspondence*: "Mrs. Montagu's concern for Sarah was genuine and practical — some time after Ralph Allen's death in 1764 she complained to Elizabeth Carter that he should have left Sarah 'a decent maintenance for life, sixty pounds a year added to what she enjoys had made her happy, for she lives retired by choice'" (xxxvi).

36. Rizzo, "The Patron as Poet Maker: The Politics of Benefaction," *Studies in Eighteenth-Century Culture* 20 (1990): 241–66. For Montagu's annuity to Fielding, see Fielding, *Correspondence*, note to letter 110 (176).

37. Linda Bree suggests a connection between *Millenium Hall* and *The History of the Countess of Dellwyn* in *Sarah Fielding* (New York: Twayne Publishers, 1996), 130, as does Rizzo in *Companions without Vows,* 310.

38. Rizzo briefly describes the Hitcham experiment in *Companions Without Vows*, 317–19, and in greater detail in the preface to *The History of Sir George Ellison*, xxvi–xxix. See also Bree, 27–28.

39. Ruth Hesselgrave's *Lady Miller and the Batheaston Circle* (New Haven: Yale Univ. Press, 1927) remains the most complete account of this neglected literary figure.

40. Burney wrote a friend that "notwithstanding Bath Easton is so much laughed at in London, nothing here is more tonish than to visit Lady Miller . . . Lady Miller is a round, plump, coarse-looking dame of about forty, and while all her aim is to appear an elegant woman of fashion, all her success is to seem an ordinary woman in very common life, with fine clothes on" (Hesselgrave, 9–10). For other contemporary reactions to Miller, see Hesselgrave, 77–85.

41. See Brewer, *The Pleasures of the Imagination*, 601–4, for a brief discussion of Seward's relationship with Miller.

42. Rizzo has also uncovered instances of Bath women sponsoring publications as individual acts of charity; "[i]n 1759 Lady Barbara [Montagu] . . . paid for the publication by Richardson of a novel by an anonymous woman, *The Histories of Some of the Penitents in the Magdalen House*; and in 1775 Elizabeth Cutts published her verses *Almeria; or Parental Advice* to benefit two indigent persons" (Preface to *Ellison,* xxiii). Dorice Williams Elliott discusses fictional enactments of female philanthropy in "Sarah Scott's *Millenium Hall* and Female Philanthropy," *Studies in English Literature* 35 (1995): 535–53.

43. For a list of Nash's "Rules to be observ'd at Bath," see Oliver Goldsmith's *Life of Richard Nash, Esq.* (Bath, 1762) in *Collected Works of Oliver Goldsmith*, ed. Arthur Friedman [Oxford: Clarendon Press, 1966]), 303–4.

44. Sarah Fielding, *Familiar Letters Between the Principal Characters in David Simple, and Some Others* (London: A. Millar, 1767), 131.

45. Penelope Corfield, *The Impact of English Towns* (Oxford: Oxford Univ. Press, 1962), 151.

46. Chronologies of Fielding's life disagree on the date of her move to Bath. I follow Battestin and Probyn who argue persuasively that she took up residence in Bath in 1754 (see Fielding, *Correspondence*, note to letter 81, 128).

47. See Fielding, *Volume the Last*, book 7, chapter 10, in which "a Gentleman" promises his protection to Cynthia and her niece Camilla. *The Adventures of*

David Simple (Oxford: Oxford Univ. Press, 1969), 428–9. The "gentleman," living in a palatial estate just outside of Bath, is almost certainly Allen.

48. Sarah Scott, *A History of Millenium Hall*, ed. Gary Kelly (Peterborough: Broadview Press, 1995), 73.

49. Ibid., 72.

50. Chandler, *Description*, 4; Smollett, *Humphrey Clinker* (London: Penguin, 1967), 75.

Material Culture of the Guild: A Study of a German Cabinetmakers' Guild Chest

ANNETTE K. WEIR

L et us keep as far as possible the views we had at the century's beginning; we may be the last representatives—with a few others perhaps—of an era that will not easily come again."[1] Johann Wolfgang von Goethe, discussing the changing face of society, prophetically expressed these sentiments in a letter written in 1825 to his friend, the master mason Carl Friedrich Zelter. By this date the guild system, which had been a vital element in German society for hundreds of years, was in the final stage of its demise. New technological, social, political, and economic forces in the nineteenth century overpowered the guilds, which often had inflexible rules and a slow, ordered way of doing things. Goethe recognized this aspect as well: "Wealth and speed are what the world admires, and what all are bent on."[2] It is an irony of the eighteenth century that the beginning of the dissolution process of the German guilds coincided with their golden age.[3]

That this final stage of the German guilds was a golden age is evident in the quality of the goods produced, artifacts that yield valuable information on the cultural and technical history of the trades. Of particular interest is a small group of objects collectively owned and used by the guilds for special purposes.[4] The guild chest is one such object, and the focus of this study is a chest located in the collections of the Detroit Institute of Arts (fig. 1). After describing and identifying the Detroit chest as the cabinetmakers' guild chest from Frankfurt am Main and giving a profile of that city and guild life within

Figure 1. Simon Ackerholm (attrib.), guild chest of Frankfurt am Main cabinetmakers (joiners), 1751. Photograph © 1998 The Detroit Institute of Arts.

it, I will explore the functions of the object. The latter part of this article will consider the form and development of the guild chest as a furniture type, the vernacular cabinetmaking tradition, and what intra-guild relationships might be suggested by the chest's iconography.

Description and Identification of the Chest

The chest entered the collections of the Detroit Institute of Arts in 1944 as a gift from an anonymous donor. The provenance of the piece is unknown. Identification of the object was made as a result of my research into the chest's rich iconography. There is also an inscription incised on the inside rim of the sunken lock housing which aids in identification; it reads: Simon Ackerholm von Christianstad in Schweden FiF [monogram] 29 May 1751. The iconography, as well as the ornamentation of the chest, is executed in marquetry of yew and rosewood with inlays of pewter, brass, ivory, and mother-of-pearl. The chest, which measures approximately 27 x 17 x 21 inches, is oak veneered with walnut and has moldings of ebony and mahogany, ormolu capitals and feet, and iron handles.[5]

Cabinetmakers differentiated themselves from other woodworkers through the technique of veneering and the iconography on the two ends of the Detroit chest depicts distinct stages of the process. The side bearing the date 1751 shows two men wearing caps and aprons, each holding the end of a frame saw (fig. 2). A tree trunk has been wedged into an open platform, and the men are cutting veneers. This activity is also illustrated in one of the most valuable eighteenth-century sources on cabinetmaking, *L'art du menuisier,* written 1769–75 by the French cabinetmaker André Jacob Roubo.[6]

A veneer is a thin sheet of wood, typically of a fine or rare kind, which is attached to a backing of a strong but less expensive wood. According to Michael Stürmer's study of the cabinetmaking trade in the eighteenth century, a high degree of skill was required in cutting veneers, whose thickness ranged from 1.5 to 2.4 millimeters, and so it was most typically done by specialists.[7] They were paid according to the pound, and veneers were frequently sold by the pound, as is suggested by the common eighteenth-century German term for veneer, *Pfundholz*—literally "pound wood." The depiction of veneer-cutting on the Detroit chest suggests that the members of this cabinetmakers' guild were skilled enough to produce their own veneers, rather than having to depend on purchased *Pfundholz.*

The next step in veneering is depicted on the other end of the chest: namely, the veneer is planed flat to a thickness of about one millimeter (fig. 3). The side to be affixed to the wood substratum is then worked with a grooved plane, thereby producing a tooth so that the glue can better adhere. In a sixteenth-century woodcut from Nuremberg there is a comparable illustration of a man planing; on the floor beside him stands a similar three-legged glue pot.[8] Of all the cabinetmakers' tools, the plane and glue pot played a special role because they distinguished this group from other woodworkers. An eighteenth-century legal case between Dresden cabinetmakers and carpenters, for example, illustrated this position: whatever required veneering—hence planing and gluing—was the preserve of the cabinetmaking trade.[9]

The tools represented on the chest, specifically in the six cartouches on the lid and the four panels on the long sides, are all used by cabinetmakers. While some of them, such as measuring or cutting tools, are also common to allied trades, a few are unique to cabinetmaking: for example, the fret saw and shoulder knife. Each group of tools located in the six cartouches and the four main panels is associated with the name of a cabinetmaker. The differentiation of tools in each group as well as the name-tools association suggest that the chest was a collective possession of cabinetmakers—that it belonged to a guild. There is a tradition of cabinetmakers' guild chests into which the Detroit chest fits. While this tradition will be discussed later, at this point it is important to note that the identity of the group largely depends on a characteristic feature: the depiction in marquetry, intarsia, or carving of wood-

Figure 2. Side view of object in figure 1 with scene of veneer-cutting. Photograph © 1998 The Detroit Institute of Arts.

working tools, specifically those of cabinetmakers. All examples in Josef Greber's landmark article on cabinetmakers' and joiners' guild chests—with one exception—depict tools without names of individuals.[10] Thus the tools serve as emblems of the trade, a custom adopted for other guild objects as well, such as silver or pewter drinking vessels used in celebrations among guild members.[11] The practice undoubtedly derives from the guilds' coats of arms as a method of identification. According to tradition, the Holy Roman Emperor bestowed coats of arms on the guilds in the fourteenth century, and they were in general use by the following century.[12] Either tools or products of a particular craft were featured in the escutcheon. Also the convention of interlacing the tools in a unified design, which is adopted by the maker of the Detroit chest but is by no means universally employed on guild objects, may trace back to the coats of arms. The tools on the Detroit chest should be viewed then in two ways: as attributes of individual cabinetmakers and, in the tradition of cabinetmakers' guild chests, as emblems of that trade. The latter view will become apparent when we consider the functions of guild chests.

Figure 3. Side view of object in figure 1, with scene of planing. Photograph © 1998 The Detroit Institute of Arts.

In two of the chest's main panels there are pairs of rifles intertwined with cabinetmaking tools. This may seem out of place, but in several German cities, such as Dresden, Brunswick, Augsburg, and Munich, cabinetmakers and gunsmiths were banded together into a single guild.[13] The explanation behind this is that the stocks of rifles were frequently veneered. Thus, these artisans were versed in the most important cabinetmaking technique. In the Frankfurt cabinetmakers' guild, for instance, there were always specialists who could produce the rifle stocks into which craftsmen from the separate metalworking guild could install the firing mechanisms.[14]

Although depictions of workshop scenes are relatively rare on cabinet-makers' guild chests,[15] identifying marks such as dates and seals or inscriptions indicating place of origin are common owing to the representative nature of the guild object. Located on the Detroit chest's lid are two seals portraying eagles and together these determine the place of origin. One seal features a double-headed eagle, which is the Habsburg imperial coat of arms, in use in this context since the early fifteenth century.[16] It is typically crowned, either each head or jointly, and holds the symbols of sovereignty: orb, scepter, and sword. The free imperial cities—those owing their allegiance directly to the emperor—emphasized this relationship by featuring an eagle in their coats of arms. But rather than Frankfurt's coat of arms, a gold-crowned eagle set in a red escutcheon, the chancellery seal of that city appears on the chest. The chancellery seal depicts an eagle carrying an *F* on its breast with two gold cloverleaf shoots extending into the wings.[17] The use of the chancellery seal among Frankfurt guilds may have been customary, as is suggested by its use in the late-eighteenth-century *Meisterbuch* of the bakers and on the *Meistertafel* of the beer brewers (1723), both objects located in the Historisches Museum, Frankfurt am Main. The seal possibly had broader use since an important chronicle of the city, written in the early eighteenth century by Achilles August von Lersner, included it on its title page.[18]

The curved corner panels of the chest feature depictions of Jacob and Rachel from the Old Testament and Tobias and Sara from the Apocrypha.[19] I have been unable to discover evidence of a patronal relationship between any of these figures and cabinetmakers. What seems more likely is that they express guild ideology by conveying something meaningful to the cabinetmakers. For example, the guild chest of Hamburg cabinetmakers (1771) depicts two allegorical female figures identified in Latin as *Veritas* and *Species*. Greber states that the ideal being expressed in this instance is that the use of honest materials produces beautiful works.[20] In general, the use of sayings, placed on objects either in the form of inscriptions or represented by figures, is common to guild culture. Any interpretation of the four biblical figures depicted on the Detroit chest should draw on an understanding of eighteenth-century guild history and especially of the Frankfurt cabinetmakers' guild; therefore, a consideration of what these figures might signify will follow discussion of these topics.

In Sibylle Banke's 1954 dissertation on Frankfurt cabinets, the author compiled a list of Frankfurt cabinetmakers from the register of citizens. Many of the names on the Detroit chest are documented and, based on Banke's list, the following conclusions can be formulated. The four cabinetmakers indicated on the chest's large panels became citizens, and hence masters in the guild, before 1751; on the other hand, the six individuals listed on the chest's lid acquired this status after 1751, suggesting that they were still journeymen when the guild chest was made.[21] The cabinetmakers identified likely constituted the leadership, and the masters would have had authority over the journeymen. The significance of having both masters and journeymen represented on the chest will be considered at the end of this article.

An inscription incised around the inside of the sunken lock housing, which is located in the chest's lid, offers further information. The inscription reads: Simon Ackerholm von Christianstad in Schweden FiF [monogram] 29 May

1751.[22] Simon Ackerholm was presumably the maker of the chest and documentation on this cabinetmaker has been located in Frankfurt's city archives. Ackerholm was baptized 14 July 1715 in Kristianstad, located in the southernmost part of Sweden. He applied to the city council of Frankfurt for citizenship in 1747. After confirmation by the council, Ackerholm took the burgher oath on 19 January 1748, at which time the administrative information and fees were recorded in the register of citizens. Ackerholm was admitted as master cabinetmaker on 18 February 1748, only six days after he married Margaretha Eva Gerhard, widow of the deceased master cabinetmaker Anton Philipp Dietz. The short entry in the guild register *(Handwerkerbuch)* recording Ackerholm's admission into the cabinetmakers' guild also includes the year of his death, 1760.[23] As Banke's list of cabinetmakers indicates—which is supported by Gerald Lyman Soliday's demographic studies—a large number of immigrants were admitted into the Frankfurt cabinetmakers' guild.[24] Ackerholm exemplified the most common way for foreigners to gain entry into a guild, that is, by marrying a former master's widow or master's daughter, thereby inheriting a workshop. There are no other known works by Simon Ackerholm, nor is there information regarding his workshop. This is not unusual considering both the paucity of records regarding individual craftsmen and that German furniture is rarely signed or stamped by its maker—the Detroit chest being an anomaly.

Frankfurt am Main and Guild Life

Lersner's chronicle of Frankfurt indicates in its title, *Der weit-berühmten freyen Reichs- Wahl- und Handels-Stadt Franckfurt am Mayn Chronica . . .,* the aspects upon which the city's position within Europe was based, that is, as an imperial, electoral, and commercial city. These aspects were largely determined by the advantageous geographical position of Frankfurt. Occupying a central location in Europe at which the major east-west and north-south roads converged, Frankfurt also had access to waterways, namely, the Main and Rhine Rivers, the latter being approximately twenty miles west of the city. Together these factors supported Frankfurt's role as an important European trade center and as a leading player in imperial politics.

The status of Frankfurt am Main as free imperial city traces back to the palatine function of the area in the Carolingian period and its eventual acquisition as imperial property.[25] All rights and privileges enjoyed by the Frankfurt citizenry were granted by the Holy Roman Emperor, and this was ceremoniously renewed by an oath of fealty upon each emperor's accession. The legal status of a free imperial city meant that its citizens were directly subject to the emperor and independent of any territorial prince.

Frankfurt was distinguished among the imperial cities because it had served as the site of the emperor's election since 1356 and coronation since 1562. The city's central location was undoubtedly a factor in its selection as host to such momentous events. Also Frankfurt was accustomed to lodging a great number of visitors through its designation—established early in its history—as a place of synods, and court and imperial diets. And above all, the city was the site of the pan-European trade fairs held semiannually.[26]

It was Frankfurt's commercial activities that defined its reputation most. The trade fairs, originating in the Middle Ages, were held each spring and fall. In the eighteenth century only Leipzig's fairs eclipsed those of Frankfurt.[27] Visitors from all over Europe assembled at the fairs, lending Frankfurt a cosmopolitan character. Although anyone—city burgher, denizen, or visitor—could rent space and sell wares, the wholesale merchants dominated the fairs, especially those that conducted the commission business for which the city was renowned, handling the goods of foreign firms on commission. Wholesale commerce was not limited to fair time, but flourished year-round and the city's economic strength lay almost exclusively in its role as a marketplace for the exchange of products made elsewhere. Frankfurt was also a financial center with important banking interests. However, as innumerable descriptions and chronicles of the city proclaimed, commerce was the soul of the city.

Three elements shaped Frankfurt society and competed politically: mercantile, aristocratic, and artisanal. The balance achieved between these elements was tenuous and this can be better understood when we consider percentages in terms of population and their respective roles in society. Commerce, upon which Frankfurt's prosperity largely depended, occupied approximately 10 percent of the permanent population on a full-time basis. Unlike Hamburg or Bremen where citizens with commercial interests were actively represented in the local government, Frankfurt's city council, the main governing body exercising judicial, executive, and legislative prerogatives, was an oligarchy controlled by members of the urban aristocracy. During the seventeenth and early eighteenth centuries members of two aristocratic societies, Alt-Limpurg and Frauenstein, and to a lesser extent the Graduate Society, dominated the benches of the council by nominating successors from their ranks.[28] In this period the Alt-Limpurg and Frauenstein societies comprised approximately forty-five families—just under 1 percent of the population. The bulk of the citizenry was organized into guilds (i.e., craft associations—see below). The artisans, however, had negligible political power or influence within the community. Their representation in the council's third bench was, Soliday notes, only a formality.[29]

There were five groups under the city council's jurisdiction: burghers, denizens, Jews, transient aliens, and the villagers located outside the city walls.[30] The burghers had full citizenship and were the core of the community. Their rights were more far-reaching than those accorded to the other groups and were guaranteed by the emperor. These rights included: to own property in the city and outlying areas; to engage in any type of economic activity, though subject to regulation by the council; and to receive special considerations with taxes and tolls. Burghers accepted the obligations belonging to their privileged position and took an oath to be loyal to the emperor, obey the city government, pay taxes, and defend the city. It is important to note that citizenship was not only required of those serving in a public office, but mandatory before entering a guild.

The burghers were not, however, a unified group. The stratification of society rested upon many factors: profession, financial means, family tradition, social standing, and religion. While the economic standing, or class, of a citizen would become increasingly important in the eighteenth century, and would play a role in Frankfurt where the commercial element was so marked, social station continued to be determined more by the non-economic factor of traditional status.[31] The concept of status, as defined by the sociologist Roland Mousnier, reflected "the estime [*sic*], honor, or dignity attached by the society to social functions which have no particular connection with the production of material goods."[32] The stratification of Frankfurt society into a hierarchy of social groups, or orders *(Stände),* was defined in police ordinances, which also provided the legal termini for the groups. The last ordinance issued in Frankfurt in 1731 indicates that artisans belonged to the fourth order. Soliday regards the organizing principle of the hierarchy as the actual or potential participation in civic government.[33] This seems reasonable since the artisans' limited political power could account for a relatively low status within the community despite their large numbers and their vital role in sustaining the community with food, shelter, clothing, and luxury goods. Demographic and economic changes sometimes increased social mobility and prompted periodic revision of the police ordinances. The most significant intermixing occurred primarily in the first three strata, while the fourth and fifth orders were relatively static. In general, an artisan's position within Frankfurt society was fixed and intractable.

The last police ordinance revision followed an important chapter in Frankfurt's history, the constitutional conflict of 1705–32.[34] The legal battle between the Frankfurt citizenry and magistracy that lasted twenty-seven years mainly sought to restore the Citizens Agreement *(Bürgervertrag)* of 1612/13, a document of constitutional validity that placed checks on the city council, but had been disregarded by that body throughout the seventeenth century. The most significant charges that Frankfurt burghers reported to the investigating imperial commission in 1713/14 are described by Soliday: "Posts in the bureaucracy were awarded according to the highest bribes; financial records were neither clear nor accurate; both regular and extraordinary taxes were increased over the seventeenth century without any consultation with the citizenry. . . ."[35] The twelve imperial resolutions issued in 1725 and 1732 primarily fell on the side of the burghers in their grievances. Among the resolutions were limits on the representation of aristocrats in the council, thereby extending participation to other leading citizens, and reforms in the city's administration, including the formation of three consultative citizen bodies that oversaw elections, finance, and the bureaucracy. Additionally, application for citizenship was made more difficult for non-Lutherans, who were permitted to stay in the city as resident aliens. Frankfurt was predominantly Lutheran, although many members of its merchant class were Calvinists; there were Catholic and Jewish populations as well, the latter being segregated from the Christian communities.[36]

Although the artisans had formed a broad base of opposition to the aristocratic government, the leadership, composed of burgher militia and merchants, made the largest gains as a result of the conflict. The reasons for this are found in the troubled history of Frankfurt's guilds. Beginning in the last quarter of the fourteenth century several unsuccessful attempts by the guilds to break the patricians' firm control of civic government progressively diminished the guilds' autonomy. The process was completed in 1616 when, following an uprising (the Fettmilch rebellion) led by a group of artisans, a decree was issued abolishing Frankfurt's thirty-eight guilds. This move was supported by the imperial government which shared the council's view of Frankfurt craftsmen as agents of insurrection. The trades were reorganized in 1617–31 into thirty-four craft associations *(Handwerke),* over which the council exercised complete control.[37] These associations possessed none of the powers of guilds: for example, they could neither make nor enforce regulations on their own, correspond freely with local trade groups or foreign guilds, or hold unapproved meetings.[38] Furthermore, members of the city council were assigned to the various craft associations in order to report on their business.

Why then were the craft associations formed? As Soliday explains, they were a way to organize a large part of the population socially and economically.[39] The rights that the council granted in 1617–31 *(Gewerberechte)* had preserved traditional practices concerning regulation of production and occupational training, and maintaining a monopoly in the local retail market. The *Gewerberechte* sought not to sweep away the past and to establish a radically new system, but endeavored to modify a preexisting one. In the case of the craft associations, the modification consisted of a loss in autonomy and a subjugation to the council's authority. A concrete example of the transformation from guild to craft association is found in the character of leadership. Before 1616 the position of guild supervisor was an elected one among guild members. In the craft associations the members no longer had the right to choose their leaders directly. Only after 1726, as an outcome of the constitutional conflict, was involvement permitted in that the guild members could nominate the candidates that were ultimately appointed by the council.[40] A leader of a craft association had the title *Geschworen*, reflecting his allegiance to the council: he was sworn to it. Through these sworn leaders of the craft associations, the council was kept informed of the groups' activities. This practice—indeed the whole structure and workings of the craft associations—endured through the eighteenth century and into the nineteenth. (The constitution governing the craft associations in Frankfurt lasted until 1864.) As leaders and official spokesmen of the cabinetmakers' craft association, the names of the sworn masters appropriately are included on the Detroit chest and occupy a place of prominence: the four large panels of the long sides. The title is differentiated in that two members are *alter Geschworen* and two *junger Geschworen* (elder and younger sworn master, respectively), indicating a hierarchy within the leadership of the craft association.[41]

The collective sense of the guilds persisted in the craft association: this was realized in policies which tried to insure that all masters had equal access to raw materials and labor supply, and the same opportunity to exploit the market. Craft association products were sold chiefly in retail shops, but also at the local market held twice weekly and at the trade fairs, an occasion when price regulations lapsed and a true competitive market emerged. The closed economic system of the craft association which reigned for the greater part of the year, however, depended on strict regulation of a number of factors: prices, production, and most important for the perpetuation of the craft, the number and quality of admissions. Unlike the elasticity of an open market, a slight increase in a trade's numbers in relation to an even demand within the community could threaten the ability of all members to make a decent livelihood *(Nahrung)*.

The concept of *Nahrung* encompassed not only the idea of a livable wage, but considered the manner in which it was earned—specifically, in adherence to a moral code. The potency and intractability of this code were considerable. The following will illustrate this. Frequently the city councils of the free imperial cities would consult one another when settling disputes involving guild matters, and their responses would reflect customs and attitudes held by that guild community. In appropriate cases the guild leadership would be asked to comment and such was the situation in 1708 when the mayor and city council of Fulda inquired whether a cabinetmaker in Frankfurt could be admitted to the guild as master if he married a woman who was born illegitimately, even if the imperial count palatine had newly pronounced her legitimacy. The leadership of the Frankfurt cabinetmakers' craft association answered that no such man could become a master.[42]

Occupational training in the craft association in the eighteenth century continued to be prescribed by the guild system. While the following discussion has the Frankfurt craftsman as its focus, it should be noted that the rules governing the three phases of a craftsman's life—apprenticeship, journeymanship, and mastership—ran similarly throughout the Holy Roman Empire. Regional differences were primarily expressed in terms of duration, fees, or test requirements. The preconditions for a young man wishing to enter a trade as an apprentice were proof of legitimate birth, well-respected sponsors, and a fee. The apprentice typically was required to spend three years under a single master, at the end of which time he was released *(Lossprechung)*. He became a journeyman after participating in an initiation ceremony of the fraternal association of journeymen for that particular trade.[43]

The journeyman's existence was marked by the *Wanderschaft,* the years of travel he was expected to undertake in order to acquire further training and experience by working with various masters. Completion of a six-year *Wanderschaft* was usual for Frankfurt craftsmen. A journeyman who trained elsewhere but wished to work in Frankfurt registered his papers with the city council, whereupon a craft supervisor placed him with a master. The journeyman lodged at a common house or inn and received a small weekly wage.

The goal of those learning a trade was to become a master. As an employer, subordinated only to the regulations of his craft association and the city council, the Frankfurt master led a settled life with enviable rights. Generally a master was limited to three workers: two journeymen and one apprentice. However, first a number of conditions had to be met in order to acquire mastership. In addition to fulfilling the required periods of apprenticeship and *Wanderschaft,* Frankfurt craftsmen were to have at least three years' experience in the city itself *(Mutzeit)*. A candidate demonstrated proficiency by producing a test piece of furniture *(Meisterstück)*. Masters' sons were favored—most conspicuously in the reduction of guild admission fees. The reasoning behind this preferential treatment was that the candidate's early familiarity with the trade contributed to the expected proficiency and, most important, that the inheritance of his father's business would not increase the number of workshops, yet would preserve the tradition of that shop.[44] As previously noted, the number of masters in a trade was an important concern: some groups even had limits on numbers. The difficulty of becoming a master in Frankfurt increased after 1616 because of the demographic and economic developments in that city. Methods of deterrence other than limiting the number of admissions per year were: a waiting period before engaging a new apprentice, lengthening the *Mutzeit,* increasing the cost of producing the test piece, and heightened standards of approval.[45]

Functions of Guild Chests

The iconography of the Detroit chest was designed to communicate the identity of its collective owner. The need for such explicitness, along with the use of expensive materials and the high level of craftmanship exhibited in this outstanding piece of rococo furniture, can be understood when we consider the functions of the guild chest. The functions of chests were similar in the various guilds throughout the Holy Roman Empire and the following discussion will largely remain generic; however, it should be noted that there were place-specific customs regarding the chest.

On a rudimentary level the guild chest was a container. It held all things necessary for the guild official(s) to execute the office and those objects deemed valuable by the guild: the seal, the register of masters, privileges, charters, or other legal documents. The imperial ordinance of 1731 *(Reichsabschied)* instituted the *Kundschaft,* an identification paper that a journeyman was required to carry. The *Kundschaft* was kept in the guild chest as long as the itinerant worked in a particular location. In many cities the chest also contained the original plan of the *Meisterstück,* the test piece which each candidate for mastership had to submit to prove proficiency in the trade.[46] The contents of the chest included a sacred object of the guild, a vessel known as the *Willkomm.* In the welcoming ceremony meant to honor new masters or journeymen, this vessel was filled with wine and passed around to guild members.[47] A cashbox was also kept in the chest, and a guild member was elected to administer the finances of the community.[48] The contents of the chest show a diversity, reflecting social and economic aspects of the group.

The words most widely used in German to designate a guild chest are *Zunftlade* and *Handwerkslade,* or, favored among guild members, *Lade.* The entry for *Lade* in the eighteenth-century encyclopedia published by Johann Heinrich Zedler, *Grosses vollständiges Universal-Lexicon . . . ,* specifies the primary usage: as a receptacle containing documents and valuables of the guild.[49] However there is another usage that is evident in guild records and is also noted in the Grimms' *Deutsches Wörterbuch:* the assembly of the guild and the guild itself is also termed *Lade.*[50] Just as the *Lade* as receptacle housed valuables that defined and established the identity of the guild community, the *Lade* as guild contained members whose status within the larger urban community depended on its existence and perpetuation.

The setting for the most important function of the chest was the plenary meeting of guild members at which legislative, executive, and judicial matters were conducted. A frequent term for such an assembly was *Morgensprache,* although there were many others; for example, in Frankfurt *Gebot* was used.[51] A description of this meeting is related in guild records. The chest was placed on a table between two burning candles and the members would seat themselves around the table according to a ranking system. A person from among the guild officials was designated to preside over the meeting. He delivered a speech that cited sanctioned behavior and prepared the assembly for what was about to transpire. He then opened the chest situated before him. This action signaled the start of the proceedings, and likewise only after closing the chest was the plenary meeting at an end. A painted scene on the underside of a purse-makers' guild chest lid from Brunswick illustrates a meeting with the open chest. The power of the open chest was considerable: it legitimized and made binding the decisions issuing from the proceedings. Those who violated the rules of conduct were punished more harshly than if the infraction occurred before the closed chest.[52] Infractions of guild rules were usually punishable by fines, either in money, wine, or beer. The sanctity of the chest is suggested by an exhortation delivered by the presider *(Ladengeselle)* at the monthly assembly of the Nuremberg journeyman tailors at the end of the eighteenth century. The speech conveyed prohibitions both sensible and subtle: before the open chest it was forbidden to swear, lie, carry an unsheathed weapon, gaze out of the window, walk to and fro in the room, and cross hands or feet over one another.[53]

In addition to the *Morgensprache,* there were other gatherings which were more social in nature, yet could still address the business of the guild. These meetings—as well as certain rites of passage such as the granting of journeyman status upon completion of an apprenticeship—also took place in front of the open chest, making each proceeding an official affair.[54] In this same ceremonial context it is possible that the guild chest of the Frankfurt cabinetmakers was seen by colleagues from other cities. Frankfurt historian Franz Lerner states that many historical documents discuss the chest of the Frankfurt cabinetmakers as the primary one *(Hauptlade)* of the German cabinetmakers, but no official municipal document confirms this (which is not surprising since the Frankfurt city council forbade its craft associations from participating in any extraterritorial federations). At the semiannual fairs, which lasted three weeks, cabinetmakers from all over the empire came to sell their wares, and Lerner convincingly conjectures that those visitors met with local cabinetmakers not only to socialize, but at times to discuss weighty matters with formality before the open chest—such as journeymen's wages or strategies to combat illicit competition.[55]

The guild chest was a communal possession and typically could not be opened by one person. Most guild chests either had many locks or a lock serviced by many keys. The latter is the case with the Detroit chest: four keys must be used to open the lock; only two of the keys are extant. It seems likely that the four master cabinetmakers, whose names are indicated on the main panels, held the four keys necessary to open the chest.[56] Many surviving guild chests exhibit a way of opening that allowed all participants of the guild meeting an equal and unchanging view of the object: by attaching two or four metal rods to the underside of the lid, and mounting corresponding guides for them within the chest, the entire lid could be lifted levelly upward. Small springs served to secure the lid at the desired height. The Detroit chest uses this method of opening.

Another function of the guild chest was a social one, whereby city residents could view the object. The chest was carried by guild journeymen in a procession, part of a festival celebration. In Frankfurt the most significant festival was Shrove Tuesday, signifying the coming of spring. While there were other ceremonial processions of the guilds—for instance, celebrating the occasion of moving into new quarters—all took the general form established by the Shrove Tuesday procession.[57] In military order the members of the guild, some bearing arms or wooden replicas of trade tools, others masquerading as stock characters such as wild men, harlequins, or farmers, wound their way through the city streets accompanied by musicians. In the wake of these characters the closed guild chest was carried and attendants with drawn swords or shouldered halberds served as escorts.[58] The sanctity of the object demanded this protection; this is made clear by a written account of the journeyman cabinetmakers' procession in Lübeck in 1768. The account includes the verbal exchange between the carriers of the guild chest and the armed attendants.

> *The two carriers spoke:*
>   Both of us carry a full load!
>   Whoever loathes this cherished chest,
>   He is not worth naming,
>   And should burn for thirst this very day.
> *Thereupon the four armed attendants replied:*
>   Rightly so, the precious chest is worth
>   as much as the cherished shield.
>   Indeed, it is worth all honor,
>   Because the authorities themselves bestowed it.
>   When this chest stands open,
>   No cabinetmaker commits a mistake.
>   In order to stick to it securely,
>   Goods, blood and life are given.[59]

It should be noted that Frankfurt craft associations needed the permission of the city council to hold such an event and this was only periodically granted.

The earliest mention of a cabinetmakers' festival procession was in 1611, although the wording of the request to the council suggests that it was an old custom.[60] Surviving municipal records document processions of the cabinetmakers in 1659, 1668, 1721, and 1744.[61] Whether less ambitious processions that did not require the permission of the council took place—ones that also featured the guild chest as part of the train—is open to question. (There is no indication in guild records as to why the processions ceased.)

The last extant document to record a cabinetmakers' procession in Frankfurt, that of 1744, specifies the occasion for the festivities: the journeyman cabinetmakers made a new chest and sign, the latter to hang outside the inn where they resided. Since the processions were a custom of the journeymen and not the masters, then this particular function does not apply to the Detroit chest, which was the possession of the master cabinetmakers. This is an assumption based on the following factors: the journeyman cabinetmakers had produced their own chest seven years before the Detroit chest; the presumed maker of the 1751 chest was a master cabinetmaker rather than a journeyman cabinetmaker; and the names of the craft association leaders of the master cabinetmakers are given prominence on the chest. (See concluding section for speculation as to why journeymen's names were included on the chest.) However it is important to outline all functions of guild chests in order to appreciate the resonance the object had for the guild community.

The sanctity of the chest expressed in the verses above, and the reverence felt for it, suggested by the portrayal of the *Morgensprache,* undoubtedly derive from the chest contents which embody the law of the guild. Given these features, the kinship between the guild chest and the Ark of the Covenant is apparent, and has already been described in these terms by Mack Walker. But while Walker recognizes that the guild chest was "a kind of ark of the guild covenant symbolizing the guild's corporate authority and autonomy," he does not consider if guild members of the eighteenth century might have viewed their chest in this way.[62]

The guilds represented a specific group in society and justified their position by tracing their origin to the biblical past. Examples of some Old Testament progenitors of trades are Adam for cartwrights, Abimelech for beer brewers, and Noah for cabinetmakers. These biblical figures were also consciously evoked by the guilds: the ark of Noah, for example, is depicted on the flag of the cabinetmakers in Frankfurt.[63] Such biblical associations were likewise enacted in guild customs in which the group's honorable, divinely ordained position was proclaimed. An account of the procession of Frankfurt butchers in 1746 illustrates this. At the head of the procession marched the masters' sons, who carried twelve illustrated placards. The inscriptions accompanying the pictures gave an account of the butchers' trade as reflected in biblical history.[64] It was fitting that the masters' sons actively participated since an important tenet of the guild system was that members were born into it. The right and compulsion to pursue the father's craft were often firm. However this closed structure defined by inheritance ensured the future of the trade in general, and the city or village guild in particular. Additionally, in the sermon *(Hobelpredigt)* of the initiation rite of a journeyman cabinetmaker the activities of the cabinetmakers in biblical times were stressed. For example, they were present at the first city built, Babylon, according to one of the sermons.[65] Given this background, it does not seem improbable that the guild community made similar associations with regard to their chest. The guild chest could have been perceived, in a general or figurative sense, as the covenant from God, who had created the trades and set them into the world order.

Form and Development of Cabinetmakers' Guild Chests

Woodworkers—which included carpenters, joiners, and cabinetmakers—were the producers of most guild chests.[66] The exceptions were tin- and locksmiths, who would make their own chests. Cabinetmakers would enlist metalworkers for hardware, and at times sculptors, turners, and painters for ornamentation.[67] Unlike the other pieces of furniture that cabinetmakers made, their guild chest was not subject to the dictates of a customer. By being both creators and users of the guild object, the cabinetmakers had the opportunity to demonstrate the skills of their craft in an unrestricted way. Thus the cabinetmakers' guild chest should not be viewed as an immutable monument to the trade, but rather as a dynamic, evolving expression of the crafting specific to that trade. Proof of the chest's representative character is demonstrated by a guild's readiness to update it by producing a replacement which conformed to the current style.[68]

The earliest extant German cabinetmakers' guild chest comes from Brunswick and is dated 1566. Greber suggests that the tendency to replace the guild chest because of stylistic changes explains nonsurvival of earlier examples (rather than assuming that the chest had not yet, or only to a limited extent, come into use).[69] Chests from other guilds surviving from the late Gothic period, such as the chest of the Bremen fishermen (ca. 1470), confirm the early existence of such objects and support Greber's reasoning, although no conclusions can be drawn concerning extent of use.

Cabinetmakers, as a group distinct from other woodworkers, are already mentioned in thirteenth-century documents.[70] In the fourteenth century, reports of woodworkers forming into guild associations increased, as did evidence that they separated into individual branches, disengaging from the parent group of carpenters. This development intensified in the fifteenth century with fundamental changes in furniture production that included rediscovery of the water-driven saw mill, capable of producing thinner boards, and a new mode of construction, frame and panel, which yielded lighter pieces. Both changes were prompted by an emergent burgher class that desired fine furniture. For cabinetmakers these developments meant liberation from their previous specialist trade, which utilized the techniques of veneering and intarsia in the production of mainly small objects. Instead they became one of the major producers of large-scale furniture. This occurred because cabinetmakers possessed the required expertise in joinery, and a refinement of planing techniques made veneering on larger objects feasible.

The historical course of Frankfurt's cabinetmakers somewhat reflects these general trends. Earlier called *Kistener* and banded with the locksmiths in the smiths' guild, the cabinetmakers of Frankfurt received their own constitution from the city council on 9 January 1487.[71] Even after abolishment of the guilds in 1616 and establishment of craft associations, the cabinetmakers retained their autonomy in relation to other woodworking groups.

Guild chests, though considerably smaller in size than chests in domestic use, are comparable in their horizontal tripartite structure of socle, middle portion, and lid. Both chest types were portable and so equipped with handles. Portability was required of the guild chest because of its role in meetings and festival processions. In general, the socle of guild chests tended to be more pronounced than those of their domestic counterparts, occupying one-third to one-half of the overall height and given further prominence by broken or stepped moldings.

While some guild chests open similarly to domestic chests, that is, to one side of the case with a flat, hinged lid, many display an alternate method, one already noted in the previous discussion of the guild meeting: by attaching metal rods to the lid and corresponding guides within the chest so that the lid could be lifted levelly upward. The adoption of the hip roof for the lid is frequently found in connection with this method of opening. Guild chests with hip roof lids were the most favored of the two types. There were most likely several reasons for its popularity. Aesthetically, the elevated form of the lid was a more effective cap to the decorative structure of the chest, and any seals or emblems placed on the sloping sides of the roof would be more visible.

Cabinetmakers favored secret compartments and concealed locks in the design of their guild chests; such features demonstrated refinement of their craft. In early examples the keyholes are exposed, but then concealment of them was desired and achieved by overlaying moveable decorative architectural elements, such as cartouches or pilasters.[72] From the beginning, the hip roof lid accommodated this inclination for mystery particularly well since it typically contained a sunken box where the lock mechanism was located. Usually a small sliding or removable flat cover concealed the lock housing. With this type, the act of inexplicably opening the chest could excite wonder.

Because guild chests were representative of their makers' skill and knowledge about current fashion, they were subject to the same stylistic developments as all types of case furniture. The regional diversity in furniture-making in Germany determined variations within a historical style. The main lincs of stylistic development from the late sixteenth century, the period of the first extant cabinetmakers' guild chest, to the mid-eighteenth century, the period of the Detroit chest, will be outlined below.

In the Renaissance period architectural forms dominated the guild chest to such an extent that it became, in effect, pure wooden architecture.[73] The dissemination of the Renaissance style in sixteenth-century Germany was affected by a device hitherto unknown on a large scale: printed patterns. Though the printed patterns were mainly produced for architects, they became equally binding for cabinetmakers.[74] The result was that the sides of the guild chest were conceived of as façades, and a gamut of architectural motifs was applied to the chest. The Renaissance style required cabinetmakers to collaborate closely with other woodworkers, especially carvers and turners. Only when surfaces were free to receive the techniques of veneering, intarsia, or marquetry did cabinetmakers utilize methods unique to their trade. However, these techniques often competed unsuccessfully with an architectural conception of furniture, in which customary architectural elements fashioned in wood by sculptors and turners were attached to the construction and came to dominate the form.

By the second half of the seventeenth century the façade style was no longer popular. The cabinetmakers' skills were now clearly displayed. Panels of the chest were veneered and no longer covered by architectural forms, but rather they were often accentuated by moldings. The role of the molding in the baroque era was redefined: in addition to delineating the form and articulating surfaces, the differentiation and accumulation of moldings introduced a new form of expression. The shape of moldings also underwent a change: based on an elliptical instead of a spherical unit, moldings acquired a sinuous yet dynamic character.

The cultural underpinnings for developments in baroque furniture-making were a deeper secularization and a refinement in social stratification that led to increasingly obvious attempts to express a more splendid lifestyle. In the eighteenth century this would become more pronounced. The eighteenth century, encompassing late baroque, rococo, and neoclassical styles, is recognized as the period in which cabinetmaking reached its apex. Not only was the furniture produced during this time incomparably elegant and artful, but cabinetmaking attained its highest technical and artistic level.

With the rococo style, curving extends not only to the moldings, but also to the body of the chest. Also typical of the style is the expanse of surface that is plain in terms of sculptural ornament, but that emphasizes veneering and marquetry. There is attention to a design that unifies all sides and the elevation as well as to technical skill in the design's execution. The brief analysis of the Detroit chest that follows will illustrate more concretely the hallmarks of the rococo style.

Most likely the immediate predecessor to the Detroit chest is located in the Historisches Museum in Frankfurt am Main (fig. 4). This chest of the city's craft association of master cabinetmakers is dated 1708. Although no documentary evidence exists explaining why the 1751 chest was produced, presumably it was made in order to stylistically update the guild object. A comparison between the two chests is one between the late baroque and rococo styles. The artistic conception of the earlier chest is inclined toward plasticity—found in the swelling of the socle, the deep concavities and convexities of the lid, the prominence of the orders, and the carving of the ivory panels. All are knitted into a heavy, dramatic unity. The relatively austere, planar quality of the later chest is relieved by the spare but selective use of sculptural ornament in the form of ormolu capitals and *rocaille* feet. Severity in the ordering of surfaces is lessened by the interplay between curved and straight forms, flat and plastic areas, and by the colorfulness of materials employed in the decorative marquetry. The underlying form of both chests is similar and there are some materials common to both, walnut and ivory. The chests' identical division of the long sides into two large fields is predetermined by a program of representation: the names of the four sworn masters, the leaders of the craft association, are indicated in these panels.

The materials and ornament of the Detroit chest mark it as a rococo piece. In the first decades of the rococo style in Germany (1730s, 1740s) there was a stronger blending of various materials and techniques than in the previous age, and by midcentury marquetry became more intricate and played a more dominant role.[75] The Detroit chest follows these trends: not only does marquetry cover the entire piece, but there is a richness and variety of materials employed: ivory, brass, tin, mother-of-pearl, rosewood, yew, and walnut. Some of these materials are used in the decorative program of the chest whose main features, the floral motifs and *rocaille,* characterize the rococo style. Other significant traits of this refined style that the Detroit chest exhibits is the curving of surfaces—in the corners of the chest as well as the moldings—and the lightness with which the piece of furniture stands.

Figure 4. Guild chest of Frankfurt am Main cabinetmakers (joiners), 1708. Photograph by Dieter Skala, reproduced with permission of the Historisches Museum Frankfurt am Main.

The Frankfurt Cabinetmaking Tradition

The guild chests of 1708 and 1751 belong to the tradition of the Frankfurt *Wellenschrank*. This type, most popular as a cabinet or wardrobe, likely originated in the late seventeenth century, although a fixed date is unknown. *Wellen* refers to the waves of wood, that is, multiple moldings set side by side that cover almost the entire surface. The resulting concavities and convexities vary in width, height, and depth so that, together with light reflecting on the highly-polished veneer, a liveliness of surface is produced.[76] While the design of both guild chests makes limited use of *Wellen,* the basic form is related to this common Frankfurt wardrobe.

Much activity of the cabinetmakers' craft association was devoted to the production of these splendid wardrobes, which only upper-class merchants and lesser nobility could afford.[77] In Sibylle Banke's dissertation researching the type, the author documents that Frankfurt cabinetmakers annually exported these pieces as far as Holland.[78] The high point of popularity for the

Wellenschrank, or *Frankfurter Schrank* as it was also called, was the first quarter of the eighteenth century, though it continued to be produced throughout the century and was subject to stylistic changes. An example from 1763 produced in part by Caspar Arzt exhibits a close resemblance to the Detroit chest: the three pilasters show the same dividers at the bottom third of the shaft; the marquetry on the pilasters features the hanging fruit motif; and unification of the socle, body, and cornice/lid is achieved by broken moldings.[79]

All master cabinetmakers in Frankfurt had to be able to produce this type of cabinet since it had been the obligatory test piece for entrance into the craft association since 1686, a circumstance which lasted until 1788.[80] However, many of the approximately 130 master-led workshops—from 1729 to the end of the century a fairly constant number was maintained[81]—were not involved in producing these costly pieces on a daily basis, for they had to provide for the entire community's woodworking needs (and much of this did not utilize the cabinetmaking technique of veneering). This included a variety of wares for all classes of society: window frames and interior paneling, cases for organs and clocks, furniture of all types and grades—in short, everything needed for life from cradle to coffin (items which the cabinetmakers also made).[82] For elderly masters and widows continuing the workshops of their deceased husbands, livelihood might consist mainly of repair work. In 1762 the city government of Frankfurt undertook a census for fire duty. Since journeymen from all trades were a major part of the fire patrol, a listing of such journeymen working in the city was undertaken. This valuable document reveals the division of the 122 journeyman cabinetmakers among the masters in the city. Approximately one-quarter of the masters had the limit of two journeymen, while almost equal numbers of the remaining masters had either one journeyman, or none assisting them in their trade.[83]

Conclusion

A more intriguing difference between the 1708 and the 1751 guild chests exists. The earlier cabinetmakers' guild chest located in Frankfurt's historical museum indicates four masters, the sworn leaders of the craft association, but no journeymen, such as those featured on the Detroit chest dated 1751. In the concluding section I will address this puzzle by considering what could be meant by the inclusion of journeymen's names on the later chest.

Journeymen of a particular trade formed an extraterritorial association, a brotherhood, which functioned as an important social net for the members with their itinerant lifestyle. For example, when a journeyman fell ill and needed financial assistance, or when he died and needed a Christian burial, it was his fellow journeymen who stepped in. Simultaneously, journeymen working in a particular locale would meet, not only socially, but to discuss the matters that affected them as they worked within a city's guild. For this a guild chest was desired to legitimize the proceedings. Therefore journeymen often had their own guild chest, separate from the guild chest of the masters. Surviving from Lübeck, Brunswick, Breslau, and other cities are guild chests from both groups which illustrate this.[84] Additionally, an important treatise on journeymen, anonymously written and published in a Leipzig journal in 1751/52, describes their meetings with such a chest. Often a guild master sat in on these meetings and at times even possessed one of the keys which opened the journeymen's chest.[85]

It is clear from the previous discussion of the festival procession that the Frankfurt journeyman cabinetmakers possessed their own chest *(Gesellenlade),* since the 1744 procession marked the occasion of them producing a new one. The journeymen's ownership of a chest lasted throughout the century, as is evidenced by a petition dated February 1801 from the craft association leaders to temporarily do away with the *Gesellenlade* and with the election of its journeyman caretaker.[86] If the master and journeyman cabinetmakers remained distinct groups in that they possessed their own guild chests, then citing six journeymen by name on the masters' chest is a provocative statement. What could the motive be? In the following section I will speculate on the inclusion of the journeymen's names.

Tensions grew between masters and journeymen in the eighteenth century, the period when the guild system began to break down. One of the main causes was the frequent economic crises, exacerbated by an increase in population, which prompted the masters to restrict admission to their ranks in order to preserve *Nahrung* of all guild members. The heart of these crises was agrarian. Unlike England, Germany did not experience significant social or technological advances in food production during the century. In years of a bad harvest, food which required the craftsman to spend one-third to one-half of his income in good times, could only be obtained for double that amount. Financial and trade crises typically followed agrarian troubles. During these periods the craftsman who produced dispensable items, such as furniture, experienced a sharp decrease in demand for his wares, while simultaneously faced rising costs. Stürmer has charted the complex forces that had short- and long-term effects on the fortunes of the craftsman. They include: fluctuations of buying power in the upper and middle classes, variable foreign trade, the volume and circulation of currency, speculation, war, the growth of population, land development, creation of credit, agrarian modernization, and the changing structure and methods of manufacturing enterprises.[87]

Another important factor creating economic hardship for the craftsman was the inability or unwillingness of the local authorities to prevent unfair competition, leaving nonguild members free to pursue the trade and illegal imports to pass unchecked through the city gates (foreign products were only supposed to be allowed during fair time). Regarding the first threat, the Frankfurt city council sometimes permitted such nonguild artisans to practice the craft under the condition that no servants, journeymen, or apprentices be used to help. To compound the problem, there were illegitimate practitioners of the trade—those artisans whose economic activity no group, guild or council, sanctioned. Another aspect of competition involved two large building commissions of the 1720s and 1730s in Frankfurt, namely the palaces of the German Order and the imperial postmaster Thurn and Taxis. Since both were not subject to the sovereignty of Frankfurt, the city council could not require them to solely use local craftsmen to build and outfit these structures. A team of foreign cabinetmakers and their accompanying journeymen arrived in the city to work on these commissions. The Frankfurt cabinetmakers complained that they did not stop there, but made furniture for the local population.[88] Regarding the danger of illegal imports, it must have been so prevalent that it prompted the cabinetmakers' craft association to periodically request that the city council reissue the ban that was part of the 1712 amendment to their constitution, specifically in 1718, 1723, 1741, 1749, 1771, and 1787.[89]

The reaction resulting from dealing with unfair competition was to restrict entrance to the craft association. This, together with the economic crises under which all suffered, put the journeymen at special risk of falling into poverty. There were strikes and general unrest among journeymen, as they believed the masters were blocking their only opportunity to achieve some level of security by attaining mastership. Notwithstanding some periodic years of poor harvests, Stürmer calls the period from circa 1730 to the start of the Seven Years' War, in 1756, the golden decades.[90] Despite this bright picture in terms of standard of living, Lerner's study of the Frankfurt cabinetmakers' craft association shows that conflicts between journeymen and masters increased as the century wore on. For example, in 1746 the journeyman cabinetmakers filed a lengthy written complaint against the leadership of the masters. The charges included interference in the election of the *Irtengeselle,* the journeyman who managed the meetings of the group, and that the leadership had the impudence *("erfrechen")* to bring matters directly to the city council that could have been settled before the chest.[91] Around midcentury— the period in which the Detroit chest was made—numerous petitions from Frankfurt journeymen to the city council made it necessary for the authorities to become more involved in the affairs of this group.[92] There does not seem to have been any event as dramatic as that which took place in Hamburg, when in 1750 difficulties between the journeyman and master cabinetmakers erupted into a strike of 135 journeymen and the ensuing imprisonment of its leaders. The Frankfurt citizenry was aware of this event since both the Hamburg city council and the journeyman cabinetmakers sent out statements to the major cities throughout the empire regarding their positions.[93] One purpose of the journeymen's broadcast was to prevent cabinetmakers from traveling there, for proximity was enough to taint the individual according to the strict code of guild ethics. I venture that the inclusion of journeymen's names on the Detroit chest is related to a troubled social and political relationship between masters and journeymen in this period. I believe the motive behind this listing was to revitalize the solidarity that journeymen and masters within one craft association should feel and manifest. Whether this was prompted by general strife, a specific incident recorded but not yet discovered, or an effort to avert difficulties such as those in Hamburg, remains open to conjecture.

The significance of including the names of the journeymen on the guild chest of the master cabinetmakers may be linked to the enigmatic figures—Jacob, Rachel, Tobias, Sara—depicted on the four corners of the chest. The narratives of these biblical characters reveal certain personal qualities that enabled Jacob to marry Rachel and Tobias to wed Sara. Jacob undertook seven years of labor in order to obtain the right to marry Rachel, and this was lengthened to an additional seven years after his father-in-law tricked him on his wedding night into lying with Rachel's older sister, Laban. (Jacob was allowed to take Rachel as his second wife at the beginning of his second term of labor.) Perseverance and patience are the traits that Jacob exhibits in this tale. Tobias' quest for Sara was less arduous, but nonetheless brave since the demon Asmodeus was intent on killing any new bridegroom of Sara's, and seven men had already fallen victim to the sorcery. However with the help of the archangel Raphael, disguised as Azariah, Tobias was able to vanquish the demon and save Sara from her despair (she was on the verge of suicide) as well as happily wed her. It is the willingness with which Tobias obeys Azariah's command that enables him to succeed. One could well imagine the master cabinetmakers exhorting the journeymen to obey the rules set forth in the guild constitution and to be patient when enduring the long years required to become a master, which in the eighteenth century seemed to become longer still. Sara and Rachel can be viewed then as the symbols of the mastership, seemingly elusive but attainable if the candidate demonstrates patience and obedience, as Jacob and Tobias readily did.

The guild chest of the Frankfurt cabinetmakers that is located in the collections of the Detroit Institute of Arts is an outstanding example of material culture. The iconography of the chest not only identifies the object, but reveals information about its users, for example, that the cabinetmakers in Frankfurt possessed the skill to produce their own veneers. The piece of furniture's special role in guild life makes it ideal for studying native cabinetmaking traditions. On another level the chest, through listing the names of both journeyman and master cabinetmakers, poses questions regarding the relationship between these two groups.

Research on the guild chest details the practical and ritualistic role the object played in guild life. The functions of the guild chest, an extraordinary artifact, were many. As a community possession, it held everything necessary for the identity and perpetuation of the guild. At assemblies, especially the *Morgensprache,* it legitimized all business of the community and thereby commanded great respect. One may even speak of an aura of sanctity with the guild chest, especially with a possible connection to the Ark of the Covenant. Above all, the chest was a potent symbol of the guild at a time when the role of the guild was clearly under threat.

NOTES

I would like to thank Professors Emeriti Nathan Whitman and Marvin Eisenberg for their comments on an earlier version of this paper. I extend my special thanks to Nancy Pear for editorial assistance and to Bonita Fike, Associate Curator of Twentieth-Century Art, Detroit Institute of Arts, who introduced me to this object and lent enthusiastic support throughout the research process. I would like to acknowledge the anonymous readers of this paper for their corrections and suggestions.

1. Goethe to Zelter, Weimar, 6 June 1825, *Letters from Goethe,* trans. M. von Herzfeld and C. A. M. Sym (New York: Thomas Nelson & Sons, 1957), no. 512. From the German: "Laß uns soviel als möglich an der Gesinnung halten in der wir herankamen, wir werden, mit vielleicht noch wenigen, die Letzten sein einer Epoche die sobald nicht wiederkehrt." *Goethes Briefe,* ed. Karl Robert Mandelkow, vol. 4 (Hamburg: Christian Wegner Verlag, 1967), no. 1300.

2. Goethe to Zelter, no. 512. From the German: ". . . Reichtum und Schnelligkeit ist was die Welt bewundert und wornach jeder strebt. . . ." *Goethes Briefe,* no. 1300.

3. I am indebted to Michael Stürmer's excellent study for the social and economic background to the German guild system in the eighteenth century: *Handwerk und höfische Kultur: Europäische Möbelkunst im 18. Jahrhundert* (Munich: C. H. Beck Verlag, 1982). Also useful is a compilation of eighteenth-century literature on guilds with accompanying essays by Stürmer: *Herbst des Alten Handwerks: Quellen zur Sozialgeschichte des 18. Jahrhunderts* (Munich: Deutscher Taschenbuch Verlag, 1979). Both books include comparative studies with England and France so that German developments are put into perspective.

4. For a pictorial overview of guild objects with accompanying explanation of their use, see Karl Gröber, *Alte deutsche Zunftherrlichkeit* (Munich: Georg D. W. Callwey, 1936).

5. Accession number 44.80, Detroit Institute of Arts. Not all of the materials are listed in the current museum registration record of the object. I have identified the metal inlays as brass and pewter on the basis of their common use in eighteenth-century marquetry, and their appearance supports this assumption. However this is a provisional identification since no analysis of the metal inlays has been conducted. The inscription is rendered as follows: SIMON: ACKER: HOLM: VON: CHRISTIANSTAD : IN : SCHWEDEN : FIF : [monogram] : 29. May : 1751.

6. The illustration is reproduced in Stürmer, *Handwerk,* 100, fig. 37. I invoke the illustration from Roubo in order to aid identification of the scene on the Detroit chest, and not to suggest that Frankfurt cabinetmakers were familiar with Roubo's publication. The four-volume work was part of the series Descriptions des arts et métiers sponsored by the Académie Royale des Sciences. The articles on *menuiserie* and *ébénisterie* in the *Encyclopédie* by Diderot and d'Alembert (Paris, 1751–65) are another valuable contemporary description of the craft.

7. Stürmer, *Handwerk,* 100.

8. The woodcut is reproduced in Josef M. Greber, "Schreiner-Zunftladen von der Renaissance bis zum Biedermeier," parts 1–19, *Schweizerische Schreinerzeitung* 62, no. 44 (1951): 540, fig. 19.

9. Gisela Haase, *Dresdener Möbel des 18. Jahrhunderts* (Leipzig: E. A. Seemann, 1983), 15, 357 n. 4. Veneering distinguishes cabinetmakers *(Kunstschreiner, Kunsttisch(l)er)* from joiners *(Schreiner, Tisch(l)er),* that is, workers who use solid wood construction. An eighteenth-century source states that craftsmen who work only with expensive woods (such as ebony, olive, or cedar), and do inlay work with woods but also nonwood materials such as ivory and tortoiseshell, are *Kunst-Tischer. Grosses vollständiges Universal-Lexikon . . .,* 64 vols. (Halle: Johann Heinrich Zedler, 1732–50), 44: 413. It should be noted that members of the Frankfurt guild (craft association post-1616) under discussion in this paper always referred to themselves as *Schreiner*—and there was no group calling themselves *Kunstschreiner.* However, veneering was a significant activity of the *Schreiner.* Not only does their evolution from *Kistener* suggest an early involvement in this specialty, but most important, the required test piece to enter the trade after 1686 was a veneered wardrobe. Franz Lerner, *Das Frankfurter Schreinerhandwerk im Wandel der Zeiten* (Frankfurt: Adalbert Eckart, 1987), 181. Therefore the knowledge of cabinetmaking was pervasive among these craftsmen— as surviving pieces of veneered furniture made in Frankfurt attest—even if many of them plied their trade daily with joinery work. I have used the term cabinetmaker throughout this paper primarily because of the difficulty of making these important distinctions when solely using the term joiner *(Schreiner).* My justification for this decision is that the Detroit chest, the focus of this study, is an example of the art of cabinetmaking whose iconography visually describes the craft.

10. Significantly the exception is a cabinetmakers' guild chest dated 1708 from Frankfurt am Main, which will be discussed later in this paper. Greber notes that the few chests without tools (Regensburg, Trier, Salzburg, Rothenburg ob der Tauber) are the exceptions to this characteristic feature. "Schreiner-Zunftladen," 62 (41), 500. My debt to Greber's article is great, since it is the only historical survey of cabinetmakers' and joiners' guild chests. (The article in *Schweizerische*

Schreinerzeitung is a serialization of the material found in Greber's book, *Die alten Zunftladen des kunstreichen Handwerks* [Zurich: VSSM-Verlag, 1952].) In addition to Greber's work, a short article by Milan Konečný on Prague guild chests ("Prager Zunft- und Innungsladen") appeared in *Weltkunst* 58 (1988): 112–13. Another source is Paul Otto's book *Alte und neue Innungsladen* (Berlin: n.p., 1937), which I have been unable to consult; a reference to it in Greber's work suggests that it focuses on twentieth-century chests and does not present a historical survey.

11. For example, a seventeenth-century silver tankard of the Stockholm joiners' guild features depictions of trade tools engraved on the lid. W. L. Goodman, *The History of Woodworking Tools* (London: G. Bell & Sons, 1978), fig. 156.

12. Gröber, *Zunftherrlichkeit,* 68.

13. Greber, "Schreiner-Zunftladen," 62 (44), 540.

14. Lerner, *Frankfurter Schreinerhandwerk,* 232. The housing for an organ was also a joint enterprise in which the Frankfurt cabinetmakers took part (146).

15. Only two cabinetmakers' guild chests in Greber's article bear workshop scenes: the chest of the Lübeck journeyman cabinetmakers, 1600, Staatliche Museen der Hansestadt Lübeck; and a lost guild chest of the Königsberg master cabinet-makers, 1613. "Schreiner-Zunftladen," 62 (37), 457, fig. 1; 62 (46), 568, fig. 25; 62 (47), 581, figs. 29, 30. Workshop scenes can also be found in south German *Flügelladen* (Gröber, *Zunftherrlichkeit,* figs. 18, 30, 31).

16. Ottfried Neubecker, "Doppeladler," *Reallexikon zur deutschen Kunst-geschichte,* vol. 4 (Stuttgart: Alfred Drucken-Müller Verlag, 1955), 157. For a study on the use of the double-headed eagle in the Holy Roman Empire, see Franz-Heinz Hye, "Der Doppeladler als Symbol für Kaiser und Reich," *Mitteilungen des Instituts für österreichische Geschichtsforschung* 81 (1973): 63–100.

17. Otto Titian von Hefner, ed., *J. Siebmacher's grosses Wappenbuch,* vol. 1, *Wappen der Souveräne der deutschen Bundesstaaten* (1856; reprint, Neustadt an der Aisch: Bauer & Raspe, 1978), 49.

18. Illustration of the chancellery seal of Frankfurt am Main in the *Meisterbuch* of the bakers is found in Gröber, *Zunftherrlichkeit,* fig. 75; and on the *Meistertafel* of the beer brewers in Franz Lerner, *Mit Gunst, Meister und Gesellen eines ehrbaren Handwerks* (Frankfurt am Main: Historisches Museum, 1987), 103. Lersner's work, *Der weit-berühmten freyen Reichs- Wahl- und Handels-Stadt Franckfurt am Mayn Chronica . . .,* was published in Frankfurt by Georg August von Lersner in 1706 (2 vols.), with a second edition appearing in 1734.

19. The inscription accompanying the figure of Rachel reads *Rahel,* which is the standard spelling in German, also in use in the eighteenth century as a contemporary source reveals (see *Universal-Lexikon,* 14: 25, s.v. "Jacob").

20. Greber, "Schreiner-Zunftladen," 62 (43), 527.

21. Because I was unable to consult Sibylle Banke's Ph.D. dissertation "Die Frankfurter Schränke: Ein Beitrag zur Stilentwicklung im deutschen Barock" (Philipps-Universität, Marburg, 1954), I relied on the publication of the lists in Heinrich Kreisel's book *Die Kunst des deutschen Möbels,* 2 vols. (Munich: C. H. Beck Verlag, 1968–70), 1: 308–9 n. 155 (for the years 1634–1720); 2:

339–40 n. 232 (for the years 1721–35); 2: 355–56 n. 685 (for the years 1736–66). The names found on the chest are: *(lid)* Jacob Mutz, Gallus Faust, Johannes Stumpf, David Menicke, Andreas Koeler, Jacob Merits, *(panels of body)* Andreas Fries, Wilhelm Keuffl, Johan Jacob Gaschuts, Johan Andreas Lippus. Only some of the names were located in Banke's list (the year that the cabinetmaker acquired Frankfurt citizenship follows the name): Joh. Jak. Mutz von Törkelweil (1752), Johannes Stumpf (1764), Joh. Andreas Köhler von (?) Langensalza (1754), Andreas Fries (1731), Wilh. Keuffel (1739), Joh. Jak. Gaschütz (1710), Joh. Andreas Lippus (1734). Each became a master after establishing citizenship.

22. (See n. 5.) In Sibylle Banke's list (in Kreisel, *Die Kunst des deutschen Möbels,* 2: 356 n. 685), the entry is given as: "Simon Ackerholm von Christianstatt aus Schonau." Schonau has been misread—it is obviously Schweden, as indicated by the inscription of the Detroit chest. Prof. Emer. Marvin Eisenberg has suggested that FiF is perhaps *fecit in Frankfurt* (made in Frankfurt).

23. All information regarding Simon Ackerholm has been obtained through the assistance of Volker Harms-Ziegler, Referenten für Personennachweis, Stadtarchiv, Frankfurt am Main (personal correspondence, 27 April 1988). The following documents are located in Frankfurt's city archives. Ackerholm's application for citizenship to the city council is in *Ratssupplikation* 1747, II, 455–56. The realization of that application is found in *Bürgerbuch* XIII, fol. 327v (entry Ackerholm), 19 January 1748. Record of Ackerholm's entrance into the guild is found in *Handwerkerbuch* 111, entry no. 207 (Simon Ackerholm), 18 February 1748.

24. Gerald Lyman Soliday, *A Community in Conflict: Frankfurt Society in the Seventeenth and Early Eighteenth Centuries* (Hanover, N.H.: Univ. Press of New England, 1974), tables 8–11.

25. For the early history of the region, see Fred Schwind, "Frankfurt vom frühen Mittelalter bis zur Mitte des 17. Jahrhunderts," in *Geschichtlicher Atlas von Hessen,* ed. Fred Schwind (Marburg: Lahn, 1984), 232–34.

26. Heinrich Voelcker, "Berufliche und soziale Gliederung der Einwohner," in *Die Stadt Goethes Frankfurt am Main im 18. Jahrhundert,* ed. Heinrich Voelcker (Frankfurt am Main: Blazek & Bergmann, 1932), 86.

27. Unless otherwise noted, the following description of Frankfurt draws upon the introduction in Soliday's book *Community in Conflict* (pp. 1–10).

28. The Frauenstein Society was not exclusively patrician but included wholesale merchants and holders of doctors' degrees. The Graduate Society comprised mostly lawyers and physicians. Soliday, *Community in Conflict,* 5.

29. Soliday, *Community in Conflict,* 140.

30. Unless otherwise noted, the following profile of Frankfurt society draws upon chapter two of Soliday's book, "The City's Inhabitants," 33–68, and especially part two thereof, "The Burghers," 40–68.

31. Soliday, *Community in Conflict,* 9.

32. This translated quotation from Mousnier's work (*Problèmes de stratification sociale* [Paris: Presses universitaires de France, 1965]) is from Soliday, *Community in Conflict,* 9.

33. Soliday, *Community in Conflict,* 64.

34. Soliday's book uses the constitutional conflict to examine the social structure of the community. For a political and administrative account of the conflict, see Paul Hohenemser, *Der Frankfurter Verfassungsstreit 1705–1732 und die kaiserlichen Kommissionen* (Frankfurt: J. Baer, 1920).

35. Soliday, *Community in Conflict,* 23. The events leading up to the conflict are summarized well in chapter one of Soliday's book, "The Constitutional Conflict, 1705–1732," 13–32.

36. Soliday, *Community in Conflict,* 5.

37. Ibid., 139–42. Between the abolishment of the guilds and the institution of the craft associations a shuffling of trades took place (cf. tables 33 and 34).

38. Soliday, *Community in Conflict,* 122.

39. Unless otherwise noted, the following information on Frankfurt craftsmen is from part one of chapter six of Soliday's book, "Artisans and Handicraft Workers: Brewers," 139–56.

40. Lerner, *Frankfurter Schreinerhandwerk,* 222–23. Soliday states that three candidates could be nominated for a post (Soliday, *Community in Conflict,* 171).

41. The guild chest of the Frankfurt butchers, dated 1731, also indicated in its program of representation the leadership of four sworn masters. Wolfgang Klötzer, "Metzgerzunftlade 1731," *Archiv für Frankfurts Geschichte und Kunst* 60 (1985): 308. This demonstrates a similarity in the character of organization between the cabinetmakers' and butchers' craft associations. Klötzer does not mention whether the term *Geschworen* was differentiated with *alter* or *junger.*

42. Lerner, *Frankfurter Schreinerhandwerk,* 201.

43. The ceremony for cabinetmakers was called *Behobelung,* in which a mock planing of the candidate took place. For a description of this ceremony, see Ch. L. Stock, *Grundzüge der Verfassung des Gesellenwesens der deutschen Handwerker in alter und neuer Zeit* (Magdeburg: Creutz, 1844), 23–28.

44. Haase, *Dresdener Möbel,* 8.

45. The waiting period *(Stillestehen)* seems to be less common, though it is documented among the Frankfurt glaziers in the second half of the seventeenth century. Lerner, *Mit Gunst,* 28.

46. Greber, "Schreiner-Zunftladen," 62 (37), 458.

47. Specifically, this ceremony was enacted when an apprentice became a journeyman, a new master first sat at the plenary meeting of the guild, and most often at the periodic assemblies of journeymen in which members new to the area were honored. Rudolf Wissell, *Des Alten Handwerks Recht und Gewohnheit,* ed. Ernst Schraepler, 2d ed., rev. and enl., 6 vols. (Berlin: Colloquium Verlag, 1971–88), 3: 259–60; 4: 382.

48. This person was named either *Ladenmeister* or *Ladengeselle,* depending on whether the corporate body consisted of masters or journeymen. Greber, "Schreiner-Zunftladen," 62 (37), 458; 62 (38), 466.

49. *Universal-Lexikon,* 16: 151–52 (s.v. *"Lade"*). The entry for *Zunfft-Lade* (64: 187) refers the reader to *Lade.*

50. I was unable to examine guild records and so relied on published works that drew heavily on such records. These were: Rudolf Wissell, *Des Alten Handwerks Recht und Gewohnheit* (see n. 47); Franz Lerner, *Das Frankfurter Schreinerhandwerk im Wandel der Zeiten* (see n. 9); and Fritz Hellwag, *Die Geschichte des deutschen Tischlerhandwerks vom 12. bis zum 20. Jahrhundert* (Berlin: Verlagsanstalt des deutschen Holzarbeiter-Verbandes, 1924). The double usage of *Lade* is clear from excerpts in the work of Wissell (1: 402; 2: 136, 497; 3: 211). See especially usages five and six in Jacob and Wilhelm Grimm, *Deutsches Wörterbuch,* vol. 6 (Leipzig: S. Hirzel, 1885), 36–38.

51. Franz Lerner, *Zeugnisse des Frankfurter Schreinerhandwerks: 500 Jahre Zunftprivileg* (Frankfurt am Main: Historisches Museum, 1987), 10. An example of the variability of names can be found in the guild book of the furriers in Wriezen an der Oder in which the following terms were used from 1641 to 1661: *Pfingstsprache, Sprache, Quartal, Hauptquartal, Schwachzeit,* and *Michalissprache.* Wissell, *Des Alten Handwerks,* 2: 193 n. 48. For the origin of the *Morgensprache* and its relation to Germanic law, ibid., 181–200, and for examples of the *Morgensprache,* ibid., 3: 335–82.

52. Wissell, *Des Alten Handwerks,* 3: 265–66. A reproduction of the purse-makers' guild chest lid from Brunswick is found in Greber, "Schreiner-Zunftladen," 62 (38), 465, fig. 3.

53. Ch. W. J. Gatterer, "Rede des Laden-Gesellen unter den Schneidern zu Nürnberg, bey ihrer vierwöchentlichen Auflage," *Technologisches Magazin II* (Memmingen, 1792), 128–31. Reprinted in Stürmer, *Herbst des Alten Handwerks,* 219–20.

54. Wissell, *Des Alten Handwerks,* 3: 265–66. For the chest's role in the journeyman initiation ceremony, see Friedrich Friese, "Wie ein Geselle gemacht wird," *Der vornehmsten Künstler und Handwercker . . .* (Leipzig, 1708), 93–136. Reprinted in Stürmer, *Herbst des Alten Handwerks,* 181–84.

55. Lerner, *Frankfurter Schreinerhandwerk,* 198–99. The conjectured examples of weighty matters are mine and not Lerner's.

56. While this assumption is the most logical, it should be noted that the number of keys varied as much as who held them. For example, one key of the journeymen's chest might have been given to a chosen master, the *Beisitzmeister,* who was required to sit in on their meetings (Wissell, *Des Alten Handwerks,* 3: 267). Also the proprietor of the inn where the journeymen lodged and assembled may have had a key (Hermann Alexander Berlepsch, "Aus dem Leben der Zünfte," in *Die Zunftlade: Das Handwerk im Spiegel der Literatur vom 15. bis 19. Jahrhundert,* ed. Bruno Brandl and Günter Creutzburg [Berlin: Verlag der Nation, 1973], 260). Another nonguild person to possess one of the keys, either of the masters' or journeymen's chest, could have been the city magistrate (Berlepsch, "Leben," 260; Greber, "Schreiner-Zunftladen," 62 [38], 465).

57. Heinz Lenhardt, "Feste und Feiern des Frankfurter Handwerks: Ein Beitrag zur Brauchtums- und Zunftgeschichte," *Archiv für Frankfurts Geschichte und Kunst,* 5th ser., 1, pt. 2 (1950): 27.

58. Lenhardt excerpts two contemporary descriptions of cabinemakers' processions (1659 and 1721) from Lersner's chronicle of Frankfurt ("Feste," 10–12). The 1659 event was recorded in an engraving by Jakob Marrel, which is reproduced on page 165 in Lerner, *Frankfurter Schreinerhandwerk.* In Marrel's engraving no guild chest is visible, though the character of the festive procession is conveyed. Lerner speculates that the absence of the guild chest was the result of confiscation of guild property after the Fettmilch rebellion and that the guild had not yet replaced it (*Frankfurter Schreinerhandwerk,* 164).

59. My translation of the following: "Wir tragen beide volle Last! / Wer diese teure Lade hasst, / Der ist nicht wert, dass wir ihn nennen, / Und soll noch heut für Durst verbrennen. / Recht so, die teure Lade gilt / So viel, als auch das teure Schild. / Ja, sie ist aller Ehren wert, / Weil sie die Obern selbst beschert. / Wenn diese Lade offen steht, / Kein Tischler einen Fehl begeht. / Drum sei, um nur dran fest zu kleben, / Gut, Blut und Leben hingegeben." Quoted in Greber, "Schreiner-Zunftladen," 62 (38), 465–66. Unfortunately Greber does not specify the source of these verses, or any other identifying material. I believe that the line "Weil sie die Obern selbst beschert" should read "Weil sie die Obern selbst bescheren" and have translated it into English accordingly.

60. Lerner, *Frankfurter Schreinerhandwerk,* 101–2.

61. Ibid., 163–66, 217, 228–29. Lenhardt cites the 1668 procession ("Feste," 11).

62. Mack Walker, *German Home Towns, Community, State, and General Estate, 1648–1871* (Ithaca: Cornell Univ. Press, 1971), 80. I am indebted to Professor Emeritus Nathan Whitman for pointing out this relationship to the Ark of the Covenant.

63. Lenhardt, "Feste," 87.

64. Ibid., 85–86.

65. The sermon is reprinted in Wissell, *Des Alten Handwerks,* 5: 461.

66. There is a surviving metal guild chest of the Frankfurt butchers that challenges this generalization. (See n. 41.) Lerner maintains though that all of the other craft associations in Frankfurt had the cabinetmakers produce their most important community posession (*Frankfurter Schreinerhandwerk,* 176).

67. Greber, "Schreiner-Zunftladen," 62 (37), 457; 62 (39), 476.

68. Greber notes that many chests made in a particular city belonging to different style epochs are extant (e.g., Brunswick, Salzburg). One can follow this tendency more readily in documents, for example, how, after styles greatly changed, new chests were commissioned (e.g., Hamburg, ca. 1600, 1724, and 1772). "Schreiner-Zunftladen," 62 (43), 527. It may be noted that the drive to be current with guild chests ran differently. For example, Greber relates that the Kassel chest from 1604 was, according to the object's inscriptions, restored twice, in 1719 and in 1856. "Schreiner-Zunftladen," 62 (47), 579.

69. Greber, "Schreiner-Zunftladen," 62 (43), 528.

70. The following information on the general development of the cabinetmaking craft is from Kreisel, *Die Kunst des deutschen Möbels,* 1: 18, 30–31, 38–41.

71. Lerner, *Frankfurter Schreinerhandwerk,* 49. This book is the best source for information on the Frankfurt cabinetmakers' guild (and craft association post-1616). See note 9 above regarding the liberties I have taken with the nomenclature of this group.

72. Greber, "Schreiner-Zunftladen," 62 (39), 477.

73. The following comments on the stylistic development of furniture are derived from Kreisel, *Die Kunst des deutschen Möbels,* 1: 77–80, 155–62.

74. This type of book continued to be used by cabinetmakers in the eighteenth and nineteenth centuries. Lerner, *Zeugnisse,* 44. For a detailed study of the use of architecture manuals and pattern books by cabinetmakers, see Reinhard Peesch, "Säulenbücher zur Antikenrezeption in den Tischlerzünften des 16. bis 18. Jahrhunderts," *Jahrbuch für Volkskunde und Kulturgeschichte* 19 (1976): 87–107.

75. Kreisel, *Die Kunst des deutschen Möbels,* 2: 165.

76. Ibid., 1: 242.

77. Lerner, *Zeugnisse,* 55.

78. Information from Sibylle Banke's dissertation was gained through Kreisel, *Die Kunst des deutschen Möbels,* 1: 242–43. (See n. 21.)

79. The cabinet by Arzt is reproduced in Lerner, *Zeugnisse,* 57.

80. Lerner, *Frankfurter Schreinerhandwerk,* 180–81, 261.

81. Ibid., 241.

82. That members of Frankfurt's craft association made humble items such as window frames is confirmed by the requirement that candidates for mastership had to produce a frame as well as a wardrobe. Lerner, *Frankfurter Schreinerhandwerk,* 181. Also conflicts with the glaziers (ca. 1613 and 1676), who also claimed the right to make window frames, demonstrate the extent to which the cabinetmakers (here practicing joinery—see n. 9) wanted to protect this lucrative activity. Ibid., 122–24, 184–85.

83. Specifically, 45 master cabinetmakers and 20 masters' widows plied the trade without the help of any journeymen (whether they had the help of an apprentice is not indicated); 52 masters and 4 widows utilized one journeyman; 32 and 6 had two; and even two masters employed three which was allowed only in the summer months (otherwise the limit was two). Lerner, *Frankfurter Schreinerhandwerk,* 242–44.

84. Greber, "Schreiner-Zunftladen," 62 (38), 466.

85. The treatise, entitled "Abhandlung von der Handwerksgesellen und ihren Zünften," appeared in *Leipziger Sammlungen . . . ,* and is reprinted in Stürmer, *Herbst des Alten Handwerks,* 201–11. For further details on the subculture of journeymen, see chapter three of Stürmer's book (Ibid., 153–224).

86. This petition precipitated lengthy proceedings and inquiries into the condition of the journeymen which resulted in a new constitution for the group in 1803. Lerner, *Frankfurter Schreinerhandwerk,* 270–74.

87. Stürmer, *Herbst des Alten Handwerks,* 264.

88. Lerner, *Frankfurter Schreinerhandwerk,* 219–22.

89. Ibid., 203.
90. Stürmer, *Herbst des Alten Handwerks,* 270.
91. Lerner, *Frankfurter Schreinerhandwerk,* 229–30.
92. Ibid., 231.
93. Max Fehring, *Sitte und Brauch der Tischler: Unter besonderer Berücksichtigung Hamburgischer Quellen* (Hamburg: C. Boysen, 1929), 96–104.

Voltaire, Fontenoy, and the Crisis of Celebratory Verse

JOHN R. IVERSON

Le plus aimé des rois est aussi le plus grand.
— Voltaire, *La Bataille de Fontenoy, poème*

Le plus aimé des rois est le plus mal chanté.
— *La Capilotade, poème ou tout ce qu'on voudra*

Voltaire's *Bataille de Fontenoy* is a perplexing document for the modern reader. In the midst of the philosophe's vast output, it seems to reveal an ambitious minion of the court, a poetizing flatterer who feverishly revised and republished—repeatedly—a somewhat mediocre text as he attempted to gain official favor. From this perspective, the poem poses a number of questions about the poet's desire and ability to manipulate the literary institutions of his time, and part of our concern in the following pages will be to address the issue of his motivations in writing and rewriting this curious, apparently atypical, work. But the interest of *La Bataille de Fontenoy* also extends far beyond Voltaire's personal machinations. For when the leading writer of the age dedicates himself to the composition of a lengthy *épinicion*, or *chant de victoire*, his actions naturally attract great national attention.[1] In celebrating the exploits of the king, he performs an important public function; the work becomes a national literary monument, erected to the glory of Louis XV. At the same time, Fontenoy sets off a tremendous outpouring of rival works that

207

challenge the authority of Voltaire's poem and throw into question the very idea of celebratory poetry. As the two lines of our epigraph—one from Voltaire and the other a parody of his text—suggest, the political event also gives rise to a poetic crisis. On the one hand, the philosophe tries to inscribe himself in literary tradition; on the other, the parodist asserts that the poetry of his age is completely inadequate to fulfill this role. From this perspective, the episode provides valuable insight into the peculiar modalities of literary exchange in eighteenth-century France and the breakdown of models from the past.

The triumph of the French army on 11 May 1745 was the most brilliant moment of Louis XV's reign.[2] After assuming personal control of the government in 1743, the young king led a successful military campaign in 1744. His recovery from serious illness at the end of that summer brought him the title "le Bien-Aimé." Thus, he was already at the height of his glory at the time of the battle. Added to this, the actual conditions of the victory at Fontenoy redoubled popular enthusiasm. In an age when open battles were a rather rare occurrence, France defeated its arch-rival England in a prolonged and bloody encounter; and at a time when most kings no longer accompanied their troops to the front, the presence of Louis XV made the affair even more remarkable.[3] Voltaire himself declared this "la journée la plus glorieuse depuis la bataille de Bovines" and later devoted a lengthy chapter of his *Histoire de la guerre de 1741* to a detailed description of the engagement.[4] Of course, from a modern perspective, we know that this enthusiasm did not last long; even before the end of the war, the king's reputation suffered terribly.[5] But, at least for a brief moment, Louis appeared willing and able to fulfill the heroic role of a triumphant, clement monarch. The victory at Fontenoy seemed to confirm French dominance on the continent.

Along with the importance of the military event, revival of court life gave Fontenoy even greater significance. As the preeminent poet of the age, Voltaire was particularly aware of the changing ambiance at Versailles and benefited greatly from it. With the d'Argenson brothers receiving ministerial appointments, the duc de Richelieu taking charge of cultural affairs, and madame de Pompadour gaining official favor, his fortunes at the court rose steadily. In 1744, Richelieu called on him to compose a *comédie-ballet* for the dauphin's wedding in February 1745. Following performances of this work, *La Princesse de Navarre*, he was named royal historiographer and given the title "gentilhomme ordinaire de la chambre."[6] Following the victory at Fontenoy, he received a second commission. *Le Temple de la gloire*, an allegorical glorification of Louis XV as Trajan, was included at the end of the year in a series of celebratory spectacles. The worldly nature of these activities has led many critics to denounce the ambitious side of Voltaire's character and to lament his willingness to demean himself as a courtier.[7] In judging him in these terms, however, such assessments completely ignore the outburst of State-sponsored literary activity at this time. Undoubtedly, Voltaire was attracted by the prospect of official titles and the security they offered; but he also responded to a wide-reaching program that hearkened to the policies of the Sun King. In the new environment at court, he could feel that he really was participating in a rebirth of the cultural brilliance of the seventeenth century. As described by Jean-Louis de Cahusac in a lengthy *Encyclopédie* article, "Fêtes de la Cour," the festivities of 1745 are inscribed in a long line of court spectacles in France. Cahusac identifies the early years of Louis XIV's reign, "l'époque de la grandeur de cet état, de la gloire des Arts, & de la splendeur de l'Europe," as the apogee of this tradition, but he devotes the greatest portion of his article to the period 1745–47, including detailed descriptions.[8] The splendor of these events appears with wonderful clarity in the images produced by Charles-Nicolas Cochin, father and son, which depict performances of *La Princesse de Navarre*.[9] Their engravings, embracing the entirety of the theatrical space, both stage and audience, capture the glory of the French nation, substantiated by military victory, transposed and sublimated in the refinement of extravagant artistic creation.

It is within this general context that Voltaire's response to Fontenoy must be situated. The monarchy's renewed support for artistic and literary activity, compounded by popular enthusiasm for the victory, virtually obligated a poet in his position to compose a celebratory work. Commentary from the period indicates that many of his contemporaries found it appropriate that he, the author of *La Henriade*, should sing the praises of Louis XV. His recent honors at the court reinforced these expectations.[10] In fact, just days after the event, he received a long letter from the marquis d'Argenson who described the battle in detail. Given the circumstances in which it was written and the respective position of the two correspondents, this letter seems to present a sort of prescriptive outline for a poem.[11] Commenting on the sort of pressure that the victory created for poets, Voltaire's rival, Alexis Piron, later remarked that, "un poëte par état eût alors passé pour un mauvais citoyen, s'il se fût tu . . . ."[12]

Already the previous year, Voltaire himself had argued that poetry was an essential element in national glory. In his *Discours en vers, sur les événements de l'année 1744*, which appeared in the *Mercure de France*, he expressed the nation's joy over recent victories and the king's miraculous recovery. At the same time, he lamented the low quality of the poetic response:

> Paris n'a jamais vu de transports si divers,
> Tant de feux d'artifice, et si peu de bons vers. (M 9: 430)

Rather than resulting in a condemnation of poetic activity, however, this complaint led him to argue for renewed literary effort. In part, this poem was a request for royal patronage. But, beyond the element of self-interest, it defined a coherent cultural politics characterized by the complementarity of royal virtue and poetic encomium. In particular, Voltaire cited the model of the *grand siècle*, an era when poetry figured at the very center of national vitality. Here, and in many other texts of the period, the legacy of the reign of Louis XIV stood as a challenge to eighteenth-century poets.[13] The extraordinary events of 1744–45 created an opportunity for them but also a burden. Their greatest hope was to equal the accomplishments of their illustrious, already-canonized, predecessors. In many ways, they, like the monarchy, felt compelled to try to reconstitute the poetic environment of the previous century. In these conditions, the new celebratory works became the object of intense scrutiny.

This conception of the role of poetry obviously informs the first lines of *La Bataille de Fontenoy*. In summoning his compatriots to admire the king, Voltaire alludes to the most famous celebratory poem of the previous century, Boileau's fourth epistle:

> Quoi! du siècle passé le fameux satirique
> Aura fait retentir la trompette héroïque,
> Aura chanté du Rhin les bords ensanglantés,
> Ses défenseurs mourants, ses flots épouvantés,
> Son dieu même en fureur, effrayé du passage,
> Cédant à nos aïeux son onde et son rivage:
> Et vous, quand votre roi dans des plaines de sang
> Voit la mort devant lui voler de rang en rang,
> Tandis que, de Tournay foudroyant les murailles,
> Il suspend les assauts pour courir aux batailles;
> Quand, des bras de l'hymen s'élançant au trépas,
> Son fils, son digne fils, suit de si près ses pas;
> Vous, heureux par ses lois, et grands par sa vaillance,
> Français, vous garderiez un indigne silence! (M 8: 383)

The opening thus has a dual mission. On the one hand, it conveys a great sense of excitement about the victory. The exclamatory "Quoi!" and the tremendous length of the first sentence are remarkably effective in creating a feeling of breathlessness. The king's noble actions accumulate in an impressive cadence that ends by stridently rebuking the mute French. On the other hand, by accepting the celebratory task, Voltaire casts himself as Boileau's successor, thereby amplifying the significance of his poem. Building on this association, he manages to construe his work as an expression of national sentiment, not simply as a spontaneous song of joy, but also as part of France's most noble poetic tradition. This link to the past is a grandiose rhetorical gesture; it also reflects the seriousness with which Voltaire later pursues revision of the work. Throughout this period his correspondence speaks of his desire to produce a text that will be a "monument" to French glory. In accordance with his ideas about the complementary relationship between power and poetry, he vows to refine his poem until it reaches a state worthy of the event: "Sans doute je corrige mon ouvrage et je le corrigeray. Je voudrois pouvoir le rendre digne, et du Roy qui l'a honoré de son aprobation, et de ma patrie à la gloire de la quelle il est consacré . . . ."[14] He sets himself a goal that far surpasses the limits of courtly flattery; his ambition is to elevate poetry and make it a worthy heroic vehicle.

Written with such high expectations, *La Bataille de Fontenoy* became what must surely be one of the most intensively revised and edited poetic works ever. Eager to display his zeal and to satisfy public interest in the event, Voltaire first issued his poem within days of the victory. Then, as new information about the battle reached the capital, he corrected and expanded it, working quickly to incorporate further details. On 31 May, in a note to his friend Cideville, he describes his most recent changes, produced during a sleepless night.[15] This highly evocative letter conveys a sense of the amazing rapidity, but also the persistence, with which the entire work was written, revised and reprinted. In fact, the poet continued to labor over the text until late that summer. Eventually, more than thirty editions appeared, presenting nearly a dozen different states of the text. Finally, Voltaire garnered considerable official recognition for his *Bataille*; he was first granted permission to dedicate it to the king and then obtained the honor of having it printed at the Imprimerie Royale.

The poet did not exaggerate, then, when he stated that "ce qui n'était d'abord qu'une pièce de cent vers est devenu un poëme qui en contient plus de trois cent cinquante," for *La Bataille de Fontenoy* was completely transformed during the course of his revisions (M 8: 375). It would be impossible to review all of the changes here, but they can be grouped in five categories that reflect their general impact.[16] First, in several cases, Voltaire added details that probably reached Paris more slowly than the news of the victory. Thus, for example, the four lines that describe a series of assaults by enemy forces at the beginning of the engagement were not introduced until quite late in the revision process.[17] Also, at this same level of detail, Voltaire corrected inaccuracies concerning the conduct of certain individuals. Frequently, he added footnotes to include this type of information. Secondly, he improved the narrative flow of the poem and gave it a more stately quality. In the poem's final version, the fine tableau of the allied army serves as an effective prelude to the action sequences (M 8:384–85). Absent in the third edition, bits of this passage were inserted in the sixth edition, before the final text appeared in the Imprimerie Royale edition. Thirdly, Voltaire altered his text to make Louis XV's role more prominent. After the exordium (quoted above), early versions quickly shifted focus to the commanding general, Maurice de Saxe, as the poet led his readers directly to the battlefield.[18] In the definitive text, he introduced an invocation that articulated the primary goal of the poem, the glorification of the king:

> O vous, Gloire, Vertu, déesses de mon roi,
> Redoutable Bellone, et Minerve chérie,
> Passion des grands coeurs, amour de la patrie,
> Pour couronner Louis prêtez moi vos lauriers. (M 8: 383)

The later versions also expanded the conclusion of the poem to include a call for peace. Only the Bien-Aimé's clement grandeur, the poet claimed, could reestablish European harmony. Fourth, Voltaire responded to specific points of criticism from his contemporaries. In some cases, this entailed replacing a word or finding a new rhyme. In others, this led to explicit rebuttals. In response to protest over a reference to English "férocité," he cited the testimony of a battle participant in an expanded note: "On m'a écrit que, lorsque la colonne anglaise déborda Fontenoy, plusieurs soldats de ce corps criaient: *No quarter, no quarter!* Point de quartier!" (M 8: 391). Finally, the poet updated his text to incorporate events that took place after the battle of Fontenoy. The capture of Oostende was such a case (M 8: 393). This process continued even while the work was being printed at the Louvre.[19]

Considered as a group, these revisions are remarkably comprehensive, and there can be no doubt that the later versions greatly improve on the earlier ones. Although longer, the text has greater coherence; it better conveys a sense of movement in the battle. The enhancement of the king's role gives the work greater political resonance. Changes in wording and rhythm give it a highly polished feel; of the many Fontenoy poems, it is certainly the most readable. But the ongoing process of correction and expansion also became an embarrassment for Voltaire. It revealed that the first editions had been issued long before the poem had reached perfection. Further emphasizing this fact, the title pages of the various editions became increasingly complex as printers sought to publicize the constant improvements. The sixth Parisian edition bore the indication, "Sixième édition, considérablement augmentée, conforme à la septième faite à Lille." As we will see, this convoluted formula proved to be an easy target for parodists. In addition, as the number of editions mounted steadily, Voltaire was accused of making slight modifications in the text in order to sell more copies. Thus, even as he moved closer to his goal of creating a worthy monument to French glory, his editorial procedures compromised the dignity of the poem.

To counteract this negative effect, Voltaire added other changes to explain why the new editions were necessary. He was forced to admit that the first version was woefully flawed, but he justified himself by claiming that public interest had demanded such hastiness. In the third edition, he remarked that he simply had not had time to gather complete information: "On n'a pû nommer les autres Lieutenans Généraux, dont les noms sont célébrés ailleurs, ou dont on a reçu la liste trop tard. . . . D'ailleurs, si on avoit pû rendre justice à tous ceux qui le méritent, il eût fallu louer tous les Officiers de l'Armée, & mettre un an à composer un ouvage qu'il a fallu faire en moins de deux jours."[20] Beginning with the sixth Parisian edition, he included a substantial "Discours préliminaire," in which he responded to several of the most common points in the criticism of his poem. In this more prominent position, he again addressed the question of the multiple printings: "Ce poëme fut composé presque le même jour qu'on apprit à Paris la victoire que le roi avait remportée à Fontenoy; et depuis on ajouta plusieurs traits à la pièce, à mesure qu'on savait quelque circonstance de ce grand événement, et qu'on faisait une nouvelle édition de l'ouvrage" (M 8: 375). The event was, in the poet's opinion, so spectacular and so popular that it required immediate celebration, yet it was also so significant that it merited an accomplished rendering. Caught between these contradictory considerations, Voltaire struggled to establish his *Bataille* as the definitive Fontenoy account.

As the editions succeeded one another, the progress of the work was also reflected in a series of paratextual reconfigurations. Again, it would be impossible to review all of them here, but the printing at the Louvre provides the most striking example of how the modifications in the poem's appearance strengthened its monumentality (fig. 1). The Imprimerie Royale edition is remarkable for its majestic title page. Eschewing the lengthy indications of edition number common in the earlier versions, this one simply announces its prestigious place of printing, with the words "Imprimerie Royale" dominating the lower portion of the page. A lovely ornament reinforces the connection with the monarchy. The image of the laurel-crowned king and dauphin, who stand proudly in the chariot of victory, replicates the commemorative medallion that was struck for the occasion. In addition, an epigraph taken from the *Aeneid* offers the poem as a lesson of virtue. Like the medallion, it alludes to the dauphin's presence at the battle and Louis's desire to educate his son in the duties of kingship. Most importantly, this edition gives the work a new title. *La Bataille de Fontenoy, poëme* is now *Le Poëme de Fontenoy*, implying that this text supersedes all other Fontenoy poems. Of

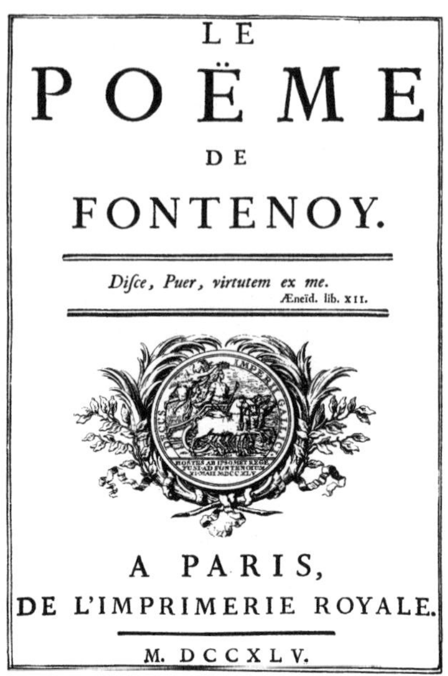

Figure 1. Title page of *Le Poëme de Fontenoy* as it was printed at the Louvre by the Imprimerie Royale. The double ruled line framing this copy was added when it was mounted in a volume along with numerous other works pertaining to the victory at Fontenoy. By permission of the Newberry Library, Chicago.

course, some of these modifications may not have resulted from direct intervention by Voltaire, but his correspondence indicates that he did play an active role in overseeing the printing of the work and made several suggestions in this area.[21]

The poet's correspondence further reveals the significance he attached to this printing: "On va faire une septième édition à Paris, et peut-être la fera-t-on au Louvre; elle est dédiée au roi; et la bonté qu'il a d'accepter cet hommage, met le sceau à l'authenticité de la pièce."[22] After obtaining authorization for this edition, he negotiated for a larger print run than usual, sent a series of additional corrections and asked that copies be distributed to prominent individuals. Exasperated by these demands, the minister Maurepas eventually exploded: "Vous n'avez pas eu intention, après trente-sept éditions, et bientôt trente-neuf, de multiplier uniquement les exemplaires: votre objet est que la beauté de ceux de l'imprimerie royale engage à les conserver et à les déposer dans les bibliothèques" (D3172, 9 July 1745). This exchange reveals that both men were quite aware that the transformation in the appearance of the poem was linked to its survival for posterity. Although Maurepas rejected this particular request, he was, in fact, sympathetic to Voltaire's perspective.[23] Indeed, when he first wrote to the king about this edition, he spoke of the advantages of printing the work on the royal presses: "Je ne crois pas qu'il y ait d'inconvénient à lui accorder la grâce qu'il désire, son objet n'étant que de faire des présents dans les pays étrangers du poème sur la bataille de Fontenoy, d'une édition plus belle et plus digne d'être envoyée."[24] By granting the poem official protection, the monarchy thus consecrated a work devoted to its celebration, crystallizing the French victory in literary form. In the end, Voltaire's efforts finally paid off; his *Bataille* became, in effect, the official version of Fontenoy.

In part, his persistence in revising the text can be explained by his desire to defend his poem against hostile critics.[25] As we have seen, he made numerous changes in the text and eventually added the "Discours préliminaire" in order to justify his characterization of the enemy, the work's long lists of names, and its failure to use allegorical figures. But, all in all, these points seem rather insignificant and hardly provide adequate grounds for Voltaire's obsessive revisionary efforts. To understand why he felt it was so important to bring his *poème de circonstance* to a state of perfection, we must return, rather, to his attachment to the idea of public poetry as a vital element in national glory.

In the remaining portion of this essay, I would like to argue that the tailoring of *La Bataille de Fontenoy* was informed by the publication of an abundant body of ephemeral literature both before and after the victory.[26] As mentioned previously, a deluge of poems greeted Louis XV when he returned to Paris at the end of 1744. Scores of poets felt compelled to express the nation's joy; writers of all ranks glorified the king's accomplishments in numerous odes, idylls and epistles. Commonly these works were short texts, written and printed in haste, issued individually, often on relatively low-quality paper. Many copies were undoubtedly distributed by the poets themselves to patrons and influential members of the court. We have seen that Voltaire counted heavily on this practice to obtain readers. At the same time, however, these works were sold by street vendors and circulated widely in the general reading public. In the case of *La Bataille de Fontenoy*, one of the Président Bouhier's correspondents, Jean-Bernard Michault, noted that this was the case: "Les colporteurs vendent la cinquième édition. Cela se débite avec le jubilé, les prières des 40 heures, les sentences à mort du Châtelet, le croquet, le muguet, etc. Le poète Roy dit que c'est vendre les muses au litron."[27] Further augmenting the visibility of these works, in at least one case, several poems were gathered to form a regular anthology; the Parisian printer David issued a *Recueil de pièces choisies sur les conquêtes & la convalescence du roy*, enhanced by a Cochin engraving.[28] More frequently, the various pieces of this literary explosion were gathered by individuals and bound together to form *recueils factices*. Even today, many of these collections of ephemeral materials survive, combining poetic works, battle accounts, engravings of fireworks displays and episcopal decrees.[29] The abundance of this celebratory literature and the care with which it was collected confirm the idea that poetry held a particularly important place in the year's glorious events.

Yet this literature was clearly haunted by a sense of failure. In its most banal form, this sentiment dictated poems in which poets despaired of adequately capturing the king's incomparable virtues. This gesture might, of course, be dismissed as simple rhetorical modesty. But other writers confirmed this idea in a number of ways. Critics issued harsh essays condemning some of the more notable works; Fréron, Gresset and Piron were all victims of such attacks. Other commentators reflected on theoretical matters, particularly the technical difficulty of the French ode.[30] In some cases, worried patriots summoned the members of the Académie Française to fulfill their official celebratory duties.[31] These observers believed that the glory of the moment was tarnished by the profusion of bad poems written by individuals who had no identifiable poetic authority. One writer cursed the "fièvre poétique" that had infected the country, while a self-proclaimed "dénonciateur du mauvais goût" spoke of collective embarrassment: "Quelle prodigeuse quantité de Vers, & d'insipides Vers! Quelle fatalité pour les Lettres! Quelle honte pour le siècle où nous vivons!"[32] Thus, Voltaire was not alone in complaining of "si peu de bons vers"; this lament formed a general chorus. Indeed, the compelling need to celebrate national glory created a widely shared feeling of poetic crisis.

Intensified by the extraordinary nature of the victory at Fontenoy, the same dynamic reproduced itself in 1745.[33] Again, huge numbers of poems congratulated the king on his successes; and again, critics deplored the low quality of these works. The noise surrounding Voltaire's poem aggravated the situation; because of his fame and the speed with which he composed his poem, his text in particular colored many of the subsequent pieces. In these circumstances, a number of writers chose to compose parodies and satirical texts; rather than glorifying the victory, they instead turned their attention to the farcical insufficiencies of contemporary literary production. In this way, they undermined the process of poetic celebration. Not that their works were subversive in an ideological sense—they typically lauded Louis XV's virtues and praised the victory—but they cast Fontenoy in a humorous light much different from the dignity Voltaire sought to communicate in his poem. These were certainly not works that could be considered "monuments" to national glory.

Even a brief examination of this body of poems reveals that they generated much of their humor by pointing out the short-comings of the more serious poems, most prominently Voltaire's. For example, they poked fun at his editorial strategies, creating endless variations on this theme. In some cases, the gesture remained simple; the *Lettre longuette à m. de Voltaire* included the comment, "Derniere Edition. Sans corrections, sans augmentation, & parfaitement semblable à la premiere."[34] In other cases, the tone became more biting: "77ᵐᵉ édition, revue, corrigée & augmentée de deux syllabes & de trois notes prises sous l'arbre de Cracovie."[35] Likewise, many of these writers included prefatory statements to justify their compositional practices. The "curé de Fontenoy," for example, directly parodied Voltaire's excuses for his over-hasty work: "Si sa Pièce paroît trop courte ou trop négligée, c'est parce qu'il n'a été que trois heures à la composer, la revoir, la corriger, & l'écrire."[36] Hostile literary theorists also discussed the multiple editions, but the effect was much different in these entertaining poems.[37] Working by allusion rather than denunciation—it was up to the reader to recognize the references to Voltaire's poem—these writers created doubts about the sanctity of the poetic process in general. (This was easy to do given the number of really awful poems produced at the time.) More than simply attacking Voltaire in a personal way, their works seemed to suggest, in a broader sense, that poetry had become an endless repetition of meaningless, metered phrases, written only to produce profits for printers.

The parodists also exploited *La Bataille de Fontenoy*'s opening exclamation, "Quoi!"[38] The word in itself provided an ideal starting point for more fun (see Appendix A). One "natif de Lille en Flandre" centered his entire "Discours préliminaire" around this "Quoi!" and then used it at the beginning of the first three stanzas of his poem.[39] "Le grand Thomas" played on its sonority:

> Quoi! restant comme un Iroquoi,
> Je ne chanterois pas le ROI,
> Tandis que tout le monde piaille![40]

Others cribbed straight from Voltaire's text, creating humorous pastiches:

> Quoi du siècle présent le plus fameux Poète
> Aura pris dans ses mains l'héroïque trompette . . . .[41]

The "maître d'école de Fontenoy" used the interjection to launch a complete review of Voltaire's literary machinations:

> Quoy du Siecle present l'Auteur Tragi-comique,
> Epique, Politique, & Critique & Lirique,

> Anglois pendant trente ans par inclination,
> Redevenu François depuis la Pension,
> Trouve bon que le ROY remporte une Victoire,
> Aux Chefs comme aux Soldats fait leur part de la Gloire;
> Ses Vers vendus un jour, refondus l'autre nuit,
> Dans sa bourse sept fois ramenent leur produit,
> Et je me tais encor![42]

In returning persistently to this device, the parodists created a circle of interconnected works and drew *La Bataille de Fontenoy* into a poetic game over which Voltaire had no control.

A second string of associations further complicated the situation. Along with the "maître d'école de Fontenoy," figures like the "barbier de Fontenoy" and the "fossoyeur de Fontenoy" established a connection between Voltaire's poem, from which they borrowed the exclamatory "Quoi," and an ever-expanding group of works authored by fictional residents of the battle-torn village (see Appendix B). The "curé de Fontenoy" instigated the cycle when he formulated his *Requête au Roy*, seeking compensation for the services he had performed for the thousands of victims. Written in the characteristic octosyllabic lines of the burlesque genre, this work went through a number of printings. The easy technique subsequently attracted many imitators; assuming the identity of other members of the Fontenoy community, they commented on the poems of their fellow village poets. As the circle expanded, the texts increasingly had less and less to do with the victory; ingeniousness became an end in itself. The goal of these works—much different from the elevated intentions of serious works like *La Bataille de Fontenoy*—was simply to prolong the dialogue, drawing material from every possible facet of the ongoing celebration of the victory.[43]

The problem for Voltaire was that he had no means of responding to these works, even though they often mocked him and his poem. Thus, he complained about one of these texts, attributing it to his enemy, the poet Pierre-Charles Roy:

> Il a fait une petite satire dans la quelle il dit de moy:
>
>> Il a loué depuis Noailles
>> Jusqu'au moindre petit morveux
>> Portant talon rouge à Versailles.
>
> On débite cette infamie avec les noms de Mr Dargenson, Castelmoron et Daubeterre en notes.[44]

Voltaire hoped that his friends would denounce this vile work to the Queen, but he himself could not descend to the level of satire to fend off the attack.

He could only argue that a celebratory poem should name prominent individuals and that his text distributed praise equitably. In effect, this was one of the points he made in his "Discours préliminaire."

But the terms in which Voltaire objected to the mistreatment of his poem suggest, in a more general sense, that he was profoundly disturbed by the levity of Roy and the other hack poets. For the injury they did was not limited to him alone; in lampooning his celebration of national heroes, they attacked French honor itself. In the mind of the poet who tried to promote his own text as a contribution to monarchical glory, these low-style parodies and contentious critiques failed to accord proper respect to public poetry. In response, Voltaire drafted the curious *Lettre critique d'une belle dame à un beau monsieur de Paris*, in which he ridiculed the comments of his critics.[45] Adopting the voice of a frivolous noblewoman, he eagerly showed that the commentaries betrayed an absence of concern for important national matters. The "belle dame" complains that,

> L'auteur du poëme prétend que nous avons beaucoup d'obligation au roi de gagner des batailles en personne, et de prendre des villes, afin que nous jouissions tranquillement à Paris du fruit de ses travaux, et des dangers où il s'expose. Quelle sottise! J'aimerais bien savoir si les dames de Londres se réjouissent moins parce que le duc de Cumberland a été bien battu.

The same attitude carries over into her assessment of the contents of the poem: "Que m'importe, à moi, que quatre ou cinq officiers de l'état-major aient été blessés? j'ai bien affaire qu'on me les nomme!" She is interested only in amorous intrigue, performances at the *opéra-comique*, and gambling. (She closes her letter, "Adieu, monsieur, le cavagnole m'attend.") As Voltaire makes these charges, he implies that they reflect the frivolity of a considerable sector of the nation. Apparently this was the attitude that spawned the perpetual stream of poetic rubbish littering the literary space of 1745. Of course, he could not publish this text, it would have compromised his role as author of the officially recognized *Bataille de Fontenoy*. But in its satirical verve, this letter conveys a sense of the importance he attached to his poem and the frustration he felt when others undermined his efforts to celebrate and perpetuate French glory.

The poetic history of Fontenoy thus yields two sorts of lessons. As far as Voltaire is concerned, his initial text and subsequent revisions reflect an extremely important characteristic of his literary practice. Throughout his career he demonstrated a fondness and a talent for reshaping works—to respond to critical commentary, to ward off threats of censorship, or to integrate new material. The intensity with which he modified and improved *La Bataille de Fontenoy* highlights certain of these mechanisms; in this respect,

the text provides an excellent case study. In addition, the Fontenoy episode
shows Voltaire attempting to position himself within a complex cultural context. Although it may seem an unusual position for this figurehead of the
philosophical movement, the events of 1745 led him to believe, at least for a
moment, that a return to the artistic policies of Louis XIV's reign was possible and that he himself might contribute to cooperation between a flourishing literary culture and a reinvigorated monarchy. As it happened, the vision
was a fleeting one. When he was asked to celebrate a new French victory, in
1747, he performed a more typical Voltairean pirouette. In his poem on the
battle of Laufeldt, he again evoked the memory of Boileau. This time, however, he sought to distinguish himself from his model:

> Je dirai tout, car tout est à sa gloire.
> Il [Louis XV] fait la mienne, et je me garde bien
> De ressembler à ce grand satirique,
> De son héros discret historien,
> Qui pour écrire un beau panégyrique,
> Fut bien payé, mais qui n'écrivit rien.[46]

Disgruntled with his experience as celebratory poet, Voltaire vowed that
henceforward he would devote his attentions to historical writing. Although
La Bataille de Fontenoy had in many ways been a great success, he would
never again attempt such a work. If the symbiosis of power, literary creation
and national glory were still to take place, it would not be in the form of
celebratory verse.

To understand why this was so, we have moved beyond the scope of
Voltaire's individual reaction to Fontenoy and looked at the tremendous outburst of celebratory and parodic literature at the time. This copious body of
poetry first responded to the victory and then fed off its own momentum to
sustain public interest for several months. It might be said that the literary
exchange overtook and subsumed the military event. At some point in the
endless cycle of poems, interest shifted definitively from what was said *about*
the battle to *how* it was said. At its most extreme, this literature became a
commentary on itself, almost entirely effacing the battle. In this way, it completely violated a traditional model of celebratory poetry. Voltaire's comments on his ambitions for *La Bataille de Fontenoy* make it seem as though
his task will be achieved if only he can revise his text sufficiently. Based on
the example set by Boileau, his idea of the literary "monument" implies a
sort of heroic model of literary reception: the brilliance of his corrected text
should eventually compel all readers, even in the future, to accept the truth it
conveys, the message of French glory. The complex literary field of eighteenth-century France did not, however, permit such a simplistic development. Public reaction and the quick pens of rival poets were less easily con-

trolled than the newly appointed royal historiographer was willing to admit.[47] Even as he labored to bring his own text to full perfection, a myriad of other writers busily undermined the notion of poetic dignity and grandeur.

NOTES

1. The *Encyclopédie* contains a short article, "Epinicion," by the Abbé Mallet: "L'épître de Boileau, le poëme de Corneille sur le passage du Rhin, celui de M. Adisson sur la campagne de 1704, & celui de M. de Voltaire sur la victoire de Fontenoy, sont de ce genre. Le poëme d'Adisson a pour objet la bataille d'Hocstet; c'est un des plus beaux ouvrages de cet illustre auteur; celui de M. de Voltaire ne mérite pas moins d'être lu; la préface que l'auteur y a mise contient des réflexions judicieuses sur ce genre de poëme, & sur l'épître de Despréaux." *Encyclopédie, ou Dictionnaire raisonné des sciences, des arts et des métiers par une Société de Gens de lettres*, ed. Denis Diderot and Jean le Rond d'Alembert, 23 vols. (Paris, 1751–73), 5: 808.

2. For more extensive commentary on the historical conjuncture and the particular significance of these years in Louis XV's reign, see Michel Antoine, *Louis XV* (Paris: Fayard, 1989), chap. 8.

3. The most recent account of the battle is Jean-Pierre Bois, *Fontenoy, 1745: Louis XV, arbitre de l'Europe* (Paris: Economica, 1996). Fontenoy long upheld the glory of French arms. Horace Vernet's monumental painting assumed a prominent position in the Galerie des Batailles at Versailles during the Restoration; see Thomas Gaehtgens, *Versailles als Nationaldenkmal* (Berlin: Frölich & Kaufmann, 1985). The battle also appeared in a variety of literary settings; it is mentioned, for example, by Diderot in both *Les Bijoux indiscrets* (1748) and *Jacques le fataliste* (1771) and by Rousseau in *La Nouvelle Héloïse* (1761). Perhaps the most striking reference to the battle and Louis XV's magnanimous conduct occurs in the conclusion of the abbé de Prades's article "Certitude" in volume 2 of the *Encyclopédie* (1752).

4. Quotations from Voltaire's works refer to *Oeuvres complètes de Voltaire*, ed. Louis Moland, 52 vols. (Paris: Garnier, 1877–85). References are abbreviated as (M volume: page). "La journée la plus glorieuse" is found in the "Discours préliminaire" of *La Bataille de Fontenoy* (M 8: 375); see also chap. 15, "Siège de Tournai. Bataille de Fontenoy," *Histoire de la guerre de 1741*, ed. Jacques Maurens (Paris: Garnier Frères, 1971), 131–54. Howard Weinbrot discusses the very different tenor of the English response in "William Collins and the Mid-Century Ode: Poetry, Patriotism, and the Influence of Context," in Martin Price and Howard Weinbrot, *Context, Influence and Mid-Eighteenth-Century Poetry* (Los Angeles: W. A. Clark Memorial Library, Univ. of California, Los Angeles, 1990), 1–39.

5. For accounts of Louis XV's precipitous fall from public favor, see Arlette Farge and Jacques Revel, *The Vanishing Children of Paris: Rumor and Politics before the French Revolution*, trans. Claudia Miéville (Cambridge: Harvard

Univ. Press, 1991); and Thomas E. Kaiser, "The Drama of Charles Edward Stuart, Jacobite Propaganda, and French Political Protest, 1745–1750," *Eighteenth-Century Studies* 30 (1997): 365–81.

6. For a full account of these events, see René Vaillot, *Avec madame du Châtelet, 1734–1749*, vol. 2 of *Voltaire en son temps*, ed. René Pomeau (Oxford: Voltaire Foundation, 1988–94), 193–258.

7. Much critical interest in *Le Temple de la gloire* has centered on the anecdote concerning Voltaire's question to the King, "Trajan est-il content?" See, for example, R. S. Ridgway, "Voltaire's Operas," *Studies on Voltaire and the Eighteenth Century* 189 (1980): 119–51.

8. *Encyclopédie*, 6: 580–85. As librettist, Cahusac participated in the creation of many of these spectacles.

9. Several of the Cochin images are reproduced in the exposition catalogue, *Voltaire et l'Europe* (Paris: Bibliothèque Nationale, 1994), 72–76.

10. His friend Cideville informed him that, just as Homer immortalized Achilles, it was his task to perpetuate Louis XV's sublime exploits: "Voltaire, pour suffire à peindre sa grande ame, / Il faloit vos talens: Poëte, Historien, / Excitez votre esprit que le sublime enflâme; / Homere trouve Achille, il ne leur manque rien." *A Monsieur de Voltaire, Historiographe de France, par Monsieur de ***. de l'Académie des Sciences, des Belles-Lettres, & des Arts, de Roüen*, in *Les Voltairiens, 2ème Série, Voltaire jugé par les siens, 1719–1749*, ed. Jeroom Vercruysse, 7 vols. (Millwood, New York: Kraus International, 1983), 6: 24.

11. D3118, 15 May 1745. All quotations from Voltaire's correspondence refer to *Correspondence and Related Documents*, ed. Theodore Besterman, 51 vols. (Oxford: Voltaire Foundation, 1968–77). Besterman notes that the poet had issued the first version of his poem before this missive reached Paris; it cannot, therefore, be considered the "source" for the work. The letter does, however, suggest that d'Argenson wished to furnish him with ample material. His letter emphasizes the King's conduct: "Le vray, le sûr, le non flatteur, c'est que c'est le Roy qui a gagné luy mêsme la bataille, par sa volonté, par sa fermeté."

12. Alexis Piron, "Anecdote comique et littéraire au sujet des deux pièces précédentes," in *Oeuvres complètes illustrées*, 10 vols. (Paris: F. Guillot, 1928–31), 8: 217; cited by Sylvain Menant, *La Chute d'Icare: La crise de la poésie française, 1700–1750* (Genève: Droz, 1981), 289.

13. For discussion of expectations surrounding serious poetry, see Menant, *La Chute d'Icare*, 273–79. Menant particularly emphasizes the importance of Boileau's episitle on the Rhine crossing as a model for eighteenth-century poets.

14. D3131, 31 May 1745, to Cideville. Voltaire relayed the story of the King's reception of the work to several of his correspondents: "J'avois mandé à M. le maréchal de Noailles que j'ofrois un bien petit tribut, que c'étoit là un petit monument de la gloire du roy. Il m'a fait l'honneur de m'écrire que le roy avoit dit que j'avois tort, que ce n'étoit pas un *petit* monument" (D3142, 13–15 June 1745, to the président Hénault). See also D3147, D3149, D3168 and D3187.

15. One morning he urged Cideville to come "chez Prault" where he was to oversee the printing of a new edition: "Après avoir travaillé toute la nuit mon cher

amy à mériter vos éloges et votre amitié, par les efforts que je fais, après avoir poussé notre bataille jusqu'à près de 300 Vers, y avoir jetté un peu de poésie, fait un discours préliminaire et ayant surtout proffité de vos avis, il faut prendre du Caffé, et c'est en le prenant que je vous rends compte de tout ce que je fais. Je viens de recevoir du roy la permission de faire imprimer l'Epître dédicatoire dont je luy avois envoyé le Modèle" (D3139, 31 May 1745).

16. Unfortunately, the volume that will contain the "Bataille de Fontenoy" has not yet appeared in the ongoing critical edition of the *Complete Works of Voltaire* (Oxford: Voltaire Foundation, 1968).

17. "Dans un ordre effrayant trois attaques formées / Sur trois terrains divers engagent les armées. / Le Français, dont Maurice a gouverné l'ardeur, / A son poste attaché, joint l'art à la valeur" (M 8: 385–86). These lines were still absent from the sixth Parisian edition by Prault pere.

18. "Aux Champs de Fontenoy, volez, accourez tous; / Voyez ce fier Saxon qu'on croit né parmi nous. . . ." *La Bataille de Fontenoy, Poëme. Troisième edition, plus correcte & plus ample que les précédentes* (Paris: Prault père, 1745), 4.

19. Voltaire writes to the printer at the Louvre, Jacques Anisson-Duperron: "Il est bien juste monsieur de ne pas oublier *Ostende* dans l'énumération des conquêtes du roy, je vous suplie d'ordonner qu'on insère le morceau suivant à la page 27" (D3175, [15 July 1745]).

20. The comment appeared in a footnote to the third edition, page 5. In later editions, this note disappeared since Voltaire made the same point in the "Discours préliminaire."

21. Notably, he wrote to Anisson-Duperron concerning the ornament: "Vous me feriez un sensible plaisir de faire mettre à la tête du poème, le côté de la médaille qui représente Le Roy" (D3204, [?25 August 1745]). The change of title also seems to have originated with Voltaire: "Je vous prie de mettre *Le poème de Fontenoy* en titre au frontispice, et en titre courant" (D3179, [20 July 1745]).

22. D3149, 17 juin 1745. This letter was addressed to the comte de Tressan, a participant in the battle who, like Voltaire, wrote a poem to celebrate Fontenoy.

23. Two weeks after scolding Voltaire, Maurepas notified Anisson-Duperron: "Vous ferés tirer, Monsieur, 800 exemplaires du Poëme de Fontenoy et vous les remettrés à M. de Voltaire; il souhaite que dans ce nombre il y en ait 200 reliés en veau et en maroquin. Comme je suis persuadé que le Roy ne désaprouvera pas cette deppense, vous voudrés bien vous charger de faire faire ces relieures; Je crois que M. de Voltaire sera content et je le désire" (D3181, 25 July 1745).

24. *Lettres de M. de Marville, lieutenant général de police, au ministre Maurepas, 1742–1747,* ed. A. de Boislisle (Paris: Champion, 1886–1905), 2: 93; cited by Besterman, D3150, [c.18 June 1745].

25. Several of these critical works are reprinted in *Les Voltairiens,* vol. 6, including Desfontaines's *Avis sincères à m. de Voltaire. Au sujet de la sixième édition de son poème sur la victoire de Fontenoi,* Dromgold's *Réflexions sur un imprimé intitulé "La bataille de Fontenoy, poème,"* and the anonymous *Apologie du poëme de M. de V**** sur la bataille de Fontenoy.*

26. Pierre Conlon registers a substantial jump in the number of works produced in 1744 and 1745 compared with previous years; in later years, the totals again drop considerably. *Le Siècle des Lumières. Bibliographie chronologique,* 17 vols. to date (Geneva: Droz, 1975), vol. 5.

27. "NE 2, 2 June 1745," in *Lettres de l'abbé Bonardy (1726–1745) et de Jean-Bernard Michault (1745),* ed. Henri Duranton (Saint-Etienne: Université de Saint-Etienne, 1977), 139.

28. This collection includes Voltaire's poem *Sur les événements de 1744* and his *Nouvelle épistre au roy, présentée à Sa Majesté au camp devant Fribourg, le premier novembre 1744.* The engraving is reproduced in Voltaire, *Histoire de la guerre de 1741.*

29. On the interest of such collections, see Albert Labarre, "Sur l'éminente dignité des *pièces,*" *Revue française d'histoire du livre* 84–85 (1994): 335–40. While discussing in a general way the preservation of ephemeral print materials, Labarre mentions specifically the copious Fontenoy production.

30. *La France consolée, ode. Par monsieur l'abbé Pellegrin. Avec un discours sur l'ode* (Paris, 1744); and the *Epître au Roy, au retour de sa campagne; avec un discours sur la critique, ou critique des critiques, par monsieur Néel* (Paris, 1744).

31. For example, *Plainte à messieurs les auteurs de l'Académie françoise* (Metz, 1744).

32. *Epître au public par un méchant poète tant en son nom, que comme portant la parole pour ses confrères, qui sont en très-grand nombre* (Paris, 1744), 2; *Le Dénonciateur du mauvais goût, et observations critiques sur l'ode de l'abbé Pellegrin* (Paris, 1744), 3.

33. Like David the previous year, the Lillois printer Panckoucke issued a *Recueil de pièces choisies sur la bataille de Fontenoy à la louange de Sa Majesté* (Lille, 1745), which he claimed was intended to satisfy "l'empressement des François pour conserver les monuments précieux de la victoire et des illustres conquêtes de notre monarque pendant cette année 1745" (verso of the title page). As in many of the *recueils factices,* Voltaire's text came first, followed by a mixture of other pieces. For general discussion of the poetic response to Fontenoy, see Menant, *La Chute d'Icare,* 285–96; and Michel Gilot, "Le Souvenir d'une belle bataille," in *L'Histoire au dix-huitième siècle. Colloque d'Aix-en-Provence; 1–3 mai 1975* (Aix-en-Provence: EDISUD, 1980), 307–28.

34. In *Les Voltairiens,* 6: 191. For general analysis of imitative modes of writing and particularly of the burlesque genre, see Gérard Genette, *Palimpsestes, la littérature au second degré* (Paris: Seuil, 1982), 78–88.

35. [F. Z. Pourroy de L'Auberivière de Quinsonas], *La Capilotade, poème ou tout ce qu'on voudra,* in *Les Volairiens,* 6: 265.

36. [Jean-Martin Marchand], *Requête du curé de Fontenoy, au Roy,* in *Recueil de pièces choisies,* item 8: 2.

37. "C'est-à-dire que vous avez fait votre Poëme *en un ou deux jours,* & que vous l'avez ensuite grossi de toutes les nouvelles vrayes ou fausses que l'on vous disoit. Mais est-ce là ce qu'on appelle composer un Poëme? N'est-ce pas travailler, comme on dit, au jour la journée?" [P. F. G. Desfontaines], *Avis sincères*

à m. de Voltaire. Au sujet de la sixième édition de son poème sur la victoire de Fontenoi, in *Les Voltairiens*, 6: 25.

38. Literary critics, too, attacked Voltaire's first sentence, since it suggested that imitation of Boileau (rather than celebration of the victory) was the poem's primary motivation: "C'est comme si quelque Poëte, sous l'Empire de Titus, eût invité tous les Romains à faire des vers à la louange de cet Empereur, parce qu'Horace avoit célébré Auguste; & cette invitation auroit été sans doute très-conséquent & très-spirituelle. . . ." *Apologie du Poëme de M. de V**** sur la bataille de Fontenoy*, in *Les Voltairiens*, 6: 4.

39. [A.-J. Panckoucke], *La Bataille de Fontenoy, poëme héroïque en vers burlesques, par un Lillois, natif de Lille en Flandre* (Lille, 1745).

40. *Le Galamathias, poesies du tems, héroïques, critiques, epiques, lyriques & comiques*, in *Recueil de pièces choisies*, item 9: 50.

41. *Epître au Roi par un Manceau* (1745), 3.

42. [P. H. Robbé de Beauveset], *Epitre du sieur Rabot, maître d'école de Fontenoy, sur les victoires du roi*, in *Les Voltairiens*, 6: 15.

43. The président Bouhier's correspondence registers the vogue of comic Fontenoy poetry: "Je ne vous parlerai point, Monsieur, de toutes les brochures poétiques dont nous sommes inondés sur la bataille de Fontenoy. Le comique a mieux réussi que le sérieux. La requête du curé de Fontenoy a remporté la palme. Elle a été faite par Mr Marchand, avocat, qui est fort de mes amis." "XXIII. 13 July 1745," in *Lettres de l'abbé Claude-Pierre Goujet (1737–1745)*, ed. Henri Duranton (Saint-Etienne: Université de Saint-Etienne, 1976), 83.

44. D3148, 16 June 1745, to Moncrif. Like many of the other parodies, the offending poem employed the opening exclamation to strengthen its ties with Voltaire: "Quoi! je serai silencieux, / Comme une huitre dans son écaille, / Lorsque la fameuse Bataille, / Met en train jusqu'aux vielleux, / Et que chacun rime ou rimaille? / Ai-je donc peur qu'on ne me raille, / D'oser faire une strophe ou deux, / Après ce Chantre si fameux, / Qui célèbre depuis Noailles, / Jusqu'au moindre petit morveux, / Portant talon rouge à Versailles?" *Vers sur la bataille de Fontenoy. par P.***, in *Recueil de pièces choisies*, item 6: 1–2.

45. *Lettre critique d'une belle dame à un beau monsieur de Paris sur le poëme de la bataille de Fontenoy* (M 8: 397–400). This text was first published in the Kehl edition in 1785; the manuscript, in Voltaire's hand, is held at the Institut et Musée Voltaire in Geneva. I thank Professor Christopher Todd, who is editing this work for the *Complete Works of Voltaire*, for this information.

46. *Epître à S.A.S. madame la duchesse du Maine, sur la victoire remportée par le Roi, à Lawfelt* (M 10: 341–42). On Voltaire's transition from poetry to history, see J. D. Leigh, "Patriotism and peace: Voltaire's responses to the War of the Austrian Succession," *Studies on Voltaire and the Eighteenth Century* 347 (1996): 643–45.

47. Of course, in other situations, Voltaire himself masterfully exploited the techniques that he deplores in the other Fontenoy poets, and with more explicit subversive intention. His adoption and simultaneous destruction of religious modes of speech is just one example of this practice. For a discussion of the monarchy's

attempts to channel information and control public response to the events of the War of the Austrian Succession, see Michèle Fogel, *Les Cérémonies de l'information dans la France du XVIe au milieu du XVIIIe siècle* (Paris: Fayard, 1989).

Appendix A. Poems that begin with "Quoi!"

In this list and in Appendix B, all poems date from 1745; many appeared with the apparently spurious place of publication, "Fontenoy." Several of the texts were included in an anthology printed by André-Joseph Panckoucke, *Recueil de pièces choisies sur la bataille de Fontenoy à la louange de sa Majesté* (see note 33). *Les Voltairiens* provides a modern reproduction of a small number of these works (see note 10). The Newberry Library (Chicago) possesses a magnificent set of ten volumes of ephemeral materials dating from the period of the War of the Austrian Succession; even this extensive collection does not, however, contain all of the items cited.

Quoi, faut-il être un Crébillon / Un Voltaire, un second Pirron? . . .
    —*Vers sur la bataille de Fontenoy . . . par m. le chevalier de C****
Quoi! Je serai silencieux / Comme une huitre dans son écaille! . . .
    — [Jean Henri Marchand], *Vers sur la bataille de Fontenoy, par P***
Quoi du Village le Barbier / A parler reste le dernier?
    —*Le Barbier du village de Fontenoy*
Eh quoi? lors que messire Jean / Qui jamais n'avait fait rimaille? . . .
    — [Jean Baptiste Carsillier], *Requeste de Gilles-Antoine Gareau, fossoyeur de Fontenoy*
Quoi, Sardis, j'entendrai chanter toute la France? . . .
    —*Complainte d'un Gascon*
Quoi du siècle présent le plus fameux Poete. . . .
    —*Epître au Roy, par un Manceau*
Quoi, dira-t-on, rien ne retient / Ton ardeur indiscrete. . . .
    —*Vers liriques sur la Bataille de Fontenoy par M. l'abbé de la ****
Quoi, restant comme un Iroquoi, / Je ne chanterois pas le Roi! . . .
    —*Le Galimathias, poésies du tems. . . par le grand Thomas*
Quoi, marchant sur les pas du *fameux Satyrique*. . . .
    —*Les Héros subalternes, poëme*
Quoi! quand tout chante le combat / Qui met Cumberland au grabat! . . .
    — [A.-J. Panckoucke], *La Bataille de Fontenoy, poëme héroïque en vers burlesques*

Quoy du Siècle présent l'Auteur Tragi-comique. . . .
  —[P. H. Robbé de Beauveset], *Epître du sieur Rabot, maître d'école de Fontenoy*
Quoi! nous sommes Vainqueurs, quoi! le bruyant François. . . .
  —[F. Z. Pourroy de L'Auberivière de Quionas], *La Capilotade, poème ou tout ce qu'on voudra*
Quoi donc j'aurai souvent en dépit de l'Envie! . . .
  —*Essay poëti-criti-heroi-comique, par le bailly de Fontenoy*
Quoi! toujours né parléra-t-on / Qué dé Bombes & dé Canon! . . .
  —[François Charles Gaudet], *La Muse gasconne, ou vers sur les succés de la campagne du Roi . . .*
Monarque, le Phenix des Rois, / Quoi, tandis que chacun gazouille? . . .
  —*Epître au Roy par Gros Jean, bedeau, carillonneur & fossoyeur*
Parlasambi notre bon Maître / Je voulons vous faire connaître. . . .
  —*Seconde piece des habitans de Fontenoy au Roy . . .*

Appendix B. Poems attributed to residents of Fontenoy

[Jean Henri Marchand], *Requête du curé de Fontenoy, au Roy.*
[P. H. Robbé de Beauveset], *Epître du sieur Rabot, maitre d'école de Fontenoy*
[Leudé de Sepmanville, or Lindet de Semonville], *Epître au Roy, par le premier marguiller de la paroisse de Fontenoy*
Epître au Roy par Gros Jean, bedeau . . .
Ode sur les victoires de Roy, par un enfant de choeur . . .
Regrets des filles de Fontenoy, sur les conquêtes du Roy . . .
Compliment des chantres de la mesme paroise à Sa Majesté
[Jean Baptiste Carsillier], *Requête au Roy, pour le curé d'Antoüin contre le curé de Fontenoy*
Néant sur la requête du curé de Fontenoy, son vicaire, le marguillier, le maistre d'école, & les enfans de choeur de ladite paroisse
Epître de mlle Javotte, nièce du curé de Fontenoy . . .
Le Barbier du village de Fontenoy
[François Charles Gaudet], *Epître ou requête de la gouvernante du curé de Fontenoy . . .*
L'Oracle ou la sybille de Fontenoy, ode, par la servante du curé
[Villerod], *Remerciement du curé de Fontenoy a l'auteur de sa requête*
Requeste de Gilles-Antoine Gareau, fossoyeur de Fontenoy . . .
Essai poëti-criti-héroï-comique, par le bailly de Fontenoy
Vers sur la bataille de Fontenoy par le vicaire du lieu

Les Habitans de Fontenoy, au Roy

Seconde piece des habitans de Fontenoy au Roy sur la suite de ses conquêtes depuis la bataille de Fontenoy

Lettre du cheval Pegaze au curé de Fontenoy

[Edmé Jacques Genet], *Lettre en vers au curé de Fontenoy, en forme de critique sur sa requête, par un curé de ses voisins*

The Inversion of Conversion: Rousseau's Rewriting of Augustinian Autobiography

PATRICK RILEY

". . . when we learn to know God we become new men in the image of our creator"

—Saint Augustine, *Confessions* 13: 22

"A l'instant de cette lecture je vis un autre univers et je devins un autre homme"

—Jean-Jacques Rousseau, *Confessions* VIII

What does it mean to convert? What are the stakes of this interruption of subjectivity for autobiography? These questions are posed forcefully by two crucial figures in the history of the genre, Saint Augustine and Jean-Jacques Rousseau. Religious conversion is the defining event in Augustine's *Confessions*: the sinner's submission to God is the experience which both legitimates the writing of an autobiography and functions as its central drama. But with Augustine conversion leads to the negation of the autobiographical enterprise: once he discovers that the value of the self lies completely in God, Augustine abandons personal narrative in favor of a reflection on the divine.

Some fourteen centuries later, Rousseau resuscitates Augustine's title and revisits the problem of conversion. That subjective violence, however, is now channeled towards a perpetual re-writing of the self. Autobiography is the inevitable outcome of the way in which Rousseau experiences conversion: as a tear in the fabric of life that only writing can mend. I will consider how Rousseau, while unquestionably recalling the structure as well as the rhetoric of Augustine's autobiography, redefines the form and meaning of conversion.[1] In suggesting what modern, secular conversion might be, Rousseau also defines modern, secular autobiography as both a reprise and a rejection of the Augustinian confessional tradition.

This study is in three parts. The first briefly suggests the critical stakes for autobiography of examining conversion. Invariably, conversion poses questions about the shape of an individual life and about the genre through which that life is represented. A relatively schematic overview of the paradoxical functioning of conversion in Augustine follows, underscoring the salient features of the religious conversionary model that will devolve on Rousseau. With these stakes and this model posited, we can turn to Rousseau's secular recasting of conversion, its reorientation away from God and toward a self so divided by experience that it can ultimately subsist only as a series of autobiographical representations.

Conversion, simply defined as radical subjective change,[2] both confirms and disrupts two of the most deeply entrenched premises about autobiography: totality and unity. The practice and critical account of post-Rousseau autobiography suggest that autobiography should possess the minimal characteristics of the realist novel (leaving aside the question of fiction):[3] a beginning and an end, and an autonomous narrative voice, as if it were possible to write one's story from a position of retrospective narrative authority beyond the life described. Autobiography's unrealizable fantasy is to write a *summa* of the self, as if the author were already dead. Hence, for example, the imagined perspective of the casket suggested by the title of Chateaubriand's *Mémoires d'outre-tombe*; hence Rousseau's repeated insistence in the *Confessions* that he is telling everything that it is possible to tell;[4] and hence Montaigne's expression in the *Essais* of his desire to portray himself "tout entier, et tout nud."[5] To this we may add the omnipresent inclusion in autobiographies of birth narratives and family genealogies which, while they obviously precede the autobiographer's self-consciousness, reinforce the illusion of a global life-narrative. As Chateaubriand puts it in an impossible sentence, "mon berceau a de ma tombe, ma tombe a de mon berceau."[6] The beauty behind the suspicious chiasmus of Chateaubriand's pronouncement is that it suggests both that the sense of a life can be assured by witnessing its beginning and its end and that there is essentially no difference between the two.

The foremost theorist of autobiography, Philippe Lejeune, proposed a definition in his 1975 *Le Pacte autobiographique,* which has become normative for numerous subsequent studies of the genre. An autobiography for Lejeune is a "retrospective prose narrative written by a real person concerning his own existence, where the focus is his individual life, in particular the story of his personality."[7] His definition supposes that the autobiographer as narrator and as protagonist are sufficiently similar to constitute two instances of the same personality.[8] Conversion, obviously, problematizes such a reading of character.[9]

Tying these two threads together, desire for totality and the demand that autobiography be a retrospective narrative of a recognizably consistent self, we arrive at a dominant generic model by which the orthodoxy of self-representational texts can be gauged. Canonical modern autobiography characterizes itself—and is by and large critically evaluated—as the pursuit of a totalizing narrative of the self that takes the broadest possible measure of the author's subjective experience. The work that refuses, fails to realize, or ironizes about this pursuit falls regularly into the genre's considerable margins.[10] What I hope to demonstrate here, however, is that even an undeniably canonical work such as Rousseau's *Confessions* to a certain extent undermines the very criteria of completeness and subjective consistency on which its canonicity is ostensibly based. No doubt this indeterminacy, or rather this determination of the *Confessions* as both canonical and potentially subversive, resides in a double game whereby Rousseau constantly *claims* unity of character, even as he simultaneously lodges the counter-claim that his life is incessantly overturned through radical change. Later, I will try to account for Rousseau's conflicting assessments of his own subjective life and their relation to his three major autobiographical works.[11]

Of course every autobiographer recognizes the fantasy of unity and totality *as* fantasy: an autobiography always comes too early and is always in some sense merely partial. And yet, when the topos of conversion is placed at the work's center, it becomes possible to write convincingly about the cradle and the grave Chateaubriand speaks of in the sentence quoted above. With its logic of death and rebirth, conversion permits the narration of a complete history because it inaugurates a radically new subjective history that closes a previous one: this is its very definition. Here and now, conversion offers a means of capturing a totalized self-image while recounting a life-narrative. At the same time, the convert risks becoming a representational schizophrenic.[12] The conversion scene defines, in a concentrated, powerful experience, everything that I believe myself to be, yet at the same time demands its wholesale denial. This is the paradox of conversion that concerns us here: by undergoing a conversion experience, I live through a death of the self which then allows me to apprehend myself as an integral totality, but at the cost that I am no longer "myself."[13]

The rhetoric of conversion plays upon what Paul de Man argues is autobiography's controlling metaphor. In "Autobiography as De-Facement," he writes: "The dominant figure of the epitaphic or autobiographical discourse is . . . the prosopopeia, the fiction of the voice-from-beyond-the-grave."[14] But the closure produced by the sealed casket is also the convert's overture: as one version of the self is buried, another is born and begins to speak. Following the prosopopeia that is the voice of the now-vanished preconvert, the voice kept alive only long enough to narrate its dislocation, there persists a language beyond the convert's epitaph, referring to a new life but not to a new name: conversion creates the literary effect of having survived oneself.

This, at least, is the scenario religious conversion establishes. Its privileged archetype in self-representational discourse is Augustine's *Confessions*, both because this text serves as an almost obsessional model in the history of the genre and because it posits the significance of conversion for autobiography in a particularly suggestive and rigorously logical way. Of the responses to the Augustinian model of conversion in the Western autobiographical tradition, Rousseau's is the most intriguing and has the furthest-reaching consequences for the development of the genre.[15]

The resonances between Augustine's and Rousseau's *Confessions* are not infrequently evoked in studies of Rousseau, but only rarely have they become the subject of an extended critical reflection, despite the powerful way in which the bishop of Hippo's confessional work clearly stands as both model and counter-model for Rousseau's autobiography. The only existing book-length study examining the two *Confessions* is Ann Hartle's *The Modern Self in Rousseau's Confessions: A Reply to Saint Augustine,* in which she argues that Rousseau, while aiming squarely at Augustine both on the level of structure and of an ideology of subjectivity, creates a radically different, modern version of the self: "the successful replacement of medieval self-consciousness by the consciousness of the modern self is what makes it necessary to convince contemporary readers that Rousseau is responding to Augustine" (10).[16] My inquiry in no way contests Hartle's assertions about the type of subjective configurations present in the two *Confessions*. However, her argument rests on demonstrating that Rousseau's *Confessions* "is *not* essentially autobiography" (9; original emphasis). Rather, in her view, the inauguration of modern selfhood is predicated upon Rousseau's construction of a quasi-fictive, universalizing "portrait" of man according to nature (9–37). While there is no question that Rousseau ascribes a paradigmatic value to his self-image,[17] I will argue that whereas Augustine's *Confessions* ultimately demand the foreclosure of autobiography, Rousseau's *Confessions*, and his subsequent *Dialogues* and *Rêveries*, suggest time and again that only autobiography is capable of salvaging the Rousseauean ideal of the autonomous self. And while Hartle de-emphasizes the role of conversion in Augustine and Rousseau, limiting her discussion to an essentially formal comparison of the conversion scenes in Book VIII of both *Confessions*, conversion lies at the center of my argument: it functions very precisely as that which ends autobiography in Augustine and as that which makes autobiography so necessary for Rousseau.

The Conversion Scenario in Augustine's Confessions

Augustine's *Confessions* are structured around two confessional forms that were already well established at the time of the text's production: *confessio peccati*, or confession of sins, and *confessio laudis*, or praise of God.[18] The constant interpenetration of these two forms constitutes the work's central tension, between a discourse of the self and a discourse of, and toward, God. The book is split roughly in half, with the first part detailing Augustine's life as a sinner and his quest for certitude, while the second is a metaphysical treatise on memory, temporality, language, and Biblical exegesis. The fulcrum upon which the division is balanced is the sinner's conversion to Christianity in Book VIII. After an interlude in which Augustine recounts his early integration into a Christian community and the death of his mother, the text ceases purely and simply to be an autobiography.[19] The irreducibility of the historical subject, whose unique experiences are coagulated in narrative, gives way to the discourse of the universal Christian subject, still emanating, of course, from Augustine's consciousness, but no longer as the mark of its subjective singularity.

The preconversional books relate Augustine's foundering in worldliness. In a desolating attempt to arrive at the simplest truth about the world, he passes through Manichean materialism, a Ciceronian exhortation to philosophy, Academic skepticism, and Neoplatonism, before finally accepting Christ in the famous conversion scene.[20] The preconversional self is inchoate and incomplete. It constantly seeks self-definition in relation to otherness, through mimetic desire. Augustine, in episode upon episode, recounts how his pursuit of certitude centers around the imitation of exemplary figures, first in the domain of rhetoric, then in philosophy, and finally in Christian history.

The drama of conversion, however, reveals the truth of the self in a sudden illumination. The exemplary figures that fueled the conversion immediately lose their significance.[21] Once it is recognized that God is the ultimate *telos* of the human soul, it becomes clear that no worldly models of imitation remain to be emulated. In this sense, conversion returns the self to itself, so that it finally becomes possible to consider selfhood as an autonomous category. Indeed, it is only after the conversion scene that Augustine poses the autobiographical question *par excellence* for the first time: "Who am I?"[22]

Conversion provides the answer to that question, but its solution generates an immediate paradox. Augustine learns "who he is" by grasping that his entire being derives from God, and that his soul will only achieve plenitude and clarity when it is reunited with its divine source upon the death of the body. Conversion also reveals "who he was," which turns out retrospectively to be nearly nothing: the preconversional self, to the extent that it is distanced from God, does not possess genuine being.[23] The sinner that the first books of the *Confessions* describe is in a sense a fiction, a false subject. The self reborn through conversion, however, can only become intelligible in direct proportion to the convert's capacity to understand God, which is inevitably limited: the convert must be "content to know without knowing, or should I say, to be ignorant and yet to know?" (12: 5, 283). Thus the latter books are an attempt to shed as much light as possible on the nature of terrestrial being by contemplating the attributes of its divine origin and destination. Self-knowledge becomes the knowledge that the self is not fully knowable, and self-representation in the *Confessions* is abruptly terminated.

Augustine's theoretical chapters (Books X–XIII) construct an image of a *deus absconditus*, the hidden God that will haunt the Port-Royal Jansenists of the French seventeenth century. Nonetheless, these chapters make it plain that the value of the redeemed soul is derived entirely from its unintelligible source, and that the entire thrust of the convert's activities is directed toward becoming worthy of joining this shadowy being, of becoming something other than a human being. The self's ideal, in this context, is its own demise as self. It is fragmentary because it is still separated from God even as conversion promises a recuperation of fullness and integrity. All subjects—of which Augustine is now only a representative—are finally reduced to a kind of nullity before the sublimity of the divine. The individuation of a sinner in the preconversional books yields to a discourse opening onto the perfect gratuity of any possible gesture of individuation. The *Confessions* must be read, therefore, as an autobiography that elides its own autobiographical content in order to demonstrate the futility of all autobiographical projects. *Confessio peccati*, the language of the fall, the space accorded to the Christian for talking about the self, is progressively subsumed by the infinite possibilities of *confessio laudis*, of talking about a God who is all the more discursively productive for being ultimately unknowable.

If Augustine finally insists that autobiography must fall silent when God enters the soul, and if the historical self disappears in anticipation of its inscription in a divine, eternal temporality existing beyond history, we nonetheless have to account for the fact that the text remains as a human artifact, as the self's durable trace marking the path to its own extinction as historical subject. This remainder, ostensibly, would point to the *Confessions*'s didactic function. The persistence of Augustine's confession as a document circulating in the world, beyond the self's disappearance as representational object, would serve as a mimetic *exemplum* for other prospective converts (just as Augustine's own conversion is sparked by a series of exemplary Christian figures). He is well aware of the superfluity of a confession addressed solely to God, since God knows every thought in the convert's mind before it even occurs (2: 3; 5: 1; and 10: 2–5). However, he seems genuinely hesitant to offer his own life as a model: at times he asserts his intention to instill the love of God in others (8: 4; and 11: 1), but he also claims on several occasions that only those who already have Christian charity in their hearts will appreciate his words (1: 6; 10: 3–4; and 10: 33).

Perhaps this is because the crucial step of conversion, the complete submission to a Big Other of whose nature the sinner is only dimly aware, involves a leap into a space in which exemplarity is impossible: the sinner cannot imitate God but simply desire Him; only those who already understand this will understand the *Confessions*. If this is the case, then the text functions not as a model for the conversion of sinners but as an edifying discourse in which the already converted see their own faith mirrored, in a doubling analogous to the superfluity of confessing to a God who has always already known what the convert's confession would contain. In either event, Augustine perceives an acute tension in the relationship between the historical narrative of his life as the memorial of a dead subject and his anticipation of a union with God. In other words, he identifies a polarity in his confession between pure retrospect and pure prospect. Autobiography recounts a self that must renounce its *textual* future when it glimpses a potential return to the eternal present of the Word. The defining characteristic of Augustine's book becomes the representation of the vanished past of a subject that never fully existed, and it emanates from a null-point in which the writing subject exists only as immanent to a fullness of being that has yet to be conferred:

> I am divided between time gone by and time yet to come, and its course is a mystery to me. My thoughts, the intimate life of my soul, are torn this way and that in the havoc of change. And so it will be until I am purified and melted by the fire of your love and fused into one with you. (11: 29, 279)

The moment of conversion is the last moment in which it is possible to live in the present: once conversion's work is completed, it is only possible to look backward through *confessio peccati* or forward through *confessio laudis*; to look directly inward is to discover a soul that is pure evanescence. Self-presence, captured as intelligible totality in the text, is precisely what Augustinian confession can never achieve in the precarious interplay between the time of lapsed historical experience and the eternity that lies somewhere beyond the time of writing. Augustine writes an autobiography whose most profound intention is to function as an index of a destination that will render both writing and retrospection meaningless. The discovery of the truth of a self that has to die in order to be grasped is also the promise of an eternal life in the radical beyond of any possible text written by a human hand.

Rousseau's Inversion of Conversion

Rousseau appropriates many of the *topoi* of Augustinian confessional discourse but shifts their function radically. In a gesture of epistemological leveling, he employs the pointed rhetoric of death and rebirth we witness in Augustine, but demolishes the metaphysical bases from which Augustinianism springs. Rousseauean conversion becomes an economy in which the place of the dialectic between God and the subject in Augustine is occupied by the equally problematic relationship between the self and its representation in the world. The self that conversion constructs in Rousseau is not an immanent subject glimpsing its own future plenitude in the light of its destination, but a self led in its encounters with the world increasingly further afield from a claimed originary, "natural" integrity. Augustinian conversion is a fortunate death promising greater life; Rousseauean conversion becomes a repeatable chain of deaths which the self always somehow survives, but from which it emerges in an increasingly disfigured guise.[24]

For Rousseau, full and self-sufficient being is a theoretical starting point, a birthright; conversion, as subjective upheaval, is the anguishing degeneration of authentic being. Augustinian conversion only occurs once: a turn to God, the moment it is accomplished, reveals itself to be the only legitimate way in which the subject can reformulate itself. In Rousseau's case, to the contrary, there are seemingly countless possibilities for the self to be overturned and refashioned into something unlike any of its previous configurations, endless ways to become a "new man." Conversion is transformed from an absolute and singular figure into a contingent and cyclical figure. In a profoundly anti-Augustinian move, Rousseau voids the notion of conversion of its positive value, wresting it, as it were, away from God, positing it as an infinitely repeatable and self-shattering experience, making it not the celebratory index of a rebirth but an elegiac lament for the death of a version of the self, and finally, making it not a subjective destination but a starting point from which a counter-discourse of the self's recuperation of its wholeness will be launched in the margins of, and beyond, the *Confessions*.

In the interval between the composition of Augustine's *Confessions* at the end of the fourth century, and Rousseau's *Confessions* fourteen centuries later, an enormous shift in the individual's self-conception has of course taken place. Augustine writes in the indistinct margin between the demise of classical antiquity and the beginnings of medieval Christianity's ascendancy, and his own conversion from classical rhetorician and student of Neoplatonism to Catholic orthodoxy bears the imprint of this movement. The individual's place in early Christendom can only be understood as relational, dependent upon its hierarchical position in a stratified Christian community, and finally, upon its subordination to God. By Rousseau's time, Renaissance humanism had already delineated a broader space for the properly human and, to a certain extent, for the personal, evident for example in the autobiographical writings of Cardano, Cellini and Montaigne. In the seventeenth century, Cartesianism had posited the sovereignty of the autonomous thinking subject, still dependent upon God's benevolent power of continuous creation for its existence, but nonetheless an intellectual and affective free agent. It is following these developments, in the rapidly secularizing and self-aware age of Enlightenment, that literary historians routinely localize the origin of modern autobiography, and just as routinely cite Rousseau's *Confessions* as the *locus classicus* of the genre.[25]

Rousseau's modernity, however, consists not in radical innovation, but rather lies in how he distances himself from a prior self-representational tradition by reformulating that tradition's tropes. While paying an odd sort of homage to Augustine, he turns the entire confessional logic of Augustinianism on its head.[26] The encounter between the Rousseauean doctrine of selfhood and the Augustinian rhetoric of spiritual conversion goes a long way toward explaining a general critical conviction that Rousseau's *Confessions* inaugurate a new direction in autobiography, yet also suggests that the originality of his autobiographical venture depends very much on its positioning—Rousseau's claims of unprecedented novelty notwithstanding—within an established generic context.

This inversion is already evident in the opening to Book I of the *Confessions*. Rousseau begins, like Augustine, with an address to God. However, God's purely tangential relation to Rousseau's concerns becomes immediately apparent: "Que la trompette du jugement dernier sonne quand elle voudra; je viendrai ce livre à la main me présenter devant le souverain juge. Je dirai hautement: voila ce que j'ai fait, ce que j'ai pensé, ce que je fus. . . . Etre éternel, rassemble autour de moi l'innombrable foule de mes semblables: qu'ils écoutent mes confessions . . ." (1: 5). God is no longer a *destinataire*, but a mere guarantor of the veracity and the sincerity of the individual's discourse, the mediator charged with insuring that Rousseau's message be relayed to his peers, who henceforth become the text's sole addressee. God is simply a more reliable reader than Rousseau's worldly peers.[27]

The passage also reveals that the judgment to which Rousseau refers is to be made not on the man, but on his book.[28] The suggestion is that the truth of the self can only be made manifest to the other through writing, one of whose functions is to recuperate and articulate what is lost in the self's encounters with the world, even though it is precisely writing that Rousseau will later identify as the agent which renders an exculpatory autobiography necessary in the first place.[29] Writing is an inoculation in reverse presented in reverse of its subjective effects, with its recuperative powers suggested before any mention is made of the disease which it caused and might also cure.

That Rousseau should require redemption is the outcome of a fatal moment of errancy in which he succumbs to the lure of authorship, the illumination on the road to Vincennes recounted in Book VIII of the *Confessions*. This key moment is emblematic of what constitutes Rousseauean conversion: it is a momentary crisis from which the self emerges completely and ostensibly irretrievably changed.[30] Before this cataclysmic upheaval, however, Rousseau has already undergone a series of also presumably irremediable crises.[31]

Throughout the text one encounters a tension between Rousseau's repeated claims that his character is unitary and consistent, in short, that he is endowed with primordially good intentions and uniform purity of feeling, and his even more frequent claims that his life is marked by unexpected reversals so powerful that they sweep him away in a kind of uncontrollable flux. The hyperbolic rhetoric employed in the description of these subjective upheavals is precisely the rhetoric of conversion, which, as I have already suggested, has the double characteristic of momentarily coagulating the subject's being in a global definition but also of marking the self's transformation into something else.

Put somewhat differently, the tension in the work between the self's unity and fragmentation echoes an ambivalence concerning the way in which Rousseau conceives the autobiographical project as such. The opening of the *Confessions*, in which he insists avidly upon complete self-disclosure, suggests that the text's primary mission is to detail the unique and irreducible historical circumstances through which the self is realized in experience. Rousseau is obsessed with the outrageous concatenations of events in which he becomes unwillingly enmeshed, and presents their narration as the basis of his enterprise, even though it is precisely these events that he sees as contrary to the unitary self-image he so fervently wishes to convey to the reader. In other words, it is what precedes conversion ontologically that Rousseau aims at eventually regaining, so that, while Augustine as convert becomes pure immanence before an other-worldly future, the repeatedly converted self in Rousseau becomes immanent to a lost version of its own essence. This is why conversion for Rousseau must be not only repeatable, but somehow *reversible:* the ultimate goal of writing autobiographies is to extricate the self from its crisis-ridden and mediate relation to its own history.

Paradoxical as the assertion may appear, Rousseau's first conversion is his birth. It subverts the hypostatized subjective ideal he has just proposed in the previous pages (in the *avertissement* to the text, the address to God, and in a narrative detailing his family origins); it also disrupts the expected order of experience: "je naquis infirme et malade; je coûtai la vie à ma mère, et ma naissance fut le premier de mes malheurs. . . . J'étois né presque mourant; on esperoit peu de me conserver" (1: 7). He describes his coming into the world as the first in a series of sudden reversals to which he will fall prey. The moment which we expect to see posited as pure origin is already a double blurring of origin: Jean-Jacques's biological source, his mother, is killed by his birth, and Jean-Jacques himself is not expected to live, existing at this point as a deathly figure and as the tragic occasional cause of his mother's demise.[32] We learn almost immediately, then, that the natural and unmediated self that Rousseau will constantly name as the pure source from which experience has excluded him, and which he seeks to recuperate, is an origin he has never known directly. Rousseau's ongoing quest for the originary self cannot find its satisfaction in a return to his earliest days, but must, we begin to suspect, be located entirely outside experience if it is to be located at all.[33]

More significant, perhaps, than Jean-Jacques's inauspicious inauguration into the world is the perverse familial role he is forced to play after he has the misfortune to survive: he has to serve as a surrogate wife to his bereaved father by staying up with him into the wee hours reading the novels she left behind. The death of his mother distorts the natural familial order; a father "more childish" (1: 8) than his own son ensures that the corruption of that order will be maintained and intensified by Jean-Jacques's participation in an attempt to resuscitate the lost maternal origin by playing her role, that is, by becoming a self whose character is dictated by the other and not by nature.[34] Before a primordial subject can constitute itself through a set of relations to the world, a debased version of the world (with the death of the mother and her simulated presence in the person of Jean-Jacques) and a fictional world (in the novels that are his mother's legacy) constitute a subject whose uniqueness is only equaled by, indeed derives from, the degree to which it deviates from immediate self-presence and autonomy.[35] The defining characteristics of the birth scene—the overturning of a dubious but cherished natural origin, the fragmentation of the self when it passes into the representational grid governed by the other—are recapitulated in a number of subsequent episodes preceding the central conversion to authorship. Since each of them repeats the presumably inimitable and irreversible moments of crisis that come before it, I will focus on just one: the broken-comb incident from Book I, which formulates the stakes of Rousseau's *bouleversements* in the clearest form.[36]

The episode comes as an abrupt end to an idyllic narrative of Rousseau's early years spent at Bossey under the tutelage of the Lamberciers, after he is abandoned by his father. The bucolic sentimentality of this narrative, its claims of a perfect adequation between environment and the self's natural proclivities, its reintegration into a natural order, are the antithesis of his "perverse" relation to the father as ersatz love object.[37] The incident is noteworthy for its banality: Rousseau is falsely accused by the Lamberciers of breaking a comb, and he puts up a heated self-defense which is finally accepted but not believed by the accusers. The entire interest of the scene lies in the extraordinary value he accords it: it becomes a moment of anguish that bowls the child over, shows him the existence of injustice in the world, and brings to a close his capacity to enjoy the supposedly pure pleasure of childhood innocence:[38]

> Qu'on se figure un caractére timide et docile . . . qui n'avoit pas même l'idée de l'injustice, et qui, pour la prémiére fois en éprouve une si terrible, de la part précisément des gens qu'il chérit le plus. Quel renversement d'idées! quel desordre de sentimens! quel bouleversement dans son cœur, dans sa cervelle, dans tout son petit être intelligent et moral! Je dis, qu'on s'imagine tout cela, s'il est possible; car pour moi, je ne me sens capable de démêler, de suivre, la moindre trace de ce qui se passoit alors en moi. . . . Là fut le terme de la serenité de ma vie enfantine. Dès ce moment je cessai de jouir d'un bonheur pur, et je sens aujourd'hui même que le souvenir des charmes de mon enfance s'arrête là. (1: 19–20)

What pains him most is the extraordinary disproportion between his own representation of himself as innocent and the contrary representation that the other has formed of him. It is as if the psychological trauma of which he speaks were caused by an inability to reconcile the two conflicting representations, so that in an instant, he no longer knows who he is; he knows only that the stunning moment of conflict he has just undergone makes him into something incomparably different.

The incident marks the end of an entire mode of being, that of a nostalgic version of innocence, but also serves as the origin of a moral sense of injustice whose traces persist at the time of writing. Every time this moral sense is engaged in the present, it is suddenly superimposed upon the childhood episode, creating the impression that Jean-Jacques's entry into the moral world encapsulates the whole temporality of his subjective experience.[39] Rousseau expresses the aftermath of the episode in an inflationary analogy to the Adamic fall when he describes the last days he and his cousin spend together at his uncle's house: "Nous restames encore à Bossey quelques mois. Nous y fumes comme on nous réprésente le prémier homme encore dans le paradis terrestre, mais ayant cessé d'en joüir. C'étoit en apparence la même situation, et en effet une toute autre maniére d'être. . . . Tous les vices de nôtre âge corrompoient nôtre innocence et enlaidissoient nos jeux" (1: 20–21).

The episode has the effect of demarcating, despite its brevity and apparent inconsequentiality, the entire scope of the child's being which, even as it is being mapped out, is forever negated through conversional change, in the same way as Adam is only able to recognize the beatitude of his prior state by its juxtaposition with the knowledge that comes with the fall. Rousseau senses a devastating loss as the direct consequence of an unsolicited confrontation with a social reality that traffics only in representations.

At the moment of autobiographical retrospection, when Rousseau looks back upon his disastrous history, he can only view his decision to place himself at the heart of communal representation by becoming an author as a moment of complete folly. Before autobiographical writing can become a potentially redemptive project, writing as such is posited as a disastrous activity that puts the self at the mercy of its purely imaginary public image, so that to become an author is to die as an autonomous self and to be reborn as the fantasy the other deduces from the author's writings.[40]

In what is perhaps the best-known passage in the entire *Confessions*, Rousseau recounts how, while walking to Vincennes to visit the imprisoned Diderot, he reads in the *Mercure de France* a question posed for an essay competition, namely, whether the progress of the arts and sciences has corrupted or purified social behavior. His response, of course, is the *First Discourse*, which results in almost overnight notoriety. What is at issue here however is not the composition of the essay itself, but the absolutely overwhelming moment of inspiration, flux, and disorientation that Rousseau experiences upon reading the question. The description of this crucial moment comes very near the text's center point, and is also its dramatic zenith:[41]

> A l'instant de cette lecture je vis un autre univers et je devins un autre homme. . . . Ce que je me rappelle bien distinctement dans cette occasion c'est qu'en arrivant à Vincennes, j'étois dans une agitation qui tenoit du délire. Diderot l'apperçut; je lui en dis la cause, et je lui lus la prosopopée de Fabricius écrite en crayon sous un Chêne. Il m'exhorta de donner l'essor à mes idées et de concourir au prix. Je le fis, et dès cet instant je fus perdu. Tout le reste de ma vie et de mes malheurs fut l'effet inévitable de cet instant d'égarement. (1: 351)

The rhetoric of this passage is scarcely different from that which Augustine uses to describe the force and suddenness of his conversion to Christ. There are also marked structural similarities between Augustine's and Rousseau's conversion experiences:[42] Augustine converts when, upon hearing a child repeat *tolle, lege*, he turns to a random passage in a Pauline epistle and sees himself troped in the text, after which he falls weeping under a fig tree. Rousseau, too, succumbs to the force of a textual message, sees himself or rather what he is about to become in that text, and collapses in tears under an oak.[43]

Nothing, however, could be more contrary to the Augustinian experience than the valence Rousseau ascribes to this conversion. The way in which he unravels the most basic implications of religious conversion far outweighs the importance of obvious structural similarities. Indeed, those similarities only succeed in inviting a comparison whose effect is to underline how greatly Rousseau's experience differs from the ecstatic discovery of God. Augustine knows that his submission to God is the beginning of genuine life and the first glimpse of his soul redeemed. Rousseau, however, sees his experience retrospectively as a shattering loss of the self-possessed soul that he could have enjoyed if only he had not succumbed to writing, to that most pernicious form of representational mediation which divorces the self from its essence.

Augustine's conversion creates the conditions under which it will no longer be necessary, nor even legitimate, to write of the self. Rousseau's, to the contrary, creates the paradoxical conditions under which the self, hopelessly fragmented in its descent into the hell of writing, and harking back to an origin that eludes its grasp, can be rehabilitated only by further writing. Each of his three major autobiographical works represents a different attempt at subjective recuperation. The *Confessions* become a memorializing discourse through the writing of a personal history explaining why Rousseau should never have become a writer. The other remaining option is writing not as retrospection but as pure prospect, from beyond the tomb of the worldly self that authorship has erected, in the dystopic delirium of the *Dialogues: Rousseau juge de Jean Jaques* and the ectopic insularity of the *Rêveries du promeneur solitaire.*

It is therefore little surprise, given the overdetermination of the role of writing in this reworking of religious conversion, that Rousseau should happen to have a pencil in his hand under the oak tree on the road to Vincennes. What he feverishly scribbles there is highly significant: he writes a text which will be incorporated into the *First Discourse*, a fictionalized prosopopeia in Fabricius's voice offering a premonitory moral discourse to the present from the distant virtue of a Plutarchan past. The gesture is an almost parodically literalized version of the prosopopeia, the "fiction of the voice-from-beyond-the-grave" that de Man gives as the privileged trope of the autobiographical genre. It is as if Rousseau sees, at the very moment he is presumably undergoing a quasi-divine inspiration to write, a figure of the death of his own self and his disfiguring rebirth as ossified author and as other, of his own en-tombment in an unwanted conversion to the discursive.[44] The ambivalent play of the death and rebirth of the self is encapsulated within the figure of Fabricius: Rousseau speaks in the appropriated voice of a dead man, ana-logically enacting a grim necroscopy of everything that he had previously been and will never be again, but at the same time resuscitating Fabricius just long enough to take his place as his living inheritor. Thus the prosopopeia admirably defines what Rousseauist conversion always leads to: the memo-rializing language that continues to flow from a self long buried, from a self ostensibly destroyed by a never-ending series of conversional lightening-strikes opening finally onto the mortality of writing.

Two problems remain to be accounted for: namely, how Rousseau justi-fies the autobiographical enterprise as an inevitable response, however para-doxical, to the violence produced by writing, and how, in the face of the *Confessions*'s seemingly self-propagating conversional logic, he can baldly affirm that his character is essentially unitary and stable. Both questions can be addressed by suggesting a deeper autobiographical intention than the stated project of full self-disclosure. There must be something beyond an historical narrative of accidents and disasters to which the *Confessions* point, if only surreptitiously.

Rousseau's retrospection reconstructs the causality of his life doubly: on the one hand, he ascribes the series of calamities that befalls him as the product of pure chance; on the other, he describes how each apparently ran-dom misfortune creates a deterministic concatenation leading to an unavoid-able outcome. What interests him far more than either his random misfor-tunes or their inevitable effects, however, is how encounters with experience's vicissitudes deform the self's natural disposition, how they corrupt the self's original language, the pre-reflective sense of innocence dictated by nature. This origin nonetheless, as we saw with Rousseau's birth, is displaced every time it is posited, to the extent that it becomes impossible to demonstrate it as an historical phenomenon. All that Rousseau is ultimately able to do, with every instance of a conversional crisis, is present the natural self he could have become had an encounter with mediation not intervened to change its trajectory. In other words, he has to content himself with suggesting a *pos-sible*, hypothetical self impervious to the aleatory that would exist if only there were no world, no other, no mediation. In this sense, the *Confessions* point to an unrealized potential self whose traces arise only sporadically in the text, during certain privileged moments in which Rousseau overcomes his own alienation and dwells briefly in a kind of beatific self-presence.

It is this underlying self-presence, when it makes itself felt precisely as that which resists crisis and change, that which resists integration into a causal-temporal frame (and thus resists narrative), that Rousseau will give as the basis of the assertion that his character is unitary and consistent. What signals and legitimates the assertion is easily overlooked, lying in insignificant proximity to the extravagant claims of totality and sincerity in the opening paragraph of the text. Marking the existence and the persistence of a self impervious to the chaos of conversion is the simple phrase "Je sens mon cœur" (1: 5), whose implicit corollary is that he feels his own goodness. Much of the autobiography that follows is an attempt to make this directly accessible sentiment as discursively transparent to the reader as it is immediately and pre-reflectively transparent to Rousseau himself.[45] Its mode, however, is derivative: it has to be excavated as a purely hypothetical reconstruction from the narrative of the historical self, since it has no other describable locus to which it properly belongs. Its existence is never more than immanent, like the state of nature postulated in the *Discourse on Inequality*.

The final scene recounted in the *Confessions* is also an assertion that Rousseau's subterranean image of the ideal self was not effectively communicated to the other. Here, he describes the effect of several private readings of a manuscript of his autobiography. Instead of the sympathetic understanding of the audience he expected, his text is met with stunned silence, which finally becomes the silence that terminates the text and silently pronounces its failure: "J'achevai ainsi ma lecture et tout le monde se tut . . . . Tel fut le fruit que je tirai de cette lecture et de ma déclaration" (1: 656).[46] If the other cannot understand Rousseau's goal of self-rehabilitation in the *Confessions*, it is no doubt because he is attempting to redress an image that the other has constructed.

Thus the most remarkable resurfacing of the kind of direct self-presence that Rousseau had hoped could be distilled from the *Confessions* occurs elsewhere, in his two subsequent autobiographical productions, the *Dialogues* and the *Rêveries*. These works directly attempt to reformulate his relation to the other. In the *Dialogues*, Rousseau posits the other—*all* others—as hostile conspirators whose greatest aspiration in life is to defame him, to corrupt his reputation before posterity by circulating counterfeit writings in his name and to force him into exile. He characterizes this as an attempt to "bury him alive," that is, to make the truth of the historical self dead to the world.[47] The fantasy is also a radicalization of his previous claims of singularity: so singular does he now become that he is pitted against the entire French nation.

The major flaw in the conspirators' method, however (Rousseau asserts), is that they have so thoroughly extricated him from the social real, by portraying him as an unimaginable miscreant, that he is now at perfect liberty to coincide with the natural self which, in the *Confessions*, experience constantly put beyond his reach. The "true" Jean-Jacques becomes so hidden from the *semblables* addressed in the *Confessions* that he can no longer be

forced into a defacement through representation. The price of this recuperation of the natural self, however, is delusion. The kind of liberation from the
other and from worldly experience it proposes comes about through a para-
noid obsession with the other's gaze: Rousseau can only claim identity with
his natural self because his public image has become so aberrant that not
even he could possibly resemble it.[48]

The *Rêveries*, on the other hand, proclaim a self whose fullness is possible because the historical world to which it is inextricably linked in the
Confessions is proclaimed to have been entirely elided: this is the sense of
the "Me voici donc seul sur la terre" (1: 995) with which the text opens, the
"donc" indicating the perfect logicality of the postulate of radical solitude.
Here, we find two beautiful examples of a recuperation of the self uncorrupted by mediation. One is from the fifth *promenade*, in which Rousseau
describes the fullness of being he senses as he drifts aimlessly across the
waters surrounding the Ile de Saint Pierre. He experiences the pleasure of
"un bonheur suffisant, parfait, et plein, qui ne laisse dans l'ame aucun vuide
qu'elle sente le besoin de remplir" (1: 1046).[49] The second is a remarkable
passage from the second *promenade* in which he describes regaining consciousness after being bowled over by a Great Dane, a passage that owes a
great deal to Montaigne's narrative of returning to consciousness after a fall
from a horse.[50] Temporarily without memory, without knowledge of the world
and of time, it is as if Rousseau witnessed his own birth as an autonomous
subject, precisely the autonomy his actual birth denied. So full is his sense of
his own being that he imagines it is the gradually resuscitating self that endows objects with life, rather than merely observes them: "Je naissois dans
cet instant à la vie, et il me sembloit que je remplissois de ma legere existence tous les objets que j'appercevois" (1: 1005).[51]

This primacy of individual feeling, this language of the heart that can only
flow in the absence of any mediative agent, is what Rousseau identifies as
the locus of genuine selfhood. His autobiographical works are an attempt to
extricate the authentic self through representation from its degraded figuring
in the public imagination and from the unexpected metamorphoses conversional change wreaks upon it. Writing an account of its truth is the only
remaining means of counterbalancing its communal co-option. The accident's
public reception is symptomatic of the other's tendency to distort reality:
"Voilà très fidellement l'histoire de mon accident. En peu de jours cette
histoire se répandit dans Paris tellement changée et défigurée qu'il étoit
impossible d'y rien reconnoitre. J'aurois dû compter d'avance sur cette
métamorphose . . ." (1: 1006–7). Furthermore, that Rousseau should speak
of the public's reaction to the incident at all indicates that his bracketing of
any concern with the other is less than entirely successful, or at least, that the

significance of solitude depends on imagining the other from whom one is absent.

The episode of Rousseau's accident nevertheless demonstrates admirably that he desires only a rebirth devoid of a prehistory, experienced not as loss but as pure repossession of autonomous being. The other conversions we have examined, born of the aleatory and corrupting confrontation between the self and social representation, are always anguishing ruptures in which a version of the self is forever extinguished. If Rousseau wants to offer not himself but his *Confessions* to the almighty judge, and if he writes the *Dialogues* and *Rêveries* as if he were already dead, it is because it is only in the autobiographical text that the primordial, irreducible Rousseauist self lives on, because of and in spite of its multiple conversions in the world.

Augustine's failure to validate the autobiographical venture lies in the fact that he allows God rather than the self to "sign" the work. That his disappearance as protagonist and the termination of narrative in the latter books of the *Confessions* are rigorously motivated by the terms of his conversion does nothing to remedy the fact that a devalued self that never truly existed has begun to speak in the dislocated voice of a self that has yet truly to exist. The writing of a non-self and the non-writing of authentic selfhood— autobiographical aporia, in other words—can only be resolved in the heavenly city. In a remarkable passage, Augustine imagines the transition from the worldly to the divine as the acquisition of the capacity to understand being without having to read its intelligibility in a text. For the angels, God's face becomes the otherworldly book in which the secrets of being are eternally revealed: "The book they read shall not be closed . . . For you yourself are their book and you forever are" (13: 15, 323). Conversion reveals that the meaning an autobiography tries to give to a life is deferred to a moment in which the autobiographer can read his truth not in his own writing but in God's face.

Rousseau attempts to shift this deferral back to writing as the locus of the truth of the self. As we move from the *Confessions* to the *Dialogues* to the *Rêveries*, however, he is increasingly obligated to cast himself as the angel capable of deciphering his own truth and as the creator who alone can restore the fullness of being that conversion continually threatens to destroy. God's power of ontological revelation devolves on autobiography itself, but there remains the anguishing risk that no one besides the autobiographer can interpret the text's message. Augustine's God becomes a different kind of eternal book for Rousseau, the flesh become word that founds modern autobiography by making it experience's ultimate end.

NOTES

1. Nowhere does Rousseau explicitly acknowledge Augustine's *Confessions* as a model; quite the contrary: he insists only on the novelty and uniqueness of his own autobiographical project. As he asserts in a preface to the *Confessions*, his is the first and will be the last true and complete work of human portraiture ever to exist. While in a strange way his claim of uniqueness may indeed be true, that uniqueness cannot be asserted on purely formal grounds. My interest here is not in trying to establish the extent to which Rousseau consciously intended to imitate or refute Augustine's autobiography, but rather to excavate the remarkable formal and above all thematic parallels existing between the two *Confessions*, and the ways in which the resemblances between the two works gravitate toward the related poles of conversion and autobiography as generic practice.

2. I am deliberately proposing this open-ended definition of conversion to allow for conversions that are religious or secular, gradual or sudden, and spiritual or intellectual. Broad and variable definitions of conversion have existed at least since the pioneering studies in the psychology of religion, at the turn of the century, of William James and E. D. Starbuck. In a Lacanian study of conversion narratives, Gerald Peters offers a useful overview of how conversion has been historically understood, ranging from the Platonic concept of epistrophe to Jungian *enantiodromia*. See *The Mutilating God: Authorship and Authority in the Narrative of Conversion* (Amherst: Univ. of Massachusetts Press, 1993), 2–6. Peters himself points to the importance of the conversion experience as a "totalizing narrative."

3. Perhaps this rigid generic rubric for traditional autobiography, borrowed as it seems to be from narrative fiction, is partially responsible for the contemporary disappearance of any meaningful distinction between autobiography and the novel over and above a purely conventional one. On this question, see Vincent Kaufmann, "Life by the Letter," *October* 64 (Spring 1993): 91–105.

4. Rousseau writes that his life is "peint exactement d'après nature et dans toute sa vérité," *Les Confessions*, in vol. 1 of *Œuvres complètes*, ed. Bernard Gagnebin and Marcel Raymond, 5 vols. (Paris: Gallimard, 1959), 3. All subsequent references to Rousseau's works are from this edition; volume number, followed by page number, will be given parenthetically in the body text). On the opening page of the *Confessions*, he claims to be presenting to his peers "un homme dans toute la vérité de la nature" (1: 5). In Book Two, he refers to his autobiographical project as "me montrer tout entier au public" (1:59). As Jean Starobinski puts it, Rousseau "va . . . énoncer discursivement toute l'histoire de sa vie" (*Jean-Jacques Rousseau: la transparence et l'obstacle* [Paris: Plon, 1957], 236).

5. Michel de Montaigne, *Les Essais*, ed. Maurice Rat, 2 vols. (Paris: Garnier, 1962), 1:1.

6. René de Chateaubriand, *Mémoires d'outre-tombe*, 3 vols. (Paris: Gallimard, 1951), 1:16.

7. Philippe Lejeune, *On Autobiography*, ed. Paul John Eakin, trans. Katherine Leary (Minneapolis: Univ. of Minnesota Press, 1989), 4. Eakin, in his foreword to

the English translation of Lejeune's *Pacte* and in his *Touching the World: Reference in Autobiography* (Princeton: Princeton Univ. Press, 1992), shows himself as an apologist of the positivistic and referential suppositions subtending Lejeune's theory of autobiography.

8. Lejeune in fact posits the problem of identity in tripartite form: "In order for there to be autobiography (and personal literature in general), the *author*, the *narrator*, and the *protagonist* must be identical" (*On Autobiography*, 5; original emphasis). Of course, in one way, Lejeune is simply offering a means of categorizing autobiography as distinct from other rhetorical forms—the autobiographical novel, for example. However, the influence of his nominalist rigor also makes itself felt in the way his reading of discursive subjectivity (which he arrives at through Benveniste's linguistic theories) is dominated by the demand for subjective consonance between experience and memory.

9. Although, curiously, in a recent study of "deconversion"—the converse of conversion read simply as a "loss of faith"—John Barbour explicitly defends and adopts Lejeune's definition of the genre even as, in my view, the narratives he analyzes directly challenge Lejeune's view of selfhood as consistent over time (*Versions of Deconversion: Autobiography and the Loss of Faith* [Charlottesville: Univ. Press of Virginia, 1994], 7).

10. One expedient for categorizing the unruly text is to consign it to the category of the self-portrait, which becomes a catch-all for texts that are autobiographical but not narrative: if the work's representational mode is not linear, it is described as simultaneous, as the pictorial metaphor suggests. On the question of the self-portrait, see, for example, Michel Beaujour, *Miroirs d'encre: rhétorique de l'autoportrait* (Paris: Seuil, 1980).

11. Starobinski writes: "Rousseau ne doute pas un seul instant de son unité, en dépit des contradictions et des discontinuités qu'il a su lui-même accuser" (*Transparence,* 236). I will read Rousseau's efforts to demonstrate subjective unity differently than Starobinski, by emphasizing the inadequacy of the *Confessions* to this task and the divergent strategies offered in the *Dialogues* and *Rêveries*.

12. Such is Augustine's fate in the *Confessions*. It is also thematized by, for instance, Saul changing his name to Paul to mark his rebirth, or by the split between "Rousseau" and "Jean-Jacques" in the *Dialogues*.

13. As John Freccero defines the importance of conversion for autobiography, "conversion as a death and resurrection provides a thematic basis for an otherwise-absurd pretense: the story of one's life is definitively concluded, yet one survives to tell the tale. Conversion is therefore not only the subject matter of confession but also the premise that makes the telling of such a story possible," "Autobiography and Narrative," in *Reconstructing Individualism: Autonomy, Individuality, and the Self in Western Thought*, ed. Thomas C. Heller, Morton Sosna, and David E. Wellbery (Stanford: Stanford Univ. Press, 1986), 20.

14. Paul de Man, *The Rhetoric of Romanticism* (New York: Columbia Univ. Press, 1984), 77.

15. In a book-length study of the relation between conversion and autobiographical narrative, I have traced the various uses to which the Augustinian conversional model is put in the French autobiographical tradition through Montaigne's *Essais*, Descartes's *Discours de la méthode*, Madame Guyon's *Autobiographie*, Rousseau's autobiographies, and Sartre's *Les Mots*. I argue that one of the most important of Rousseau's reworkings of the Augustinian model is the shift from spiritual to esthetic conversion, in the sense that with the illumination on the road to Vincennes, Rousseau is converted not to God but to writing. One of the general transformations conversion and autobiography undergo in the history of the genre in France is to become circular, to the extent that conversion to writing culminates in autobiographical writing centering on how writing defines the self. Rousseau is the first major figure to point to the vertiginous, quasi-Proustian possibility of writing determining a life lived fully only in writing.

16. Ann Hartle, *The Modern Self in Rousseau's* Confessions*: A Reply to Saint Augustine* (Notre Dame: Univ. of Notre Dame Press, 1983), 10. The relation between Augustine and Rousseau is also examined in Paul J. Archambault's "Rousseau's Tactical (Mis)reading of Augustine," *Symposium* 41 (1987): 6–14. Archambault investigates some of the ways Rousseau deliberately bends Augustinian doctrine through out-of-context quotation, disingenuously false interpretation, and pastiche, "as a refutation, however veiled, of a specifically Catholic and Augustinian conception of man" (6). In this respect, Archambault's project is similar to Hartle's even though he quickly dismisses her study for its "obviousness" and unwillingness to engage both texts in an interpretive juxtaposition (12 n. 2). However, Archambault, an Augustinian scholar, is essentially engaged in this article in a polemical apologetics for Augustine's *Confessions*. Hartle, on the other hand, is more interested in how an Augustinian conception of selfhood is transformed, or rather submerged, by its Rousseauean counterpart.

17. In the *avertissement* to the *Confessions*, as I have mentioned in a different context (above, n. 1), Rousseau refers to his autobiography as a unique and veridical "portrait of man"; he further asserts that this portrait is useful as a "comparison piece" (1: 3) for a general anthropology. It should not be forgotten, however, that on the very next page, at the beginning of Book I, Rousseau insists that he is absolutely unique in human history; the paradigmatic status he grants to his autobiographical portrait is, then, ambiguous at best.

18. For a discussion of these two major Christian rhetorical modes, and Augustine's use of them, see Karl Joachim Weintraub, *The Value of the Individual: Self and Circumstance in Autobiography* (Chicago: Univ. of Chicago Press, 1978), 18 ff. Also see Robert McMahon, *Augustine's Prayerful Ascent: An Essay on the Literary Form of the* Confessions (Athens: Univ. of Georgia Press, 1989), 4, 10.

19. There is a substantial critical tradition of attempting to provide a satisfactory explanation for Augustine's abrupt elision of autobiographical content in the *Confessions*. Two of the most cogent interpretations are Eugene Vance, "Augustine's *Confessions* and the Grammar of Selfhood," *Genre* 6 (1973): 1–28, and Robert

Elbaz, *The Changing Nature of the Self: A Critical Study of the Autobiographic Discourse* (Iowa City: Univ. of Iowa Press, 1987), 17–45. Both of these authors argue that the break in the *Confessions* between autobiography and treatise is in fact a logical, if not formally organic, consequence of the nature of the relation between the self and God as Augustine comes to understand it.

20. For an analysis of the itinerary leading to Augustine's conversion to Catholicism (whose principal steps have themselves been termed—misleadingly, in my view—"conversions" by several critics, as the titles of their studies suggest), see J.-M. Le Blond, *Les Conversions de Saint Augustin* (Paris: Aubier, 1950); Leo C. Ferrari, *The Conversions of Saint Augustine* (Villanova: Villanova Univ. Press, 1984), Pierre Courcelle's magisterial *Recherches sur les* Confessions *de Saint Augustin* (Paris: Boccard, 1950); and Robert J. O'Connell, *Images of Conversion in St. Augustine's* Confessions (New York: Fordham Univ. Press, 1996).

21. In the space of some eleven pages preceding the conversion narrative, for instance, Augustine is told about nine Christian figures and seven conversions. Moreover, many of these conversions themselves arise through imitation of other conversions, creating a mimetic avalanche. On the question of mimesis as a basis for conversion in Augustine, see John Freccero, "The Fig Tree and the Laurel: Petrarch's Poetics," *Diacritics* 5 (1975): 34–40, and Geoffrey Galt Harpham, "Conversion and the Language of Autobiography," in *Studies in Autobiography,* ed. James Olney (New York: Oxford Univ. Press, 1988), 44–48.

22. Saint Augustine, *The Confessions*, trans. R. S. Pine-Coffin (Harmondsworth: Penguin Books, 1961), 9: 1, 181. All subsequent references to the *Confessions* are from this edition. Book number, followed by chapter and page numbers, will be given parenthetically in the body text.

23. In 7: 11–12, Augustine proposes a hierarchy of degrees of being based on proximity and similarity to God. The closer one is to God, the more goodness one possesses, and consequently the more "being." Augustine the sinner has as little goodness as possible in him, and hence as little being. It is almost as if the recognition of one's past sins is the recognition that the sinner was never "really" a subject. On this question, see Elbaz, *Changing Nature of the Self*, 24 ff., and James F. Anderson, *St. Augustine and Being* (The Hague: Nijhoff, 1965).

24. In this entire section, the reader will recognize my debt to classic studies of Rousseau: Starobinski, *Transparence*, for the importance of autobiography as an affirmation of global innocence and a means of attaining absolution and regaining subjective wholeness; Jacques Derrida (*De la grammatologie* [Paris: Minuit, 1967]) and Paul de Man (*Blindness and Insight: Essays in the Rhetoric of Contemporary Criticism* [New York: Oxford Univ. Press, 1971]) on Rousseau's ambiguous relation to writing and on the question of subjective origins. My goal here is to integrate some of the well-known positions, above all from the domains of psychoanalysis and discourse analysis (since my argument centers on writing and the self), into a new perspective on Rousseau's autobiographies examined through the generic and the ideological lens of conversion as it is articulated—paradigmatically—by Saint Augustine.

25. Weintraub's *Value of the Individual* (see above, n. 18) does an exemplary job of tracing the historical development of the notion of autonomous individuality through an analysis of a large number of autobiographical works, and ends with Rousseau's *Confessions* and Goethe's *Dichtung und Wahrheit,* which he takes as consummate representatives of the modern conception of selfhood. Many critics posit Rousseau's *Confessions* as the generic origin of modern autobiography. Among them may be counted Roy Pascal, Georges May, Georges Gusdorf, Francis Hart, Philippe Lejeune, and Michael Sheringham, whose *French Autobiography: Devices and Desires* (Oxford: Clarendon Press, 1993) is the most recent historical study of the genre in France.

26. The great Augustinian scholar, Pierre Courcelle, did not fail to notice Rousseau's inversion of Augustine: "Rousseau . . . présente ses propres *Confessions* comme 'une entreprise qui n'eut jamais d'exemple.' Elles sont pourtant l'exacte antithèse de celles d'Augustin" (*Les* Confessions *de Saint Augustin dans la tradition littéraire: antécédents et postérité* [Paris: Etudes augustiniennes, 1963], 459). Courcelle goes on to note that, despite this "challenge" to Augustinian doctrine, Rousseau has probably nonetheless taken the sixteen year-old Augustine of the *Confessions* as a psychological and representational model for the narration of his own adolescence. This hypothesis, coupled with the identification of the two *Confessions* as ideologically antithetical, suggests that the relation between the two works turns on structural and rhetorical parallels masking fundamentally different worldviews. Unfortunately, Courcelle goes no further than a single paragraph alluding to the play of similarity and difference in the two *Confessions.* The present essay may be thought of as an attempt to unpack the implications of Courcelle's laconic juxtaposition.

27. Put somewhat differently, God and Rousseau become structural parallels, in that they are the only beings capable of a perfect comprehension of the *Confessions*'s message.

28. Rousseau here goes one step beyond Montaigne. The latter insists on the inseparability of life and book—on their "consubstantiality," to use Montaigne's term ("Du dementir," *Essais* 2: 18, 69). In Rousseau's case, the book has become a stand-in for the individual it portrays, and the man is no longer able to speak of himself as eloquently as his work. From the very outset, then, Rousseau is acutely aware that intelligibility is only conferred on a life *represented,* to the extent that even God has to read the truth of the self as a book.

29. On the question of autobiography as obsessional self-defense, see Starobinski, *Transparence;* on the destructive yet paradoxically recuperative power of writing, see Derrida, *Grammatologie*; and de Man, *Blindness and Insight.*

30. There are of course numerous critical readings of this scene in the *Confessions*; see, for example, Starobinski, *Transparence,* 60–61; Robert Elbaz, *Changing Nature of the Self,* 102–5; and Dennis Porter, *Rousseau's Legacy: Emergence and Eclipse of the Writer in France* (New York: Oxford Univ. Press, 1995), 30. Starobinski insists on Rousseau's contradictory feelings of both inspiration and damnation; Elbaz, on the other hand, stresses the essentially tragic tenor of the episode; and Porter

compares Rousseau's illumination, in a first instance, to the conversions of Paul and Augustine, but also to the Althusserian concept of interpellation.

31. William Spengemann underlines the stunning regularity with which claimed turning points arise in the *Confessions*, and indeed continue well beyond Rousseau's illumination on the road to Vincennes (*The Forms of Autobiography: Episodes in the History of a Literary Genre* [New Haven: Yale Univ. Press, 1980], 67).

32. On the originary significance of Rousseau's birth and prehistory—the "family romance" of Jean-Jacques's parents—see Jean-François Perrin, *Le Chant de l'origine: la mémoire et le temps dans les* Confessions *de Jean-Jacques Rousseau* (Oxford: Voltaire Foundation, 1996), 13–20.

33. On the question of the "floating" origin, which Rousseau taxes with containing the uncorrupted fullness of being, see de Man, *Blindness and Insight*, 115.

34. For a discussion of Rousseau's birth, and particularly, the dynamic of his relation to the father, see Thomas M. Kavanagh, *Writing the Truth: Authority and Desire in Rousseau* (Berkeley and Los Angeles: Univ. of California Press, 1987), 1–5. He argues astutely that the *Confessions* as autobiographical text are not merely the positive representation of the self as product and finitude, as the culmination of its own history, but also as a subject whose textual inauguration coincides with the elision of its own origin. What also interests me here, in addition to the blurring of origin, is the aftermath of its loss, the modalities the self is forced to adopt as it survives itself in the bizarre occasionalism of son-as-mother and son-as-wife, since, after all, the loss of an origin is only the beginning of a life-narrative punctuated by further transformations of the self into something other than its natural birthright.

35. This uniqueness, we should recall, is inscribed at the text's very inception, in the opening of Book I: "Je ne suis fait comme aucun de ceux que j'ai vus; j'ose croire n'être fait comme aucun de ceux qui existent. Si je ne vaux pas mieux, au moins je suis autre. Si la nature a bien ou mal fait de briser le moule dans lequel elle m'a jetté, c'est ce dont on ne peut juger qu'après m'avoir lu" (1: 5). There are two poles posited here, "natural" uniqueness and the uniqueness that can only be seized and appreciated after a complete reading of the text. What I am suggesting is that Rousseau's uniqueness, at least inasmuch as it applies to early childhood, has little to do with the "mold in which nature has cast him," but rather that the singularity he ascribes to himself arises from a displacement of nature into a mediative matrix in which Rousseau serves as a surrogate for someone else while his consciousness is nourished by the imaginary.

36. On the incident of the broken comb, see: Starobinski, *Transparence,* 18–21; Lejeune, "Le peigne cassé," *Poétique* 25 (1976): 1–29; E.S. Burt, "Developments in Character: Reading and Interpretation in 'The Children's Punishment' and 'The Broken Comb,'" *Yale French Studies* 69 (1983): 192–210; Elbaz, *Changing Nature of the Self,* 79–80; and Huntington Williams, *Rousseau and Romantic Autobiography* (Oxford: Oxford Univ. Press, 1983), 130–35.

37. Several critics have underlined the way in which Rousseau casts the Bossey interlude as a mythical narrative of earthly paradise enjoyed and painfully lost. See, for example, the first chapter of Starobinski, *Transparence;* Marcel Raymond, *Jean-Jacques Rousseau, la quête de soi et la rêverie* (Paris: Corti, 1962); Michel Launay,

"La structure poétique de la première partie des *Confessions,*" *Annales de la société Jean-Jacques Rousseau* 36 (1963–65): 49–56; and chapter 1 of Lejeune, *On Autobiography.* Lejeune summarizes the arguments of the previous three studies and attempts a more nuanced exposition of the structure of Book I. A significant component of the presumably natural environment at Bossey, which Rousseau describes as an expedient that paradoxically saved him from greater corruption later, is the displaced sexual pleasure he derives from childhood spankings. This early foray into masochism, "précisement . . . contraire à ce qui devoit s'ensuivre naturellement" (1: 15), is a reinscription of the mediate in the midst of Rousseau's idyll of naturalness, but one whose relation to his previous experiences of representational mediation he passes over entirely.

38.   The narrative sequence immediatcly preceding the broken-comb incident describes the "punition des enfants," the spankings that Rousseau received from Mlle Lambercier at Bossey, and tells of the masochistic pleasure Rousseau took in them, which he does not fail to characterize as a "gout bisarre" (1: 16). Clearly, then, the purity he ascribes to the Bossey sojourn is suspicious, even to him. It is, however, strategically useful for him to maintain this fiction in order to maximize the sense of reversal in the episode of the broken comb which follows: it is precisely this radicalization of the rupture that makes the incident conversionary.

39.   Not only does the episode function as a temporal synecdoche but also its meaning for Rousseau broadens from the specificity of the original event to become a generalized ethical principle (1: 20): the stakes of this episode are nothing less than the entire Rousseauean theory of empathy elaborated in the *Discourse on Inequality.*

40.   This critique of writing and the institution of authorship is already present in Rousseau's general attack on cultural production in his first theoretical work, the *Discours sur les sciences et les arts.* A more specific condemnation of writing (as opposed to speech) is to be found in the *Essai sur l'origine des langues,* a text upon which Derrida's reading, in the *Grammatologie,* of logocentrism in Rousseau is largely based.

41.   It is no doubt less than accidental that this incident is recounted in Book VIII of Rousseau's *Confessions,* just as Augustine's conversion in the garden at Milan is recounted in Book VIII of his autobiography. The placement of the conversion scenes in the two *Confessions* is compared in Hartle, *Modern Self,* 25–26.

42.   Both experiences, of course, are also echoes of Paul's conversion on the road to Damascus, with Rousseau's obviously paralleling Paul's in its physical staging.

43.   For a discussion of the formal and thematic parallels between the two *Confessions* and the place of conversion within each text, see Hartle, *Modern Self,* 24–28. Her discussion of Augustine's and Rousseau's conversions is structural rather than interpretive, and suggests the extent to which Rousseau adopts Augustine as a formal model for conversion. She does not, however, focus on the extraordinary transformation conversion undergoes in Rousseau's autobiography.

44.   Dennis Porter argues that Rousseau founds the modern conception of the writer—a conception in which life and writing, public and private, are essentially conflated and which is only now being seriously threatened as the dominant model

of authorship. Although Porter's focus is more on the valorization of the concept of "the writer" than on the anguishing subjective loss authorship entails for Rousseau, he nonetheless insists on the unbreakable bond between subjectivity and writing (*Rousseau's Legacy*, 27).

45. This is one of Starobinski's central arguments in his reading of the *Confessions*'s autobiographical project. It is also, of course, a goal that Rousseau himself suggests. Thus he writes, in an almost Cartesian passage at the end of Book IV: "Je m'applique à bien déveloper par tout les prémiéres causes pour faire sentir l'enchainement des effets. Je voudrois pouvoir en quelque façon rendre mon ame transparente aux yeux du lecteur, et pour cela je cherche à la lui montrer sous tous les points de vue, à l'éclairer par tous les jours, à faire en sorte qu'il ne s'y passe pas un mouvement qu'il n'aperçoive, afin qu'il puisse juger par lui-même du principe qui les produit" (1: 175). It is significant that Rousseau points to the reduction of the entire "enchainement des effets" to a single principle. For a cogent reading of Rousseau's "enchainements" that attempts to synthesize the causal (historical) and affective (ahistorical) concatenations he points to, see Michael Sheringham, *French Autobiography*, 31–66.

46. On the question of his audience's response to his private readings of the *Confessions*, see Catherine A. Beaudry, *The Role of the Reader in Rousseau's* Confessions (New York: Peter Lang, 1991), 1, 17–20; see also Robert J. Ellrich, *Rousseau and His Reader: The Rhetorical Situation of the Major Works* (Chapel Hill: Univ. of North Carolina Press, 1969), 73–83.

47. For a basic overview of the plot, see Robert Osmont, introduction to the *Dialogues* in Rousseau, *Oeuvres complètes*, 1: xlv ff.; see also James F. Jones, Jr., *Rousseau's* Dialogues: *An Interpretive Essay* (Geneva: Droz, 1991). Michel Foucault provides a very suggestive reading of the conspiracy in his *Introduction aux Dialogues*, in ed. J. Rivelaygue, *Rousseau* (Paris: Didier, 1970), 163–71.

48. For an analysis of Rousseau's obsession with the other's judgment and his autobiographical strategies for recuperating the other's approbation in the *Dialogues*, see Eugene L. Stelzig, "Autobiography as Resurrection: Rousseau's *Dialogues*," *a/b: Auto/biography Studies* 10, (Fall 1995): 39–51. Stelzig argues that the *Dialogues* are a more elaborate form of apologetics for the self than even the *Confessions*.

49. Georges Poulet provides a reading of the relation between solitary *repos* and plenitude of being in "Le Sentiment de l'existence et le repos," in *Reappraisals of Rousseau: Studies in Honor of R. A. Leigh*, ed. Simon Harvey, Marian Hobson, Davis Kelley, and Samuel S. B. Taylor (Manchester: Manchester Univ. Press, 1980), 37–45.

50. "De l'exercitation," *Essais* 2: 6, 408–14.

51. Shaun Irlam, in "Showing Losses, Counting Gains: 'Scenes' from Negative Autobiography," *MLN* 106 (1991): 997–1011, offers a reading of lacunae of consciousness in Augustine, Montaigne and Rousseau. Beginning with Augustine's "remembrance" of forgetfulness described in the *Confessions*, Irlam goes on to analyze the scene in which Montaigne is knocked unconscious after falling from his horse, a finally the scene in the *Rêveries* that so closely resembles Montaigne's.

Irlam's argument is that while one of autobiography's central concerns is the representation of positive indices of the fullness of being, these seminal incidents turn, to the contrary, on temporary absences of the autobiographer's consciousness of existence. His focus with the passage from the *Rêveries* is thus on Rousseau's temporary interruption of being, on its characteristic of absence. My interest in the scene is essentially the opposite: I read the lacuna Rousseau experiences as entirely subordinate to the sensation of full self-possession that his "rebirth" into a world that his own mind seemingly creates *ex nihilo* produces. Thus, I would argue that it is not absence *per se* that captures Rousseau's interest, but the sudden consonance between self and world that he perceives, because, in the vague moments of regaining full consciousness, it appears that the world derives entirely from what the self projects on it. The true wonder of the moment is that the other's capacity to mediate between the self and the world is disabled: what arrives fortuitously here is precisely what the *Rêveries* are constantly trying self-consciously to achieve with their refusal of any social address.

"A Sawce-box and Boldface Indeed": Refiguring the Female Servant in the Pamela-Antipamela Debate

SCARLETT BOWEN

I

Shortly before Pamela's marriage to Mr. B in Richardson's first novel, Mrs. Jewkes tells Pamela that she should alter her style of address to Mr. B and desist from calling him "master." The once-assertive Pamela now demurely answers, "He shall always be my Master; and I shall think myself more and more his Servant."[1] This remark and others like it elicit from most feminist critics a quizzically-arched eyebrow as it becomes clear that Pamela's potentially revolutionary class ascent paradoxically entails greater subordination from her as a wife to her husband than was required from a servant by her master. Expressing a view often repeated by subsequent critics, Terry Castle notes, "Much of the interest in [*Pamela*] . . . lies precisely in the way the heroine's private discourse—which up to a point is basically spirited and self-respecting—modulates into a fairly embarrassing political statement: a paean to womanly subjugation—marriage with the 'master.'"[2] *Pamela*'s conservative political ending seems to confirm not only gender but also class hierarchies. Christopher Flint, for example, asserts that "Pamela's history, while it registers the exhilaration of class ascent, also stresses the anxieties accompanying radical change, seeking, in the end, to forget what it first appears to celebrate" by revealing Pamela's once-genteel background and by marking her as more exceptional than exemplary.[3]

Revisionist feminist scholars, notably Nancy Armstrong, have provocatively argued that Richardson's "forgetting" of class distinctions in favor of an apolitical construction of virtuous femininity led to the subtle yet decisive consolidation of middle-class values, which concomitantly empowered middle-class women.[4] Revisionist feminist criticism has also, however, taught us to be suspicious of endings, and asks, in the words of feminist film critic Miriam Hansen, "to what extent is closure effective"?[5] Resisting a teleological reading of both novelistic narrative and the narrative of bourgeois class legitimation, this essay will revisit the portrayal of the "basically spirited and self-respecting" servant girl who rules the first half of Richardson's novel. In resisting the novel's naturalization of a radical misalliance and its uneven depiction of Pamela as "always already" a lady, I find myself making a surprising alliance of my own with those eighteenth-century authors, readers, and social commentators known then and now as "antipamelists."[6] Long before narrative theorists began to question the ideological effectiveness of narrative closure, these readers and writers refused to accept the conclusion of Richardson's story, and they refused to participate in the general amnesia about the eponymous heroine's status as a "spirited" servant girl.

A quick survey of eighteenth-century readers' responses to *Pamela* reveals that class distinctions between women did matter in the mid-eighteenth century. Those who celebrated Pamela's virtues were able to do so only if they suppressed her class affiliation.[7] In a prefatory letter included in the second edition of *Pamela*, the Reverend William Webster at first records being "astonished" that a young girl "in the low Scene of Life and Circumstance" should resolve to "return to her primitive Poverty, rather than give up her Innocence." Webster abates this astonishment by reading Pamela as transcending her class and viewing the novel as a *vade mecum* for women of the leisured classes: "I doubt not *Pamela* will become the bright Example and Imitation of all the fashionable young Ladies of *Great Britain*" (8). Those critical of Pamela, however, emphasize her class identification, assuming in particular a class-specific sexuality. The author of "Critical Remarks on *Sir Charles Grandison*, *Clarissa*, and *Pamela*" observes that Pamela "was not of that rank or situation in life which could entitle her to those notions of honour and virtue, which are extremely proper and becoming in Clarissa."[8] In other words, servant women, and laboring women in general, were perceived as willing to provide sexual favors in order to escape exigent circumstances and as excluded from the degree of bodily self-respect that the intention to preserve one's chastity requires. What is significant about these two readers' responses is that although they share the same fundamental recognition of servant women's difference from leisure-class women, neither of them is able to bring celebratory attention to this difference. The celebration of Pamela is made possible only when she is interpreted as a "lady" and her status as a lady's *maid* is conveniently forgotten.

Yet, as modern critics such as Terry Castle and Christopher Flint aver, part of the pleasure of reading *Pamela* stems precisely from its sympathetic and lively portrayal of a defiant female servant who staves off and converts the tyrannical and sexually harassing Mr. B. To recuperate and contextualize the relative powers of the laboring-class femininity deployed in Richardson's novel, I have found eighteenth-century antipamelist texts to be a rich resource. The antipamelists, after all, were most threatened by what they saw as the novel's propensity to extol and reward a rebellious servant maid, and they were the readers who refused Richardson's narrative coercion to "forget what [the novel] first appears to celebrate." Drawing on conduct manuals for servants, antipamelist critical commentary, and two antipamelist fictions, Henry Fielding's *Apology for the Life of Mrs. Shamela Andrews* (1741) and Eliza Haywood's *Anti-Pamela: or Feign'd Innocence Detected* (1742),[9] I will read these texts against their classist, parodic and satiric grains in order to excavate some of the specificities and powers of servant women in particular, and of their laboring-class female peers in general.[10] For the most part, the antipamela texts show that class distinctions between women mattered for conservative purposes: so that social hierarchies and household order could be maintained, and so that the exploitation of servant women could be justified. But class distinctions also mattered in a somewhat progressive way, in their acknowledgement of the vibrant, assertive roles of servant and laboring women. Indeed, reading *Pamela* through its parodies helps us to remember what is lost in the transition from lady's maid to lady as well as what is elided in interpretations of *Pamela*'s socially ambiguous heroine as representative only of the newly emerging ideology of domestic femininity.

Pamela's hybrid social character reflects the novel's hybrid textual production as well as Richardson's different didactic investments for women. *Pamela* grew out of Richardson's endeavor to write a collection of model letters to be used by the laboring classes. While the publication of *Familiar Letters* was delayed, he developed the letters of a servant maid writing home to her parents by embellishing upon a supposedly true, albeit unusual, report he had heard of a lady's maid who resisted her master's sexual advances until the master made his intentions honorable by marrying her. As we can surmise from the novel's detailing of the rules of conduct for married women at the end of the novel, Richardson invested as much in the portrayal of a dutiful leisure-class wife as he did in the portrayal of a virtuous servant maid. In fact, Richardson often uses the role of the latter to emphasize the proper duties of the former. Robert Folkenflik justifiably remarks that Richardson "suggests powerfully that the good wife is in many ways the good servant" (268). Yet this is only one of the stories *Pamela* tells. As the opening quotation illustrates, the other story, in an almost chiasmatic contradiction with the first, details the ways in which a good servant, one who is headstrong, verbally assertive, and "artful," *does not* make a good wife. The last half of Richardson's novel thus distances Pamela from those very attributes of her servant identity by placing her in stark contrast to Mrs. Jewkes, a monstrous and bawdy version of laboring or plebeian femininity.

Even so, in exploiting this ideological slippage between female servants and ladies, Richardson inadvertently fueled existing anxieties about the social ambiguity of servants and particularly about servant maids. In theory, servants, far more than any other class of laborers, were expected to abdicate all claims to independence and privacy, conforming entirely to their masters' wills. J. Jean Hecht, the first to make eighteenth-century servitude the subject of a book-length study, quotes a reverend who delivers this imperative to servants in one of his sermons:

> your time and strength are no longer your own, when you are hired; they are your master's, and to be employed in his service; and consequently you cannot employ them as you please, but as he directs: nor can you misemploy them, or with-hold them from him without manifest fraud and injustice.[11]

Bridget Hill describes how this imperative played out for female servants; they were stripped of their identity, taken away from their families, forced to don clothing incongruent with their background, and sometimes required to take on different names.[12] The upper classes required such suppression of identity not only to subordinate the servants, but also to increase their own social prestige. The better the servants were dressed, the better their manners, the more prominence was ascribed to their employers.

This use of servants to display status had some undesirable effects, however. There are numerous accounts in eighteenth-century social commentary of people mistaking lady's maids for ladies when maids, as Pamela frequently does, wear the cast-off clothes of their mistresses.[13] Employers also worried that upper servants themselves would confuse emulation and deference with entitlement to upper-class privilege. As Eliza Haywood's *Present for a Servant Maid* (1743) shows, many of the conduct books for servants devoted considerable attention to chiding female servants for forgetting their place. She writes, "The greatest Pleasure you take is in being called *Madam* by such as do not know you; and you fear nothing so much as being taken for what you are."[14]

Thus while Richardson in *Pamela* seemed to be saying that upper-class ladies should model themselves after their servant maids,[15] the rest of the employer classes were complaining that servant maids were modelling themselves too much after their mistresses. For antipamelists, one fearful consequence of servant maids' emulating or being mistaken for their mistresses was that servant maids would aspire beyond their social class. In Haywood's *Anti-Pamela: or Feign'd Innocence Detected*, Haywood rewrites Richardson's novel in order to critique lower-class families for grooming their daughters for a higher social station, spending money on haircuts instead of meals, or not allowing the daughter to wash dishes for fear of "spoiling her Hands" (6). She blames the parents for their daughters' fall into sexual vice by their "flattering themselves that by breeding them like Gentlewomen, . . . the [young women] shall be able to make their Fortune by Marriage"—the consequence of which, as she warns in her counter-fiction, can be a sentence in Newgate prison for prostitution, fraud, and a host of other criminal activities. The anonymous author of the pamphlet "Pamela Censured: in a Letter to the Editor" concurs, as he protests *Pamela*'s implicit message that "every Maid Servant from what low Stock soever she sprung, if she is pretty and modest, and etc., has an undoubted Right to attempt to entice her Master to Marriage."[16]

Yet female servants' upward social mobility, instances of which were actually quite rare,[17] probably troubled antipamelists and the employer classes less than servants' increased economic agency at this point in the century. Hecht observes that urban domestic service was undergoing important changes: one was the movement toward wage labor, and the other was a situation in which demand exceeded supply: "A variety of economic developments and resulting social changes created a steadily increasing demand for domestics throughout the period; multiple sources furnished a constantly increasing, though generally inadequate, supply" (1). The great opportunity for employment gave servants a particular economic self-determination, as they would sooner quit and take their services elsewhere than put up with unreasonable masters. Patty Seleski notes that "women servants were, in fact, notorious for their habitual changes of employment."[18] She gives evidence of maid servants' quitting their jobs in order to take more suitable ones, or in order simply to live off their earnings—in effect giving themselves a paid holiday (151).

The preponderance of employers' criticisms of "insubordinate" servants found its basis in just this sort of assertion of independence. Hecht gives a representative example from a note written by a discontented female servant to the Reverend Richard Lardner in 1745:

> I think it is proper to speak to those who dress your victuals, and not to
> them as have nothing to do with it. . . . I knew what business was before I

came to you and more than what you have to do, and though I cant please you, I dont doubt but I shall please other people very well . . . I will not stay with you, to be found fault with for nothing. (78)

The cook's strong sense of agency in this note stems from two particularly significant resources available to the servant classes at this time, one being her recognition of other opportunities—"I shall please other people very well"—and the other being her understanding of proper master/servant relations—"I think it is proper . . . . I knew what business was." The note thus expresses both the new contract form and the old paternalistic form of service. The cook's latter assertion, "I knew what business was," conforms to E. P. Thompson's description of plebeian protest, in which he asserts that "plebeian culture is rebellious, but rebellious in defense of custom."[19] In other words, resistance does not take the form of usurping upper-class privilege, but rather it often calls for the reestablishment of proper paternalistic treatment of the lower classes. The cook's temerity in educating her master about the proper way to inform her about the quality of her work and her assertion of her own expertise indicates a fluency with a set of codes by which she agrees to work. The economic conditions are favorable enough that if her master refuses to abide by these codes, she has plenty of other opportunities to find one who does.

Such social and economic factors help explain why *Pamela* sparked such tremendous controversy. Benefitting from an increase in economic self-determination and a tradition of rightful resistance, servants posed a threat to social and household order, a threat that left its psychic traces on the literary productions of the employer classes. Critical discussions of the *Pamela/antipamela* debate, therefore, must go further than Bernard Kreissman's misogynist formulation that "an attentive reading of [Richardson's] novel reveals behind the Pamela who minces across its pages the Shamela whom Fielding exposed."[20] *Pamela* caused such a stir because it gave a positive portrayal of a rebellious servant who not only got her way but who also was rewarded with social advancement. In their attempt to discredit Pamela and her laboring-class attributes, the antipamelist texts illuminate the battleground on which class distinctions between women were formulated. These sites of contestation take place over the subjectivity, body, and sexuality of servant women, often submerging the material and economic grounds which inform these contestations.[21] It will be my aim in the next section of this essay to examine some of these material and economic grounds as well as to acknowledge the specific powers and agencies of the servant woman which Richardson and the antipamelists both invoked and suppressed.

II

In creating a powerful female character who could stave off and out-scheme Mr. B, Richardson pays tribute to those hallmarks of laboring femininity which antipamelists seek to malign. One of the reigning critiques of Richardson's heroine is the charge of her duplicitousness, a familiar charge regarding eighteenth-century servants, and one that most likely had its basis in actual master/servant dynamics. Desiring to be both deferential and self-assertive, servants were often put in the position of saying one thing while wishing they could say another. Richardson not only depicts Pamela engaging in such doubleness, but he also shows Pamela using this ability in a positive way to defend herself. "O the little Hypocrite, said he! she has all the Arts of her Sex" (45), retorts the originary antipamelist, Mr. B. Richardson's narrative style, through which readers have access to Pamela's innermost thoughts, does little to revise this understanding of Pamela's character, as he details her conflicting outward speech and inward thoughts. In one of her confrontations, for instance, she writes, "*I* ashamed to see *you!* thought I; Very pretty indeed!—But I said nothing" (44). In another example, she describes trying to hide her rebellious thoughts: "I said something mutteringly, and he vowed he would hear it. . . . Why then, said I, if your Honour must know, I said, That my good Lady did not desire your Care to extend to the Summer-house and her Dressing-room" (63). This sharp wit on the one hand, and her crying, "curcheeing" (curtsying) and blushing (31–32) on the other, enables Pamela to remain dutiful in her position while at the same time being defiant. Richardson shows the value of Pamela's artfulness by demonstrating it was all necessary to protect her chastity; the converted Mr. B explains, "Tho's she is full of her pretty Tricks and Artifaces, to escape the snares I had laid for her, yet all is innocent, lovely, and uniformly beautiful" (255).

Antipamelists, however, refuse to assign value to this familiar trope of servitude. As in Richardson's text, the lady's maid in antipamela literature is portrayed as having a hidden subjectivity, yet for these writers, the ability to dissimulate is seen as a threat.[22] They fear that behind her gentlewomanly facade lurks a laboring woman's motives and desires for economic enfranchisement. Haywood's *Anti-Pamela* shows how her heroine, aptly named Syrena Tricksey, learns at an early age the necessary arts of dissimulation. Affecting a faint as well as an honorable character, she at one point retorts, as Pamela does, "I preferr'd my Honesty in Rags, to all the Splendor in the World, when it must be the Purchase of Vice and Infamy" (59), and at another can "burst into a rage" (151) and give herself "an Air of Insolence, as indeed is more to natural to [her]" when the man she attempts to engage eludes her (153). Henry Fielding's *Shamela* turns its jokes on parodying Richardson's epistolary narrative style, revealing not the virtuous mind of a girl writing home to her parents, but the boisterous and mercenary thoughts of a careful schemer and of her like-minded mother. Fielding's Shamela, true to her namesake, celebrates her artfulness at every turn: "I pretended to be shy," "I pretended to be Angry" (10).

In a tradition that goes back at least to Defoe's *Moll Flanders,* laboring women are often depicted as being driven by desires for material gain. For Fielding, Pamela's protestations of sexual virtue can be understood only as a bargaining chip. Shamela proclaims her virginity—while carrying on an affair with Parson Williams—and refuses to give in to Booby until the deal is made: "nothing under a regular taking into Keeping, a settled Settlement, for me, and all my Heirs, all my whole Life-time, shall do the Business—or else cross-legged, is the Word" (15). Once married, Shamela lets her material desires run rampant: "I believe I shall buy every Thing I see. What signifies having Money if one doth not spend it" (44).

Like Fielding, Haywood similarly defines Syrena as a materialistic being who pursues economic gain not by work, but by sexual and romantic labor. Syrena and her mother are only interested in work that can further Syrena's pursuit of a wealthy man, so when her more well-to-do relatives suggest that she be a milliner or mantua-maker, she refuses, as "sitting all Day to run Seams" would put her "out of Fortune's way"(5), or beyond the gaze of a viable suitor. Economic and business metaphors abound in descriptions of Syrena's intrigues. Syrena sees every man in terms of his cash value. She sizes him up, wondering "whether something may be made of him, for he must be rich; he goes as fine as any Lord, and has a Man that waits upon him" (14). Syrena's mother coaches her, "Now your Business is by an artful Management to bring this *Liking* up to *Love,* and then it will be in your power to do with him as you please" (18). Indeed, Syrena is described consistently as being incapable of feeling love, unless it is love of money: "The pains she took for this Interview may very well be taken for the Effect of Love, as indeed it was; but not of the Man, tho' something belonging to him" (39).

The focus on servant women's avaricious pursuits of men serves to distinguish them from their mistresses and justify their subordination. As Ian Watt notes, for both leisure-class women and servant women, marriage was a priority.[23] Bridget Hill writes that "most young domestic servants saw marriage as their goal and, almost certainly, as the only escape route for them from service."[24] Given the similarity between the situation of servant women and that of leisure-class women, eighteenth-century writers reinforce servant women's inferior status by showing that servant women's motives for marrying are base and material.

The antipamela fictional representations of servant women as mercenary also function to depict negatively their economic agency. While I do not wish to glamorize the life of a servant—this occupation did require the sacrifice of much personal and social autonomy—we should not dismiss the fact that servant and other laboring women managed their own financial affairs, a capability denied to many leisure-class women. D. A. Kent's study of female servants at mid-century convincingly argues that the large numbers of middle-aged and older women who chose not to marry and to remain in service points to the possibility that "service was sufficiently attractive for some women to choose it as a way of life rather than simply as a stage in their life-cycle."[25] Fielding and Haywood, in presenting servant women whose only goal is to entice a wealthy man into marriage, seek to disavow and divert attention away from this economic self-sufficiency. Yet in acknowledging this aspect of servant women's lives as threatening, they inescapably point to its power.

Another much-criticized, and therefore formidable, attribute of servant women was their capacity for verbal defiance. Usually, eighteenth-century employers were vehement about controlling servant women's speech. Not only did they seek to control their gossiping about the affairs of the household, but they also sought to curb any expression of opposition: Haywood writes in a *Present for a Servant Maid,* "It is also very becoming in you to be modest and humble in your Deportment, never pretending to argue the Case, even tho' your Mistress should be angry without a Cause, *A soft Answer puts away Wrath,* says Solomon" (23). In *Pamela,* the unreformed Mr. B displays this intolerance for servant women's unruly speech in the many epithets he hurls at Pamela: "Boldface," "Sawce-Box," "Insolent." Pamela is not alone in this characteristic—the cook is known for being "snappish and cross" (51), and of course these are the same slurs Pamela uses to attack Mrs. Jewkes.

Antipamelists have quite a bit of fun with this aspect of servant women's unruliness, but not without a conservative agenda. Fielding's Squire Booby follows suit in his attacks on Shamela: "Bold face," "Saucy Chops," "saucy Sow," "Saucebox." And Shamela gives ample cause for them. She does not hesitate to be "impudent" with Mr. Booby, telling him to "kiss [her] A—" (13) or "D—n you" (16) when he asks her to forgive him. As a "Servant of Spirit," she believes it is her prerogative to give "saucy answers" (17) and she and her fellow female servants often let out a "violent laugh" (14) at

Booby's expense. Of course, Fielding and Haywood depict the servant women in this way in order to prove their heroines as irredeemably low-class and socially dangerous. Shamela and Syrena defy aristocratic authority in order to turn the social order topsy-turvy and gain money and power. As Richard Gooding argues, "for Richardson's detractors, the getting of power is the primary motivation for all members of the lower orders, and the only real cultural problem is that of keeping the upstart poor in their place" (130). Both Fielding and Haywood end up castigating these expressions of laboring women's assertiveness, as both fictional spin-offs conclude either with the servant woman's sentencing to Newgate or her being found out and cast into the street.

Thus it is all the more remarkable that Richardson gives so many lively descriptions of servant women's "saucy" speech, not simply to exploit it for comic or disciplinary purposes, but to portray it as necessary for Pamela's physical protection. At one point, for example, Pamela describes servant women as foreign to her in their sexual promiscuity, but she then admits their similar positions and the advantages of being a "boldface":

> . . . what Sort of Creatures must the Womenkind be, . . . to give way to such Wickedness? Why, this it is that makes every one be thought of alike: And . . . it is grown more a Wonder that the Men are resisted, than that the Women comply. This, I suppose, makes me such a Sawce-box, and Boldface, and a Creature; and all because I won't be a Sawce-box and Boldface indeed. (73)

In the last sentence, Pamela acknowledges not only the laboring-class heritage but also the advantages of her verbal shrewishness. A sharp tongue in a woman has many valences—it can mean that she is sexually "forward," but it can also mean that she's standing up for herself, and it is this latter meaning which Richardson's Pamela consciously embraces. Richardson in this passage shows an identification between Pamela and other servant women, as she acknowledges their shared plight in that they, too, are probably being coerced into sexual relations by the "Arts and Strategems these Men may devise to gain their vile Ends . . . . For you see by my sad Story . . . what Hardships poor Maidens go thro', whose Lot is to go out to Service" (73).

In addition to her verbal assertiveness, Pamela's frank observations about sexual matters and their consequences reveal her affiliations with other servant and laboring women. Richardson unconventionally adopts the commonplace notion of laboring women's familiarity with sexual matters for the purposes of protecting Pamela's virtue. He depicts her as being quite aware of the consequences of giving in to Mr. B:

> He may condescend, may-hap, to think I may be good enough for his Har-
> lot; and those Things don't disgrace Men, that ruin poor women, as the
> World goes. And so, if I was wicked enough, he would keep me till I was
> undone, and 'till his Mind changed; for even wicked Men, I have read,
> soon grow weary of Wickedness of one Sort, and love Variety. Well then,
> poor Pamela must be turn'd off, and look'd upon as a vile abandon'd Crea-
> ture . . . . (49)

Not only does Pamela know how "the World goes," but she is also aware of
the pervasiveness of sexual relations between masters and servants: "There
is 'Squire Martin in the Grove, has had three Lyings-in, it seems, in his
House, in three Months past, one by himself; and one by his Coachman; and
one by his Woodman; and yet he has turn'd none of them away" (72). While
Richardson portrays Pamela using such knowledge to strengthen her resolve
to resist Mr. B, Richardson's detractors could not imagine a female servant
knowing so much and still remaining virtuous.

For most of eighteenth-century society, sexual knowledge and behavior
provided an important marker of class distinctions between women. Women
of the lower ranks were perceived as more sexually active and conversant in
sexual matters, whereas unmarried leisure-class women, at least "proper"
ones, were thought to be sexually chaste and innocent. This notion that sexual
morality was more permissive among the laboring class than it was among
the middling to upper classes was not entirely unfounded. Anna Clark's careful
study of plebeian sexual morality from 1780 to 1820 shows that later in the
century, at least, a wide range of sexual choices existed for members of the
lower orders.[26] Common-law marriages were prevalent; some plebeians felt
premarital sex was acceptable as long as there was a marriage proposal,
some adhered to "respectable religiosity" in eschewing premarital sex, and
some condoned births out of wedlock "if men and women lived up to their
responsibilities" (44–47). She notes that "in plebeian culture, chastity was
not necessarily the most important female virtue: whatever their sexual situation, women could be valued as industrious workers, affectionate mothers,
kind friends, and good neighbors" (49). Furthermore, "the boundaries between 'respectable' women, unmarried mothers, and prostitutes were often
blurred" (50), as plebeian women sometimes, in order to supplement their
wages, engaged in part-time sexual commerce.

Antipamelists brought to Richardson's novel an oversimplified understanding of laboring female sexuality, which for them translated as general sexual
willingness and availability. This assumption also played right into their acceptance of sexual relations between masters and servants. Sarah Maza,
writing about eighteenth-century French servants, says that "the sexual favours

of [the master's] female domestics were part of the privileges of a patri-arch."[27] Because of this understanding of male ruling-class sexual privilege, many female servants were forced into sexual relations with their masters, yet it is also possible, as Bridget Hill argues, that "Many [female servants] voluntarily entered into sexual liaisons."[28] Certainly antipamelists held to the latter belief. Their attitude toward Pamela's defense of her virtue is mir-rored in Richardson's novel itself, in the view of the neighboring gentleman in Lincolnshire, who sees nothing wrong or troublesome about Mr. B's ab-duction and seduction of Pamela: "Why what is this . . . but that the 'Squire our Neighbor has a mind to his Mother's Waiting-maid? And if he takes care she wants for nothing, I don't see any great Injury will be done her. He hurts no family by this" (122). Thus in Haywood's and Fielding's fictions, servant women are portrayed as being quite distinct from leisure-class women in that they are sexually desiring and willing to engage in sexual relations outside of marriage. Haywood's Syrena, for example, takes a liking to a man she sees and is "struck at first Sight of him . . . . she shew'd herself without Disguise, and was all the Libertine" (162). Likewise, Fielding has Shamela comically remark several times on how appreciative she is of Parson Williams's physi-cal charms: "O Parson Williams, how little are all the Men in the World, compared to thee" (32).

With this understanding of sexual permissiveness among the lower ranks, antipamelist writers present sexual virtue among servant women as nothing more than an act, one which upper-class men would be foolish to believe. In the subplot of *Anti-Pamela* that most mirrors Richardson's narrative, Haywood portrays the youngest son of an upper-class family, Mr. L, who falls for Syrena while she works as a lady's maid. He soon learns that while "in the Morning [he] thought himself happy in the Possession of a beautiful innocent creature, that loved him with the extremest Tenderness, [he] found himself before the Sun went down, the Wretched Property of a presuming, mercenary, betraying, perjur'd and abandon'd Prostitute" (102). Similarly, many contemporary critics interpreted Pamela as sexually knowing and ex-perienced despite her protestations of sexual virtue. The author of "Pamela Censured," for example, asserts that Pamela feigns innocence of sexual mat-ters, yet "with all the Inconsistence imaginable expresses herself as cun-ningly and knowing upon the Subject as the best bred Town Lass of them all could have done."[29] According to this critic, Pamela's knowledge of sexual consequences and of the double standard of sexual conduct automatically locates her in the lower ranks of women, specifically in the realm of town prostitute ("Town Lass"). This conversancy with sexual matters makes her morally suspect as it implicates her in plebeian sexual morality, thereby pre-cluding her from leisure-class virtue.

Without doubt, Pamela's recourse to the rhetoric of virtue in resisting Mr. B sets her apart from popular contemporary representations of laboring or plebeian women and functions in Richardson's text as the main justification for Pamela's elevation to the gentry. As Ian Watt remarks, "there is, of course, nothing inherently new in making a fictional heroine regard her chastity as a supreme value; what was new was that Richardson attributed such motives to a servant girl" (165–66). Nancy Armstrong also attributes particular significance to this aspect of Richardson's heroine:

> The fact that Mr. B tries and fails to seduce Pamela on so many occasions tells us that this woman possesses some kind of power other than that inhering in either the body of a servant or in that of a prominent family. . . . When in the history of writing before *Pamela*, we might ask ourselves, did a female, let alone a female servant, have the authority to define herself so? (113)

For Armstrong, Pamela's resistance as well as her claim to a virtuous subjectivity heralds a new form of bourgeois femininity. Yet I would argue that Armstrong is only partly right, for in Richardson's depiction of Pamela's resistance to Mr. B, and in his illustration of the ways she is able to maintain her virtue, Richardson does draw on the specific powers employed by and granted to women of the servant and laboring classes. Armstrong and Watt are correct to note that a servant girl's recourse to the class-coded rhetoric of virtue is new, but the act of her resisting her master is not new, even in the realm of sexual relations.

The ideology of servant-keeping held that servants were the master's property. This belief sometimes led to the justification of masters' supposed rights to sexual relations with their servants, but there also existed another tradition within paternalism, which held that the master was also bound to protect, not harm, his dependents. As early as 1720, conduct manuals for servants show that servant women had a right to resist their master's sexual advances. Thomas Seaton's *The Conduct of Servants in Great Families* says that servant women must make all attempts to avoid rakish masters—if avoiding him or screaming don't work, they are to "by all Means quit the Service, however profitable; and not expose themselves to the Chance of being surprized in an unguarded hour."[30] Even Haywood's *Present for a Servant Maid,* which continually promotes self-abnegation for female servants, focuses a great deal of attention on the specific right of servant maids to resist their masters' sexual advances. She encourages them to appeal to their masters' duties as patriarchs of the household, to tell the master how "cruel it is to go about to betray a Person whom it is his Duty to protect" (46). Haywood categorically tells servant girls to quit if the master persists.

Richardson's novel upholds this tradition of servants' right to resist, especially if doing so maintained proper social hierarchies. Pamela, for example, invokes a sense of social propriety when she resists Mr. B's sexual advances. She attempts again and again to insist on the proper boundaries between master and servant and argues that by his being "so free to a poor Servant," he "lessn's the Distance that Fortune has made between [them], by demeaning himself" (35). She strives to preserve the social hierarchy rather than transgress it, and feels justified in being defiant when Mr. B fails to do the same. When he accosts her in the summer-house, she states, "I lost all my Fear, and all Respect, and said, Yes, I do [forget to whom I'm talking], Sir, too well!—Well may I forget that I am your Servant, when you forget what belongs to a Master" (35). Richardson echoes his approval of such defiance when he addresses the behavior of other servants in the novel. Pamela instructs Mrs. Jewkes, for instance, that "a Person should know how to judge between Lawful and Unlawful. And even the Great, . . . tho' at present angry when they are not obey'd, will afterwards have no ill Opinion of a Person for withstanding them in their unlawful Commands" (362). And at the very end of the novel, Richardson points out the lesson from the "double Conduct of poor John," that "lower servants may learn . . . how to distinguish between lawful and unlawful Commands of a Superior" (410).

No celebrator of social chaos, Richardson certainly limits the agency of servants in favor of hierarchy. Yet his fictional renderings of what Janet Todd calls Pamela's "pride of servitude" and "self-respecting lowliness" (137) paradoxically create a version of laboring femininity that wields more power than its leisure-class counterpart. Nowhere is this paradox more striking than in the novel's implicit comparison and contrast of Pamela with Sally Godfrey, a "deserving good Girl" (357) "of a good Family" (394) who ends up being seduced by Mr. B. Sally in many ways exemplifies the tropes of leisure-class femininity in her passivity and compliance to both her mother and Mr. B; significantly, her agency is completely submerged into either Mr. B's "naughty" desires (395) or her mother's contrivances to entangle Mr. B in a marriage. While Sally Godfrey embodies the same qualities that Richardson, through Mr. B, lists as ideal qualities in his "faint Sketch of Conduct" for a leisure-class wife, such as sweetness, complaisance, and forbearance (367–68), these are not the traits which kept Pamela from becoming "Sally Godfrey the Second" (399).[31] In depicting Pamela's successful resistance of Mr. B, Richardson exploits Pamela's hybrid social identity, highlighting the strengths—artfulness, verbal assertiveness, and a practical and informed stance about sexual relations—that she derives from her position as a servant and from her connections to laboring-class femininity. It is this transgressive energy which antipamelists deplore and which Richardson's novel must "forget" in order to transform Pamela into a proper leisure-class wife.

III

The final section of this essay examines both Richardson's effacement of Pamela's servant identity towards the end of the novel and the antipamelists' refusal to allow such an erasure. In order to convince readers that Pamela deserves to be elevated into the gentry, Richardson must dissociate Pamela from the very specificities and powers of laboring femininity that he at earlier parts of the narrative seems to embrace. Yet the particularities of servant women's social and sexual identities continue to be represented by the other female servant characters, who provide a necessary foil to Pamela. The depictions of Pamela's relations with the other servant women provide another valuable source of information about the role of servant women in eighteenth-century culture. Moreover, these representations show that eighteenth-century writers still held fast to notions of class-specific expressions of femininity despite the new construction of domestic femininity as a universal ideal.

The justifications of Mr. B's marriage to Pamela that recur in the last part of the novel involve constructing Pamela as an exemplary woman who transcends the limitations of class. Upon Mr. B's announcement of his marriage to Pamela, Lady Davers expresses the concerns of many of Richardson's readers when she goads her brother about starting a new trend of misalliance: "I'd have you . . . publish your fine Reasons to the World, and they will be sweet Encouragements to all the young Gentlemen that read them, to cast themselves away on the Servant-wenches in their families" (349). Lady Davers does not want to give up the importance of a woman's social status, which Mr. B seems to dismiss when he replies that Pamela is naturally "so inrich'd with the Beauties of Person and Mind, so well accomplish'd, and so fitted to adorn the Degree she is raised to" (350) that censurers will be persuaded that she deserves marriage into the upper classes. Indeed, in the last paragraph of the novel, Richardson proclaims that Pamela has a character "worthy of the Imitation of her Sex, from low to high Life" (412). As Armstrong asserts, these arguments suggest the triumph of an apolitical virtuous femininity which elides class distinctions between women. The force of this conclusion was so powerful that Richardson had explicitly to revoke its levelling implications in *Pamela II* by having Pamela remark, "It is my absolute opinion, that degrees in general should be kept up; although I must always deem the present case an happy exception to the rule."[32]

Yet to perform its literary and ideological work, *Pamela* must at the same time assert both universal femininity and class-specific distinctions between women. This paradox is crucial to justifying Pamela's marriageability into the upper classes while maintaining the class subordination of other servant women. An important part of the plot of *Pamela*, one which ultimately prepares her for marriage to Mr. B, is her abduction and imprisonment at the estate in Lincolnshire. In Lincolnshire, Pamela not only becomes divorced from her context as a servant, but she is also placed in stark opposition to Mrs. Jewkes, another upper servant. Richardson elevates the delicate and chaste Pamela largely by contrasting her to Mrs. Jewkes's grotesque physicality and sapphic sexuality. Charlotte Sussman, critical of the empowering rhetoric of universal femininity evoked in Richardson's text, reminds us to stay attentive to "the ways in which exemplary images of femininity are constructed in relation to the other kinds of women who inhabit the novel."[33] Sussman makes this point about Pamela's relation to Sally Godfrey, but it seems even more applicable to Pamela's relation to Mrs. Jewkes. Seeing Pamela in contrast to Mrs. Jewkes reveals that exceptional, virtuous femininity is actually class-specific; it is, in fact, specific to leisure-class femininity. In upholding some of the predominant markers of class differences between women, namely the body and sexuality, Richardson is actually in alignment with his antipamelist critics. The main point of departure for Richardson and writers like Fielding and Haywood is that the antipamelist writers refuse to accept the potential "lady" in the "lady's maid." While Richardson asserts Pamela's superiority to Mrs. Jewkes, Haywood and especially Fielding illustrate her continued affiliation with servant women's physicality and voracious sexuality; in the words of Fielding's Mrs. Jervis, the antipamelists show that Pamela and her fellow servants "hang together . . . as well as any Family of Servants in the Nation" (19).

For all of Richardson's novel's appreciative attention to Pamela's mind and virtue, there is much descriptive detail about her physical beauty and attributes, which in the eighteenth century conveyed class distinctions. Ian Watt aptly describes the construction of the leisure-class woman's body and the use Richardson makes of this construction:

> since middle-class wives tended to be increasingly regarded as leisure exhibits engaging in no heavier economic tasks than the more delicate and supervisory operations of housewifery, a conspicuously weak constitution was both an assertion of a delicately nurtured past and a presumptive claim to a similar future. It is true that Pamela's humble birth hardly entitles her to this trait; but in fact her full possession of it only shows that her total being has been so deeply shaped by ideas above her that even her body exhibits—to invoke the assistance of a neologism for which there is in any

case a regrettable need—a not uncommon form of what can only be called sociosomatic snobbery. (161)

This "sociosomatic snobbery" helps Richardson construct Pamela as worthy of marriage into the upper classes.[34] From early on in the novel, we are told of Pamela's beauty and at least on one occasion it is suggested that such beauty denotes an upper-class heritage: Lady Brooks remarks to Mr. B about Pamela, "See that Shape! I never saw such a Face and Shape in my Life; why she must be better descended than you have told me!" (59). As other critics have often remarked, Pamela's frequent fainting also indicates a delicacy and frailty that further support her rise to ladyhood.

These suggestions of Pamela's natural suitability for upper-class femininity, however, are not as convincing as her direct contrast to other servant women. In the description Pamela gives of Mrs. Jewkes, Pamela's physical difference from her is pronounced:

> She is a broad, squat, pursy, fat Thing, quite ugly . . . about forty Years old. She has a huge Hand, and an Arm as thick as my Waist, I believe. Her Nose is flat and crooked, and Brows grow over her Eyes; a dead, spiteful, grey, goggling Eye, to be sure, she has. And her Face is flat and broad; and as to Colour, looks like as if it had been pickled a Month in Salt-petre: I dare say she drinks!—She has a hoarse man-like Voice, and is as thick as she's long; and yet looks so deadly strong, that I am afraid she would dash me at her foot in an Instant, if I was to vex her. (107)

Like her innkeeper family, Mrs. Jewkes laughs heartily, she drinks, "she curses and storms . . . like a Trooper" and talks "nastily . . . like a vile London Prostitute" (158). Mrs. Jewkes' body and manner in its excesses recalls the grotesque body of Rabelais' world, so famously described by Bakhtin, yet here the grotesque body has lost its Rabelaisian "deeply positive" meaning and serves only to reify class difference.[35]

Richardson in the description of Mrs. Jewkes has chosen to emphasize a typical trope of laboring femininity, in that plebeian women's physiques are generally depicted as robust and hearty. Yet his choice is also strategically designed to separate Pamela from Mrs. Jewkes, for most upper female servants, such as housekeepers and lady's maids, were hired on the basis of their physical attractiveness and neatness as well as their competence as workers since they were most often in public view. As such, upper female servants often defied neat class distinctions based on the body, a material fact which evoked some anxiety in employers and is evidenced in the conduct books for servants. Haywood's *Present for a Servant Maid,* for example, illustrates employers' resentment of this form of social blurring and reasserts the construction of the upper female servant's body as a laboring woman's body:

> The affectation of following your Mistress's Example, has corrupted but too many of you; you imagine it shews a Delicacy, and looks pretty in you to be able to breakfast on nothing but Tea and Coffee, whereas both these Liquors, especially the former, diminish your Strength, waste your Time, and, for the most part, draw on a more pernicious Consequence, which is Dram-drinking. (10)

Haywood reprimands female servants for imitating leisure-class femininity by referring to the specifics of a laboring woman's body, one which is valued on the basis of its "strength" and productive time, and one which must be disciplined for its propensity to indulge physically, in such as activities as "dram-drinking." Unlike in leisure-class women, "delicacy" in servant women was not a positive trait.

Consistent with conduct literature's strategy of maintaining distinctions between ladies and female servants, the antipamelist fictions by Fielding and Haywood insist on Pamela's continued affiliations with laboring women by emphasizing her physical strength, control, and assertiveness. In *Shamela,* for example, Fielding exploits this tradition for comic purposes with slapstick descriptions of fighting among the servant women. Shamela's mother, an innkeeper and orange-seller, writes to her daughter, "I have sprained my right hand, with boxing with three new made Officers.—Tho' to my Comfort, I beat them all" (21). When Mrs. Jewkes picks a fight with Shamela, Shamela "flew at her and scratched her Face, i'cod, 'till she went crying out of the Room" (25). Haywood's heroine Syrena rarely gets into fights, but she can throw an angry fit and use her strength to get away from sexual intrigues that are progressing too quickly; when a gentleman grabs her and tries to pull her into a tavern; she, "frighted now in good earnest, . . . snatches [her] Hand away with more Strength than could be expected from [her]" (16). Like Richardson, Fielding and Haywood are "sociosomatic snobs," but they are more interested in exposing the robust laboring femininity disguised behind the proper-looking lady's maid.

In their attacks on *Pamela,* Haywood and Fielding's representations seek to expose upper female servants' overlap with leisure-class femininity as nothing more than effective acting and to instruct their readers that bodies aren't always a reliable signifier of social standing. Syrena, for instance, surpasses "the most experienc'd Actresses on the Stage" (3); she can imitate a female delicacy and sensitivity that equals any lady, as she can affect "her whole Frame, Agitations adapted to the Occasion, her Colour would come and go, her Eyes sparkle, grow Languid, or overflow with Tears, her Bosom heave, her Limbs tremble; she would fall into Faintings, or appear transported . . . and all this so natural, that had the whole College of Phycians [sic] been present, they could not have imagin'd it otherwise than real" (3). Similarly, Shamela pretends lady-like embarassment and inexperience in sexual matters: she fools Booby with a blush "by holding [her] Breath, and squeezing [her] Cheeks with [her] handkerchief" (42). Just as easily, she dupes him on their wedding night: "I acted my Part in such a manner, that no Bridegroom was ever better satisfied with his Bride's Virginity" (43). The authors delineate the particularities of laboring women's bodies—that they are strong and most likely sexually experienced—in order to discredit Richardson's portrayal of a lady's maid who possesses a leisure-class body and manner.

Antipamelists simply did not accept that a "servant wench" could prove a respectable wife to a man of the upper ranks. Not only did they fear her rampant material desires and ability to dissimulate, but most of all they feared what they perceived as her "unruly" sexuality. For Richardson, proving Pamela's exceptionality in the realm of sexual proclivity and behavior is perhaps the greatest challenge to making her marriage to Mr. B acceptable. As the author of "Critical Remarks" illustrates, eighteenth-century society held that in order to keep "families, inheritances, and distinctions of ranks and orders" intact, "the chastity and continence of women are absolutely and indispensably necessary," yet for the lower orders, chastity "for obvious reasons, exerts no great influence" (29–30). Antipamelists believed permissive plebeian sexual morality to be incompatible with the sexual fidelity required of upper-class women. Fielding thus depicts Shamela as continuing her affair with Parson Williams after her marriage to the duped Squire Booby until, as the last postscript to *Shamela* reports, "Mr. Booby hath caught his Wife in bed with Williams; hath turned her off, and is prosecuting him in the spiritual Court" (59).

Contrasting the chaste Pamela to the lascivious and sapphic Mrs. Jewkes allows Richardson to elevate Pamela while still maintaining classist attitudes toward servant women.[36] In the portrayal of Mrs. Jewkes, Richardson does not diverge very much from his detractors' views of the housekeepers in the novel. The author of "Pamela Censured," for instance, compares both to keepers of bawdy houses. He calls Mrs. Jervis a "procuress in Ordinary though indeed she doth not prove so pac'd an One as Mrs. Jewkes doth afterwards" (46); and Mrs. Jewkes "enters into the Business with all the Assurance of an experienc'd Bawd" (49). Similarly, in *Pamela,* the heroine calls Mrs. Jewkes "the vile procuress" (176), and indeed, the sexual freedom and licentiousness Jewkes represents makes her the perfect bawd for Mr. B. As his minion, she parrots B's sexual libertinism; she tells Pamela, "are not the two Sexes made for one another? And is it not natural for a Gentleman to love a pretty Woman? And suppose he can obtain his Desires, is that so bad as cutting her throat?" (104). In the attempted-rape scene, when Jewkes pins Pamela down for Mr. B, Jewkes' laboring-class traits—her physical strength, bawdiness, and cunning—are all used in service to Mr. B's desires.

Commonly in the eighteenth century, descriptions of madams indicate that the procuress has her own sexual interest in the young woman to be debauched, either out of genuine desire or of vengeance for her own "fallen" state. Robert Erickson in *Mother Midnight,* for example, notes that "the bawd was in the business of breaking young women into the trade by the services of hired 'bullies,' and women thus broken, or lost, were thought to desire the same fate for others."[37] He quotes one male observer as saying

> I cannot help remarking that the Fair Sex are far more indebted for their ruin to female friends than male foes. There is a lust in a woman who has once lost her reputation, to bring every other upon a level with herself, that her prid e may not be hurt with reproach . . . Thus has many a virtuous Young Female been debauched by Woman-kind. (39)

The author is able to absolve men of their responsibility for the sexual exploitation of young women by shifting the blame to the female bawd. Significantly, this passage also registers the troubling nature of the bawd's role in procuring women. A woman whose business it is to view, evaluate, and treat women as sexual objects, even for the purpose of giving them over to men, is threatening in that she challenges the culture's assumptions about male sexual privilege. Although in this quotation there is a move to reframe the experienced woman's desire for the young virgin as a way to bring innocent women down to her level, the phrasing—"there is a lust in a woman"—keeps the sapphic sexual valence at play.[38]

The antipamelists readily exploit this sexual ambiguity, registering their anxiety about lower-class women's sexual agency, which they believe can be directed at women just as easily as men. In *Shamela,* Fielding plays with the underlying sexual tension between Mrs. Jervis and Shamela. Wishing herself in Booby's position, she privately admits her attraction to Pamela; she muses, "If I was to keep a House a thousand Years, I would never desire a prettier Wench in it" (18). As the two women are scheming to attract Squire Booby and get him either to propose marriage or to draw up a sizeable settlement, Mrs. Jervis imagines Shamela through Booby's eyes to determine how best to make Shamela attractive to him, yet her identification with this aristocratic male role soon gives her an outlet for her own desire. She says,

> 'my dear Honeysuckle, I have one game to play for you ; he shall see you in Bed; he shall, my little Rose-bud, he shall see those pretty, little, white,

round, panting—and offer'd to pull off my Handkerchief.' '—Fie, Mrs. Jervis, says I, you make me blush, and upon my Fackins, I believe she did.' (14)

Significantly, Shamela's blush is the only sincere one in the entire parody—on all other occasions, Fielding makes sure we know Shamela is faking a blush by pinching her cheeks. Fielding is making a concerted effort to highlight the same-sex desire expressed here, and to show that this is the only form of desire that might unsettle or embarrass even the sexually experienced and savvy Shamela. Moreover, the housekeeper's fantasy about possessing Pamela takes the form of seeing herself as a master seducing his servant maid—in effect adopting conventional male ruling-class sexual privilege. Laboring women's sexuality is figured as especially threatening, in that the housekeeper fantasizes about usurping not just male privilege, but also class privilege, in seducing the beautiful lady's maid.

In *Pamela,* Richardson likewise acknowledges the threatening sexual agency of laboring women, but he deploys it very differently. Mrs. Jewkes' unruly and sapphic sexuality serves to secure Pamela's chaste sexual identity as well as to diminish Mr. B's role in Pamela's attempted rape. Jewkes' prurient interest in Pamela serves as a kind of litmus test of sexual inclination:

> Every now-and-then she would be staring in my Face, in the Chariot, and squeezing my hand, and saying, Why, you are very pretty, my silent Dear! And once she offer'd to kiss me. But I said, I don't like this Sort of Carriage, Mrs. Jewkes; it is not like two Persons of one Sex.
>
> She fell a laughing very confidently, and said, That's prettily said, I vow; then thou hadst rather be kiss'd by the other Sex? If'ackins, I commend thee for that. (102)

In Richardson's novel, this depiction of Mrs. Jewkes's desire for Pamela serves to illustrate more than laboring women's sexual agency; the dialogue between Mrs. Jewkes and Pamela also serves to evidence Pamela's heterosexual desires, even while she remains sexually virtuous.

Because plebeian and servant women were thought to be sexually permissive, Richardson has to make clear that in resisting the advances of Mr. B, Pamela is not like the sapphic Mrs. Jewkes. This ironic slippage between heterosexual chasteness and same-sex desire was not missed by antipamelist critics. The author of "Pamela Censured" states, "There are at present, I am sorry to say it, too many who assume the Characters of Women of Mrs. Jewkes's Cast, I mean Lovers of their own Sex, Pamela seems to be acquainted with this, and indeed shews so much Virtue, that she has no Objection to the Male Sex as too many of her own have" (50–51). According to the author, Pamela is more virtuous than Mrs. Jewkes because she desires men—although he's still having a joke about this. Throughout the tract, he sketches a continuum of sexual immorality and sexual virtue, with same-sex desire associated with the lowest immoral pole, promiscuous heterosexual activity in the middle, and chaste heterosexual relations as the highest form of virtue. Yet how do eighteenth-century men know that in fending off men, women are not just indulging a preference for other women? Is sexual virtue just another name for sexual perversity? Richardson dispels this potential confusion by having Pamela recoil at Mrs. Jewkes's overtures.

In order to make narrative, moral, and social sense of the transition from a master's attempted rape of his servant maid to the marriage of an exemplary couple, Richardson must not only secure Pamela's sexual virtue, but also he must divest Mr. B of his libertine sexuality. Mrs. Jewkes' sapphic role, often construed in the text as masculine, again becomes useful. From the first sight of Jewkes, Pamela notices her "hoarse man-like Voice" and reacts as if she has met her debaucher: "I am undone, . . . for she is very, very wicked" (107). Although Mrs. Jewkes is said to be following Mr. B's orders to imprison Pamela and "prime" her for Mr. B's arrival, Richardson makes a point to emphasize Jewkes' own investment in debauching Pamela. Mrs. Jewkes, also like Fielding's Mrs. Jervis, envisions herself in her master's shoes, asserting her superior expertise and efficiency in seducing Pamela: "if I was he, I would not be long away!—What means the Woman, said I?—Means! . . why I mean, I would come, if I was he, and put an End to all your Fears—by making you as happy as you wish" (114). A couple of pages later, she says, "Well, well, Lambkin . . . if I was in his Place, he should not have his Property in you long questionable. Why, what would you do, said I if you was he?—Not stand shill-I, shall-I, as he does; but put you and himself both out of your Pain" (116).

Richardson gradually divests Mr. B of responsibility for the attempted rape and places it all on Mrs. Jewkes. During the attempted rape, Pamela lies pinned between Mrs. Jewkes and the cross-dressed Mr. B, who is impersonating the other servant, Nan. Jewkes shifts from being Mr. B's accomplice, to being the instigator of the rape. Pamela writes,

> . . . the guilty Wretch took my Left-arm, and laid it under his Neck, as the vile Procuress held my Right; and then he clasp'd me round my Waist!

> Said I, Is the Wench mad! Why, how now, Confidence? thinking still it had been *Nan*. But he kissed me with frightful Vehemence; and then his Voice broke upon me like a Clap of Thunder. . . .

> Said she, (O Disgrace of Womankind!) What you do, Sir, do; don't stand
> dilly-dallying. She cannot exclaim worse than she has done. And she'll be
> quieter when she knows the worst. . . . (176)

Just as Mr. B pauses in his attack, Jewkes, with no sympathy for the distressed Pamela, urges him to complete his attempt. The shift in blame is further confirmed by Pamela's assertion that Mrs. Jewkes is worse than Mr. B: "O what a black Heart has this poor Wretch! So I need not rail against Men so much; for my Master, bad as I have thought him, is not half so bad as this Woman!" (212). Even Mr. B notes that "Mrs. Jewkes carry'd her Orders a little too far" (255). Mrs. Jewkes' unruly and transgressive sexuality becomes a convenient scapegoat for libertine masculinity.[39] In fact, laboring female sexuality as a whole becomes scapegoated and almost emblematically yoked to sapphic desire. It is no accident of plot that in the pivotal scene of the novel, in which Pamela's virginity is most under threat, that what we purportedly have is three servant women in bed together. Mr. B's impersonation of the drunken Nan most overtly signifies the appropriation of "unruly" transgressive sexuality of laboring women. Furthermore, Pamela's ability to mistake Mr. B for Nan serves to highlight the ways in which eighteenth-century society, as it understands female identity in terms of sexual passivity, begins to view laboring women and their complex sexuality as masculine. Pamela, for instance, supposedly has no problem believing that Nan's body and the imposing masculine body of Mr. B are one and the same, until Mr. B speaks.

Much to the chagrin of antipamelists, Jewkes is redeemed by Pamela's forgiving her and by her role in assisting proper heterosexual relations. At the wedding ceremony, Pamela requests her presence: "I said to Mrs. Jewkes, Don't leave me; pray, Mrs. Jewkes, don't leave me; as if I had all Confidence in her, and none where it was most due. So she kept close to me" (289). In details that bring to mind the bedroom scene, Pamela takes hold of her arm and leans on her (289). Now there can be no misinterpretation of their physical affection: "Mrs. Jewkes would have kissed my Hand at the Chapel Door; but I put my Arms about her Neck, for I had got a new Recruit of Spirits just then, and kissed her; and said, Thank you, Mrs. Jewkes, for accompanying me" (290). And Nan guards the door (289), not to hide an illicit sexual affair, but a legal marriage.

Richardson's evocation and domestication of Jewkes' unruly and sapphic sexuality points to the central role of plebeian female sexuality in Richardson's project to "set Virtue in its own Amiable Light" (3). The novel on the one hand promotes a new ideal of domestic virtuous femininity, yet on the other hand betrays the necessity of defining leisure-class femininity against its laboring-class counterpart. Richardson invokes the grotesque, laboring female body in order to appropriate its transgressions and give evidence of Pamela's moral superiority. Stallybrass and White describe this phenomenon on a wider scale in the eighteenth century:

> The grotesque body of carnival was being re-territorialized, it was being appropriated, sublimated and individualized to code refined identity, to give the eighteenth-century nobility and the bourgeoisie masks and symbols to think with at the very moment when they were repudiating the social realm from which those masks and symbols came.[40]

The antipamelists exhibit the same tendency to evoke, appropriate, and repudiate laboring female sexuality; but according to their interpretation, Pamela is just as complicit in such sexual behavior as the other servant women in the novel. Instead of domesticating laboring-female sexuality, they exploit it for all of its unruly potential in order to prove that while a servant maid may be a master's mistress, she should by no means be made a master's wife. The end result is not all that different—both Richardson and antipamelists end up discrediting laboring female sexuality, a move which importantly belies Richardson's claims to a universally available female virtue.

Paraphrasing from R. P. Utter and G. B. Needham's *Pamela's Daughters,* Ian Watt delineates "the emergence of a new, fully developed and immensely influential stereotype of the feminine role" which the publication of *Pamela* ushered into being: "the model heroine must be very young, very inexperienced, and so delicate in physical and mental constitution that she faints at any sexual advance; essentially passive, she is devoid of any feelings towards her admirer until the marriage knot is tied—such is Pamela and such are most of the heroines of fiction until the end of the Victorian period" (161). In this formulation, Watt illustrates the way that *Pamela,* perhaps because of her abundant progeny, has been read too much not only in terms of her descendants but also in terms of the novel's own ending. While the last half of the novel may leave readers with the memory of a leisure-class version of Pamela, this is not the Pamela who during the first half of her history uses her saucy and audacious servant identity to fend off Mr. B; nor is it the Pamela who raises the ire of so many of Richardson's contemporaries. Enlisting the unlikely help of the antipamelists to re-read *Pamela* allows us insight into the traces of Pamela's laboring-class characteristics as well as illuminates the continued appeal—and apprehensiveness—of these qualities for eighteenth-century readers and writers. Raymond Williams argues that in order to understand "the complexity of a culture," we must attend to its "residual" as well as its "emergent" and "dominant" discourses.[41] Both Richardson's novel and the antipamelist responses record the "residual" discourses of class-specific gender and sexual ideologies, and in doing so they inadvertently betray some of the powers of servant and plebeian women, powers that needed to be maligned or suppressed as the dominant discourse of domestic femininity triumphs, and as Pamela becomes elevated from lady's maid to lady.

NOTES

I would like to thank several colleagues who assiduously read various versions of this essay and offered invaluable suggestions about both content and form: Lance Bertelsen, Lisa Moore, Beth Hedrick, George Boulukos, Jenneken Van Keppel, Jennifer M. Bean, and Zjaleh Hajibashi.

1. Samuel Richardson, *Pamela: or, Virtue Rewarded*, ed. T. C. Duncan Eaves and Ben D. Kimpel (Boston: Houghton Mifflin, 1971), 257. Hereafter all page citations to this edition are in the text.

2. See Terry Castle, *Clarissa's Cyphers: Meaning and Disruption in Richardson's "Clarissa"* (Ithaca: Cornell Univ. Press, 1982), 169. Several other critics have noted the novel's reactionary feminist politics: see Terry Eagleton, *The Rape of Clarissa: Writing, Sexuality and Class Struggle in Samuel Richardson* (Oxford: Basil Blackwell, 1982), 36–37; Janet Todd, "Pamela, or the Bliss of Servitude," *British Journal for Eighteenth-Century Studies* 6 (1983): 139; Robert Folkenflik, "*Pamela*: Domestic Servitude, Marriage, and the Novel," *Eighteenth-Century Fiction* 5 (1993): 268; Bridget Hill, *Servants: English Domestics in the Eighteenth Century* (Oxford: Clarendon Press, 1996), 224.

3. Christopher Flint, "The Anxiety of Affluence: Family and Class (Dis)order in *Pamela: or, Virtue Rewarded,*" *Studies in English Literature* 29 (1989): 489.

4. Nancy Armstrong, *Desire and Domestic Fiction: A Political History of the Novel* (Oxford: Oxford Univ. Press, 1987), 59–95.

5. Miriam Hansen is drawing from Ann Kaplan's work on the film *Stella Dallas.* See Hansen's "Pleasure, Ambivalence, Identification: Valentino and Female Spectatorship," *Cinema Journal* 25, no. 4 (Summer 1986): 9–10. I'd like to thank Jennifer M. Bean for bringing this article to my attention.

6. Several critics have recently addressed the "Pamela Vogue" phenomenon, yet all of these studies share a striking omission: nowhere do critics acknowledge that the flurry of responses to the novel had to do with the eponymous heroine's status as a servant girl and the more general contest being waged in the culture at large over the class identities of servants. See Terri Nickel, "*Pamela* as Fetish: Masculine Anxiety in Henry Fielding's *Shamela* and James Parry's *The True Anti-Pamela,*" *Studies in Eighteenth-Century Culture* 22 (1992): 37–49; James Grantham Turner, "Novel Panic: Picture and Performance in the Reception of Richardson's *Pamela,*" *Representations* 48 (Fall 1994): 70–96; Richard Gooding, "*Pamela,*

Shamela, and the Politics of the *Pamela* Vogue," *Eighteenth-Century Fiction* 7 (1995): 109–30.

7. This revision of Pamela's class is also present in pamelist fictions. Richard Gooding in his *"Pamela, Shamela,* and the Politics of the *Pamela* Vogue," notes that even the most faithful imitations of the novel, John Kelly's *Pamela's Conduct in High Life,* uses romance conventions to elevate Pamela's birth. For Gooding, this means that "Pamelist literature is marked by incomprehension of—or resistance to—Richardson's interest in the kinds of confrontation that can occur between the conscientious individual and the hereditary stewards of political and social authority" (121). Richardson himself in *Pamela II,* while not going so far as to revise Pamela's class origins, certainly did his best to obscure them; see Terry Castle, *Masquerade and Civilization: The Carnivalesque in Eighteenth-Century English Culture and Fiction* (Stanford: Stanford Univ. Press, 1986), 139–51.

8. "Critical Remarks on Sir Charles Grandison, Clarissa, and Pamela" (London: J. Dowse, 1754), 35.

9. I have selected the Fielding and Haywood fictions because they do not attempt to alter Pamela's class status or her gender. Hereafter all references will be to the following editions: Henry Fielding, *An Apology for the Life of Mrs. Shamela Andrews* (1741; reprint, New York: Garland Publishing, 1974) and *Anti-Pamela: or Feign'd Innocence Detected,* published anonymously but attributed to Eliza Haywood (1742; reprint, New York: Garland Publishing, 1975).

10. I have tried to keep the categories of "servant" and "plebeian" or "laboring class" distinct, but this is not entirely possible, as the writers tend to view the servant classes as representative of the laboring classes. As Hill in *Servants* notes, service "provided the only close contact most of the middle and upper classes had with the labouring class" (5).

11. As quoted in J. Jean Hecht, *The Domestic Servant Class in Eighteenth-Century England* (London: Routledge and Kegan Paul, 1956), 72.

12. Bridget Hill, *Women, Work, and Sexual Politics in Eighteenth-Century England* (Montreal and Kingston: McGill-Queen's Univ. Press, 1994), 146–47.

13. Daniel Defoe, for example, records his annoyance when he kisses a chamber maid who he assumed was a member of the family. See *Every-Body's Business Is No-Body's Business* (London, 1725), 13.

14. Eliza Haywood, *Present for a Servant Maid* (Dublin: Reprinted by and for George Faulkner, 1743), 24–25. Subsequent page references will be to this edition.

15. In his list of moral observations at the end of the novel, for example, Richardson writes, "From the Oeconomy she purposes to observe in her Elevation, let even Ladies of Condition learn, that there are Family Employments in which they may, and ought to, make themselves useful" (411).

16. "Pamela Censured: in Letter to the Editor" (London: J. Roberts, 1741), 18.

17. Hill in *Servants* notes that "while some servants married fellow servants, lesser tradesmen, or craftsmen, and enjoyed a modest standard of living, it was rare for them to leave their own class" (213).

18. Patty Seleski, "Women, Work and Cultural Change in Eighteenth- and Early Nineteenth-Century London," in *Popular Culture in England, c. 1500–1850,* ed.

Tim Harris (London: Macmillan, 1995), 149. Of course, it is possible that lady's maids, who required more education and depended upon a more select group of wealthy employers, may not have been as mobile as other types of servant maids. This does not significantly alter my argument, however, because the antipamelists tend to gloss over the distinctions between different types of female servants. In their imaginations, female servants are usually collapsed into one general occupational category, often defined by the lowest servant rank.

19. E. P. Thompson, *Customs in Common: Studies in Traditional Popular Culture* (New York: The New Press, 1993), 9.

20. Bernard Kreissman, *Pamela-Shamela: A Study of the Criticisms, Burlesques, Parodies, and Adaptations of Richardson's "Pamela"* (Lincoln: Univ. of Nebraska Press, 1960), 7.

21. One of the most obvious class distinctions between women that is notably absent in Richardson's novel and the antipamelist literature is the labor that upper female servants perform. Pamela holds the position of lady's maid, a position which becomes obsolete once her mistress dies. In this position, Richardson describes her as doing bookkeeping and needlework, but also reading, singing, dancing, drawing, and, of course, writing. These duties match what we know about the position of lady's maids; as Hecht explains, upper female servants performed mainly supervisory roles and possessed special skills in bookkeeping and sewing, while the lower female servants did more of the manual labor of cleaning, marketing and cooking (60–69). On the whole, though, Richardson follows suit with the antipamelists in downplaying servant work and instead in representing female servants mainly as romantic and sexual beings. Fielding, for example, does not mention Shamela working at all, and in *Anti-Pamela*, Haywood mentions servant women's work just enough to prove female servants are lazy and incompetent. Her heroine Syrena notes that as a lady's maid "I have so little to do, and am so much respected by the inferior Servants, that I can scarce think I am a servant myself" (49). Later, when Syrena is hired as a housekeeper by an older man who is taken with her beauty, she admits that she is "ignorant enough how to order the Affairs of a Family" (188). This marginalization or devaluing of servant women's labor serves to hide the central importance of and demand for domestic labor at this time in English society, and it also reveals an underside of domestic service for women—their treatment as sexual commodities.

22. While Armstrong credits conduct literature for leisure-class women and Richardson in *Pamela* with inventing a female subjectivity that is specifically bourgeois (108–134), I contend that *Pamela* and its parodies illustrate that female subjectivity plays a crucial part in the representations of servant women, in order to make more nuanced distinctions between servants and ladies.

23. Ian Watt, *Rise of the Novel* (Berkeley and Los Angeles: Univ. of California Press, 1957), 148.

24. Hill, *Servants,* 108.

25. D. A. Kent, "Ubiquitous but Invisible: Female Domestic Servants in Mid-Eighteenth-Century London," *History Workshop Journal* 28 (Autumn 1989): 112. Kent argues that urban domestic service offered many advantages to single

women, such as economic security, the guarantee of diet and lodging, and independence. As Kent states, the female servant "was valued because of her unmarried status. Her wages may have been low, as they were for all women workers, but they were the wages of an independent woman and not those of a supplementary wage-earner" (115).

26. Anna Clark, *The Struggle for the Breeches: Gender and the Making of the British Working Class* (Berkeley and Los Angeles: Univ. of California Press, 1995), 42–62.

27. Sarah Maza, *Servants and Masters in Eighteenth-Century France* (Princeton: Princeton Univ. Press, 1983), 138.

28. Hill, *Servants*, 63.

29. The author refers to the passage quoted above in which Pamela reflects on what would happen if she should submit to Mr. B; see "Pamela Censured," 32. For an example of how this class bias is also present in twentieth-century critics of the novel, see Eagleton in *The Rape of Clarissa*, where he writes, "The premarital Pamela is an engagingly realistic woman, shrewd, practical and humorous, and it is precisely this which makes her absolutism about sexuality seem so contrived" (34).

30. Thomas Seaton, *The Conduct of Servants in Great Families* (1720; reprint, New York: Garland Publishing, 1985), 145.

31. For a discussion of Lady Mary Wortley Montagu's interesting intimation that women of the lower classes are better prepared than leisure-class women for courtship and marriage decisions, see Cynthia Lowenthal, *Lady Mary Wortley Montagu and the Familiar Letter* (Athens: Univ. of Georgia Press, 1994), 175–77.

32. Samuel Richardson, *Pamela, Part Two*, ed. Mark Kinkead-Weekes, 2 vols. (London: Everyman's Library, 1963), 2: 168.

33. Charlotte Sussman, "'I Wonder Whether Poor Miss Sally Godfrey Be Living or Dead?': The Married Woman and the Rise of the Novel," *Diacritics* 20, no. 1 (1990): 90.

34. While Armstrong argues that in the creation of domestic femininity, "male desire is redirected away from the surface of the body toward its depths" (120), I would argue that attractions of the female body persist, especially in representations of leisure-class women. Tassie Gwilliam also critiques this point of Armstrong's in *Samuel Richardson's Fictions of Gender* (Stanford: Stanford Univ. Press, 1993), 17.

35. Mikhail Bakhtin, *Rabelais and His World*, trans. Helene Iswolsky (Bloomington: Indian Univ. Press, 1984), 104.

36. In my discussion of the ways in which Mrs. Jewkes' sapphic sexuality butresses Pamela's identity as sexually virtuous, I am indebted to Lisa Moore's *Dangerous Intimacies: Toward a Sapphic History of the British Novel* (Durham: Duke Univ. Press, 1997), in which she argues that "The sexual category of feminine virtue, then, is crucially predicated on various colonial violences: slavery, the extermination of indigenous peoples, the exploitation of Europe's poor as indentured servants and transplanted laborers, revolution at home, and wars of imperial dominion abroad. The sexual Other of the virtuous bourgeois woman is often her slightly sapphic female friend; the unconscious logic of these texts links

that freakish figure with a variety of characters drawn from nationalist and colonial discourses: decadent French and Italians, sensuous barbaric Turks, simple but savage Africans, sexually aberrant Indians, slaves, monsters, and voodoo witches" (12).

37. Robert Erikson, *Mother Midnight: Birth, Sex, and Fate in Eighteenth-Century Fiction (Defoe, Richardson, and Sterne)* (New York: AMS Press, 1986), 39.

38. While there were a number of other eighteenth-century terms to express homoeroticism between women, I employ the term *sapphic* because it was used more commonly. For further discussions of eighteenth-century vocabulary used to discuss female homosexuality, see Randolph Trumbach, "London's Sapphists: From Three Sexes to Four Genders in the Making of Modern Culture," in *Body Guards: The Cultural Politics of Gender Ambiguity,* ed. Julia Epstein and Kristina Straub (New York: Routledge, 1991) and Moore's *Dangerous Intimacies.*

39. Robert Folkenflik has also noted the way that Mrs. Jewkes is scapegoated; he writes that both Jewkes and Colbrand "will eventually serve as scapegoats for Mr B.'s behavior, but their threatening sexuality helps to keep the temperature of the novel high" (265).

40. Peter Stallybrass and Allon White, *The Politics and Poetics of Transgression* (Ithaca: Cornell Univ. Press, 1986), 104.

41. Raymond Williams, *Marxism and Literature* (Oxford: Oxford Univ. Press, 1977), 121.

"This Theatre of Monstrous Guilt":
Horace Walpole and the
Drama of Incest

PAUL BAINES

Horace Walpole completed his tragedy *The Mysterious Mother* in 1768, and it has remained mysterious ever since. Whereas Walpole's *The Castle of Otranto* (1764) has never been out of print, *The Mysterious Mother* has hardly ever been in it. All scholars accept that *Otranto* stands as the inaugural text of the Gothic novel; fewer scholars are aware of the foundational and influential status of *The Mysterious Mother* in Gothic drama.[1] The play has remained oddly secret long after political or gender-based criticism might have been expected to recover it. The reasons for neglect are partly to be located in the scandalous nature of the action itself, as even the briefest plot summary will indicate: the "mother" of the title is the widowed Countess of Narbonne, who has banished her son Edmund for a supposed sexual misdemeanor with her maid; sixteen years later he returns, with a fellow-soldier named Florian, to confront his mysteriously contrite mother, and marries a beautiful orphan, Adeliza. Through the machinations of a villainous priest, Benedict, it is discovered that Adeliza is actually the offspring of Edmund's original transgression, which took place not with Beatrice the maid (as he had assumed) but with his own mother; he has thus unwittingly married his own sister/daughter. The Countess, who has borne the knowledge of this truth all along, stabs herself.[2]

It is an extreme version of incest narrative, even in literary terms, and this portrayal of a family in ruins has always had the potential to lead readers back to Walpole's own family life. The youngest son of the seemingly immovable and all-powerful Prime Minister of England, brought up as a weakling by an adored and adoring mother while the father maintained a separate and quite public establishment with his mistress, and rumored on occasion to be not actually Sir Robert Walpole's son at all, Horace Walpole could have found ample material for melodrama in the illegitimacies, divorces, and sexual disasters of his own immediate family circle. A gendered or sexualized approach is found in early accounts of the play: in 1821 Byron saw Walpole as "the 'Ultimus Romanorum,' the author of the *Mysterious Mother*, a tragedy of the highest order, and not a puling love play. He is the father of the first romance, and of the last tragedy in the language, and surely worthy of a higher place than any living writer, be he who he may."[3] A "seminal" author, then, as "father of the first romance," Walpole's Roman virtues are specifically masculine ones: "puling" is a word which the play itself uses to indicate effeminacy (Benedict contemptuously calls Adeliza a "puling moppet" [5.1], and Edmund describes himself as a mere "puling boy" before his mother's authority [2.1]), so the play becomes defined as highly masculine. On the other hand, Coleridge's rawest nerve seems to have been touched by the play, and Byron's commendation of it, and he vigorously contested its author's personal masculinity: "The *Mysterious Mother* is the most disgusting, detestable, vile composition that ever came from the hand of man. No one with a spark of true manliness, of which Horace Walpole had none, could have written it."[4]

Modern biographers and defendants of Walpole have commented, often with a certain embarrassment, on the supposed connection between *The Mysterious Mother* and Walpole's own sexual character. W. S. Lewis notes:

> The twentieth century has been initiated into the mysteries of the unconscious and needs no gloss on *The Mysterious Mother,* but one point should perhaps be noted. . . . When Walpole came to arrange his works for posthumous publication he printed his "Epitaph on Lady Walpole," with its praise of her sensibility, charity, and unbigoted piety, immediately after *The Mysterious Mother.*[5]

Psychoanalytic criticism of the play has occasionally followed this lead. Betsy Harfst decodes the play as a "punishment dream" through which Walpole purges unresolved Oedipal tensions and other latent personal stresses (such as guilt about the element of parricidal wish-fulfillment in *The Castle of Otranto,* and attachment to the elderly Madame du Deffand, who doubled both as mother-figure and daughter-figure); Martin Kallich confirms it as "a fascinating psychological palimpsest wherein the outlines of the author's life at a time of crisis may be deciphered."[6] The temptation to use the play in the service of psychobiography continues. In the most recent biography of Walpole, Timothy Mowl comprehensively (if rather punitively) "outs" his anti-hero as an unambiguous homosexual, and straightforwardly anchors the tragedy to a fear of heterosexual pressure.[7]

I have no wish, however, to extend this tidy homology between public and private any further; my intention is rather to try to reconfigure it along less personalized sexual and textual lines. While I do not deny that some of the play's energy may derive from personal conflict, a psychoanalytic reading can do nothing except use the play to analyze Walpole's personality (which can then of course be reinscribed as the "source" of authoritative meaning). I seek instead to offer a reading of the play's Oedipal dynamics of sex and power which does not depend on a direct identification of the play with Walpole's personal sexuality. Secondly, I wish to explore the slow-burning revelation of the play's textual history in relation to the tension between disclosure and concealment through which the play dramatizes its sexual content. Here the consequences are in an obvious way personal to Walpole as the play's author: though not everyone was as unnerved by the play as Coleridge, Walpole knew well enough (and at a conscious level) the sort of scandal that would attach to him for having written it. The playtext's own emergence from self-censorship and clandestine circulation, its oscillation between public and private status in its reception and textual history, re-enacted a kind of Oedipal pattern in the Sophoclean or dramatic sense of a secret whose teasing out is the source of theatrical tension. Its transgressive stance within the order of print is overlaid by its gradual absorption into the wider family of Walpole's audience, realigning the notion of a private sexual crime in more social terms. While the Countess's original sin cannot quite be redeemed in the world of the play, the regret which accompanies that failure becomes transferred to the textual redemption of Walpole's 'sin' in having authored it. The process by which this happens cannot simply be mapped onto the confession or sublimation of a private fantasy.

I

The Mysterious Mother revisits with more explosive effect many of the scenes of family tension explored in Walpole's *The Castle of Otranto*. In the novel, the Gothic setting offers an atavistic, archaizing and yet privileged space for the playing out of a scenario of patriarchal tyranny, rapacity, divorce and incest, ending not (as in so many later texts in the genre) in virtue rewarded or domestic bliss, but in childless domestic melancholy, the hero united with a second-best wife. Steeped in Walpole's reading of Jacobean drama, *Otranto* is dramatic in various ways and in 1781 it was adapted for the stage by Robert Jephson under the title of *The Count of Narbonne*—a title which more properly belongs to the hero of Walpole's unperformable attempt to invent Gothic drama. In adapting *Otranto* for a theatre which *The Mysterious Mother* would never reach, Jephson relegated much of the novel's supernatural machinery to narrative passages, perhaps learning from the instinct for the visual and performable which Walpole had demonstrated in his own play. For the nature of Gothic, as Walpole imagines it theatrically, is internal; supernatural forces become psychological ones. While providence and prophecy drive *Otranto* towards a revelatory conclusion through preternatural events and apparitions, all the active forces in *The Mysterious Mother* are internal ones, linking the play with the spirit-world fantasies of later closet dramas. Though the events of the play occur on the anniversary of the original crime, and thus may appear to be part of a celestial pattern, the notion of anniversary is something which the Countess herself has organized in yearly mourning for her dead husband, and the return to the moment is at least as much the product of individual consciousness as of any divine plan. The storm which shatters the Countess's penitential statue of her dead husband appears ominous and vengeful only to the priests and the comic and superstitious porter, notionally the guardian of the private domestic space of the castle, who accompanies the Countess on her trip to encounter the elements in 2.3. The Countess deliberately exposes herself to patriarchal vengeance in the shape of the thunderbolt, but soon realizes that a sense of doom is always internal, not cosmic:

> Omens and prodigies are but begotten
> By guilt on pride. We know the doom we merit;
> And self-importance makes us think all nature
> Busied to warn us when that doom approaches. (3.1)

"'Tis from within / I tremble," she tells Benedict (1.4). The real "thunderbolt" is the projected vision of "Conscience's flaming lance" which she experiences in 4.3. In this play the "supernatural" is only the invention of hypocritical priestcraft, exerted to further the powers of the malign confessor Benedict; the reality of it is a wholly psychological phenomenon, the haunting presence of a dead, vengeful spouse, which the Countess produces through the activities of conscience. Benedict's whole strategy, indeed, is to "sound" the Countess's "inmost soul, / And mould it to the instant of projection" (1.3); his success, ironically, derives from the strength of her inner virtue rather than the providential discovery of her weakness.[8]

This general internalization is mapped onto a recasting of the Oedipus story, which Walpole uses as a literary analogue to legitimize his shocking drama. *The Mysterious Mother* is an Oedipal drama which out-Hamlets *Hamlet* by rendering the desire for incestuous union between son and mother a conscious and consummated wish (at least on the mother's part). The language is full of allusions to riddles, oracles and so on, which signal the Sophoclean source, and both *Oedipus Tyrannos* and *The Mysterious Mother* end with the exile of the contaminated son to await death after the suicide of the guilty mother. But there are major differences, most obviously in the lack of a supernatural machinery to reveal the latent sexual crime, but also in the more private domestic scope of the drama. Though aristocrats, the Narbonne family have no stake in the state, and for Edmund to go and fight in the national wars is precisely an extreme form of exile: Gothic is domesticated here into a single family trauma. Conceived partly as a star vehicle for a (perhaps conveniently) unavailable actress, and inventing, as female, the sort of monolithic, wounded character of charisma and exclusion later to dominate "Byronic" drama in male guise, the play refocuses attention on the mother rather than the son. In this it resembles treatments of the Phaedra legend by Euripides (*Hippolytus*) and Racine (*Phèdre*); Voltaire's *Sémiramis*, another highly exotic version of mysterious mothering which Walpole saw in Paris in 1766 and admired, is another possible source.[9] It would be easy enough to construe the basic plot of *The Mysterious Mother* as a displacement of male incestuous desire onto a guilty mother, rendering the son innocent (as with Hippolytus); the Countess could be read as disruptively sensual, usurping patriarchal authority over sexual situations with catastrophic results, for which she is punished by death. Mystifying the Mother would then be a relatively familiar process of collapsing a venerated idol into a castrating witch. Yet one of the most controversial or culpable elements of the play, as Walpole understood it, was exactly its failure to demonize the Countess in this way.

Walpole departs from dramatic convention in abandoning the gendered and hierarchical division between men and women in the "Persons" or Dramatis Personae and listing the Countess at the top. In the play, she possesses real power: as the widow of Narbonne, she bears (in Edmund's phrase) "Narbonne's sceptre" (3.4). Benedict may be her confessor but she is his boss, resisting confession and absolution (his means to power) and silencing him on several occasions with the play's unambiguous approval (for example, in 3.4). He can only refer to the absent institutional authority of "Holy Church," which he also pointedly characterizes as female (4.1) and which the Countess simply ignores. Economically, in the sense of running the law of the home, the Countess is unimpeachable: Benedict and Edmund acknowledge that she scrupulously pays the revenues of the estate to her son (1.3, 2.1), reserving a portion for Adeliza and charitable provision; at the same time she evinces an authority over both her confessor and her rebellious, self-consciously masculine son, before which they both wilt:

COUNTESS: Thou art my son, and I will prove a mother.
But I'm thy sovereign too. This state is mine.
Learn to command, by learning to obey.
Tho' frail my sex, I have a soul as masculine
As any of thy race. This very monk,
Lord as thou thinkest of my ductile conscience,
Quails - look if 'tis not true - when I command.
. . . .
EDMUND (*alone*): Why, this *is* majesty. Sounds of such accent
Ne'er struck mine ear till now. Commanding sex!
Strength, courage, all our boasted attributes,
Want estimation; ev'n the preheminence
We vaunt in wisdom, seems a borrow'd ray,
When virtue deigns to speak with female organs.[10]

It is true that the Countess neglects the forms of architectural mastery which normally house and embody male power: Edmund complains that the castle (the crumbling site of the family *oikos* or "House") is no longer maintained in the baronial manner of his heroic forefathers (2.1), and Benedict castigates the Countess's failure to repair the fabric of the church (4.5). But Edmund's feudal ambitions are immediately and convincingly ridiculed as a return to primitive brutishness by his fellow-soldier, Florian (2.1) and the play as a whole, in line with Walpole's Whig credentials, is manifestly anti-sacerdotal.[11] The Countess voices proto-Protestant sympathies against the corruptions of the Church which the play very obviously seconds (she is backed up by Florian, and by references to the incipient Reformation in which the action is set), leaving her as a sort of icon for an imagined future liberty of conscience (if not of action). If she is a threat to patriarchy, the play cannot characterize her as a wholly unwelcome one.

Nor is the Countess's sexuality threatening in itself to the male figures who claim an interest in it. Benedict, misogynistically prone to discover sexual aberration in women as a means to dominion over them, is convinced of her unassailable sexual probity:

BENEDICT: . . . She own'd to me,
That, tho' of nature warm, the passion love
Did ne'er anticipate her choice. The count,
Her husband, so ador'd and so lamented,
Won not her fancy, till the nuptial rites
Had with the sting of pleasure taught her passion.
This, with such modest truth, and that truth heighten'd
By conscious sense, that holds deceit a weakness,
She utter'd, I would pawn my order's credit
On her veracity.[12]

Edmund sees his mother as a "sensual woman" (2.1) but (ostensibly at least) only in the sense that she had a right to her sexual pleasures, as he had a right to his. Walpole himself commented in the postscript to the play that "I have endeavoured to make her very fondness for her husband in some measure the cause of her guilt," and the Countess's explanation of the incestuous moment, in the penultimate scene (5.6) argues a real case for the plausibility of this apparently catastrophic fall. She reveals how her husband's death on the way home from a long absence left her with a disappointed sexual longing which found for its object the person who most resembled him: his son.[13] Incest is thus not some sort of demonic visitation, still less a thoroughgoing corruption, but an adjunct of marriage and motherhood, stimulated by the very domestic scene it violates.

Moreover, the play does not simply concentrate on the Countess's aberrant desire. The entropic consequences of these Oedipal resemblances are very fully worked out in the libidinous economy of the play, since Adeliza falls in love with her father-brother exactly because of his "parental" address to her (3.2); a mother-figure, the Abbess under whose tutelage she has lived, dies just before she marries Edmund, and the Countess, mistaking Edmund's involvement for Florian's, imaginatively, even seductively, repeats what she guesses to be the lover's words of wooing, in order to hasten the match.[14] Edmund is besotted with what Florian ironizes as Adeliza's "fruitful" and "matron-like" air (2.1), but on attempting to consummate the marriage, as Florian reports, these signs reveal something closer to home:

> FLORIAN: . . . With a voice
> Appall'd and hollow like a parricide's,
> He told me he was wedded.
>
> . . . .
> . . .   As he urg'd
> His suit, the maiden's tears and shrieks had struck
> On his sick fancy like a mother's cries!
> Th' idea writhing from his brain, had won
> His eyeballs, and he thought he saw his mother! (5.3)

At the moment of marriage, Edmund intuitively conceives of sex as a forbidden parricidal desire for the mother: the ceremony takes place on the sixteenth anniversary of the original adolescent crime, and thus recapitulates that rite of passage.

The play indeed concerns itself as much with male desire as female; the Count's fatal wish to go hunting a stag instead of returning to his wife's bed, for example. We hear it suggested that the Count's attitude to premarital sex was a good deal more lax than the Countess's, further confirming Edmund's genetic inheritance.[15] The originating sexual motor in the play's story is actually that of Edmund's desire for the maid, Beatrice: making arrangements to sleep with your mother's maid on the night your father has been killed by a stag might raise even a psychoanalytic eyebrow. Florian, though "of morals loose enough" (2.1), is somewhat taken aback by the directness of the link; his father is dead too (2.4) and it is he who describes Edmund's post-marital voice as parricidal.[16] Edmund's collapse of authority before his mother, his inquisitive searching of the "weeping Magdalene" as he calls her (2.1), and his knowing estimate of her sexuality all indicate that Walpole wanted to suggest a Hamlet-like interest which is not innocent of incestuous desire. This is how he retells the story of his banishment to Florian and complains of his mother's refusal to compromise on the issue of sexual continence:

> EDMUND: . . . she herself was woman then;
> A sensual woman. Nor satiety,
> Sickness and age and virtue's frowardness,
> Had so obliterated pleasure's relish—
> She might have pardoned what she felt so well. (2.1)

It is tempting to ask here how Edmund knows this, for the simultaneously easy and appreciative recourse to a stereotype of female lubricity is not merely a momentary dramatic irony. The Countess's final confession to Edmund (5.6) is intercut with a drastically truncated version of Oedipus's self-discovery, from the anathematization of the "black passions" and "shocking images" of what he takes to be his mother's fantasy, to an instinctive guess at what is about to be revealed—it is less a surprise than it ought to be.

The other male characters are also implicated: the porter, Peter, confesses to having desired Beatrice as well (1.2). Even Florian, the only character to come from outside the original domestic zone, finds himself flirting with the enigmatic Countess he has come to interrogate (2.4 and 5), for she in turn finds that he resembles "my Narbonne" in his martial sentiments and fatally understands him, rather than Edmund, to be Adeliza's lover. As for Benedict, a grander Inquisitor, his sexuality is technically renounced for the Church ("for her I have forgot I am a man" [4.1]), but the Countess has already told him she does not believe that his outfit really smothers desire: "she wills me / Ask my own breast, if cowls and scapularies / Are charms all powerful to subdue desire?" (1.3). She is right to do so: Benedict figures as a diminished Gothic tyrant (reminiscent of Manfred in *Otranto*), seeking mastery and forbidden knowledge, and his sexuality has turned into a crusading and malign pursuit of the Countess's mysterious secret, which turns out (despite his conviction of her sexual continence) to be nothing less than her sexuality. He is the first to guess, and in the moral logic of the play, it is so much the worse for him.

Thus no one escapes from the "theatre of monstrous guilt" (as Edmund puts it in 5.6), the space of penitence established and maintained for sixteen years by the Countess. It is true that the Countess is singled out as the only onstage figure who dies within the confines of the play — on Edmund's sword, which he has found himself, in despite of the Oresteian role open to him, unable to inflict on her. But this is no straightforward poetic justice; her final usurpation of phallic power (if that is what the use of Edmund's sword connotes) is in one sense her own judgment, which a patriarchal religion and wronged spouse have been unable to inflict. No one else has the physical or moral authority to enforce it, and iconographically the suicide is as much the gesture of Lucretia, or Juliet, as any more guilty heroine; a Roman virtue. There is a sense of loss in her compulsory and compulsive defeat, leaving Benedict as the more obviously hissable villain.

II

The Mysterious Mother is not, of course, as one-sided as this reading might suggest. Far from offering the coherence of a punishment dream, it shows signs of deep compromise and division. I would not propose that the Oedipal scheme is wholly lucid, or that its implications could be brought fully to even a private consciousness at the time it was written. If it desires a future of enlightened tolerance, it does so on the basis of an already-projected past of patriarchal brutality which will inevitably defeat it within the play. The incest taboo is not, in any sense, being undermined. But its violation is being recognized, with a certain shock, as a fundamental element in domestic situations: the "Domestic bliss" which Edmund imagines to be his with Adeliza (2.1) generates its own exemplary horrors, in what the prologue terms a "tremendous picture of domestic woe."

In a recent article on Diderot's *Le Fils Naturel* (1757) Suzanne Pucci argues that imagined incest quite specifically constitutes the affective mode by which the emergent bourgeois family nucleates and binds itself together, grafting onto the principle of family resemblance the privilege of passion which it otherwise lacks. What she terms the "script of family devotion" is borrowed, apparently catachrestically, from the language of sentimental romance, and this element of romance is never quite filtered out even when the potential incest is discovered and normative marital arrangements take over. Pucci contrasts this reading of incest dramas with other accounts, which cast incest as a pathological alterity used to define normal family relations by a principle of exclusion, a lack or negativity which invites completion along lines of domestic symmetry (marrying to *avoid* the horror of incest).[17] But neither kind of reading would be possible for *The Mysterious Mother*, which notably plays down any potential definition of the Edmund-Adeliza marriage as sibling incest and concentrates instead on the generational model (mother/son, father/daughter) in which issues of power and inheritance are more to the fore than in the quasi-romance of brother and sister. There simply are no other models of the family available in the play beyond the incestuous one: we have an orphanage, peopled through some unaccountable process by "children of both sexes, neatly clothed in a white and blue uniform" (2.2), the celibates who have resigned sexuality altogether to become sexless fathers, mothers, brothers and sisters, and the participants in the rite of incest. In the analogue of the story which Walpole cites in his postscript, the son/daughter marriage is regarded as guiltless (because unwitting) and allowed to continue, producing new generations as if in the normal way, with the mother under the tutelage of the church, but everyone in the play is gathered into the Oedipal vortex.[18] The Countess's plan to marry Adeliza off to Florian is thwarted, Adeliza is returned to the convent (thereby fulfilling one of Hamlet's analogous desires for Ophelia), and Edmund returns with Florian to the wars: there is no genetic future for this family, because there is no genetic future at all. The bourgeois family cannot be "inaugurated" here, as in Pucci's account of Diderot's play, because the incest motif which might set a limit on its normality, or lend it affective strength, has here completely consumed it.

Insofar as this depiction of irredeemable marital crisis might be read (as Pucci reads *Le Fils Naturel*) as a general account of family relations, it required certain kinds of internal censorship; even an aristocrat with a private press might be shocked by the extent of his own imagining. Walpole's play is unusually frank, but this licence is granted on the basis of a good deal of conventional moralizing. Moreover, the various antinomies on which the play appears to be constructed shift alignment markedly in the course of the play, giving it a much more complex set of dynamics than the model of the play as censored punishment dream allows for. In one sense, the Countess is an Enlightenment figure: she relies on conscience and rationality, refusing to enclose herself in the Gothic space of the confessional. She is nonetheless Gothic ("mysterious") in her resistance to disclosure and revelation. As Benedict has predicted, her internalization of conscience results in hysterical projections of external vengeance and she becomes intermittently open to traditional characterizations of femininity as chaos, fragmentation, madness and pathology, however pitiable, and however sane her final act of defiance.[19] Benedict's ruinous Gothic mythology of female depravity is perversely vindicated: he is the only one to gain from disclosure, and yet public knowledge is after all a rationalist and Enlightenment virtue. The space which the play imagines for itself is no less labile. The action is set against the backdrop of a decrepit castle and several moribund religious institutions, yet the spatial movement of the play is away from the "Platform before the Castle" (1.1) to "A small Garden within the Castle, terminated by a long Cloister, beyond which appear some Towers" (3.1); the ineluctable transition from private to public somehow works itself into a recess. The gate to the castle is notionally policed by the loyal but superstitious porter, Peter, who is however unable to say whether Beatrice, the object of Edmund's early desire, is inside the castle, or outside it (2.3); he is also unable to understand how Edmund gets into the castle without his knowledge (5.2). Walpole often uses stage directions which complicate the relation between inside and outside: Peter himself is made to "retire" to an ambiguously liminal position from which he is never rescued.[20]

This spatial uncertainty is in marked contrast to Sophocles's *Oedipus Tyrannos*, where revelation is always public, against the conspicuous "inner" portion of the Greek stage. While a tension between interrogation and confession is of course vital to that play, there is a further contrast to be drawn between the two modes of revelation. While Oedipus takes most of the drama to understand that the parricide he has condemned is himself, despite being told exactly this early on by the priest-figure Tiresias, the Countess has *always* known the truth, and has suppressed it for sixteen years. In the play she is caught between a confessional urge for disclosure ("Be known my crimes!" [3.1]) and a desire to screen Edmund and Adeliza from social stigmatization and its internalized aspects. Hearing from Florian that Edmund and Adeliza are married, she demands to know both more ("when? where? how?") and less ("Quick, unsay / The monstrous tale" [5.5]). When she eventually confesses to them (Adeliza faints halfway through, missing the worst), she protests, "it must be known, the fullness of my crime" against Edmund's uncompleted utterance "swallow th' accurs'd sound, / Nor dare to say—" (5.6). Nevertheless, disclosure is still only partial, for when the remnants of this latter-day Thebes turns up to fulfil their choric function, she cries "conceal our shame—Quick, frame some legend" (5.6) and Edmund cannot actually speak the truth: "rot my tongue 'ere the dread sound escape it" (5.7).

Like the servant who fits the final piece into Oedipus's puzzle, characters in the play are always "close to terrifying speech."[21] Their attentions to the dangerous performances of language are characteristic not only of the tension between disclosure and concealment in the play but of its relentless foregrounding of linguistic acts in general. In a play where sexual activity has become prohibited, sexual energy is displaced into language, and a sexualized potential is repeatedly discovered in diction. Language is the public agent of memory and revelation: "Not a word / Can 'scape me, but will do the work of thunder," says the Countess (5.6), realizing the Zeus-like destructive potential of language to administer what natural supernaturalism (the storm) will not.[22] Words occur throughout the play as named and powerful agents: vows, charms, hymns, incantations, spells, riddles, prayers, blessings, curses. The lexicon of speech acts is rich to the point of clotting: characters are said to proclaim, praise, swear, converse, attest, decree, excuse, "war with words," preach, wrangle, chant, plead, implore, revile, command, urge, rebuke, scoff, forbid, upbraid, insult, sneer, deride, or mock. Sounds are babbled, chirped or warbled. Characters try to decipher "half-told woe," the voice of the storm, misery's "proper language" or "sin's despairing accent"; truth lives on their lips. There is cant, harangue, gossip, "flow'ry dialect," innuendo, jargon, heresy, prophecy; the "babbler Fame" is not to be trusted, words are solemn, unjust, unwelcome or uncharitable (as well as sweet); tongues are licentious or profane, breath is unhallowed, sounds can be silver, joyous, powerful, or (indeed) incestuous, lectures are saucy, reproaches are lewd, suggestions are impure, language is nauseous. The play is full of explosive verbal ironies, as when Edmund comments on his mother's sensual nature in relation to his own: "she might have pardoned what she felt so well" (2.1). Revelation is hastened by a number of apparently random verbal triggers, as when Adeliza desires to call the Countess "mother" or suggests that Edmund might take his father's place and "woo thee to be happy" (4.4).

These catachrestic but unavoidable borrowings from marital discourse cannot be purified for the domestic scene, and here act as double suggestions which unhinge the Countess and cause her to release more "broken phrase / In phrensy dropp'd" (4.1) for the hermeneutic reconstructions of Benedict. And though virtue may deign "to speak with female organs," as Edmund bizarrely puts it in submitting to his mother's commands (3.4), predominantly language in the play, whoever speaks it, is phallic and wounding, a sting, brand, or scorpion. Edmund refuses to reveal the catastrophe to Florian because he "must not violate / Thy guiltless ear" (5.7), but Florian has already managed to "wound your reverence's saint-like organs" in making a bawdy remark to Peter, which the latter significantly translates into a violation of the castle's closed entrance: "Yon mould'ring porch for sixteen years and more / Has not been struck with such unhallow'd sounds" (1.2). It is as if sexuality now so much permeates language that saying something is tantamount to doing it: Beatrice's role in the original crime was to pass on Edmund's "message" to his mother. For that reason psychoanalytic criticism might look not so much to Freud as Lacan, for the kind of ritual we have here seems to require the latter's somewhat less personalized categories: a not sufficiently unconscious desire for union with the mother (or reunion, in Edmund's case) might be said to have resulted in an unusually direct and literal acknowledgement of the phallic nature of the symbolic order and law of the father as Lacan conceives them.[23] In purely dramatic terms, however, we have in the persistent attention to language something like a discourse of theatricality, a self-conscious speech which merges with occasional metadramatic moments such as the Countess's sense of herself as the "spectatress of this last of horrors" in a "frightful scene."[24] The secret is somewhere in the words, the "half-told woe" which must be "unriddled." Language figures as the public and present manifestation or reconfiguration of a private and past sexual transgression, and so there is a certain unease, even horror, about the act of speaking: the play's tense and ambivalent exchanges between disclosure and concealment all hinge on the idea of blasphemous speech.

To a purely personal reading of the play, however, the horror of speech might be associated with Walpole's own "utterance" as a dramatist, and a fear of the potential "performance" of the play: "acting" means both pretending and doing. To have given material expression to a forbidden desire, in however morally censorious terms, was an act which could figure as a kind of sexual crime within Walpole's self-constructed cultural cloister or "house," his own "castle of my ancestors."[25] On several occasions Walpole referred to his play (as to his other works) as a child or baby, while his friend William Mason indulged at one point in their discussion of the play in an extended and disturbing trope on the idea of male authors and female texts in which *The Mysterious Mother* became Walpole's mother and his daughter at once.[26] While the link between paternity and authorship is *façon de parler* in the eighteenth century, it perhaps takes on a special charge in the case of a childless bachelor like Walpole, and in the case of a play dominated by a sexual dynamic. This "theatre of monstrous guilt," as Edmund describes the scene in his final speech, might have the potential to overspill its dramatic bounds and "unriddle" the sphere of Walpole's privacy. In the final section of this essay we will examine the largely external forces which made this threat gradually recede.

III

Having conceived this extraordinary psychosexual drama, an illegitimate take on the classic Oedipal scene, Walpole did not keep it to himself for any length of time, but immediately began a form of publication. He showed the manuscript to two close friends, John Chute and Thomas Gray, in the summer of 1768, before printing fifty copies of the play at his private press at Strawberry Hill. Some of these copies were then distributed, in a highly select manner, and always with some sort of health warning. Walpole thus contrived a closet circulation for the play which policed the instinct to publish with the injunction to censor, keeping in tension the already ambivalent relation between Gothic and Enlightenment enacted by the play itself.[27] On the title page Walpole printed the motto: "sit mihi fas audita loqui," or, "may it be lawful for me to speak the things I have heard" (my translation). This is from Virgil *Aeneid* 6.266, a narratorial interjection at the point where Aeneas is on the brink of the underworld, and here a wish, displaced onto an unimpeachably classic author, that it might not be blasphemous to utter a report from a different kind of underworld: a visit of the Muses to "Tartarus," a "black inspiration" discovering the "dark secrets of humanity" as various early critics put it.[28] Walpole equipped the printed text with a postscript in which he set out the ambivalent position, both repelled and celebratory, on the value of the play which he was to maintain for the next thirty years: that its subject or idea was "disgusting" but that the "execution" had some formal literary merit. The idea is separated from the activity of giving it form, in an apparently self-protective strategy of denial. Fearful of the potential for social condemnation of the play insofar as it was represented by its heroine, Walpole argued that it conformed to Aristotelian requirements for pity and terror, it observed the unities almost perfectly, and was in truth more moral for its Shakespearean disdain of French theatrical decorum (a theme he also explored in the undated prologue to the play). Nonetheless, Walpole's desire to instigate a "revolution in the passions" of the spectator, and the detailed concessive explanation of how he had tried to create a defensible, even admirable Countess, could not be wholly pallisaded by the vocabulary of moral condemnation. "The villainy of Benedict," we learn, "was planned to divide the indignation of the audience, and to intercept some of it from the Countess"; he has quite deliberately set out to "palliate the crime, and raise the character of the criminal"; he has delayed the revelation of the secret until the penultimate scene, "and bestowed every ornament of sense, unbigoted piety, and interesting contrition, on the character that was at last to raise universal indignation; in hopes that some degree of pity would linger in the breasts of the audience; and that a whole lifetime of virtue and penance might in some measure atone for a moment, though a most odious moment, of a depraved imagination." It is momentarily unclear here whose imagination is being specially pleaded for, but there is a compromising reluctance to abandon the mysterious mother to the fate of "universal indignation."

That reluctance and sympathy remained, as Walpole knew it would, a source of potential damage to his reputation. His work of, as it were, depraved imagination began to make its way in the world under limiting conditions; it was secretly copied in manuscript many times, and its relation to

Walpole became an increasingly open secret among London literati. Scholars such as Isaac Reed, and journalists like Henry Samson Woodfall, variously tried to get extracts into print, but Walpole put a stop to it each time. Fearing a piracy in 1781 (for which confirmatory evidence is lacking, so it may be a fantasy of violation and disclosure), Walpole got a trade bookseller, James Dodsley, to print a less inward edition of the text, in which the emotive and highly charged postscript was replaced by a curt prefatory "Advertisement" of disavowal—defense here being placed in advance of the reading. Neither this nor the supposed piracy were actually published, and nor was the text Walpole prepared for an abortive edition of his works in 1770.[29] From 1781 Walpole began to circulate the trade edition, rather than the Strawberry Hill original. Yet in 1791 when a bookseller from Dublin, always regarded as the definitive home of the illegitimate book trade, ventured to issue an edition, and Walpole's aristocratic friends had it suppressed, Walpole asked that it be allowed to go ahead, with a friend correcting the proofs; it was immediately pirated at London (with a further piracy in 1796). Finally, it was incorporated, with footnotes explaining the classical and other allusions, in the 1798 arrangement of his *Works* edited by Mary Berry, whom he had befriended and housed: the posthumous, legitimate, canonical text of Walpole's literary corpus and legacy includes the guilty play in a perfectly prominent position.[30]

The rather tame surfacing of the play late in Walpole's life is in marked contrast to the dynamics of revelation in the play itself, though one should not underestimate the prurience with which it was regarded: Coleridge's comment was yet to be made. What I want to draw attention to in this final section is the ways in which the play, unlike the Countess, can become socialized, adopted, and shared. The oscillation between private and public, between dissociation and the embrace of authenticity, was negotiated in various practical ways which perhaps facilitated eventual publication by making the text itself, or at least the printed copy for which there exists no holograph manuscript, less crucially personal. Three aspects will illustrate the gradual redistribution of ownership which the play underwent: performance, illustration, and annotation.

There was even a point at which Walpole had not realized that his play was unperformable in public because of its content. "I am not yet intoxicated enough with it, to think it would do for the stage," Walpole wrote to George Montagu, in the first enthusiasm of having completed it, "though I wish to see it acted: but as Mrs Pritchard leaves the stage next month, I know nobody could play the Countess."[31] The ideal, unavailable performer is contrasted with the all-too-available and detestable David Garrick, the master of the stage whose corrupt management and editorial incursions Walpole disdained

with aristocratic hauteur. The play seems never to have been publicly performed, and it is unlikely that it could have been licensed for performance
without very significant rewriting. Laetitia-Matilda Hawkins tells a long story
about how she and her father, the magistrate Sir John Hawkins, got the Archbishop of London to block Walpole's proposal to have the play acted, but
like the later rumors of a public performance of the play in Ireland, it soon
begins to sound like someone else's fantasy being woven round Walpole's
play.[32]

Instead, Walpole contrived in-house, closet performances, as he described
to Montagu: "Mr. Conway, Lady Ailesbury, Lady Lyttleton and Miss Rich
are to come hither the day after tomorrow, and Mr Conway and I are to read
my play to them, for I have not strength to go through the whole alone."[33]
This presents an interesting set of possibilities for the division of parts: did
Walpole read (was he not strong enough to read) the Countess, or Edmund,
or both? Clearly there is a desire to control and limit performance of the play,
and to keep under control the precarious metaphor of "acting"; at the level of
verisimilitude, a mixed audience might have managed something like one to
a part. Walpole seems often to have sent copies to male friends and read
selections to female friends, further controlling the kind of reception the play
might meet with. While control could not be total, Walpole's limits were
often reinstituted in other contexts, as when some of Walpole's correspondents also organized miniature, male-voiced readings. Horace Mann, having
at long last been given a copy of the play in 1779, told Walpole how he and
his nephew recited the play in a pleasantly Gothic setting which did not however exceed the bounds of domestic routine. "My nephew and I continually
talk of it with ecstasy. He had almost got it by heart in his journey, and
frequently recites passages out of it as we walk together in my little garden
by moonlight before supper. I shall soon be as perfect in it as he is."[34] This
"delicious entertainment for the closet" was also performed by Montagu and
his "boys":

> We read the acts amongst us, after my lungs could not Pritchard it through.
> They left off quinze, gambling and claret, and were the Florians of your
> play. The churchman indeed looked grave, but they threw him his ten com-
> mandments and bottle of port and amused themselves without. They would
> have got it by heart. However, a few similes they have retained, and cap
> with one another some of the lines that struck them most.[35]

Even so clubbish and collectively masculine a performance, however, could
make Walpole uneasy, and Montagu had to promise to keep the play locked
up. Readings without Walpole's express permission could be more problematic: Walpole probably never knew about a disastrous reading of the play
organized, with many courteous precautions which came to seem comic in

the light of the catastrophe of the actual event, at Windsor castle by Fanny Burney in 1786.[36]

Nonetheless, collective reading partially tapped the instinct for performance, and kept alive a notion of the stageworthiness of the play (which has no lack of appropriate stage directions). Another strategy was offered by one of Walpole's correspondents, William Mason. A clergyman, and a dramatist of some contemporary repute, Mason wanted to make the play fit for the stage by rendering the Countess's incest unwitting, and moving the time of the Count's death to after the consummation, thus disguising its parricidal aspect. This act of censorship, however, he also felt necessary "from a strong conviction that something ought to be done, in this way, to fit it even for the closet."[37] Walpole saw at once that this sublimatory strategy destroyed the play's dramatic tension, though under the rules of polite correspondence he could not say so; through the rest of their friendship the performability of the play in Mason's collaborative version was a continuing subject for discussion. A more satisfactory closet for the play to inhabit came in physical form. In August 1775 Lady Diana Beauclerk began to draw seven scenes from the play, and Walpole went into raptures which suggest that an outlet for his own internal admiration for the play had finally been found: "If the subject were a quarter as good as the drawings, [they] would make me a greater genius than Shakespeare, as she is superior to Guido and Salvator Rosa. Such figures! such dignity! such simplicity!"[38] In 1776 Walpole built one final addition on to his personalized Gothic castle at Strawberry Hill to house the drawings. The Beauclerk Tower, as it was from the outside, lay at the North West end of Strawberry Hill; Walpole described it as an "extinguisher" or candle snuffer, and its truncated spire broke up the line of the roof both conspicuously and comically. The Beauclerk Closet, the 9' 5" diameter hexagonal room inside the tower, was less visible to spectators, and seems to have been reserved for "his most particular friends" as Mary Hamilton put it in 1783.[39] It is oblique of access, up the back stairs, and appears to rest on nothing. Here, in the controlled environment of this comic excrescence on the prefabricated Gothic of Strawberry Hill, visitors could see in fossilized, sentimental postures, the Aristotelian "pity and terror" of the play. Mary Hamilton reported the kind of mental process engendered by this new arrangement: "the story is the most horrible to be conceived, but these drawings, though they recall to mind the horrid subject, are most affectingly interesting."[40] Walpole poured out gratitude and praise to Lady Diana for producing an acceptable, feminized spectacle, from his otherwise shocking play (though as Lady Diana, like many of Walpole's female artist friends, had something of a "past" herself, not everyone was happy with her involvement here).[41] In *A Description of the Villa of Mr. Horace Walpole* (1784), in which Walpole carefully publicized his privacy, he guided the visitor (or reader) round each of the scenes on the walls, praising with enthusiasm Lady Diana's fluency and sublimity at the implicit expense of his own. Sensibility wins out over not only prurience, but horror. The gaze of the spectator is not here allowed to see itself as the supplement to a felt lack in the scenario, as is sometimes the case in dramatic tableaux: the spectator is appealed to for communion, not required to act as an external moral authority. By representing present emotions rather than past crimes, a sentimental seal is given to the potential danger of the forbidden scene.

This was not a locus of pure contemplation, for in this "mouse" (as Walpole also termed it) he had stored ten other pictures, a tea-service, a tea-chest, four stools, a locket of Mary Tudor's hair, a watch, and an illuminated manuscript. But at the center of the room stood:

> A writing table of Clay's ware, highly varnished: it is black, with blue and white ornaments in a gothic pattern, designed by Paul Sandby. In one of the drawers the play of the Mysterious Mother, to explain the drawings, bound in blue leather and gilt.

This lusciously detailed combination of aesthetic advertisement and sensual secrecy seems to have formed Walpole's most stable solution to the problem of his own transgressive text as it might emerge in non-textual forms.

But if we seem to have returned here to Walpole's private relation to the text, it will be worth emphasizing the social nature of even this locale. Writing to Mason on 15 July 1780, from the Beauclerk closet, Walpole once more expatiated on the "ingredients, passions, graces, horrors, scenes, [and] expressions" of the drawings, and went on:

> I am writing in their own closet, and it is having the continence of Scipio to say no more about them though you know them so well; but how infinitely pleasanter if you was sitting here and talking them over. What shackled conversations are letters when one gasps for effusion! You can rhyme your sensations and stamp them immortal, and gulp them, and they half choke me; pray breathe for me, and send me something to help me—as the apothecaries say—expectorate.[42]

Here, in the utmost privacy of the closet, simultaneously flaunting and concealing the secret of the bachelor citadel or childless "house," with all the inner/outer tensions of the play's internal dynamic and its external circulation resolved aesthetically and architecturally, writing on the table which conceals his tragedy in blue leather and gilt, Walpole turns outwards once more to a kind of sociality, of a charged, if defensively humorous, kind.

Subject to conflict and uncertainty as the various mediations of the play were, they increasingly rendered the play a known and acceptable quantity among a fit audience, however few; the socialization of the play as an item on the tour of Walpole's own domestic space, or to be read among friends, gradually removed the stigma of personal authorship. A final illustration of this process returns us to William Mason, one of the many friends who knew the play who tried to place it within a kind of general human history. As well as citing Sophocles in the postscript, Walpole had identified as his notional source a story he had heard "when very young" about a case of conscience of much the kind that his play enacts which a guilty mother had brought to Archbishop John Tillotson. Having transposed the story to a different "past" and region in the way of Gothic romance, Walpole then discovered through his friend John Chute what he calls the "origin of the tradition" in a sort of folk tale or collective myth within *L'Heptaméron* of Marguerite de Navarre. Oddly enough, from Walpole's perspective, this story contained many coincidences of dating and location with his own invented version.[43] Thereafter, many male friends began to discover odd resemblances, collisions between fiction and archetype, which they forwarded to Walpole. William Cole sent him a reference to a medieval manuscript with a story of St Albanus containing an incest motif; Michael Lort sent an analogue for the "case of conscience" version, with its redemptive priest figure, from a text by Joseph Hall of 1650 (it also occurs in Luther's *Table-Talk*, which Mason sent, as well as in the writings of William Perkins, from whence it was reprinted in the spurious ninth volume of *The Spectator* in 1715). Topham Beauclerk noted a French epitaph telling a similar story, and Mason further sent "an old play," probably *The Fatal Discovery* (1698), which happens to match his own sublimated version of the story. Isaac Reed and John Pinkerton began to comment on the sources of this strange tale, and Walpole himself noted another epitaph in this line in his *Miscellany* for 1792.[44] Most telling perhaps is the comment of Horace Mann, writing in 1779 just after receiving a copy of the play: "I have heard that something of the same kind and very like your subject happened some years ago in the Ecclesiastical State. If I can get the particular circumstances and be assured of the veracity of them, I will inform you of them."[45] He never did, and there is an obvious air of automatic invention about the vague memory: as if such a powerful tragedy requires a source in firmer reality.

The analogues which Walpole's male correspondents supplied all served to assure Walpole of the collectivity of his folk-tale 'tradition', even of the actuality of its occurrence. Like the other strategies for collective interpretation or aestheticization of the tragedy, they diffused the personal investment Walpole had in the play and negotiated a wider, though not completely open, space for the mental performance of the play. By connecting the play through art or analogue to a broader set of human schemata, the play becomes shared; if the dynamic antagonisms of repression and translucence, inner and outer, Gothic and Enlightenment, could not be coherently resolved within the play, the processes by which the text was actualized in reading and reception redeemed it from the status of private fantasy or covert confession. While a psychoanalytic or personal reading of the play can only envisage it as a direct expression of Walpole's mental life, conscious or unconscious, the realization of the play as a collective document should stress to us that the play is open to different kinds of engagement. Its intense portrayal of family trauma, its fascination with verbal power, and its intertextual fusion of Greek and French dramatic material in a new Gothic form should point us beyond the temptation to reduce the play to a document of self-recognition towards a more public kind of textual genealogy and literary analysis.

NOTES

1. See however Bertrand Evans, *Gothic Drama from Walpole to Shelley* (Berkeley and Los Angeles: Univ. of California Press, 1947), and Edward Burns, "'The Babel Din': Theatre and European Romanticism," in *Romantic Literature: A Guide to Romantic Literature: 1780–1830*, ed. Geoff Ward (London: Bloomsbury, 1993), 51–57. Quotations from the play are from *The Works of Horatio Walpole, Earl of Orford*, 5 vols. (London: G. G. and J. Robinson, 1798), 1: 37–129; references by act and scene (the text is not lineated) will be placed where possible in the text.

2. I paraphrase this from the much longer summary in Charles Beecher Hogan, "The 'Theatre of Geo. 3,'" in *Horace Walpole: Writer, Politician, and Connoisseur*, ed. Warren Hunting Smith (New Haven: Yale Univ. Press, 1967), 227–40.

3. George Gordon, Lord Byron, preface to *Marino Faliero* (1821), reprinted in *Horace Walpole: The Critical Heritage*, ed. Peter Sabor (New York: Routledge and Kegan Paul, 1987), 147.

4. *Specimens of the Table Talk of the late Samuel Coleridge* (1835), reprinted in *Walpole: The Critical Heritage*, 148.

5. W. S. Lewis, *Horace Walpole* (London: Rupert Hart-Davis, 1961), 163; see also the comments of R. W. Ketton-Cremer, *Horace Walpole: A Biography* (London: Duckworth, 1940), 281–84.

6. Betsy Perteit Harfst, *Horace Walpole And The Unconscious: An Experiment in Freudian Analysis* (New York: Arno Press, 1980), 108–95; Martin Kallich, *Horace Walpole* (New York: Twayne, 1971), 105–17 (quotation from 117).

7. Timothy Mowl, *Horace Walpole: The Great Outsider* (London: John Murray, 1996), 218–22. Mowl is more sympathetic to *The Mysterious Mother* than Walpole's other works.

8. The Porter and the Orphans are shown to be subject to superstitious fears which Florian in each case satirizes (1.2 and 2.2); the monks, ironically, fear a mysterious voice of warning in 4.2 which turns out to emanate from a religious ceremony.

9. See Walpole's "Paris Journals" for 8 April 1766; *Horace Walpole's Correspondence*, ed. W. S. Lewis and others, 48 vols. (New Haven: Yale Univ. Press, 1937–83), 7: 312. Madame du Deffand reminded Walpole of Voltaire's play shortly after he finished his own (to Walpole, 21 March 1768, ibid., 4: 49), and he recommended it to Robert Jephson (letter of late February 1775, ibid., 41: 294).

10. This is the very end of act 2 (scene 4), and may be the point at which Walpole stopped writing for two years (see "Short Notes", in *Correspondence*, 13: 43); at any rate it is the high point of the Countess's ability to control herself and others as "subjects." For Edmund's conception of his own "masculine" inheritance see 2.1 and 3.4.

11. As his friend the Reverend William Cole noted; see *Correspondence*, 1: 186 n. 7. For encounters of this sort in the play see especially 2.2 and 5.3.

12. 2.2. There may of course be a certain irony in Benedict's "pawning" of his order's credit, but the irony is against him not the Countess.

13. The likeness is established as early as 1.2, and confirmed by the Countess in 3.4: "there spoke his sire. How my soul yearns / To own its genuine offspring!"

14. The Countess tends to see Adeliza's sexuality as a guilty inheritance; see 1.3, 3.1 and 4.3.

15. 1.2; see also 3.4 and 5.5.

16. For further comments on Florian's sexuality see 1.2 and 5.5.

17. Suzanne R. Pucci, "The Nature of Domestic Intimacy and Sibling Incest in Diderot's *Fils Naturel*," *Eighteenth-Century Studies* 30 (1997): 271–87.

18. Walpole cites a "case of conscience" brought to Archbishop John Tillotson as the "event in real life" on which the tragedy is based; he also draws attention to a story in Marguerite de Navarre's *L'Heptaméron*, where a similarly tolerant conclusion is reached. The sources and analogues for the tragedy are discussed further below.

19. The play does not confine this propensity to the Countess, for in the final scene Edmund also hallucinates the figure of the dead Count Narbonne.

20. See the end of 5.4; for more examples of Peter's odd spatial coordinates see 1.2 and 2.3.

21. Sophocles, *Oidipous Turannos* 1169–70 (my translation), in *Sophoclis Fabulae*, ed. A. C. Pearson (Oxford: Clarendon Press, 1975), unpaginated.

22. In 2.2 the thunder is alleged by the priests to be heaven's warning against the sins of heresy, an allegation fiercely contested by Florian.

23. The Gothic Mother might then be construed as the realm of the Imaginary. For the theories of Jacques Lacan in this connection see his *Ecrits* (Paris: Seuil, 1966).

24. 5.5 and 3.1; for similar moments see 2.1 ("specious theatre"), and 5.3 ("theatre of holy interludes").

25. For the phrase see Walpole to George Montagu, 11 June 1753, *Correspondence*, 11: 149; and more generally, David D. McKinney, "The Castle of My Ancestors: Horace Walpole and Strawberry Hill," *British Journal for Eighteenth-Century Studies* 13 (1990): 199–214.

26. See Mason to Walpole, 1 December 1772, *Correspondence*, 28: 55–56; for other examples see Walpole to Mason, 11 May 1769, to Lord Hardwicke, March 1773, to Lady Ossory, 6 February 1789, ibid., 28: 16–17, 41: 191, 34: 37.

27. The tension between the contrary desires for publication and suppression which ensued once Walpole had written the play has been expertly analyzed by Peter Sabor: "'An old tragedy on a disgusting subject': Horace Walpole and *The Mysterious Mother*," in *Writing and Censorship in Britain*, ed. Paul Hyland and Neil Sammells (New York: Routledge, 1992), 91–106. In covering some of the same ground in this different context, I hope nonetheless to offer some additional insights.

28. The motto additionally underscores the play's dramatization of the illicit possibilities of speech. For the early critics quoted here see *Walpole: The Critical Heritage*, 184, and "Character and Writings of Horace Walpole," *New Monthly Magazine* 38 (August 1833): 422–32.

29. For the bibliography of the play see Allen T. Hazen, *A Bibliography of the Strawberry Hill Press* (New Haven: Yale Univ. Press, 1942), 79–85. For the other events noted here see *Walpole: The Critical Heritage*, 137–39; Walpole to Woodfall, 8 November 1783, Walpole to William Mason, 6 and 22 May 1781, *Correspondence*, 42: 85–86, 29: 139–40, 143.

30. It was thereafter republished in an anthology, *The Modern British Drama*, 5 vols. (London: William Miller, 1811), in an edition with *The Castle of Otranto* edited by Montague Summers (London: Constable and Co., 1924), and edited by Janet Dolan, "Horace Walpole's *The Mysterious Mother:* A Critical Edition" (Ph.D. diss., Univ. of Arizona, 1970). A new edition, edited by Paul Baines and Edward Burns with four other plays of the period, will appear in the World's Classics series in 1999.

31. Walpole to Montagu, 15 April 1768, *Correspondence*, 10: 259–60. Hannah Pritchard had a reputation for strong female roles, including the title character in Samuel Johnson's *Irene* as well as Lady Macbeth, and intriguingly, Hamlet's mother. Walpole also envisioned the "low comic" actress Kitty Clive in this connection, writing a bizarrely comic epilogue for her in character (*Works of Horatio Walpole*, 4: 397–98) in which she is made to describe herself as strutting like a turkey-cock, thus giving an additional spin to the problem of gender in the play. Clive was a close friend and neighbor of Walpole's and John Pinkerton describes how on 20 September (the key date of the play) 1784, Walpole left him alone in the Gothic setting of Strawberry Hill to read *The Mysterious Mother* while he himself went off to visit Clive; a characteristic double accent: *Walpoliana*, 2 vols. (London: R. Phillips, 1799), 1: 27.

32. Hawkins, *Anecdotes, Biographical Sketches and Memoirs* (1822), cited in *Walpole: The Critical Heritage*, 299–306; and see *Correspondence*, 28: 17 n. 3.

33. Walpole to Montagu, 15 April 1768, *Correspondence*, 10: 259–60.

34. Mann to Walpole, 25 September 1779, *Correspondence*, 24: 517.

35. Montagu to Walpole, 18 September 1769, *Correspondence*, 10: 297; and see Walpole's reply, 16 October 1769, ibid., 298.

36. Fanny Burney, journal entry, 29 November 1786, reprinted in *Walpole: The Critical Heritage*, 139–41. Burney thought Walpole contaminated himself by wilfully imagining the story.

37. Mason to Walpole, 15 May 1781, *Correspondence*, 29: 142; for the proposed alterations see Mason to Walpole, 8 May 1769, ibid., 28: 9–16.

38. Walpole to Lady Ossory, 27 December 1775, *Correspondence*, 32: 289.

39. Mary Hamilton, journal entry, 5 July 1783, reprinted in *Correspondence*, 31: 206.

40. Mary Hamilton, journal entry, 21 June 1784, reprinted in *Correspondence*, 31: 216.

41. See Hawkins, *Anecdotes*, reprinted in *Walpole: The Critical Heritage*, p. 304.

42. Walpole to Mason, 15 July 1780, *Correspondence*, 29: 71.

43. See Walpole to Conway, 9 August 1768, *Correspondence*, 39: 102.

44. Cole to Walpole, 3 August 1768, Lort to Walpole, 5 July 1775, Mason to Walpole, 23 February 1778, Beauclerk to Walpole, 19 August 1775, Mason to Walpole, 7 October 1778, *Correspondence*, 1: 186, 16: 165, 28: 363, 41: 308, 28: 444; Isaac Reed, *Biographia Dramatica* (1782), reprinted in *Walpole: The Critical Heritage*, 137–39; *Horace Walpole's Miscellany 1786–95*, ed. Lars E. Troide (New Haven: Yale Univ. Press, 1978), 127.

45. Mann to Walpole, 25 September 1779, *Correspondence*, 24: 517.

Burke, Radical Cosmopolitanism, and the Debates on Patriotism in the 1790s

EVAN RADCLIFFE

Early in her *Vindication of the Rights of Men* (1790), Mary Wollstonecraft makes a passionate argument against what she calls Edmund Burke's "servile reverence for antiquity" in his *Reflections on the Revolution in France* (1790). As part of her argument, she asserts that this reverence would implicitly sanction traditional practices that are deeply immoral, practices such as the "inhuman custom" of the slave trade. But, surprisingly, her attack on Burke does not home in on what she sees as an implicit defense of slavery. Instead, she directs her polemic in a different direction. What she attacks him for is making a link between slavery and patriotism; and what she focuses on is not slavery but patriotism. Her primary objection is that Burke's tendency to bind up certain traditional practices with "the love of our country" will have the pernicious effect of degrading the noble ideal of patriotism. Wollstonecraft criticizes Burke by maintaining that his kind of patriotism is not a truly public ideal, but instead a "selfish principle" to which "every nobler one is sacrificed." She contrasts his version of patriotic feeling to a more broadly human identity, asserting that in Burke "[t]he Briton" or "the citizen"—by which she means one's artificial identification with one's country—overcomes the deeper and more important identities of "the man" or "the image of God." In her view, Burke replaces the old Greek and Roman "enthusiastic flame" of public concern with a debased version of patriotism in which "self is the focus."[1]

Wollstonecraft's concern with Burke's version of patriotism is typical of the British debates about the French Revolution. The Revolution controversy raised questions about all kinds of loyalties and connections, and it focused to a remarkable extent on the nature and value of love of country, seen in both political and broadly moral terms. Politically, conservatives encouraged a patriotism that, in order to condemn reform, associated reform with French principles; in turn, this conservative form of patriotism generated strong resistance from radicals. But the partisan debate about love of country went beyond political issues, for from its beginning it involved questions inherited from previous moral discourse, questions that often dealt with the eighteenth-century problem of egoism. Hence, along with the issue of who could effectively claim patriotism for his or her side, came other questions: Is love of country a truly public affection, or just an extension of love of self? What is the relation between love of country and more extensive connections, such as a universal link to humanity (a link at which Wollstonecraft is glancing with her contrast between "the man" and "the Briton")? And what exactly is the basis for love of country? Burke was at the core of the controversy over these questions. Exploring the debates with an eye toward the relation and potential conflict between patriotism and universal attachments—and also toward earlier moral discourse—can not only shed light on the debates, but also reveal more precisely where Burke's individuality and originality lie.

Burke's arguments, as we will see, are particularly his,[2] but the problems to which he was responding were not individual to him. What political writers in the 1790s were all wrestling with were the potentially troublesome relationships between love of country and other attachments, both those that are more extensive, like universal benevolence, and those that are less extensive, like love of self or family. These are relationships which have been overlooked by modern scholars. Although historians have recently illuminated the role played by the rhetoric of and ideas about patriotism in eighteenth-century Britain, their analyses slight an important dimension of radical ideology in the 1790s, and thus of the conservative response to it. What they leave out is the radicals' belief in the precedence of universal attachments and affections, a belief invested with moral as well as political significance, and one which was a center of controversy in the decade. Scholars have noted the radicals' advocacy of the universal rights of man[3] (an advocacy which connects them to modern political thought), but this doctrine of rights is distinct from the universalism that was most central to many radicals. These radicals would have described their universalism principally in terms of benevolence—an idea which is part of the British sentimental tradition (but not of our modern political discourse), and which is not necessarily implied in the language of the rights of man. Thomas Paine, for example, does not refer to universal benevolence, although he does talk of the rights of man.

But for most radicals (in contrast to Paine) it was benevolence, conceived of as an inclination of our affections rather than a theoretical doctrine of rights, that counted.[4] And these radicals tended to assert cosmopolitan views that made a comprehensive loyalty superior to a limited connection to one's country, though still usually compatible with it (indeed, before the 1790s the potential conflict between broad connections and narrower ones had not been seen as particularly pressing or as having immediate political implications). In contrast, conservatives sought to discredit reformers and their thinking by driving a wedge between universal connections and national loyalty; during the Revolution controversy, conservative discourse on patriotism was in large part a reaction to radical cosmopolitanism. On either side, when controversialists defined a proper love of country, they almost always had to do so by stating its relationship to the ideal of universal benevolence or (as it was often formulated) the figure of the citizen of the world. The debate, significant in itself, is also a crucial context for Burke's comments on love of country. Because doctrines of universal attachment seriously threaten what he takes as the basis of society, they spur him to a full articulation of his views of patriotism.

Burke's discussions of patriotism are always complex, often unconventional, and sometimes apparently self-contradictory. He asserts that our apparently most extensive affections are actually selfish; he also seems to contend that love of country is noble when it's British but fundamentally flawed when it's French. He treats patriotism both as something basic in the lives of British citizens but also as something that they need to relearn. He insists on the importance of history to patriotism, but (unlike most conservative patriots appealing to history) does not use history as a source of heroic examples that will reveal British preeminence. Most fundamentally, he constructs a form of patriotism that is specifically British but also remarkably un-chauvinistic; Burkean patriotism is both British and also appropriate to Europe in general. If Burke's patriotism has an "other," that "other" is not the usual British suspects (such as France or Catholicism) but the abstraction of universal benevolence.

II. *"Consider yourselves more as citizens of the world"*

British supporters of the French Revolution continued to make the claim of patriotism that reformers had made throughout the eighteenth century: they asserted that they were the true patriots because it was only they who would serve the general public good and preserve constitutional liberties. But the cosmopolitan path that supporters of the Revolution took was new, and would not have been easily predictable to a participant in earlier eighteenth-century British politics. Although many opponents of the government in the 1790s had expressed universalist views before the Revolution controversy, nevertheless the opposition to the government earlier in the century had been largely chauvinistic; reformers employed a rhetoric of patriotism imbued with hostility to France and other nations.[5] But when the French Revolution seemed to offer a spur to progressive changes in Britain, radicals—while not discarding their claim to be true patriots—began to appeal frequently to universal benevolence, the idea that benevolence and sympathy can be extended to all humanity. This idea was actually not as revolutionary as it might have been; it could have been used as a levelling doctrine that extended benevolence and solidarity across class lines, but instead it was seen as reaching primarily across geographical distances. This geographical extension was crucial to the radicals' program, for if they wanted reform in France to become a model for reform in Britain, they needed to accomplish two ends. First, they needed to build links to France; as the radical London Corresponding Society wrote in a letter to the French National Convention, "we, instead of natural enemies, at length discover in Frenchmen our fellow citizens of the world."[6] Second, they needed to combat traditional British distrust of what the French did, especially after Britain went to war with France; they had to have a way of opposing conservative calls to patriotic solidarity against the French.

The cosmopolitan views that many British supporters of the French Revolution held had two distinct sources: not only universal benevolence, which had been explored by eighteenth-century British moral philosophers, but also the figure of the citizen of the world, which had its roots in Stoic philosophy (and was common among Enlightenment *philosophes*). These sources correspond to the two chief emphases of cosmopolitanism—detachment from lesser connections (the citizen of the world), or strengthening of greater connections (universal benevolence). Although the distinction between these orientations was usually unnoticed, it had practical political implications.

Being a citizen of the world implied that one had achieved a comprehensive view by disentangling oneself from prejudices and partial attachments; although one could have attachments to particular people or places, these attachments could carry weight only if they were based not on prejudice, tradition, or mere accident, but rather on reason—and in any event such attachments should not be too strong. Indeed, since detachment was crucial, one could be a citizen of the world—an unbiased philosopher, a neutral scientist, a detached historian, an impartial judge (to use common images)—

without asserting any significant interest in the welfare of humanity at large. In contrast, universal benevolence was in practice the British radicals' preferred term precisely because it made a stronger case for concern for others; it implied not divestment, but an active extension and strengthening of ties and affections. The radicals of the 1790s inherited this version of the cosmopolitan ideal from British moral philosophers such as Francis Hutcheson and Lord Shaftesbury, who, in the eighteenth-century debate about how extensive our affections and loyalties can be, had argued that we can and should seek universal benevolence.[7]

Thus radicals could draw on the eighteenth-century concern with egoism. A central goal of British moral philosophers had been to criticize the egoistical theories of human behavior set out by Hobbes and Mandeville—"the selfish system," as it was sometimes called—[8] and the attack on egoism had also formed part of political rhetoric, often by way of charges of unpatriotic selfishness levelled against political figures (usually of the Court party).[9] Having inherited the view that egoism was the great enemy, British supporters of the Revolution sought to put it to their own use. Sometimes they followed the most uncompromising of commentaries on the selfishness of patriotism, the one made by Jonathan Edwards in colonial New England. To Edwards, patriotism was simply an extension of self that did not share the nature of true virtue: love of country, if it wasn't part of universal benevolence, was as flawed as "any other private affection," even if it extended "to a system that contains thousands of individuals."[10] A few radicals in the 1790s built on this extreme view, none more consistently than Edwards's admirer William Godwin. Godwin blames love of country for "a spirit of hatred and all uncharitableness towards the countries around us," because most people have "a kind of selfish impulse of pride and vain-glory, which assumes the form of patriotism, and represents to our imagination whatever is gained to our country as so much gained to our darling selves."[11]

But patriotism retained enough of the aura of public spirit that it had had during most of the eighteenth century for most radicals to want to claim a true patriotism for themselves, just as earlier reformers had.[12] Accordingly, they usually represented patriotism as potentially but not inherently and irretrievably selfish, and sought to define a proper patriotism in a particular way. Some opposed the selfishness that was potential to patriotism by using the idea of reason, arguing that only "rational" patriotism, as distinct from "natural" patriotism, was valuable.[13] As Hazlitt put it during a later phase of the debate, "our country . . . is not a natural but an artificial idea," and patriotism cannot be "the offspring of physical or local attachment."[14] Indeed, anyone who advocates the stance of the citizen of the world cannot accept a narrowly national partiality as natural and inevitable, and the radicals took a position that was an echo of earlier cosmopolitan writers. These earlier writers, while acknowledging that geographical attachment had some power, argued that one could and should become more deeply attached to proper principles; thus, to Hutcheson, in an extreme case—for example, if one's country becomes tyrannous, or unjust, or corrupted—one could even give up one's national love.[15] In his opposition manifesto *The Idea of a Patriot King* (written 1738, published 1749), Bolingbroke (who praises cosmopolitanism) asserts that "[p]atriotism must be founded in great principles."[16]

Since radicals who supported French principles had to oppose British chauvinism, they pursued this line of argument, as when Richard Price wrote in his *Discourse on the Love of Our Country,* "by our country is meant . . . not the soil or spot of earth on which we happen to have been born; . . . [but] that body of companions and friends and kindred who are associated with us under the same constitution of government, protected by the same laws, and bound together by the same civil polity" *(Discourse,* 2–3). A few writers in the 1790s went even further than this, however, following to their logical end the possible implications of an attachment to principles instead of geography. When Joseph Fawcett spells out the duties of what he calls "the Patriot of the Christian school," he sees that they may include turning against one's own country "if his fellow-countrymen oppose the rights, [or] set their face against the welfare, of his fellow-men; if they engage in unrighteous war, [or] if they go out to unjust battle."[17] Godwin makes a similar point in *Political Justice,* arguing that the attachment of a person to the well-being of his countrymen "will be to the cause, and not to the country. Wherever there are men who understand the value of political justice and are prepared to assert it, that is his country. Wherever he can most contribute to the diffusion of these principles and the real happiness of mankind, that is his country" (515 [5.16]; see also 627 [6.4]).[18]

Many supporters of the Revolution, however, found the key to proper love of country not solely or directly in principles or reason, but rather in a truly unselfish affection—universal benevolence. Universal benevolence, that is, could serve to overrule a potentially misguided patriotism. Here radicals followed a lead of Hutcheson's, who had suggested that we expect of humankind "that their general benevolence should continually direct and limit, not only their selfish affections, but even their nearer attachments to others . . . ."[19] Thus Richard Price asserted that "we must remember, that a narrower interest ought always to give way to a more extensive interest. . . . we ought to consider ourselves as citizens of the world . . . " (*Discourse,* 10). To Price, a test for true lovers of country should be the question, are you "always considering yourself more as citizens of the world than as members of any particular community?" (*Discourse,* 44). Similarly, Fawcett maintained that "the partiality of the affections to any particular community" is a good thing only if "restrained from offending against the laws of universal benevolence" (*Sermons*, 2: 157).

As these comments suggest, John Dinwiddy's point that radical patriotism "became paradoxically tinged with cosmopolitanism" ("England," 57) is misleading. Cosmopolitanism was crucial for many radicals, and although there is a potential conflict between patriotism and universalism—a conflict on which conservatives insisted—radicals had a clear idea of how the two ideals might cooperate.[20] As Samuel Romilly put it, "The true interests of a nation never yet stood in opposition to the general interests of mankind, and it never can happen that philanthropy, and patriotism can impose on any man inconsistent duties."[21]

III. *"The Friend of every Country—but his own"*

As part of their resistance both to British radicalism and to the implications of French principles for Britain, conservatives thus needed to attack cosmopolitanism. They saw that the elevation of the cosmopolitan ideal could undermine the power of British patriotism—a patriotism that they hoped would be an effective weapon against French ideas (which they often saw as a greater threat than French military power). Accordingly, conservatives, led by Burke, both attacked universal benevolence and defended patriotism. But these were not straightforward tasks. Conservatives needed to redefine universal benevolence, which might seem to be a great and worthy ideal, as actually selfish—as a morally flawed, treacherous, and destructive "phantom" or seductress (Parr, *Spital Sermon*, 2: 375, 365). And they also needed to define patriotism as the ideal that would both challenge cosmopolitanism and evoke support of the current British government.

To oppose the particular strain of cosmopolitanism represented by universal benevolence, conservatives could (and sometimes did) follow the opponents of Shaftesbury and Hutcheson in the eighteenth-century philosophical debates. Writers such as Hume, Adam Smith, and Lord Kames had contended that because we always feel far more for those close to us than for those distant from us, universal benevolence is beyond our capabilities; they had added that love of country is the utmost affection of which we are capable, and that it should thus be our crucial public loyalty. But while conservatives did pursue t his avenue, they found an easier path in assailing the figure of the citizen of the world. Because of the frequency of this figure in the writings of French *philosophes*, conservatives could link radicals to those suspect French writers, regardless of how distinctive the British radicals really were. And although advocates of the citizen of the world could assert that this stance included a concern for all the world, their position was open to attack on the score of self-involvement. This conservative attack, which echoed ancient denunciations of the Stoics,[22] gave the conservatives their own way of occupying the high moral ground of true unselfishness and public concern. They denied that universal benevolence lay within human capabilities, and they also went further; they sought to show what belief in it must really mean, and why it mattered. They contended that if universal attachments could not really exist, then the cry of universal benevolence must conceal some selfish design. Thus they pursued earlier hints that a cosmopolitan stance might actually be a cover for personal selfishness and indifference to others.

Before the 1790s, attacks on the citizen of the world had usually accused him chiefly of indifference, as in Gibbon's assertion that "I will not be a citizen of the world, I reject with scorn that proud title under which philosophers conceal an equal indifference to the whole human race."[23] But in the 1790s "indifference" easily slid into "selfishness," and the tale of the radicals' selfishness is everywhere in conservative writings of the decade.[24] Samuel Parr noted that philosophers other than Socrates assumed "[t]he title of 'Citizen of the World' . . . to gratify . . . their vanity," and added that on several occasions he had seen "a resemblance" between such philosophers and "some modern writers upon ethics" (*Spital Sermon*, 2: 502 n. 61). Robert Fellowes referred to "the too often affected appellation of a citizen of the world; a name frequently abused to disguise a base insensibility to the best affections of the human heart."[25] Hannah More's Mr. Fantom becomes a philanthropist precisely because he is selfish, and this "boundless selfishness and inordinate vanity converted a discontented trader into a turbulent politician," with the result that "the more the word benevolence was in his mouth, the more did selfishness gain dominion in his heart."[26]

The conservatives also added a new dimension to the attack on selfishness. They insisted that, however the radicals actually praised patriotism, their true goal was to destroy local and national attachments. Hume, earlier, had not worried about the potential destruction of patriotism. Hume notes that Plutarch had contended that because "[m]an is not a plant, rooted to a certain spot of earth," "[t]o change one's country . . . is little more than to remove from one street to another" (see "De exilio," in *Moralia*). But while Hume does see that this perspective, if people could truly adopt it, might "destroy all their attachment to their native country," he doubts people could indeed take it seriously: "The reflections of philosophy are too subtle and distant to . . . eradicate any affection."[27] Yet with this topic as with others that had once seemed only academic, the heightened tensions created by the French Revolution led Hume's case to be taken seriously. The *Anti-Jacobin* calls the philanthropist "A steady Patriot of the World alone, / The Friend of every Country—but his own."[28] Parr describes "a kind of fashion, which prevails among some writers, to deprecate the love of our country, to represent it as interfering with the principles of general benevolence, and to resolve it into prejudice, vanity, jealousy, or weak and inglorious selfishness" (*Spital Sermon*, 2: 463 n. 44). When Hannah More's Tom asks, "What is a *patriot* according to the new school?", Jack answers, "A man who loves every other country better than his own, and France best of all" (*Village Politics*, in *Complete Works*, 1: 367).

IV. *"Engaging the affections on the part of the commonwealth"*

These attacks all lead back to Burke, who established the conservative pattern of presenting patriotism and universal benevolence as opposites. As Hazlitt put it, he set "[t]he two noblest impulses of our nature, the love of country and the love of kind . . . in hostile array."[29] Burke points to selfishness, for example, both in the French and in "the whole clan of the enlightened among us" who have an "attachment to their country in itself" only as an instrument to their goals—"only so far as it agrees with some of their fleeting projects."[30] And he sees around him "perverted minds, which have no delight, but in contemplating the supposed distress, and predicting the immediate ruin, of their country" (*Letters on a Regicide Peace* [1795–97], Third Letter, in *WSEB*, 9: 371; see also *An Appeal from the New to the Old Whigs* [1791], in *FR*, 157). But although others followed Burke's lead, his persistence and passion were unmatched, and not only because of the personal talents which even his opponents acknowledged. Equally important was that his principles and mode of thinking were particularly hostile to universal benevolence. His powerful mistrust of philosophical abstractions and theoretical speculation, which he saw as disengaging us from our habitual affections and sentiments, made it for him already a damning indictment that (in his view) universal benevolence could exist only abstractly, only in theory. And Burke's mistrust was deepened by contemporary identifications: "citizen of the world" had become nearly synonymous with "philosopher" and philosophical detachment, and abstract or visionary theory was seen as a crucial characteristic of French revolutionary principles.[31]

Because of the comprehensiveness of the threat Burke saw in radical ideology, a threat embodied in the way universal benevolence challenged traditional affections, he needed to go beyond the pattern of previous political debate on patriotism; he needed a deeper defense of British society than could be provided by arguing only that the current government would best defend the public good and constitutional liberties. And old views of the sources of patriotism also would not serve his purposes. In the early days of the Revolution, France was not a clear military threat, so Burke could not easily call up the kind of patriotism that Adam Ferguson had described—a national or communal spirit based on the need for protection or security. (Indeed, Ferguson suggests that in modern states, which are civilized and commercial, "the national spirit . . . cannot be exerted," and consequently he cannot see how national affections might arise.)[32] Further, Burke could not use the view that had seen love of country as largely a matter of birth and land.[33] While this kind of patriotism might work against any potential love of France, mere geography gave no way to foster loyalty to the current arrangements in Britain. (In fact, as Conor Cruise O'Brien notes, Burke's own geographical origins—his Irish Catholic background—could make his patriotism suspect; Horace Walpole, for example, "ridiculed the idea that Burke could be any kind of patriot.")[34] Geography also could not be the basis of loyalty insofar as Burke thought not simply of England but of the widespread British empire. When he sought to point out the links between Britain and the American colonies, for example, what Burke underscored was "the close affection which grows from common names, from kindred blood, from similar privileges, and equal protection," as well as "the spirit of English communion" (*Speech on Conciliation with the Colonies* [1775], in *PRW*, 265). Burke could use a variation of the geographical argument, one which connects love of country to our affections for the people in our vicinity, those with whom we have grown up; still, he acknowledged that "[t]he idea of a people . . . is wholly artificial," a "legal fictio[n]" *(An Appeal from the New to the Old Whigs*, in *FR*, 163).

Since older views of patriotism were inadequate to any attempt to oppose the abstraction and malignant results of universal benevolence, Burke had to assert his own definition of patriotism. This definition enabled him to argue both critically and constructively. Critically, it enabled him to attack universal benevolence (and French patriotism, which he saw as closely related). Constructively, it enabled him to forge a case for supporting the current government and social arrangements of Britain—an important result, especially since patriotism in the past had often been a weapon used against the government by the opposition.[35] He achieved these ends by defining patriotism with reference to its sources; he altered the former connection of love of country to geography, and gave a new significance to the idea of history or time in patriotism. Ultimately, he made national allegiance and loyalty a matter not chiefly of self-interest, or of particular policies, or of attachment based on abstract principles (such as a contract theory of governmental obligations, a favorite theme of radicals), but of deep affections.

The ideas of time and history, along with associated ideas like inheritance and tradition, are what keep Burke's position from collapsing into that of the reformers who contended that love of country can be a free choice based on rational principles. Rather than rational principles, Burke argues, we are attached to institutions and arrangements that have endured through time. Whereas Hazlitt, opposing a conservative selfish patriotism, sees love of country as properly the result of "reason and reflection" ("Illustrations of Vetus," in *Complete Works*, 7: 67), Burke takes it to be a profound result of time. And this point is crucial to understanding how Burke could make a distinction, in 1793, between "the moral France"—the *ancien régime* that no longer exists—and "the geographical" France, which has repudiated the ancient order *(Remarks on the Policy of the Allies*, in *WSEB*, 8: 465).

Burke's argument, for which Hume was probably a precursor,[36] is partly a notion of habit—what "holds [men] together" in a country is the "secret, unseen, but irrefragable bond of habitual intercourse" (*Regicide Peace*, First Letter, in *WSEB*, 9: 247)—but it also involves time in a more historical sense: "Our country . . . consists, in a great measure, in the ancient order into which we are born. . . . The place that determines our duty to our country is a social, civil relation" (*Appeal from the New to the Old Whigs*, in *FR*, 161).[37] Hence the loss of old customs and practices, and a new civil order, means a different country. It is a mistake, Burke writes in 1795, to refer to "France"; what now inhabits the location of that former nation can be called *France* only by way of "the hocus-pocus of *abstraction*" (*Regicide Peace*, Fourth Letter, in *WSEB*, 9: 50). Our country is constituted largely by our ways of life; to transform them is to create a different country. And Burke draws a further implication from this connection between our ways of life and our country: wanting to change our country must reflect not true patriotism, but hatred for everything around us. "You began ill," he says to the French, "because you began by despising every thing that belonged to you"; "your leaders . . . despise all their predecessors, and all their contemporaries" (*Reflections*, 122, 124; see also 135).[38] For Burke, French cosmopolitanism implies both selfishness and the devaluation of other affections. In addition, the despising of predecessors enables Burke to reemphasize his central point that the French have discarded all tradition (a portrayal in keeping with his view of the Revolution as something unprecedented).

The disrespect of the French for tradition (and thus for their country, in Burke's eyes) is something Burke is able to use straightforwardly to oppose the Revolution. But his use of tradition against his British opponents has to be more complex, because he knows that the British radicals (unlike the French) are not making a clean break with the past. As Don Herzog points out, radicals like Richard Price did indeed appeal to past events (such as those of 1688) and to native traditions. Burke's response includes presenting his own version of the past events, a version that argues against innovation; his response also includes trying to undermine the traditions to which British radicals appeal. He repeatedly reminds Price that his predecessor Hugh Peters, the seventeenth-century revolutionary, was executed; in Herzog's words, "Burke cannot resist taunting Dr. Price with the fact that he too has a tradition, he too has his precursors."[39] But a more important dimension of Burke's use of tradition against the radicals (a dimension Herzog overlooks) is the great weight he puts on the continuing force of the tradition, as manifested in the way it has shaped current arrangements. Burke in effect opposes a lived tradition, something which is parallel to prescription or continuous possession, to mere precedent (in the sense of something that simply happened in the past). He suggests that the appeal to precedent made by someone seeking change, like Price, is almost an abstract appeal, inasmuch as it must necessarily refer to a strand of tradition that is not dominant in the present. In thus portraying tradition as manifested in our ways of life, and invoking our affections for those ways of life, Burke seeks to give his use of tradition a strategic advantage.

It might seem that Burke's account has a weakness in its dependence on continuity, on a line that extends from the past without breaks, since (as he knows) this is not a picture that would automatically command wide assent. But to some extent his success depends less on the persuasiveness of his historical account than on his ability to invoke the texture of his audience's lived experience. His true goal is to create a picture of the current order, and of the tradition it embodies, that brings to life or reinforces his audience's affections for their lives. Thus Burke seeks to show what love of country is not principally by defending the historical legitimacy of the British government (a point which would have little relation to our affections) but by describing his own vision of British society. For similar reasons, Burke is unlike most conservative advocates of patriotism in tending not to invoke heroic figures or military exploits from the past.[40] His final point of reference is the present (albeit a present that has been forged by traditions). As he remarks in another context, "[o]ld establishments are tried by their effects. If the people are happy, united, wealthy, and powerful, we presume the rest" (*Reflections*, 285). Burke's strategy is to use his picture of British society to help defeat the threat of the Revolution by reinforcing a love of country that he hopes already exists, unreflectively.

Nevertheless, we should be careful not to see love of country for Burke as primarily deriving from, and hence secondary to, an antecedent affection for our ways of life. In his view, love of country does not just grow from love for these ways of life; love of country also helps to underpin them. Patriotism comes close to being the foundation of a country, or (more precisely) of any modern nation. To Burke, the orderly social existence of modern Europe depends on national affections; this kind of society cannot function without a reverence or even love for institutions and practices as its foundation. Mere principles or abstractions like universal benevolence are unable to provide such a foundation; all that political speculation will do is to loosen "all the ties, which . . . attach mankind to their old, habitual, domestic Governments" (*Regicide Peace*, Fourth Letter, in *WSEB*, 9: 83). Nor can this social foundation be a system of laws or sanctions. Burke objects to the new French system partly because of its heavy reliance on the threat of punishment: in Revolutionary France, "at the end of every visto, you see nothing but the gallows. Nothing is left which engages the affections on the part of the commonwealth" (*Reflections*, 171–2).[41] It is precisely these affections upon which society must be built: "public affections, combined with manners, are required sometimes as supplements, sometimes as correctives, always as aids to law." Public affections, and chiefly patriotism, are a crucial social feeling, and the prominence of patriotism in Burke's writings of the 1790s stems from his conviction that if radical cosmopolitanism undermines patriotism, it also undermines the modern nation.

By connecting national affections to institutions, Burke seeks to merge government and nation (in contrast to opposition attempts to separate them).[42] He criticizes not only the way the French state destroys affections that are connected to traditional ways of life, but also its blindness to the ways in which our affections need to be engaged by our institutions—an engagement achieved by means of great national figures or personifications, who are, crucially, linked to tradition. In the French system, Burke asserts, "institutions can never be embodied . . . in persons[,] so as to create . . . love, veneration, admiration, or attachment" (*Reflections*, 172). In the British system, however, "[w]e procure reverence to our civil institutions on the principle upon which nature teaches us to revere individual men." This reverence has nothing to do with merit or efficacy, on which Burke is silent here (established governments are to be supported regardless of their policies, except in extreme cases); rather, we revere individual men, and thus institutions, "on account of their age; and on account of those from whom they are descended" (*Reflections*, 121). Institutions, that is, are not only personified; this personification is connected to age—to history.[43] Again, Burke connects national affections to time, and builds an argument on his belief that abstract principles cannot inspire deep affections.

This belief appears not only in Burke's explanation of why the French must rely on the threat of the gallows, but throughout his writings on the Revolution: the revolutionaries' disregard of national affections seems to him to be such an obviously deep flaw that he often proceeds as if his invocation of national affections will automatically score a point in his favor. At such times he tends to refer to "natural" feelings, feelings which must recoil from revolutionary acts. But Burke also knows that the very familiarity of such feelings can reduce their power; as he puts it in the *Enquiry into the Sublime and Beautiful*, "it is the nature of things which hold us by custom to affect us very little whilst we are in possession of them" (103 [pt. 3, sec. 5]). Further, the Revolution showed Burke, more clearly than ever before, that abstractions like universal benevolence can indeed exert a powerful influence,[44] and at times he acknowledges that people can turn aside from their "natural" responses: "Opinions . . . frequently guide and direct the affections; and men may become more attached to the country of their principles, than to the country of their birth" (*Regicide Peace*, Third Letter, in *WSEB*, 9: 310).[45] Hence Burke cannot just appeal to natural feelings but must attempt to reclaim them,[46] and this aim is epitomized in his portrait of Marie Antoinette in the *Reflections*.

Burke's treatise on the sublime and the beautiful (1757) suggests that a chief reason why he concentrated more on the Queen than the King was that she could more easily be a focus of affection;[47] she would not be the imposing figure of authority that the King would (or ought to) be. As Burke observes in his treatise, kings are associated with power, not affection: "[s]overeigns are frequently addressed with the title of *dread majesty*" (*PE*, 67 [2.5]). Love and the affections are connected to the beautiful, and associated with women and vulnerability, while the sublime involves a fear which precludes these "softer" emotions: "[t]he authority of a father . . . hinders us from having that entire love for him that we have for our mothers" (*PE*, 111 [3.10]).[48] The Queen's role is not that of a dreaded ruler; she is not part of the machinery of government, but rather is (or should be) a focal point for national reverence and love, which serve a unifying function. Her role is symbolic; to use the language of the passage quoted earlier, she is one of those persons in whom "institutions" are "embodied . . . [,] so as to create . . . love, veneration, admiration, or attachment" (*Reflections*, 172). And this role stems largely from her occupying a position exalted by tradition (what Burke refers to in a letter as her "high Rank" and "great Splendour of descent)."[49] She stands, ultimately, for a traditional and time-honored national way of life.[50] Through his emotionally-laden descriptions of the Queen, Burke seeks to revive in his readers traditional responses to monarchs and to chivalric representations of female vulnerability.[51]

In a similar way, Burke seeks to recall his readers to their habitual feelings for national institutions, and hence to promote critical responses to the institutions of the Revolution. Anyone who "admires, and from the heart is attached to national representative assemblies," he says, "must turn with horror and disgust" from the revolutionary National Assembly (*Reflections*, 161). But it is the Queen who serves as Burke's centerpiece, because his highly literary portrait of her allows him to invoke traditional aesthetic and moral responses, responses which often are allied for Burke. Indeed, in his writing language itself seems to support traditional national affections, as when he says, "[t]o make us love our country, our country ought to be lovely" (*Reflections*, 172). David Bromwich calls attention to this rhetorical scheme of elaborating meanings "by disposing a single root-word into different parts of speech," and argues that "[i]f one has become a member of a moral community that persists over time, even the linguistic usage by which one registers approval or disapproval will wear the look of something precedented, undiscovering, almost circular in its obviousness." As a result, the effect of Burke's nearly-tautological sentences "is of a mere memory or confirming echo which seems nevertheless to involve a recognition."[52] Burke thus invokes with specific reference to love of country what he sees as stable traditions of aesthetic and moral taste, traditions that are relatively resistant to political theorizing.

What Burke reminds his readers is that time has (in a word he uses repeatedly) "consecrated" the established state. In a pivotal passage of the *Reflections*, in which he argues that the consecration of the "commonwealth" keeps its current members mindful that they are only "temporary possessors and life-renters in it," Burke illustrates his point with the image of generations within a family (192–3). The illustration is crucial, for central to Burke's argument about national affections is his use (in this as in many other cases) of the image of family. In this argument, family plays a part far more important than it does in the associationist model common in the eighteenth century, a model which portrayed love of country as developing outward from the family in a series of concentric circles of loyalty.[53] Although Burke does make use of this model (see *Reflections*, 135, 315), for him family affections are not only the source of national affections, a developmental step, but also a paradigm or image by which we understand national affections.[54]

Family affection serves Burke as an image for national affections first because he sees it as un-theoretical or even anti-theoretical. Affections within a family seem unreflective, unplanned, and beyond doctrine; they grow largely from experience over time, as a result of living in a family. We grow up with our traditions, practices, and institutions, just as we grow up with our families; we don't evaluate them before we can care for them, and we don't make deliberate choices of whom to love.[55] And if our feeling for our country is like our feeling for our family, Burke thinks, we will be strongly anti-radical; like the private affections we feel within our families, national affections—our attachments to traditional institutions and practices—should be resistant to, and discredit the value of, political speculation and innovations.

Burke also sees family as a model for tradition, and not only because the unreflective way in which family affections grow resembles how a tradition develops. More deeply, it is fundamental both personally and politically to Burke that family implies inheritance[56]—a familial link to time—and thus he repeatedly uses family as the mediator and link between love of country and time. Inheritance is his paradigm for the handing down of practices, affections, and beliefs in the national realm. As he puts it:

> the people of England well know, that the idea of inheritance furnishes a sure principle of conservation, and a sure principle of transmission . . . . we receive, we hold, we transmit our government and our privileges, in the same manner in which we enjoy and transmit our property and our lives. . . . In this choice of inheritance we have given to our frame of polity the image of a relation in blood; binding up the constitution of our country with our dearest domestic ties; adopting our fundamental laws into the bosom of our family affections. (*Reflections*, 119–20)

Thus, if we are truly attached to our country, our attachment is not simply to a particular society at an isolated moment ("a nation is not an idea only of local extent, and individual momentary aggregation"),[57] nor does it arise simply because we are accustomed to a way of doing things, to a tradition of manners and habits. Our feeling goes beyond mere attachment; what we feel for our country is love, and Burke suggests that we feel that affection partly because our country resembles ("by the spirit of philosophic analogy," 120) our family.

V. *"The end of local patriotism"*

Given the vehemence of Burke's defense of patriotism, however, what is he to do with love of country in France—an especially important question when the aggressive renewal of patriotism by the revolutionaries posed a threat to Britain. It might seem that he would be able to oppose the French manifestation of love of country only by means of a chauvinistic inconsistency. But Burke's approach is to portray French patriotism as being not genuine love of country, but rather a variation on universal benevolence; it is the insubstantial creature of mere doctrine. Burke's true opponent, the "other" of his patriotism, is not a particular country or group, but cosmopolitanism: cosmopolitanism threatens all patriotism, and French cosmopolitanism threatens all European countries. And the way that Burke seeks to link French patriotism to cosmopolitanism is by depicting it as based only in theory; it is the result of the work of neither time nor local connections. Thus his belief in prescription, in the importance of continuity over time as against the present-minded emphasis of revolutionary theory, has a territorial equivalent in his belief in continuity between the local and the national. Against what he perceives as the abstraction of universal benevolence, Burke insists that any extensive affection must be based not on theoretical connections but on concrete local attachments.

Burke could argue that French patriotism was a "homicide philanthropy" precisely because it signalled the end "of *local* patriotism" (*Regicide Peace*, Third Letter, in *WSEB*, 9: 303). The French Revolution, like other revolutions "of doctrine and theory," makes connections between people depend on *"doctrine and theoretick dogma,"* on *"other interests . . . than those which arose from their locality and natural circumstances"* (*Thoughts on French Affairs* [1791], in *FR*, 208 [emphasis in original]). Historical experience, says Burke, has shown that such connections, "if they did not absolutely destroy, at least weakened and distracted the locality of patriotism" (*Thoughts on French Affairs,* in *FR,* 209; cf. 211). Thus, although the French boast "that all local ideas should be sunk, and that the people should no longer be Gascons, Picards, Bretons, Normans, but Frenchmen," Burke asserts that "instead of being all Frenchmen, the greater likelihood is, that the inhabitants of that region will shortly have no country" (*Reflections,* 315).[58]

By "have no country," Burke means not that those "inhabitants" will lack any state or linking principle, but rather that what they have will look nothing like the "scheme of relations" (*Regicide Peace,* Second Letter, in *WSEB,* 9: 303) to which the French—or any modern Europeans—have been accustomed. To do away with local connections is like doing away with traditions (indeed, each act implies the other), and if a country is in large part constituted by such connections and traditions (as Burke argues), a patriotism that does away with them in effect does away with the country itself. What is left is only "the dust and powder of individuality," "an unsocial, uncivil, unconnected chaos of elementary principles" (*Reflections,* 194–95). Being a "people," and having what Burke calls the "pretended *rights of man,*" "are things incompatible": "The one supposes the presence, the other the absence of a state of civil society" (*An Appeal from the New to the Old Whigs,* in *FR,* 179).

French patriotism is a "homicide philanthropy" also because a society constructed by considering human beings simply as individuals, "stripped" (as Burke writes in a different context) "of every relation, in all the nakedness and solitude of metaphysical abstraction" (*Reflections,* 90), leads as well to the paradoxical result of wiping out individuals. Burke portrays a

France in which the individual "is as nothing. Individuality is left out of their scheme of Government" (*Regicide Peace,* Second Letter, in *WSEB,* 9: 288). By this Burke seems to mean two things. Most directly he means that when "[t]he state is all in all," when the traditions and local attachments that function as limits on central power disappear, "personal liberty" is drastically reduced (*Regicide Peace,* Second Letter, in *WSEB,* 9: 287–88). (In part Burke has in mind the ways in which the "diversity of members and interests" secures "general liberty," and makes "all the headlong exertions of arbitrary power . . . for ever impracticable"—*Reflections,* 122). Individuals cannot be as individually distinct when they are prevented from pursuing "the infinite variety of human concerns" (*Reflections,* 193; see also *Regicide Peace,* Second Letter, in *WSEB,* 9: 287). In Burke's view, traditions and local attachments do not limit our individuality, but rather help to create the conditions that make exercising our individuality possible.

I would argue further that, since for Burke our traditions and local attachments in some sense *constitute* what we are individually, he is also envisioning a more profound way in which individuality is threatened in France.[59] In a system like the French, Burke thinks, "all love to our country, all pious veneration and attachment to its laws and customs, are obliterated from our minds" (*An Appeal from the New to the Old Whigs,* in *FR,* 176). As a result, we fall prey to what Edward Shils calls "civil amnesia";[60] what we once were as persons will be lost, for in being naked individuals, acting without the guidance of "antient opinions and rules of life" (*Reflections,* 172), without the direction provided by traditions and customs, we can hardly be the same *kind* of individuals. Even our "moral sentiments" will be destroyed; they are "so nearly connected with early prejudice as to be almost one and the same thing," and they "will assuredly not live long under a discipline, which has for its basis the destruction of all prejudices . . . " (*An Appeal from the New to the Old Whigs,* in *FR,* 193). As J. G. A. Pocock summarizes Burke's "central doctrine":

> We cannot be fully human unless we clearly inhabit a society and a culture, which furnishes us with the context in and on which we must act, and with the moral and practical reasons for acting in and on it. It follows that we cannot possibly destroy and replace the whole fabric of society without destroying our own intelligences and our capacity to replace it, since we shall be destroying the only reasons for acting, and even living, which we can possibly have.[61]

In Burke's view, then, traditional individuality is destroyed by excessive individuality—not quite the same as the familiar villain of selfishness, but closely allied to it. As he does with British universal benevolence, Burke claims to expose only self-concern underneath French patriotism. It is "a selfish temper and confined views" that spark "[a] spirit of innovation" (*Reflections,* 119). And if loving "the little platoon we belong to in society, is the first principle . . . of public affections," then a "profligate disregard" of the position we share with others—like that of French patriots—is "[o]ne of the first symptoms . . . of a selfish . . . ambition" (*Reflections,* 135). In Burke's analysis, radical selfishness is revealed as a particularly virulent will-to-power.

This was a powerful attack. Yet it required Burke to go on the defensive as well. By relying on local attachments as the proper foundation for a true patriotism, Burke faced the accusation that the local attachments he championed might themselves be selfish. Indeed, Catherine Macaulay, after quoting Burke's comment on the "little platoon we belong to in society," retorted that we should not "confound those *narrow affections* which bind small bodies together by the mutual ties of a personal interest, to that *liberal benevolence,* which, chearfully sacrifices a *personal interest* to the *welfare* of the community" (*Observations,* in *Political Writings of the 1790s,* 1: 133).[62] But Burke had already worked out what his defense would look like when he had responded in the 1760s to the denunciation of political factions. In *Thoughts on the Cause of the Present Discontents* (1770), he had had to acknowledge the force of criticisms made by moral philosophers as well as political controversialists: "I admit that people frequently acquire in such confederacies a narrow, bigoted, and proscriptive spirit; that they are apt to sink the idea of the general good in this circumscribed and partial interest" (*PRW,* 185). In response, he defended limited attachments on several grounds. First he makes a restricted point, based on the requirements of practical political activity: small political groupings are "essentially necessary for the full performance of our public duty" (*PRW,* 185). Then, he asserts that selfishness is not an inevitable quality of small groups; they are only "accidentally liable to degenerate into faction" (*PRW,* 185). Finally, he confronts the accusation of selfishness more directly, using his favored image of the family. He states that small groups are like families, and if we criticize such groups "we may as well affirm, that our natural regards and ties of blood tend inevitably to make men bad citizens" (*PRW,* 185). Family subsequently slides into friendship, as Burke instances the Romans, who took small groups as a sign of a valuable sociability: "They believed . . . that friendship was no mean step towards patriotism" (*PRW,* 186).[63]

In making this argument, Burke had to pass over the important difference between family attachments, which are to a given group, and friendships and party loyalties, which are chosen,[64] because in the 1760s parties and factions had been what was deeply in question. They had been seen as limited loyalties, while patriotism had been contrasted to them as the broader and more valuable public affection.[65] But in the 1790s Burke did not need to concentrate on the difficult task of showing that party loyalty could indeed be part of a broad concern for national welfare. He was able more easily to link patriotism to other limited loyalties and to argue that the menace lay precisely in a broader loyalty, the broader loyalty of cosmopolitanism, which he portrayed as a menace to patriotism in particular. Thus Burke defended patriotism and other limited loyalties together.

Hume had not been so sanguine about limited loyalties; for him, even family affections are an example of our "confin'd generosity," which "instead of fitting men for large societies, is almost as contrary to them, as the most narrow selfishness."[66] But most writers followed the same line as Burke, and in his writings on the Revolution, Burke repeats this point that local attachments are not selfish but rather the basis of our broadest public affections. "No cold relation is a zealous citizen"; we need links to "our families . . . our neighbourhoods, and our habitual provincial connections." Although "this subordinate partiality" might seem likely to extinguish or overshadow "[t]he love to the whole," Burke argues that it will not; rather, it is more likely to be "a sort of elemental training" to love of an "extensive" country (*Reflections,* 315). Being "attached to the subdivision . . . is the first link in the series by which we proceed towards a love to our country" (*Reflections,* 135). Supporters of the Revolution did not let this argument pass; James Mackintosh argued in 1791 that it was the *ancien régime* that had fomented French selfishness and had set the national at odds with the local: "Every thing tended to inspire *provincial,* and to extinguish *national* patriotism."[67] But by the end of the century, Mackintosh had undergone a highly public conversion to Burke's point of view, a conversion that explicitly involved a renunciation of "general benevolence" in favor of "the particular affections."[68]

Burke's visions of Revolutionary horrors and of traditional British virtues were crucial in creating a conservative consensus. Yet he and other opponents of the Revolution had a strong ally in the course of French events themselves. The Terror, regicide, imperialism—especially the invasion of republican Switzerland in 1798—made it difficult to uphold ideals associated with the Revolution, particularly in a repressive Britain that was, for much of the time between 1793 and 1815, at war with France. The ideals of universal benevolence and of the citizen of the world had been given an infusion of energy by the Revolution; they then became its casualties. For most of the nineteenth century, radicals were still able to assert a patriotism in opposition to the established order, often by invoking ancient rights rooted in the English past; thus radical patriotism could coexist with the powerful British nationalism of the century.[69] But the failure of the French Revolution and the rise of nationalism were too much for radical cosmopolitanism to be able to survive.

NOTES

1. *A Vindication of the Rights of Men,* 2nd ed., vol. 5 of *The Works of Mary Wollstonecraft,* ed. Janet Todd and Marilyn Butler (London: William Pickering, 1989), 14–15. Burke actually opposed slavery, although that opposition may not matter to Wollstonecraft's point about the tendency of Burkean prescription. (I should note that the Burkean doctrine of prescription that Wollstonecraft is attacking also emphasizes security of property.)

2. With only a few exceptions (for example, J. C. D. Clark, *English Society, 1688–1832: Ideology, Social Structure and Political Practice during the Ancien Régime* [Cambridge: Cambridge Univ. Press, 1985], 250), most scholars have noted Burke's intellectual originality in turning the tide of British public opinion against the Revolution. But although Burke is often linked to the later development of British nationalism, the significance of his contribution specifically to the debate over patriotism has been little discussed. Stella Cottrell does observe briefly that the broadsheet propaganda of 1803 "was permeated with [Burke's] ideology"—"The Devil on Two Sticks: Franco-phobia in 1803," in *Patriotism: The Making and Unmaking of British National Identity,* ed. Raphael Samuel, 3 vols. (London: Routledge, 1989), vol. 1: *History and Politics,* 264; see also 269). And although in one essay David Eastwood passes over Burke when he focuses on Southey's role in developing a conservative language of patriotism ("Robert Southey and the Meanings of Patriotism," *Journal of British Studies* 31 [1992]: 265–87), he does elsewhere take note of some ways in which Southey follows or diverges from Burke: see "Robert Southey and the Intellectual Origins of Romantic Conservatism," *English Historical Review* 104 (1989): 309, 315–16.

3. For example, see David Eastwood's references to the "implied internationalism of 'the rights of man,'" in "Southey and the Meanings of Patriotism," 268; see also 267, 272.

4. The cosmopolitanism of the radicals is also distinct from the comprehensive knowledge John Barrell discusses in *English Literature in History, 1730–1780: An Equal, Wide Survey* (New York: St. Martin's, 1983). Universal benevolence does not depend on wide knowledge, or knowledge at all; one need not comprehend the expanse of life (the difficulty of which is one of Barrell's central themes) before one can subscribe to universal benevolence. Indeed, to proponents of universal benevolence, one of its virtues is the way in which it is open to all persons. As an incidental point, it is notable that Richard Rorty's recent argument against "human rights foundationalism" has eighteenth-century roots; he takes Hume, along with the contemporary Hume scholar Annette Baier, to be our best advisors in "sentimental education." See "Human Rights, Rationality, and Sentimentality," *Yale Review* 81.4 (1993): 1–20.

5. John Dinwiddy, "England," in *Nationalism in the Age of the French Revolution,* ed. Otto Dann and Dinwiddy (London: Hambledon, 1988), 55–56; Linda Colley, "Radical Patriotism in Eighteenth-Century England," in *Patriotism,* ed. Samuel, 1: 171–76. On patriotism in the eighteenth century generally, see as well John Brewer, *Party Ideology and Popular Politics at the Accession of George III* (Cambridge: Cambridge Univ. Press, 1976), 96–111; Colley, *Britons: Forging the*

Nation, 1707–1837 (New Haven: Yale Univ. Press, 1992); Hugh Cunningham, "The Language of Patriotism," in *Patriotism*, ed. Samuel, 1: 57–89; Gerald Newman, *The Rise of English Nationalism: A Cultural History* (New York: St. Martin's, 1987); Anne E. Brownlow, "Eighteenth Century English Patriotism and the French Revolution," *History of European Ideas* 15 (1992): 289–96; and Kathleen Wilson, *The Sense of the People: Politics, Culture and Imperialism in England, 1715–1785* (Cambridge: Cambridge Univ. Press, 1995).

6. Quoted in Cunningham, "Language of Patriotism," 71.

7. For further discussion of the radicals' position, and of some ways in which the debates of the 1790s about universal benevolence drew upon eighteenth-century British moral philosophy, see Evan Radcliffe, "Revolutionary Writing, Moral Philosophy, and Universal Benevolence in the Eighteenth Century," *Journal of the History of Ideas* 54 (1993): 221–40. In his book *The Cosmopolitan Ideal in Enlightenment Thought: Its Form and Function in the Ideas of Franklin, Hume, and Voltaire, 1694–1790* (Notre Dame: Univ. of Notre Dame Press, 1977), Thomas J. Schlereth tends to pass over the distinctiveness of British thinkers. He notes neither the British writers' emphasis on universal benevolence nor their need (which I discuss below) to oppose the selfish system. In fact, British writers often seek to distinguish themselves from the French, whom they view as exemplars of the selfish approach. See for example the third edition of Godwin's *Political Justice* (1798), ed. Isaac Kramnick (Harmondsworth: Penguin, 1978), 377–78 (bk. 4, ch. 10); in the first edition, Godwin had gone even further, linking the selfish system to monarchical societies in general (*An Enquiry Concerning Political Justice* [1793; reprinted Oxford: Woodstock, 1992], 431 [5.6]). All subsequent references to *Political Justice* are to the first edition.

8. David Hume, *An Enquiry Concerning the Principles of Morals* (1751), ed. L. A. Selby-Bigge, 3rd ed. rev. P. H. Nidditch (Oxford: Clarendon Press, 1975), 295–302 (app. 2); Samuel Parr, *A Spital Sermon, . . . Preached April 15, 1800*, in *The Works of Samuel Parr*, ed. John Johnstone, 8 vols. (London, 1828), 2: 363.

9. See Eastwood, "Southey and the Meanings of Patriotism," 266–67.

10. Edwards, *The Nature of True Virtue* (1765), in *Ethical Writings*, ed. Paul Ramsey (New Haven: Yale Univ. Press, 1989), 612.

11. Godwin, *Thoughts Occasioned by the Perusal of Dr. Parr's Spital Sermon* (1801), in *Uncollected Writings by William Godwin (1785–1822)*, ed. Jack W. Marken and Burton R. Pollin (Gainesville: Scholars' Facsimiles and Reprints, 1968), 322. See also the comments of Richard Price in the speech that started the whole Revolution controversy, *A Discourse on the Love of Our Country*, 6th ed. (London, 1790), esp. 2, 5.

12. For example, see the responses to Burke by Catherine Macaulay (*Observations on the* Reflections [1790]) and Thomas Christie (*Letters on the Revolution of France* [1791]), both reprinted in Gregory Claeys, ed., *Political Writings of the 1790s*, vol. 1: *Radicalism and Reform: Responses to Burke, 1790–1791* (London: Pickering, 1995). Macaulay insists on referring to Richard Price as a patriot (122, 126), while Christie asserts that "every real British patriot" should study the French

constitution; he says, moreover, that this advice is "my mode of proving my love to England" (180). See also Colley, "Radical Patriotism," 182, and "Whose Nation? Which Class? Class and National Consciousness in Britain, 1750–1830," *Past and Present* 113 (1986): 116; Cunningham, "Language of Patriotism," 61–62; Dinwiddy, "England," 56–57.

13. The source of this distinction is probably William Adams (a friend of Price), in his sermon "On the Love of Country" (1774) (quoted in D. O. Thomas, *The Honest Mind: The Thought and Work of Richard Price* [Oxford: Clarendon Press, 1977], 297–98).

14. Hazlitt, "Illustrations of Vetus," in *Complete Works of William Hazlitt*, ed. P. P. Howe., 21 vols. (London: J. M. Dent, 1930–34), 7: 68, 67.

15. See Hutcheson, *An Essay on the Nature and Conduct of the Passions and Affections*, 3rd ed. (1742), 159 (sec. 5, art. 10, sub-art. 3); *An Inquiry Concerning Moral Good and Evil*, Treatise 2 of *An Inquiry into the Original of Our Ideas of Beauty and Virtue, in Two Treatises*, 4th ed. (1738; reprinted Glasgow, 1772), 149–50 (sec. 2, art. 12).

16. *Political Writers of Eighteenth-Century England*, ed. Jeffrey Hart (New York: Knopf, 1964), 208.

17. Fawcett, *Sermons Delivered at the Sunday-Evening Lecture, for the Winter Season, at the Old Jewry*, 2 vols. (London, 1795), 2: 166–67.

18. See also John Thelwall's comments in "On the Prospective Principle of Virtue," in *The Tribune* (1795–96), vol. 1, reprinted in *The Politics of English Jacobinism: Writings of John Thelwall*, ed. Gregory Claeys (University Park: Pennsylvania State Univ. Press, 1995), 97.

19. Hutcheson, *Illustrations on the Moral Sense* (1742), ed. Bernard Peach (Cambridge: Belknap Press of Harvard Univ. Press, 1971), 181 (sec. 6, art. 4).

20. Limiting the sources of the cosmopolitanism of the 1790s to Condorcet and Paine, as Dinwiddy's brief comment does ("England," 63), is another indicator of how the sources and importance of universal benevolence have been overlooked.

21. Romilly, *Thoughts on the Probable Influence of the French Revolution in Great-Britain* (London, 1790), 6.

22. On the Stoic origins of cosmopolitanism, see Schlereth, *Cosmopolitan Ideal*, pp. xvii–xxi, and Alan D. McKillop, "Local Attachment and Cosmopolitanism— The Eighteenth Century Pattern," in *From Sensibility to Romanticism*, ed. Frederick W. Hilles and Harold Bloom (New York: Oxford Univ. Press, 1965), 191–218.

23. Quoted in Parr, *Spital Sermon*, 2: 382.

24. The link between Godwin's supposedly egoistical system and utilitarian thinking—Hazlitt called him "the first *whole-length* broacher of the doctrine of *Utility*" (*Complete Works*, 16: 404)—in part accounts for the particular form taken later by attacks on nineteenth-century utilitarians. See J. B. Schneewind's argument that Godwin is "the original" of "the picture of the utilitarian which we find again and again": "the monster of abstract rationality, basically selfish, denying the importance of family, friends, country, laws, traditions . . ."—*Sidgwick's Ethics and Victorian Moral Philosophy* (Oxford: Clarendon Press, 1977), 139.

25. Quoted in Parr, *Spital Sermon*, 2: 498 n. 59.

26. More, "The History of Mr. Fantom, the New-Fashioned Philosopher" (1794), in *The Complete Works of Hannah More*, 7 vols. (New York, 1855), 1: 3, 4. For conservatives, the egoism of the radicals is partly displayed in their reliance on their own speculations, as opposed to conventional social wisdom.

27. Hume, "The Sceptic," in *Essays Moral, Political, and Literary*, ed. Eugene F. Miller (Indianapolis: Liberty Classics, 1987), 175, 172.

28. "New Morality," in *Poetry of the Anti-Jacobin*, 2nd ed. (London, 1800), 224 (no. 36; 9 July 1798).

29. Hazlitt, *Life of Napoleon*, in *Complete Works*, 13: 50. For Burke's role as leader of the attack on universal benevolence, see Radcliffe, "Revolutionary Writing," 233–38.

30. Burke, *Reflections on the Revolution in France*, ed. Conor Cruise O'Brien (Harmondsworth: Penguin, 1968), 183–84. When possible I have quoted from easily accessible texts of Burke. For Burke's other writings, I have used these editions: *Further Reflections on the Revolution in France*, ed. Daniel E. Ritchie (Indianapolis: Liberty Classics, 1992), hereafter abbreviated as *FR*; *Pre-Revolutionary Writings*, ed. Ian Harris (Cambridge: Cambridge Univ. Press, 1993), hereafter *PRW*; *A Philosophical Enquiry into the Origin of our Ideas of the Sublime and Beautiful* (1757; 2nd ed., 1759), ed. James T. Boulton (London: Routledge and Kegan Paul, 1958), hereafter *PE*; *The Writing and Speeches of Edmund Burke*, gen. ed. Paul Langford (Oxford: Clarendon Press, 1981–), hereafter *WSEB*; *The Works of the Right Honourable Edmund Burke*, 8 vols. (London: Bohn's British Classics, 1872), hereafter *Works*.

31. Schlereth, *Cosmopolitan Ideal*, 191 n. 3; David Simpson, *Romanticism, Nationalism, and the Revolt Against Theory* (Chicago: Univ. of Chicago Press, 1993), 64–83. For the identification of theory with internationalism in general (something else Burke mistrusted), see Simpson, 59, 178–81.

32. Ferguson, *An Essay on the History of Civil Society* (1767), ed. Louis Schneider (New Brunswick: Transaction, 1980), 220 (pt. 5, sec. 3); see also 19 (1. 3), 21 (1. 4), 25 (1. 4), 59 (1. 9), 101 (2. 3). It is true, however, that others— such as John Reeves and his Association for the Preservation of Liberty and Property—called on this defensive spirit (Eastwood, "Southey and the Meanings of Patriotism," 273).

33. McKillop notes that, from the seventeenth century on, discussions frequently connected love of country to geographical roots; the great exemplars of this love of country were the Swiss, who simply loved the place where they had been born and lived ("Local Attachment," 193–98). But as Burke would say, "Our country is not a thing of mere physical locality" (*Appeal from the New to the Old Whigs*, in *FR*, 161).

34. O'Brien, *The Great Melody: A Thematic Biography and Commented Anthology of Edmund Burke* (Chicago: Univ. of Chicago Press, 1992), 90.

35. See esp. Cunningham, "Language of Patriotism," 60–61. Cunningham notes that it was the increasing success of radical appeals to patriotism that led to Dr.

Johnson's famous definition of patriotism, in the 1775 edition of his *Dictionary*, as "the last refuge of a scoundrel" (61).

36.   The relations between Burke's position on love of country and the similarly conservative positions of not only Hume but also Adam Smith, both of whom Burke admired, are complex. Hume comes closest to Burke's view of the importance of antiquity in sanctioning established governments (see "Of the First Principles of Government," "Of the Original Contract," and "Idea of a Perfect Commonwealth"—*Essays*, 33, 474–77, 512–13), but Burke develops and makes more conservative what in Hume are only hints. Burke's emphasis on history, in his doctrine of prescription, is original; as Harvey C. Mansfield Jr. says, in the area of political philosophy "prescription is [Burke's] special discovery"—Introduction to *Selected Letters of Edmund Burke* (Chicago: Univ. of Chicago Press, 1984), 20. For an important discussion, see Paul Lucas, "On Edmund Burke's Doctrine of Prescription; or An Appeal from the New to the Old Lawyers," *The Historical Journal* 11 (1968): 35–63. See also H. T. Dickinson, *Liberty and Property: Political Ideology in Eighteenth-Century England* (New York: Holmes and Meier, 1977), 299–302; J. G. A. Pocock, *Politics, Language, and Time: Essays on Political Thought and History* (New York: Atheneum, 1971), 202–32; and Francis Canavan, *Edmund Burke: Prescription and Providence* (Durham: Carolina Academic Press, 1987). Of the many treatments of Hume and Smith, especially relevant in this context are Frederick Whelan, *Order and Artifice in Hume's Political Philosophy* (Princeton: Princeton Univ. Press, 1985); Sheldon Wolin, "Hume and Conservatism," in *Hume: A Re-evaluation*, ed. Donald W. Livingston and James T. King (New York: Fordham Univ. Press, 1976), 239–56; and Donald Winch, *Adam Smith's Politics: An Essay in Historiographic Revision* (Cambridge: Cambridge Univ. Press, 1978). For Adam Smith's discussion of patriotism, see especially *The Theory of Moral Sentiments* (1759; 6th ed. 1790), ed. D. D. Raphael and A. L. Macfie (Oxford: Clarendon Press, 1976; reprinted Indianapolis: Liberty Classics, 1982), 227–37 (pt. 6, sec. 2, ch. 2–3).

37.   See also Burke, *Regicide Peace* (First Letter), in *WSEB*, 9: 253: "Nation is a moral essence, not a geographical arrangement."

38.   It is typical of Burke to link unhappiness and "speculations" (*Reflections*, 124); as he notes, "The bulk of mankind . . . are not excessively curious concerning any theories, whilst they are really happy" (*Letter to the Sheriffs of Bristol*, in *Works*, 2: 31).

39.   Herzog, "Puzzling Through Burke," *Political Theory* 19 (1991): 346.

40.   For the ways Admiral Vernon was used in debates about patriotism in the 1740s, see Wilson, *Sense of the People*, 142–52, 160–62; for Southey's use of Nelson, Wellington, and Marlborough, see Eastwood, "Southey and the Meanings of Patriotism," 279–82, 286–87; and for the cult of George III, see Linda Colley, "The Apotheosis of George III: Loyalty, Royalty, and the British Nation, 1760–1820," *Past and Present* 102 (1984): 94–129. Burke's exclusion of military exploits is all the more notable in light of Thelwall's description of how the English are taught to love their country by way of tales of "glorious" English "butchery": "On the Prospective

Principle of Virtue (second lecture)," *Tribune,* vol. 1, in *Politics of English Jacobinism,* 107.

41. This objection recalls Burke's attacks on Warren Hastings' use of fear as the chief tool of government in India; see Frans De Bruyn, "Edmund Burke's Gothic Romance: The Portrayal of Warren Hastings in Burke's Writings and Speeches on India," *Criticism* 29 (1987): 415–38, esp. 433.

42. In *The Rights of Nature* (1796), one of his replies to Burke, John Thelwall contends that "separating the government from the nation" is not "a new-fangled Jacobinical artifice," as Burke and others claim, but rather a Burkean tactic; he adds that this separation is caused whenever "governments set up an interest opposite to that of the people" (*Politics of English Jacobinism,* 392 n). For an earlier debate about the relation of state to nation, see Wilson, *Sense of the People,* 278–80.

43. Wollstonecraft specifically criticizes Burke's appeal to personifications as a rhetorical means of heightening affections; she also argues that a government inspires affections in a people not through symbols, but through proper actions (see *Vindication of the Rights of Men,* 48, 17). See also Thelwall's "Report on the State of Popular Opinion," *Tribune,* vol. 2, in *Politics of English Jacobinism,* 236.

44. See Iain W. Hampsher-Monk, "Rhetoric and Opinion in the Politics of Edmund Burke," *History of Political Thought* 9 (1988): 474. Burke writes, "It must always have been discoverable by persons of reflection, but it is now obvious to the world, that a theory concerning government may become as much a cause of fanaticism as a *dogma* in religion" (*An Appeal from the New to the Old Whigs,* in *FR,* 182).

45. Catherine Macaulay points to this conflict in Burke, referring to his "entering into such contradictions, as at *one time* to represent the excellencies of the English constitution as *obvious* . . . and so sensibly felt by its subjects as *unanimously* to bind their affections . . . : and *at another, trembling* lest if the question of the abstract rights of men were brought before the eyes of the people, the most *dreadful* confusions might follow . . . ."—*Observations,* in *Political Writings of the 1790s,* 1: 135.

46. As David Bromwich puts it, "For Burke, the work of taste appears as a kind of *resumption*—a restoration . . . of an accustomed former continuity of moral sentiments"—*A Choice of Inheritance: Self and Community from Edmund Burke to Robert Frost* (Cambridge: Harvard Univ. Press, 1989), 67.

47. Catherine Macaulay notes that the "high colouring" of Burke's description of the Queen is "adapted . . . to *enslave* our affections"—*Observations,* in *Political Writings of the 1790s,* 1: 138.

48. In the 1790s, moreover, Burke presents monarchs in a milder light than before; he tends to reserve the language of the sublime for the Revolution. See Steven Blakemore, *Burke and the Fall of Language: The French Revolution as Linguistic Event* (Hanover: Univ. Press of New England for Brown Univ. Press, 1988), 61, 70–71. I am indebted generally to Blakemore in my comments on Burke's use of the sublime and the beautiful, but I cannot accept Blakemore's contentions that for

Burke "[t]ime mellows the sublime into the beautiful" and that this mellowing applies to institutions (61; see also 49, 64). Blakemore cites as evidence Burke's comment that in contrast to what we feel for our fathers, "we generally have a great love for our grandfathers, in whom this [parental] authority is removed a degree from us, and where the weakness of age mellows it into something of a feminine partiality" (*PE*, 111 [3.10]). But this passage seems not to hinge on time. The reduced power of a grandfather's authority depends not on the passage of time in any direct way, but on the interposition of a figure of more immediate authority (the father), and on the likely debility of the grandfather. Further, these considerations cannot apply to institutions, since Burke suggests neither that something interposes between us and them, nor that, as time passes, we treat them with less awe because they are weaker.

49. *The Correspondence of Edmund Burke,* gen. ed. Thomas W. Copeland, 10 vols. (Cambridge: Cambridge Univ. Press, 1958–78), 6: 90; to Philip Francis, 20 Feb. 1790. See also *Reflections,* 168.

50. The need for reverence toward the Queen helps explain why Burke, while showing her vulnerability and lack of power, does not emphasize her frailty to the extent we might expect from the treatise, which makes weakness a crucial dimension of female beauty. She does not "counterfeit weakness," which Burke had seen in the treatise as natural to and proper for women, but shows the strength to bear with "serene patience" (*PE,* 110 [3.9]; *Reflections,* 169). The description of the Queen as controlling her suffering, as "suffer[ing] well" (*Reflections,* 169), recalls less the treatise than it does the stoicism of Adam Smith's *Theory of Moral Sentiments:* "We reverence," says Smith, the "reserve" and "silent and majestic sorrow" of those who "exert that recollection and self-command which constitute the dignity of every passion" (*TMS,* 24 [1. 1. 5. 3]; for Smith's explanation of the psychology of these responses, see *TMS,* 21–22 [1. 1. 4. 7–8]).

51. This image of the lady in distress which Burke uses here is common to him; see De Bruyn, "Edmund Burke's Gothic Romance," and Linda M. G. Zerilli, "Text/ Woman as Spectacle: Edmund Burke's 'French Revolution,' *The Eighteenth Century: Theory and Interpretation* 33 (1992): 47–72.

52. Bromwich, *Politics By Other Means: Higher Education and Group Thinking* (New Haven: Yale Univ. Press, 1992), 147.

53. The best-known expression of this commonplace is in Pope's *Essay on Man* (4: 363–68). One reason why family plays a central role in this model is that it elides the problem of moving from self to others—although family is part of the private domain, it already involves more than one person, and thus moves toward the public.

54. In his analysis of how Burke construes our relationship to tradition, Stephen K. White refers to Burke's recognition of the difference between affections that are part of our "first nature" (such as those toward parents) and those that we choose and make our "second nature" (such as those toward a political inheritance). But White does not take note of how Burke's treatment of the growth of our national affections minimizes the role of choice (as I argue below), nor does he discuss the specific ways in which Burke thinks national affections are fostered. See "Burke on

Politics, Aesthetics, and the Dangers of Modernity," *Political Theory* 21 (1993): 507–27, esp. 518–19.

55. Wollstonecraft recognizes this Burkean argument, and argues that family affections are indeed dependent on proper actions on a parent's part (thus recalling earlier advocates of universal benevolence, such as Hutcheson—see Radcliffe, "Revolutionary Writing," 226). She draws the implications for national affections: "A government that acts in this [unjust] manner cannot be called a good parent, nor inspire natural (habitual is the proper word) affection . . ." (*Vindication of the Rights of Men,* 17).

56. "In his own life Burke was absorbed, one can truly say obsessed, with the idea of bequeathing an estate to a successor in the next generation, and to an illimitable posterity thereafter" (Bromwich, *Choice of Inheritance,* 52).

57. Burke uses this phrase in a speech that he never delivered, dated from May 1782; quoted in Pocock, *Politics, Language, and Time,* 226. In replying to Burke's sense of the nation, Thelwall writes that by *Britain* he does not mean some "mysterious, allegorical thing," but rather "the aggregate of British population," and adds, "That is my idea of a country, or a state" (*Rights of Nature,* in *Politics of English Jacobinism,* 403n).

58. Although Burke in a letter shifted some of the blame for this result to the monarchy itself, he remained consistent on the need for local connection: "To strengthen itself the Monarchy had weakend [*sic*] every other force: To unite the Nation to itself, it had dissolved all other ties. When the chain, which held the people to the Prince was once broken, the whole frame of the commonwealth was found in a State of disconnection" (*Correspondence,* 6: 242; to the Chevalier de la Bintinaye, March 1791).

59. As J. G. A. Pocock puts it in another context, Burke appeals to "ancient and venerable traditions, habits established so deeply in the past of mankind as to make them part of human nature itself"—Introduction to *Reflections on the Revolution in France,* ed. Pocock (Indianapolis: Hackett, 1987), xv. See also Bromwich, *Choice of Inheritance,* 45.

60. Shils, *Tradition* (Chicago: Univ. of Chicago Press, 1981), 327.

61. Pocock, Introduction to *Reflections,* xliv.

62. See also Wollstonecraft, *Vindication of the Rights of Men,* 22.

63. On the analogy of parties and friendship, and generally the relation between the private and the public in Burke, see Harvey C. Mansfield Jr., *Statesmanship and Party Government: A Study of Burke and Bolingbroke* (Chicago: Univ. of Chicago Press, 1965), 183–90.

64. I owe this point to David Bromwich.

65. Thelwall was to echo a theme of these attacks in relation to the French, noting that "one of the first misfortunes of France" was that leaders "formed themselves into factions, (parties as they are called here!). . . which have an inevitable tendency to produce a selfishness of character"—"On the Prospective Principle of Virtue (third lecture)," *Tribune,* vol. 1, in *Politics of English Jacobinism,* 120.

66. Hume, *A Treatise of Human Nature* (1739–40), ed. L. A. Selby-Bigge, 2nd ed. rev. P. H. Nidditch (Oxford: Oxford Univ. Press, 1978), 499 (bk. 3, pt. 2, sec. 2), 487 (3. 2. 2); see also 534 (3. 2. 7), 602 (3. 3. 3). For discussion of the relation between family and society in Hume, see Whelan, *Order and Artifice,* 220–21, 244–46; see also Whelan's comments generally on artificial virtues as distinguished from natural virtues. In sharply distinguishing between family affections and the foundations of society, Hume is making a stronger point than the more common argument, which is only that from the standpoint of impartial justice, family preferences may skew our judgments.

67. Mackintosh, *Vindiciae Gallicae* (1791; reprinted Oxford: Woodstock, 1989), 236.

68. *Memoirs of the Right Honourable Sir James Mackintosh,* ed. R. J. Mackintosh, 2nd ed., 2 vols. (London, 1836), 1: 116. For discussions of Burke's influence on Mackintosh's conversion and of the ways in which Mackintosh was taken as a representative figure, see Seamus Deane, *The French Revolution and Enlightenment in England, 1789–1832* (Cambridge: Harvard Univ. Press, 1988), 43–57.

69. See generally Cunningham, "Language of Patriotism"; Dinwiddy, "England"; and Newman, *Rise of English Nationalism,* 229–30. On how "nationalist sentiment was the agent . . . of class-conscious popular politics at mid-century," see Margot Finn, "'A Vent Which Has Conveyed Our Principles': English Radical Patriotism in the Aftermath of 1848," *Journal of Modern History* 64 (1992): 637–59. On the dominance in radical politics of appeals to constitutionalist reasoning, and how this dominance was partly a result of the defeat of British Jacobinism, see James A. Epstein, *Radical Expression: Political Language, Ritual, and Symbol in England, 1790–1850* (Oxford: Oxford Univ. Press, 1994), 3–28.

Writing Women into History:
Defining Gender and Citizenship in
Post-Revolutionary America

PETER C. MESSER

In March of 1805, as Mercy Otis Warren contemplated the preface to her *History of the Rise, Progress, and Termination of the American Revolution,* she found herself in the awkward position of having to defend her decision to write a history. Warren began by acknowledging that "there are certain appropriate duties assigned to each sex," and that the task of writing the history of wars was generally believed to be best suited to "the nervous style of manly eloquence." She persisted in her efforts, however, upon "recollecting that every domestic enjoyment depends on the unimpaired possession of civil and religious liberty, [and] that a concern for the welfare of society ought to glow in every human breast." What stands out in Warren's justification is not the connection she drew between history and the preservation of civil and religious liberty, a typical view of the role of history-writing in the eighteenth century, but her insertion of gender into her defense. Warren not only informed her readers that she was commenting on contemporary politics and culture, but that she was doing so as a woman.[1]

For the most part, historians have argued that the republican ideology surrounding the American Revolution discouraged women such as Warren from taking an active role in the debates over politics and culture that divided the new nation. Even the discourse of republican wives and mothers, these authors have argued, ultimately justified the exclusion of women from such discussions.[2] As Ruth Bloch has pointed out, however, "the increasing participation of early nineteenth-century women in the teaching profession, religious benevolent associations, and voluntary reform societies—activities that led directly to the early women's rights movement—suggest another side to the story."[3] In order to explore the "other side of the story" this paper approaches the question of gender in early America from a narrative, or storytelling perspective.[4] Instead of focusing primarily on how masculinity and femininity were perceived I will explore how the stories people told about their past reveal who could take on these characteristics and with what consequences for society. After independence, historians such as Warren began portraying women as having made significant contributions to the creation of the nation by entering into the masculine world of public affairs. As a result, these histories created a collective memory that encouraged readers to accept women taking an active role in public life, even while the gendered language of virtue discouraged them from doing so.

When compared to all of the changes that the American Revolution did not bring to women's lives—the vote, property ownership, or easier divorce to name three—the changes in how people wrote and remembered history may seem insignificant. Such an assumption, I believe, would be a mistake. Eighteenth-century historians envisioned their accounts of the Revolution as a means of promoting national unity and encouraging the development of those values which they saw as essential to the survival of the republic.[5] As a result, changes in the way these authors portrayed women acting in history, particularly in the history of the Revolution and the formation of the United States, would have signaled an attempt to change how people understood women's relationship to civil society. While these histories may not have caused the changes described by Bloch, they do illustrate the emergence of a way of thinking that both legitimated and encouraged new roles for women in the creation and maintenance of the republic. In most histories this transformation in women's roles appeared in their new-found ability to take on the masculine characteristics of a republican citizen—a prospect colonial authors had found unsettling at best. Mercy Warren, however, went even further. She challenged the traditional association of femininity with political incompetence and argued that it endowed women with an ability to perceive problems facing the republic that masculine eyes alone would miss.[6]

Women were not absent from the histories of America written prior to independence, but they appeared primarily as passive actors who were almost entirely devoid of any independent agency. In the descriptions of the founding and establishment of the New World communities women appeared primarily in the background. They inhabited a domestic world that was completely divorced from the political and economic spheres in which men determined the success or failure of the colonies. In Robert Beverley's *History and Present State of Virginia* (1709), for example, women arrived in the colony only when men "grew sensible of the Misfortune of wanting Wives," and after they had rejected native women as "Pagans, and for fear they shou'd conspire with those of their own Nation, to destroy their Husbands." In this account, women played no part in helping the men of Virginia secure their plantations beyond agreeing to go to the colony and presenting their prospective husbands with a "Certificate of their Modesty and good Behavior."[7] Although men realized that women were necessary for the survival of the colony, they saw their necessity as almost entirely biological. The importation of virtuous women would ensure that the planters begot legitimate heirs, but Beverley made no effort to connect this process to the establishment of a viable political or economic community in Virginia. They did bring a sense of security with them, but this arose primarily from their disengagement with public concerns. The wives imported from England, unlike Native American women, would *not* be drawn into the ongoing disputes between the Indians and the settlers and thus they would *not* contribute to the destruction of the colony. Beverley made no mention of the ability of English wives to make a contribution to the economy or to impart values or ideals to either the planters or their children that would independently contribute to the longevity or prosperity of Virginia society.[8]

Thomas Prince's *Chronological History of New England* (1736) offered a slightly different portrait of the women who accompanied their husbands to Plymouth Colony; however, they remained the passive observers of history and not its active creators. Prince described "Mrs. John Winthrop," for example, as "a desirable consort," who "cheerfully left her parents to serve the Lord Jesus with her husband in a terrible wilderness."[9] If Mrs. John Winthrop made any contribution to the decision to go to New England, or to her husband's activities once there, Prince made no mention of it. As a result, we are left with an image of a man acting as the founder of the colony, accompanied, but in no obvious way aided, by his wife, whose praiseworthiness rested entirely on her acceptance of her dependence on Jesus and her husband. Puritan theology may have emphasized the importance of family governance and partnership between husband and wife but these shared responsibilities did not extend beyond the walls of the household.[10] The world inhabited by women remained separate from the public debates that their husbands engaged in over the creation and maintenance of New England society.

Women, of course, did play an essential role in the establishment of the New World colonies, both as the helpmeets of their husbands and as the producers of goods and services that their families needed to survive.[11] The manner in which colonial historians acknowledged these contributions tended to minimize rather than celebrate their importance to the community. John Lawson, a surveyor employed by the proprietors of North Carolina and author of *A New Voyage to Carolina* (1714), lamented "that Colony might now have been in far better Condition than it is," but for the lack of industry among the men. Significantly, North Carolina remained in this underdeveloped state despite the best efforts of its women, whom the surveyor praised as "the most industrious Sex in that Place."[12] According to Lawson, women acting on their own, no matter how diligently, could not overcome masculine weakness, incompetence, or bad luck. Women, according to this portrait, suffered through history according to the actions of their male relations, and had little, if any, independent power to improve either their own lives or their communities.

Not surprisingly, in this context, colonial historians judged the entry of women into the masculine public world as a dangerous and ultimately destructive act. Daniel Neal, in his *History of New England* (1742), described Anne Hutchinson, one of the leaders of the dissident Antimonian movement, as a woman possessing a "bold and masculine spirit" whose actions subverted the good order of the colony.[13] Neal extended his criticisms to include not only Hutchinson but also the "Licentious women" who discussed her ideas with their husbands. In this account, women who took up and discussed religious questions, whether in public or in private, violated established gender roles and consequently threatened the stability of the community. Similarly, Thomas Prince argued that the Puritan migration from England to the colonies had it roots in "the rising power of the young queen [Henrietta Maria], a very zealous and active Papist, the extreme fondness of the king [Charles I] for her, and the persecuting spirit of bishop Laud under her."[14] The contrast between Henrietta Maria and Mrs. Winthrop is particularly telling. The young queen of England had zealously embraced the anti-Puritan crusade of Archbishop William Laud, imposing her will on both the nation and her husband. The wife of the Puritan leader was the antithesis of the queen, uninterested in public affairs and concerned only with obeying the wishes of her husband and Jesus. Comparing the roles these two women played in Prince's history suggests that he saw the exclusion, or voluntary withdrawal, of women from public life as one of the defining characteristics of New England—something that made it superior to a corrupt Old England.

The American Revolution forced authors to reconsider the stark divide they had created between the civic affairs of men and the domestic responsibilities of women. In the 1760s and early 1770s colonial resistance to British policies consisted primarily of attempts to curb colonial consumption of British goods. This strategy effectively politicized women's domestic responsibilities as the purchasers of imported goods and the coordinators of home manufacture.[15] Patriot authors, as a result, set about convincing Americans that the survival of their rights and liberties depended on encouraging women to take an interest in public affairs. Thomas Paine's "An Occasional Letter to the Female Sex," published in the *Pennsylvania Magazine,* condemned "that morose man, [who] while he imposes duties upon women, would deprive them of the sweets of public esteem, and in exacting virtues from them, would make it a crime to aspire to honour." In a striking reversal from the narrative offered by Prince and Neal, Paine chided all who would discourage women's aspirations for the "sweets of public esteem" and "honour." The "morose" men in America stood in marked contrast to those of more enlightened countries where "public honours have been paid to women. Art has erected [to] them monuments, Eloquence has celebrated their virtues, and History has collected whatever could adorn their characters."[16] Thus the maturity or legitimacy of New World society now depended on encouraging, rather than discouraging, women to take an interest in public affairs and celebrating the achievements of those who did.

As the struggle against Great Britain continued, Patriot authors proved increasingly willing to accord women the public role called for by Paine. The *United States Magazine,* for example, offered its readers a description of the "Paradise of Female Patriotism" to illustrate the important role women had played, and must continue to play, in the Revolution. The inhabitants of this garden included notables such as "Mrs. John and Samuel Adams" as well as "those unhappy maids that are yet, from the bias of connection, under wrong impressions of their country's cause" but who would gain admittance by future "virtuous deeds."[17] The last lines are the most indicative of a transformation in the representation of women's public roles. The "unhappy maids" described by this author would eventually come to understand their nation's political cause by overcoming the biases imparted to them by either their parents or husbands. The success of the Revolution, according to this author, depended in no small part on women entering the public world of revolutionary politics unencumbered by the beliefs of their husbands, fathers and brothers. Women, in this account, had the ability not only to understand and act on political questions, but also to do so on their own terms. While the author's reference to Mrs. John and Samuel Adams indicates that women still derived their identity from their male connections, this status no longer precluded their involvement or interest in the public affairs of the community.

The writings of Loyalist historians offer us an indication of the degree to which the Revolution encouraged its supporters to reconsider the public role of women. For these authors the participation of women in the Revolutionary movement became an indication of the absurdity of the Patriot cause. One proponent of such a view was Peter Oliver, a justice on the Supreme Court of Massachusetts Bay Colony. His personal and vitriolic account of the origins of the American Revolution used the Whigs' politicization of women and their domestic sphere to lampoon the revolutionaries. Oliver pointed out that the regulations the Sons of Liberty imposed on funerals had worked largely because they enabled "the Ladies . . . to exhibit their Share of Spite, & their Silk Gowns." Similarly, he described how as tarring and feathering became a common means of punishing suspected collaborators with the British "the fair Sex threw off their Delicacy, and adopted this new Fashion."[18] Women, in both of these examples, appeared to be far more concerned with fashion than with any political question. The "fair Sex" embraced the Patriot cause because it allowed them the opportunity to display their finery or participate in what they saw as fashionable activity. Consequently, according to Oliver, the colonists' cause rested on feminine whim as much as on reasoned argument, and was thus exposed to the world as the morally bankrupt movement he believed it to be.

While not as impassioned as Oliver's account, the histories written by other Loyalists reflected a similar point of view. As with the colonial accounts, women primarily appeared in the background of these histories as wives and mothers and emerged in the public world only to create unrest. One of the few women to appear in Alexander Hewatt's history of South Carolina and Georgia was an Indian, married to a white trader, who led a revolt of the Creek nation in South Carolina. Similarly, Samuel Peters argued that New Haven's "Blue Laws" threatened to subvert social order by allowing women to testify against their husbands. Anne Hutchinson did become a tragic figure in George Chalmers's *Introduction to the Causes of the American Revolt* (1781), but only because her fate revealed the hypocrisy of the Puritans, and their willingness to mimic "the popish clergy in the darkest ages." Thomas Hutchinson, in his *History of the Colony and Province of Massachusetts Bay* (1764) was not so kind to his great-great grandmother. His account of the Antimonian controversy echoed Neal's condemnation of "Mrs Hutchinson," whose "meeting of the sisters" proposed "doctrines and opinions which involved the colony in disputes and contentions" which "had like to have produced ruin in both church and state."[19]

In short, Loyalist historians shared their colonial counterparts' hesitancy to describe women as positive public agents in the formation of the colonial society. At best the appearance of women in public revealed their helplessness in a misguided male society. And at worst, it was a prime indicator of disordered communities and misplaced priorities. In contrast to at least some of their Whig counterparts, Oliver, and the other Loyalists, did not have to come to grips with an expanded role for women as a precondition for the success of their political agenda. Support for the Crown did not hinge on women's observance of boycotts, and to the extent that it required women to operate farms or businesses while husbands were away, it did so only as a result of the disruptive actions of the Patriots. In other words, Loyalist authors had no need to reconsider the role of women in public life in their histories and thus did not.

Among the Patriots, on the other hand, women's active participation in the struggle against Great Britain forced the supporters of American independence to reconsider how they saw women in both the present and the past.[20] A contributor to the *Pennsylvania Packet,* for example, argued that American women had made an invaluable contribution both to the Revolution and to the cause of women the world over:

> It is needless to repeat the encomiums that have already been given to the females for their exertions. Every whig mind must be sensible that they deserve the highest praise. Even those who are enemies to the cause must admit, that the means of serving it do honour to the sex. The women of every part of the globe are under obligations to those of America, for having shewn that females are capable of the highest political virtue. Those of posterity will also acknowledge that they deserve happiness and glory from them.[21]

The author's argument that women had demonstrated "political virtue" worthy of commemoration to posterity seems particularly important. Virtue, in the language of classical republicanism, was the civic-minded pursuit of the public good, an activity almost always the exclusive domain of men.[22] Now women were entering the public world and taking on masculine characteristics without threatening to undermine the good order of the state, as they had in the colonial and Loyalist accounts. On the contrary, women's willingness and ability to embrace these qualities had contributed to the success of the Revolution; hence they were worthy of emulation by other women, not only in America but also in "every part of the globe."

The histories of America that appeared following independence continued to develop and promote the image of women taking an active part in the public life of the new nation that had emerged during the Revolution. The most basic demonstration of this change in attitude from the colonial period appeared in historians' willingness to politicize family life. James Sullivan, in his *History of the District of Maine* (1795), argued that the ultimate viability of the republican experiment in the United States depended on properly founded families. "Where we find the public opinion well established in favour of the permanency of marriage compacts, and in favour of female chastity," he informed his readers, "there we find the bounds of civil government commensurately strong, and property well secured."[23] In this case we find that the viability of civil law and the security of private property dependent on permanent marriage and female chastity. In contrast to Beverley and Prince, Sullivan explicitly argued that the survival of the nation's political and economic institutions depended on Americans' willingness to create families. The roles of wife and mother took on an political dimension that transformed women into both the dutiful helpmeets of their husbands and the guardians of the republic. In short, Sullivan was articulating the ideals of republican wifery and motherhood in which the fair sex participated in the creation of the nation rather than simply observing that process as they had in earlier histories.[24]

When historians moved on to recounting the events of more recent times, women took on an even more active role in the founding and defense of the American nation. William Gordon's *The History of the Rise and Establishment of the Independence of the United States of America* (1788), for example, portrayed colonial resistance to Great Britain as a familial exercise in which all members of that venerable institution played a vital role:

> Handling the musket and training, are the fashionable amusements of the male inhabitants, while the females encourage them to proceed . . . Husbands and wives, parents and children, brothers and sisters, lovers, the young and the old, seem possessed of, or rather to be possessed by a martial spirit, and are fired with an enthusiastic zeal for liberty.[25]

The responsibility for defending the colonies' "liberty," in this account, did not fall exclusively on men, but instead on husbands, wives, sisters, and brothers, acting in concert, each fulfilling their assigned roles. As with the earlier account that had appeared in the *Pennsylvania Packet,* Gordon praised women for embracing masculine qualities, for becoming "possessed by a martial spirit" and "fired with an enthusiastic zeal for liberty." Both the military ardor and the political sensibility described by Gordon had long been attributed to men. Yet in his account of the Revolution it was only when women also embraced these virtues that America secured its independence. The founding of the nation, in other words, had depended on women embracing republican values usually reserved for men.

To be sure, as Ruth Bloch has pointed out, the histories also contained a considerable number of episodes in which women appeared as helpless virgins and vulnerable wives dependent on the vigorous actions of men to save and protect them.[26] Mercy Warren's description of the English invasion of

New Jersey in 1776, for example, recounted how the invaders had targeted helpless women and children:

> Many unfortunate fathers, in the stupor of their grief, beheld the misery of their female connections, without being able to relieve them, and heard the shrieks of infant innocence, subjected to the brutal lust of British grenadiers or *Hessian Yaughers*.[27]

When read in the context of the politicization of the family in the years following independence this episode offers more than an illustration of feminine helplessness. The British assault on the sanctity of both marriage and female chastity revealed first and foremost their inhumanity and hostility to the principles of republicanism. If the rule of law and the security of property hinged on the sanctity of marriage and female chastity, this account implied, the behavior of the royal army indicated that the King and Parliament respected neither. The story thus served to remind the readers of the stark divide that separated the two sides in the struggle for American independence and, ultimately, of the necessity of the Revolution.

Postwar historians' willingness to celebrate instances of women's vigorous defense of the Patriot cause suggests that neither atrocity stories in particular nor histories in general were intended to reinforce an ideal of female passivity. The works of William Gordon and David Ramsay, among others, reveal a clear shift in women's roles away from what Bloch describes as either mothers passively offering their children's lives to the cause or as assaulted virgins. Gordon noted that when "the American daughters of liberty in Philadelphia, were desirous of sharing with the gentlemen in the splendors of patriotism," they gathered donations in order to supply the Continental Army with food and clothing.[28] In this case, Gordon pointed out that women, acting on their own in order to "share in the splendors of patriotism," had made a vital contribution to the defense of the nation. Additionally, they had done so at a time when the nation's political leaders in Congress had been unable to supply the army, and taxpayers and merchants had proven unwilling to aid the Patriot cause. Such an account stands in stark contrast to that of John Lawson, who described the industrious women of North Carolina as powerless to overcome the difficulties created by masculine indolence, incompetence, or bad luck. Far from being trapped by the limitations of the male leaders of the Revolution the women of Philadelphia had taken matters into their own hands and made a vital contribution to the American struggle for independence.

An even more striking example of the agency that authors began to grant women appeared in David Ramsay's *History of the Revolution in South*

Carolina (1785). In his account of the disastrous effects on the Patriot cause of the 1781 British capture of Charleston, South Carolina, Ramsay reversed the traditional gender roles assigned to men and women:

> In the height of the British conquests, when poverty and ruin seemed the unavoidable portion of every adherent to the independence of America, the ladies in general discovered more firmness than the men. Many of them, like guardian Angels, preserved their husbands from falling in the hour of temptation, when interest and convenience had almost gotten the better of honour and patriotism.[29]

In this case the men were weak, easily swayed, concerned only with money and ease of living, characteristics earlier authors, notably Oliver, had associated with women. The "ladies," on the other hand, demonstrated firmness in support of independence and prevented their husbands from falling into temptation and being seduced into abandoning the Patriot cause. Far from appearing as the potential weak link in the America camp, the women of Charleston had proven, under considerable adversity, to be among the most virtuous republicans in America. Consequently, far from reinforcing an ideal of female passivity and dependence Ramsay's portrayal of women's active role in the Revolution offered a vision of women overcoming weak and corrupt men in order to promote the public good.

Audience reaction to these first histories of the United States indicates that some members of the reading public embraced their portrayals of women's active part in the war, and, implicitly, their potential contributions to the peace. One reviewer of Gordon's work remarked that "[o]n reading Gordon's *History to the American Revolution*, I was pleased to find that he has noticed the patriotic conduct of the American women, at a period when their virtuous exertions rendered essential services to their country." The reviewer went on to emphasize to readers that they should recall that "[o]n the commencement of actual war, the women of America manifested a firm resolution to contribute as much could depend on them, to the deliverance of their country."[30] The reviewer's praise of Gordon's inclusion of women in his history reveals that, for some, celebrating female participation in Revolution was vital to understanding its significance. When viewed in the context of history's didactic mission, this attitude suggests a growing belief that women had an important public role to play in the survival of the United States.

Another example of audiences embracing a larger role for women in the usually masculine public world appeared in a review of Hannah Adams's *A Summary History of New England* (1799). The reviewer in the *Monthly Magazine* began his appraisal of Adams's work by lauding the study of history "because its lessons are of indispensable use in teaching us our duty as citizens of a free state, as guardians of our own liberty and happiness." By beginning the review in this manner, the author immediately conceded that Adams was making a contribution to the ongoing public debate over the future of the republic. He went on to argue that her take on the republic's past was particularly important because it signaled the awakening of a political consciousness in a member of the female sex:

> It is surely no small addition to the credit which belongs to the present writer, to observe that she is a woman. So many causes beyond what are incident to the other sex, combine to divert female industry and ambition into frivolous or improper channels, that the same attainments are unspeakably more meritorious in a woman than in men.

While hardly an unqualified compliment, this sentiment reveals a clear belief that women should be encouraged to direct their industry and ambition into the affairs of politics usually reserved for men. The author reinforced this message by stressing that too often women were allowed to divert their energy into frivolous and improper channels because of their "rigorous exclusion from all political offices, and by that prejudice in the other sex which banishes political discussions from mixed circles." Adams's work, as a result, was particularly praiseworthy because it demonstrated both the possibility and desirability of collapsing these boundaries that needlessly, and dangerously, divided the masculine and feminine worlds, excluding the latter from the public life of the nation.[31]

The praise that these reviews extended to Gordon's illustrations of female patriotism and Adams's interest "in the sciences of policy and government" reveals a significant transformation in how some Americans viewed women in society. Unlike colonial and Loyalist authors, these writers saw women's entry into the masculine world of public affairs, as observers and discussants if not full participants, as an indication of social stability rather than impending chaos. While not all readers would have shared these views, the efforts of both the historians and the reviewers to incorporate them into the founding myth of the nation suggest an increasingly receptive audience. The simple fact that between 1785 and 1799 both authors and reviewers saw an expanded role for women as a necessary element of the histories that they envisioned guiding the nation's future development implies a growing acceptance of female activism in the public interest. In other words, accounts of politically active and informed women making a positive contribution to the political life of the nation were being both promoted and accepted as vital to understanding the origins of the American republic, and by extension, how to ensure its future survival.

The potential for a serious rethinking of the role of women in American society inherent in these new histories appears most clearly in the writings of Mercy Warren. In her *History of the Rise, Progress, and Termination of the*

American Revolution (1805) Warren challenged the idea that femininity was incompatible with participation in the public life of the nation. While Ramsay, Gordon and the various reviewers had all included women in their histories of the Revolution, they remained deeply skeptical of femininity. In their accounts, women had contributed to the cause of independence and could help maintain the republic by renouncing their feminine characteristics in favor of masculine republican virtues. Warren, on the other hand, rejected their implicit argument that femininity somehow disqualified women from either understanding or participating in public life. Instead, she argued that it offered a uniquely valuable perspective on contemporary affairs.

In her private correspondence, Warren made it clear that she observed no innate difference between men and women in their ability to understand or comment on politics. In a letter to John Adams, for example, she reminded her correspondent first of his own insincerity, then her own ability, before offering the political advice he had jokingly sought from her:

> Your asking my opinion on so momentous a point as the form of government which ought to be preferred by a people, about to shake off the fetters of monarchic and aristocratic tyranny may be designed to ridicule the sex for paying any attention to political matters. Yet I shall venture to give you a serious reply.[32]

Warren clearly resented Adams's implication that her "sex" automatically disqualified her from any serious consideration of "political matters." Her decision to offer her ideas about the form of government Americans should establish despite his mockery was designed to disabuse Adams of this notion. Despite her persistent belief in her ability to participate in affairs of state, however, Warren never advocated that women entirely abandon the domestic sphere in favor of the public arena of politics. Women, according to Warren, needed to strike a balance between public and private that preserved many aspects of their traditional responsibilities as wives and mothers. She emphasized these sentiments in a letter to "A very young lady," whom she advised to "by no means acknowledge such an inferiority as would check the ardour of our endeavors, to equal in all mental accomplishments, the most masculine heights"; yet she further urged her to ponder "how miserable must that woman be, who, at the same time she has both genius and taste for literary enquiry, cannot cheerfully leave the pursuit to attend to the daily cares of the prudent house-wife."[33]

Warren's reluctance to call on women to renounce their traditional roles undoubtedly reflected her own willingness to abide by established gender conventions and what Rosemarie Zagarri has described as the lack of "an ideology of feminism."[34] Warren's attempt to combine her fervent interest in politics with the realities of the life of an eighteenth-century woman, however, led her to create a new political language in which femininity enabled, rather than inhibited, women's participation in the public life of the nation. In a letter to Catherine Macaulay, for example, Warren attacked the idea that the feminine world was incompatible with understanding public affairs:

> When the observations are just and honorary to the heart and character, I think it very immaterial whether they flow from female lips in the soft whispers of private friendship or whether thundered in the Senate in the bolder language of the other sex.[35]

Warren's argument began by affirming that men and women operated in different worlds, the former in "the soft whispers of private friendship" the latter in the public forum of the Senate. From this starting point she then denied that these different circumstances prevented either sex from developing an equal understanding of political issues. Women she insisted did not need to aspire to manly republican virtues in order to make a contribution to society because they already possessed the necessary qualities to participate in public life.

Warren used her history to illustrate the sentiments she expressed in her letter to Macaulay. Rather than seeking to minimize either her femininity or that of her heroines, she chose to accentuate it, and, in the process, reveal how it allowed women to make valuable contributions to the public good. The women whom Warren held up for praise in her history, unlike her male counterparts, were noteworthy for their ability to blend their femininity with an ardent support for the American cause. In recounting the siege of Charleston, Warren praised the "ladies" of the city for providing examples of "feminine fortitude" during the British occupation by secluding "themselves from the gaieties of the city . . . while with a charitable hand, they visited and soothed, whenever possible, the miserable victims crowded on board prison ships, and thrust into jails."[36] Unlike Ramsay, Warren did not juxtapose effeminate men with virtuous women in order to praise the latter. On the contrary, the women of Charleston retained their feminine characteristics and used these as an effective means to resist the British occupation.

A more complete insertion of feminine qualities into the masculine world of politics and governance, and an indication that Warren could conceive of women as more than just republican wives even if she never aspired for such a role herself, appeared in her treatment of Catherine the Great of Russia. The example is particularly telling because, unlike other European rulers, the Czarina did not rush to aid the Americans. Warren, nonetheless, held her up as a model of a strong and competent ruler, despite the empress's tepid reaction to the Revolution: "Determined to maintain her independent dignity, and hold the neutral position she had chosen . . . she concluded the business with the policy of the statesman, the address of her sex, and the superiority of the empress Catherine."[37] Warren's praise was carefully calculated to draw the reader's attention to the virtues of this powerful, independent, female monarch. From Warren's perspective, unlike the authors of the account of the "Paradise of Female Patriotism," the stand that the empress took on the American Revolution was of decidedly secondary importance to her ability to effectively govern a state. Catherine successfully combined the "policy of a statesman" with the "address of her sex" in order to advance the best interests of her nation. The Czarina's femininity, far from hindering her ability to play the roles of the statesman, actually infused her decisions with an added dimension that defined "the superiority of the empress Catherine."[38]

While Warren may never have called on women to embrace such overtly political roles as Catherine the Great's, she did insist that their femininity was consistent with an interest in, and ability to comment on, political and cultural issues. She began her history by noting, in terms similar to those with which she addressed Catherine Macaulay, that it was produced by "a mind that had not yet yielded to the assertion, that all political attentions lay out of the road of female life."[39] Warren's words made it clear that she was capable of understanding political concerns, that she did not have to renounce her femininity in order to do so—it already being within the "road of female life."

Very carefully, almost demurely, Warren transformed this defense of her innate abilities into an argument that her feminine perspective made her history particularly useful and insightful. She introduced this theme by way of an apology for her occasional digressions from a strict recounting of the political and military conflicts of the Revolution:

> Observations on the moral conduct of man, on religious opinion or persecutions, and the motives by which mankind are actuated in their various pursuits, will not be censured when occasionally introduced. They are more congenial to the taste, inclination, and sex of the writer, than a detail of the rough and terrific scenes of war. Nor will a serious or philosophic mind be displeased with such an interlude, which may serve as a temporary resting-post to the weary traveler, who has trodden over the field of carnage, until the soul is sickened by a view of the absurdity and cruelty of his own species.[40]

Warren began by apologizing for her comments on the moral nature of man, explaining them as a natural product of her sex. Her apology, however, quickly became a commentary on the interests and actions of the other sex. The moral reflection produced by the tastes and inclination of the female mind, she argued, was of greater value to a serious or philosophic mind than "the rough and terrific scenes of war" that were the natural product of men writing history. Such accounts, she stated, only left the reader sickened by "the absurdity and cruelty of his own species." Her reflections on "the moral conduct of man," on the other hand, would "prepare a rational agent for some higher stage of existence, when the drama on this tragic theatre is finished."[41] Traditional masculine history, in other words, only led readers to despair, where a history penned from a feminine perspective prepared the reader for the coming of a republican millennium. Far from being an impediment, Warren's femininity, in her mind, better enabled her to understand the issues facing the new nation and to formulate solutions to its problems.

Warren's take on history was not universally applauded. While her literary agent assured her that it "would meet with a favorable reception from a large part of the community," others disagreed.[42] The one published review of Warren's history conceded that it "will be read with pleasure by those, who can be satisfied without entering into the minutiae of cruelty and carnage; and the devout mind will be gratified by the author's repeated acknowledgment of God, and its frequent interpositions in our favour." The reviewer, however, went on to question much of what Warren had included in her history, with particular reference to those elements of the text that revealed the gender of its author. The "narratives (and those rather copious) of transactions which had no connection with the revolution" that Warren had seen as the natural inclination of the female sex, he argued, were one of the history's greatest shortcomings. Similarly, the reviewer criticized the work because "a freedom is used in some instances which a gentleman would not, perhaps, have thought prudent." Ultimately, he concluded, by advising Warren that "we all have our appropriate duties," even "'aged women' have a sphere of usefulness," but that she should consult the gospel of Paul to remind herself of "the duty of women generally."[43] Clearly, some members of the reading public rejected Warren's claim both that she had a duty to enter public discussions of politics and that her feminine qualities made her particularly capable of doing so.

Warren may have had the last laugh in the debate over women's roles in the public life of the new republic. After all, even as the discourse of republicanism and republican virtues evolved to emphasize women's domestic qualities and highlight their inability to operate as rational agents in the public sphere a new wave of female activism was building. As previously mentioned, the nineteenth century witnessed the growing presence of women in debates over slavery, temperance, health and educational reform and saw many take on new careers outside of the home as teachers. Additionally, women played prominent roles in the waves of religious revivals that swept through the nation in the early nineteenth century. These movements used the unique feminine qualities associated with women to legitimate their participation in the ongoing debate over the future of the nation, and ultimately led to the formation of the first women's rights movement. In all of these cases, both the female activists and those who responded to their agitation clearly embraced the image of women concerned with the moral and political health of the nation introduced by the American Revolution and celebrated in the histories of that struggle. While not all Americans accepted these new assertive roles for women, both their persistence and influence point to a growing belief that gender did not preclude participation in the public life of the American republic.

Neither the Revolution nor the histories commemorating it can alone account for the increase in women's political and social activism in the nineteenth century.[44] At the same time, however, it would be a mistake to ignore their potential role. As anthropologists, historiographers and literary critics have all pointed out, human action is in some ways defined and limited by the stories a society tells about itself.[45] Thus, by introducing a new series of stories about the roles of women in public life, the American Revolution altered how people understood their world. By including these new stories in their histories commemorating and celebrating the war, historians effectively institutionalized the image of women taking an active interest in public affairs in the collective memory of the nation. As a result, I would suggest, it became easier for some women and men to challenge the nineteenth-century ideal of female passivity because a narrative, or system of didactic stories, existed within the popular discourse that legitimated such challenges. Thus Mercy Warren's feminine perspective on history and Ramsay's and Gordon's republican heroines helped provide a foundation for future change by making women's active participation in the creation and maintenance of the republic a vital part of its history.

NOTES

The author would like to thank Philip Gould and Toby Ditz, both of whom commented on earlier drafts of this essay. It is much better as a result of their thoughtful suggestions.

1. Mercy Otis Warren, *History of the Rise, Progress, and Termination of the American Revolution* (Boston: Manning and Lorring, 1805) 1: iv.

2. Caroll Smith-Rosenberg, "Dis-Covering the Subject of the 'Great Constitutional Discussion,' 1786–1789," *Journal of American History* 79 (1992): 841–73;

Lawrence J. Friedman, *Inventors of the Promised Land* (New York: Alfred A. Knopf, 1975); Ruth Bloch, "The Gendered Meanings of Virtue in Revolutionary America," *Signs* 13 (1987): 37–59; Jan Lewis, "The Republican Wife: Virtue and Seduction in the Early Republic" *William and Mary Quarterly,* 3d ser., 44 (1987): 689–721; Linda Kerber, *Women of the Republic: Intellect and Ideology in Revolutionary America* (Chapel Hill: Univ. of North Carolina Press, 1980).

3. Similarly, other scholars have described how women changed the way they viewed themselves in society, becoming more assertive of their own interests and less deferential to traditional stereotypes. Joy Day Buel and Richard Buel in *The Way of Duty: A Woman and Her Family in Revolutionary America* (New York: W.W. Norton, 1984); Laura Thatcher Ulrich, *A Midwives Tale: The Life of Martha Ballard Based on Her Diary, 1785–1812* (New York: Alfred A. Knopf, 1990); Nancy F. Cott, "Passionlessness: An Interpretation of Victorian Sexual Ideology, 1790–1850," *Signs* 4 (1978): 219–36; Cathy N. Davidson, *Revolution and the Word: The Rise of the Novel in America* (New York: Oxford Univ. Press, 1986).

4. A discussion of the linguistic or rhetorical approach to the image of women in Revolutionary ideology appears in Smith-Rosenberg, "Dis-Covering the Subject," and Kerber, "Forum: Beyond Roles, Beyond Spheres: Thinking About Gender in the Early Republic," *William and Mary Quarterly*, 3d ser., 46 (1989): 565–58.

5. For a general discussion of how a nation forms around the imagined bonds among otherwise disparate populations see, Benedict Anderson, *Imagined Communities: Reflections on the Origin and Spread of Nationalism* (New York: Verso, 1991). A considerable historiography exists on the use of history, in particular, to promote nationalism and the political agendas in the period following the Revolution, including Ralph N. Miller, "American Nationalism as a Theory of Nature," *William and Mary Quarterly,* 3d ser., 12 (1955): 74–95; Sidney Kaplan, "The History of New Hampshire: Jeremy Belknap as Literary Craftsman," *William and Mary Quarterly,* 3d ser., 21 (1964): 18–39; William Raymond Smith, *History as Argument: Three Patriot Historians of the American Revolution* (The Hague: Mouton, 1966); Arthur Shaffer, *The Politics of History: Writing the History of the American Revolution, 1783–1815* (Chicago: Precedent Publishing, 1975); Charles E. Modlin, "The Loyalists Reply," in *American Literature 1764–1789; The Revolutionary Years*, ed. Everett Emerson (Madison: Univ. of Wisconsin Press, 1977), 59–71, and Cecilia Tichi, "Worried Celebrants of the American Revolution," in the same volume, 275–91; Lester Cohen, *The Revolutionary Histories: Contemporary Narratives of the American Revolution* (Ithaca: Cornell Univ. Press, 1980).

6. Contemporary anthropology, communication theory and historiography, have come to similar conclusions concerning the importance of history as a guide to establishing the boundaries of acceptable behavior and influencing who is allowed to participate in civil society. See for example, S.N. Eisenstadt, "Some Observations of the Dynamics of Traditions," *Comparative Studies in Society and History* 11 (1969): 451–75; Eisenstadt, "Post-Traditional Societies and the Continuity and Reconstruction of Tradition," *Daedalus* 102 (1973): 1–27. Walter Fisher, *Human Communication as Narration: Toward a Philosophy of Reason Value, and Action*

(Columbia: Univ. of South Carolina Press, 1987); Edward Shils, "Tradition," *Comparative Studies in Society and History* 13 (1971): 129; Hayden White, *Metahistory: The Historical Imagination in Nineteenth-Century Europe* (Baltimore: The Johns Hopkins Univ. Press, 1973).

7. Robert Beverley, *History and Present State of Virginia* (1705), ed. Louis B. Wright (Chapel Hill: Univ. of North Carolina Press, 1947), 286–87.

8. Of course the image of white women in Virginia as passive and uninvolved in no way corresponded to the reality of the situation. If anything, Beverley's account represented an attempt to create an ideal past that would impose order on the disorderly women of the present. For a discussion of the prominent and controversial role women played in early Virginia see Edmund Morgan, *American Slavery, American Freedom: The Ordeal of Colonial Virginia* (New York: W.W. Norton, 1976); Kathleen Mary Brown, *Good Wives, Nasty Wenches and Anxious Patriarchs: Gender, Race, and Power in Colonial Virginia* (Chapel Hill: Univ. of North Carolina Press, 1996).

9. Thomas Prince, *Chronological History of New England* (1736; reprint, London: Cummings, Hilliard, and Co., 1826), 376.

10. Edmund S. Morgan, *The Puritan Family: Religion and Domestic Relations in Seventeenth-Century New England* (New York: Harper and Row, 1944).

11. For a discussion of the complicated and important roles women played in colonial society see Laura Thatcher Ulrich, *Good Wives: Image and Reality in the Lives of Women in Northern New England, 1650–1750* (New York: Oxford Univ. Press, 1980).

12. John Lawson, "A New Voyage to Carolina" (1714), in *Lawson's History of North Carolina,* ed. Francis Latham Harriss (Richmond: Garrett and Massie, 1937), 85.

13. Daniel Neal, *The History of New England*, 2nd ed. (London: A. Ward, 1742), 1: 183.

14. Prince, *Chronological History,* 422.

15. Kerber, *Women of the Republic,* 37–41.

16. "An Occasional Letter to the Female Sex," *Pennsylvania Magazine* 1 (1775): 364.

17. *United States Magazine,* 1 (1779): 122–24.

18. Peter Oliver, "The Origin and Progress of the American Rebellion," in *Peter Oliver's Origin and Progress of the American Rebellion,* ed. James Adair and Douglas Shutz (Stanford: Stanford Univ. Press, 1961), 97–98.

19. Alexander Hewatt, *Rise and Progress of the Colonies of South Carolina and Georgia* (1779; reprint, Spartansburg: The Reprint Company, 1971), 2: 152–65. Samuel Peters, *A General History of Connecticut,* 2nd ed. (London, 1782), 197–99. George Chalmers, *An Introduction to the History of the Revolt of the American Colonies* (1845; reprint, New York: Arno Press, 1972), 1: 54. Thomas Hutchinson, *History of the Colony and Province of Massachusetts Bay* (1764), ed. Lawrence Shaw Mayo (Cambridge: Harvard Univ. Press, 1936), 1: 50. In one of the few appearances by a woman in William Smith Jr.'s *History of the Province of New York,* the wife of governor William Cosby "clandestinely brought about" the marriage of

her daughter to Lord Augustus Fitzroy while "on his travels through the colonies." William Smith, Jr., *The History of the Province of New York* (1826), ed. Michael Kammen (Cambridge: The Belknap Press, 1972), 2: 23.

20. For a discussion of women's participation and leadership in riots to protest food prices and shortages see Barbara Clark Smith, "Food Rioters and the American Revolution," *William and Mary Quarterly,* 3d ser., 51 (1994): 3–38; for a general discussion in the ways in which women participated in the resistance to Great Britain see Alfred E. Young, "The Women of Boston: 'Persons of Consequence' in the Making of the American Revolution, 1765–1776," in *Women and Politics in the Age of Democratic Revolution,* ed. Harriet B. Applewhite and Darlene G. Levy (Ann Arbor: Univ. of Michigan Press, 1990), 181–226.

21. *Pennsylvania Packet,* November 4, 1780.

22. Bloch, "The Gendered Meanings of Virtue," 18.

23. James Sullivan, *History of the District of Maine* (Boston: I. Thomas and E.T. Andrews, 1795), 90.

24. Lewis, "Republican Wife"; Kerber, *Women of the Republic.*

25. William Gordon, *The History of the Rise and Establishment of the Independence of the United States of America* (London: Charles Dilly, 1788), 2: 380–81.

26. Bloch, "The Gendered Meanings of Virtue," 49.

27. Warren, *History of the Rise,* 1: 352.

28. Gordon, *History of the Rise and Establishment,* 3: 377.

29. David Ramsay, *History of the Revolution in South Carolina, From a British Province to an Independent State* (Trenton: Isaac Collins, 1785), 2: 124.

30. Supplement to volume three of the *Columbian Magazine or Monthly Miscellany* (1791): 759.

31. *Monthly Magazine and American Review* 1 (1799): 446–47.

32. Warren to John Adams, March 1776, in the Mercy Warren Papers in the Massachusetts Historical Society; hereafter MWP. Warren expressed similar sentiments on numerous occasions, suggesting her surprise to Hannah Lincoln that "any gentleman of you acquaintance should caution you not to entertain any particular subject when we should meet" and in another letter asking "as every domestic enjoyment depends on the decisions of the mighty contest, who can be an unconcerned and silent spectator?" Warren to Hannah Lincoln 12 June 1774, and to Lincoln 3 Sept. 1774, MWP.

33. Warren to "A very young lady," undated, Mercy Warren Letter Book, hereafter MWLB, in MWP.

34. Rosemarie Zagarri, *A Woman's Dilemma: Mercy Otis Warren and the American Revolution* (Wheeling: Harlan Davidson, 1995), xvii.

35. Warren to Catherine Macaulay, December 20, 1774, MWLB, in MWP.

36. Warren, *History of the Rise,* 2: 347–348.

37. Ibid., 2: 310–12.

38. Ibid., 2: 303.

39. Ibid., 1: iv.

40. Ibid., 2: 225.

41. Ibid., 2: 226.

42. James Freeman to Warren, 22 Feb. 1803, in MWP. On Freeman's role as Warren's agent see Lester Cohen, introduction to *History of the Rise, Progress and Termination of the American Revolution*, by Mercy Otis Warren (Indianapolis: The Liberty Fund, 1990), 1: xxvi.

43. *The Panoplist*, 2 (1807): 429–32.

44. Rosemarie Zagarri has suggested that women had begun to cultivate a more active role for themselves as republican wives and mothers well before the outbreak of the Revolution. Zagarri, *A Woman's Dilemma*, 28.

45. Michel Foucault, "Nietzsche, Genealogy, History," *Language, Counter-memory, Practice*, ed. Donald F. Bouchard (Ithaca: Cornell Univ. Press, 1977), 139–64, argues that one purpose of history is to define and place limits on what actions society will accept. Likewise, Clifford Geertz, "Ideology as a Cultural System," *The Interpretation of Cultures* (New York: Basic Books, 1973), 193–233, argues that the success of any effort at social change depends on the degree to which it fits within a person's comprehension of "the universe of civic rights and responsibilities in which one finds oneself located." Literary theorists such as Hans Robert Jauss (see his "Literary History as a Challenge to Literary Theory," *New Literary History* 2 [1970]: 7–37) have also argued that the reader's understanding of a text hinges on it conforming to his or her "horizons of expectations," suggesting readers will only accept arguments that are presented in recognizable surroundings. Thus, as with Geertz, before people can accept an argument or a series of actions they must first recognize them as legitimate.

Vitalizing Nature and Naturalizing the Humanities in the Late Eighteenth Century

PETER HANNS REILL

In 1946 Max Horkheimer claimed in an essay that "the collapse of a large part of the intellectual foundation of our civilization is to a certain extent the result of technical and scientific progress."[1] Horkheimer located the origins of this demise—whose process he characterized as "the self-destructive tendency of Reason"—in the Enlightenment. This line of analysis, further elaborated by Horkheimer and Adorno in the *Dialectic of the Enlightenment*, was later expanded and amplified by many commentators: post-modernists who rebel against the so-called "hegemony of enlightenment rationality," and analyze the knowledge/power dyad that gave rise to the intrusive, all controlling pan-opticon of modern social control: some feminists who decry the Enlightenment's supposed elevation of universality over distinctness, and "converted" philosophers of science, such as Stephen Toulmin, who seek to uncover Modernity's dangerous and outmoded hidden agenda by searching out the political and social forces that led to its inception.[2] Despite the vast differences separating these critics and the multiple tones of major and minor they sound, the indictment is clear. The Enlightenment in its fascination with science and universalizing reason sired such movements as gender and racial discrimination, colonialism, and totalitarianism. Naomi Schor in a recent article summarizes this critique, though in a radical manner.[3] She sees the Enlightenment as a crucial episode in the forging of the discourse of universality and scientism, with its "dangerous tendency to slide from assertions of universal kinship to increasingly lethal forms of totalitarianism ranging from the Spanish inquisition to the gulags and genocidal massacres of our own blood-soaked century."[4]

These are strong words. For students of the Enlightenment there seems to be a radical breech between what is meant by the central signifiers in this critique and what we perceive. Clearly, the major focus in these attacks is the Enlightenment's supposed worship of science, reason, and universality, of a form of power/knowledge, that is invariably characterized in the singular. And we all know what that singular suggests: the triumph in and by the Enlightenment of a mathematically based science, founded upon certain essential presuppositions concerning matter, method and explanation whose reign has lasted until today. Stephen Toulmin characterized this macrohistorical movement as follows:

> In choosing the goals of Modernity an intellectual and practical agenda that . . . focused on the 17th-century pursuit of mathematical exactitude and logical rigor, intellectual certainty and moral purity, Europe set itself on a cultural and political road that has led both to its most striking technical successes and to its deepest human failures.[5]

Yet when one begins to query what was really implied beneath this all-powerful engine of cultural and social change, the picture becomes much more hazy, complicating and confusing the new master narratives that are now being forged and opening, I believe, fascinating alternatives to evaluate what is often called the Enlightenment project.

This is certainly true for the manner in which nature was interpreted in the Enlightenment and how those interpretations were deployed in discourses dealing with human activities. Recently historians of eighteenth-century science have begun to question the assumption that the natural philosophy of the period can be reduced to mathematical mechanism.[6] It is usually conceded that during the first half of the Enlightenment, roughly from the late 1680s to the 1740s this form of science, usually called Newtonianism, became dominant. During that period, the central project of natural philosophy had been to incorporate the methods and assumptions of formal mathematical reasoning into explanations for natural phenomena. Its overriding impulse was to transform contingent knowledge into certain truth, to reduce the manifold appearances of nature to simple principles. In this process leading proponents of the mechanical philosophy of nature proposed a new definition of matter, established methodological and explanatory procedures to incorporate this definition into a viable vision of science, and evolved an epistemology that authorized these procedures. Matter's essence was streamlined and simplified: it was defined as homogeneous, extended, hard, impenetrable, movable, and inert. The result, in Horkheimer's words, was that "Nature lost every vestige of vital independent existence, all value of its own. It became dead matter—a heap of things."[7]

By the middle of the eighteenth century, however, some of the core assumptions of this new language of nature were no longer considered satisfying or self-evident. For many younger intellectuals mechanism's very success made it suspect, for, as Margaret Jacob and Aram Vartanian have shown, the brave new world of seventeenth-century mechanism was very easily adapted to serve as a support for political absolutism, religious orthodoxy and established social hierarchies.[8] Joined to that was an increasing crises of assent, expressed in a wave of mid-century skepticism directed against the spirit of systems, against a one sided reliance upon abstract reasoning in constructing a coherent picture of reality. For leading thinkers of the late Enlightenment, deductive philosophy was deemed incapable of accounting for nature's vast variety. Hume announced this theme in the opening paragraph of his essay on "the skeptic."

> There is one mistake, to which philosophers seem liable, almost without exception; they confine too much their principles, and make no account of that vast variety, which nature has so much affected in all her operations. When a philosopher has once laid hold of a favorite principle, which perhaps accounts for many natural effects, he extends the same principle over the whole creation, and reduces to it every phenomenon, though by the most violent and absurd reasoning. Our own mind being narrow and contracted, we cannot extend our conception to the variety and extent of nature; but imagine, that she is as much bounded in her operations, as we are in our speculation.[9]

Hume's skeptical analysis of causation was but one instance, though perhaps the most radical, of the re-evaluation of mechanical natural philosophy. Buffon's attack upon the introduction of mathematical principles into the core of natural philosophical reasoning was probably more typical. In the introduction to the *Histoire naturelle*, Buffon drew a distinction between abstract and physical truths. The first were imaginary products of human invention. The second were real: they existed in nature and were the object of human inquiry. Mathematical proofs belonged to the first category, which were founded upon arbitrarily accepted logical principles. These, in turn, were used to generate equally arbitrary, though more complex principles. All were joined by a method of definition whereby consistency was maintained by rigorously excluding anything that did not agree with the first abstract principle. Physical truths, in contradistinction, were based on things that have actually occurred. They were more than mere constructs of human reason, forever open to manipulation. "They do not stand in our power."[10] In order to understand physical truths, the researcher had to compare and observe similar sets of past occurrences. Science, according to this view, was the description and understanding of real things that have taken place in the world. For both Buffon and Hume, understanding connections in nature was based upon repeated historical observations of succession. In Hume's definition, cause "is *an object, followed by another, and where all the objects, similar to the first, are followed by objects of the second.*"[11] In late eighteenth-century terms, the new science was to be a science of facts, observation and controlled inference.

The mid-eighteenth-century skeptical critique of hypothetical thinking elevated the contingent over the coherent. It became a commonplace that all human knowledge was extremely constricted, both because of its reliance upon sense impressions and its limited scope. If humans were endowed with reason, its power to pierce the veil of the unknown was greatly circumscribed. At the same time, many late Enlightenment thinkers surrendered the idea that nature's operations could be comprehended under the rubric of a few simple, all encompassing laws. Variety and similarity replaced uniformity and identity as the terms most associated with nature's products. Hume made this clear in his *Enquiry Concerning Human Understanding* where he denied all concepts of inherent identities. What is identical appears so only because we have been accustomed by habit to consider them so. "But there is nothing in a number of instances, different from every single instance, which is supposed to be exactly similar; except only, that after a repetition of similar instances, the mind is carried by habit, upon the appearance of one event, to expect its usual attendant, and to believe, that it will exist."[12] Nature not only was seen as complex, it also was considered to be in continuous movement. As an anonymous author stated, "the world is a theater of continual revolutions,"[13] in which old forms of existence are replaced by new ones. In short, nature had a history. This triple movement—the limiting of reason's competence, which produced a wide ranging epistemological modesty; the expansion of nature's complexity; and the historicization of nature—set a new agenda for late Enlightenment natural philosophers. To paraphrase Hume, they were required to rethink the meaning of the terms *"power, force, energy* and *connexion."*[14]

Generally, one can discern two broad late eighteenth-century strategies designed to satisfy the objections raised by the skeptical critique of reductive rationalism and uniformity. The first, and best known, was formulated by neo-mechanists such as D'Alembert, La Grange, La Place and Condorcet, and usually guided by the physical sciences. Though retaining the mechanists' definition of matter as inert, they limited mathematics' role in describing nature to an instrument of discovery instead of considering it a model of reality. In so doing, they put aside those debates concerning the ultimate composition of matter (was it made up of atoms, monads, or immaterial points[15]) or the definition of force (the *vis viva* controversy)[16] that had animated early eighteenth-century thinkers. Rather, they developed the mathematics of probability as the surest guide to direct observational reason, while maintaining an epistemological modesty concerning the truth claims of these activities.

The second response to the skeptical critique was proposed by a loose group of thinkers, less frequently studied, though extremely numerous, whom I call, for want of a better term, Enlightenment vitalists. Their inquiries usually centered on the fields of chemistry, geology, the life sciences and natural history. Unlike the neo-mechanists, they sought to reformulate the concept of matter, along with those of force, power and connection in their construction of a science that respected natural variety, dynamic change, and the epistemological consequences of skepticism.

For the vitalists, the basic failure of mechanism was its inability to account for the existence of living matter. Mechanists had posited a radical separation between mind and matter that only the intervention of God could heal, either as the universal occasion for all phenomena or as the creator of a preestablished harmony between mind and matter. This mind/body dichotomy was, according to Stephen Toulmin, the "chief girder in this framework of Modernity, to which all the other parts were connected."[17] Enlightenment vitalists sought to dissolve this dichotomy, to dismantle modernity's girder, by positing the existence in living matter of active or self-activating forces, which had a teleological character. Living matter was seen as containing an immanent principle of self-movement whose sources lay in the active powers which resided in matter itself. Thus, we encounter natural philosophers vitalizing the world with living forces such as elective affinities, vital principles, sympathies and formative drives, reminiscent of the living world of the Renaissance. Rather than considering nature to be Horkheimer's "heap of things," Enlightenment vitalists envisioned it as a teeming interaction of active forces revolving around each other in a developmental dance. A typical example was provided by the German physiologist, comparative anatomist and anthropologist Johann Friedrich Blumenbach. In the complex composition of organized matter (the term usually assigned to living matter), he discerned a number of "*common* or *general* vital energies because they exist, more or less, in almost all, or at least in a great many, parts of the body."[18] The foremost of these was the *Bildungstrieb,* which Blumenbach defined as a power which directs the formation of bodies after the miracle of conception, prevents them from destruction and compensates them through reproduction from any mutilations the body may incur.[19] In addition to these vital powers, Blumenbach posited another vital energy, "namely the *vita propria*, or *specific life:* under which denomination I mean to arrange such powers as belong to certain parts of the body, destined for the performance of peculiar functions."[20] According to him, "virtually every fibral in the living body possessed a vital energy inherent in itself."[21] An organized body consisted of a complex conjuction of energies and forces of varying intensities and functions that could not be reduced to a single dominating principle. It was a constituent assembly of forces.

The re-introduction into nature of active, goal-directed living forces such as the *Bildungstrieb* led Enlightenment vitalists to reassess the basic methodological and analytic categories of scientific investigation and explanation. The new conception of matter dissolved the strict distinction between observer and observed, since both were related within a much larger conjunction of living matter. Relation, *rapport* or *Verwandschaft* replaced aggregation as one of the defining principles of matter. Identity and non-contradiction were substituted by degrees of relation and similarity. The world of living matter consisted of a circle of relations, which looking at it from the human vantage-point, radiated out to touch all forms of matter. The constituent parts of living matter formed a "synergy" in which each conjoined particle was influenced by each other and the habitus in which it existed.[22] By emphasizing the centrality of interconnection, Enlightenment vitalists modified the concept of cause and effect. In the world of living nature, each constituent part of an organized body was both cause and effect of the other parts. All forces were symbiotically linked. Furthermore, with the re-introduction of goal into living nature, Enlightenment vitalists made it the efficient cause of development. An explanation for something's existence took the form of a narrative modeled upon the concept of stage-like development or epigenesis, in which a body evolves through stages from a point of creation effected by the merging of male and female seminal fluids. Unique creation and true qualitative transformation were central to the vitalitist vision of living nature.[23]

These shifts in natural philosophic assumptions challenged Enlightenment vitalists to construct an epistemology capable of justifying and validating them. True to the skeptical critique of causation and forces, the vitalists agreed that active life forces could not be seen directly, nor could they be measured. They were "occult powers" in the traditional sense of the term, not as modified by Newton who insisted on their quantification.[24] At best they were announced by outward signs, whose meaning could only be grasped indirectly. This language of nature reintroduced the topos of locating real reality as something that lurked within a body. That which was immediately observable was considered superficial. Understanding entailed a progressive descent into the depths of observed reality, using signs as the markers to chart the way. Thus, Enlightenment vitalists reintroduced the idea of semiotics as one of the methods to decipher the secrets of nature.

The basic epistemological problem was to understand the meaning of these signs and how to perceive the interaction of the individual yet linked active forces, powers and energies without collapsing one into the other. To resolve this problem Enlightenment vitalists called for a form of understanding that combined the individualized elements of nature's variety into a harmonic conjunction that recognized both nature's unity and diversity. The methods adopted to implement this program were analogical reasoning and comparative analysis.

Analogical reasoning became the functional replacement for mathematical analysis. With it one could discover similar properties or tendencies between dissimilar things that approximated natural laws without dissolving the particular in the general. The fascination for analogies was strengthened by a general preference for functional analysis, in which actual outward form was subordinated to activity. Comparative analysis reinforced the concentration upon analogical reasoning. It allowed one to consider nature as composed of systems having their own character and dynamics, yet demonstrating similarities not revealed by the consideration of outward form. Comparison's major task was to see similarities and differences and mediate between them, finding analogies that were not immediately apparent.

However, in pursuing a program based upon analogical reasoning and comparative analysis, a further epistemological problem arose. If nature was unity in diversity, how could one choose which element to emphasize? When should one concentrate upon the concrete singularity and when should one cultivate generalizing approaches? The proposed answer was to do both at once, allowing the interaction between them to produce a higher form of understanding than provided either by simple observation or by discursive, formal logic. This type of understanding was called divination, intuition or *Anschauung*. Its operation was based on the image of mediation, of continually moving back and forth from one to the other, letting each nourish and modify the other. Buffon described this practice in the introduction to his *Histoire naturelle:* "the love of the study of Nature supposes two seemingly opposite qualities of the mind: the wide-ranging views of an ardent mind that embraces everything with one glance, and the detail-oriented laboring instinct that concentrates only on one element."[25] Seventy-two years later, Wilhelm von Humboldt attested to the appeal of this logic of mediation in his description of how one obtained historical knowledge. "Thus two methods have to be followed simultaneously in the approach to historical truth; the first is the exact, impartial, critical investigation of events; the second is the connecting of the events explored and the intuitive understanding of them which could not be reached by the first."[26]

In many ways, this act of mediation was supposedly mirrored in the physical world through the action of the life forces. Thus, for example, Blumenbach argued that the *Bildungstrieb* successfully mediated between the "two principles . . . that one had assumed could not be joined, the teleological and the mechanical."[27] Friedrich Schiller, who was trained as a physician, made a similar claim in his first medical dissertation, written in 1779, for a force that mediated between mind and matter. He described it as "a force [that] in fact exists between matter and mind. This force is quite distinct from the world and the mind." It was, he claimed, "a force which is spiritual on the one hand and material on the other, an entity that is penetrable on the one hand and impenetrable on the other."[28] Correct understanding formed an analogue to this force as it moved from the concrete to the intellectual and back, mediating in a manner that simple logic would deny.

In this movement, however, understanding passed through a third, hidden and informing agent that was, in effect, the ground upon which all reality rested. In eighteenth-century vitalist language, this hidden middle element, opaque, un-seeable, yet essential was called by such terms as the internal mould (Buffon), prototype (Robinet), *Urtyp* (Goethe) or *Haupttypus* (Herder). Some writers used the image of a magnetic field to give it visual representation. It was constituted by the magnetic poles and yet united them without submerging them in a reductive unity. The area of its greatest effect was the middle, where the field encompassed the largest area.

For us, this model of apprehension is difficult to perceive, for it flies in the face of what we consider rational, logical or scientific. I believe it points to an attempt to answer the skeptical critique of rationalism by seeking to go beyond binary systems of logic and explanation. Binary systems assume that the distance between signifier and signified can be collapsed, that reason can look at the world and it would look back reasonably. What these late Enlightenment thinkers seemed to prefer was a ternary system, which introduced something between sign and signified, what Herder called the *Mittelbegriff,* through which everything was refracted but which could never be seen, grasped, or directly identified. In short, they were arguing for a harmonic view of nature that organized reality around the figures of ambiguity and paradox central to the skeptical stance, a position that was reluctant to reduce one thing to another but allow them to be allied to each other. This harmonic ideal often was expressed through the use of creative oxymorons such as Buffon's "internal mold," or Schiller's concept of "material ideas," which verbally reconstructed the paradoxical *rapports.*

But how did the Enlightenment vitalists validate this theory of understanding? What allowed them to proclaim that the tools of analogical reasoning, comparison and internal, intuitive understanding were scientifically objective. The problem was especially acute because of the blurring between object and observer. But it was precisely this mingling that served as the justification for this approach to science. It was argued that because humans were part of living nature, they could, through the act of sympathetic understanding, acquire a living knowledge of nature's processes. Similarity and relationship were the vehicles of understanding, which by passing through the extended middle ensured the truth values of these endeavors.

This harmonic view of reality formed the core and essence of the late Enlightenment vitalists' vision of nature and humanity, differentiating it from early eighteenth century mechanism and later Romanticism. It accounted for its fascination with extremes—boundaries and limits—and its hoped for mediations. It was not a dualistic vision of nature and humanity, for real reality always lay between extremes. Harmony, the joining of opposites within an expanded middle generated by reciprocal interaction, served as the norm and desired end of each natural process, though that dynamic was continually in motion, leading to ever changing harmonic combinations. Living nature then was the place where freedom and determinism merged. Its description invoked images and metaphors drawn either from the moral sphere or directly applicable to it. Horkheimer had claimed that the "the inner logic of science itself tends towards the idea of one truth which is completely opposed to the recognition of such entities as the soul and the individual."[29] The science envisioned by Enlightenment vitalists sought to reintroduce entities such as soul and individuality into the inner core of scientific thinking.

For that very reason, Enlightenment vitalism had definite appeal to late Enlightenment thinkers who strove to create what we would call the humanistic sciences by naturalizing their objects of inquiry and explanatory strategies. These elective affinities were further strengthened by the fact that scientific questions were central to the discourse of time. The "great analogy of nature," as Herder termed it, was considered the essential reference point for discussions concerning truth, beauty, and human organization. As Steven Shapin has argued, "this was not because of 'mere' metaphysical glossing, but because in these (and later) cultural contexts nature and society were deemed to be elements in one interacting network of significance."[30] Therefore any substantial change in a philosophy of nature implied an equally strong realignment of social, political, religious and cultural sensibilities.

Given the restrictions of space it would be foolhardy for me to try to demonstrate how the language of vitalism informed the many attempts to create humanistic disciplines in the late Enlightenment. I debated whether to focus on the construction of a single discipline or to present a few select cases where the convergence can be seen. I opted for the former, hoping that a loss of comprehensive coverage will be compensated by more analytic precision, for it is my intention not just to show that the humanities borrowed a number of metaphors from vitalism, but translated that model to serve the ends of constructing a humanistic science. I have decided to focus upon history, though I could easily have chosen the other areas I am now exploring, namely aesthetics, anthropology and linguistics.

Buffon, in the introduction to the *Histoire naturelle* and also in his *Les Epoques de la nature* drew a direct analogy between natural history and the history of civil society. Both followed analogous methods in attempting to fix specific points in space and time and to chart the moral and physical revolutions that took place on the earth.[31] Throughout the late eighteenth century, historians would take up this analogy and proclaim it their duty to compose a "natural history" of human endeavors, as Herder's definition of universal history illustrates. "The whole of human history is a pure natural history of human powers, actions, and drives located in space and time."[32] The analogy's appeal was founded on the shared belief that everything in the world was ordered by eternal principles. As Herder proclaimed: "The power that thinks and acts in me is according to its nature so eternal a power as that which holds the sun and stars together."[33]

But the laws that governed the human world were not those of physics, which just dealt with what Horkheimer called "heaps of things." Ferguson described the nature of this system and the connection of its parts as follows: "parts that constitute the system of nature, like the stones of an arch, support and are supported; but their beauty is not of the quiescent kind. The principles of agitation and of life combine their effects in constituting an order of things, which is at once fleeting and permanent. . . . The whole is alive and in action: the scene is perpetually changing; but in its changes exhibits an order more striking than could be made to arise by mere position or description of any forms entirely at rest."[34] The goal then was to understand and describe this order of things. How was this to be done? Let us listen to Ferguson again. For him the material world was a system of "signs and expressions," created by God, but calling for human interpretation. "It is a magnificent but regular discourse, composed of parts and subdivisions, proceeding, in the original or creative mind, from generals to particulars; but in the observer, to be traced by a laborious induction from the indefinite variety of particulars, to some notion of the general mold of forms in which they are cast."[35] Included in this vast semiotic field were the past actions and creations of mankind. Herder sounded the same theme when he called for the development of a "semiotics of the soul."[36] It was the historian's task to order and make sense of these signs, to place them within a system of meaning, and to evolve an adequate way of presenting these hard-won insights.

In late eighteenth-century language this imperative clearly implied that history was to be made scientific, for to systematize was to scientize. To quote Ferguson again, "the love of science and the love of system are the same."[37] But what constituted this system? The German historian August Ludwig Schlözer attempted to answer it. As Ferguson, Schlözer drew a distinction between two types of ordering procedures, which he called an *Aggregate* and a *System*. An *Aggregate* arises when "the whole human race is cut up in parts, all of these parts numbered, and the available information about each is correctly presented."[38] This was unsatisfactory. "A picture cut up into parts in which each part is treated separately does not give a living representation of the whole."[39] This cut-up picture corresponded to Ferguson's order of stones in an arch and evokes Horkheimer's "heap of things." All described a mechanistic principle of order and explication. One had to go beyond mechanism, Schlözer argued, and create a true system. This is achieved by looking at things with "a generalizing vision that encompasses the whole; this powerful vision transforms the aggregate into a system, brings all the states of the earth together in a unity."[40] Schlözer's ideal was modeled upon Buffon's characterization of the generalizing view of the natural historian, which, while paying close attention to the particular, encompasses everything in one glance.[41] The goal for both was to establish a real connection, that would make clear the "natural, immediate, and obvious connections" between events.[42]

The vitalist call for constructing a natural system describing real connections was adopted and complemented by its program of proceeding from outward signs to inner reality, designed to achieve a comprehension of the unseen, active and penetrating forces of living nature and ultimately to acquire an apprehension of the "general mold of forms," an English translation of Buffon's *moule intérieur*. In a similar sense, Herder argued that the historian's goal was to apprehend "the great drama of active forces."[43] But this was not easy to observe, for the major players were hidden from view, performing on a stage located within the depths of living matter. "The ground of the observable lies in the inner, for everything is formed through organic forces which develop from the inner outwards."[44] Real reality could only be perceived through analogical comparisons whose efficacy and truth value were guaranteed according to Herder by two things: 1) the universal circle of similarities and interconnections validated our projection of self upon other. The human was, in effect, a composite of all the types of living things that have existed. Humans recapitulated the history of organized life and hence were able to project their understanding on to these forms. 2) This projection was true because it was refracted through and reflected the extended middle, the invisible but organizing *Haupttypus*.[45] For these two reasons analogies became our most powerful analytic tools; they alone gave us the "key to penetrate into the essence of things."[46]

In constructing their research and explanatory agendas late Enlightenment historians sought to mediate between the dual operations of investigating structure and process, place and time. Structural analysis located the object of inquiry within the total field of external and internal synchronic relations, while the inquiry into process dealt with the "history of the species."[47] According to the first assumption every social body was influenced by the physical and social environment in which it existed. Thus, historians would look to climate, soil, geography, social and economic organization, government, religion, "opinions", and culture as those elements which form and limit the body social.[48] The specific configurations of cultures and societies that resulted from this mediation were treated as "acquired characteristics" or habits. They were ingrained determinants that defined the "characteristics" of a social body, but were not essential qualities. They could be changed.

These external categories did not directly imprint themselves upon the "organized body." Rather they were redirected or mediated by the active principles residing within that body. Such active powers were seen as analogues to the specific forces in an individual body. Sometimes they were defined as the principles of an activity (e.g. commerce, language) or as the spirit of a group (middle class). In cultures as a whole these powers were considered to reside in those peoples or groups whose activities were hidden from normal observation, neglected by traditional historical discourse. Schlözer provides us with an insight into which groups the late Enlightenment historians considered active. Expanding on the theme of conjunction and universal interconnection, Schlözer exclaimed: "All peoples of the world have always been connected with one another, though in most cases very indirectly . . . . The universal historian does not seek, as had previously been done, for these connections along highways, where armies and conquerors have marched to the beat of the drum, but rather along byways, where merchants, apostles, and travelers silently and unobtrusively have wandered."[49] Apostles, traders, travelers, along with craftsmen and farmers, scholars, writers, artists and poets did the real work that kept the body alive and hence were equivalent to the "hidden" active powers in the organized cultural body.[50] On the other hand, the more conventional subjects of historical writing— nobles, monarchs, and warriors—represented the external characteristics of a state's history: to concentrate on them was to fall into the dual dangers of reductionist classification and mechanistic analysis; both had elevated the obvious and most superficial aspect of an organized body to an essential characteristic.

In emphasizing the action of unseen hidden powers, Enlightened historians argued that living matter contained an immanent principle of self-movement which acted directionally. Hence all organized bodies were, as Ferguson called them, "progressive natures." "Progressive natures are subject to the vicissitudes of advancement or decline, but are not stationary, perhaps in any period of their existence. Thus, in the material world, subjects organized, being progressive, when they cease to advance, begin to decline . . ." By analogy, intelligence and human society were also "progressive natures," continually advancing or declining, and should be analyzed as such. Unlike stationary (mechanical) bodies which "are described by the enumeration of co-existent parts . . . subjects progressive are characterized by the enumeration of steps, in the passage from one form of state or excellence to another." This explanation is clearly modeled upon the vitalist theory of epigenesis in which a body evolves through stages from a point of creation effected by the merging of male and female fluids. Each stage in the process had its own integrity, none more privileged or revealing than the other. As Ferguson stated: "The natural state of a living creature includes all its known variations, from the embryo and the foetus to the breathing animal, the adolescent and the adult, through which life in all its varieties is known to pass."[51]

But not all progressive development was continuous. At critical junctures it proceeded through a series of changes, "revolutions" in which outward form was altered drastically, followed by gradual development in the newly formed shape. The critical transitions in this process were marked by "astonishing revolutions in almost the whole economy of its system."[52] The image often used for these revolutions was metamorphosis. Schlözer confirmed these views. "The best periodization in the history of states is, without a doubt, the genetic, which details the step-like growth and decline of states (their metamorphoses)."[53]

Late eighteenth-century historians found the idea of epigenesis fascinating because it assumed the dual existence of individuality and regular order, without collapsing one upon the other. The "progression" or "degeneration" of a social body was not arbitrary. Rather, it followed a pattern analogous to that of all living entities. These were shaped by regulative patterns such as the internal mold and directed by formative principles such as the *Bildungstrieb,* hidden within the depths of organized matter. The regulative patterns became the functional equivalents of general laws. They insured the ordered step-by-step progression or regression of a social body. But these patterns differed from axiomatic laws, for they were not sufficient to account adequately for individual appearances. They dealt only with form, not with specific manifestations, not with the multiplicity of life, not with individuality.

In history, these patterns of change were assumed universal because they were founded upon inherent human drives. However, since drives could only be understood in relation to an object, so too could these descriptive forms only have meaning when placed within a context. As in the world of nature these forms were "empty," that is, they could never predict the specifics of any organic entity. The laws of history were, at best, directional markers that allowed one to use the tools of analogy and comparison to explicate similar forms. Real history had to unite the form with the content and in so doing preserve both the unity and diversity of historical analysis.

Given this interplay between regular form and individual uniqueness, historians of the late Enlightenment could venture into areas of inquiry where documentary evidence was slim or non-existent. The early history of peoples, the history of religion, of myth, of ritual, even of language were fields they cultivated with enormous energy, driven on by the allure of analogical reasoning and guided by assumptions founded upon the idea of "progressive development." The results were certainly mixed, but all believed they could undertake such generalizations precisely because of the time and situation-bound nature of each formulation. Thus, for example, poetic effusions could still be grasped as "individual" or "original" products of a specific society, results of the active human spirit restructuring the external world. This insight encouraged late Enlightenment historians to use poetry as a tool to probe a culture's characteristics, even to reflect upon the political history of the society in which it appeared. From Homer's epics through the *Niebelungenlied,* the troubadours, *Ossian,* and the Roman *Carmina,* historians attempted to extract historical meaning from them based upon the assumption of the relation between the general and the specific, place and time.

The analogy of the step-like "progression" of organized bodies was also applied to individual subjects such as art (Winckelmann),[54] economics (Smith), or religions (Semler, Spittler),[55] to problems such as colonization (Schlözer, Heeren),[56] or relations of dominance between males and females (Millar),[57] and to specifically human activities such as language (Schlözer, Adelung, Herder, Humboldt).[58] And, of course, the most common example was to extend the analogy of organized bodies to nations and civilizations (Adelung, Herder, Robertson, Ferguson).[59]

According to these explanatory procedures, specific content could only be apprehended by investigating the action and interaction of an organized entity—be it an individual, a language, or a nation—existing within a specific environmental context. Historical understanding was seen as combining a sense for the formal pattern of development with an acute awareness of the unique force field of historical and environmental determinants existing at a given moment. Synchronic and diachronic studies were to nourish each other. Schlözer summed this idea up in his definition of history and synchronic studies, called "statistics" by late eighteenth-century German historians. "A history is a continuously moving statistics, a statistics is a halted history."[60]

These specific positions were constructed upon the interpretive figures of mediation. These, in turn, were authorized and unified by the appropriation of vitalist epistemology. Both provided a convincing and compelling justification for the mediating explanations late Enlightenment historians favored. The epistemology offered a theory of understanding founded upon similarity and conjunction rather than upon identity and separation. It proposed a methodology of investigation and a procedure of explanation in which analogical reasoning and comparative analysis were considered as primary. Understanding was made possible through sympathy and "intuition," procedures that were sanctioned by assuming a correspondence between observer and observed; that is, by collapsing the strict distinction between mind and body, subject and object.

Even more than translating specific elements of Enlightenment vitalism into history, many historians adopted what I would call vitalism's mental stance, its pre-figuring imperative, which played a more subtle but perhaps even greater role in establishing the contours of late Enlightened historical thought. Its most compelling aspect was to elevate paradox or the harmonic juxtaposition of opposing pairs to a primary mode for structuring reality. This formulation refused to assume the possibility of knowing directly that which united the antinomies—the extended middle that lay between both extremes. Late Enlightenment historians who adopted vitalist explanatory models reintroduced the opacity between sign and signified.

Historians' acceptance of this pre-figuring mental stance can be seen in Schlözer's definition of history and his description of the generalizing vision the historian was to employ. They were reinforced by works that investigated the question of the connection between imagination, research and historical reconstruction.

This line of inquiry reached its culmination in Wilhelm von Humboldt's classic essay, "On the Tasks of the Historian," written in 1821, supposedly marking the theoretical beginning of German historicism. Rather than being the beginning of a new idea of history, it represents the distillation of late Enlightenment thought about history, derived in a large part from the assumed analogy between history and natural history. Humboldt focused upon the problem of combining creative imagination with precise research, related it to the problem of historical representation and evolved a theory of historical understanding that, despite the years that separated his essay from the first volume of the *Histoire naturelle,* corroborated Buffon's basic assumptions. In Humboldt's essay, the same interpretive *topoi* form the core of his argument. These included the following; that there is a basic analogy between natural and human history; that synchronic and diachronic analyses must be correlated; that concentration upon outward phenomena and the use of the techniques of aggregation were insufficient for historical understanding; that one must proceed from outer form to inner powers; that these powers were joined in an internal "Mittelpunkt"; that this middle point could not be apprehended by reason, formal philosophy, or simple empiricism; and that its perception as well as all historical understanding was built upon the creative interplay between active investigating force and the object to be investigated, between creative imagination and precise analysis of the particular. These positions supposedly confirmed the two primary principles that the object of historical analysis was "the wonder of creation," and its steplike "formation," and that the task of historical representation was a "creative imitation of nature," an imitation of its "organic form."[61] In effect, in this essay Humboldt completed a project initiated by the late eighteenth century historians who drew their arguments, methods, and epistemology from the vitalist restructuring of the sciences.

When Humboldt's essay appeared, the only professional historian to sing its praises was Arnold Heeren, one of the last representatives of German Enlightenment historiography. For by then, the science that underpinned Humboldt's historiography had been supplanted by what we now call Romantic *Naturphilosophie.* Though they sometimes appear related, a major difference separated Enlightenment vitalism from *Naturphilosophie.* Vitalism was nourished by and within the late eighteenth-century skeptical critique of absolute solutions and reductive rationalism. It could thrive as long as ambiguity and paradox were seen as productive, not considered either dangerous or ineffective. With the tensions generated during the last decade of the eighteenth century and the first two of the nineteenth that epistemological modesty was destroyed by the desire for absolute answers. Disdainful of science "stuck in the rubbish dump of sensory reflection,"[62] (Steffens) *Naturphilosophie* aimed, as Nicholas Jardine has recently written, "at a total history, one that would encompass the entire differentiation of the cosmos from the original oneness, through the formation of the solar system and the earth, the proliferation of the three kingdoms of nature . . . to the culmination of the universe in humankind."[63] In this all-encompassing view, built upon the philosophic concept of identity (*Identitätsphilosophie*), the late Enlightenment's epistemology modesty was cast aside in favor of types of systems often seen by postmodernists as having being forged in the Enlightenment.

This is the final irony. For a careful look at the late Enlightenment might reveal a way of thinking and doing that is much more sympathetic to postmodernism than Romanticism. In its project of seeing nature not just as a heap of things, of creating a place for soul and the individual, of avoiding the rush to reductionism, the late Enlightenment, at least in part, envisioned an order of things that stood in strong contrast to the instrumental reason often associated with it. If there is such a thing as the Enlightenment project—rather than, as I believe, a set of competing positions that rehearse in their own context questions we still confront—it included a healthy respect for differentness, free movement and creation. Adam Ferguson made this explicit in 1767:

> Our notion of order in civil society is frequently false: it is taken from the analogy of subjects inanimate and dead; we consider commotion and action as contrary to its nature; we think it consistent only with obedience, secrecy, and the silent passing of affairs through the hands of a few: The good order of stones in a wall, is their being properly fixed in places for which they are hewn; were they to stir the building must fall: but the order of men in society, is their being placed where they are properly qualified to act. The first is a fabric made of dead and inanimate parts, the second is made of living and active members. When we seek in society for the order of mere inaction and tranquillity, we forget the nature of our subject, and find the order of slaves, not of free men.[64]

NOTES

1. Max Horkheimer, "Reason Against Itself: Some Remarks on Enlightenment," in *What is Enlightenment: Eighteenth-Century Answers and Twentieth-Century Questions,* ed. James Schmidt (Berkeley: Univ. of California Press, 1996), 359.

2. Stephen Toulmin, *Cosmopolis: The Hidden Agenda of Modernity* (New York: Free Press, 1990).

3. I would like to thank Dena Goodman for calling my attention to this article.

4. Naomi Schor, "French Feminism Is a Universalism," *Differences: A Journal of Feminist Cultural Studies* 7 (1995): 15.

5. Toulmin, *Cosmopolis,* x.

6. For an excellent analysis of this tendency see Simon Schaffer, "Natural Philosophy," in *The Ferment of Knowledge: Studies in the Historiography of Eighteenth-Century Science,* ed. George S. Rousseau and Roy Porter (Cambridge: Cambridge Univ. Press, 1980), 53–91.

7. Horkheimer, "Reason Against Itself," 361.

8. Margaret C. Jacob, *The Radical Enlightenment: Pantheists, Freemasons, and Republicans* (London: Allen and Unwin, 1981); Aram Vartanian, *La Méttrie's l'Homme Machine: A Case Study in the Origins of an Idea* (Princeton: Princeton Univ. Press, 1960).

9. David Hume, *The Philosophical Works,* ed. Thomas Hill Green and Thomas Hodge Grose, 4 vols. (London, 1883), 3: 213–4.

10. Georges Leclerc, comte de Buffon, *De la manière d'étudier & de traiter l'Histoire Naturelle* (1749; reprint, Paris: Bibliothèque Nationale, 1986).

11. David Hume, *An Enquiry Concerning Human Understanding,* in *Works*, 4: 63.

12. Hume, *Works*, 4: 62.

13. *Traité des Extremes ou élements de la science de la réalité* (Amsterdam: Darkstee & Merkus, 1768), 232.

14. Hume, *Works*, 4: 51.

15. The disinclination to engage in the regnant questions of the early eighteenth century was made evident by the German mathematician Wilhelm Johann Karstens in his discussion of the earlier disputes concerning matter, where he dismissed the whole controversy concerning these issues as useless. Karstens, *Physische-chemische Abhandlung, durch neuere Schriften von hermetischen Arbeiten und andere neue Untersuchungen veranlasset,* 2 vols. (Halle, 1786, 1787), 2: 69.

16. On the *vis viva* controversy see Thomas L. Hankins, "Eighteenth-Century Attempts to Resolve the *Vis Viva* Controversy," *Isis* 56 (1965): 281–97; Carolyn Iltis, "D'Alembert and the *Vis Viva* Controversy," *Studies in History and Philosophy of Science* 1 (1970): 135–44; "The Decline of Cartesianism in Mechanics: The Leibnizian-Cartesian Debates," *Isis* 64 (1973): 356–73; "The Leibnizian-Newtonian Debates: Natural Philosophy and Social Psychology," *The British Journal for the History of Science* 6 (1973): 343–77; "Madam du Chatelet's Metaphysics and Mechanics," *Studies in History and Philosophy of Science* 8 (1977): 29–48. See also David Papineau, "The Vis Viva Controversy: Do Meanings Matter?" *Studies in History and Philosophy of Science* 8 (1977): 111–42; and the following by Giorgio Tonelli, "Analysis and Syntheses in Eighteenth-Century Philosophy Prior to Kant," *Archiv für Begriffsgeschichte* 20 (1976): 178–213; "Critiques of the Notion of Substance Prior to Kant," *Tijdschrift voor Philosophie* 23 (June 1961); "The Philosophy of d'Alembert: A Sceptic beyond Skepticism," *Kantstudien,* 67 (1976): 353–371.

17. Toulmin, *Cosmopolis,* 108.

18. Johann Friedrich Blumenbach, *Elements of Physiology,* trans. Charles Caldwell, 2 vols. (Philadelphia, 1795), 1: 33.

19. Ibid., 1: 22.

20. Ibid., 1: 33

21. Ibid., 1: 22

22. The term synergy was coined by Georg Stahl and then used extensively by Paul Barthez in his theory of vital physiology.

23. Kant was much more influenced by this explanatory model than is usually supposed. For an excellent discussion of the vitalistic influences on his philosophy

see: Wolfgang Krohn and Günther Küppers, "Die natürlichen Ursachen der Zwecke: Kants Ansätze der Selbstorganisation," *Selbstorganisation: Jahrbuch für Komplexität in den Natur-, Sozial- und Geisteswissenschaften* 3 (1992): 7–15.

24. Both Blumenbach and Barthez called their respective concepts of the *Bildungstrieb* and the *Princip Vital* occult powers and both turned to the authority of Newton. Yet both acknowledged that the only way the powers could be recognized was by their effects and these were beyond quantification.

25. Buffon, *Histoire Naturelle, general et particuliere*, 44 vols. (Paris, 1749–88), 1: 4: "l'amour de l'étude de la Nature suppose dans l'esprit deux qualités qui paroissent opposées, les grandes vûes d'un génie ardent qui embrasse tout d'un coup d'oeil, & les petites attentions d'un instinct laborieux qui ne s'attache qu'à un seul point."

26. Wilhelm Humboldt, "On the Historian's Task," *History and Theory* 6 (1967): 59.

27. Johann Friedrich Blumenbach, *Ueber den Bildungstrieb und das Zeugungsgeschäfte* (Göttingen, 1781), 65–66 n.

28. *Friedrich Schiller: Medicine, Psychology and Literature with the first English edition of his complete Medical and Physiological Writings,* ed. Kenneth Dewhurst and Nigel Reeves (Berkeley: Univ. of California Press, 1978), 152.

29. Horkheimer, "Reason Against Itself," 364.

30. Simon Schaffer, "Social Uses of Science" in Rousseau and Porter, *Ferment of Knowledge,* 101.

31. "Comme dans l'Histoire civile, on consulte les titres, on recherche les médailles, on déchiffre les inscriptions antiques, pour determiner les époques moraux; & des révolutions humaines, & constater les dates des évènemens de moraux; meme, dans L'Histoire Naturelle, il faut fouiller les archives du monde, tirer des entrailles de la terre les vieux monumens, recueillir leurs débris, & rassembler en un corps de preuves tous les indices des changemens physiques qui preuvent nous faire remonter aux différens ages de la Nature. C'est le seul moyen de fixer quelques points dans l'immensité de l'espace, & placer un certain nombre de pierres numéraires sur la route éternelle du temps. Le passé est comme la distance; " Buffon, *Les Époques de la nature,* ed. Jacques Roger (Paris: Editions du Muséum Paris, 1998), 4.

32. Johann Gottfried Herder, *Ideen zur Philosophie der Geschichte der Menschheit,* in *Herders Sämmtliche Werke,* ed. Bernhard Suphan, 33 vols. (Berlin, 1877–1913), 13: 154.

33. Herder, *Sämmtliche Werke,* 13: 16.

34. Adam Ferguson, *Principles of Moral and Political Science,* 2 vols. (Edinburgh: Univ. of Edinburgh Press, 1972), 1: 174.

35. Ibid., 1: 275.

36. Herder, *Sämmtliche Werke,* 13: 184.

37. Ferguson, *Principles,* 1: 278.

38. August Ludwig Schlözer, *Vorstellung seiner Universal Historie,* 2 vols. (Göttingen: J. C. Dieterich 1772), 1: 15.

39. Ibid., 1: 15.

40. Ibid., 1: 19.

41. "les grandes vues d'un génie ardent qui embrasse tout d'un coup d'oeil." Buffon, *Histoire Naturelle,* 1: 4.

42. Schlözer, *Vorstellung,* 1: 46.

43. "Vom Erkennen und Empfinden der menschlichen Seele: Bemerkungen und Träume," Herder, *Sämmtliche Werke,* 8: 169.

44. Ibid., 13: 129.

45. Ibid., 13: 123.

46. Ibid., 8: 170.

47. Buffon, *Histoire Naturelle,* 1: 20.

48. This program was often derived from Hippocrates. Both Judith Shklar and George Armstrong Kelly show how Montesquieu's analysis of space was derived from Hippocrates. Judith Shklar, "Virtue in a bad climate: Good men and good citizens in Montesquieu's *L'esprit des lois,*" in *Enlightenment Studies in Honour of Lester G. Crocker,* ed. Alfred J. Bingham and Virgil W. Topazio (Oxford: The Voltaire Foundation, 1979), 316. George Armstrong Kelly, *Mortal Politics in Eighteenth-Century France* (Waterloo: Univ. of Waterloo Press, 1986), 43.

49. Schlözer, *Vorstellung,* 2: 272–3.

50. These groups became the focus of historical research, while those who profited from them without contributing to society were relegated to minimal importance. Rulers, generals, aristocrats were, as a rule treated with disdain. Here Schlözer and Herder, though bitter enemies, agreed, though Schlözer probably would not have gone as far as did Herder in the assertion that "die beruhmtesten Namen der Welt sind Würger des Menschengeschlechts, gekrönte oder nach Kronen ringende Henker gewesen." Herder, *Sämmtliche Werke,* 13: 380. A wholescale skepticism about court, cabinet, and military history was developed even when the courts and cabinets, the rulers, aristocrats, and generals still wielded immense power and authority.

51. Ferguson, *Principles,* 190–92.

52. Blumenbach, *Elements of Physiology,* 2: 203.

53. Schlözer, *Vorstellung,* 2: 358.

54. Johann J. Winckelmann, *Geschichte der Kunst des Altertums* (Darmstadt: Wissenschaftliche Buchgesellschaft, 1972).

55. See Johann Salamo Semler, *Zur Revision der kirchlichen Hermeneutik und Dogmatik* (Halle, 1788); Ludwig T. Spittler, *Grundriss der Geschichte der Christlichen Kirche,* Vol. 2 of *Sämmtliche Werke* (Stuttgart, 1827).

56. See Arnold Heeren, *Historische Werke,* vol 6. (Göttingen, 1823), August Ludwig Schlözer, *Versuch einer allgemeinen Geschichte der Handlung und Seefahrt in den ältesten Zeiten* (Rostock, 1761).

57. John Millar, *Observations Concerning the Distinction of Ranks in Society* (London, 1771).

58. See August Ludwig Schlözer, *Allgemeine Nordische Geschichte* (Halle, 1771); Johann C. Adelung, *Mithridates oder die allgemeine Sprachkunde* (Berlin, 1806); Herder, *Ideen zur Philosophie der Geschichte der Menschheit* (Leipzig, 1821); Wilhelm von Humboldt, "Ueber die Verschiedenheit des menschlichen Sprachbaues und ihren Einfluss auf die geistige Entwicklung des Menschengeschlachts," in *Wilhelm von Humboldt Werke,* 5 vols. (Stuttgart: J. G. Cotta, 1980) 3: 368–756.

59. See Johann C. Adelung, *Versuch einer Geschichte der Cultur des menschlichen Geschlechts* (Leipzig, 1782); Herder, *Ideen;* William Robertson, *The History of Scotland during the Reigns of Queen Mary, and of King James VI till his Accession to the Crown of England with a review of the Scottish History previous to that Period* (London, 1761); Robertson, *The History of the Reign of the Emperor Charles V with a View of the Progress of Society in Europe from the Subversion of the Roman Empire to the Beginning of the Sixteenth Century* (London, 1769); Adam Ferguson, *An Essay on the History of Civil Society* (Edinburgh: Edinburgh Univ. Press, 1966).

60. Schlözer, *Vorstellung,* 1: 11.

61. Humboldt, "Ueber die Aufgabe des Geschichtschreibers," in *Werke,* 1: 597.

62. Nicholas Jardine, "Naturphilosophie and the kingdoms of nature," in *Cultures of Natural History,* ed. Nicholas Jardine, J.A. Secord and Emma C. Spary (Cambridge: Cambridge Univ. Press, 1996), 233.

63. Jardine, "Naturphilosophie," 232.

64. Ferguson, *Civil Society,* 268–69.

Contributors to Volume 28

Paul Baines is Lecturer in the Department of English Language and Literature, University of Liverpool, United Kingdom. He has published many articles on eighteenth-century subjects and is the author of *The House of Forgery in Eighteenth-Century Britain* (Ashgate Publishing, 1998). He has edited Walpole's *The Mysterious Mother* for an anthology, *British Romantic Plays* (co-edited with Edward Burns), published by Oxford University Press in the World's Classics series.

Scarlett Bowen is Assistant Professor of English at William Paterson University and is currently working on a book-length study of prose representations of working women in the British eighteenth century.

Elizabeth Child is a graduate student in English at the University of Maryland, where she is working on a dissertation entitled "Local Attachments: Geography, Gender, and Print Culture in England's Provincial Towns, 1660–1788." She has an article forthcoming in the essay collection *Female Communities, 1600–1800* (New York: St. Martin's Press). The present article was the recipient of the 1997 Catherine Macaulay Prize, presented by the Women's Caucus of ASECS.

Lisa Forman Cody is Assistant Professor of History at Claremont McKenna College. She is currently finishing a book-length project with the working title "Reproduction: Science, Culture, and Childbirth in Britain, 1660–1870." She is also working on two other book-length projects, one on representing "pregnant men" in European art and literature, the other on the intersection of the body and medicine with the marketplace and finance in eighteenth-century Britain.

John R. Iverson is Assistant Professor of French at the University of Missouri-Columbia. He recently completed his dissertation on Voltaire and notions of glory and heroism in eighteenth-century France. He has also been involved in building the electronic *Encyclopédie* for the ARTFL Project at the University of Chicago. His paper was originally presented at the ASECS meeting in Nashville.

Suzanne Kiernan is Lecturer in the Department of Italian at the University of Sydney, Australia.

Peter C. Messer is Assistant Professor of History at Texas A&M University at Commerce. The paper was first presented at the 1997 ASECS conference in Nashville, and revised while the author was a postdoctoral fellow participating in the Sawyer Mellon Seminar on National Cultures and the Construction of the Modern World at the Johns Hopkins University. This essay grew out of his dissertation, "Stories of Independence: Eighteenth-Century Narratives" (Rutgers University, 1997) which explored the ways in which eighteenth-century Americans used history as a way of defining themselves, first as members of the British empire and later as the founders of an independent republic.

Judith C. Mueller is Associate Professor of English at Franklin and Marshall College. She has published several articles on Jonathan Swift, and is currently working on a book-length study of male sexuality in the Restoration and early eighteenth century.

David Porter is Assistant Professor of English at the University of Michigan. He is currently completing a book on European responses to various aspects of Chinese culture during the eighteenth century, and has previously edited two Routledge volumes, *Between Men and Feminism* and *Internet Culture*. His essay was presented at the 1996 MWASECS conference in Indianapolis.

Evan Radcliffe is Associate Professor of English at Villanova University. He has published articles on the 1790s and on Romantic literature, and is currently working on a study of Wordsworth's narrative poetry in relation to the debate over the French Revolution.

Peter Hanns Reill is Professor of History and Director of the Center for Seventeenth- and Eighteenth-Century Studies and the William Andrews Clark Memorial Library at University of California-Los Angeles. His paper was originally presented as a plenary address at the 1997 ASECS meeting.

Patrick Riley is Assistant Professor of French at Colgate University. He works on Enlightenment and Autobiography, and is currently completing a book tracing the relaton between conversion and autobiographical narrative from Saint Augustine to Sartre.

Eleanor F. Shevlin currently teaches writing, literature, and book history courses at the University of Maryland College Park. The paper was presented at the 1997 ASECS conference in Nashville. She is working on a book-length project tentatively entitled "The Makings of a Genre: Titles, Property, Law, and the Construction of the Eighteenth-Century English Novel, 1688–1789." She serves as the Society for the History of Authorship, Reading, and Publishing (SHARP) liaison to ASECS.

James Grantham Turner is Professor of English at the University of California, Berkeley, and has taught at Oxford, Sussex, Liverpool, Virginia, Northwestern, and Michigan. In addition to editing *Politics, Poetics and Hermeneutics in Milton's Prose* (Cambridge, 1990) with David Loewenstein, Robert Paltock's *Life and Adventures of Peter Wilkins* (Oxford, 1990) and *Sexuality and Gender in Early Modern Europe: Institutions, Texts, Images* (Cambridge, 1993), he has written numerous articles on seventeenth- and eighteenth-century culture and two books: *The Politics of Landscape: Rural Scenery and Society in English Poetry, 1630–1660* (Oxford, 1979) and *One Flesh: Paradisal Marriage and Sexual Relations in the Age of Milton* (Oxford, 1987; 2nd edition 1994).

Annette K. Weir is an independent scholar who works as a librarian as well as pursuing her scholarly interests in art history. The present essay was originally presented at the 1996 MWASECS meeting in Indianapolis. She is currently working on an analysis of the late sixteenth-century portrait collection of Ferdinand II, Archduke of Austria.

Executive Board 1997–1998

President: **Margaret C. Jacob,** Professor of the History and Sociology of Science and Professor of History, University of Pennsylvania
First-Vice President: **Carol Blum,** Research Professor of Humanities, State University of New York at Stony Brook
Second-Vice President: **Ruth Perry,** Professor of Literature, Massachusetts Institute of Technology
Past President: **J. Paul Hunter,** Barbara E. and Richard J. Franke Professor and Director of the Chicago Humanities Institute, University of Chicago
Treasurer: **Catherine Lafarge,** Professor of French, Bryn Mawr College
Executive Secretary: **Byron R. Wells,** Professor of Romance Languages, Wake Forest University

Members-at-Large
Dena Goodman, Professor of History, Louisiana State University
Anita Guerrini, Professor of History, University of California at Santa Barbara
Susan S. Lanser, Professor of Comparative Literature and English, University of Maryland
Howard D. Weinbrot, Ricardo Quintana Professor of English and William Freeman Vilas Research Professor, University of Wisconsin
Julia Douthwaite, Professor of Romance Languages and Literatures, University of Notre Dame
Lawrence E. Klein, Professor of History, University of Nevada at Las Vegas

Administrative Office
Office Manager: **Vickie Cutting,** Wake Forest University
Publications Manager: **Hailey Brady**

For Information about the
American Society for Eighteenth-Century Studies, please contact:
ASECS
PO Box 7867
Wake Forest University
Winston-Salem, NC 27109-7867
Telephone: (336) 727-4694
Fax: (336) 727-4697
E-mail: asecs@wfu.edu
Web Site: http://www.press.jhu.edu/associations/asecs

Patron Members 1997–1998

Paul Alkon
Mark S. Auburn
James G. Basker
Barbara Becker-Cantarino
R. Bernasconi
Carol Blum
Theodore E. D. Braun
Peter M. Briggs
Patricia Brückman
Michael Burden
Joseph A. Byrnes
Marilyn Carbonell
Louis Cornell
Margaretmary Daley
Roland Desne
Margaret Anne Doody
Frank H. Ellis
Roger J. Fechner
Jan Fergus
Dustin H. Griffin
Joan R. Gundersen
Phyllis Guskin
Basil Guy
Robert H. Hopkins
Lynn A. Hunt

Margaret C. Jacob
Annibel Jenkins
Gary Kates
Shirley Strum Kenny
David H. Koss
Thomas W. Krise
J. Patrick Lee
Nancy M. Lee-Riffe
Geoffrey Marshall
H. W. Matalene
Helen Louise McGuffie
Alan T. McKenzie
Donald C. Mell, Jr.
John H. Middendorf
Earl Miner
Dennis Moore
Frank Palmeri
Jane Perry-Camp
R. G. Peterson
John Valdimir Price
Ralph W. Rader
John Radner
Ronald C. Rosbottom
Treadwell Ruml II
Roseann Runte

Harold Schiffman
William C. Schrader
Richard Sher
English Showalter
John Sitter
Patricia Meyer Spacks
Barbara Stafford
Susan Staves
Mary M. Stewart
Ann T. Straulman
Masashi Suzuki
Mika Suzuki
Diana M. Thomas
Connie C. Thorson
James L. Thorson
Raymond D. Tumbleson
Bertil Van Boer
David F. Venturo
Howard D. Weinbrot
David H. Weinglass
James A. Winn
James Woolley
William J. Zachs
Lisa M. Zeitz

Sponsoring Members 1997–1998

Paula Backscheider
Jerry C. Beasley
David Blewett
Thomas F. Bonnell
Martha F. Bowden
Leo Braudy
Leslie Ellen Brown
Morris Brownell
Martha L. Brunson
Chester F. Chapin
Jonathan C. D. Clark
Katharine Clark
Ralph Cohen
Thomas M. Columbus
Michael J. Conlon
Brian Corman
Howard J. Coughlin, Jr.

Patricia B. Craddock
Robert DeMaria
Alix S. Deguise
Pierre Deguise
William F. Edmiston
JoLynn Edwards
A. C. Elias, Jr.
Antoinette Emch-Deriaz
Clarissa C. Erwin
Timothy Erwin
David Fairer
Bernadette Fort
Hans Gross
Isobel Grundy
Diana Guiragossian-Carr
Madelyn Gutwirth
Roger Hahn

Karsten Harries
Phillip Harth
Donald M. Hassler
Daniel Heartz
Charles H. Hinnant
J. Paul Hunter
Kathryn Montgomery Hunter
Adrienne D. Hytier
Regina Mary Janes
Thomas Jemielity
Loftus Townshend Jestin
Claudia L. Johnson
Carol Kay
Frederick M. Keener
Oscar Kenshur
Charles A. Knight
Gwin J. Kolb

Colby H. Kullman
Catherine Lafarge
Susan Lanser
John E. Larkin, Jr.
David Lee
April London
David D. Mann
John A. McCarthy
David McNeil
Shirley McNerney Rendell
Linda E. Merians
Michael Mooney
Judith Moore
Nicolas H. Nelson
Melvyn New
Felicity Nussbaum
Mary Ann O'Donnell
John H. O'Neill
Hal N. Opperman

Douglas Lane Patey
Harry Payne
Virginia J. Peacock
Ruth Perry
Stuart Peterfreund
J. G. A. Pocock
James Pollak
Thomas R. Preston
Irwin Primer
Tom Prins
Ruben D. Quintero
Thomas J. Regan
Walter E. Rex
John Richetti
Albert J. Rivero
Betty Rizzo
Raymond Rizzo
Peter Sabor
J. T. Scanlan

Barbara B. Schnorrenberg
Gordon J. Schochet
Robert G. Schwartz
Frank Shuffelton
Donald T. Siebert
Stephen Soud
Robert Spector
G. A. Starr
Joan Koster Stemmler
Damie Stillman
A. G. Tannenbaum
Dennis Todd
Linda Veronika Troost
Randolph Trumbach
Jack Undank
Peter Wagner
Tara Ghoshal Wallace

Institutional Members 1997–1998

American Antiquarian Society
Arizona State University Library
Brown University-John Carter Brown Library
University of California
Carleton University Library
Case Western Reserve University-Freiberger
    Library
Colonial Williamsburg Foundation Library
University of Connecticut-Homer Babbidge
    Library
Dalhousie University Library
Emory University-Robert W. Woodruff Library
University of Evansville Library
Florida Atlantic University-Wimberly Library
Folger Institute
Fordham University
Georgia State University-William Russell
    Pullen Library
Hamilton College-Burke Library
Harvard College
Herzob August Bibliothek
Indiana University
Johns Hopkins University-Milton S. Eisenhower
    Library
University of Kansas
University of Kentucky-Young Library
Luther College
Massachusetts Institute of Technology
McMaster University
Metropolitan Museum of Art-Thomas J. Watson
    Library

Mount Saint Vincent University Library
University of North Carolina-Davis Library
Northwestern University
University of Notre Dame-Hesburgh Library
Ohio State University
Omohundro Institute of Early American History
University of Pennsylvania
Primary Source Media
University of Rochester
Rutgers University-Alexander Library
SUNY at Binghamton
SUNY at Buffalo
Smith College-W. A. Neilson Library
Smithsonian Institution
University of Southern California
Swarthmore College Library
University of Tennessee
University of Texas at Austin
Towson State University
University of Tulsa-Farlin Library
University Press of Kentucky
University of Victoria-McPherson Library
Washington University-Olin Library
Westfalische Wilhelms University Englisches
    Seminar
William Andrews Clark Memorial Library
Williams College
Yale Center for British Art
Yale University-Sterling Memorial Library
York University-Scott Library

Index

Every effort has been made to include in this index all identifiable persons named in essays who lived during or before the long eighteenth century, as well as a small number of widely cited twentieth-century theoreticians. Readers seeking a complete list of contemporary critics should however consult the endnotes of individual essays.

Ackerholm, Simon, 178, 179
active forces, 365–67, 371–72
Adams, Hannah, review of *A Summary History of New England*, 350–51
Adams, William, 333n. 13
Addison, Joseph, 107–8, 114–16, 122, 147
Adelung, Johann C., 374
Adventures of a Kidnapped Orphan, The, 140–41
advertising, 103–23
American Revolution: effects on women, 344–45, 347, 356; histories of, 348–50, 353–54; opposition to, 345–47
analogy, analogic reasoning, 367, 371–72, 374–76
Annesley, James, 133
Anodyne Necklace, 104, 113–17, 120–21
Anti-Jacobin, The, 318–19
Ape-Gentle-Woman, or the Character of an Exchange-Wench, The, 84n. 32
Arcadian Academy (*Accademia degli Arcadi*), 1–17
architecture: garden 37–38, 40; Gothic, 292, 303. *See also* landscape gardening; Parrhasian Grove.
Aristotle, 138, 300, 303
Augustine, Saint, 87, 98n. 11, 229–30, 232–37, 241–42, 246, 250n. 24

Austrian Succession, War of, 207–21
autobiography, theories of, 230–31; Western tradition of, 232

Barthez, Paul, 378n. 22, 379n. 24
Baudelaire, Charles, 14
Benjamin, Walter, 14
Beauclerk, Lady Diana, 303–4
Beauvais tapestries, 35–37, 40, 45
Beckford, William, 30
Behn, Aphra, 57, 70, 92
Bentham, Jeremy, 131, 133, 148, 153n. 37
Berry, Mary, 301
Beverly, Robert, *History and Present State of Virginia*, 343
Blackstone, William, 133, 135–40, 142, 148, 153n. 37
Blumenbach, Johann Friedrich, 365–66, 368
Bolingbroke, Henry St. John, Viscount, 316
Bowdler, Jane, 156, 162–63
Brooke, Henry, *The Fool of Quality*, 143
Buffon, Georges Leclerc, comte de, 363–64, 367–68, 370–71, 376
Burke, Edmund, 311–39
Burney, Frances, 156, 162, 303
Byron, George Gordon, Lord, 288

cabinetmakers, 175, 189–90
Canevari, Antonio, 2–4